National Character and Public Spirit in Britain and France, 1750–1914

In this detailed comparative study, Roberto Romani considers the concept of 'national character' in the intellectual histories of Britain and France. Perceptions of collective mentalities influenced a variety of political and economic debates, ranging from anti-absolutist polemic in eighteenth-century France to appraisals of socialism in Edwardian Britain. Romani argues that the eighteenth-century notion of 'national character', with its stress on climate and government, evolved into a concern with the virtues of 'public spirit' irrespective of national traits, in parallel with the establishment of representative institutions on the Continent. His discussion of contemporary thinkers includes Montesquieu, Voltaire, Hume, Millar, Burke, Constant, Staël, and Tocqueville. After the middle of the nineteenth century, the advent of social scientific approaches, including Spencer, Hobson, and Durkheim, shifted the focus from the qualities required by political liberty to those needed to operate complex social systems, and to bear their psychological pressures.

ROBERTO ROMANI is Research Associate at the Centre for History and Economics, King's College, Cambridge. His publications include *L'economia politica del Risorgimento italiano* (1994).

National Character and Public Spirit in Britain and France, 1750–1914

Roberto Romani

CAMBRIDGE UNIVERSITY PRESS

PUBLISHED BY THE PRESS SYNDICATE OF THE UNIVERSITY OF CAMBRIDGE
The Pitt Building, Trumpington Street, Cambridge, United Kingdom

CAMBRIDGE UNIVERSITY PRESS
The Edinburgh Building, Cambridge CB2 2RU, UK
40 West 20th Street, New York, NY 10011–4211, USA
477 Williamstown Road, Port Melbourne, VIC 3207, Australia
Ruiz de Alarcón 13, 28014 Madrid, Spain
Dock House, The Waterfront, Cape Town 8001, South Africa

http://www.cambridge.org

First published 2002

Printed in the United Kingdom at the University Press, Cambridge

Typeface Times 10/12 pt.   *System* LATEX 2$_\varepsilon$ [TB]

A catalogue record for this book is available from the British Library

Library of Congress Cataloguing in Publication Data
Romani, Roberto.
National character and public spirit in Britain and France, 1750–1914 / Roberto Romani.
    p.   cm.
Includes bibliographical references and index.
ISBN 0 521 81000 0
1. National characteristics, British – History.   2. National characteristics, French –
History.   3. Public interest – Great Britain – History.   4. Public interest – France –
History.   5. Great Britain – Intellectual life.   6. France – Intellectual life.   I. Title.
DA470 .R66   2002
941.07 – dc21   2001037399

ISBN 0 521 81000 0 hardback

Contents

Acknowledgements   *page* vii
List of abbreviations   viii

Introduction   1

Part I   1750–1850

France

1   All Montesquieu's sons: the place of *esprit général*,
    caractère national, and *mœurs* in French political
    philosophy, 1748–1789   19

2   After the Revolution: Staël on political morality   63

3   From republicanism to industrialism and national character:
    Melchiorre Gioja, Charles Dupin, and Continental political
    economy, 1800–1848   93

4   The French Restoration dispute over mores
    and Tocqueville   122

Great Britain

5   Between Whiggism and the science of manners: Britain,
    1750–1800   159

6   British views on Irish national character, 1800–1846   201

Part II   1850–1914

7   The demise of John Bull: social sciences in Britain,
    1850–1914   231

vi

8   Durkheim's collective representations and their background   271

9   Socializing public spirit, 1870–1914   305

    Conclusion   335

Index   344

Acknowledgements

This book was conceived, and most of the research behind it carried out, while I was a Leverhulme Fellow of the Centre for History and Economics of King's College, Cambridge, and a Research Fellow of Darwin College, Cambridge. I am very grateful to both the Directors of the Centre, Emma Rothschild and Gareth Stedman Jones, and the then Master of Darwin College, Geoffrey Lloyd, for providing me with the ideal environment in which to work. I also wish to express my gratitude to the Leverhulme Trust for financing my research, and to the John D. and Catherine T. MacArthur Foundation for supporting its final stage. Earlier versions of chapters 1 and 6 first appeared, under the same titles, in article form: chapter 1 in *Studies on Voltaire and the Eighteenth Century*, 362 (1998), pp. 189–235, and chapter 6 in *History of European Ideas*, 23 (1997), pp. 193–219. I thank the Voltaire Foundation and Elsevier Science for their permission to reproduce this material. I have received advice and encouragement from many people during my work on this book. My thanks are especially due to Eugenio Biagini, Emma Rothschild, and Donald Winch, who have discussed, criticized, and supported my project over the course of five years. Among the friends and colleagues who have helped me by commenting on earlier versions of parts of the book are Eugenio Biagini, Robert Collison Black, Geoffrey Lloyd, Emma Rothschild, Philippe Steiner, Richard Whatmore, and Donald Winch. But my greatest debt in this respect is to Michael Bentley, who has read the whole script and made a number of fruitful suggestions for corrections and improvements. Of course, I accept full responsibility for any errors which remain in the book, and for its many shortcomings. I am glad of this opportunity to recognize the various kinds of help I have received from Daniela Donnini Macciò, Manolo Ferrante, Inga Huld Markan, Maurizio Isabella, Susanne Lohmann, Asha Patel, Amy Price, Massimo Rubboli, Rupert Wilkinson, and Carlo Zappia. Andrew Cresswell has checked my English, patiently and resourcefully. I dedicate this book, with gratitude, to Aurelio Macchioro, who, as a historian, a partisan against the Nazis and fascists in 1943–5, and a public-spirited citizen, embodies many of the civic virtues which are the subject of this book.

Abbreviations

Periodical publications

AS	*L'année sociologique*
BM	*Blackwood's Edinburgh Magazine*
CE	*Le censeur européen*
ER	*Edinburgh Review*
LG	*Le globe*
MF	*La Minerve française*
MR	*Monthly Review*
QR	*Quarterly Review*
RE	*Revue encyclopédique*

Montesquieu

EDL	*De l'esprit des lois*, ed. V. Goldschmidt (1748; 1757 edn, 2 vols, Paris, 1979)
LP, followed by letter number	*Lettres persanes*, ed. J. Starobinski (1721; 1758 edn, Paris, 1973)
OC	*Œuvres complètes*, ed. R. Caillois (2 vols., Paris, 1949–51)
OCL	*Œuvres complètes*, ed. E. Laboulaye (7 vols., Paris, 1875–9)

Adam Smith

TMS	*The Theory of Moral Sentiments* (1759), ed. D. D. Raphael and A. L. Macfie
WN	*An Inquiry into the Nature and Causes of the Wealth of Nations* (1776), ed. R. H. Campbell, A. S. Skinner, and W. B. Todd

References to these works, which are to be found in *The Glasgow Edition of the Works and Correspondence of Adam Smith* (6 vols., Oxford, 1976–87), follow the paragraph system.

Tocqueville

TOPC *Œuvres, papiers et correspondances*, ed. J.-P. Mayer et al.
(16 vols., Paris, 1951–)

DA *De la démocratie en Amérique* (1835–40), ed. J.-P. Mayer, *TOPC*,
I, in two books

Collected works

BCW *The Collected Works of Walter Bagehot*, ed. N. St John-Stevas
(15 vols., London, 1965–86).

BOC L. de Bonald, *Œuvres complètes* (3 vols., Paris, 1864)

BWS *The Writings and Speeches of Edmund Burke*, ed. P. Langford et al.
(7 vols., Oxford, 1981–)

CO Condorcet, *Œuvres*, ed. A. Condorcet O'Connor and F. Arago
(12 vols., Paris, 1847–9)

COC F.-R. de Chateaubriand, *Œuvres complètes* (5 vols., Paris, 1836)

DOC D. Diderot, *Œuvres complètes*, ed. R. Lewinter (15 vols., Paris,
1969–73)

GOM M. Gioja, *Opere minori* (17 vols., Lugano, 1832–7)

HCW W. Hazlitt, *Complete Works*, ed. P. P. Howe, A. R. Waller, and
A. Glover (21 vols., London and Toronto, 1930–4)

MCC Mably, *Collection complète des œuvres*, ed. G. Arnoux
and P. Friedemann (1794–5; 15 vols., Darmstadt, 1977)

MOC J. Michelet, *Œuvres complètes*, ed. P. Viallaneix
(21 vols., Paris, 1971–)

MCW *The Collected Works of John Stuart Mill*,
ed. J. M. Robson et al. (33 vols., Toronto and London, 1963–91)

SOC Mme de Staël, *Œuvres complètes* (18 vols., Paris-Bruxelles,
1820–1)

SSO C. H. de Saint-Simon, *Œuvres* (6 vols., Paris, 1966)

TO *Œuvres de Turgot et documents le concernant*, ed. G. Schelle
(5 vols., Paris, 1913–23)

VOC Voltaire, *Œuvres complètes*, ed. L. Moland (52 vols., Paris,
1877–85)

Introduction

1 The ambiguities of national character

This book deals with the history of national character in European political and economic thought, c.1750–c.1914. It considers British, French, and, to a lesser extent, Italian authors – the latter being included to provide a comparison with a viewpoint originating from circumstances very different from those of Britain and France, where national unification and consolidation were achieved much earlier. The names of Montesquieu, Hume, Staël, Tocqueville, Carlyle, Mill, Taine, Durkheim, or Marshall suffice to demonstrate that national character was a cornerstone of social thought in the period in question. Attention has often been paid to the relevance of the theme in single authors, but national character has not become a standard point of reference to assess their contributions, and an overarching treatment, which narrated the vicissitudes of the idea rather than those of its exponents, has so far been lacking.[1]

Regarding an initial definition of national character, the one offered by Ernest Barker is only apparently banal: 'a mental organization connecting the minds of all the members of a national community by ties and connections as fine as silk and as firm as steel'.[2] Barker suggests the strength of national character, seemingly paradoxical in view of its non-materiality. I would go further by arguing that it benefits from a radical abstractness, which derives from the impossibility of assessing with any precision either its attributes or the range and efficacy of its effects. Even the most refined analyses carried out by social scientists today cannot make the idea any less elusive.[3] It is in its elusiveness that

---

[1] That is not to say that the last few decades have been barren. Apart from contributions by historians on single authors and those by social scientists, chiefly social psychologists and business studies scholars, on national attitudes, the works dealing with the Victorian version of character are particularly notable; see esp. S. Collini, 'The Idea of Character: Private Habits and Public Virtues', in his *Public Moralists* (Oxford, 1991), pp. 91–118. For a survey of French thought on a subject closely related to national character, see T. Todorov, *Nous et les autres: la réflexion française sur la diversité humaine* (Paris, 1989). A book to which I am most indebted, similar to my own for inspiration and method but for the lack of a comparative approach, is G. Bollati, *L'Italiano: il carattere nazionale come storia e come invenzione* (Turin, 1983).

[2] E. Barker, *National Character and the Factors in Its Formation* (1927; London, 1939), p. 4.

[3] See, e.g., D. Peabody, *National Characteristics* (1985; 2nd edn, Cambridge and Paris, 1988).

the secret of the fortunes of national character lies: as potentially all-embracing, it is able to be all-powerful, or at any rate decisive as a final and independent cause. Yet the constant attraction of national character to social thinkers would be unimaginable if it was not real at least to an extent. It is an intriguing notion because, for example, it would be foolish to deny that the English are different from the French only because we are unable to determine precisely, on empirical grounds, the manifestations, degree, and consequences of their difference. Although I could not agree more with Max Weber's statement that 'the appeal to national character is generally a mere confession of ignorance', there is indeed a grain of truth in the conventional wisdom about the various dispositions of peoples.[4] The size of this grain, and especially what to make of it, is another matter.

It is a peculiarity of national character that it is as likely to surface in a piece of communitarian critique as in a commentary on a football game, or in a text-book on international competition as in journalistic tirades about Frenchness or Englishness. Even a widely exploited catchword like 'national identity', which nowadays sounds more 'modern' than the stereotype-laden 'national character', often amounts to the same old stuff and proves equally over-comprehensive, and, in the end, equally elusive. In the spheres of academia, journalism, and politics, concerns with the character and the quality of citizens (either fellow citizens or those of other countries) variously recur, matched by the versatility of national character as a folk notion: something ordinary people resort to in order to account for the most disparate facts, from a country's parking habits to its military proficiency, from the efficiency of its tourist facilities to the tone of its political life.[5] It is my belief that national character needs historical concep-tualization in order to be dealt with more consciously by those who care about intellectual discipline and clarity – in view of the support the idea may give to xenophobia and nationalism, this is no trivial task.

Having said that national character is an inherently abstract concept, natu-rally tending to comprehensiveness, some specifications of the book's scope are needed. First, I am interested in the ways in which a depiction of a national character was put to use, rather than in national character in itself or its va-lidity as an explanatory tool. My goal is not to trace successive portraits of, say, English character but to show how a certain idea of the English worked within a definite framework of thought, and, in particular, to spotlight the pur-poses it served. Generally (and also relatively) speaking, highbrow depictions of national characters have not varied much over the centuries and have been close relatives of lowbrow national stereotypes. Traditional images of peoples,

---

[4] M. Weber, *The Protestant Ethic and the Spirit of Capitalism*, trans. T. Parsons (1904–5; London and New York, 1958), p. 88.

[5] I was moved to write this book by a search for answers to questions like these (yes, even regarding parking habits which put me, as a cyclist in Florence, in constant danger), at the time that the magnitude of corruption in the Italian political system was unearthed (1993–5).

in some cases dating back to the early modern era or even the Middle Ages, may be traced at the base of the observations of even the most sophisticated pre-1914 social scientist. That is not to say that no alteration in national portraits occurred in the period of relevance here, but that it was marked by continuity rather than change; variations were usually subtle, and always maintained a link with the previous depiction. What did in fact change was the portion of the population taken to represent the national character. Typically, while the French philosophers of the eighteenth century limited their analysis to the leisured classes, thought to be the whole *nation*, post-revolutionary authors progressively extended their perspective to encompass all ranks. This extension, and the ways in which it occurred, is one of the major strands of my narrative.

The second specification follows from the first, and regards the variety and range of problems encompassed by 'national character'. Linking certain places to certain attitudes has been a constant preoccupation of the human mind since the Greeks at least. This is one of the discursive practices weaving Western civilization, covering a number of topics and standpoints touching on geography, politics, philosophy, medicine, and so on. Evidently then, because of geographical and chronological boundaries as well as politico-economic focus, the book considers only a fraction of a mammoth story. But this fraction has distinctive traits which mark it out, in spite of the long ancestry of the problem which lies at the core of writing on national character in the period 1750–1914: the relationship between a free government (and/or a market economy) and the quality of citizens. In other words, to return to a previous statement, national character was prevalently put to use in political and economic thought to assess this relationship. This is the essential viewpoint, albeit a very general one, which defines the subject matter of this book. National character was a vehicle, though one that entailed certain arguments and viewpoints to the exclusion of others. The book's main thread is variation in the discussion of national dispositions conveying the issue of peoples' suitability for liberty.

The following chapters are intended to explore two related contentions. The first is that, in the wake of Pocock and Skinner, the viewpoint of citizens' aptness for liberty should be distinguished from the specific idioms in which it was expressed. Republicanism of Machiavellian or Harringtonian origin should not subsume it; considering republicanism as an episode, albeit widely influential, seems in effect legitimate.[6] The issue of civic qualities (or civic virtues, or public spirit, and all other possible synonyms) has a history which is in itself larger than any particular strand of thought. That is, this history is complex and multifaceted, with each phase of it involving more than a single idiom – for instance, both that of civic humanism and that of climatology

---

[6] On republicanism, see esp. J. G. A. Pocock, *The Machiavellian Moment* (Princeton, 1975). See chapter 3 below for a fuller discussion.

in the case of eighteenth-century France – and with the relevance of definite idioms in the articulation of public spirit themes progressively fading in the face of novel historical scenarios and problems. Bringing in Montesquieu's *esprit général* and Hume's 'national character' as the starting points of analysis places civic qualities in fitting discursive contexts, allowing for a richer variety of motifs. My second contention is the pervasiveness of the issue of citizens' dispositions over the period under consideration. In spite of the widespread abandonment of civic republican tenets after the French Revolution in general and the Terror in particular, the question of the intrinsic relationship between government and citizens' attitudes gained momentum throughout the nineteenth century, when representative institutions were set up in France and other Continental countries. Later in the century, the focus shifted towards the adequacy of the human material to the demands of a mass society.

In the eighteenth century, a tradition of thought about national character, with its stress on climate, human physiology, and type of government as factors, intertwined with another tradition, that of civic humanism, whose leitmotivs were virtue, independence, and participation. The two traditions sometimes coexisted in the same writer, in spite of the potential contrast between the situated outlook of the former and the universalism of the latter. Yet the frames of reference were not the same on the two sides of the Channel. The presence in Britain of an indigenous idiom, that of Whiggism in its pre- and post-Burkean incarnations, introduced major differences between the two countries. In France, there progressively developed a concern with 'public spirit' – that is, social discipline, responsibility in electoral choices, a sense of interdependence and belonging, and the willingness to operate and develop the institutions of self-government – as an indispensable element for the effective workings of free institutions and a complex society. From this angle, the crux of the matter was not the temperament of a people derived from race or history (its peculiarly 'national' traits), but a set of attitudes of potentially universal application. The full emergence in Restoration France of this perspective, following the popularity of classical republicanism among the eighteenth-century *philosophes*, drawing inspiration from the pugnacious tradition of British Whiggism, and preceding the theories of citizenship of late Victorian and Edwardian Britain, provides an essential point of reference within the book. In accordance with my first contention above, I regard the 'civic' thinking running through the nineteenth century as an original intellectual phenomenon, motivated by the political and social problems of the day, in spite of its obvious antecedents. One of these was eighteenth-century Whiggism: the belief in the suitability of the English for liberty, and in their determination to defend it, effectively conveyed 'public spirit' themes. Yet the nature of Whiggism was strictly insular, resting as it did on a disparaging judgement of the French as a complement to national self-assurance.

In documenting the gradual emergence of a separate 'civic' standpoint from national character discourse, the book shows that other approaches addressing citizens' dispositions were not dismissed altogether over the nineteenth century. There was, on the one hand, a racial or racialist standpoint, and on the other, there were various forms of the environmentalist stance, like the climatological, the political–institutional, or the sociological; and sometimes racial and environmental viewpoints were inextricably mixed. It is only an apparent paradox that in the final decades of the nineteenth century the boost to the establishment of the social scientific approach, with its refined forms of environmentalism, came from evolutionary biology. The effect of Darwinism was nothing less than a new conceptualization of man, resulting from a fresh emphasis on the collective dimension of life coupled with a richer and more momentous notion of environment. Durkheim, whose 'collective representation' represents the most thorough effort of the social scientific approach, built on this basis.

A useful criterion for discriminating among writers is whether national character was seen as an effect of institutions and in particular of government (a perspective endorsed by many, but not all, eighteenth-century writers), or a cause of the establishment and performance of institutions (as many, but not all, nineteenth-century authors believed). Even some of those who in principle acknowledged the interplay of the two elements may on close scrutiny show a preference for one view or the other.[7] At first sight, this criterion may look quite odd: for it is a very plausible supposition that within a country the interaction of citizens and institutions induces a parallel and mutual determination, so that the two elements would be, in practice, inextricable. Yet this picture may suit England, where representative government in the modern sense originated; elsewhere, setting up free institutions entailed in most cases a break with the past, from which there arose the possibility of a mismatch between political machinery and dispositions.

Given the book's aim to provide a narrative of the lines of development in the perception of peoples' and citizens' attitudes, two difficulties arise. First, the broad scope of the issue, as well as its popularity over the period, make an attempt at a complete treatment impossible. It follows that the plan of the book might have turned out differently. Other stories, with other protagonists and other plots, may equally be on the mark, not least in view of the limitations I have set myself. Highly educated opinion as expressed by political philosophy and the social sciences has been dealt with, but of course the subject

---

[7] For a formulation of these two main approaches approximating my own, although posited with the analysis of civic virtue in view, see Q. Skinner, *The Foundations of Modern Political Thought* (2 vols., Cambridge, 1978), I, pp. 44–5. Skinner juxtaposes Hume as the greatest exponent of the primacy-of-institutions outlook with Machiavelli and Montesquieu, who most authoritatively spread the idea that 'it is not so much the machinery of government as the proper *spirit* of the rulers, the people and the laws which needs above all to be sustained', p. 45.

recurred in popular culture, as well as in travel reports, a form of literature situated between the two extremes. To limit the ground to cover and to spotlight the Anglo-French connection, the issues stemming from the encounters with extra-European peoples have been excluded from consideration. The 'race' figuring most in the book is the Celtic, or perhaps the Teuton, one, and not, say, the Black. Furthermore, research has been limited to published material, including posthumous pieces written for publication (or the classroom) but excluding those connected with personal life; a public discourse, like that addressed in this book, is not necessarily reflected by private correspondence or diaries. To give a significant example, the chapter on British opinion on the Irish would have delineated a significantly different picture if private papers had been taken into account. Finally, in a book devoted to national character the lack of specific and lengthy consideration of John Stuart Mill, the advocate of 'ethology', may appear surprising. But in view of the amount of recent literature on Mill and character, it should not. Mill is in fact called into play twice, in chapters 7 and 9.

The second and more substantial difficulty encountered in achieving the objective of providing a connected narrative, rather than a collection of essays, is the relevance of contexts. Besides the unquestionable existence of recognizable threads running from the *Esprit des lois* to 1914, it is equally unquestionable that the history of the idea of national character (in my sense) owes much to specific, circumscribed debates, where the combination of particular events and situations with old or new arguments determined stances affecting successive views of collective mentalities and habits. Yet it would be wrong to believe that national character was discussed either in abstract terms – as a concept of social and political thought, that is – or in order to tackle specific and situated questions, since the two perspectives regularly merged. For instance, Montesquieu's idea of *esprit général* was intended to support the claims of the *noblesse de robe*; the 'Whig' picture of the English served egregiously to defend the post-revolutionary arrangement first, and to foster the enlargement of the franchise later; Hobson's model personality was thought of as a response to new social pressures; in spite of all its social scientific refinement, Durkheim's concept of collective representation originated from a reflection on France's instability; and so on. National character was a matter of both conceptualized thought and situated interests and power, as all chapters illustrate, albeit in different degrees.

A first consequence of this twofold level of discourse is that some minor authors, and even sets of anonymous articles, have been considered to complement the contributions coming from the *maîtres à penser*. More fundamentally, there arises in principle a choice between a treatment focused on issues – say, notions of Englishness in the debate over the first Reform Act, or changing views of French mentality between the Jacobins and Napoleon, or the linkages established between economic performance and peoples' attitudes in the reports about the industrial exhibitions – and a treatment focused on authors. I have been led to prefer the latter approach by, first, my prevalent interest in high culture, and, second, by my concern with the theme of the shift from national character to 'civic' views, a concern calling for a treatment as co-ordinated as possible. Given this option, the Irish chapter amounts to an exception, grounded in the view that Ireland was the crucial battlefield for British literati at a time when the images of both Englishness and Frenchness were so firmly established in British culture as to make their further investigation unpromising; on the other hand, many eminent authors of the age, from the economists to Carlyle and Macaulay, wrote on Irish character. Although the book does not deal with all possible contexts or specific issues, all the writers considered are set within their historical milieux.

As for the watersheds of my story, which account for the division of the subject matter into two parts, the French Revolution figures as the focal point of the period 1750–1850, and then there is the consolidation of procedures and patterns of thought into the 'social sciences' during the second half of the nineteenth century. It is relevant to specify that the character spoken about was that of men, not of women. From Montesquieu onwards, the attitudes of the latter were thought to be part of the national mind only to the extent of their influence over men. Incidentally, many authors of the eighteenth and early and mid nineteenth century, especially in Britain, regarded the mere existence of this influence as a symptom of a faulty national character. Although men's view of women changed much within the period, the absolute prevalence of men as objects of evaluations of collective mentalities remained until at least 1914.

2   Climate and government: the discourse on national character

The roots of the connection between liberty and national character stretch back for centuries. The Greeks came to define their civilization and themselves in terms of liberty, in contrast with the 'despotic' kingdoms of Asia; since that time, the qualities required from the citizenry of a free community have provided a fundamental focus for national character discourses. The use of the term 'discourse', reminiscent of Foucault and Skinner, is not casual. National character as a political notion was talked about according to customary patterns for a very long time, spanning from antiquity to the end of the eighteenth century. This was a 'discourse' in the sense that the same arguments recurred, differently assembled, in spite of the variation of contexts and writers' intentions over the centuries. Authors introduced substantial innovations neither in viewpoint nor in the causal chains used to account for national characters, although they did stretch the meaning and implications of the traditional motifs.

With regard to the themes and approaches formulated before Montesquieu, with whom my treatment begins, it is impossible here to make more than a few sketchy remarks about the crucial dualism of climate and government – of physico-geographical and political motifs, that is – as factors of collective character.[8] Antiquity abounds with statements about the efficacy of both. Greek ethnology was marked by the belief that racial and cultural differences were caused by climate, a view refined by the Hippocratic school of medicine with its investigations of the effects of 'airs, waters, and places' on peoples' characters.[9] Aristotle distinguishes between the suitability for liberty of peoples living in cold, hot, and mild climates; in the same *Politics*, one also finds passages about the need for public education to mould the citizen in accordance with the form of government: 'for each government has a peculiar character which originally formed and which continues to preserve it'.[10] The demoralization and humiliation of subjects is shown to be a chief means for the perpetuation of a tyranny; conversely, in *Nicomachean Ethics* it is said that the true statesman makes citizens good and law-abiding.[11] Plato's *Laws* contains themes which will recur again and again in my book, like the effects of climate and natural environment on the character of citizens, the necessity of laying down laws that do not fly in the face of such influences, and the political importance of unwritten rules and customs.[12] Generally speaking, Greek and Roman political thinking pointed out the power of laws and institutions to change attitudes, the Lycurgan constitution being cited ceaselessly as an instance of laws establishing customs; yet Solon was equally popular as champion of the argument that dispositions should determine legislation.

These patterns of thought maintained their power and vitality until the eighteenth century; hence there was established an unbroken tradition about the characteristics of peoples, whose recurrent motifs passed on from one author to the other. In early modern times it became a sort of axiom that Northern peoples were liberty-loving, in parallel with the revival of the theory about the softening effects of an overly generous nature.[13] As Machiavelli for instance illustrates,

[8] A fundamental reference is C. J. Glacken, *Traces on the Rhodian Shore: Nature and Culture in Western Thought from Ancient Times to the End of the Eighteenth Century* (Berkeley, 1967).
[9] As vehicles of ethnological knowledge, see, e.g., Herodotus' histories, some of the dramatists' works, and the Hippocratic corpus. Thucydides' comparison between the collective mentalities of Spartans and Athenians is a celebrated early piece of evidence of the explanatory potential of national characters: *History of the Peloponnesian War*, trans. C. Foster Smith (4 vols., London and New York, 1919), I, bk I, lxx–lxxi.
[10] *The Politics*, trans. J. Barnes (Cambridge, 1995), 1260b10–20, 1276b15–35, 1288a5–20, 1310a10–20, 1327b20–38, 1337a10–30; the quotation is on 1337a15.
[11] *ibid.*, 1313a20–1314a30; *The Nicomachean Ethics*, trans. J. A. K. Thomson and H. Tredennick (Harmondsworth, 1976), 1102a5–12, 1103a14–26.
[12] *The Laws*, trans. T. J. Saunders (Harmondsworth, 1975), esp. 704–8, 747, 788, 793. For civic virtue as the purpose of education, see 643–5.
[13] Glacken, *Traces*, pp. 429–60.

some argued that laws could offset the undesired consequences of the natural environment; they should be devised with that aim in view.[14] It is hardly necessary to mention how Machiavelli's political construction, elaborating on the Roman moralists', focused on the interrelatedness between laws and citizens' patriotic virtues (their *bontà*: orderly behaviour, prudence, determination, martial spirit, honesty). From a standpoint very different from that of Machiavelli, Saint Augustine had already construed the worldly success of the Romans as a reward from God for their qualities of character.[15] The continuing success of ideals of public virtue well into the French seventeenth century is testified by Fénelon's *Télémaque*. Here the focus was on the king's capacity to create good *mœurs* (sobriety, frugality, industry, patience, attachment to liberty, martial courage, and modesty in women) through laws.[16] Bodin, a fundamental influence on Montesquieu and an authoritative advocate of the theory of humours as channels of climatic causes, held the same view as Machiavelli on the potential of laws over the natural environment.[17] From authors like Machiavelli, Bodin, Fénelon, Fontenelle, Du Bos, and Arbuthnot, Montesquieu inherited a combination of Hippocratic inspiration, climatological determinism, insights into the limits of government action, civic values, and an awareness of national character.

This 'paradigm', so to speak, came under progressively intensifying attacks in the second half of the eighteenth century, and did not survive the Revolution. With particular respect to France, it is arguable that the years 1789–1815 opened a new phase, in which the traditional clusters of argument gave way to fresh departures. It is true that these departures may have reworked the civic humanist legacy, but the straitjacket of a conventional set of motifs had gone, together with the feeling of continuity with the ancients, at a time when public morality appeared to many French of increasing importance but also dangerously out of control. As was often observed over the first decades of the nineteenth century, the Revolution had not only impaired the traditional sources of allegiance (the prestige of the monarch and religion, essentially), but had also jeopardized the very notion of social hierarchies. The people's frenzy during the Terror, which haunted the ruling classes for decades, posed questions about the political dispositions of the mass of the French which Napoleon's authoritarian regime left unanswered. It is not surprising, then, that the Restoration witnessed a debate on national character and public spirit, a debate which presents original features.

---

[14] *Discorsi sopra la prima deca di Tito Livio* (1513–21), in N. Machiavelli, *Il Principe ed altre opere politiche*, ed. S. Andretta (Milan, 1997), bk I, ch. 1, pp. 105–8.
[15] *The City of God*, trans. H. Bettenson (413–26; Harmondsworth, 1972), bk V, chs. 15–16.
[16] *Les aventures de Télémaque*, ed. J.-L. Goré (1699; Paris, 1994). My thanks to Emma Rothschild for first indicating to me the relevance of Fénelon to the French Enlightenment.
[17] Glacken, *Traces*, pp. 434–47.

At this juncture speaking of an established 'discourse' on national character is no longer appropriate, because post-revolutionary writers perceived the problems of the age as radically novel, and, although their predecessors could give inspiration, they could no longer offer a set of ready-made conceptual frameworks. A major casualty of this recognition was natural environmentalism of classical origin, and faith vacillated even apropos the educational power of liberty – now conceived as embedded in representative institutions. The social world came to be construed as rapidly changing, in contrast with the static perception of the previous ages; this understanding could not but undermine the explanatory relevance of climate. The creation of representative governments in France caused bitter frustration and bewilderment, since they proved incapable of guaranteeing social discipline and participation. The political settings ushered in at first by the Revolution and then by the Restoration ought to have entailed that civic virtues, which had been a literary and philosophic ideal throughout the eighteenth century, turned into a mass practice. That this did not happen had the effect of shifting the focus from free institutions to the underlying qualities making up 'public spirit'. As regards Britain, where no constitutional discontinuity occurred, a post-revolutionary break in the traditional discourse on national character is less easily discernible, not least because of its features there. Climate, for instance, had been regularly dismissed throughout the second half of the eighteenth century, and the Scottish philosophers had introduced new social environmentalist approaches. However, while Burke's *Reflections on the Revolution in France* did determine a shift in the national self-image in obscuring its defiant, 'republican' traits, military and economic dominance allayed previously widespread fears of moral decline of civic humanist origin.

The French Revolution itself can be seen as a consequence of profound social changes affecting the whole of Europe. It is arguable that, at the basis of the loss of grip of civic humanist patterns, there lay the rise of 'commercial society'.[18] The turning point, in perception if not in actual fact, came over the course of the eighteenth century in Britain, and during the revolutionary and Napoleonic years in France. In a traditional community, centred on the possession of real property as the criterion of independence and leadership, large family units involving relations of dependence, strong neighbourhood relations, and service in the militia, civic virtues naturally stemmed from feelings of affection as well as the self-interest of each freeman. A share in local government could look like an extension of the role of household master, while martial bravery was dictated by

---

[18] Notable contributions to the definition of this concept are: P. G. M. Dickson, *The Financial Revolution in England: a Study in the Development of Public Credit 1688–1756* (1967; Aldershot, 1993); I. Kramnick, *Bolingbroke and His Circle* (1968; Ithaca and London, 1992); I. Hont and M. Ignatieff, eds., *Wealth and Virtue: the Shaping of Political Economy in the Scottish Enlightenment* (Cambridge, 1983); J. G. A. Pocock, *Barbarism and Religion* (2 vols., Cambridge, 1999), I, *The Enlightenments of Edward Gibbon*, esp. pp. 95–109.

the fact that the family, fortune, and liberty of each combatant were at stake in a war.[19] In contrast, a commercial society is composed by definition of individuals pursuing their own private businesses; they are as separate from each other as everybody is separate from public concerns. In obeisance to the social division of labour, militias are replaced by standing armies, while the dynamics of the modern economy corrode the structure of ranks and tend to sever communal relations. As they no longer entail a direct participation in the life of the polity, so the concepts of freedom and virtue are changed in the directions of, respectively, freedom from restraint and personal honesty. Self-interest does not include participation when each citizen is engrossed in economic activities, nuclear families relate to the private sphere, and international laws make defeat less momentous for the individual. However, one of the main contentions of this book is that not only prudence and commercial probity were insisted upon within the framework of commercial society. The necessity of updated civic virtues (namely, of what is here labelled 'public spirit') for the efficient and just workings of free institutions continued to be affirmed throughout the nineteenth century, albeit in the awareness of the problematic nature of these virtues in the age of individualism and equality.

3   La Bruyère, Shaftesbury, and Muralt

Although closely interrelated, the histories of France and Britain differ remarkably, with the former country preoccupied with the faults of the national mind which made liberty so fragile after 1815, and the latter sanguine about the mental dispositions which guaranteed the solidity and continuation of representative institutions. This is why in the first part more attention is paid to France (chapters 1–4) than Britain (chapters 5–6). In France, as in Italy, the relevant thinkers found themselves in opposition to governments, and their countries in constant institutional turmoil; hence there was a more pressing, and more anxiously posited, concern with the traits of one's own national character. If on the Continent there were recurrent waves of self-criticism, these had no counterpart in Britain, at least in the second half of the period covered in part I.[20] For the formation of the self-image of the English as 'noble and free' by history and providential design, the seventeenth century represents of course a turning point: then, to adopt the idiom of the time, the original and natural rights of the

---

[19] See Q. Skinner, 'The Idea of Negative Liberty: Philosophical and Historical Perspectives', in R. Rorty, J. B. Schneewind, and Q. Skinner, eds., *Philosophy in History* (Cambridge, 1984), esp. pp. 217–19.

[20] Even when the English were labelled as 'stupid' by radicals like J. S. Mill or Bulwer Lytton, or by Bagehot, these writers were actually taking up a traditional motif, which, in the form of the Englishman's practical nature or stubbornness, accompanied rather than denied the positive image of John Bull. For the oscillations of a radical, see the treatment of Hazlitt in chapter 5 below.

English people retaliated against the Norman yoke. In the revolutionary tracts, the people were being presented as a repository of virtues trampled on by tyrants, and as the single legitimate source of power. These motifs, of radical origin, came in a sense to be confirmed by Locke's *Two Treatises of Government*, where the right of resistance to unjust political authority was made to depend on the judgement of each individual adult. For Locke, a ruler had the right to command his subjects only in so far as these agreed; in the case of England, the people had demonstrated they possessed a mature political judgement by resisting irresponsible and unjust kings by force. By contrast, in an absolute monarchy like France, similar understanding and determination were unable to take root.[21]

At the turn of the seventeenth century, three famous texts reveal a great degree of unanimity in the attitudes towards liberty of the French and the English, respectively. Written in 1688, La Bruyère's attack on the courtier morality of *les grands* – displaying servility, frivolity, a taste for pomp and luxury, and a habit of intrigue – anticipated the eighteenth-century philosophers. La Bruyère was an early instance of a French writer alienated from his own fellow citizens; he consciously and explicitly judged them by totally alien criteria, and it could not be otherwise, he wrote, since 'there is no *patrie* under a despotism'. La Bruyère's 'external' viewpoint fed on his adoption of the ancients as standard-setters in moral matters. Although the passions of ruling men have not changed since the time of Athens, its citizens were free, and this made all the difference with respect to moral attitudes. Athens was a republic of equal citizens, who led simple lives rather than imitating one another at a court; they socialized in the public spaces of the city, combining business and learning with pleasure; and government was their own concern – La Bruyère exclaimed, finally: what a people, and what a city! Like Montesquieu's *Lettres persanes*, *Les caractères* rested on an acute awareness of the historical and geographical relativity of French mores, that is to say, of how odd and unnatural they seemed when assessed from a vantage point.[22] In the eighteenth century, French *mœurs* would be the subject of discussion in all Europe, with fashion, brilliance and ease in conversation, and a new social role for women, taken to represent a new facet of civilization, however this facet was judged.

Shaftesbury, too, was critical of his countrymen, whom he accused of being prone to excessive 'enthusiasm' – that is, religious fanaticism – and lack of refinement. But, at bottom, he had no doubts about either the public virtues of Englishmen or the substance of their liberties. In *Characteristics*, a key relationship is established between 'public spirit' and a free government; namely,

---

[21] *Two Treatises of Government*, ed. P. Laslett (1689; Cambridge, 1967), esp. II, secs. 138, 223, 228, 230, 240. See J. Dunn, *Locke* (Oxford, 1984), pp. 22–59.

[22] *Les caractères ou les mœurs de ce siècle* (1688–94; Paris, 1993), esp. 'Discours sur Théophraste', pp. 18–21, and ch. 12, pp. 285–6; quotation in ch. 10, p. 221; the eulogy of Athens is paraphrased from the 'Discours sur Théophraste', pp. 20–1.

'morality and good government go together'. On the one hand, a sense of part-nership can only spring from political equality and the rule of law; on the other, a free constitution needs a public opinion that expresses just views on 'the balance of power and property'. The whole political process is essentially underlain by moral sentiments, on the grounds that the 'real love of virtue' requires 'the knowledge of public good', and this knowledge is based in turn on a 'common sense' of moral origin.[23] For Shaftesbury, the difference between a people and a multitude lies in the citizens' perception of a common good, and in the correlative application of the moral truths 'so firmly established in Nature itself' to operate the constitution.[24] England is animated by a 'noble ardour', pointing to 'a right disposition in our people towards the moral and instructive way'. Accordingly, English literature is not as polite or fashionable as French literature, but it has 'solid thought, strong reasoning, noble passion, and a continued thread of moral doctrine, piety, and virtue to recommend it'.[25] Shaftesbury advocated a notion of patriotism grounded on 'our political and social capacity' resulting from the Revolution, and he criticized 'the patriots of the soil' for their attachment to a physical idea of England. This is a 'Patria', he summarized, not a mere 'country'.[26]

The third example comes from the pen of a Swiss writer, the Berne aristocrat Béat-Louis de Muralt. His *Lettres sur les Anglois et les François* (1725) put the seal on the images of both peoples with an authority enhanced by Muralt's expected neutrality (actually, together with figures like Haller and Bodmer, he was seeking to strengthen Swiss identity against French influence). The book is a denunciation of French manners and habits, which are viewed as an aberration, a strange collective folly which warped the laws of nature and set in their place the artificial *par excellence* – the dictates of fashion. England serves as a positive standard of comparison, being depicted as the land of common sense and reason, of science, of a fierce independence, and especially of a spirit of liberty fuelled by a residue of ancient ferocity; whereas France is characterized by the dreary uniformity of custom, a passion for *esprit* which turns out to be vanity, a cult of exteriority, corruption of sexual mores, and political servility. What the French really care about and admire is 'l'esprit, la vivacité, la politesse, les manières' – here 'trifles rule', is Muralt's conclusion.[27] Although, quite clearly, he is depicting the aristocracy, he asserts that these traits are shared by 'the multitude'. Whereas in France everybody is a courtier 'by

---

[23] *Characteristics of Men, Manners, Opinions, Times, etc.*, ed. J. M. Robertson (1711; 2 vols., London, 1900), 'On the Freedom of Wit and Humour', I, pp. 72–3.
[24] *ibid.*, 'Miscellany III', II, pp. 244–5, fn.; 'Miscellany V', II, p. 344.
[25] *ibid.*, 'Advice to an Author', I, pp. 179–81, quotation on p. 180.
[26] *ibid.*, 'Miscellany III', II, pp. 244–50, quotation on p. 248.
[27] *Lettres sur les Anglois et les François et sur les voiages* [*sic*] (n.p., 1725), 'Lettres sur les François', pp. 177, 196.

inclination', in England the upper classes do not depend on the court, while the lower ranks neither depend on the rich and powerful nor fear and admire them.[28] Muralt saw a high degree of accord in the character and tastes of all classes of Englishmen, including the lower ones.[29]

In the *Lettres* as well as the other two texts considered, a necessary relationship between the morality of the citizens' everyday behaviour and good government is established; this relationship is a pillar of Western political thought, albeit usually an implicit one. When discussing national characters, the assumption that moral individuals are needed in a free and just state becomes momentous (less obvious, one is tempted to say), since it is intended that certain peoples are less suitable than others. The following chapters will show the ways in which this assumption was formulated and put to use in the differing contexts of France, Britain, and Italy.[30]

[28] See, e.g., *ibid.*, 'Lettres sur les Anglois', p. 7.
[29] *ibid.*, 'Lettres sur les Anglois', pp. 19–20, 76.
[30] A few practicalities should be settled before starting. All translations are my own unless otherwise indicated. As a rule, I have used the original French texts rather than the existing translations, to which additional reference is made only when longer passages are quoted. *Mœurs* has been customarily translated as 'mores' rather than 'manners', since the latter term has a particular association with the Scottish 'science of manners' of the second half of the eighteenth century. I have usually adopted each author's usage concerning the English/British terminology.

Part I

1750–1850

France

1 All Montesquieu's sons: the place of *esprit général, caractère national*, and *mœurs* in French political philosophy, 1748–1789

1 Introduction

This chapter does not focus on the multifaceted meaning of terms so widely used as *mœurs, manières*, or even *caractère national*.[1] Nor does it consider all aspects of the relevant literature. Montesquieu is taken as lodestar, following the early criticism of the *Esprit des lois* (1748) as well as the easily recognizable traces that this work left in later writings. The choice of Montesquieu is unsurprising, considering that the interpreters of the French Enlightenment have traditionally seen his work as seminal in many respects. Yet we must be on our guard against assuming any innovation, watershed, or sharp break within the tradition of thought about national characters – Montesquieu's masterpiece is no exception. The *Esprit des lois* was a universal reference for following writers, but this was neither because of its author's views on the influence of climates, nor because of his views on the effectiveness of political factors. It was clearly the frame and not the picture that made the difference. Montesquieu had turned the relationship between government and people's attitudes into an element within a comprehensive vision of politics, and this accounts for the lasting impression that the book made on contemporaries.

The *Esprit des lois* may be considered as the beginning of a fruitful tension within French pre-revolutionary thought between the postulates of classical political theory and in particular of civic humanism – which centred on citizens' virtues as both cause and effect of good government – and some tentative

---

[1] As regards the working meaning of these terms: *mœurs* relate to internal convictions and *manières* to external behaviour, but an intimate connection was thought to exist between the two. See A. M. Wilson, 'The Concept of *mœurs* in Diderot's Social and Political Thought', in W. H. Barber et al., eds., *The Age of the Enlightenment: Studies Presented to Theodore Besterman* (Edinburgh, 1967), pp. 188–99, where *mœurs* are defined as 'the internalization of control' (p.194). For a definition of *caractère national*, see the anonymous entry 'Caractère des nations' in *Encyclopédie, ou Dictionnaire raisonné des sciences, des arts et des métiers* (17 vols., Paris, 1751–65), II, p. 666: 'Le caractère d'une nation consiste dans une certaine disposition habituelle de l'âme, qui est plus commune chez une nation que chez une autre, quoique cette disposition ne se rencontre pas dans tous les membres qui composent la nation.'

explorations into the study of society and its dynamics.[2] The sway of the *Esprit des lois* was so wide that it might be tempting to characterize these decades through a contrast between Montesquieu's concept of *esprit général* and *mœurs*, where the former was a manifestation of the new 'science' of comparative politics, and the latter amounted to the traditional complement to republican government. These two strands of thought can be distinguished only for the sake of argument, however, even in Montesquieu's case; and, while *mœurs* were not only a component of the civic humanist discourse but also a notion used to describe and represent French society, Montesquieu's *esprit général*, if it did point to the relationship between government and society, was constructed with classical material. Although a line of development towards a social focus is indeed traceable, the scene appears far from straightforward because new insights were usually grafted onto old ones. The legacy of the past was manifold, with at least the climatic argument to be placed alongside civic humanism, and was remarkably vital. At the same time, the traditional frames of reference happened to convey 'social' topics like public opinion or criticism of *salon* mores. Additionally, the *philosophes* were progressively devising perspectives which could be subsumed within neither *esprit général* nor the classical patterns of political discourse. All this determined a situation where political idioms blended and interacted.

To give a momentous instance of this mix of languages, it is indisputable that civic humanism lay at the basis of the widely held opinion that there was neither national character, nor *patrie*, nor public virtues when the country was oppressed by despotism, because general interests were neglected in favour of private pursuits. But the moral effects of tyranny came also to be viewed from another standpoint, and probably an equally popular one. From Montesquieu's picture of Asian rule onwards, 'despotism' as a form of government was inextricably linked to the demoralization of the subjects under it, a sort of lethargic apathy that effectively made people able to bear the regime but which proved ruinous when the qualities of citizenship had to be practised. The concept of despotism, which in Montesquieu had strong associations with natural causes like climate and geographical location, became a crucial reference throughout the French Enlightenment by virtue of the perception of a political degeneration following the age of Louis XIV. The civic humanist approach smoothly

---

[2] On the revival of the classical and especially Roman republican theory of citizenship in Renaissance Europe and after, see esp. Q. Skinner, *The Foundations of Modern Political Thought* (2 vols., Cambridge, 1978), I; J. G. A. Pocock, *The Machiavellian Moment* (Princeton, 1975); and, by the same author, *Virtue, Commerce and History* (Cambridge, 1987). On the wide currency of themes like corruption of morality, depopulation, the moral depravity of towns, the idealization of the countryside, and patriotism in eighteenth-century France, see H. Chisick, *The Limits of Reform in the Enlightenment: Attitudes toward the Education of the Lower Classes in Eighteenth-Century France* (Princeton, 1981), esp. pp. 190–244. On the admiration for Spartan virtue in France, see E. Rawson, *The Spartan Tradition in European Thought* (Oxford, 1969), pp. 220–300.

combined with Montesquieu's notion of despotism – and, more generally, with climatology. Both helped to substantiate a critique of the nation's mores which is a kind of hallmark of the period. On the one hand, the patriotism, frugality, and independence of republican citizens served as a standard, and on the other, there emerged a view of France as a 'mild' despotism, with all its moral implications. It will be documented how a few definite structures of discourse were mixed in various and original ways under the stimulus of discontent. The notion of national character played a role in all the perspectives that gradually emerged over the period of interest: apart, that is, from *esprit général,* philosophical history, radical naturalism in both Rousseau's and Diderot's versions, and the utilitarian approach.

The authors considered made extensive use of the adjective 'national', attaching it to the expressions they employed to define the moral condition of people. Yet this terminological practice did not entail an endorsement of the characteristically nineteenth-century idea of nations as singular polities, predetermined by unique language, shared beliefs, history, or destiny. Rather, it was the typology of forms of government inherited from antiquity that provided French writers with *prima facie* criteria for the appraisal of countries, including their own. The philosophers' 'nations' were usually the peoples inhabiting existing states, whereas states themselves were often regarded as necessary but strictly utilitarian political devices.[3] Even state borders were often neglected in their assessments of collective manners and habits. Climate, for instance, when taken as a criterion for evaluating a people's character, was usually applied to vast areas of the globe (continents, for example) rather than to particular countries. The basic distinction within the climatological argument was more between North and South than between established states. That is not to say that there was an absence of patriotism in France – though I would point to its potentially universal rather than strictly French content.[4] At any rate, since the question of whether a French national identity existed before 1789 is still far from resolution, it is appropriate to say that my view chiefly rests on the evidence supplied by the *philosophes.*[5] Other sources may convey a different impression. One feature of 'nation', pointed out by some interpreters as one of its defining traits, namely, its original association with the process of enlargement of the political

---

[3] See T. J. Schlereth, *The Cosmopolitan Ideal in Enlightenment Thought* (Notre Dame, Ind., 1977).

[4] 'Typically, the "patriot" of eighteenth-century France was a man who had done something to promote the common good, such as, for example, writing a book on agriculture, or education, or ethics, or who had performed a signal act of beneficence.' Chisick, *The Limits of Reform,* p. 223.

[5] See D. Bell, 'Recent Works on Early Modern French National Identity', *Journal of Modern History,* 68 (1996), pp. 84–113. Bell notes the often varying use in recent historical literature of terms like 'nation', 'nationalism', 'national identity', etc.; as these terms happen to mean different things to different historians, the subject has become 'nebulous' (pp. 86–8).

community to previously excluded sectors of the population, will serve as the thread of the chapter.

2   Montesquieu

'Oh! Oh! Is he Persian? What a most extraordinary thing! How can one be a Persian?', wondered Parisian persons of fashion.[6] The whole of Montesquieu's work can be regarded as a search for a reply to his contemporaries' sardonic astonishment and open contempt. Concern about the *mœurs* of peoples lies at the base of his intellectual trajectory: first, in the *Lettres persanes*, French manners are the target of Montesquieu's literary talent. Next, in the *Grandeur et décadence des Romains*, irony turns into a historical inquiry into the effects of virtue and vice. Finally, the *Esprit des lois* traces the operation of the natural laws that rule the moral world. Besides these milestones, *Mes pensées* and Montesquieu's other unpublished papers further document his intellectual evolution from the literature of mores to what, in comparative and relative terms, can be called its science.

What Montesquieu depicts in the *Lettres persanes* (as well as in his other writings) as the French character is, in effect, that of the upper classes only, something which is obvious enough considering that 'the mass of the population are an animal which can see and hear, but never thinks'.[7] Consequently, no traits could be exclusive to the French populace in comparison with their counterparts in other countries. As was customary at the time, discussing the moral attitudes of the leisured class meant both dealing with what was peculiarly French and taking into account the whole *nation*, the *société* itself.

Montesquieu's prime concern was the moral and political condition of France – the two facets could hardly be taken in isolation. The core of contemporary French character was a blend of honour and 'gaieté'; but the former showed itself in the practice of duelling, and the latter in an outrageous habit of intemperate 'jest [*badinage*]'.[8] Sound values (that is, family ones) were neglected in favour of the arts of appearance and vain pleasures: the lifestyle of courtiers had become a model for all. 'That unfortunate vivacity of our nation', Montesquieu erupted, 'which lets fashion affect even financial projects, the decisions of councils, and the government of provinces!' Fashion rules the country unopposed – 'it is the standard by which they judge everything that happens in other countries: they always think that anything foreign is ridiculous'. Yet this applies only to 'bagatelles', for French politics is managed in accordance with foreign laws and principles (he had in mind Roman law and Popish ultimatums).

---

[6] *LP*, XXX, p. 83 (*Persian Letters*, trans. C. J. Betts (Harmondsworth, 1977), p. 83).
[7] *LP*, CXI (variant reading, 2nd edn, 1721), p. 441.
[8] *LP*, XC, pp. 215–16, and LXIII, p. 163.

Turned into a people of post-seekers, the new deity of the French is 'influence [*la faveur*]', whose priests are the ministers.[9] Montesquieu's portrait of France is that of a country where virtue is mocked, where witty but empty 'gens du bel-air' triumph in the *salons,* and political intriguers dictate state policies from the halls of the powerful.

Besides the ethical motifs which are inherent to the natural law philosophy, Montesquieu's moral roots are firmly planted in classical models, in a nostalgic regret of the moral side of republican civic humanism. Classical examples provided him with the terms of comparison he needed in order to deal with 'disorder' in French manners. Conscious as he was that republican government was unthinkable in modern times, the relationship between freedom and virtue, on the one hand, and despotism and vice, on the other, was nonetheless a cornerstone of his thought – the whole of *Romains* may be regarded as *Lettres persanes* turned upside down, with the Romans' virtues as the counterpart of French vices. D'Alembert shrewdly observed that Montesquieu 'had made himself foreign to his own country' in order to make a better assessment of its moral life.[10]

In the process of transition from *Lettres persanes* to *Esprit des lois,* a notable shift of emphasis occurred in the account of the causes of national character. This holds true even if signs of Montesquieu's later beliefs can be found in both the *Lettres* and the *Romains.* The explanation put forward in *Lettres persanes* to account for the corrupted French *caractère général* was a political one. The latest vicissitudes of French character appear as a logical consequence of Louis XIV's absolutist regime, as well as of the great power and riches of Catholic priests. Two further minor factors were avarice and, ultimately, the social mobility brought about by the failure of Law's experiment and the insufficient degree of paternal authority allowed by French laws.[11]

To the extent that royal power increased, the aristocracy abandoned its estates. This was the principal cause of the change in *mœurs* which occurred in the nation. The simple *mœurs* of former times were rejected in favour of the vanities of towns; women stopped knitting [*quittèrent la laine*] and began to despise all amusements which were not pleasures.[12]

Within this political and social process, the bad moral examples set by kings and ministers played a salient part: 'the sovereign imposes his attitudes on the

---

[9] 'Mes pensées', *OC,* I, p. 1337; *LP,* C, pp. 232–3 (*Persian Letters,* pp. 184–5; trans. modified), and LXXXVIII, p. 213.
[10] D' Alembert, 'Eloge de M. le président de Montesquieu' (1755), in *EDL,* p. 77.
[11] *LP,* XCII, p. 218; XCIV, p. 221; for religion, see CXVI–CXVII, pp. 262–7; Law's influence is dealt with in CXXXVIII, pp. 306ff., CXLII, pp. 321ff., CXLVI, pp. 335–7; and paternal authority in CXXIX, pp. 287–8.
[12] 'Mes pensées', p. 1146.

court, the court on the town, and the town on the provinces'.[13] The growing influence of women acted as both cause and effect of moral crisis, whereas luxury figures as a powerful agent of corruption only in *Grandeur et décadence des Romains*. A contrast between England and France is sketched. After asserting that 'not all nations of Europe are equally submissive to their rulers', Montesquieu maintained that 'the restive disposition of the English hardly give their king the time to assert his authority'. If the main feature of French character was its inconsistency, the English were certainly greedy but also hardheaded and self-reliant. Montesquieu always commended the manly qualities of the English, but he regarded the feverish spirit that had made them free as the cause of perpetual unrest and anxiety and, consequently, unhappiness.[14]

Montesquieu's later account of *esprit général* was based on the revelation on the part of the philosopher of the concealed action of natural laws, culminating in his rediscovery of the influence of climate over men's attitudes. Therefore, in *Esprit des lois*, the political factor may, and sometimes does, appear to be a trifling one that can be neglected without inconvenience. The will of kings has regularly proved impotent in the face of given 'things' and 'situations' as well as collective dispositions and interests.[15] Yet nature and politics interact in Montesquieu's perspective, and this makes any sharp distinction between them out of place, as demonstrated by the persistence of political polemics within the natural law framework.[16]

In both his early books, Montesquieu had asserted the existence of 'immutable, eternal, and general laws'; from the writing known as 'De la politique' (1725) onwards, there is a recurrence in his writings of remarks of a deterministic kind about the effectiveness of the 'common character' of societies, that is, a sort of collective soul 'which is the effect of an infinite chain of causes, which multiply and combine over the centuries'.[17] The term *esprit général* itself is used

[13] See *LP*, XCIX, pp. 231–2 (*Persian Letters*, p. 184; trans. modified); CXLVI, pp. 335–7; see also the following texts by Montesquieu: *Considérations sur les causes de la grandeur des Romains et de leur décadence*, ed. J. Ehrard (1734; Paris, 1968), ch. 21, p. 167; 'Lettres de Xénocrate a Phérès' (1723–4), *OC*, I, pp. 517–18; 'Mes pensées', p. 1327 ('J'appelle *génie d'une nation* les mœurs et le caractère d'esprit de différents peuples dirigés par l'influence d'une même cour et d'une même capitale').

[14] *LP*, CIV, p. 239 (*Persian Letters*, p.190). On English character see *LP*, CIV, pp. 239–40; CXVII, p. 266; CXXXVI, p. 303; 'De la politique' (1725), *OC*, I, p. 114–15; 'Notes sur l'Angleterre', *OC*, I, pp. 876–7, 878, 883; 'Mes pensées', pp. 1334–7. On Spanish and Portuguese character see *LP*, LXXVIII, pp. 194–7; 'Essai sur les causes qui peuvent affecter les esprits et les caractères' (1732–6?), *OC*, II, pp. 59–60. Dutch character is dealt with in 'Voyage de Gratz à la Haye', *OC*, I, pp. 863–4, 869.

[15] As instances of earlier remarks about the limited effectiveness of politics, see 'Analyse du Traité des devoirs' (1725), *OC*, I, pp. 108–11, and 'De la politique', pp. 112–19.

[16] See Jean Ehrard's interpretation of Montesquieu in his *L'idée de la nature en France dans la première moitié du XVIIIe siècle* (Paris, 1963), and also M. Richter, *The Political Theory of Montesquieu* (Cambridge, 1977), pp. 1–110.

[17] The first quotation is from *LP*, XCVII, p. 227 (and see also *Grandeur des Romains*, ch. 18, p. 145, and 'Mes pensées', p. 1129); the second is from 'De la politique', p. 114 (and see also 'Réflexions su les habitants de Rome' (1732), *OC*, I, pp. 910–12).

in *Romains* in order to account for the Romans' rise and fall: 'several examples accepted in the nation formed its *esprit général* and created its *mœurs*, which rule as imperiously as laws'.[18] A pivotal theme of the *Esprit des lois*, oriental tyranny, with effeminacy as its concomitant, was commonplace for the readers of *Lettres persanes* and *Romains*. Neither were they neglectful of the two reasons for which French monarchy differed from oriental despotism: first, in France manners and religion still hindered the absolute will of kings, and, second, punishment was in proportion to crime, where the latter feature 'is as it were the soul of a state'.[19]

Another element had to be added in order to make up the *Esprit des lois*. This was the power of climate over men's character, a point made several times since Aristotle and which, since the sixteenth century, had been through several attempts at secularizing, generalizing, and systematizing.[20] Montesquieu mentions the effects of climate in many pre-1748 writings, but the theme is only given full treatment in his 'Essai sur les causes qui peuvent affecter les esprits et les caractères'.[21] This unpublished text is divided into two parts dealing with the influence on character of physical and moral factors respectively. The former applies best, he says, to homogeneous groups of people like nations. He ascribes 'the different force of passions' to the 'different constitution of the body [*la machine*]', as it is through this that air temperature and 'thinness [*subtilité*]', nourishment, soil, and wind 'infinitely contribute to altering the spirit'. Physical impressions are transmitted to the soul by means of 'nervous fibres': the thicker and harder they are, the less sensitive one is. Notwithstanding the tributes he paid to observational sciences, in practice Montesquieu still adhered to Cartesian views and methods – this means that his physiology appears purely fictional to modern eyes.[22] The following example of Montesquieu's way of reasoning is by no means an isolated one:

It is not well known what arrangement of the brain is required for a lively spirit, but one can speculate about it. For instance, it is known that the vivacity of the eye is often a

---

[18] *Grandeur des Romains,* ch. 21, p. 167; see also ch. 15, pp. 116–17ff.
[19] *LP,* CII, pp. 235ff.
[20] See J. Dedieu, *Montesquieu et la tradition politique anglaise en France* (Paris, 1909), esp. pp. 192–225; R. Mercier, 'La théorie des climats des *Réflexions critiques* à *L'esprit des lois*', *Revue d'histoire littéraire de la France,* 53 (1953), pp. 17–37, 159–74; R. Shackleton, 'The Evolution of Montesquieu's Theory of Climate', *Revue internationale de philosophie,* 9 (1955), pp. 317–29; R. Shackleton, *Montesquieu: a Critical Biography* (Oxford, 1963), pp. 303–19; Ehrard, *L'idée de la nature,* pp. 691–717; C. J. Glacken, *Traces on the Rhodian Shore: Nature and Culture in Western Thought from Ancient Times to the End of the Eighteenth Century* (Berkeley, 1976), pp. 427–60, 551–65; G. Abbatista, 'Teoria dei climi e immagine del Nord in Montesquieu', *Antologia Viesseux,* 19 (1983), pp. 13–23; C. Borghero, 'Dal "génie" all' "esprit": fisico e morale nelle *Considérations sur les Romains* di Montesquieu', in A. Postigliola, ed., *Storia e ragione* (Naples, 1987), pp. 251–76.
[21] See *LP,* XXVI, p. 94; XXXIII, p. 108; XLVIII, p. 130; CXVIII, p. 268; CXXI, p. 271; CXXXVII, p. 304; and *Grandeur des Romains,* ch. 5, p. 54; ch. 20, p. 157.
[22] See M. H. Waddicor, *Montesquieu and the Philosophy of Natural Law* (The Hague, 1970), pp. 22–9; Borghero, 'Dal "génie" all' "esprit"', pp. 255–7; a different interpretation is offered by S. Goyard-Fabre, *Montesquieu: la Nature, les Lois, la Liberté* (Paris, 1993), pp. 55ff.

sign of that of the mind. Now, peoples from cold climates seldom have animated eyes. As there is humidity in excess in their brains, the transmitting nerves are constantly wet, and therefore become loose; it follows that they are incapable of producing the swift and sharp vibrations which make eyes bright.[23]

The main outcome of Montesquieu's physiology is the typology of national characters drawn along the North–South axis which has been rendered famous by *Esprit des lois*. But it is undeniable that, in all his texts, moral causes go hand in hand with the physical ones.[24] In the paper in question, the *caractère général* that he recognizes in each nation amounts to the effects of both climate and a combination of moral causes such as laws, religion, manners, habits, and the example of the court. 'The complexity of the causes that shape the *caractère général* of a people is great indeed.' He goes on to maintain that moral influences usually prevail over the force of climate.[25]

The 'Essai sur les causes' is a preface to the full treatment of national character given in the *Esprit des lois*. This is a well-known passage:

Many things govern men: climate, religion, laws, the maxims of the government, examples of past things, mores [*mœurs*], and manners [*manières*]; a general spirit [*esprit général*] is formed as a result. To the extent that, in each nation, one of these causes acts more forcefully, the others yield to it. Nature and climate almost alone dominate savages; manners govern the Chinese; laws tyrannize Japan; in former times mores set the tone in Lacedaemonia; in Rome it was set by the maxims of government and the ancient mores.[26]

Besides assertions like this, there are also statements which emphasise the predominant role played by climate. That national character is, nevertheless, the product of a blend of various causes is ultimately demonstrated by the comprehensive, flexible way in which Montesquieu constructs his arguments.[27] As a rule, he maintains that the more people's dispositions are harmed by the climate, the stricter the laws must be. The task of a wise legislator is to counterbalance or favour the social outcome of climate: 'if it is true that the character of the spirit and the passion of the heart are extremely different in the various climates, *laws* should be relative to the differences in these passions and to the differences in these characters'.[28] Climate is a major example of the 'nature des choses' which

---

[23] 'Essai sur les causes', p. 43.

[24] The twofold approach is applied in various contexts; see, e.g., 'Mes pensées', pp. 1015, 1303; 'Essai sur le goût dans les choses de la nature et de l'art' (1753–7), *OC*, I, pp. 1240–3.

[25] 'Essai sur les causes', pp. 58–9, 60–2. Among moral causes he also lists the influence of the people one lives with (p. 62) and that of one's profession (pp. 64–5).

[26] *EDL*, bk XIX, ch. 4, p. 461 (*The Spirit of the Laws*, trans. A. M. Cohler, B. C. Miller, and H. S. Stone (Cambridge, 1989), p. 310).

[27] While book XVI relates the condition of women to climate, book VII shows its connections with political principles; the whole of book IV explains the inner relationship that links education to forms of government; and the spirit of commerce has no relation whatsoever with climate (book XX).

[28] *EDL*, bk XIV, ch. 1, p. 373 (*The Spirit of the Laws*, p. 231); but see the whole bk XIV, pp. 373–88.

legislators have to take into full account. The relationship between climate and laws exemplifies the kind of regularity that appeared to many contemporaries as the essence of the new form of social and political knowledge. Climate, existing mores, religion, and established laws and principles of government make up the *esprit général*, which is the true basis for legislation. Whatever the form of government, rulers should avoid interfering with *esprit général* and, when forced to do so, should act slowly and with the utmost care. 'The government most in conformity with nature is the one whose particular arrangement best relates to the disposition of the people for whom it is established.'[29]

Montesquieu was offering a lesson in moderation and prowess in legislative engineering founded on the discoveries of philosophers. The anti-absolutist implications of a position like this were unmistakable at the time, but to understand them now, in their full historical significance, it is pertinent to refer to the gradual process of legal and political separation between state and society. As documented by Tocqueville, 'society' as the private sphere of individual action progressively emerged in the second half of the eighteenth century as a result of the policies pursued by the Bourbon monarchs, which made the French state occupy the public sphere with a monopoly of the powers of legislation, police, warfare, justice, taxation, and administration.[30] Montesquieu, who was elaborating a philosophical reply to the loss of French aristocratic power as a result of absolute rule, was fighting a battle deeply conservative in nature. He strongly opposed the trend just mentioned through the advocacy of intermediary powers as constituting the true nature of monarchical government – in this sense he can be represented as an ideologist of the *noblesse de robe*.[31]

While many philosophers borrowed crucial ideas from Montesquieu, none of them took up the socio-political stance whose support those ideas had been intended for, and many turned them against that stance. The fortunes of the *noblesse* were, unquestionably, not a matter of concern for Voltaire, Rousseau or Diderot. A generation after Montesquieu French philosophers were engaged in the intellectual process of separating society from political structures and organization. The consideration of civil society meant something

---

[29] *EDL,* bk I, ch. 3, p. 128 (*The Spirit of the Laws,* p. 8). As regards *forms* of government, Montesquieu maintains, for instance, that civic virtue is required in republics, while fear is required under despotic rule – connections like these being treated as laws of nature. The form of government is clearly one of the moral factors that contribute to the shaping of *esprit général.* In books IV, V, and VII, he establishes a link between the three forms of government and types of education, laws, and luxury respectively. But the mould in which peoples are cast by forms of government amounts to a sort of ideal type. The fact that, for instance, frugality is required in republics merely shows one of the conditions of existence of republics according to the nature of things, whereas national character is effectively shaped within the much larger horizon of *esprit général.*

[30] A. de Tocqueville, *L'Ancien Régime et la Révolution* (1856), *TOPC,* II.

[31] See, e.g., M. Cranston, *Philosophers and Pamphleteers: Political Theorists of the Enlightenment* (Oxford, 1986), pp. 30–3.

more than the appreciation of its inner dynamics, and the identification of its agents: in the face of a government monopolizing and centralizing power, and one which most philosophers came to oppose, society became the seat of healthy energies almost by default. Namely, it is arguable that this appreciation did not rest on a view of the virtues of the French middle ranks, as one might expect, but rather on the English example of political courage and entrepreneurial spirit. Whatever its source, a new perspective slowly took over, which increasingly saw society as the proper starting point of any political inquiry. Once divested of their aristocratic overtones, Montesquieu's arguments were such that, in the following decades, they would contribute to the emergence of the new standpoint. In particular, the origin of the relentless polemics that philosophers on both sides of the Channel waged against the *homme à systèmes*, that is, the thinker or politician who aimed to apply abstract schemes to the living bodies of societies, lies in the *Esprit des lois*. The debate assumed various overtones according to circumstances and the group against which it was directed, with the Physiocrats providing a regular target. There was, nevertheless, a general assumption underlying the philosophers' stance that even kings should respect the basic structures on which the life of a community depends. The intellectual emergence of civil society in France resulted from a steadily growing aversion to government policies; the only possible bulwark against these policies was the identification with social interests.

Montesquieu's famous distinction between the peoples of the North and the peoples of the South is that, in short, cold climates make men self-confident, brave, and persevering, whereas warm ones have an enervating and morally debasing effect.[32] On Montesquieu's stage the chief players are the Asian peoples, the English, and the slaves. All were traditional objects of climatological reflections, and his treatment adds nothing new. In the case of the Asians, Chardin's *Voyage en la Perse* and Du Bos's *Réflexions critiques sur la poesie et sur la peinture*, among other works, had spread a belief in their climate-induced effeteness and softness. For Montesquieu, hot climates made the Asians physically weak but imaginative, and 'a certain laziness of the spirit, naturally bound with that of the body' resulted. For this reason, and because of sharp contrasts in climate and hence character between neighbouring nations, which facilitated invasions, Asia was condemned to eternal despotism. Europe, on the other hand, thanks to a milder climate, developed a 'spirit of liberty'.[33] However, despotism was not in principle limited to hot countries. Despotism was one of the three types of government he envisaged (the others being the republican and the

---

[32] *EDL*, bk XIV, pp. 373–88; compare Aristotle, *The Politics*, trans. J. Barnes (Cambridge, 1995), 1327b20–38.
[33] *EDL*, bk XIV, ch. 4, p. 378; bk XVII, chs. 1–6, pp. 425–31. For the chorography of Asia and Europe in relation to the size of nations, see bk XVII, ch. 6, pp. 430–1.

monarchical). Actuated by fear, despotism presupposed education of a peculiar kind: the subject had to be ignorant and broken in spirit.[34]

While substantially confirming the analysis of the English character already sketched, in the *Esprit des lois* Montesquieu not only adds that they have a tendency to commit suicide because of 'a failure in the filtering of the nervous juice', but also provides a number of insights into the influence that English laws can have on national mores and character. The essence of his argument, which takes up a long chapter in book XIX, is that citizens' passions – from envy to ambition and political fervour – can be freely expressed under English government; the ultimate result of the social mobility thus prompted is a universal love of the country. Granted that the rise of the middling ranks brings the nation great riches, Montesquieu notes that the English show 'a substantive luxury [*un luxe solide*]' based on real needs as well as a certain spiritual 'grossièreté'. He remarks that Englishmen are too involved in politics to live with women, so that the latter are 'modest' and 'timid'.[35]

In dealing with slavery Montesquieu is led to a sort of justification by his philosophical eagerness to apply natural laws to everything. This happens partly on climatological grounds:

there are countries where the heat enervates the body and weakens the courage so much that men come to perform an arduous duty only from fear of chastisement ... But, as all men are born equal, one must say that slavery is against nature, although in certain countries it may be founded on a natural reason.[36]

Montesquieu made much use of an assumption which would become a recurrent motif of later discourses about national character: it could be called the 'no pain, no gain' argument. Mild climate and fertile soil, associated as they are with the easy satisfaction of needs, make peoples idle, and careless of the stimuli brought about by freedom. By contrast, those placed in a harsh environment are compelled to work hard and to reap freedom's economic advantages. The expected vices and virtues result. Montesquieu applies this theory to Europe as a corollary of the North–South divide.[37] Even if disguised in climatological clothing, the moral implications of the 'no pain, no gain' argument seem obvious.

The rest of the chapter will explore the ways in which *esprit général* themes, in conjunction with the new centrality of the concept of despotism, served as the essential point of departure for younger writers, who recognized the suggestion of civil society latent in the *Esprit des lois*. Montesquieu's significant innovation was the depiction of polities as structures where forms of government were

---

[34] *EDL*, bk IV, ch. 3, pp. 158–9.
[35] *EDL*, bk XIX, ch. 27, pp. 477–86.
[36] *EDL*, bk XV, ch. 7, pp. 394–5 (*The Spirit of the Laws*, p. 251).
[37] See, for instance, *EDL*, bk XVIII, chs. 4–7, pp. 435–7; bk XXI, ch. 2, pp. 28–9.

inherently associated with characteristic social organizations, involving a refusal to reduce one element to the other.[38] This standpoint lends credibility to the view, so often put forward, that the *Esprit des lois* marks a turning point in the prehistory of the social sciences. On a plane closer to eighteenth-century concerns, Montesquieu's approach entailed a conscience that a change in government policies was not sufficient to restore a sound moral environment in France.

Despite its innovation, however, Montesquieu's political theory entertained close links with the political horizon of antiquity. All the basic components of *esprit général* date back to the classical age. The inspiration as well as most of the contents of Montesquieu's theory of climate derive either directly from Plato, Hippocrates, Aristotle, Polybius, Strabo, and the like, or from their more modern interpreters, with Hippocrates and Galen providing Montesquieu with a model of physiology which effortlessy harmonized with that of Descartes. The idea that Asiatic peoples were political slaves by nature was a commonplace in antiquity and was allied to the widely accepted assumption of a fundamental difference in the national characters of Northern and Southern peoples. Even the 'no pain, no gain' argument was a common feature of the ancients' political thought, where it was illustrated, as in the *Esprit des lois*, with reference to the cases of fertile and barren countries. In Greek and Latin authors the appeal to the influence of natural causes was often associated with assessments of the significant role of governments in the shaping of habits, manners, and collective characters; the opposite influence was also emphasized, however, for in Plato's words 'the unwritten customs' are 'the bonds of the entire social framework'.[39] Many other apposite parallels might be cited, although it would suffice to recall Montesquieu's excerpts from Hippocrates' *Airs, Waters, Places* as evidence of his favourite sources, which account for the astonishing similarities in argument which the construction of *esprit général* shares with the classical world.[40]

The most notable consequence of Montesquieu's incomplete emancipation from the ancient models of political thought is the lack of a proper dimension of social progress. His approach in the *Esprit des lois* seems synchronical even when episodes of the past are illustrated (the historical account of French feudalism looking more like an appendage than a component part of the book). This matches what Callot has called 'the imposing immobility' of Montesquieu's conception of nature.[41] As is demonstrated by the role played in it by climate,

[38] M. Richter, 'Despotism', in P. P. Wiener, ed., *Dictionary of the History of Ideas* (5 vols., New York, 1973), II, p. 9.

[39] *The Laws*, trans. T. J. Saunders (Harmondsworth, 1975), 793. Montesquieu's borrowings from the ancients are scrupulously listed in L. M. Lewin, *The Political Doctrine of Montesquieu's 'Esprit des Lois': its Classical Background* (New York, 1936).

[40] The excerpts are in Montesquieu, *Œuvres complètes*, ed. A. Masson (3 vols., Paris, 1950–5), III, pp. 712–13. I am grateful to Geoffrey Lloyd for drawing my attention to Montesquieu's debts to antiquity in general and to Hippocrates in particular.

[41] E. Callot, *La philosophie de la vie au XVIIIe siècle* (Paris, 1965), p. 147.

esprit général thoroughly reflects the static character of Montesquieu's system. *Esprit général* could hardly lend itself to theories of social development on the Scottish model.

3   Major and minor critics of the *Esprit des lois*

Early commentators focused on climate, which they separated from the general texture of the work, thus usually ignoring the complexity of *esprit général*. 'In the *Esprit des lois*, climate is what motion is in the Universe, that is, the universal cause of everything', as J. De La Porte wrote. There was even a poem that mocked the idea that 'climate alone is the arbitrator / of Gods and govern-ment', which was 'all the politics of our anonymous Solon'.[42] As mentioned above, many striking statements in Montesquieu's work could easily convey the idea that he had ascribed an undisputed force to climate. The climatological theory was heavily attacked by Catholic critics as a fundamental element in Montesquieu's moral and religious relativism, whose open contrast with any view of the primacy of religion in history was apparent. 'What is the point of these reflections but to say that, if religion intends to take roots or continue to exist, it has to adjust itself to climate?'[43] The main bones of contention were the climatological explanation of polygamy, divorce, the diffusion of religions, suicide in England, and luxury. Even those who argued in support of the work showed some embarassment at defending Montesquieu's treatment of these topics.[44] Such criticisms were fully on the mark, in so far as they signalled that Montesquieu's approach implicitly legitimized the existence of societies (as well as religions) of different types. He had explained that each society was made up of parts that were interconnected in a way which was not accidental (with religion as one of these parts), and social organizations could be accounted for thereby on a purely rational basis. Many early reviewers were scathing about Montesquieu's heavy reliance on the dubious evidence supplied by the classics as well as by controversial travel reports. It was convincingly demonstrated, well before Voltaire, that Montesquieu's climatological theory lacked a sound factual basis. As regards its inner logic, many pointed to the decisive impact on collective characters of moral factors like education, shared social values,

---

[42] [J. de La Porte], *Observations sur l'Esprit des Loix, ou l'Art de lire ce livre, de l'entendre et d'en juger* (Amsterdam, 1751), pp. 88, 112; Bonneval, *L'Esprit des Lois en vers*, OCL, VI, pp. 245–6. But there were also those who, like d'Alembert, rejected this simplistic interpreta-tion: see his 'Climat (Géog.)', in *Encyclopédie*, III, p. 534.

[43] [Abbé La Roche], 'Réponse à la défense de l'Esprit des Lois' (1750), OCL, VI, p. 226. See also J. B. L. Crevier, *Observations sur le livre de l'Esprit des Loix* (Paris, 1764).

[44] See A. de la Beaumelle, *Suite de la défense de l'Esprit des Lois ou Examen de la Réplique du gazetier ecclésiastique a la défense de l'Esprit des Lois* (1751), OCL, VI, pp. 247–312; [F. Risteau], 'Réponse aux observations sur l'Esprit des Loix' (1751), in Montesquieu, *Lettres familières à divers amis d'Italie* (Rome, 1773), pp. 215–347. See also P. L. M. de Maupertuis, *Eloge de monsieur de Montesquieu* (Amsterdam, 1756), p. 24.

the example set by rulers, and so on. What a strange idea, one commentator remarked, to impute everything to physical causes 'and nothing to passions, taste,
prejudices, education, and fashion', that is, 'to man!'[45] Furthermore, historical
evidence of the fact that national characters do change over time was easy to
collect, and was actually cited by many reviewers.

The effectiveness of physical factors was questioned by Turgot. In addressing
an audience of young *Sorboniques*, he argued that 'education' – that is, all our
sensations and ideas – encompasses the influence of climate. The single thing
that we can speak about with any certainty is that climates have a moral influence
'through the objects which they present us with'. It would be important to assess
the 'hidden principles' that act as links between climate and national character,
but any natural difference in men's souls 'will always be unknown to us as it
can never be the object of our reasonings'. Consequently, one should resort to
physical causes only when the moral ones have proved ineffective in explaining
facts. Turgot seems to turn to Montesquieu's *esprit général* when he maintains
that the characters of peoples are shaped by 'a sort of general education' made up
of language, manners, religion, laws, government, and 'circumstances'. Once
so created, 'mœurs' (intended as 'inner laws') play a very effective part in
politics; they are 'the most powerful restraint [*frein*] for men and almost the
single one for kings'. What is inconceivable is that 'a happy proportion of body
fluids' could ever make men virtuous.[46]

Turgot tends to make mores depend on stages of civilization, at least when
dealing with the early stages.[47] During the phases of hunting and animal hus-
bandry, mores are seemingly shaped by the mode of production, but as the agricultural stage is reached and real governments and states can be established,
societies turn into complex mechanisms with the effect that the economic factor loses its primacy. At that point, the comprehensive concept of education
referred to above seems to become not only an autonomous force, but also a
decisive factor, through the achievements of science, in social development.[48]
That his stadial theory was intended mainly as a key to the understanding of
the past is evidenced by his full acceptance of Montesquieu's portrayal of the
kind of mores brought about by education under despotic rule. The demoralizing

---

[45] La Porte, *Observations*, pp. 87–8.
[46] In *TO*, I, see 'Recherches sur les causes des progrès et de la décadence des sciences et des arts'
(1748), pp. 139–40; 'Discours sur les avantages que l'établissement du christianisme a procurés
au genre humain' (1750), pp. 212–13; 'Lettre à Madame de Graffigny sur les Lettres d'une
péruvienne' (1751), p. 253; 'Plan d'un ouvrage sur la géographie politique' (1751?), p. 262;
'Plan de deux Discours sur l'histoire universelle' (1751), pp. 293–4, 304. Turgot's references
to language had an antecedent in Condillac's remarks about the connection between language
and national character: 'Essai sur l'origine des connoissances humaines' (1746), in Condillac,
Œuvres philosophiques, ed. G. Le Roy (3 vols., Paris, 1947–51), I, pp. 98–104.
[47] R. L. Meek, *Social Science and the Ignoble Savage* (Cambridge, 1976), pp. 68–76.
[48] 'Plan d'un ouvrage', pp. 259ff.; 'Plan de deux Discours'; and 'Pensées et fragments', *TO*, I,
pp. 326, 330–1.

consequences of despotism affect both the private and the public sphere; 'despotism perpetuates ignorance and ignorance perpetuates despotism'; so that, gradually, fear and subservience become a habit. Turgot's Oriental 'mollesse', as resulting from slavery and polygamy, is derived from Montesquieu.[49]

Voltaire repeatedly and harshly criticized the *Esprit des lois* for its lack of internal structure and, above all, for its misuse of historical sources. As regards *esprit général*, Voltaire took sides with the advocates of moral causes. It is true that he ascribed some basic features of peoples to climate, believing, like Montesquieu, that the passions had a physical basis; and that his own practice of history made him occasionally resort to climatological assertions.[50] But when he came to discuss the force of climate, he concluded that its influence was dwarfed by that of government. 'Climate has some force, but government one hundred times more; religion associated with government is even more forceful.' Climatological theory fully exemplified to Voltaire's eyes Montesquieu's carelessness at handling history (and logic), and he seemingly regarded some of those propositions as an affront to reason. According to Voltaire, misleading reasoning had been the true pillar of oppressive regimes throughout history; behind climatological fables there lay a betrayal of the moving forces of the Enlightenment.

To account for the effects of climate, Montesquieu tells us that he made a sheep's tongue freeze . . . But a sheep's tongue will never explain why the struggle between the secular and religious powers has outraged Europe and covered her in blood for more than six hundred years . . . Government, religion, and education are the causes of everything with the unfortunate mortals who crawl, suffer, and reason on this globe. Nurture the reason of men in the surroundings of mount Vesuvius, and along the rivers Thames and Seine; and, as a result, you would see no Konradin [of Hohenstaufen] handed over to the executioner to follow a pope's advice; no Mary, Queen of Scots, dying after the last torture; and no catafalques set up by white penitents for a young Protestant guilty of suicide.[51]

In the *Lettres anglaises*, Voltaire does not indulge in those generalizing contrasts that constitute the irreducible content of national character literature, and we know that this was intentional. The draft of one of the letters (1728) shows how uneasy Voltaire felt about the sweeping statements so often made by travellers about national characters. Voltaire thought that 'such general ideas are liable to too many exceptions', whereas no mere traveller can grasp more than the surface of national life. In addition, national characters change over time: 'truth in one age is error in another'.[52] These views relate to his own later

---

[49] 'Plan de deux Discours', pp. 290–7. The excerpt entitled 'Les caractères nationaux' in 'Pensées et fragments', pp. 338–9, is mistakenly attributed by the editor to Turgot, whereas it is a translation of the beginning of Hume's essay 'Of National Characters'. For Turgot's *Mémoire sur les municipalités*, see chapter 4 below.

[50] See, as instances of climatological remarks, *Essai sur les mœurs* (1756), *VOC*, XII, ch. 143, p. 370; XII, ch. 157, p. 439; XIII, ch. 183, p. 96.

[51] 'Commentaire sur l'Esprit des Lois' (1777), *VOC*, XXX, pp. 456–7; see also pp. 442–5.

[52] 'Projet d'une lettre sur les Anglais à M***' (1728), *VOC*, XXII, pp. 17–18.

writing of history, which he intended as a sort of political economy of mores. The opening sentences of *Essai sur les mœurs* are striking. What deserves to be brought to light by the historian, Voltaire argued, is not the sequences of kings and their battles, but 'the spirit, the mores [*mœurs*], and the customs [*usages*] of the principal nations, drawn upon facts which one cannot afford to ignore'. He was opposing the disgusting tales of the 'barbarous centuries' built on a basis of 'appalling lies' to a bottom–up historiography of the civilization process, that is a historiography centred on institutions and beliefs.[53] In pointing to the progressive implications of the latter, Voltaire was putting forward a history of the opinions of peoples as the true counterpart of establishment history. The idea behind Voltaire's declaration of intent was that it was opinion that ultimately ruled the world. The oppositional content of an idea that rapidly became a cornerstone of the French Enlightenment is apparent. In *Remarques pour servir de supplément à l'Essai sur les mœurs* (1763), he argued that the thread of modern history was the war between the empire and the papacy, and that it was a war in which one of the sides relied only on the power of belief. 'Therefore, it is the history of opinion that is needed; once viewed through it, the chaos of events, factions, revolutions, and crimes becomes deserving of the consideration of the wise.' There are opinions that have dramatically changed the behaviour of men. History is a theatre where the struggle between 'fanaticism' and 'reason' is eternally represented, and it is the philosopher's duty to enlighten men through an authentic depiction of the horrors brought about by fanaticism.[54]

Once viewed in this context, Voltaire's references to national characters figure as historically grounded observations expressing his eagerness to depict civilization as dependent on the slow march of reason – in its incarnations as 'opinion' or 'spirit'. Both are called into play, for example, to account for the striking differences that had occurred in the development of the French and English governments over the centuries. For, besides its favourable geographical situation, England owed its liberty to its 'spirit': 'the English have something more solid, more thoughtful, more obstinate about their spirit than certain other peoples'. Thanks to this attitude, they managed to break with popish rule, while the French, 'less serious [*plus léger*] people', have been dancing with their own shackles. The contrast between the two nations recurs in Voltaire's texts to the point that even the shared experience of seventeenth-century political unrest

---

[53] *Essai sur les mœurs,* XI, foreword, pp. 156–7; XII, ch. 81, p. 53. See also 'Remarques pour servir de supplément à l'Essai sur les mœurs et l'esprit des nations' (1763), *VOC,* XXIV, pp. 543–7, and *Le siècle de Louis XIV* (1751), in Voltaire, *Œuvres historiques,* ed. R. Pomeau (Paris, 1987), pp. 616–20.

[54] 'Remarques pour servir de supplément', pp. 547, 554, 569. Ceremonies, as well as belief, make up a religion, and whereas the former element can be accounted for on climatological grounds, the latter depends on 'l'opinion, cette reine incostante du monde': 'Climat' (1771), in *Questions sur l'Encyclopédie, VOC,* XVIII, pp. 200–2.

seemed to him to reflect their different 'characters'. The Glorious Revolution, in which 'iron decided everything', had witnessed 'a melancholic energy and a reasoned fury', whereas the French 'plunged into sedition at whim and for fun: women led factions; love both formed and broke up cabals'. At present, the main trait of English character is 'love of freedom'.[55]

But, if opinion may mould politics, government, regarded as part of a broadly intended educative process, seems to be a decisive factor in the shaping of public opinion itself. Voltaire believed that government was largely responsible for the attitudes of the French upper classes, whereas the mass of the people did not count, being thought of as incapable of rational thinking. Reason must first and foremost replace fanaticism 'among the leading men'; later, it would progressively gain possession of the minds of the others, going down to 'the people [*peuple*] themselves, who, though they do not know it, can see the moderation of their superiors and learn to be moderate themselves'. Voltaire's *peuple* has very little to do with *les honnêtes gens*. 'The spirit of a nation', he argued, 'always lies in the few who set the many to work, and feed and rule them.' As an example of the government's influence over mores, he ascribes the celebrated French *politesse* to Louis XIV's benevolent politics. But the French government is implicitly blamed when Voltaire regrets that, in contrast with their English counterparts, French aristocrats neglect commercial activities. More generally, in France, talents were neither appreciated nor rewarded.[56]

In the entry for 'France, François, Français' (1771) in the *Dictionnaire philosophique*, Voltaire is able to depict a less bleak portrait of French character, but in order to do so he is forced to resort to the virtues of climate. Providing that 'each people has its own character, likewise each man', national character is made up of two groups of elements: 'climate and soil' provide its unchangeable basis, whereas governments, religions, and education determine its variable parts. The 'kernel' of French character is still as Caesar found it, that is, the Frenchman is 'prompt to make up his mind, ardent about a fight, impetuous in attack, easy to put himself off'. If, now, French character looks remarkably different, it is because of the established illiberal regime, which has made any political participation by the citizens impossible – 'liveliness itself, which will survive forever, nowadays has nothing but the charms of society as

---

[55] 'Gouvernement' (1771), in *Dictionnaire philosophique, VOC*, XIX, pp. 292–7 (*Political Writings*, trans. D. Williams (Cambridge, 1994), p. 59); *Le siècle de Louis XIV*, p. 652; *Essai sur les mœurs*, XIII, ch. 180, pp. 61, 66–8; *Lettres philosophiques* (1734), *VOC*, XXII, pp. 104–5 ('Sur le parlement').
[56] *Le siècle de Louis XIV*, pp. 996, 979–80ff., 1063 (*The Age of Louis XIV and Other Selected Writings*, trans. J. H. Brumfitt (Washington, 1966), p. 239; trans. modified); *Dictionnaire philosophique*, pp. 279 ('Goût'), 383–4 ('Homme'); *Essai sur les mœurs*, XII, ch. 155, pp. 433–4; *Lettres philosophiques*, p. 111 ('Sur le commerce'), 179–82 ('Sur la considération qu'on doit aux gens de lettres').

its object'.[57] Clearly enough, Voltaire adopted a climatological stance in order to make his political criticism more effective.

This duality of approach was typical of the French scene: while climatological remarks provided a sort of learned foundation, the political polemic was being brought increasingly to the fore.[58] National character themes played a substantial part in the French philosophers' discourse ultimately because they feared that the moral roots of society were in danger; this implied a dialectic between a reinvented original identity of France (through its history as well as the indestructible properties of its soil and climate) and its present corruption. Images taken from the civic humanist tradition, on the one hand, and memories of past greatness, on the other, were simultaneously called into play in an attempt to mark out the contrast with the current situation. This is shown, for instance, by abbé Coyer's famous dissertations on *Patrie* – 'we have forgotten the idea which was linked to this great word' – and *Peuple* – our ancestors wisely gave the people representation in the *états-généraux*.[59] Here, once again, Montesquieu had paved the way, in so far as almost the whole of the sixth part of the *Esprit des lois* is devoted to a historical analysis of feudalism in France.[60] If all this discussion may look very abstract, its protagonists intended it as a sort of battlefield for political agitation. What the chapter deals with are excerpts from a militant literature.

The climatological explanation was not entirely dismissed, notwithstanding its apparent flaws, since it was able to contribute to the reconstruction of French history, and, in particular, to the delineation of a standard of Frenchness prior to absolutism. The most common pattern of thought about the causes of collective character emerged as a blend of both moral and physical factors. The philosophers who, in their various ways, put the two kinds of determinants together were d'Alembert, Morelly, Goguet, Condillac, Mably, Diderot, Chastellux, Rousseau, Holbach, and Raynal.[61] In associating climate with

[57] 'Franc ou Franq; France, François, Français', in *Dictionnaire philosophique*, pp. 178–82.

[58] See H. Vyverberg, *Human Nature, Cultural Diversity, and the French Enlightenment* (Oxford, 1989), pp. 64–87.

[59] [abbé Coyer], *Dissertations pour être lues: la première, sur le vieux mot de patrie: la seconde, sur la nature du peuple* (The Hague, 1755), pp. 15, 63–4.

[60] See E. Carcassonne, *Montesquieu et le problème de la constitution française au XVIIIe siècle* (Paris, 1927). As regards history as capable of legitimizing the demands of the 'nation', see F. Furet and M. Ozouf, 'Deux légitimations historiques de la société française au XVIIIe siècle: Mably et Boulainvilliers', *Annales ESC*, 34 (1979), pp. 438–50.

[61] The first four writers mentioned will not be dealt with in what follows: see d'Alembert, 'Analyse de l'Esprit des Lois' (1755), in *EDL*, I, pp. 99–100; d'Alembert, 'Climat (Géog.)', p. 534; Morelly, *Essai sur l'esprit humain* (1743; Geneva, 1971), pp. 4–5, 13–19; Morelly, *Essai sur le cœur humain* (1745; Geneva, 1970), pp. 14–16; Morelly, *Code de la nature*, ed. G. Chinard (1755; Paris, 1950); A.-Y. Goguet, *De l'origine des lois, des arts et des sciences, et de leur progrès chez les anciens peuples* (1758; 3 vols., Paris, 1820); Condillac, 'Essai sur l'origine des connoissances humaines', p. 98. The anonymous author of 'Caractère des nations' in *Encyclopédie*, II, p. 666, can be added to the list. La Mettrie unreservedly supported

government as causes of national character, most of these authors drew heavily on Montesquieu, demonstrating that the hints that he had made about the sort of protection that *esprit général* should guarantee to society when confronted by government by no means constituted seed fallen on stony ground.

4   A French historian: Mably

Mably's *Observations sur l'histoire de France* (1765) can be taken as an example of a standard sentiment. 'Je suis historien, je suis Français', so I feel that it is my duty to tell my fellow citizens some unpalatable truths. In Mably's account, early Frenchmen had been 'supremely [*souverainement*] free', but they lost their liberty because of the affluence which resulted from the conquests they made. French character emerged from the struggle of kings against the anarchic rule of feudal barons – while in the same period the English were engaged in limiting the prerogatives of kingship.

There developed different political views and different characters in the two countries. Their goals were opposite, as the royal power, with the support of public opinion, made as much progress in France as liberty in England. States take up habits to which they cling mechanically. If the English sometimes forgot their liberty, their distraction could not last long. Equally, if the French became irritated against the king, this would be nothing but a temporary effervescence, from which habit would soon lead them again under the yoke of monarchy.[62]

The *esprit général* of England may effectively remedy many of the flaws in its political constitution; on the other hand, the same spirit of freedom could be severely impaired by the moral corruption brought about by avarice and luxury. The French case is different, as Frenchmen were forced by absolutist rule to relinquish 'the tradition of their customs', the most notable of which was the *états-généraux*. As an unfortunate result, the French people acquired 'a character in conformity with our government', that is, of an acquiescent type.[63] The French soul is now 'crushed [*affaissé*]', since liberty is a necessary requirement for citizens' courage and industry.

the climatological argument, depicting man as 'une Plante ambulante': *L'Homme Machine* (1748), in J. O. de La Mettrie, *Œuvres philosophiques*, ed. F. Markovits (2 vols., Paris, 1987), I, pp. 72–3. Another advocate of the effects of climate, Buffon, remained strictly within the boundaries of natural history when dealing with national characters: he makes no mention of types of government, and the relationship he is eventually concerned with is the influence of *mœurs* on men's physical attributes and not the reverse. See Buffon, *De l'homme*, ed. M. Duchet (1749; Paris, 1971), pp. 270–1, 308–9, 311.

[62] *Observations sur l'histoire de France* (1765), *MCC*, II, pp. 249–50.
[63] *ibid.*, pp. 254–85, 338–50. Elsewhere, he wrote that in France certain limits were set to monarchical power by the parliaments, an independent clergy, a proud aristocracy, and the arts and sciences: *De l'étude de l'histoire, a Monseigneur le Prince de Parme* (1765), *MCC*, XII, pp. 134–7.

The vision of the persistence and effectiveness of historically determined national characters lay at the root of Mably's deep concern with the French political state of affairs.

> Great nations never behave out of reflection. They are moved, pushed ahead, held back, or agitated by a sort of interest which is the product of the habits they have taken up. This national character is so heavy that it carries everything away; and once it has been formed over time, it becomes even more unlikely that it may change in the essentials, because it is very rare that events as momentous as to affect the whole mass of citizens may occur, and consequently give them, with a new general interest, a new way of seeing and thinking.[64]

The interplay of absolute rule and subjects' demoralization as expressed by the decline of French character made Mably suspect that any purely political solution would prove inadequate. Just after advocating the convocation of the *états-généraux*, he phrased the dilemma as follows: 'if the nation, through insufficient love for liberty and political enlightenment, is unable to take advantage of this event, the new *états-généraux*... will not solve our present problems, nor will it allow us to hope anything favourable for the future'.[65]

Mably, like other French philosophers, often expressed the connection between political and moral crisis in another, less direct and apparently more universal, way. If the single ruling power in the country is the absolute will of kings, no real national character can establish itself because their changing passions are the exclusive criterion of mores. Lacking a true collective dimension, people cannot help resorting to individual struggles for wealth and recognition, and this results in the predominance of 'mollesse' via avarice and luxury as well as of a 'servile ambition'. This 'philosophical' mode of argument fully reveals that the fading of French character is implicitly equated to the loss of what was traditionally meant by republican virtues. Mably's historical relevance lies in his dissemination of the language of republicanism and, in particular, of its typical assessment of *mœurs*. Within that pattern of thought, the stress on the absolute importance of mores as a necessary complement to laws went hand in hand with his firm belief in the ability of governments, disguised as Roman censors, to create and implement dispositions and habits.

It is in *Du cours et de la marche des passions dans la société* (1775) that Mably couples civic humanism with the climatological thesis. Once he had adopted a sense-based theory of knowledge as well as a Montesquieu-like physiology, the influence of climate over passions became an obvious inference. His main climatological tool is Montesquieu's typology of Northern and

---

[64] *Observations sur l'histoire*, III, p. 304.
[65] *ibid*. Montesquieu, too, had maintained that 'la liberté même a paru insupportable à des peuples qui n'étaient pas accoutumés à en jouir'. *EDL*, bk XIX, ch. 2, pp. 459–60.

Southern characters, through which he aims to account for the great variety of habits, mores, laws, and collective characters 'which mark out all the countries of the universe'. Mably fully endorses the 'no pain, no gain' argument, warning against the moral dangers of the 'almost spontaneous produce of too fertile soils', and claiming that the establishment of Asian despotism through subjects' 'mollesse' was the best instance of his point. He draws much attention to the potential that legislators have to redress the effects of the 'imperious influence' of climate. But it seems that governments can lead peoples to virtue only on condition that, besides inhabiting the temperate areas of the globe, they are white. Blacks and native Americans appear to suffer from irremediable frailty of the brain. In practice, it is in Europe that consistent and climate-conscious policies can effectively direct citizens' minds towards new interests, thus developing 'new passions and new ideas'.[66] Mably draws his examples mainly from ancient history, taking sides with Spartan laws which, in his view, successfully counteracted the native 'vagrant [*vagabonde*] reason', a consequence of Southern European climate. His option for Sparta reveals his desiderata for France, since France is to be found among the list of Southern countries like Greece, Spain, and Italy, where the legislators' task is 'to moderate, direct, and regulate the imagination, which quickly grows tired of all things for which it has suddenly developed a passion'. Although the reason of individuals is 'sublime' in France, it desperately needs associating with 'the public and general reason' which is the product of wise laws. But often governments do not acknowledge the effective workings of climate, and favour the vices that it brings about.[67]

5   Rousseau between *mœurs* and nationalism

Rousseau's remarks about the untimeliness of Peter the Great's reforms were phrased in national character jargon: 'his first wish was to make Germans or Englishmen when he ought to have begun by making Russians'. The rationale of Rousseau's view was that the timing of peoples' growth differed in each case; the Russians were still in a barbarous state and thereby not mature for *la police*. The paragraph under consideration hints at the peculiarity of each people (in the mentioned respect), possibly envisaging a quasi-natural, organic pattern of growth. Besides arousing Voltaire's fury, these comments have contributed to the reading of Rousseau as a forerunner of nineteenth-century

---

[66] *Du cours et de la marche des passions dans la société* (1775), *MCC*, XV, pp. 270–3, 280, 296–9, and *passim*.
[67] *ibid.*, pp. 304–11, 382–5; overall, climate is dealt with on pp. 265–389. Critical discussions of climatological arguments can be found in *De la législation ou principes des lois* (1776), *MCC*, IX, pp. 26–7, and *De l'étude de l'histoire*, pp. 96–8. Mably's first important work, not included in *MCC*, shows a precocious predisposition to treat national spirits as the true subjects of history: *Paralléle des Romains et des François, par rapport au Gouvernement* (2 vols., Paris, 1740).

cultural nationalism.[68] Since Rousseau inserted his views on national character in a comprehensive political philosophy, some preliminary questions need to be addressed before entering into an evaluation of this claim.

A few pages of *Lettre à d'Alembert sur les spectacles* summarize, in an exemplary way, the relationship between laws, mores, and opinion. Laws, Rousseau asserted, are far from being omnipotent: if it were so, then enacting 'edicts upon edicts, regulations upon regulations' would be the remedy for all evils. But the secret to a legislator's success does exist, and, as Solon had taught, it is to be found in a skilful tuning of laws to the peculiarities of the people at hand, in order that their enforcement 'ensues from the single combination of these peculiarities'. This means that lasting governments are founded on a beneficial alliance of laws and mores, of which Sparta was a major instance. As for the origin of mores, Rousseau sees it lie in public opinion: 'when one does not live alone but in contact with others, their judgements regulate everything; nothing looks good or desirable to individuals but what the public has judged such, and the only pleasure [*bonheur*] most people are acquainted with is being deemed happy'.[69]

Public opinion is the real ruler of the world because even monarchs are subject to its yoke. The legislator may significantly affect it, and *mœurs* with it, only at the time when government is first established (in which case it brings about a 'civil religion' as documented in *Contrat social*). Rousseau underlines that a nation-people have to fulfil certain prerequisites in order to be 'suitable for legislation' – he mentions the existence of social bonds, the docility and vigour of the people, the weakness of customs and superstitions, an appropriate size, a favourable geo-political position, and a material standard of living ensuring independence. However, the legislator's task is so difficult that only a few states are well constituted; this is because of the 'impossibility of finding the simplicity of nature associated with social needs'. In so far as *mœurs* are established, government not only 'no longer has the power to change them', but it also

---

[68] Rousseau's remark about Russia is in *Du contrat social*, ed. P. Burgelin (1762; Paris, 1992), bk II, ch. 8, p. 70 (*The Social Contract and The Discourses*, trans. G. D. H. Cole, J. H. Brumfitt, and J. C. Hall (London, 1973), p. 217; trans. modified). Those who have pointed to Rousseau's precocious nationalism include A. Cobban, *Rousseau and the Modern State* (London, 1934), pp. 151–91; A. Choulguine, 'Les origines de l'esprit national moderne et Jean-Jacques Rousseau', *Annales de la société Jean-Jacques Rousseau*, 27 (1937), pp. 7–283; R. Derathé, 'Patriotisme et nationalisme au XVIIIe siècle', *Annales de philosophie politique*, 8 (1969), pp. 69–84; F. M. Barnard, 'National Culture and Political Legitimacy: Herder and Rousseau', *Journal of the History of Ideas*, 44 (1983), pp. 231–53. The same view is shared by almost all students of nationalism, from Kohn to Chabod to A. D. Smith. The image of Rousseau as prophet of nationalism is rejected by T. Todorov, *Nous et les autres: la réflexion française sur la diversité humaine* (Paris, 1989), pp. 206–11, and M. Barberis, 'Quel che resta dell'universale: l'idea di nazione da Rousseau a Renan', *Filosofia politica*, 7 (1993), pp. 5–28.

[69] *Lettre à d'Alembert sur les spectacles* (1758), in J.-J. Rousseau, *Discours sur les sciences et les arts. Lettre à d'Alembert sur les spectacles*, ed. J. Varloot (Paris, 1987), pp. 221–3; quotation on p. 223 (*Politics and the Arts*, trans. A. Bloom (Glencoe, Ill., 1960)). See also *Du contrat social*, bk II, ch. 8, pp. 68–9; bk II, ch. 10, p. 76; and bk IV, ch. 7, p. 156.

finds it difficult to preserve them from the inevitable and natural alterations which occur over time: 'public opinions, although very difficult to govern, are in themselves very fluid and liable to change'.[70] Government being ruled out, it is different modes of production as well as the dynamics of urbanization that have significant effects on mores and opinions.

Up to this point, nothing really novel has emerged from Rousseau's treatment. Echoes of Montesquieu's *esprit général* are clearly discernible. Solon's rule and the consequences drawn from it were philosophers' bread and butter, ultimately amounting to an expression of the primacy of society. Rousseau elaborates on the final frailty of despotism, reminding tyrants that their power depends on the prejudices of subjects, and that 'they have only to change their way of thinking, and you are forced to change your course of action'.[71] Chapter 8 of book III of *Du contrat social* is entitled 'That all forms of government do not suit all countries', and reveals itself as a noteworthy application of Montesquieu's climatological theory, despite the fact that no mention is made here of a physiology underlying it. Rousseau's starting point is that 'liberty, not being a fruit of all climates, is not within the reach of all peoples. The more this principle, laid down by Montesquieu, is meditated on, the more its truth is felt; the more it is combated, the more chance is given to confirm it by new proofs.'[72] The focus, here, of Rousseau's observations on the power of climate is the fertility of different soils, for 'the civil state can subsist only so long as men's labouring brings them a return greater than their needs'. He maintains that there is an inner relationship between the surplus that soils of different quality can produce and forms of government: for instance, a monarchy, which is the regime where the heaviest taxes are imposed, can be established only in countries whose favourable climate makes them plentiful. Free governments can be established only in mild climates, since cold areas are the proper seat of 'barbarism', for 'all polity is impossible', whereas despotism is the natural fate of warm fertile countries, where much produce is obtained with little effort. After drawing some unoriginal corollaries from all this, Rousseau comments, in a style that recalls Montesquieu, that there probably are exceptions, but these confirm the rule, as 'sooner or later they produce revolutions which restore things to the natural order'.[73]

Again, even if there is probably an element of novelty in the connection established between climate and taxation, remarks like the above, high-sounding as they are, were little more than platitudes at that time. Nor does Rousseau's treatment of climate elsewhere add anything incompatible with that of

---

[70] *Lettre à d'Alembert*, p. 232; *Du contrat social*, bk II, chs. 8–10, pp. 68–76, esp. ch. 10, pp. 75–6.
[71] *Emile ou de l'éducation*, ed. M. Launay (1762; Paris, 1966), bk II, p. 98 (*Emile*, trans. B. Foxley (London, 1974), p. 47).
[72] *Du contrat social*, bk III, ch. 8, p. 106 (*The Social Contract*, p. 247; trans. modified).
[73] *ibid.*, bk III, ch. 8, p. 108 (*The Social Contract*, p. 249).

Montesquieu.[74] The originality of Rousseau's contribution can be traced, instead, to his idea of 'original characters of peoples', which runs especially through *Emile* and *Projet de constitution pour la Corse*. Granted that 'every nation has its own specific character', which can be grasped by means of observation and comparison, this 'primitive character' results from natural features like race, climate, and soil. Land of a poor quality in a hilly or mountainous environment, for instance, makes people become shepherds, and moulds their minds accordingly, while they are as hardworking as the temperature goes. The notion of original character supplies Rousseau with an additional weapon in his polemic against modernity. He contends that these natural differences are threatened by the looming uniformity brought about by civilization, as is apparent especially in towns – 'to my eyes, Paris and London are the same city'.

The Frenchmen of today are no longer the big fair men of old; the Greeks are no longer beautiful enough to serve as an artist's model; the very face of the Romans has changed as well as their character; the Persians, originally from Tartary, are daily losing their native ugliness through the intermixture of Circassian blood. Europeans are no longer Gauls, Germans, Iberians, Allobroges; they are all Scythians, more or less degenerate in countenance, and still more so in conduct [*mœurs*].[75]

Rousseau refers to two factors of dreary uniformity in particular, factors which are closely bound to each other. These are, first, the mixing of peoples due to migration, increased communication, and trade since the fall of Rome, and second, the all-pervasive force of 'corruption'. But even elements of an environmental type are called into play: cleared forests, drained marshes, and universal cultivation of land. Rousseau's advice is to look for original national traits 'in remote provinces' – by doing so, we would discover that national characters (that is the peoples themselves) are as good as they are close to nature. Original characteristics seem to be important to Rousseau as a reminder of past natural purity, as a term of comparison, and as a bulwark against oppressive cultural influences, whether they came from abroad or from the eulogists of commercial society.

The text where the dualism between original characters and the corrupting effects of civilization is most clearly presented is *La nouvelle Héloïse*. Although

---

[74] See *Emile*, bk I, p. 56; bk II, p. 161; bk IV, pp. 278–9, 301–2; and bk V, p. 594. In *Emile*, the influence of physical causes is sometimes seasoned with scattered hints at physiological features, which, for example, are resorted to in the famous relationship between the cruelty of the English and their large consumption of animal flesh: bk II, pp. 196–7.

[75] *ibid.*, bk V, p. 594 (*Emile*, p. 417; trans. modified); see also pp. 591–2. See also *Considérations sur le gouvernement de Pologne* (1771), in J.-J. Rousseau, *Discours sur l'économie politique. Projet de constitution pour la Corse. Considérations sur le gouvernement de Pologne*, ed. B. De Negroni (Paris, 1990), pp. 171ff.; *Projet de constitution pour la Corse* (1765), in Rousseau, *Discours sur l'économie politique*, pp. 117–24. Elsewhere, 'les premières mœurs' are ascribed to modes of production, which, at any rate, are natural as well: J.-J. Rousseau, *Essai sur l'origine des langues*, ed. C. Porset (1756?; Bordeaux, 1970), pp. 97–107.

the portrait of Parisians as phony socialites given by Rousseau's spokesperson Saint-Preux is evidently reminiscent of Muralt, it serves eminently to illustrate the attitudes of men in urban settings where *esprit*, luxury, and commerce are cherished in place of independence, *retraite*, domestic virtues, and agriculture. Rousseau neatly poses the difference between 'original' characters, namely the 'natural inclinations' of peoples which are to be looked for in the provinces, and the effects of a 'numerous and tightly-knit [*resserrée*] *société*', apparent in all capital cities.[76] The crux of the matter is Rousseau's belief that Nature does not make mistakes and therefore 'all the vices we attribute to the original mould [*au naturel*] are actually the effect of the bad forms it has received'.[77] Saint-Preux makes explicit that the object of his travels is not to study national characters but man in general as shaped by various forms of social relations, and, in Paris, it is the *société* that immediately captures the eye. By positing the rural household of Julie and Wolmar as the positive counterpart of mores in large towns, *La nouvelle Héloïse* in fact amounts to a discussion of modern *mœurs* rather than national identities, in spite of many passages about the British, the Swiss, the Chinese, etc. Observing the moral consequences of social settings, Saint-Preux remarks, could actually lead to the knowledge of individual peoples, but by a route so long and tortuous that in practice 'I shall not be likely to comprehend any single people in my lifetime.'[78] A momentous conclusion stemming from Rousseau's premises is that, since men socializing at courts and in *salons* become mere 'masks', the peculiar traits of each people are those of the middle and lower ranks.[79]

Rousseau's vision of national character is no evidence at all of his being a forerunner of nineteenth-century nationalism. Rather, he thought of the attitudes of the peoples of his times – that is, as developed from benevolent Nature's mould through history – in the customary terms of virtue and corruption. Although his terminology was not bereft of inconsistencies, Rousseau employed the expression 'caractère national' and its synonyms in order to define the changing outcome of the relationship between the original traits of peoples and the sphere of civic virtue and *patriotisme*. When, in *Considérations sur le gouvernement de Pologne* and in *Projet de constitution pour la Corse*, he spoke of the necessity of giving a national character to a certain people, he meant that

---

[76] *Julie ou la nouvelle Héloïse*, ed. M. Launay (1761; Paris, 1967), part II, letter 14, pp. 163–7; letter 16, pp. 171–2; letter 21, pp. 189–99.

[77] *ibid.*, part V, letter 3, p. 426 (*Julie, or, The New Heloise*, trans. P. Stewart and J. Vaché (London, 1997), p. 461; trans. modified).

[78] *ibid.*, part II, letter 16, pp. 171–2; see also part I, letter 23, pp. 46–7; letter 60, p. 111; part IV, letter 3, pp. 308–11; part V, letters 2–14, pp. 413–82; and part VI, letters 1–5, pp. 485–505. On French character, and on Rousseau's attitude towards it, there are revealing passages in *Les confessions*, ed. B. Gagnebin, M. Raymond, and C. Kœnig (1782–9; Paris, 1998), pp. 213, 238–40.

[79] *Julie ou la nouvelle Héloïse*, part II, letter 14, p. 166.

that people had to turn from the pursuit of mere private interests to the pursuit of public interests, that is, to *patriotisme*. A *patriote* is for Rousseau, as well as for all his fellow philosophers, 'one who, under a free government, cherishes his *patrie*, and finds his happiness and glory in zealously supporting it as his means and faculties permit'.[80] Legislators instil civic virtue in the citizens' minds by resorting to an idea of *patrie* that simply amounts to good government, that is, government by laws. Rousseau's circular reasoning, which in itself was no novelty at all, can be summed up by connecting two of his aphorisms. 'There can be no *patrie* without liberty', he maintained, 'nor liberty without virtue, nor virtue without citizens', but at the same time 'peoples become in the long run what the government makes them' by means of laws and public education.[81] The possible contradiction between virtue as the condition of possibility of *patrie* and *patrie* as the source of virtue is attenuated, if not overcome, by the fact that these are Rousseau's two writings that deal with the establishment of a government, in agreement, therefore, with the previous point about both the legislator's constraints and the healthy condition of the people required for its successful intervention. The gist of the matter is that Rousseau clearly indicates the interaction between government and citizens as a vital requisite of the political realm, emphasizing the moral tension that should substantiate it.

In *Considérations sur le gouvernement de Pologne*, the famous 'jeux d'enfants', which he advocates to establish Polish character, entertain no link whatsoever with something like the irreducible cultural identity of Poland. They would suit any country in the same circumstances as the Poland of the time. Rousseau suggested a programme of national celebrations with the explicit aim of counteracting, on a spiritual plane, a possible invasion by Russians; in doing so, he made appeal to factors of social identity that amounted to patriotism, without attaching any 'nationalistic' meaning to it. If you cannot stop Russians from invading you, 'see to it, at least, that they shall not be able to digest you'. It is true that this entailed making the Poles different from other peoples, namely, giving their souls 'a national outlook [*physionomie*]' through a set of national institutions, a revival of old Polish *usages*, and the creation of new ones, peculiar to the country. But the single event of Polish history he refers to is a military victory as recent as 1770, which he invites the citizens to celebrate; and the single *usage* he mentions, and of which he recommends the diffusion, is a national dress.[82] For the rest, Rousseau speaks in general of the necessity of public games, outdoor mass spectacles, and patriotic honours and rewards – on the model of the ancient Greeks and Romans. This is patriotism, not nationalism:

---

[80] [de Jaucourt], 'Patriote', in *Encyclopédie*, XII, p. 124.
[81] 'Discours sur l'économie politique' (1755), in *Discours sur l'économie politique*, pp. 69, 77–8 (*The Social Contract*, pp. 139, 149–50; trans. modified).
[82] *Considérations sur le gouvernement de Pologne*, pp. 170–7. For the role of education, see pp. 177–82.

his frame of reference is in the republican tradition and thereby is universal in character. As other texts of his show, popular celebrations suit republics apart from any reference to national identity.[83] In Poland as elsewhere, mores are an inherent element of the polity, but, as shown, they draw their true importance from their relationship to a government, that is, from their being instrumental in the making (and development) of a *patrie*. Rousseau's problem is to secure 'the Republic in the hearts of the Poles'; in this perspective, good *mœurs* relate essentially to what, in Poland as elsewhere, are the basic components of good government: civic virtue, laws, and liberty.

I assumed that I was addressing myself to a people that, though not wholly free from vices, still possesses some energy and certain virtues; and, on that assumption, my project is a good one. But, if Poland has, in this regard, already reached a point where all is deep-seated venality and corruption, then it can only fail in its attempt to reform its laws and retain its liberty; it should abandon the whole venture and bow its head under the yoke.[84]

The question can be addressed from another viewpoint. The measures advocated in *Considérations* were aimed at the 'passions' rather than the reason of the Poles. Unsurprisingly in view of his assertion of moral sentiments, Rousseau's republican citizen is to be led to virtue through the arousing of intense feelings of belonging, which should permeate his life as a whole. This is why to Rousseau there is no gulf between the public and the private spheres – a stance entailing that the reform of public mores must begin with that of domestic life.[85] It is arguable that, in both spheres, the problem is how to create 'enthusiasm', since the goal is to win over 'the hearts' of men, in order, respectively, to establish the laws and to gain the love and loyalty of relatives, servants, and employees. *La nouvelle Héloïse* is revealing in this respect, for the idyllic household of Julie provides a small-scale model of games, public honours, celebrations, and spectacles intended to 'make' honest servants and contented peasants. The secret of Julie and Wolmar is 'the language of heart', consisting of good examples, humanity, and a sensitive management of passions.[86] It emerges, then, that the 'jeux d'enfants' are of universal application because the language of heart is so – a not unexpected conclusion considering the universal nature of the principles and concerns by which Rousseau was driven.

As regards Rousseau's references to patriotism as an exclusive and anti-cosmopolitan kind of passion, he explained it by saying that it was natural

---

[83] See, e.g., *Lettre à d'Alembert*, pp. 297–312.
[84] *Considérations sur le gouvernement de Pologne*, p. 240 (*The Government of Poland*, trans. W. Kendall (Indianapolis and New York, 1972), p. 92; trans. modified).
[85] See, e.g, *Julie ou la nouvelle Héloïse*, appendix, p. 582: 'S'il y a quelque réforme à tenter dans les mœurs publiques, c'est par les mœurs domestiques qu'elle doit commencer.'
[86] *ibid.*, esp. part IV, letter 10, pp. 339–52, and part V, letter 7, pp. 456–62.

to love those who are closer more forcefully – a banal point, perhaps, yet rather commonplace in the writings of Scottish philosophers, and one that has certainly nothing to do with nineteenth-century nationalism.[87] It seems to refer much more to the *vexata quaestio* of the size of republics: Rousseau advocated a republic where 'each member can be known by everybody else'. The nation, according to Rousseau, must become a *patrie*; but the reverse is unperceived in his perspective.

6   The *Histoire des deux Indes* and radical naturalism

Raynal's bulky *Histoire des deux Indes* offers a treatment of all the patterns of thought surveyed (for example, the contrast between Northern and Southern peoples and the 'no pain, no gain' argument), which is hardly surprising given its collective authorship. Moreover, the national characters of most of the known peoples are depicted, chiefly on the grounds of climate, government, and religion.[88] The vicissitudes of French genius are discussed in some depth. Like Mably, Raynal outlines the story of a French character that was bold, proud, and freedom-loving, but which faded when France fell under absolutist rule. Now, 'inconsistency' seems natural to a nation which is 'gay and lively like children'. It is argued that this capricious attitude, coupled with a remnant of the spirit of liberty, has played a crucial role in softening the most brutal facets of the regime. 'The national character' made 'a sort of balance of power' possible by directing the attention of kings and courtiers to 'the frivolous entertainments which they idolized', by prevailing over the plans of certain 'despotic ministers', and by safeguarding what remained of the ancient dignity of the subjects. The discrepancy between the nation's 'mœurs et manieres' and the form of its government accounts for the fact that contemporary Frenchmen show traits that are thought of as contradictory (for example, they are 'effeminate, but brave'), and that ultimately result in an attitude which is 'thoughtless [*léger*] and superficial'.[89]

Among many other things, the *Histoire des deux Indes* suggests something like a recipe for catching up with Great Britain, that is to say that even

---

[87] Rousseau's stance emerges very clearly from 'Discours sur l'économie politique', pp. 72–4. Denunciations of national prejudices are not rare in *Emile*: see bk IV, pp. 329–30; bk V, pp. 590ff., 617.

[88] Although it is now realized that Raynal's part in the actual writing of the *Histoire* was small, I consider it (in the second edition, 1774) as it appeared to its first audience, that is as a work by a single author. When considered in this light, this patchwork of ideas assumes a special interest as a genuine, even if unintentional, product of the *Zeitgeist*. Consequently, this discussion only takes occasional account of the actual authorship (when known) of the passages referred to. The contribution of Diderot has been precisely identified by M. Duchet, *Diderot et l'Histoire des Deux Indes ou l'écriture fragmentaire* (Paris, 1978).

[89] *Histoire philosophique et politique des établissemens et du commerce des Européens dans les Deux Indes* (1770; 2nd edn, 7 vols., The Hague, 1774), I, p. 26; IV, pp. 108–9; VII, pp. 239–43. The passage about French contrasts recalls J. Brown, *An Estimate of the Manners and Principles of the Times* (1757; 2 vols., Dublin, 1758), I, p. 88.

unenlightened concerns with European and colonial supremacy are given some thought. Raynal recalled the age of Louis XIV with some bitterness:

What could the French genius have done under the single influence of laws, since it dared to do such great things under the rule of the most absolute of kings? In appreciating how much energy patriotism has given the English, in spite of the non-existent stimulus of climate, consider what it would have produced in France, where a mild sky invites a lively and sensitive people to create and enjoy! France is a country where, as in the Greece of old, there are ardent spirits able to invent, under a sky which warms them with its most beautiful rays; and there are also quick and skilful hands [*des bras nerveux*], in a climate where the cold itself stimulates work.[90]

The character of the English is depicted along the lines drawn by both Montesquieu – their 'fervent spirit' is the ultimate reason for their liberty – and Mably – that spirit is due to their sensitivity to misrule, developed over centuries of monarchical oppression. British government is a creation of that 'national character'. Great Britain was the object of mixed feelings, as Raynal and his associates noticed not only the political virtues of its people but also the aggressiveness of the economic policies it pursued.[91]

The *Histoire des deux Indes* confirms the view that French philosophers dealt with national character themes in a comprehensive and flexible way, synchronically taking several different factors into account. Either direction of influence between government and *mœurs* could easily be reversed.[92] On the other hand, the *Histoire* raises reasonable suspicions of meaningless inconsistency, because of its catholic approach as well as the innumerable contradictions that mar its pages. Even 'a polyphonic text', however, may have its points. Unambiguously, the view that made the Blacks born for slavery because they were ignorant, sly, and mean is reversed: the reason they were like this is because they were enslaved.[93]

The *Histoire*, at least from its second edition onwards, is marked by a tension between human nature and human history. The authors constantly referred to a

---

[90] *Histoire des Deux Indes*, VII, p. 392; on the question of catching up with Great Britain, see V, pp. 392–402.
[91] *ibid.*, I, pp. 26–7; IV, pp. 97, 105, 112–13; V, pp. 254–6, 372–3, 392–3; VII, pp. 229–33.
[92] 'Les bonnes loix se maintiennent par les bonnes mœurs; mais les bonnes mœurs s'établissent par les bonnes loix': *ibid.*, VII, p. 421. This remark, which was common in eighteenth-century France as Rousseau in particular indicates, originally came from Machiavelli: see *Discorsi sopra la prima deca di Tito Livio* (1513–21), in N. Machiavelli, *Il Principe e altre opere politiche*, ed. S. Andretta (Milan, 1997), bk I, ch. 18, p. 156 (where the stress is on the influence of *mœurs* on laws).
[93] I am referring to a passage quoted in W. R. Womack, 'Eighteenth-Century Themes in the *Histoire philosophique et politique des Deux Indes* of Guillaume Raynal', *Studies on Voltaire and the Eighteenth Century*, 96 (1972), p. 168, from the third edition of the *Histoire* (1780). Inspiration on this specific point may have been drawn from Buffon: *De l'homme*, pp. 283–4. See M. Duchet, 'L'*Histoire des deux Indes*: sources et structure d'un texte polyphonique', *Studies on Voltaire and the Eighteenth Century*, 286 (1991), pp. 9–16.

hidden reality which lay behind the miseries recorded in the annals of humanity. These writers opposed the concept of a rational natural man to man as shaped by centuries of oppression. The following passage is distinctively Diderotian.

It is sufficient for a powerful and not very enlightened nation to adopt an initial erroneous position, which ignorance gives credence to: this error soon becomes general, and serves as a basis of the whole moral and political system. Soon, the most honest tendencies [*penchants*] come to contradict duties. In order to follow the new moral order, it is necessary to deny violently the physical order. This constant struggle will give birth to the most astonishing contradictions in mores; the nation will be reduced to a mere assemblage of miserable people, who will spend their lives tormenting one another, while complaining of nature. This is the portrait of all existing peoples, with the exception, perhaps, of a few republics of savages.[94]

From a standpoint like this, a call for government, mores, and religion in accordance with natural laws inevitably emerges. The fascination with an uncorrupted 'natural man' – the inner baseness of modernity is contrasted with the purity and innocence of early societies – conveys with the utmost clarity an awareness of the inextricability of political and moral reform.

The admirers of the *bon sauvage* were carrying to a paradoxical extreme the same plea which ran through Voltaire or Montesquieu's texts, namely the primacy of society over government. What the authors grouped around Raynal ultimately say is that the latter has to accommodate to the former; what differs is simply that they do not refer to a present or past community but to a mythical one which they call natural and rational. The ascendancy-of-society perspective, well expressed by the common request 'to set up governments made for men' and not the reverse, was coupled with a moral connotation of society. It has been shown how many philosophers writing about the corrupt mores of the age were unable to do without some notion of a previous period of national history when virtues had been upheld. The need for a moral yardstick was generally felt, and sought either in historical time, or in an ideal state of nature, or even in the life of surviving primitive tribes. The abstractness of this position is thus apparent. As said earlier, the primacy of society was a claim drawing its impact from political protest, rather than from the acknowledged emergence of a virtuous middle class in France. The middle ranks were hardly focused on, and thereby hardly differentiated from the aristocracy, the regular target of philosophers' strictures. As Mably wrote, 'the third state is nothing in France', because, in line with the 'national spirit', nobody wants to be included in it.[95] The widespread appeal of the French past, the English example, or Roman and Greek models, resulted from this view of the French middling ranks as exclusively preoccupied with social climbing.

---

[94] *Histoire des Deux Indes*, I, pp. 70–1.
[95] Mably, *Observations sur l'histoire*, III, p. 313.

Considering that Diderot was a major contributor to the *Histoire*, it is no wonder that in his other writings he showed a similar approach, relying on a visionary physiology (*Elémens de physiologie* is particularly astonishing) that went hand in hand with the invention of a primeval purity of manners. If the secret of man's fate must be looked for in his physical organization (variously influenced by climate) and not in education, as he asserted against Helvétius, civilization too may be assessed by means of organic analogies. In full agreement with the *Histoire*, Diderot argued that European societies suffered from an 'old disease, almost incurable', that is, the contrast between natural and enacted laws. The divergences between the natural, the civil, and the religious codes had made the practice of mores consistent with each of the three domains impossible, and thereby induced a state of frustration and alienation. '*Mœurs*', he stated in *Supplément au voyage de Bouganville*, are in fact 'a general obedience to laws, either good or bad, and such conduct as follows from that obedience'; so that if laws are good, mores are good, but, if laws are confused, mores are non-existent.[96]

The starting point of his evaluation of the role that national characters play can be found in the distinction he drew between 'young' peoples, which, because of their naiveté, were still capable of endorsing a set of coherent principles, and those that appeared to be irretrievably lost. The inhabitants of Tahiti, as well as the Russians, were numbered among the 'young' group. The organic metaphor, once handled in this way, might result in a view of the course of history. But Diderot is, to say the least, a disconcerting writer: his pages are often obscure and his *œuvre* abounds with conflicting statements. Take for instance his position on Russia. In advising the Tsarina, Diderot declared the Russians fit for liberal laws, notwithstanding the unfavourable climate (as Montesquieu himself had argued). Its influence was 'great' but not decisive. The problem is that passages like this fly in the face of his advocacy of physical causes:

Mores are everywhere the result of legislation and government; they are not African or Asiatic or European. They are good or bad. You are a slave under the Pole where it is very cold, and a slave in Constantinopole where it is very hot: but everywhere a people should be educated, free and virtuous. If what Peter I brought to Russia was good in Europe, then it should be good everywhere. Without denying the influence of climate on mores, it is clear from the current condition of Greece and Italy, and it will be clear from the future condition of Russia, that good or bad mores stem from other causes.[97]

Diderot was reacting to what had become a major tenet of social knowledge, namely the unsuitability of harsh climates to civilization. He went as far as

---

[96] *Observations sur l'Instruction de Sa Majesté Impériale aux députés pour la confection des lois* (1774), *DOC*, XI, pp. 233–4; *Supplément au voyage de Bouganville* (1773–4), *DOC*, X, p. 240.
[97] *Observations sur l'Instruction*, p. 214 (*Political Writings*, trans. J. H. Mason and R. Wokler (Cambridge, 1992), pp. 85–6).

rejecting Solon's principle that the constitution should be adapted to the characteristics of the people, on the grounds that the legislator can 'make' the national spirit when, as in Russia, the government holds an absolute power and the people are 'slavish and barbarous'.[98]

Tentatively, it may be argued that most of Diderot's remarks on the decisive influence of physical factors over men concerned the character of individuals, and especially of talented ones, rather than collective identity; to him, multitudes were in themselves a passive and depressing *tabula rasa*, which was effectively shaped by laws and government.[99] Diderot's discourse on historical man revolves around more familiar horizons as he elaborates on the theme of demoralization brought about by despotism.[100] As regards the French, he observes that those who are inferior in rank customarily mimic their immediate superiors, with the effect that the boundaries of all social groups become blurred in the name of a fatal 'luxury of imitation', which amounts to vulgar ostentation in a few cases and to the mask of misery in many.[101]

Diderot's contribution to the *Histoire des deux Indes* features a particular use of 'national spirit'. He considers this spirit, resulting from a blend of physical and historical causes, as inherently related to a concern with the common good, in so far as it is only when the nation's 'speculative principles' and 'physical situation' match that collective progress is guaranteed and a proper 'national spirit' emerges. National character in this sense should preside over the government, but it does not always do so. As for society, individuals in practice follow their own passions and interests regardless of the public dimension, even if in words national spirit is eulogized. There is hardly one 'who would not build his own prosperity through public ruin'. This self-interested attitude becomes blatant in the case of colonists: 'beyond the Equator a man is neither English, Dutch, French, Spanish, nor Portuguese. He retains only those principles and prejudices of his native country which justify or excuse his conduct.'[102] Passions are stronger than any national version of public morality. On a different plane, Diderot's use of primitive man as a standard by which to assess the advantages and disadvantages in the life of modern man led him to a social and economic account of moral propensities, which sapped the foundations of any

---

[98] *ibid.*, p. 232.

[99] *Réfutation suivie de l'ouvrage d'Helvétius intitulé, L'Homme* (1783–6), *DOC*, XI, pp. 506, 586–7; 'Project d'un traité', *DOC*, XIII, pp. 910–11. Conversely, the concept of genius plays an important role in Diderot's moral perspective: see A. Strugnell, *Diderot's Politics* (The Hague, 1973), pp. 73–89.

[100] *Supplément au voyage*, p. 240; *Observations sur l'Instruction*, p. 234; *Réfutation*, pp. 573–5. See also the extracts from the *Histoire des Deux Indes* collected in Diderot, *Political Writings*, pp. 190–1, 194–5.

[101] *Réfutation*, p. 576; see also pp. 609–10.

[102] See the third edition of the *Histoire des Deux Indes* (10 vols., Geneva, 1780), V, pp. 2–3 (*Political Writings*, pp. 177–8, where 'esprit national' is translated as 'national character').

rigid notion of national character. This passage concerns a European settlement in South America:

> The scraps and dregs of civilised societies can sometimes form a well ordered society. It is the iniquity of our laws, the unjust distribution of goods, the burdens and pains of poverty, the insolence and impunity of the rich, the abuse of power, which frequently make rebels and criminals. Bring together these unfortunate men, whom an often exaggerated severity has banished from their own homes; give them a bold, generous, humane and enlightened leader; and you will make out of these ruffians an honest, docile, reasonable people.[103]

7 The widening of *société*: Helvétius, Mably again, and Holbach

When the connections between the incipient awareness of civil society and the themes relating to national character are focused on, the relevant authors appear to differ remarkably in their viewpoints. Mably stretches the potential of civic humanism to the limit, whereas Helvétius and Holbach dismiss crucial elements of the classical legacy in favour of a distinctively novel approach based on utilitarian tenets. Another difference is that the importance of Helvétius from the 'social' perspective is to be ascribed to his mould-breaking role in terms of the general mode of approach to national character, rather than to any specific contribution.[104]

Climate was Helvétius's *bête noire*. He viewed the notion of its influence as stemming from a philosophy of knowledge which emphasized the role of human physiology ('la machine') in determining personality, whereas he advocated the effectiveness of education. The whole of *De l'Homme* and many sections of *De l'Esprit* are devoted to a multisided attack on the philosophic background of the climatic doctrine. Helvétius was one of the few authors who entirely rejected climatological suggestions, even if a trend that progressively leant towards the limitation of climatic views and in favour of political factors is recognizable in the 1770s and 1780s. Besides its broad philosophical and pedagogical implications, his opposition rested on the justification for despotism that the climatological thesis could provide. 'The laziness and negligence' of governments could be validated by the climatological approach.

If the physical organization determines almost entirely what we are, what grounds are there to reproach the teacher for the ignorance and stupidity of his pupils? Why, it may be argued, impute the shortcomings of nature to education? How to reply? And, once a principle is admitted, how to deny its immediate consequence? On the other hand, if it is proved that talents and virtues can be acquired, the industry of the teacher will be

---

[103] *ibid.*, V, p. 139 (*Political Writings*, p. 179).
[104] Helvétius retained parts of the republican discourse, especially in *De l'esprit*, to an extent undocumented in the following treatment.

stimulated and his negligence prevented: he will become more conscientious, both in stifling the vices and in nurturing the virtues of his disciples.[105]

A broadly intended education, especially as embodied in laws, was the sole effective influence on the shaping of both individual and national characters: 'in each country there are some objects which education brings to the attention of everybody, and the uniform impression of these objects produces in the citizenry the resemblance of ideas and sentiments which is called national spirit and character'.[106] Helvétius's utilitarian philosophy sets pleasure and pain as the moving forces of human passions, and this leads him to maintain that *all* men have the same capability of achieving, by means of education and favourable circumstances, 'spiritual superiority'. His discovery was that 'talents and virtues can be acquired'. The elimination of fictional physiology and its related climatological suggestions, together with the adoption of utilitarianism, brings a breath of fresh air. Utilitarianism entails a view of the 'nation' as made up of all ranks, even if, according to Helvétius, not all of these should be educated in the same way.

As the character of individuals is, in practice, to a great extent shaped by their social status, so that of nations depends on the form of government and the kind of public education it accordingly provides. But 'the form of government under which we live is always part of our education', Helvétius argues, adding that as a consequence moral philosophy should turn into the science of the legislator.[107] The rule is that 'it is always the degree of absurdity of laws that everywhere accounts for the degree of stupidity or nastiness of citizens'.[108] Government's influence works through the rewards ('riches and honours') that it attaches to actions; men's love of pleasures can be effectively directed by wise legislators towards the common good. Helvétius makes a case for a system of rewards that ultimately develops social virtues, so that 'under an excellent legislation the only corrupt ones will be the fools'. This simple framework – 'reform of *mœurs* should begin with reform of law' – enabled Helvétius to develop some polemical motifs, always taking as his lodestar, especially in *De l'Esprit*, the paralysing effects of despotism and superstition.

Helvétius rejected the belief that certain nations, like the Asiatic ones, were either indifferent to or unfit for the passions of glory and virtue. Once it is admitted that 'national characters are liable to assume all sorts of shapes', national stereotypes become false and even ridiculous. He opposes the traditional image of the French as lively and enjoyable to be with: lack of welfare and political,

---

[105] *De l'Homme, de ses facultés intellectuelles et de son education* (2 vols., London, 1773), I, p. 5.
[106] *ibid.*, I, p. 326, fn.
[107] *ibid.*, I, pp. 230–7; *De l'Esprit* (1758), in C. A. Helvétius, *Œuvres complètes* (1795; repr. edn, 14 vols., Hildesheim, 1967–9), II, pp. 236–51.
[108] *De l'Homme*, I, p. 269.

administrative, and religious oppression could not fail to change their genius. People acquire the character that is esteemed and rewarded under the existing government, and consequently the contemporary French show a spirit which is 'superficial [*léger*] and frivolous'. That 'the body of the French nation becomes more stupefied [*s'abrutit*] by the day' is a reflection of the nature of their government, rather than a permanent national trait. Helvétius's frame of thought proves a vantage point from which to criticize such national prejudices, which he calls the 'mutual contempt' of nations. Peoples misrepresent the cause of their nation's superiority by ascribing it to natural factors, and fail to perceive 'the ridicule of which the nation is the object to the eyes of reason', because of national vanity and intolerance.[109]

To return to Mably, there is a third standpoint discernible, besides history and climate, from which he addressed national character themes. This is his obscure perception of the role of the masses in politics. The absence of the modern concept of nation and the ongoing discovery of civil society have been said to constitute the context of French reflections. The two terms, 'nation' and 'society', were inextricably linked. As students of nationalism have convincingly argued, the rise of modern nations meant that all orders of society were identified with the national community; the 'people', which came to be seen as the central object of loyalty, was only superficially divided along the lines of class and status.[110] This makes all the difference when one compares most eighteenth-century French philosophers to nineteenth-century writers. The former neglected consideration of the habits and mentalities of the lower orders, that is, of those that bore no political character within the *ancien régime*. The character that the philosophers mainly discussed (and thought of as 'national') was that of the upper strata only, even if occasional reference was made to that of the middling ranks, usually to assimilate it into the dispositions of *les grands*. The mores, habits, and psychological traits of the lower ranks usually played no part whatsoever.[111] However, a shift of emphasis occurred with regard to the political significance of *le peuple* in the period from Montesquieu to Holbach.[112] A novel acknowledgement of the lower strata was an essential component of the enhanced distinctness of the whole society. In so far as all elements of political power had been drained from the upper classes of society (from the *états*) to be concentrated in the hands of the state, with the consequence that now

---

[109] *De l'Esprit,* V, pp. 69–73, and III, pp. 70–92; *De l'Homme,* I, pp. VI, 234–5, 316, fn.; II, p. 64.
[110] The point is forcefully made by L. Greenfeld, *Nationalism: Five Roads to Modernity* (Cambridge, Mass., 1992), pp. 3–26; see also E. Gellner, *Nations and Nationalism* (Oxford, 1983).
[111] That is not to say that the wretched living conditions of the lower strata and especially of the peasants went unremarked, as many instances demonstrate, from La Bruyère to Diderot.
[112] 'Pour appartenir au peuple, tel qu'il est défini en 1765 par Jacourt dans l'*Encyclopédie,* il faut associer *pauvreté* et *labeur*': J.-P. Gross, 'L'idée de la pauvreté dans la pensée sociale des jacobins. Origines et prolongements', *Annales historiques de la Révolution française,* 248 (1982), p. 207.

no other allegiance was legitimate, foundations had been laid for recognition of the equality of all citizens in the sight of the law. This paved the way for a political perspective that involved all the groups that made up society. To delineate the clash between this incipient consciousness as far as it is discernible in Mably and his republicanism, the relevant text is *Du cours et de la marche des passions dans la société.*

Mably's confidence in the power of laws has already been pointed out: 'nothing is impossible to a skilful legislator', he wrote, 'he holds our heart and our spirit in his hands, so to speak; he can make new men'. This belief is closely related to his view of the course of history as a struggle between reason and passions, as a battlefield where 'I have seen the passions like as many Furies' indefatigably engaged in corrupting *mœurs*. Laws exist in order to restrain passions and enforce reason. 'National character' comes into play as a concise expression of the ruling passions of societies. Mably goes so far as to argue that national character in this sense becomes the essential tool of policy-makers, because it enables them to predict the fate of society, which depends on 'the fortifications that a people has set up against its own meanness, ambition, luxury, and effeminacy, as well as against tyranny and anarchy'.[113]

But, 'I say it with regret', vigorous passions have also been the moving force of civilization, the unexhausted sources of both vices and virtues. The stirring of passions is a necessary requisite of the 'practice of great and heroic virtues', yet Mably fears that 'this agitation' may itself cause troubles and finally decline. Free communities are agitated by many passions simultaneously, which 'mutually contain themselves', whereas under despotic rule passions follow one another according to the will of kings.[114] A free society is, thus, a problematic and fragile arrangement, and Mably points to civic morality – that is, a positive tension between citizen and polity – as the only possible inner force of social dynamic. However, he shows a growing concern that the progressive trend could be reversed. Mably had in mind the republican tradition of thought, with its notion of cyclical recurrence, when he depicted the decline of a nation as a decline in its public spirit:

A general state of confidence would soon be followed by contented and lazy indolence ... The spirit of the government influences the citizens, but, in turn, the spirit of citizens influences the government. Thus, the stirring sentiment that, through the blend of various powers and their reciprocal action, excites emulation, multiplies *lumières*, and strongly binds [*attache*] both the magistrates and the citizens to *patrie* and liberty, would alter bit by bit, because it is the nature of men to view with indifference the good things we are not afraid of losing.[115]

---

[113] Mably, *Du cours et de la marche des passions*, pp. 207–8, 473.
[114] *ibid.*, pp. 406–7, 412–13.
[115] The quotation is from *ibid.*, p. 256; what precedes is from *De la législation*, p. 268, and *Du cours et de la marche des passions*, pp. 430, 472–4.

A main character on the stage of history set by Mably is the much despised mass of the people, 'the mad or imbecile multitude that covers the earth'. People at large are unable to think clearly and cannot detach themselves from present circumstances, thus being ruled by conflicting passions that ultimately result in basic and fleeting pleasures. The savage stupidity of multitudes may sometimes alarm, Mably comments, but in the end it is government's laws that provide them with the sets of passions required by the polity at a given moment.[116] But Mably had difficulty in coming to terms with the irrationality of the masses, since his intellectual framework was inherently unfit for the task. If there really was a growing perception in France of the progressively enlarging boundaries of society, it could hardly be interpreted with reference to republican virtues – how could it be suggested that the doubtful morality of tradesmen, or even peasants, would add to the martial courage, public spiritedness, and frugality of Frenchmen?

It is true that Mably confidently asserted that existing laws and circumstances moulded the passions of the masses so well that they acted as the most effective conservative element in societies. In this case, 'national character' amounts to the aggregate of the opinions shared by citizens to which they stick 'almost by instinct', and which they ultimately see as reason itself. Mably emphasizes the actual force of this 'national genius' – 'the empire of *mœurs* and public opinions' – over the behaviour of citizens.

From it, there necessarily results a kind of confidence, of security or habitual composure, which prevents the fiery outbursts of passions, or, at any rate, calms them down with little effort. In these circumstances, nations are less tempted to shake off the yoke of laws and customs [*coutumes*]. An event that, at another time, would bring about a revolution, will just excite a short-lived riot, which will leave no trace afterwards.[117]

The course of history was determined by collective passions restrained by law. It was the ambition of the Romans, for instance, that shaped them into a conquering and powerful people; behind the events of Roman history lay the hidden force of national character 'which became a political system' and led them almost inadvertently to glory. Governments, Mably repeats, can direct the mind of the 'populace' at will: as a result, 'its routine and ignorance will mould mechanical heroes'.[118]

On the other hand, national character as people's mental horizon vanishes during times of persistent social or political crisis; in such circumstances, the citizen, 'displaced and dragged away from his habits', will follow the leader who 'knows how to flatter his passions'. Since the allegiance of *le peuple* has no rational basis, it is hardly surprising that they are depicted as incapable of

---

[116] *Du cours et de la marche des passions,* pp. 166–7 and *passim.*
[117] *ibid.,* pp. 198–9.
[118] *ibid.,* pp. 200–23, 244–5, 436–7, 444–5; and see *De la legislation,* pp. 252ff.

defending the established regime – what is actually striking is the violence of Mably's comments overall.

The people [*peuple*], used to mechanical obedience by fear as well as the example of their superiors, no longer know whether they are men of the same species as them, and eventually come to think that their deplorable situation is their natural state. They come to regard their stupidity as the foundation and the pledge of their tranquillity, and of public security: they would deem themselves unfortunate if they were allowed to move on. If, by chance, their misery is relieved for a while, they view it as a favour [*une grâce*], and, carried away by the cheerfulness of their gratitude, will not fail to burden themselves with new shackles.[119]

If a despot seizes power, the people are led by their ignorance, idleness, and rashness not to resist.

Happy with the most trifling satisfaction, even after the most severe injuries [*injures*], in order to be consoled of an afflicting present the people [*peuple*] do not demand anything more than a hope of a better future: you would say that they love to be wrong, and that the flimsiest promises suffice to calm them.[120]

When, and if, the people shake off their habit of torpid passiveness, they quickly grow tired of the effort, and, having forgotten what set them in motion, blame themselves for their imprudence and temerity. Eventually, they are eager to return to their routine, now even more cherished.[121]

In a revealing passage, Mably correlates the fall of Rome and Sparta, that is, of his true models of polity, with the *peuple*. How could the low passions required to rule the masses fail to affect the republic's magistrates? 'In order to be liked by the ignorant multitude, whose ridiculous and capricious expressions of praise should instead be despised, will not the magistrates be flattered by their acclaim?'[122] The reason why so many nations have failed to establish enlightened governments is the ascendancy of the multitude over their natural superiors, or, in other words, of blind passions and temporary pleasures over reason.[123] In warning the American patriots against the dangers of democracy in 1784, the inherent barbarity of the multitudes represents the boundary at which laws, policies, and regulations designed to improve *mœurs* have to stop. Legislators can cope with the corruption brought about by economic development, but unenlightened multitudes are an unpleasant fact of nature, that is, impervious to change. Consequently, Mably advocated an aristocratic government for the United States.[124] This censure of *le peuple* is less relevant than the

[119] *De l'étude de l'histoire*, pp. 90–1.
[120] *ibid.*, p. 90.
[121] *Du cours et de la marche des passions*, p. 167.
[122] *ibid.*, p. 403.
[123] *ibid.*, p. 402.
[124] *Observations sur le gouvernement et les lois des Etats-Unis d'Amérique* (1784), *MCC*, VIII, pp. 339–485.

fact that he at least deemed the lower ranks worthy of consideration, a posture stemming from the prominence he ascribed to the notion of passions, which had in the people their natural seat.

Holbach's sensitivity to a wider dimension of politics was unquestionably greater than Mably's, mainly thanks to his sharper cognizance of society. In the civic humanist perspective, society is defined and synthesized through its *mœurs*, which, at the same time, help to constitute the political domain in general, as well as being an essential point of reference for law-making in particular. Holbach, too, makes much of the relationship between government and *mœurs*, but these tend to be viewed as separate from politics. Government simply borrows its powers from society, and is created to meet its needs. Society has rights that are absolutely original and that dictate the political agenda. Holbach took a step forward in the slow appraisal of society that marks the French Enlightenment.

In order to be useful, Politics should draw its principles from nature, that is to say, to adapt [*se conformer*] to the essence and goals of Society. This is a whole formed by the gathering of a large number of families and individuals, whose aim is to meet more easily their mutual needs, to get the things they desire, to support each other, and in particular to enjoy with security the goods supplied by nature and industry. It follows that the Politics intended to preserve society should adopt its goals, make the attainment of the means easier, and remove all the obstacles which could cross its path.[125]

The essential political goods – liberty, property, and security – have the benefit of society as their object, and their provision represents the only possible criterion of legitimacy for a government.

A society whose rulers and laws do not yield any good to its members loses its rights over them; the rulers who harm society lose the right to govern it. There is no *patrie* without well-being; a society without equality contains only mutual enemies, and an oppressed society contains only oppressors and slaves; slaves cannot be citizens; it is liberty, property, and security that make *patrie* dear, and it is the love of *patrie* that makes a citizen.[126]

Social distinctions, honours and rewards should be awarded on the exclusive basis of social utility, society being 'a chain of services' where 'no one is contemptible as long as he is really useful'.[127]

Holbach, in wondering by what standard to assess the justice, that is, utility, of laws, made appeal to the universally acknowledgeable criteria of nature and reason. All people are capable of distinguishing between good and evil in

---

[125] *Système de la Nature ou des loix du monde physique et du monde moral* (1770; repr. edn, 2 parts, 1 vol., Geneva, 1973), part I, p. 140 (see also pp. 141ff.). What precedes the quotation is from *La politique naturelle ou discours sur les vraies principes du gouvernement* (1773; repr. edn, 2 parts, 1 vol., Hildesheim, 1971), part I, pp. 110ff.

[126] *Système de la Nature*, part I, p. 143.

[127] *La politique naturelle*, part I, pp. 44, 171–3.

society, if 'passion, interest, or prejudice' have not blinded them. He believed in the possibility, and necessity, of educating the masses. Yet, the citizenry may actually be blind, since it is by no means rare that despots win the allegiance of a people. Often, peoples show an 'almost invincible attachment' towards tyrannical regimes and their pillars like unnatural religions, primeval habits, ancient laws, and the prejudices on which aristocracy is founded. It follows that 'the mistaken opinions of men are the real sources of their misfortunes'. Although the point in itself was hardly novel, Holbach forcefully stresses it in parallel with his fuller appreciation of the social dimension; together, these elements point to a shift in perception. In many harshly phrased passages, Holbach puts the blame for political evils on the peoples themselves, all ranks included, for their lack of understanding and proneness to obey. Dominated by habit, people misapprehend the sources of public well-being, namely, that which constitutes social utility. Yet any individual pursuit of power, riches or pleasure is doomed to failure if consideration of the social environment is neglected: it is in fact impossible to be 'exclusively happy'. The decisive factor of well-being, both individual and collective, is for Holbach the people's correct perception of social relationships.[128]

If political regimes result from the eternal struggle between 'l'erreur' and reason, the crucial feature of free governments is the promotion of a public opinion in accordance with reason, via laws, education, economic policies, and the good example of rulers. In particular, governments are in charge of the moral elevation of those who apply themselves to 'hard and necessary toil'. Holbach's picture of the lower ranks would be, in itself, close to Mably's – both judge them incapable of conducting themselves consistently – but Holbach is able to perceive the causes behind the effects.

The unjust harshness of arbitrary power and the vexations and contempt of the Grand, the Wealthy, and the People in office, take away from the common man [*l'homme du Peuple*] any feeling of honour and self-esteem. Therefore, he is willing to do anything to emancipate himself from the misery into which, very often, oppression has plunged him. His state of dependence forces him to conform to the corruption of those whom he needs to survive, or of those whose benevolence has become necessary to him. Thus, he easily agrees to sacrifice to them a feeling of honour to which he does not attach any importance; he has no idea of what a virtue is; he sells his conscience in exchange for either money or protection; and, from a distance, he imitates the vices and foibles of those whom he thinks luckier than himself.[129]

Holbach thought that in a free country people at large could effectively choose worthy representatives for political assemblies, on the grounds that even the

---

[128] *ibid.*, part I, p. 162, and part II, pp. 123–4; *Système de la Nature*, part I, pp. 136–43, 330–1, 339–40, and *passim*.

[129] *Système social ou principes naturels de la morale et de la politique* (3 vols., London, 1774), III, pp. 35–6.

least enlightened worker knew whether he was happy or not and that he was able to relate his own situation to the behaviour of the people in office.[130]

By saying that people's *mœurs* should be the primary concern of free governments, Holbach expressed something more than the usual reliance on the effects of laws over characters. Granted that enlightened governments must enforce reason, which was defined as the knowledge of what was useful to mankind, against despotism, which amounted to the prevalence of individual or group interests, the real battleground apparently shifted away from soundness of governments and towards social confrontation. In each nation the contrast is between two social passions that are natural to men, the will to dominate and the love of independence, both being fuelled by doctrines and opinions. In parallel, there is a struggle between the 'fits of enthusiasm' of society and the wisdom embedded in a rational government. Legislation and government policies 'should be even-tempered [*calme*], bereft of passions and prejudices', supplying people with various means of education about general interests: 'the function of politics is to direct, temper, and rectify the passions and opinions of peoples; it would be very dangerous if politics were their slave'.[131] However, Holbach also affirmed that if the wisest of rulers was carrying on the most beneficial policies, but against the will of the citizen, he should give up – 'no man can acquire the right to rule a nation against its will'.[132]

France's upper ranks are depicted by Holbach as an unmistakable example of the moral effects of despotism in its soft variant. In contrast with the lethargy caused by Oriental tyrannies, milder degrees of oppression make subjects 'vain, absent-minded, and dissipated', living in a state of perpetual delirium and excitation due to tireless pursuit of futile pleasures. Holbach compares the 'bonne compagnie' to children who plunge into a 'perpetual whirlpool [*tourbillon*]' as a result of their refusal to come to terms with grim realities. Frenchmen flatter themselves on being free because there are no visible chains at their feet, and because they imagine sharing with rulers a chimerical feeling of honour, whereas their 'good-natured [*débonnaires*] despots' efficiently soften subjects' wills by stimulating their lust for luxuries and spectacles. A ridiculous vanity is the ultimate result of social life in a nation which reminds Holbach of a 'theatre of illusions and cheap tricks, in which actors appear only to be booed'. Reason is necessary to put a just price on things, and the French are 'insensible, or contented, slaves' because they have lost the sense of what is important in the pursuit of amusements and trifles.[133]

---

[130] *La politique naturelle*, part I, pp. 180, 185.
[131] *ibid.*, part I, pp. 180–2; part II, pp. 7–9, 122–5, 130, 164, 187–8. The final quotation is from part II, p.124.
[132] *ibid.*, part I, pp. 44, 172–4ff., 166–7.
[133] *Système social*, III, pp. 88–104; *La politique naturelle*, part II, pp. 34, 37–43, 88–91, 101–2, 244–7. Holbach, too, made room for a certain much limited influence of climate over characters; see esp. *Système de la Nature*.

8   Before the Revolution: Chastellux and Condorcet

A notably original feature of Chastellux's thought is his open opposition to those who thundered against the corrupted mores of contemporary France. He believed that this attitude concealed the real problems, which were financial and political in character. Chastellux accordingly sought to show that the past – Greek and Roman as well as French – could not teach Frenchmen any lessons: 'the *good old days* are a moral superstition'. In particular, the ancients' patriotism was spoilt by xenophobia, the exaltation of force and glory, and a neglect of justice and private duties.[134] Chastellux's standpoint was that of a peaceful and rational pursuit of social interests as well as of individual well-being, in contrast, allegedly, with the warlike, despotic, and greedy governments which had followed one another over the centuries. Rome was his most telling example. France was not an especially flagrant case of misrule and corruption, but, like all other European countries, a nation whose government originated from conquest and for this reason suffered from many evils, with fiscal oppression as the most momentous.[135] Britain being by far the most advanced country, France too was slowly fighting its way, against despotism and superstition, towards the fulfilment of the ideal of 'the greatest happiness [*bonheur*] for the greatest number'.[136] Chastellux believed in a science-led progress of civilization which was unstoppable, and which therefore could not fail to advance the principles of government as well.[137]

Even if there is no myth of the past in Chastellux, there is the acknowledgement of the 'original and primitive' character of nations. In his major work, *De la félicité publique*, Chastellux states that nations form under the hallmark of a 'national character', for 'peoples existed before laws'. Such collective attitudes are regarded as ultimately indelible, and legislators should not only recognize their existence but also enact laws accordingly: 'whatever modification one wished to see introduced in the governments of Tyre, Sparta, and Athens, it is certain that the spirit of commerce should have presided over the first, that of equality in the second, and that of independence in the third'.[138] The topic is dealt with at some length in his *Voyages dans l'Amérique Septentrionale*, where Chastellux establishes, as a general rule, that 'legislators, like doctors, should never flatter themselves on being able to give political bodies a particular temperament, but, on the contrary, set out to know the one they already have, to struggle against its shortcomings, and to multiply its

---

[134] *De la félicité publique, ou considérations sur le sort des hommes dans les différentes époques de l'histoire* (1772; 2 vols., Bouillon, 1776), I, pp. 11–13, 28–9, 50–88ff.
[135] *ibid.*, II, pp. 3–5, 308–9.
[136] *ibid.*, II, p. 82.
[137] *ibid.*, II, pp. 69–82ff.
[138] *ibid.*, I, p. 151.

possible advantages'.[139] Here, the theme of national character verges on the already mentioned criticism of the man of system, the politician who neglects any consideration of appropriateness and timeliness in his eagerness to apply his favourite abstract scheme *in corpore vivo*. The recurrence of this criticism is so wide that, besides the rhetorical function that it probably fulfilled, it highlights a genuine concern which matches the slow, but visible, emergence of a logical primacy of society over government. This holds true even when, as in Chastellux's formulation, there are echoes of Machiavelli and classical republicanism which evidently rival Montesquieu's influence. Once represented as the sphere of purely private interests, society could be most effectively talked about in economic terms. Chastellux's discussion of the incidence of taxes on peasants – a combination, as it is, of refined economic modelling and climatological typologies – is strikingly modern, both for its realistic views of labourers' living conditions and for Chastellux's sincere concern with their material and psychological welfare.[140]

Chastellux's 'national character' results from the political, economic, and social circumstances existing at the time of the first gathering of men into a certain society. Climate as well as 'example' and 'habit' also play a part in the formation of a definite collective identity. He argues against Machiavelli that, if this original character comes to clash with the national interests as spontaneously ripened over time, it is wise not to bring the nation back to its 'first principles'. Chastellux is unreservedly confident in the 'natural progress of *lumières*', that is, in the actual working of a 'principle of perfectibility' (which can be summarily identified with science and *lettres*) to be associated with a laissez-faire government. No particular ethical value is attached to the original character of peoples. It is improved 'legislation and morality' that he recommends, rather than a return to former habits and values, in order to make a people 'happy'.[141]

With Condorcet's pre-revolutionary writings a new perspective takes full shape. This implied a critique of Montesquieu's relativism. His language of moderation and institutional engineering was rejected by Condorcet in the name of a vision of unrestrained universal application of natural rights. *Esprit général*, which Condorcet depicts as built around the effectiveness of climate, soil, 'physical constitution', and finally 'national spirit', appears as nothing less than the last bulwark of oppression. Laws, he contends, must not change according to variations in temperature and types of local customs, and this because good laws are first and foremost applied reason. It follows that the same laws could and should be enacted everywhere – 'what relationship could the Tartar or

---

[139] *Voyages dans l'Amérique Septentrionale dans les années 1780, 1781 & 1782* (2 vols., Paris, 1786), II, pp. 133–41, 262ff.; the quoted lines are from pp. 137–8.
[140] *De la félicité publique*, I, pp. 30–49.
[141] *ibid.*, I, pp. 40, 153, fn.; II, pp. 4, 57, 252–3, 300, 308–9.

Chinese ceremonial have with the laws?' – and that men's characters are fully determined by the degree of congruence to reason of the existing laws.[142]

Since truth, reason, justice, the rights of men, and the interests of property, liberty, and security are the same everywhere, it is difficult to understand why all provinces of a state, and for that matter all states, should not have the same criminal laws, the same civil laws, the same laws regulating trade, etc. A good law must be good for all men, in the same way that a correct clause is correct for everybody.[143]

Together with the teachings of Montesquieu, what Condorcet's approach denied was the criterion originally put forward by Solon, namely the necessary adaptation of legislation to the moral state of a people. This criterion had been a breeding ground for the political relevance of national character throughout the centuries; it had constituted one of the main patterns of thought on the relationship between government and citizens. In principle, Condorcet's coherent universalism expelled the notion of national character from Western political discourse, and, in doing so, stigmatized national character as an inherently conservative idea. It should be rational principles, rather than *mœurs*, that made up the knowledge base of the lawgiver.

In line with Helvétius, Condorcet contends that peoples are lazy only where governments take away the fruits of labour, and that citizens are honest, patriotic, sensitive, and noble when their rights are respected. But to argue that complicated balanced constitutions are in reality designed to oppress *le peuple* is quintessential Condorcet. The transparent nature of human rights called for a simple government like that of the United States, based on a small number of straightforward principles.[144] The equality of all men turned into an operational principle. Two developments can be cursorily mentioned. The first regards the black slaves (whose owners, he reports with bitter satisfaction, at times defend themselves from criticisms by quoting passages from the *Esprit des lois*). Stating that the black slaves undergo demoralization because of their situation was not new; but the straightforward view that nature created the Blacks 'to have the same spirit, the same reason, and the same virtues as the Whites' challenged the common assumption.[145] Secondly, he acknowledges that, providing that 'no situation [*condition*] is demoralized by an unjust opinion, or oppressed by bad laws', virtues like pride and honour can be manifested by men of all ranks.[146]

---

[142] *Réflexions sur l'esclavage des nègres* (1781), *CO*, VII, p. 83; *De l'influence de la Révolution d'Amérique sur l'Europe* (1786), *CO*, VIII, p. 18; *Sur les assemblées provinciales* (1788), *CO*, VIII, p. 496; *Observations sur le vingt-neuvième livre de l'Esprit des Lois* (1780), in D. de Tracy, *Commentaire sur l'Esprit des Lois de Montesquieu* (Paris, 1819), pp. 420–3.

[143] *Observations sur le vingt-neuvième livre*, p. 420.

[144] *Réflexions sur l'esclavage*, p. 83; *De l'influence de la Révolution d'Amérique*, pp. 13, 18.

[145] *Réflexions sur l'esclavage*, p. 98, fn. 63.

[146] *De l'influence de la Révolution d'Amérique*, pp. 19–21.

2 After the Revolution: Staël on political morality

Germaine de Staël is often given the credit, along with Burke, for bridging the cultural gulf between the eighteenth and the nineteenth centuries. But the attention given to Burke's political thought contrasts with the neglect of that of Staël, who until recently was considered largely in the light of her literary performance.[1] And, paradoxically, the remarkable blossoming of Constant studies in the last two decades has obscured her relevance as a political thinker rather than spotlighting it. At the time in question, however, their roles were reversed, with Constant being dominated by Staël's personality and fame and appearing to be her *protégé*.[2] As both an opponent of the Napoleonic regime and an essayist and novelist, Staël's prestige and authority were in constant growth from *De la littérature* (1800) and *Delphine* (1802) right up to her death in 1817.[3]

Francis Jeffrey, the editor of the *Edinburgh Review* and a pivotal figure of British intellectual life in the first decades of the century, wrote in 1813 that he knew of no other author who 'has thrown so strong a light upon the capricious and apparently unaccountable diversity of national taste, genius, and morality, by connecting them with the political structure of society, the accidents of climate and external relation, and the variety of creeds and superstitions'.[4] According to another respected writer of the age, James Mackintosh, Staël possessed an unsurpassed genius for 'tracing the peculiarities of usages, arts, and even speculations, to their common principle in national character', and

---

[1] Notable exceptions are S. Moravia, *Il tramonto dell'Illuminismo: filosofia e politica nella società francese (1770–1810)* (Bari, 1968), and G. E. Gwynne, *Madame de Staël et la Révolution française* (Paris, 1969). See also M. Berger, 'Introduction', in *Madame de Staël on Politics, Literature and National Character*, ed. M. Berger (London, 1964), pp. 1–69; and G. A. Kelly, 'Liberalism and Aristocracy in the French Restoration', *Journal of the History of Ideas*, 26 (1965), pp. 509–30.

[2] Gwynne, *Madame de Staël*, esp. pp. 1–50; G. A. Kelly, *The Humane Comedy: Constant, Tocqueville and French Liberalism* (Cambridge, 1992), pp. 13–14.

[3] 'Il fallait être le vainqueur d'Austerlitz pour exiler l'auteur de *Corinne*': C. de Rémusat, 'La Révolution française' (1818), in his *Passé et présent: mélanges* (2 vols., Paris, 1847), I, p. 114. But there is plenty of contemporary evidence, ranging from the volumes of *Staëlliana* published after her death to Quinet's recollections in *Histoire de mes idées*.

[4] F. Jeffrey, 'Mad. de Staël – *Sur la Literature* [*sic*]', *ER*, 21 (1813), pp. 2–3.

for 'placing a nation, strongly individualized by every mark of its mind and disposition, in the midst of ancient monuments, clothed in its own apparel, engaged in its ordinary occupations and pastimes amidst its native scenes'.[5] By raising intriguing questions not only about Staël but also about her reception in Britain, statements like these point to Staël as the acid test of post-revolutionary thinking on a European scale. The chapter has two main parts: while the first (sections 1–4) examines Staël's views on public spirit and national character, the second (section 5) shows how these reacted with contemporary British opinion.

1   Staël in the 1790s

'Are the French made to be free?', Staël wondered in *Considérations sur la Révolution française*. It was not a rhetorical question: the relationship between government and institutions, on the one hand, and the attitudes and beliefs of citizens, on the other, lay at the heart of her political thinking since *Réflexions sur la paix* (1794) and *Réflexions sur la paix intérieure* (1795). It emerges from these works that Staël did not ascribe the Terror only to the aberrations of the Jacobin frame of mind, as commentators customarily maintain; Jacobin activists certainly mobilized the people by a political programme but depended crucially on the latter's will. The lower ranks, she argued, have in fact become an independent political force, which regards even leaders like Robespierre as 'means'.[6] It is true that the Jacobins hold some sway over the masses, but only by appeasing 'their vile passions and their absurd opinions', in particular their craving for property. Popular rule cannot but amount to arbitrariness and ultimately 'crime'; the Terror is still looming because 'it has its natural and permanent source in the lower classes'.[7]

In her moral treatise *De l'influence des passions sur le bonheur des individus et des nations* (1796), Staël maintained that politics amounted to the management of citizens' passions, and, following in the footsteps of Hume, Helvétius, Holbach, and a number of other eighteenth-century writers, paid lip service to the educative potential of governments. But the awareness that long-standing theories could hardly account for France's revolutionary turmoil loomed large. The relationship between government and 'nation' was construed so that the former was equated with 'reason', exerting restraint on the 'passions' of the latter – passions which, taken together, made up a collective 'character' like that

---

[5] J. Mackintosh, '*De l'Allemagne, par* Mad. de Staël', *ER*, 22 (1813), pp. 204–5.
[6] *Réflexions sur la paix, adressées à M. Pitt et aux français, SOC*, II, pp. 36–7; *Réflexions sur la paix intérieure, SOC*, II, p. 81 and fn. For a comment, see Gwynne, *Madame de Staël*, pp. 64–5; and P. Michel, *Un mythe romantique: les Barbares 1789–1848* (Lyon, 1981), pp. 45–58, esp. pp. 55, 57.
[7] *Réflexions sur la paix intérieure*, pp. 119–24, 133. 'Ne serait-il donc pas singulier d'appeler les non-propriétaires à la garde de la propriété?', p. 121.

of an individual. Rather oddly, ambition, love, envy, vanity (the 'esprit général' of France), avarice, glory, and so on were equally stigmatized, on the grounds that all passions led to an imbalance between desires and the capacity to meet them. The more effective the government's checking action, the purer political liberty can be, she contended.[8] This depiction of the political mechanism accorded with the features of the phase succeeding the Terror, when, to the eyes of a moderate like Staël, popular passions were still raging and the government alone championed order and liberty. However, it cannot be excluded that the idealization of the role of government was to a certain extent instrumental, since at the time of writing *De l'influence des passions* she was exiled and trying to win the favour of the Directory.[9] At any rate, it is hard to trace an optimistic note in the book. The problem was that passions were 'indestructible', on the one hand, and that the ultimate basis of liberty was 'the way in which peoples conceive the social order', on the other.[10]

In Directorial France, the government was confronted with 'the ferocious enthusiasm of the rabble [*populace*]'. From a horrified posture, Staël depicted the Jacobin Terror as the eruption of evil and unfettered passions, and in particular of 'esprit de parti'.[11] This passion, which had taken up new resonances under the circumstances, was emblematic of the moral monstrosities the Revolution had created, and which aroused in Staël awe and fear. The spirit of party is an ideological frenzy, an uncompromising resolve to impose one's own idea; but, she added, it *ne tient point à la nature de son objet*, it is unrelated to any idea in particular as it can be a vehicle of all. In fact, both aristocrats and Jacobins are dominated by it. The clash of contrasting, but equally 'imaginary' (extreme, that is) party visions results in a loss of contact with reality; hence an abstract fervour comes about.[12] It is possible to advocate atheism with the intolerance of superstition, and to preach liberty with the fury of despotism. This aspect of the spirit of party is the most disquieting: 'it is the single sentiment that associates wicked actions with an honest soul; the most frightening torture imaginable originates from this contrast'.[13] The real subject of *De l'influence des passions* is the tragic divorce which occurred between the Revolution and public morality, and the ensuing confusion between virtue and crime.

The nature of partisan frenzy was rational, in the sense that, given a total disregard for the affections of the heart, the single bonds between party men were the 'bonds of opinion' determined by their blind devotion to an idea.[14]

[8] *De l'influence des passions sur le bonheur des individus et des nations, SOC*, III, pp. 10–15, 35.
[9] Gwynne, *Madame de Staël*, pp. 34–6.
[10] *De l'influence des passions*, pp. 12, 15.
[11] *ibid.*, pp. 70ff., 89ff., 129–58, 236–7.
[12] *ibid.*, pp. 136–40.
[13] *ibid.*, pp. 129–48, quotation on p. 146.
[14] *ibid.*, pp. 134, 141–2.

The sectarians were 'assassins raisonneurs, qui marchent au crime par la métaphysique';[15] in contrast to them, Staël posited a moral conception focused on pity (*pitié*) as the sentiment which should inform conduct in the present collapse of the 'social state'. While the morality of pity looks like a mirror image of the Jacobin attitude, the underlying belief was far from banal. Staël was seeking 'any moral instinct whatever' to reunite the French into a social body, in the awareness that there was nothing in the world as divisive as reason.[16] Pity could serve this purpose, in conjunction with the moral code supplied to the masses by religion, and to superior persons by natural morality.[17] That Staël's reliance on instinct rather than reason contradicts the function ascribed to government is less important than the later developments of her stance which that reliance foreshadows. Although possibly reminiscent of Scottish philosophy, the primacy of instinct had Rousseau as its main source. In spite of the critique of all passions contained in this treatise (a critique which was not subsequently taken up), in the *Lettres sur les ouvrages et le caractère de J.-J. Rousseau* of 1788 she had enthusiastically approved of this great figure who combined reason with sentiment, and made virtue 'a passion'.[18]

As noted by commentators, the *idéologues* exerted a strong influence on Staël in the 1790s, and this is of particular significance from my point of view.[19] The *idéologues* were in fact specially responsible for raising the issue of the reformation of national mores as a precondition for the transition to a republican government. As the constitution-building of the early years of the Revolution gave way to civil war, the regeneration of *mœurs* seemed to many to be the only way to ensure the success of constitutions. In order not only to extinguish the monarchical manners and deferential habits of the Old Regime but also to curb the 'excesses' of the lower classes' 'enthusiasm', a series of educational and political schemes were devised by Rœderer, Condorcet, and other republican writers. Their eventual collision with the Jacobins was the tragic outcome of a division of a fundamental kind. The *idéologue* Daunou, in a memoir written in prison in 1794, portrayed the contrast between Robespierre and the *parti philosophique* in terms of their divergent views of the *peuple*: just and wise by

---

[15] *ibid.*, pp. 236–7.
[16] *ibid.*, p. 237.
[17] *ibid.*, pp. 177–88.
[18] *Lettres sur les ouvrages et le caractère de J.-J. Rousseau* (1788; 2nd edn, 1798; repr. edn, Geneva, 1979), esp. pp. iv, 5–12ff., 43–4, 72–5. On the cult of Rousseau as a masterful writer on sentiments, and the eruption of the 'romantic' sensibility in pre-revolutionary France, see S. Schama, *Citizens: a Chronicle of the French Revolution* (Harmondsworth, 1989), pp. 145–74. But Staël rejected Rousseau's political thought: *Lettres sur les ouvrages*, pp. 76–85. Staël's fascination rested on *Emile* and especially *La nouvelle Héloïse*, rather than on *Du contrat social*.
[19] For an account of Staël's kinship with the *idéologues*, see Gwynne, *Madame de Staël*, part III. On Staël as a leading representative of the *parti philosophique* in the Directory years, see Moravia, *Il tramonto dell'Illuminismo*, esp. pp. 233–8, 282–90ff., 462–79ff.

very nature for the Rousseauist Robespierre, the impulsive prey to passions for the heirs of Condillac and Helvétius.[20]

Although the relationship between government and citizens' virtues is no field for proper breakthroughs, a shift of emphasis occurred at this juncture. From Montesquieu's celebrated picture of Asian rule onwards, it had been a universally shared belief that despotism invariably brought about the demoralization of its subjects, and, by explicit or implicit extension, that a free government entailed good *mœurs*. The Revolution put this argument to the test. The *idéologues*, although not openly opposing it, tended to debunk it implicitly, by coupling legislative reform with a constantly reiterated concern over the existence of the attitudes necessary to carry it through; they allowed for a flexible interaction between *mœurs* and institutions. As Condorcet put it in *Fragment de justification*, it would be dangerous to force the pace of reform at the risk of alienating 'common opinion' from institutions which it would welcome in due course. The gap between projected change following the precepts of reason and *esprit public* should be bridged, in Garat's words, by 'the art of thinking made popular'.[21] By acting and writing along these lines, these republicans of the 1790s paved the way for the primacy of mores over government, a perspective which would gather momentum after 1815. Staël, at times listed as an *idéologue* herself, drew fundamental inspiration from the mores controversy of the 1790s although she did not carry the new perception to extremes.

The main contention of Staël's next major work, the then unpublished *Des circonstances actuelles qui peuvent terminer la Révolution* (1798), is the unpreparedness of French *esprit public* for a republican government, which is 'founded on universal consensus'; hence the violence and coercion of the Terror, as well as the fragility of the Directorial government.[22] Representative institutions needed a correlative public spirit to work properly, and 'the nation in 1789 was just ready for a temperate monarchy'. Basically, Staël was positing a model of progressive and voluntary development of the 'habits of liberty' in the mass of the French in opposition to the Jacobin practice of imposing coercive measures. 'It is in the many anonymous actions', she maintained, 'that I find the signs [of public opinion, a term synonymous with public spirit for all practical purposes], and this national opinion forms habits which are the main

---

[20] Daunou, *Extraits d'un mémoire destiné à ses commettants* (1794), quoted in Moravia, *Il tramonto dell'Illuminismo*, pp. 198–9. For the *idéologues* on mores, Moravia's book is essential reading; see also R. Whatmore, *Republicanism and the French Revolution: an Intellectual History of Jean-Baptiste Say's Political Economy* (Oxford, 2000), pp. 85–107.

[21] Condorcet, *Fragment de justification* (1793), *CO*, I, p. 575; J. D. Garat, *Mémoires historiques sur M. Suard* (1820), quoted in Moravia, *Il tramonto dell'Illuminismo*, p. 201.

[22] *Des circonstances actuelles qui peuvent terminer la Révolution et des principes qui doivent fonder la République en France*, ed. L. Omacini (Paris and Geneva, 1979), esp. pp. 33–9. See also *Réflexions sur la paix intérieure*, pp. 85, 106. A similar point is made in B. Constant, *Des réactions politiques* (Paris, an V [1797]), pp. 1–2.

support of free governments.' A government is despotic when it either antici-
pates or resists opinion. By shattering all social bonds, the Terror had debased
citizens' characters, bringing about 'a barbarous selfishness'.[23] To make things
worse, centuries of hierarchical oppression had induced the 'depravity' of the
lower classes, which Staël saw as a revengeful and ferocious force, capable of
destroying but not of rebuilding.[24] At any rate, Staël accepted the republican
status quo and committed herself to reinforcing its moderate orientation.

How to overcome 'the silence of the nation' and create public spirit becomes
therefore Staël's priority. The traditional appeals of republicanism to political
participation were judged ineffective. This was because among the citizenry
the vast majority were largely indifferent to political strife, their main concerns
being social order and the unconstrained pursuit of business. The achievements
of the Revolution would never be secured until those needs were met.

I think that the possibility of living apart from public affairs is a major benefit to most
of the people. This repose [*repos*], unknown to the ancients, is made possible by larger
communities, and amounts to an additional chance of happiness [*bonheur*] given to a
wide range of characters. Legislators and rulers should take this fact into full account,
and therefore not rely, in a nation of this kind, on the type of patriotism which fuelled
the ancient republics.[25]

Clearly enough, to advocate 'the type of patriotism which fuelled the ancient
republics' meant to run the risk of rekindling popular extremism.[26] At that
moment in time, the citizenry wanted to recover from the Terror; and, in any
case, political participation was for the few, not for the many. The first requisite
of 'public spirit' was the cessation of illegal rule, which even the ongoing war
could not justify.[27] Next, Staël pointed to a moderate, 'aristocratic' constitution
as the proper framework for the full exercise of justice and security. In particular,
she advocated the defence of property, the consideration of individual interests
as the ultimate determinants of politics, administrative decentralization, and the
independence of judges.[28]

[23] *Des circonstances actuelles*, pp. 321–2, 324–5, 160. On the relationship between public opinion
and *mœurs* from Montesquieu to Tocqueville, see Kelly, *The Humane Comedy*, pp. 46–9.
[24] *Des circonstances actuelles*, pp. 33–9.
[25] *ibid.*, pp. 109–10. Staël noted that in antiquity military defeat entailed the economic ruin of
each citizen and often enslavement, while assemblies were all-powerful; hence 'les calculs
personnels ne pouvaient jamais être indépendants'. See also *Réflexions sur la paix, adressées
à M. Pitt*, pp. 40–1, and *Réflexions sur la paix intérieure*, p. 124.
[26] See 'A quels signes peut-on connaître quelle est l'opinion de la majorité de la nation?' (1792),
SOC, XVIII, p. 276: 'Il y a deux forces toutes puissantes dans la nature morale comme dans la
nature physique: la tendance au repos, et l'impulsion vers la liberté; l'une ou l'autre tour à tour
l'emporte; mais c'est de la combinaison de toutes les deux que résulte la volonté permanente
et générale: c'est à la solution de ce problème qu'il faut aller l'attendre, et qu'on est sûr de
l'obtenir.'
[27] *Des circonstances actuelles*, pp. 321–3.
[28] *ibid.*, pp. 326–8. See also *Réflexions sur la paix intérieure*, pp. 123–4.

But Staël did not limit herself to these constitutional recommendations – this is only the practical, purely political side of her thought. There is a more philosophical and abstract stratum in her text. Now that equality had been established, a stricter morality was required as the bedrock of public spirit. Morality should be 'the constituent power' (*le pouvoir constituant*) of the republic. Morality and republican equality were seen to share the characteristic of being 'natural' and original: a political system whose foundations were to be traced back to 'simple', 'primitive' ideas of momentous consequence could not but be inherently associated with the moral sphere.[29] 'The kind of liberty I love', she had said in 1788, 'is that which does not allow other distinctions among men than those marked by nature.'[30] Granted that in the new society much would be devolved to individual choices and voluntary actions, nothing but a rigorous morality could be an enlightened replacement for the older forms of social and political control. Staël's goal was to form 'a sort of pact of souls' among the citizens as a preliminary to any social contract.[31] Religion was resolutely, if rather instrumentally, called on to substantiate public morality, and not only that of the lower classes.[32] The component elements of Staël's religion-informed morality were personal dignity, the striving after the improvement of human spirit, the love of public esteem, self-confidence, and the dignified endurance of adversities and persecution.[33] An 'austere morality' would eventually form to replace the notorious *légèreté* of French character inherited from the Old Regime. In the end, and this is typical Staël, she stuck to a rationalistic faith in the future of civilization in spite of all the suffering and the moral wounds she constantly exhibited. The advance of *lumières* called for a parallel advance of morality as a necessary, inevitable occurrence – therefore, with all its violence and wrongs, the Terror amounted to a mere episode.[34]

Two characteristics of Staël's position should already be clear. First, the relevance of the human element – the citizens' beliefs and actions – in their interaction with institutional engineering; second, her debt to the Enlightenment *philosophes* as well as the *idéologues*. Basically, she developed the views of the latter in order to provide an explanation of that astonishing and frightening phenomenon, Jacobin France, arguing that, if public spirit had not been fit for a republican government in 1792, a legal and moderate version of it would bring about suitable *mœurs* in the course of time. No mention was made of any effect of climate on them, nor was any substantial concession made to the classic republican mode of discourse. So far so good, even if Staël finds it difficult to

---

[29] *Des circonstances actuelles*, pp. 38–9.
[30] *Lettres sur les ouvrages*, p. 82; see also *Réflexions sur le procès de la Reine* (1793), *SOC*, II, p. 22.
[31] *Des circonstances actuelles*, esp. pp. 222–3, 341–2.
[32] *ibid.*, pp. 222–38.
[33] *ibid.*, pp. 225–6.
[34] *ibid.*, pp. 341–4.

keep her argument within the boundaries of politics and, by introducing the idea of public morality, seems at times to debunk the effectiveness of the political factor itself. This idea differs from that of public spirit, with its civic humanist echoes, on the grounds of its greater comprehensiveness and, it might be said, profundity. Staël had in mind a metapolitics where what was involved was the person as a whole, with all his sentiments and passions, in the ultimate belief that in the relationship between citizens and government a place should be found for the noble and the sublime. If private virtues stemmed from a confrontation with 'malheur' – the moral sufferings intrinsic to life[35] – then public virtues could not have a different origin, as they were an extension, though projected upon a larger stage, of the sensitivity, fortitude and courage cultivated in the private sphere. What she opposed with the utmost force was the separation between private and public morality which the Jacobin mentality represented – the Terrorists were said to have a personality which was 'the most inconceivable moral problem which has ever existed'.[36] Morality was a wide-ranging force to her, inseparable from the dynamics of political life and, under the circumstances, required to heal the injuries caused by the Jacobins in the social fabric. In spite of all this moralization of politics, in *Des circonstances actuelles* the interaction between institutions and *mœurs* is relatively straightforward (and is also brilliantly and thoroughly conceived).

2   *De la littérature* and *De l'Allemagne*

Staël's line of argument becomes subject to alterations and oscillations in her successive writings, the hugely influential *De la littérature* and *De l'Allemagne*. Their contents are wide-ranging to say the least: in the former and shorter of the two, for instance, a system of politics, a manifesto of a new literature, a philosophy of history, and a set of moral sentiments of possible practical use to individuals are distinctively traceable, and constantly interacting. One principle seems to stand out: *mœurs* are the product of government, not of climate or religion.

It cannot be denied, that the legislation of a country is all-powerful in its influence over the habits, taste, and talents of its inhabitants; since Lacedaemon existed by the side of Athens, in the same century, under the same climate, with nearly the same religion; and yet nothing, it must with truth be observed, could be more different than their mores [*mœurs*].[37]

---

[35] See esp. *De l'influence des passions*.
[36] *Essai sur les fictions*, ed. M. Tournier (1795; Paris, 1979), p. 49.
[37] *De la littérature*, ed. G. Gengembre and J. Goldzink (1800; Paris, 1991), part I, ch. 1, p. 101 (*The Influence of Literature upon Society* (2 vols., London, 1812), I, p. 98). For similar statements in *De l'Allemagne*, see *De l'Allemagne*, ed. S. Balayé (1810–13; 2 vols., Paris, 1991), I, part I, ch. 2, p. 63; ch. 18, p. 137; II, part III, ch. 5, p. 119; ch. 11, pp. 177–80.

The chain of cause and effect, as applied especially in *De la littérature*, is this: the type of government (despotic, aristocratic, or democratic, in conjunction with the varying degrees of liberty it allows) dictates *mœurs*, and in turn these inform the tone and subjects of literary creations (Staël considers both fiction and philosophy under the heading of literature). This mechanism is put to work in the cases of Greek, Roman, and contemporary Italian, British, and French literature. The rule is that a free government induces a literature which is 'philosophical', realistic, and useful. The German writers, deeply moral and dedicated to the pursuit of truth under governments feudal but mild, fall within the same pattern, but only just, as an interpreter has noted.[38]

There is, however, a distinction between the North and the South of Europe which overlaps the effects of government in both texts. Bent on inventing 'Romanticism', Staël takes Britain and Germany as specimens of Northern nations, with France, Italy, Spain, and Greece as representatives of the South. This distinction entails specific personality traits (like bravery, energy, melancholy, and imagination in the Northerners, and immorality, epicureanism, and superficiality in the Southerners) as well as different literary cultures. It is worth emphasizing that, whereas Southern *volupté* is ascribed to the final corruption of the Roman empire, no full-fledged explanation is given of Northern primeval energy and vibrant passions; though here and there, climate as a factor of national literature and character is surreptitiously introduced (that is, alongside statements about the primacy of governments and laws).[39] In strict logic, the North–South divide would entail nothing less than the overturning of the previous perspective: for here it is certain given characteristics of the Northerners, like pride, a detachment from life, independence, and self-reliance that make them fit for liberty. However, Staël's is only a particularly blatant example of a practice – combining government with physical factors – quite common in the French Enlightenment.

Staël's invention of a literature of enthusiasm and sombre passions served a twofold political purpose. On the one hand, there was the suggestion of a new style of French public morality and political communication, a suggestion developed especially in the second part of *De la littérature*; on the other, and interconnectedly, there was a renewed focus on citizens' 'enthusiasm'. As 'the love of beauty, the elevation of soul, the enjoyment of devotion', enthusiasm was the antithesis of egoism.[40] It was by an appeal to moral sentiments and passions, rather than reason or interest, that the French masses could be attached to

---

[38] J. C. Isbell, *The Birth of European Romanticism: Truth and Propaganda in Staël's 'De l'Allemagne', 1810–1813* (Cambridge, 1994), pp. 33–4.

[39] See *De la littérature*, esp. part I, ch. 8, pp. 162–6; ch. 10, pp. 191, 196–9; ch. 11, pp. 203–12; and *De l'Allemagne*, esp. I, 'Observations générales', pp. 45–7; part I, ch. 5, pp. 75–6; II, part III, ch. 2, pp. 93–5; ch. 5, pp. 119–20; ch. 7, pp. 151–2.

[40] *De l'Allemagne*, II, part IV, ch. 10, pp. 301–2.

the republican cause (in *De la littérature*), and the European peoples could over-throw Napoleon (in *De l'Allemagne*). Although Staël's handling of the notion of passions is oscillating and confused, both republican 'enthusiasm' and national 'patriotism' should be regarded for all practical purposes as crystallizations of passions,[41] and in fact interpreters agree that it is somewhere near the linkage between reason and passions that the bedrock of her thinking lies.[42] As Staël argued in her first published writing, passions have a firm grip on souls because they unite reason with instinctive energy; examples of powerful passions being patriotism, love, and religion.[43]

But Staël's conceptual grid is more complex than that. The worst enemy of enthusiasm, Staël tirelessly repeated, was the French propensity for vanity and self-love, which invariably resulted in the derision of virtues and a habit of insensitivity and superficiality. The Germans, in contrast, abounded in enthusi-asm, which was 'the capacity to feel and think'; but they lacked 'character' – the wellspring of public and political deeds. The function fulfilled by the former was the choice of ends, which, to be achieved in practice, required the in-tervention of the latter.[44] The distinction between enthusiasm and character, not introduced before *De l'Allemagne*, may serve to clarify the difficulty in the causes of national character signalled above: potentiality for 'enthusiasm' would in effect be geographically determined but a free government would be required to develop them into a 'character'. (However, this would once more seal the fate of Southern peoples.) Unquestionably, she maintained that an ac-tive public morality could be created by free institutions alone. In commenting on the excellent state of higher education in Germany, Staël remarked:

How is it then that the nation is wanting in energy, that it appears generally dull and confined, even while it contains within itself a small number of men, who perhaps are the most intellectual in all Europe? It is to the nature of its government, not to education, that this singular contrast must be attributed. Intellectual education is perfect in Germany, but everything there passes into a theory: practical education depends solely on things actually existing; it is by action alone that the character acquires that firmness which is necessary to direct the conduct of life. Character is an instinct; it has more alliance with nature than the understanding, and yet circumstances alone give men the opportunity of developing it. The government is the real instructor of the people; and public educa-tion itself, however beneficial, may create men of letters, but not citizens, warriors, or statesmen.[45]

---

[41] See P. Bénichou, *Le sacre de l'écrivain 1750–1830* (Paris, 1985), pp. 228–45.

[42] Gwynne, *Madame de Staël*; J. Roussel, *Jean-Jacques Rousseau en France après la Révolution 1795–1830* (Paris, 1972), pp. 338–47; S. Balayé, *Madame de Staël: lumières et liberté* (Paris, 1979).

[43] *Lettres sur les ouvrages*, esp. pp. 5–6, 8–9, 22ff., 43, 70ff. Compare *De l'influence des passions*, the work where Staël argued that passions were the main obstacle to both private and public happiness.

[44] *De l'Allemagne*, I, part I, ch. 2, pp. 55–73; II, part III, ch. 11, pp. 177–80; part IV, ch. 10, pp. 301–4.

[45] *ibid.*, I, part I, ch. 18, p. 137 (*Germany* (3 vols., London, 1813), I, pp. 171–2; trans. modified).

A perhaps more straightforward escape from the above-mentioned difficulty, and one which does have some indirect textual support, would be to confine 'character' to politics and 'enthusiasm' to literature – as before, the former would depend on political and the latter on physical causes. But at least two considerations militate against this solution. First, in Staël the geographic divide is also a normative one, burdened with either explicit or implicit political and religious implications. Second, however vague its meaning, enthusiasm itself has an evident political side, which would be overshadowed by a sharp separation from 'character'. In short, any attempt to separate politics from literature is fraught with failure because Staël did not regard them as two distinct spheres; on the contrary, she aimed to indicate their necessary connection. Bombastic as it may sound, Staël was engaged in redesigning the European consciousness as a whole by taking the Revolution as the turning point after which nothing could any longer be the same. Staël makes a number of interconnected moves, like declaring the end of French supremacy in matters of taste and style, pointing to German ideas, rejecting utilitarianism, refreshing religious feeling, exalting 'mélancolie' and enthusiasm, assessing the good and the bad in Shakespeare and dozens of other writers, depicting national characters, revitalizing patriotism, and showing the pertinence of all this to contemporary politics.

The following passage applies the notion of character to Britain:

> The extension of knowledge in modern times only serves to weaken the character, when it is not strengthened by the habit of business and the exercise of the will. To see all, and comprehend all, is a great cause of uncertainty; and the energy of action develops itself only in those free and powerful countries where patriotic sentiments are to the soul like blood to the veins, and grow cold only with the extinction of life itself.[46]

The English national character is the best possible example of the effects of a free government on the right natural raw material. As their literature abundantly mirrors, the English are proud of their liberty, virtuous, practical, and thoughtful when the polity is concerned.[47] To adopt Staël's terminology, they exemplify the combination of enthusiasm and character which is the hallmark of free peoples.[48] An Anglophile like many *philosophes*, including her father, she abundantly relies on the *Esprit des lois* when depicting the English, in much the same way as the *Lettres persanes* (together with a number of unflattering eighteenth-century national self-portraits) lie at the root of her views on French *mœurs*. But though Staël does not significantly add to the traditional national stereotypes, her use of them as weapons in her campaign to regenerate France remains remarkable.[49]

---

[46] *ibid.*, I, part I, ch. 2, p. 64 (*Germany*, I, p. 36; trans. modified).
[47] *De la littérature*, part I, chs.13–17, pp. 216–55.
[48] *De l'Allemagne*, II, part IV, ch. 10, p. 303.
[49] But, as Isbell has argued, Staël did change the French image of the Germans: *The Birth of European Romanticism*, pp. 40ff. See F. Rosset, 'Coppet et les stéréotypes nationaux', in

Chapter 18 of part I of *De la littérature* is entitled 'Why did the French nation have more grace, taste, and gaiety than any other European nation?' Because of the institutions and circumstances shaping the character of the upper classes, she answered. Devoid of power but keen on honour, French aristocrats practised their total submission to the king with grace and politeness; it was a 'necessary politics' at a court where 'to please and displease was the actual source of all the punishments and rewards which fell outside the domain of law'.[50] The body of the nation imitated *les grands* in 'this universal desire to please'. Independent judgement and behaviour became rarities as everyone was subservient to the opinion of everyone else. Vanity, frivolity, self-love, and pride banned energy and commitment as the means of gaining a position.[51] There grew up a 'mocking spirit' directed at those who were serious and dedicated, believed in genuine sentiments, and dealt with weighty matters – directed, that is, at those who showed signs of enthusiasm.[52] The French national character with its 'pleasant *légèreté*' comes from here, from the effects of arbitrary rule upon aristocratic *mœurs*; and the Revolution, Staël added, has not decisively changed it. Recent events confirmed both the bravery in war of the French, where they act as a mass, and their pusillanimity in civil struggles, where personal fortitude is required.[53]

Having delved into Staël's terminology, it should be added that 'morality', 'virtue', 'passions', '*mœurs*', 'public spirit', and finally '*lumières*' all look at times like interchangeable names to refer to a kind of politics fundamentally alternative to government's violence and oppression. Staël regularly appeals to the eventual ascendancy of virtues over wicked forces, and seems to seek consolation in postulating an ever-improving march of civilization. Besides being often directly evoked and discussed, the shock caused by the Terror lurks in many of the pages of these major works as well. As indicated above, the peculiarity of Jacobin despotism when compared with the traditional, Montesquieuvian view, and at the same time the very reason for its sinister fascination, was its 'reasoning' character; the Terror was not founded on force alone but on an ideology 'deadly fatal for the empire of *lumières*'. Additionally, Jacobin fanatics associated the proneness to crime that naturally came from popular passions with a misguided enthusiasm, and it was the latter element that made them so effective.[54] Staël's own advocacy of enthusiasm could hardly leave this precedent out of account. Arguably, it was largely due to its responsibility in the creation of

---

S. Balayé and K. Kloocke, eds., *Le groupe de Coppet et l'Europe 1789–1830* (Lausanne and Paris, 1994), pp. 55–66.

[50] *De la littérature*, part I, ch. 18, pp. 271–3, quotation on p. 272 (*The Influence of Literature*, II, p. 49; trans. modified).

[51] *ibid.*, part I, ch. 18, pp. 274–8.

[52] *ibid.*, part I, ch. 18, p. 276; part II, ch. 2, pp. 302–6 (and also part II, ch. 5, pp. 342–7ff.); *De l'Allemagne*, I, part I, ch. 9, pp. 94–5; II, part IV, ch. 11, pp. 306–7.

[53] *De l'Allemagne*, I, 'Observations générales', pp. 46–7; part I, ch. 11, pp. 107–8.

[54] The citation is from *De la littérature*, part II, ch. 8, p. 396.

the Jacobin outlook that Staël made her attack in *De l'Allemagne* on eighteenth-century utilitarian and materialist philosophy.[55] It was not by chance that she embraced a radically anti-Machiavellian posture: 'an unjust act has never been useful to a nation'. After endorsing the idea of a political science based on *analyse* as spread by the *idéologues*, she adds nonetheless that moral laws are placed above *calcul*, which therefore must be guided by the rights of the individual that morality safeguards. Morality is 'a sentiment', differing from 'well-understood interest' because it makes room for *belles actions*, 'sacrifices of virtue'. When men refuse to view God as the maker of morality, morality itself should be deified, she commented.[56]

Even the model of political communication proposed in *De la littérature* can be seen as a response to the challenge of Jacobinism. Whereas the idea that the new French republic would provide the conditions for the emergence of a type of literature suited to a free country (dealing with serious topics, informed by patriotism, and austere in tone) is quite simplistic and naive, it is noteworthy that in Staël's depiction a writer or orator would be capable of arousing enthusiasm – an 'ivresse de la vertu' – in his audience. On the one hand, the public function of literature would exalt and inspire authors, and this in an almost 'supernatural' way; on the other, political communication in a free state was a matter of sentiments and passions, of moral conviction turned into energy.[57] In her ideal world, superior, generous men would dominate assemblies with the pathos of their speeches in defence of the weak. Her favourite form of political communication was in fact eloquence, whose 'natural realm' was 'the power of sentiments over our souls' and not *calcul* – 'if you talk to human nature, it will respond'. For this reason, eloquence was the ultimate bulwark of liberty. Characteristically, she viewed melancholy as a vehicle of profundity and strength in eloquence.[58]

Staël's basic suggestion was to mingle politics with morality as closely as possible, so that there would be no possible gulf between public and private life.[59] In a republic, 'it is necessary that each man of talent is an additional obstacle to political usurpation'.[60] In contrast with the 'vulgarity' of language,

---

[55] *De l'Allemagne*, II, part III, esp. chs. 12–13, pp. 181–94. See also *De la littérature*, part II, ch. 6, pp. 372–80. In *De l'Allemagne*, II, part III, ch. 4, pp. 113–17 (the chapter is entitled 'Du persiflage introduit par un certain genre de philosophie'), Staël considers the damage done to French morality and religiosity by the 'scepticisme moqueur' of eighteenth-century philosophy.

[56] *De la littérature*, part II, ch. 6, pp. 374–80.

[57] *ibid.*, part I, ch. 20, pp. 293–5; part II, ch. 2, pp. 306–11; ch. 5, pp. 351–62. 'Il fait servir l'émotion à quelques grandes vérités morales', p. 352.

[58] *ibid.*, part II, ch. 8, pp. 393–406; quotations on pp. 400, 403. On melancholy and eloquence, see p. 403. As Kelly has noted, 'this was still a culture of the spoken word, in public or in private', and Staël enjoyed a 'divine sense of *la parole*': Kelly, *The Humane Comedy*, p. 23. On the 'esprit de conversation', see *De l'Allemagne*, I, part I, ch. 11, pp. 101–10.

[59] *De la littérature*, part II, ch. 6, pp. 375–6.

[60] *ibid.*, part II, ch. 2, p. 311.

mores, and ideas brought about by the Revolution, she advocated an aristocracy of *mœurs*, and by that term she meant education, talent, *politesse*, and higher moral sentiments, to create a 'tribunal of opinion' irrespective of political cleavages. Simply, the best men would rule. Unlike the Old Regime, the republic would pay tribute to solid talent and merit; unlike the Jacobin dictatorship, it would require urbanity of *mœurs* from its statesmen, not only because conventions were 'the image of morality' but also because they worked as social bonds.[61] It was immaterial to close the gap between political opinions if there remained differences in *esprit* and sentiments.[62] To build the republic of *mœurs*, the humanity, generosity, and tenderness of women were indispensable, because 'they are the only beings who, being separated from political interests and cultivating no ambition, can despise immoral actions, mark out ingratitude, and pay tribute to one disgraced whose fall has been caused by noble sentiments'.[63]

The ideal of a republic of *mœurs* was intended for the upper classes, where superior moral natures were more likely to be found; to complete the picture, Staël set out to outline a morality for the masses ('la force ignorante'), whose role in revolutionary politics she could not ignore. Now, she warned, thousands of people exercise their own judgement when they take a stand on political matters. It is therefore necessary for the educated to impart sentiments and affections which are more efficacious than mere opinions in influencing people's minds. Having mentioned that a reasonable amount of basic instruction should be imparted, she pointed to the feelings of devotion and admiration for rulers as the key. The goal was 'to attach the people to the idea of virtue'. This could be effected through the examples of great men, who, by performing glorious deeds, would eventually form a pride-inspiring national tradition. Classic models of virtue, like Cato opposing Caesar, were at the basis of Staël's construction.[64] Politics is elevated to morality through a literature (in her sense) aimed at inspiring virtue. Basically, *De la littérature* and *De l'Allemagne* are an application of what Staël had found so revealing in the *Nouvelle Héloïse* in 1788: the unmistakable truth of the beliefs and perceptions originating from the inner self.

3   Enthusiasm, Northern and Southern

Corinne ou l'Italie indicates better than any other writing of hers that Staël's distinction between Southern and Northern peoples is drawn in a spirit which is not that of Montesquieu. This is a novel in which, obviously, Staël's concern is

---

[61] *ibid.*, part II, ch. 2, pp. 306–7, 314–19 ('la politesse est le lien que la société a établi entre les hommes étrangers les uns aux autres', p. 314), esp. p. 319. See also *Réflexions sur la paix intérieure*, ch. 2. For a comment on 'l'aristocratie des talents', see Gwynne, *Madame de Staël*, pp. 68–77.

[62] *De la littérature*, part II, ch. 2, p. 319.

[63] *ibid.*, part II, ch. 4, p. 336.

[64] *ibid.*, part II, ch. 3, pp. 327–31.

neither the correlation of politics with literature, as it was in the two writings just examined, nor any other openly political subject. *Corinne* features a contrast between characters as an existential dilemma, a matter of a difficult choice between two ways of thinking and feeling. The work tells the love story between the Scottish Oswald, Lord Nelvil, and Corinne, an Italian poet of British origin. The setting is that of the Italian *grand tour* – Rome and Naples, Venice and Florence – in 1795.

Oswald and Corinne are idealized embodiments of the personality traits allegedly characterizing Britain and Italy, with the French d'Erfeuil, a product of the Parisian *salon*, as an example of national frivolity, vanity, egoism, and ignorance.[65] The figure of d'Erfeuil serves to highlight, by way of contrast, the dispositions of Oswald and Corinne. Both encapsulate forms of 'enthusiasm' in Staël's sense, but these forms differ fundamentally. Oswald embodies British morality, courage, good sense, practical spirit, self-control, melancholy, and reluctance to give vent to his feelings. Corinne is a high priestess of beauty and sentiments, a woman inspired by the flames of nature, artistic imagination, and passion. As the title of the novel suggests, the link established between individual and national attitudes is pivotal; the fascination and drama of the plot depend largely on it. Accordingly, the book abounds with descriptions of places, collective characters, and works of art, as well as philosophic and moral reflections.

If Oswald's virtues originate from public life, Corinne's traits spring from a life devoted to art. Corinne describes herself as dominated by a poetic 'vibration [*ébranlement*]', which is the source of artistic beauty, of religion 'in lonely souls', of generosity in heroes, and of altruistic feelings in mankind.[66] Corinne's Italy is not only a land graced with a balmy and bountiful climate but the land of beauty *par excellence*, both natural and artistic, stimulating a taste and imagination with which all Italians are imbued. Poetry is in Italy like 'the echo of nature'.[67] In recalling her British girlhood, Corinne censures the conformism of mores which oppress and suffocate women's lives there. The 'froid mortel' she felt in Britain referred to both climate and human contact.[68] As for Oswald, he is a sensitive and noble man, broken by his father's death, for which he feels responsible. His generous nature, as well as his otherness relative to the Italians, are suggested in a peculiar fashion. In one of the initial chapters, Oswald saves the town of Ancona from a great fire through a series of heroic actions; as the representative of a superior culture and morality, he comes to the rescue of the

---

[65] On d'Erfeuil, see *Corinne ou l'Italie*, ed. S. Balayé (1807; Paris, 1985), esp. pp. 33–9, 70–80, 505–10. Besides d'Erfeuil, the characters of Madame d'Arbigny and de Maltigues also encapsulate French vices: see pp. 305–36. Conversely, see a favourable depiction of Parisian life in 1791, pp. 305–8.
[66] *ibid.*, pp. 85–6.
[67] *ibid.*, pp. 83–4; see also pp. 141, 218–19, 242.
[68] *ibid.*, pp. 360–90, quotation on p. 368.

Jews as well as the inmates of an asylum against the will of a superstitious mob.[69] His tour of Italy with Corinne imperils his intention to marry his compatriot Lucile, as his father wanted him to do. In spite of his love and admiration for Corinne, he knows well that a woman like her 'accords little with the English way of living'.[70] In the end, Oswald and Lucile get married, and Corinne dies of grief as a consequence. There is a strong sense that cultural differences of a collective nature are at the origins of this tragic conclusion.

Corinne speaks of Italy in the then customary terms of a contrast between a glorious past and a miserable present, in which the nation's sole remaining distinction is that of 'imagination'. When Corinne asks Oswald whether he agrees with her that Italian artistic eminence would deserve a nobler national destiny, his answer is resolute: nations always deserve their fate, whatever it is. Although Italian governments are so weak, they very effectively enslave spirits, Oswald holds. Artistic genius is no compensation for the want of human dignity.[71] In visiting the Colosseum in Rome, Corinne goes into raptures about the magnificence of the remains, whereas Oswald, to whom moral judgement is paramount, sees only 'the luxury of the master and the blood of slaves'. His kind of 'enthusiasm' is that of personal sacrifice in defence of one's own opinions, principles, or duties – this is for him the highest form of virtue.[72] Corinne's Catholicism and Oswald's Protestantism follow from the two lovers' different moral premises. He criticizes the empty formalism of Catholicism, while she favours a religion of love and happiness over one of duty and sacrifice. Corinne's outburst is telling: 'Dear Oswald, let us then mingle everything, love, religion, genius, with sunshine, perfume, music, and poetry; atheism exists only in coldness, selfishness, and baseness.'[73]

Oswald's jealousy at a ball takes the shape of a criticism of Italian mores, which are the subject of an ensuing exchange of letters. Oswald considers true feelings of love and devotion impossible in a country where mores are free, public opinion is non-existent, and social constraints consequently far too lax. If Italy is the country of carnal and fugitive love, Britain is said to be 'the shrine of decency and delicacy'. Life in Italy amounts to mere escape from pain, regardless of dignity and sound merit.[74] Corinne's reply makes much of the view that 'governments shape the character of nations'. This is especially true with respect to Southern peoples, because they are indolent and inclined to resignation, while the delights of nature make up for the lack of a proper public sphere. Qualities like energy, honour, and pride can flourish only in 'free

[69] ibid., pp. 39–46.
[70] ibid., p. 144; see also pp. 166, 171.
[71] ibid., pp. 96–7, 103–4; see also pp. 447–9.
[72] ibid., pp. 115–16; see also pp. 225–6.
[73] ibid., pp. 268–77, quotation on p. 273 (*Corinne, or Italy*, trans. S. Raphael (Oxford, 1998), p. 179; trans. modified).
[74] ibid., pp. 152–8, quotation on p. 153.

and warlike' nations; in Italy, men have no collective goals to aim at. On the plane of private life, Corinne is at pains to contend that the Italians differ from the French. Her very Rousseauesque point is that the absence of *société* has benefited the former. In Italy, 'there is neither *société*, *salon*, or fashion, nor the little, everyday means of making an impression'. For this reason, while Italians can be ambitious and self-interested, they are not frivolous, namely, proud and vain. Actually, they are spontaneous, sincere, and loyal. They do not conceal their natural passions, because they are unafraid of disapproval from *société*.[75] The book features Corinne's lengthy defence of Italian literature against the claims of Oswald and d'Erfeuil, each of them arguing for the superiority of his own national literature.[76]

Although Staël clearly identifies with Corinne, this means neither that she also identifies with the South, with Catholicism, nor that she levels a comprehensive criticism at British mores. The dramatic impact of the story springs from the equal nobility of both morals, in spite of the questionable aspects of each. The different histories and natural endowments of North and South have determined different characters: for Staël this is a fact, amounting to a fundamental distinction within the European mind. The North–South divide is a category of thought, a device for the assessment of national histories, cultural products, and individual or collective personalities, which she shared with other members of the Coppet circle like Sismondi and Bonstetten. *Corinne* signals a shift in the use of this traditional dichotomy. In Montesquieu, North and South referred to a difference in the physiological base, and were assessed from the point of view of the legislator. Staël's frame of reference is much broader, because the psychological and cultural motifs are not subsumed within the political concern but are given independent relevance. Her ultimate political allegiance was to the passions of 'enthusiasm', regardless of their geographic variants.

4　Staël as diarist and historian of the Revolution

The Russian character figures prominently in Staël's diary *Dix années d'exil*, the part which is of interest here having been written in 1812 and published in 1820. Staël's account of the Russian character was candidly ambivalent, since, on the one hand, the Russians had been under the supposedly corrupting heel of despotism for centuries, but, on the other, were bravely fighting Napoleon. Her explanation was that only those involved in politics and administration had been 'depraved', but the masses of peasants (at the moment turned into soldiers) were

---

[75] *ibid.*, pp. 159–65, quotation on p. 161; see also pp. 106, 290–4, 422–7, 559–62. Staël speaks of 'l'indolence naturelle au climat', p. 183, and she accounts for the laziness of Neapolitan *lazzaroni* in terms of the ease of satisfying basic needs in a very favourable climate, p. 290. For Rousseauesque passages blaming civilization for the obliteration of natural diversities of customs and mores, see pp. 39, 110, 429.

[76] *ibid.*, pp. 173–200.

patient, able to endure severe hardship, hospitable, and even 'doux'. Added to which, the Russian 'nature' was Oriental (rather than Northern European), and hence rich in contrasts, and with more than a touch of barbarian passion and violence. What Staël really praised was that Russians of all ranks were driven by a 'public spirit' consisting essentially of religion and patriotism, two forms of 'enthusiasm' which were leading to great deeds.[77]

The damage done to the Russian mind by despotism became apparent through the faulty attitude of the *bonne compagnie*. More used to dissimulation than reflection, and to distrust and suspicion than intimacy and cultured conversation, the Russian aristocracy suffered from 'the defects of slavery', only partially compensated for by an almost barbaric energy.[78] There was no question of the Russians attaining 'moral perfection', because this could only be the result of a free constitution, as the English demonstrated.[79] However, Staël made herself very clear: one could not afford to criticize too harshly a people and a ruling class whose virtues underlay the successful resistance to Napoleonic aggression.[80]

Considérations sur la Révolution française is a posthumous work, which, while again focused on French *mœurs* in their relationship to a free government, gives the impression that Staël's optimistic standpoint was, at least to an extent, due to the hope of contributing to the consolidation and extension of representative institutions in France. At the time of writing (1816), Staël had successfully created her own myth, and her fame as both a literary authority and a victim of Napoleon's tyranny was at its peak. As will be explained in detail in chapter 4, in Restoration France a bleak view of the attitude of the French towards free institutions could not but serve the conservative platform, especially in the years immediately following 1814–15, which were marked by the *Ultras*' attacks on the new order. At such a time, as an opinion maker of the liberal camp, she could hardly concede the national character argument to her adversaries.

The main thread of the book is the attempt to parallel the French to the English Revolution as expressions of the same trend towards representative government. From my angle, the work revolves around the first chapter of the sixth part, entitled 'Les François sont-ils faits pour être libres?' This question was often raised at the opening of the Restoration, and not only by the *Ultras*: Charles Comte for example answered it in the negative in the *Censeur européen*.[81]

---

[77] *Dix années d'exil*, *SOC*, XV, pp. 262–90. As regards serfdom, Staël maintained that the absence of a middle class in Russia had given class relations a somewhat paternal character; Russian serfdom was 'tout à fait défavorable aux lumières des premières classes, mais non pas au bonheur des dernières', p. 276.

[78] *ibid.*, pp. 296–7, 307–8, 315, 317, 326–7, 344.

[79] *ibid.*, pp. 288, 304–6, 337–8.

[80] *ibid.*, pp. 277, 315. On Russian character and Russian politics, see also Staël's *Considérations sur la Révolution française*, ed. J. Godechot (1818; Paris, 1983), pp. 429–30.

[81] C. Comte, 'Considérations sur l'état moral de la nation française, et sur les causes de l'instabilité de ses institutions', *CE*, 1 (1817), pp. 1–92. See chapter 3 below.

Staël opposed an optimistic stance to contrary claims which, she writes, came from both the French *Ultras* and sectors of British opinion. Actually, there was not much in her recent record to nourish confidence in the French people.[82] Here, her evaluation of the causes of the lower classes' ferocity during the French Revolution is oscillatory, and the justifications she puts forward conflict with other passages.[83] Yet she had never given up her belief in the unstoppable progress of *lumières*, with the result that, both revolutionary unrest and despotic rule having come to an end, she could contend that in each nation 'there is always what makes representative government not only possible but necessary'; in France, it was only by 'destroying the *lumières*' that the resurgence of liberty could be avoided.[84]

Her defence of the French is carried out along lines we already know: government shapes a nation's *mœurs*; the Old Regime is responsible for French frivolity; and the virtues of liberty, that is 'public spirit', would mature as long as liberal institutions were set up and lasted for long enough.

It is in free countries only that the true character of a woman and the true character of a man can be known and admired. Domestic life inspires all the virtues in women; and the political career, far from habituating men to despise morality, as an old tale of the nursery, stimulates those who hold public functions to the sacrifice of their personal interests, to the dignity of honour, and to all that greatness of soul which the habitual presence of public opinion never fails to call forth. Finally, in a country where women are at the bottom of every intrigue, because favour governs every thing, the morals of the first class have nothing in common with those of the nation, and no sympathy can exist between the persons who fill the drawing-rooms and the bulk of the people. A woman of the lowest order in England feels that she has some kind of analogy with the Queen, who has also taken care of her husband, and brought up their children . . .[85]

The infamous *légèreté* of the French was in reality limited to the people in power and those close to it. Marriage, the institution on which 'mores and freedom rest', was more respected since the Revolution.[86] A certain bashing of the English character, now deemed impetuous and prone to sectarian violence, is meant to support Staël's position.[87]

---

[82] She made clear both in *De la littérature* and in *De l'Allemagne* that the corrupted manners originating from the court and the aristocratic circles had held sway over all classes. And even in the *Considérations* there is no lack of disparaging comments on French character: see e.g. pp. 271, 290, 337, 365, 601. On Staël's 'propagandist agenda' in relation to *De l'Allemagne*, see Isbell, *The Birth of European Romanticism*.

[83] Staël explains popular excesses on the grounds of previous oppression and distress in *Considérations*, pp. 96, 146, 304; but elsewhere in the book she describes the *peuple* as an utterly unjustifiable homicidal and bloodthirsty mob: see pp. 273, 278ff., 301.

[84] *ibid.*, pp. 523, 587.

[85] *ibid.*, pp. 591–2 (*Considerations on the Principal Events of the French Revolution* (3 vols., London, 1818), III, pp. 366–7).

[86] *ibid.*, pp. 590–1.

[87] *ibid.*, pp. 512–13ff.

Whatever the degree of instrumentality of Staël's text, there is a deeper layer in it which is worth considering. On the historical side, her reconstruction is straightforward. By turning feudal lords into courtesans, Richelieu, at bottom a foreigner (like Napoleon), had suffocated the seeds of French liberty, and, with it, the loyalty, candour, and independence of the 'original' French character.[88] There ensued a shameful history of court intrigues, reflecting the 'absence of principles' in the rulers. Nonetheless, she argues against Blackstone and more generally British opinion, despotism was opposed by Frenchmen on numerous occasions. It remains true, however, that France was never ruled by laws but rather by customs and the whims of kings.[89]

Staël accepts Burke's interpretation of the Revolution as flawed by abstract rationalism, combining it easily with the political Anglophilia of her father Necker. The architects of the revolutionary project were way off the mark even from the standpoint of national character. The 'abstract equality' they preached was in conflict with the principle of 'emulation' to gain places and honours which suits the French so well, and which Napoleon a few years later exploited on a large scale.[90] The passion for ideas is alien to their character. The French are a practical, pleasure- and power-oriented people; the kind of equality they love is that of property and rank.[91] What Staël especially stigmatizes is the cowardice of the people, always ready to join the winning party and shift allegiances when necessary. From the Constituent Assembly to Napoleon, the French, bereft of principles as a consequence of the absolutism of the Old Regime, followed only their vanity and self-love.[92] Napoleon is depicted as a despot who ruled by corrupting opinion (made to focus on war rather than liberty) and morality (through a network of interests).[93] It ensued from all this that, when the Bourbons were restored, the French were 'dull by despotism', and the only citizens active in the public sphere were place-hunters.[94]

At this point begins the real challenge for Staël: to postulate, against both the evidence she herself has presented and the claims of the *royalistes*, that the French are fit for liberty. She contends that it is impossible for a people 'to have the virtues of liberty before achieving it'; and liberty is established either through a 'happy circumstance' or through the 'strong will' of a leader.[95] Now, France has 'energy' and 'force', the qualities which first appear in the transition to a representative government; but in order to be transformed into

---

[88] *ibid.*, pp. 74–5.
[89] *ibid.*, pp. 115–22.
[90] *ibid.*, pp. 223, 337.
[91] *ibid.*, pp. 244, 397, 465.
[92] *ibid.*, pp. 271, 285, 290, 304, 464, 475, 478.
[93] See, e.g., *ibid.*, pp. 354, 365–7, 410, 412.
[94] *ibid.*, p. 478.
[95] *ibid.*, pp. 243, 510. See also the whole of ch. 10 in part VI, entitled 'De l'influence du pouvoir arbitraire sur l'esprit et le caractère d'une nation', pp. 586–93.

reliable virtues, they must be cultivated by free institutions gradually inculcating 'public spirit'.[96] Her argument derives support from a reconstruction of English history prior to 1688, which highlights the frivolity, corruption, and violent impetuosity of the population.[97]

But Staël makes a point which imperils the straightforwardness of her stance. She evokes the necessity, and the effectiveness, of public spirit as a polity-building force. Two statements are relevant in this respect. First, she says that a people made to be free is such because it wants to be free; and she continues: there are no examples in history of peoples that failed to establish their will, for the reason that when institutions are below the existing level of *lumières*, institutions tend to rise up to that level. During the Old Regime, *lumières* flourished and government declined. Even if here she was talking about philosophic *esprit* rather than public spirit, which is questionable, the impression is that men make institutions, and not the reverse. The Revolution would appear as the attempt to create institutions adequate to the increased fondness of the French for liberty. In the following paragraph, Staël adds almost incidentally that the task of establishing a suitable government may meet with 'great obstacles'.[98] The second statement concerns citizens' participation, as she contrasts the small number of Frenchmen involved in public businesses with the English situation, where many people practise 'political virtues'. 'One of the marvels of English liberty is the large number [*la multitude*] of people who take an interest in the affairs of each town and each province, and whose spirit and character are shaped by the occupations and duties of citizenship.'[99] In England public spirit is the 'soul' of the constitution.[100]

In the *Considérations* the will to support the liberal cause made Staël posit public attitudes as a matter of cause and effect: the question was to state as convincingly as possible that institutions were the cause and attitudes the effect. Yet the *Considérations* can be assessed from another viewpoint as well. To put forward a broad generalization, there is a difference in kind between an approach in terms of the causes of national character and one in terms of public spirit. The goal of the former approach is to apprehend the influence of factors like climate or government, and, if an interaction between national character and institutions is contemplated, its forms and relevance largely depend on the selection of factors. By contrast, the public-spirit approach focuses on that interaction by

[96] *ibid.*, pp. 510–12. See also p. 601, where Staël criticizes the conservative argument that the French were riotous and subversive: 'Après avoir vu la servilité avec laquelle Bonaparte a été obéi, on a peine à concevoir que ce soit l'esprit républicain que l'on craigne en France.'
[97] *ibid.*, pp. 513–23.
[98] *ibid.*, pp. 509–10.
[99] *ibid.*, p. 511.
[100] *ibid.*, p. 545. For a eulogy of the public spirit, morality, religiosity, and literature of contemporary England, see pp. 523–75. Staël argues that in that country political liberty serves to link interest to morality, p. 554.

making public spirit a necessary complement of the establishment of a (representative) government. What counts here is not the cause of a certain disposition but its functioning in a given institutional context. The *Considérations* can be seen as a specimen of the public-spirit standpoint, because, while it was taken for granted by Staël that public dispositions depended on government, the indispensability of public spirit to the workings of free institutions figured as the underlying theme of the treatment. The point to note, however, is that the whole of her quest for public morality may be seen in the same light. The many differences between the two approaches just sketched will be examined in due course from various angles. With respect to the relationship between civic humanism and 'public spirit' in my sense, Staël's awareness that the kind of patriotism of the ancient republics could not be transposed to commercial nations is worth recalling. The aim of this chapter has been to recognize through the example of Staël that the functional outlook of public spirit emerged in France in the wake of the Revolution. In Britain, a 'civic' line of argument was incorporated in the Whiggish pride in the 'matchless' constitution pervading the eighteenth century. Historically, a linkage is traceable between the establishment of representative institutions and an approach in terms of public spirit.

It has been shown how even climate, the most static of factors, was not utterly dismissed by Staël; a fact which confirms the relative nature of all broad statements about my subject. At the same time, its very richness and complexity should not obscure the gradual formation of certain lines of argument and their rise to a prominent position, albeit not unchallenged. Constant's *Principes de politique* (1815) is a good early document expressing the necessity of public spirit, a stance which would inform French liberal culture up to the publication of Tocqueville's *Ancien régime* at least. Staël's *Considérations* appeared in 1818, and certainly the stress she placed on the human factor in politics contributed significantly to the adoption of that stance by Restoration liberals. But Staël was too close to the revolutionary events to give more than occasional thought to the issue of citizens' participation, viewed by later authors as the most effective means of creating public spirit. If I had to characterize her own brand of public spirit in the light of the *Considérations*, I would point to the importance she ascribed to time, namely, she advocated a 'habit of liberty' and a balance of passions which only long experience could bring about. This position clearly served the main thesis of the book, and at the same time had distinct Burkean echoes.

How, then, had the Revolution moved things on from Montesquieu and Helvétius? Discussing *mœurs* in abstract terms and in relation to a typology of the forms of government which dated back to Aristotle was of little use in the face of the Revolution, which had altered the way in which the relationship between morality and politics was perceived. A free, representative government could be either republican or monarchical, but it did not matter which because 'free' *mœurs* were required in any case, and, above all, were not mechanically shaped by government. Politics having eventually delivered basic liberty and equality, morality had to be stressed and strengthened. The overall legacy of the Revolution was the enhancement of the role of *mœurs* in the face of institutional engineering – Staël sought answers to the question of how to harmonize the French with institutions unsupported by pre-existing social relationships, traditions, or religion. In outline, Staël and the other Restoration liberals were bedevilled by a paradox: liberty and equality could not exist without free *mœurs*, but free *mœurs* were created by liberty and equality. A dynamic perspective, which made much of anticipations and delays in the relationship between *mœurs* and institutions, served to loosen the grip of the paradox, as Staël's *Considérations* have shown. But whose were the *mœurs* talked about? The political role of *le peuple* in the Revolution could not but induce a shift of meaning. If it had been possible in the eighteenth century to affirm the similar features of the *bonne compagnie* in all countries, adding that it was in the *peuple* that true national traits should be looked for in a cultural or even ethnological sense, in the Restoration the *peuple* not only became the nation itself but a political entity *par excellence*.[101]

Once set against this background, Staël stands out as a transitional figure, who associated clear hints of the new perception with a dull reassertion of the infallible sway of political institutions over people's attitudes. Staël's reflections on public morality, by developing the line of argument inherited by the Enlightenment, and by taking the Revolution and in particular the years 1793–4 as a point of no return for the European mind, contributed momentously to the shaping of the spiritual climate at the beginning of the new century. It must be conceded, if one wishes to measure her standing against the common yardsticks of political thought, that she cannot bear comparison with, say, Constant. Her thinking is neither sharp, nor particularly acute; her handling of concepts is approximate and her writings abound with obscurities and contradictions. But *De la littérature* and *De l'Allemagne* are superb examples of popular politics, texts where a political message – focused on personal liberty and public morality – is conveyed by an evocative flux of moral sentiments.

5   Staël reviewed, or national identity evoked

In 1776 Staël, then aged ten, was in England; she returned in 1793, with a brigade of fellow exiles who scandalized the Surrey neighbourhood with their open liaisons (like that of Staël and Narbonne) unsanctified by marriage, and the rumours of their past flirtations with 'Jacobinism'. During 1813–14, she returned once more into English exile, but this time as a public-figure heroine

---

[101] For Staël on *salon* society and *peuple*, see *De l'Allemagne*, I, part I, ch. 1, p. 99; *Dix années*, p. 342.

acclaimed by both Tories and Whigs. With all her relevant works translated and in some cases republished, she was fêted during this last period of stay both as a freedom fighter and as an author of European stature.[102] James Mackintosh, who had studied with Constant at Edinburgh, was appointed her guide to visit the London *salons*; he wrote in a letter to his daughters: 'I am generally ordered with her to dinner, as one orders beans and bacon; I have, in consequence, dined with her at the houses of almost all of the Cabinet Ministers.'[103]

Staël's literary fortunes in Britain were heavily influenced by the changing tides of the political and intellectual climate – which included an element of fashion. Until the triumphal sojourn of 1813–14, which coincided with the publication of *De l'Allemagne*, only *Delphine* and *Corinne* had been reviewed; but at the peak of her popularity editors rushed to catch up by commissioning reviews of *De la littérature*.[104] In 1803, the *Edinburgh Review* defined *Delphine* 'dismal trash', a boring peroration in favour of 'adultery, murder, and a great number of other vices'.[105] In *Corinne*, reviewers did find things to praise, especially Staël's talent as an 'enlightened traveller', a painter of men and places. Indeed, that Staël was unbeatable in depicting national characters was to become a *Leitmotiv* of successive journalism. Two points recurred: the reviewers' approval of Staël's political determination of national attitudes, especially as applied to the English; and disagreement about the role of climate, which many thought she had overestimated. On the basis of this twofold stance, a reviewer of *Corinne* set the record straight:

[102] R. Escarpit, *L'Angleterre dans l'œuvre de Madame de Staël* (Paris, 1954), part I. According to Mackintosh, 3,500 copies of the English version of *De l'Allemagne* were sold in six weeks: *Memoirs of the Life of the Right Honourable Sir James Mackintosh* (2 vols., London, 1835), II, p. 265. After the first edition was destroyed by Napoleon's police in 1810, *De l'Allemagne* appeared in French in London in 1813, and it was translated into English during the same year. For an assessment of the contemporary significance and Europe-wide impact of the book, see esp. I. A. Henning, *L'Allemagne de Mme de Staël et la polémique romantique* (Paris, 1929), and Isbell, *The Birth of European Romanticism*. The power of Staël's pen should not be underestimated, as the Prince Regent, for one, was induced by his ministers to pay her a visit because it was good politics to make her write well of England: H. Kurtz, 'Madame de Staël and the Duke of Wellington 1814–1817', *History Today*, 13 (1963), p. 735. There circulated the dictum that in 1814 there were only three powers left in Europe: England, Russia, and Madame de Staël.

[103] *Memoirs*, II, p. 264. For Mackintosh's enthusiasm for *Corinne*, see *Memoirs*, I, pp. 405–8. On Mackintosh and Staël, see N. King, 'Lettres de Madame de Staël à Sir James Mackintosh', *Cahiers Staëliens*, 10 (1970), pp. 27–54. Of the many recollections, the vividness and pungency of Byron's are unsurpassed: *The Complete Miscellaneous Prose*, ed. A. Nicholson (Oxford, 1991), pp. 184–6, 221–4.

[104] Actually, there appeared notices of *De l'influence des passions* and *De la littérature* in the *British Critic* in 1798 and 1800 respectively, but neither was original. I have taken advantage of P. H. Dubé, *Bibliographie de la critique sur Madame de Staël 1789–1994* (Geneva, 1998).

[105] S. Smith, 'Mad. de Staël's *Delphine*', *ER*, 2 (1803), pp. 172–7. As all articles in the British press were anonymous, the names of authors cannot always be given. The title indicated is the running title.

'an Englishman bears a much greater resemblance to a Roman, than an Italian of the present day'.[106]

Jeffrey's account of *De la littérature* appeared in the *Edinburgh Review* in 1813 (the *Monthly Review* had preceded the Whig journal by a year). Although marked by its rejection of the theory of perfectibility, Jeffrey's piece is a balanced discussion, in which he agreed with Staël's fundamental distinction between North and South: 'she is right in saying, that there is a radical difference in the taste and genius of the two regions'. Yet he did not follow Staël in tracing its causes, for he ascribed most weight to the educational effects of Protestantism and in particular to the reading of the Bible; in doing so, Jeffrey denied the validity of geographical divides and affirmed the primacy of cultural and historical determinants.[107] Jeffrey, like many other reviewers of Staël's books, was naturally led by her choice of subjects to take a stand on what constituted the identity of the English.[108] In effect, Staël's overall praise of English politics and character permitted journalists to go beyond merely defensive, Pavlovian reactions, and thereby cast veritable light on the self-image of the English at a crucial juncture of their history. Basically, all reviewers proudly cherished national literature and politics; what differed, and it was no immaterial difference, was tone and style.

Staël's approval of things English not having been without reservations, Jeffrey proudly settled the old Racine-versus-Shakespeare controversy in this way:

Now, we humbly conceive it to be a complete and final justification for the whole body of the English nation, who understand French as well as English and yet prefer Shakespeare to Racine, just to state, modestly and firmly, the fact of that preference; and to declare, that their habits and tempers, and studies and occupations, have been such as to make them receive far greater pleasure from the more varied imagery – the more flexible tone – the closer imitation of nature – the more rapid succession of incident, and vehement bursts of passion of the English author, than from the unvarying majesty – the elaborate argument – and epigrammatic poetry of the French dramatist.[109]

Jeffrey equally defended English philosophy and eloquence. As regards Staël's poor estimate of British humour and 'talent for pleasantry', he retorted by saying that busy people enjoyed themselves in ways which were different from those proper to men 'who have nothing to do with their time but to get rid of it

---

[106] J. Playfair, 'Madame de Staël's *Corinne*', *ER*, 11 (1807), p. 194. On p. 183 Playfair, a mathematician and geologist, wrote: in this book 'the difference of national character is the force that sets all in motion'. See also *MR*, 54 (1807), pp. 152–9.

[107] '*Sur la Literature*', pp. 41–2.

[108] Although a Scotsman, Jeffrey almost unvariably spoke of England and the English even when he meant Britain and the British. I follow his use when dealing with him.

[109] '*Sur la Literature*', p. 44. For a more sympathetic interpretation of Staël on Shakespeare, see the review of *De la littérature* in *MR*, 68 (1812), pp. 449–59.

in amusement'.[110] As for politics, he mildly rebukes the elitism of Staël's view of the use of literature. Granted that 'all men have not the capacity of thinking deeply', and 'the most general cultivation of literature will not invest every one with talents of the first order', there is a need to educate 'the greater multitude' since liberty is related to 'intelligence'. As he writes, 'it is in the intelligence of the people themselves that the chief bulwark of their freedom will be found to consist, and all the principles of political amelioration to originate'. Characteristically, the task of the people is to resist the encroachments of arbitrary power.[111] It is important to note that Jeffrey was no blind eulogist of his country, for in the same article, there figures a very bleak portrait of working-class life in manufacturing districts.[112]

There were six analyses of *De l'Allemagne* at the time of its appearance, usually containing a careful blend of praise and blame.[113] Whereas nobody liked Staël's attack on utilitarianism and inductive philosophy, her descriptions of national mores and characters met with universal praise. In spite of his disinclination to endorse the 'racial' distinction between Latins and Teutons, Mackintosh spoke of her genius as a 'national painter' and a 'moral painter of nations', while the writer in the *Scots Magazine* took the opportunity to reassert the legitimacy of such portraits.[114]

To draw national character well is a nice and delicate task. It is an idle common-place to assert, as is currently done, that such distinctions originate merely in fancy or prejudice. It does by no means follow, indeed, that the character drawn of a people will apply to all the individuals that compose it. Such sweeping conclusions have been made, and justly ridiculed. There are in every nation the grave and the gay, the sober and the dissolute, honest men and rogues. Still, on a careful inspection we shall discover that some virtues and some faults are more prevalent in one nation than in another. Qualities even substantially the same are more or less varied and modified by the reigning spirit. To distinguish these shades of human thought, requires indeed a rare union of qualities. It demands at once comprehensive views and delicate discrimination. These requisites the present author seems to possess in a very high degree, and there never perhaps was an abler picture drawn than is here exhibited of the German people.[115]

Mackintosh considered national spirit and character the most important things to be observed in a country, but, he remarked, these could neither be numbered

---

[110] '*Sur la Literature*', pp. 46–7.
[111] ibid., pp. 6–7, 23–4.
[112] ibid., pp. 21–4.
[113] But see M. Butler, *Romantics, Rebels and Reactionaries: English Literature and Its Background 1760–1830* (Oxford, 1981), pp. 120–1.
[114] Mackintosh, too, stressed the importance of the Catholicism–Protestantism divide in the shaping of national literatures, with the former religion amounting to 'festal shows and legendary polytheism'. But he conceded that the adoption and preservation of the two religions was likely to have been due to the 'original characters' of the peoples concerned: '*De l'Allemagne*', p. 207.
[115] 'Mad. Staël's *Germany*', *Scots Magazine and Edinburgh Literary Miscellany*, 75 (1813), pp. 921–2.

nor measured. What struck him (and Jeffrey) in Staël was the 'philosophical' nature of her descriptions. She had managed to combine sympathy for German sentiments and a talent for observation with historical, literary, and philosophical insight, and the result was a 'grand historical painting' where phenomena were subsumed under general causes.[116] In Jeffrey's words, 'by combining the past with the present, and pointing out the connexion and reciprocal action of all coexistent phenomena', she had developed an 'harmonious system' which was a sample of 'the generalizing spirit of true philosophy'.[117]

Both the *Monthly* and the *Quarterly* reviewers were content with England classed as a 'Teutonic', 'Germanic', or 'Gothic' civilization. In their view, this entailed a specific religion and specific political institutions and 'domestic habits', in addition to a literature and a literary taste of 'autochthonous growth'. 'It is justly observed that certain features of civilization, inherited from the Romans, are common to the Italian, Spanish, and French nations, while certain other features of domestic habit and political institution are common to the German, Scandinavian, and English nations.' But within the Gothic family there were differences: the *Quarterly* saw England – 'more active and ambitious' than Germany, 'more studious and contemplative' than France – 'as an intermediate link' between those two extremes, although there was 'still so much general likeness of character and feeling' between England and Germany.[118] Actually, France was 'to be feared', for 'their rashness in the sudden application of their theories' in the political realm, and for the immoral effects of Catholicism on domestic life in the private sphere.[119] The French, the *Quarterly* went on, were irremediably frivolous and thereby slaves of the majority opinion, whereas the Teutons showed 'a peculiar cast of humour' consisting of originality of character and independence of sentiments. At bottom, the difference lay in the fact that the Englishman 'is conversant not with terms but things'.[120]

---

[116] Mackintosh, '*De l'Allemagne*', pp. 204–5.

[117] Jeffrey, '*Sur la Literature*', pp. 2–3.

[118] 'Mad. de Staël on Germany', *MR*, 72 (1813), p. 423 (from which the long quotation is taken), and 74 (1814), p. 364; 'Madame de Staël Holstein's *L'Allemagne*', *QR*, 10 (1814), pp. 360–2ff. Among other things, the English and the Germans shared a love for nature and animals, habits of comfort, and hospitality: 'Staël Holstein's *L'Allemagne*', pp. 363–6; for similarities in their literatures, see pp. 378–9. That the English mind was at mid point between the French and German ones was also Staël's opinion, as reported by H. Crabb Robinson, *Diary, Reminiscences, and Correspondence* (3 vols., London, 1869), I, p. 175.

[119] 'Mad. de Staël on Germany', *MR*, 73 (1814) p. 67; 'Staël Holstein's *L'Allemagne*', *QR*, pp. 368–9.

[120] 'Staël Holstein's *L'Allemagne*', *QR*, p. 372. See also 'Baroness Staël Holstein's Germany', *British Critic*, n.s., 1 (1814), pp. 510, 647, 657. The dichotomy between the English and 'things', on the one hand, and the French and 'abstractions', on the other, was a recurrent motif from at least the mid eighteenth century onwards, to be eventually elaborated by Carlyle with reference to the Irish and other peoples. Carlyle published two pieces related to Staël, articles which testify, as he wrote, to the importance of *De l'Allemagne* 'as the precursor, if not parent, of whatever acquaintance with German literature exists among us': see 'Jean Paul

When reviewers take a Francophobic tack, Staël may still be hailed as a great author but is also likely to be reminded of her three handicaps: being French, being a woman, and leading an immoral life.[121] Apart from Staël's persona, and the extremes to which the advocates of a Protestant and anti-French idea of Englishness sometimes carried their arguments, journalistic culture, both Tory and Whig, was undergoing momentous changes in these years, not necessarily in the direction of progressive or cosmopolitan stances.[122] Traditional self-celebratory motifs were reformulated and rejuvenated. Burke's interpretation of the Revolution had diffused a bleak depiction of the French as riotous, prone to abstractions, frivolous, and in general unprepared to change. An idea that seems to have been shared throughout the political spectrum, and which the response to Staël well documents, is the close relationship said to exist between English or British character and the national government; often, the primacy of character over institutional machinery was asserted. Legislation, wrote one commentator, should be 'the faithful reflection of some moral reality'.[123] The association of, respectively, British virtues with British liberty, and French immorality with the French sequence of illiberal governments, was regularly put forward.[124]

When the *Considérations* appeared, the war was over, and Staël's pen could no longer exert an influence upon politics. However, the conjunction of a writer of her renown with a topic as hot as the Revolution could not but stimulate reflections deeply informed by political positions. To the question about the ability of the French to be free, the *Edinburgh Review* and the *Eclectic Review* answered in the negative, while the *Monthly Review* was more open. To support the argument that 'regulated freedom' would be unattainable to them for a long

Friedrich Richter's Review of Madame de Staël's *Allemagne*', *Fraser's Magazine*, 1 (1830), pp. 28–37, 407–13, translated and edited by Carlyle, and 'Schiller, Goethe, and Madame de Staël', *Fraser's Magazine*, 5 (1832), pp. 171–7.

[121] Staël went to England with her lover Rocca (besides her son and daughter), although the couple lived apart. For a consideration of the moral problem raised by Staël's writings, see, e.g., *MR*, 76 (1815), pp. 443–4. Although both Tory and Whig reviewers talked of Staël's 'masculine mind' as the best of praises, the two groups differed in their reactions to a woman entering a man's domain, with the Tory press readier to speak of her faults as a writer as being typically feminine.

[122] On the press in early and mid Victorian decades and the rise of 'philosophical criticism', see E. Halévy, *La formation du radicalisme philosophique* (3 vols., Paris, 1901–4), III, pp. 326–30; J. Clive, *Scotch Reviewers: the 'Edinburgh Review', 1802–15* (London, 1957); J. O. Hayden, *The Romantic Reviewers 1802–1824* (London, 1969); B. Fontana, *Rethinking the Politics of Commercial Society: the 'Edinburgh Review' 1802–1832* (Cambridge, 1985).

[123] 'Mad. de Staël on the French Revolution', *Eclectic Review*, 11 (1819), p. 324.

[124] The most explicit instances are the MR review of the *Considérations*, in 88 (1819), pp. 1–16, 138–54, esp. pp. 143–5, 151–3; the quoted 'Mad. de Staël on the French Revolution' in *Eclectic Review*, 11 (1819), pp. 201–18, 316– 44, 488–503; and Jeffrey's *ER* review of the *Considérations* dealt with below. For the position of the *Edinburgh Review*, with its complex interplay of Whiggish pride for Britain's political achievements and the bragged 'superiority of a man derived from having a share in the system of government', see Clive, *Scotch Reviewers*, pp. 176–9.

time, Jeffrey argued that the parallel with England put forward by Staël was inappropriate, because 'England had a Parliament and a representative legislature for 500 years before 1648.' That was to say that in England 'opinion' was now fully formed – to Jeffrey, who faithfully subscribed to Hume's view, it was on opinion that all governments were founded in the final analysis – and therefore rulers were unlikely to be grossly mistaken about it. But in France, where no 'previous training' had taken place, public opinion could 'neither be *formed, collected,* nor *expressed* in an authentic or effectual manner'; consequently, there was no possible basis for a stable government, let alone a free one. In England,

there were no such novelties to be hazarded, either in 1640 or in 1688. The people of this country have had an elective Parliament from the earliest period of their history – and, long before either of the periods in question, had been trained in every hamlet to the exercise of various political franchises, and taught to consider themselves as connected, by known and honourable ties, with all the persons of influence and consideration in their neighbourhood, and, through them, by an easy gradation with the political leaders of the State . . . [125]

It is a necessity for any government to conform to the will of those who have the power to overturn it; in a modern, civilized country, what counts is the opinion of 'that larger proportion of the people who can bring their joint talents, wealth and strength, to act in concert when occasion requires'.[126] But their power remains virtual until they acquire a consciousness of their common views as well as of the strength resulting from their union. The problem with France is that a representative assembly does not create, but merely channels public opinion. This gradually forms 'in the villages and burghs' through associations, local magistracies, and political elections. Being new to all this, the French for a long while cannot have 'the power of enforcing and resisting' which a representative government requires.[127]

The 1820s witnessed a mania for Staël in France, fuelled by the appearance of her complete works including previously unpublished material.[128] But in England the *London Magazine* wrote in 1821 that 'we may possibly give great offence to Edinburgh philosophers, but it does appear to us that the English public have had almost enough of Madame de Staël'.[129] However, *pace* the *London Magazine*, both the new writings and a biographical sketch by Staël's

---

[125] 'Mad. de Staël sur la Revolution Françoise [*sic*]', *ER*, 30 (1818), pp. 281–5, quotation on p. 285; see also pp. 315–16.
[126] *ibid.*, p. 283.
[127] *ibid.*, pp. 284–5.
[128] See Henning, *L'Allemagne*.
[129] 'Madame de Staël', *London Magazine*, 4 (1821), p. 394. This article amounts to little more than abuse of Staël. For a reply, see 'Mde. de Staël's Ten Years' Exile', *Eclectic Review*, 16 (1821), p. 416. Obituaries, too, were hardly complimentary.

cousin Necker de Saussure occasioned another round of reviews, many of which were favourable. Her historical role as interpreter of the events of 1789–1815 was acknowledged, together with the wide influence of her writings; thanks to her, one wrote, liberal ideas had become 'the genteel opinions of her age'.[130] Yet, by observing that Jacques Necker should be 'contented to be known to posterity chiefly as the father of Madame de Staël', Jeffrey made, all things considered, a wrong prediction. He was probably closer to the truth when he argued that 'a great deal of what startled the Parisians by its novelty, in the writings of Mad. de Staël, had long been familiar' to the thinkers of Britain and Germany, and here he was referring not only to literature but also to 'politics' and 'metaphysics'.[131] What did strike Jeffrey, however, was the vivacity of Staël's personality, a trait 'of which we have no idea in this phlegmatic country' and which was, to many Britons, quintessentially French. This contrast forms the final component of the idea of Englishness (or Britishness) that emerges from the reviews of Staël's texts. Her flamboyant nature, so well reflected in her works, seems in fact to have been an object of curiosity for many British, who regarded themselves as more quiet, self-controlled, and considerate. In Jeffrey's case, his mixed feelings about her character are revealed by the overt ambiguity of this description: 'her great characteristic was an excessive movement of the soul – a heart overcharged with sensibility, a frame overinformed with spirit and vitality'.[132]

---

[130] 'Mad. de Staël's Life, and Treasures of Thought', *MR*, 92 (1820), pp. 243, 253. See also *MR*, 102 (1823), pp. 256–64. As for her literary achievements, she was regarded as the best woman writer of all ages even by those who had little sympathy for her: see, e.g., 'On the Writings of Madame de Staël', *British Critic*, 13 (1820), pp. 390, 393.

[131] 'Madame de Staël', *ER*, 36 (1821), pp. 56, 67. See also 'Complete Works of Madame de Staël', *MR*, 97 (1822), p. 540. But it was also asserted that Staël, like Lavoisier or Smith, had created a 'new science', namely the analysis of 'the spirit of nations' and of 'the springs which move them': 'The Chateau of Coppet', *BM*, 6 (1818), p. 278. For a late assessment of Staël's work as a whole, see T. H. Lister, 'Madame de Staël', *Foreign Quarterly Review*, 14 (1834), pp. 1–30. Staël's talent to sketch national characters continued to be appreciated; see, e.g., A. Alison, 'Modern French Classics, I, Madame de Staël and Chateaubriand', *BM*, 41 (1837), pp. 718–19, 726.

[132] 'Madame de Staël', pp. 58–9.

3 From republicanism to industrialism and national character: Melchiorre Gioja, Charles Dupin, and Continental political economy, 1800–1848

1 Introduction

Can two authors, unquestionably minor in many respects, be taken to represent a breakthrough in European thought? The answer is yes, if their inferior status when judged by posterity rests on a relative lack of brilliance, but contrasts with both the great esteem in which they were held by contemporaries and the wide sway they exerted. Additionally, when the scholar concentrates on the underlying structures of thought, the so-called 'minor' writers may prove more representative than the 'major' ones. In the aftermath of the French Revolution, the Italian Melchiorre Gioja (1767–1829) and the Frenchman Charles Dupin (1784–1873) provide exemplary evidence of that most un-English intellectual product, early and mid-nineteenth-century Continental political economy. The focus of the chapter is on the clues to the shift from 'virtue' to 'industry' which can be gained from the two authors. The second section is devoted to a short profile of Gioja, while the third deals with Dupin; subsequently, it will be argued that some key aspects of their approach are discernible in other Italian (section 4) and French (section 5) economists of the first half of the century. The main issues raised are reconsidered in the concluding remarks (section 6). The parallel treatment of two national cases is intended to highlight not only the similarity of responses that the demise of revolutionary Rousseauism induced, but also the differences.

The relevance of classical political economy to the subject of this book is twofold. First, as a refined form of social knowledge which aspired to be scientific, political economy was a medium for national character arguments, especially on the Continent, where it often acted as a general theory of modernization. In particular, national character comparisons played an important role within the economic thought of Chevalier, Faucher, and other French writers. Second, political economy, predictably enough, highlighted economic virtues, a matter of the utmost concern in an age witnessing an unusually rapid pace of growth. But it is apparent that the validity of the patterns of human character set as standards by political economy went much beyond the economic sphere. These patterns of behaviour, and this is the hypothesis the chapter sets out to verify, looked in France and Italy like an escape from the revolutionary dead end.

As will be documented, the contrast between 'virtue' and 'industry' touches on a variety of issues relating to the specific features of Continental classical political economy, such as a predominant concern with social stability, an equally pervasive desire to catch up with Britain, a neglect of analysis in comparison with the attention paid to policy issues, and the view of economic growth as the proper route to nation building in the modern era. Underlying the work of the economists, there was a widespread appraisal of the age as *par excellence* economic, involving a clear awareness of the growing importance of the economic sphere and its science in accounting for post-revolutionary change, and providing answers to the political questions of the times.

In the previous chapters 'republicanism' and 'civic virtue' were not the focus of attention; here systematic reference will be made to them. There is hardly the need to repeat that 'republicanism' (a term which suits my current argument better than 'civic humanism') is the line of thought about the government of republics initiated by Aristotle; and that 'civic virtue' is one of its elements, that is the idea that a responsible and active participation of citizens in political life, or at least their abiding by the republican written and unwritten laws, would guarantee the republic's permanence. In interpreting these terms, however, context is everything. For this reason the sizeable literature on seventeenth- and eighteenth-century republicanism in the Anglo-Saxon world cannot in justice be transposed to other cases. The type of republicanism this chapter is concerned with is Rousseau's, Mably's, and even Montesquieu's, all of whom dressed up in their revolutionary garb; there is no room here for Harringtonesque utopias, the realm of virtue having materialized under the Jacobins. The experience of Jacobin rule decisively shaped contemporary views of republicanism on the Continent. Approximately speaking, post-Terror French and Italian onlookers came to perceive republicanism in the light of two distinguishing features. First, its institutional dimension: a republican *patrie* would generate a virtuous citizenry by its institutions, rather than the reverse.[1] Second, revolutionary republicanism emphasized that economic equality was to be achieved through agrarian laws, confiscations, progressive taxation, etc. Violent and authoritarian methods seemed quintessential to the doctrine; the various strands of turn-of-the-century Thermidorians identified this Rousseauism-with-teeth with revolutionary excesses.

---

[1] See N. Hampson, *Will and Circumstance: Montesquieu, Rousseau and the French Revolution* (London, 1983), and, by the same author, 'La Patrie', in F. Furet and M. Ozouf, eds., *The French Revolution and the Creation of Modern Political Culture 1789–1848* (3 vols., Oxford, 1988), I, pp. 125–37.

2   Gioja

The French Revolution, as imported into Italy by Napoleon's army in 1796, marked a watershed for Italian intellectuals. Faced with the sudden establishment of a representative government, Italians felt that the old system of social control had irremediably collapsed. New strategies were urgently needed in view of the liberation of the political potential of the lower classes brought about by the Revolution. Chief among Italians rising to the new historical challenge was the Milan-based Melchiorre Gioja.

The economic thought of Gioja was marked by his enthusiastic participation in the political life of the short-lived Cisalpine Republic (1796–9). In fact, even if Gioja's main economic work is *Nuovo prospetto delle scienze economiche* (1815–17), the story of his distinctive approach to economics should begin with his first political writings and especially with the *Dissertazione su quale dei governi liberi meglio convenga alla felicità dell'Italia* of 1796. In this work – later to be hailed as a fundamental text of the Italian *Risorgimento* – Gioja's greatest concern is 'how to rally all social classes around the Republic through self-interest and reason'.[2] Any republic, he unoriginally maintained, rests ultimately on mores (*costumi* in Italian).[3] But the times of Cicero had long gone: the discouraging amount of civic virtue observable in the Cisalpine Republic represented a major obstacle to a straightforward application of republican tenets. It is true that Gioja typically suggests that a limit should be set on the amount of land owned, because great wealth entails corruption of all social values; and that patches of land should be assigned to poor families as a moralizing measure.[4] But, overall, he realized that the classical republican framework could hardly deal with the Cisalpine lower classes' persistent hostility to the new regime, the distance between elites and populace conjuring up the frightening images of a Vendéan Terror.

Gioja's recurrent portraits of the lower classes, the *popolo*, show 'a weak pupil devoid of judgement', prone to excesses, and incapable of a steady and reflexive attitude. In itself, an evaluation like this was hardly new, but its bearing had dramatically changed after the revolutionary ratification of universal liberty and equality. Gioja makes it explicit: now, each man is the unique judge of what is good for him, any coercion being ruled out by 'the holy rights of nature'.[5] Since 1789, rulers have had to come to terms with 'public opinion', which in the

---

[2] M. Gioja, *Dissertazione sul problema dell'amministrazione generale della Lombardia: quale dei governi liberi meglio convenga alla felicità dell'Italia* (1796), in A. Saitta, ed., *Alle origini del Risorgimento: i testi di un 'celebre' concorso (1796)*, (3 vols., Rome, 1964), II, p. 101. My sketch of Gioja is largely taken from R. Romani, *L'economia politica del Risorgimento italiano* (Turin, 1994), pp. 48–73.
[3] *Dissertazione*, pp. 115ff.
[4] *ibid.*, pp. 42–5.
[5] *ibid.*, p. 18.

Cisalpine is unfortunately controlled by the Catholic priests. The advancement of reason has been very slow, he lamented – and not surprisingly under the circumstances, the *popolo* seems obscurely menacing. In the face of the fragile Cisalpine government, haunted by lack of 'public spirit', in the *Dissertazione* Gioja advocated a cautious policy of appeasement over the short term, and of republican education over the medium term. In spite of his own declarations of principle, he maintained that the 'superstition' of the lower classes should be revalued and put to good use, and the new political ideas connected to the old. In this way, grass-roots priests might become the most effective propagandists of republican feelings, through their closeness to the hearts of the lower classes. This should be associated with the material incentives made possible by free trade, the 'spirit of enterprise', and fair taxation. Gioja's recommendations hinge upon the criticism of 'the man of system' put forward by many in the eighteenth century. Against those who cultivate abstract 'ideas of perfection', he asserts that the masses 'attain the truth only after passing through all degrees of error'.[6]

Successive writings show that Gioja became obsessed with what he thought of as the idleness, depravity, and readiness for revolt shown by the Lombard people. He even wrote that 'the Lombard peasant is naturally inclined to theft and robbery'.[7] The *popolo* confuses freedom with licence; demands economic equality; and is duped by the priests but abhors religious tolerance. Gioja's resentment is here and there expressed in utilitarian language: the people do not know where their good really lies. In short, he bitterly noticed the persistence of the old mentality and its associated habits, as confirmed by the warm welcome the Austrians received in Northern Italy in 1799 (when the revolutionary 'Triennium' came to an end). Gioja was elaborating at length on a theme which was common knowledge among the Italian 'patriots', as the supporters of the new regime called themselves. The people's attitude quickly became the most credited explanation for the failure of the republics of 1796–9. The patriots coined the term 'passive revolution' to define a change that had occurred without the participation, and often against the will, of the bulk of the people.[8] Even if the Napoleonic regime later established over most of Italy guaranteed against uprisings, the deep cleavage revealed in 1796–9 haunted Italian reformers for decades.

This situation can be considered as the moving force behind Gioja's thought, the cornerstone on which he built his understanding of society. The context in which he set the study of political economy is apparent from his first economic writing, *Sul commercio de'commestibili* (1802):

---

[6] *ibid.*, esp. pp. 106, 113.
[7] See the articles collected in *GOM*, vols. I and III.
[8] See, among many possible commentaries, R. De Felice, *Italia giacobina* (Naples, 1965), pp. 9–58.

People laugh at monarchies and republics, to the great outrage of both; when the kings manifest their paternal unselfish love, people reply by asking to eat; when republics (candidly as usual) talk about their rights, people say that they want more bread and less rights; people have ever maintained that the best government is that under which a plentiful subsistence is obtained with little effort; when faced with change, either important or ludicrous, people's only hope is cheaper bread.[9]

An attitude like this suggests the absolute relevance of the economic sphere for purposes of political and social control. Republicanism now appears to Gioja as inextricably linked not only to the French excesses of 1793, but also to an unreasonable under-consumptionist ethic.[10] The completion of Gioja's intellectual universe is marked by the statistical works of 1803–8. Once he had become the official historian and statistician of the Napoleonic regime which followed the interlude of 1799, he found no difficulty in sharing the new ideological posture. I turned to statistics, he writes, as a reaction against the dangers involved in the vague sentimentalism of Rousseau and Mably.[11] The operational character of his research is shown by his definition of statistics: 'the science which describes a country with the aim of presenting the advantages and disadvantages of each object'.[12] Bentham's utility is the principle of efficiency applicable to all the sectors of society; Gioja spreads the liberating word that 'virtue is the eldest daughter of pleasure'. The focus of the statistical investigation of two Lombard districts is on the economic activities that he regarded as in need of rationalization. Nothing escapes from Gioja's rationalizing plan – in fact, in the course of his career he paid great attention to what could be termed with Foucault the 'microphysics of power'. (Furthermore, he often sums up his prescriptions in tables, an example of a peculiar mania for cataloguing that Foucault would surely have liked.) Thus, Gioja discusses the most economical way of cooking or the closing time of taverns as well as the introduction of machinery in manufactures, and advocates productivity wages and measures against idleness.[13] Now the whole of Lombard society and not just the lower classes was under his utilitarian scrutiny, logically enough considering that in his views all men are 'naturally lazy'. The agency in charge of reform was the government, whose range of intervention was thought as a rule to depend on the relative backwardness of a country. 'Peoples become what the governments want' once the proper incentives are activated. In the case of Lombardy, there was much work to do because strong forces were opposing

[9] *Sul commercio de'commestibili e caro prezzo del vitto* (1802), *GOM*, XII, p. 17.
[10] *ibid.*, pp. 306–10.
[11] *Indole, estensione e vantaggi della statistica* (1808), *GOM*, VII, p. 155; *Tavole statistiche ossia norme per descrivere, calcolare, classificare tutti gli oggetti d'amministrazione privata e pubblica* (1808), *GOM*, VIII, p. xii.
[12] *Indole, estensione e vantaggi della statistica*, p. 68.
[13] *Discussione economica sul dipartimento d'Olona* (Milan, 1803); *Discussione economica sul dipartimento del Lario* (1804), *GOM*, XV, pp. 3–278.

'the best direction of private interests': 'ignorance', 'prejudice', 'indolence', 'habits', 'badly advised compassion', 'caprice', and so on.

As Gioja puts it, a people's 'character'– namely, the sum of its 'economic and moral habits' – is one of the factors affecting economic performance. He distinguishes between habits which reduce production, and those leading to wasteful forms of consumption, as well as others of a similar kind. In practice, he censures things as disparate as a night's sleep longer than six hours, primitive ways of working, socializing on weekdays, unconcern for the maintenance of roads, river banks, etc., an excessive number of servants, pipe-smoking in young people, irrational religious beliefs, proverbs praising idleness, and so on. In general, a national character is sound when it is based on the prevalence of 'interest' over idleness and 'caprice'. Gioja's conclusion is that 'morality is a branch of the economy', and that statistics teaches how to evaluate its influence on production and consumption.[14]

As regards the *Nuovo prospetto delle scienze economiche*, composed of six volumes making 1,800 pages, its title refers to economics, but it was conceived as a handbook of public administration. Some principles of economic analysis are set forth at the beginning of the work; but, page after page, they are put aside in favour of an enormous number of different topics, such as population figures and the death rate, several 'historical digressions', accountant-like calculations of both interest on money and the value of land, and, last but not least, a translation into Italian of the whole of *The Way to Wealth* by Benjamin Franklin. Nevertheless, policy issues remain at the core of the work. Gioja was an advocate of both industrial production organized in big, machinery-equipped factories sited in towns, and capitalist agriculture.[15] He believed that, given Italian backwardness, an industrial take-off could be guaranteed only by government intervention. Traditional ways of promoting manufacturing, such as high duties, tax exemptions and the supply of capital, went with the 'small' measures we have found in the statistical works. He even proposed regulating the type of goods to consume, either by means of the law or by means of persuasion.[16] Underpinning the role of the state, there was the idea, expressed for instance by the rejection of the distinction between productive and unproductive labour, that society was a 'great enterprise'. Each element of it had an economic function, which the government was entitled to supervise and if necessary to implement, thanks to its superior know-how. Not surprisingly, the invisible Smithian hand is countered on the grounds of citizens' 'insufficient forward thinking, will, and power'.[17]

---

[14] *Tavole statistiche*, pp. 210–20.
[15] *Nuovo prospetto delle scienze economiche ossia somma totale delle idee teoriche e pratiche in ogni ramo d'amministrazione privata e pubblica* (6 vols., Milan, 1815–17), esp. vol. II.
[16] *ibid.*, VI, pp. 2–119.
[17] *ibid.*, IV, pp. 148–9, 150–63, 209.

Gioja did not assume that factory discipline managed to improve workers' habits. Manufactured goods, not factory toil, were essential to social order. What he values is the continuous supply of new goods made possible by industrial production; he regards the goods as the incentive to make people work. Consumption is the reward for production. Only new unsatisfied needs would make men determined to overcome their own natural laziness. This, he wrote, is the core of civilization. In enthusiastically upholding luxury, he not only unremittingly mocks Rousseauesque self-denial but also comes to ascribe Roman greatness to the flow of refined goods.[18]

Given a focus on consumption, the repression of idleness, and state control over the citizens' lives, the economic sphere was thought of by Gioja as the appropriate form of politics to follow the point of no return of 1792–4. After the revolutionary turmoil other Italians pointed to work as the modern incarnation of civic virtue, pleasure and pain being the new moral basis of society; what marks Gioja out is his totalitarian application of the principle. It was discovered that the route to industrial development was the same as the route to a well-ordered society, a viewpoint that undermined the ethos of civic excellence derived from Machiavelli's Florence or Rousseau's Geneva. As if under Napoleon it had suddenly awakened, the revolutionary generation found republicanism irremediably archaic, an oddity made possible only by frenzy, misplaced enthusiasm, or sinister interests. The language of civic virtue was dismissed in favour of an economic language, which transformed fellow citizens into 'hands', frugality into acquisitiveness, economic equality into functional social inequalities, and non-dependent agricultural tenure into industrial capitalism. Hence, 'national character' became a concise expression of a people's productive attitudes, whereas citizens' 'virtue' appeared related to a set of controversial political tenets as well as to an outdated economic framework. Mores remained of crucial importance, but they underwent a decisive transformation by being inserted within a perspective which focused on the relative economic backwardness of Italy.

3 Dupin

Talented in mathematics and geometry, Dupin entered the *Ecole polytechnique* in 1801 and studied under the direction of Gaspard Monge and Lazare Carnot. In recollecting those days, Dupin waxed lyrical. His recognition of the illiberal character of the Napoleonic regime never troubled his enthusiastic view of a time when science served to defend France against the whole of Europe. Thanks to the 'superior men' who taught there, the *Ecole polytechnique* was the hotbed of science applied to military engineering. Over a period when, he

---

[18] See e.g. *ibid.*, I, p. 257; III, pp. 232–5; IV, pp. 1, 58–77, 86.

tirelessly maintained, careers were open to merit and patriotism worked miracles, Dupin's attitude and beliefs took a turn destined to last. 'Happy soil of France', he wrote in 1819, which ever nurtures *lumières* and talents! The Napoleonic years witnessed the blossoming of a 'new republic of the letters, arts, and sciences', so that France was as unbeatable on battlegrounds as she was unrivalled in civilization.[19] Dupin, greatly affected by the attainment of this 'twofold prize of glory', pledged his scientific knowledge to the goal of national eminence.

Upon leaving the *Ecole*, he worked for the French navy as an engineer, and was finally dispatched to the Ionian Islands in 1808. The speeches he delivered at the newly founded *Académie Ionienne* present a curious blend of modern and classical arguments. Dupin had a profound knowledge of classical authors, to the point of having his 1810 translation of Demosthenes published in 1814. His recipe for Greece's development revolved around manufacturing ('les arts', 'l'industrie') and the applied sciences, on the one hand, and the reform of *mœurs* through public education, on the other. The latter measure, however, was the ultimate cornerstone of the social edifice:

If men are the outcome of education, citizens are the outcome of public education. It imbues them with the love of *patrie*, as well as with a higher moral tone which makes them capable of achieving great things. It also induces a firm character, which is the true courage of the enlightened man. Public education ... also gives pupils the need for public approval and the love of glory, the love which forces them to go beyond themselves in order to win public opinion.[20]

Wealth without *mœurs* is 'an element of weakness and corruption', as Greek and Roman history proves at length: both peoples were defeated when they were rich, as they had been triumphant when the sword was their only resource. What is needed to halt the degeneration of the Greek *patrie* is virtue, knowledge, and a sensitivity to shame and glory, while the 'physical utility' of wealth takes second place. Any attempt at economic progress should rest on the human stuff, that is, on citizens 'worthy of the name' who alone can guarantee the power and duration of the state.[21] In such a context, Dupin's claim that in modern times prosperity is necessarily linked to industrial production, and that this in turn depends on 'exact knowledge', sounds out of place.[22] At any rate, these two themes – citizens' qualities and science-driven industry – were to remain

---

[19] *Essai historique sur les services et les travaux scientifiques de Gaspard Monge* (Paris, 1819), esp. p. 62; 'Notice nécrologique sur M. Delambre', *RE*, 16 (1822), pp. 437–60, esp. pp. 440–2. For Dupin on Napoleon, see esp. his review of Koch, *Mémoires pour servir à l'histoire de la campagne de 1814*, *RE*, 15 (1822), pp. 250–62. The *Ecole* was the alma mater of a number of Saint-Simonians.

[20] 'Sur la régénération de la Grèce' (1808), in C. Dupin, *Discours et leçons sur l'industrie, le commerce, la marine, et sur les sciences appliquées aux arts* (2 vols., Paris,1825), I, p. 18.

[21] 'Sur l'éducation publique des Grecs' (1809), in *Discours*, I, pp. 32–4.

[22] 'Sur la régénération de la Grèce', pp. 19–20.

Dupin's core topics, even if in later writings civic humanism would be dropped, and the context of *mœurs* would be transformed in such a way as to render the conjunction of public morality and manufacturing a possibility. Although Dupin had joined the cause of the emperor in 1815, the Restoration found him assigned to the arsenal in Dunkirk. His visits to Britain in 1816–19 gave him the materials for his celebrated three-volume *Voyages dans la Grande-Bretagne* (1820–4), which in succession reported on the army, navy, and commercial organization of Britain. He rapidly became an authority not only on military and especially naval matters, to which he could apply his brilliant technical and scientific expertise, but also in the field of economic and statistical enquiries. Dupin was eventually appointed professor of mechanics and applied geometry at the *Conservatoire des arts et métiers* (1824). His lectures, attended by a public of mechanics and craftsmen, were published and translated into eight languages. He was made a baron in 1825, and began a long career in politics when elected to the Chamber in 1827. He welcomed the July Monarchy, to which he rendered important service in the Chamber, the Council of State, the Council of the Admiralty, and the Council of Agriculture. In 1837 he was elevated to the peerage. He published extensively on a host of economic questions, like French trade and industry, colonies, child labour, and the condition of the working class. His *Forces productives et commerciales de la France* (1827), a two-volume account of the French economy, was widely acclaimed.[23]

In his writings after 1815 Dupin kept faith with patriotism, but to a large extent this was made to fall within the economic domain. As the most important means of increasing national wealth, power, and prestige, industrial development became his overriding concern. Industrial production being brought forth by science and inextricably linked to better technical and moral education of the workforce, science and productive effort were now the vehicles of virtue and glory. Monge and James Watt became favourite examples of the new brand of heroism which added to 'the welfare of citizens'.[24]

Finally the age comes when admiration is the reward for benefactors of the public, when men who contribute to the well-being of citizens are not regarded as inferior to those who are the instruments of celebrated injuries, suffered by nations, and which have long

---

[23] For biographical accounts, see *Nouvelle biographie générale* (46 vols., Paris, 1855–85), XV, cols. 316–26 (by A. Legoyt); E. L. Newman, ed., *Historical Dictionary of France from the 1815 Restoration to the Second Empire* (2 vols., Westport, Conn., 1987), I, pp. 356–9 (by R. Brown). See also parts of R. Chartier, 'Les deux France: histoire d'une géographie', *Cahiers d'histoire*, 22 (1978), pp. 393–415.

[24] *Essai historique*; review of Chaptal, *De l'industrie française*, *RE*, 2 (1819), p. 30; 'Progrès de l'industrie française, depuis le commencement du XIXe siècle' (1823), in *Discours*, II, pp. 71–123; 'Analyse des discours prononcés dans l'Assemblée tenue pour l'érection d'un monument en l'honneur de James Watt' (1824), in *Discours*, I, pp. 174–227. See also 'Influence du commerce sur le savoir, sur la civilisation des peuples anciens et sur leur force navale' (1822), in *Discours*, I, pp. 228–80.

been thought of as exclusively glorious. Happy are the nations which reach this stage of wisdom and humanity!²⁵

On the one hand, history demonstrates that commercial peoples are not inferior in moral disposition and bravery; on the other, industry and commerce are directly opposed to the conquering and plundering spirit which has so disastrously marked the centuries. Political economy shows that commerce benefits all sides. Clearly enough, the customary point after Smith and Constant, that is, the contrast between peaceful commerce, which calls for tolerance and liberty, and warlike attitudes, was endorsed by Dupin.²⁶ But with a difference. Not all conquests had been synonymous with spoliation. If Rome repeatedly takes the blame for having been predatory and tyrannical, a blueprint for the wrong way of acquiring wealth, ancient Greece and Napoleonic France introduced enterprise and noble *mœurs* to the defeated peoples (incidentally, Dupin goes to great lengths to defend the looting of Italian art masterpieces by the French). The two peoples 'showed themselves to be the enlightened friends and the benefactors of human spirit'.²⁷

Once manufacturing had been identified as the decisive factor of civilization, the universalist tone soon gave way to a concern with *revanche*. This was not uncommon: that Waterloo had been a victory of Britain's economic supremacy was clear to everybody in 1820s France, to the effect that considerations of national power lay behind much of French 'industrialist' thinking of the first half of the century. Industry could be viewed as the continuation of the Napoleonic wars by other means, as Dupin convincingly shows. Whether in peace or at war, France and Britain will always fight each other, he argued. Dupin never ceased to scorn English declarations in favour of free trade and international partnership; conversely, the civilizing mission of France over the world could not but clash with English attempts at eradicating both foreign manufactures and the free governments that make manufactures possible.²⁸

---

²⁵ 'Analyse des discours prononcés dans l'Assemblée', pp. 183–4.
²⁶ 'Influence des sciences sur l'humanité des peuples' (1819), in *Discours*, I, pp. 63–88, esp. pp. 77–8; 'Influence du commerce'.
²⁷ 'Influence des sciences', pp. 69–70, 87; 'Influence du commerce', esp. pp. 254–6 and fn.; *Essai historique*.
²⁸ Review of Chaptal, *De l'industrie française*; review of De Pradt, *Parallèle de la puissance anglaise et russe*, *RE*, 20 (1823), pp. 65–90, 309–26. For these themes see J.-C. Perrot, 'Les effets économiques de la Révolution: trente années de bilans (1795–1825)', in G. Faccarello and P. Steiner, eds., *La pensée économique pendant la Révolution française* (Grenoble, 1990), pp. 561–95, and F. Crouzet, *De la supériorité de l'Angleterre sur la France: l'économique et l'imaginaire XVIIᵉ–XXᵉ siècles* (Paris, 1985). Although Dupin's defence of French protective policies basically sprang from his idea of a 'social solidarity' existing among the various components of the economy, those policies were intended as an anti-British weapon too. See Dupin's parliamentary speech of 14 April 1836, in *Le moniteur universel*, 106 (15 April 1836), pp. 741–3.

The view of industry as the 'new path to peoples' power, peace, and true glory' rested nonetheless on English example. Mass production made possible by updated machinery, Dupin asserted, is the key not only to higher productivity and hence to higher real wages but also to increased employment. Machinery makes work lighter and creates opportunities for more skilled jobs.[29] He takes on the usual accusation against urban manufacturing that it foments immorality, arguing that education and instruction can make the difference in any situation.[30] Yet there is a social concern in Dupin, manifested not only by his direct involvement in workers' education, but also by his condemnation of excessive workloads for children and by his interest in savings banks and other protective measures.[31] The fact is that for him labour was a social function charged with political and moral significance. The 'social question' was far from being a matter of social order or welfare, purely and simply, but involved a broad perspective deriving from the identification of industrial production with the national cause. Granted that Dupin's patriotism is now indistinguishable from the needs of French industry, there exists a mass 'heroism', defined by eagerness to work and manufacturing ability nourished by industrial education. Middle-class place hunters are contrasted with that model figure, the manual worker who invents or perfects machines, and who in due course succeeds in becoming a workshop owner.[32] A wise capitalist entrepreneur would not only strive to harmonize his interests with those of the workers through a judicious organization of labour; he would also assume a paternal role, and hence he would praise and blame, reward and punish his employees on the basis of concern for their welfare.[33] Mutual support between all those involved in productive activities is Dupin's overall recommendation. And he never forgets that operatives were soldiers in the recent past and were liable to be soldiers in the future, a viewpoint making even the most rebellious of them partake of the moral credit and respect which Napoleon's armies earned.[34] More generally, manual

---

[29] See, e.g., *Considérations sur quelques avantages de l'industrie et des machines, en Angleterre et en France* (Paris, 1821); 'Cours de géométrie et de méchanique appliquées aux arts' (1824–5), in *Discours*, II, pp. 289, 349; 'Introduction d'un nouveau cours de géométrie et de méchanique appliquées aux arts' (1824), in *Discours*, II, pp. 172–7ff.; *Forces productives et commerciales de la France* (2 vols., Paris, 1827), I, p. 133. Dupin thought that traditional French luxury staples should be associated with coarser goods to provide a sufficient manufacturing base: 'Progrès de l'industrie', pp. 86–7, 104.

[30] 'Introduction d'un nouveau cours', pp. 179–81ff., 200–3; *Forces productives*, I, p. 133.

[31] *Du travail des enfants qu'emploient les ateliers, les usines et les manufactures* (2 vols., Paris, 1840–7); *Constitution, histoire et avenir des caisses d'épargne de France* (Paris, 1844).

[32] See esp. *De l'influence de la classe ouvrière sur les progrès de l'industrie* (Paris, 1835).

[33] See, e.g., 'Introduction au cours de méchanique appliquée aux arts' (1820), in *Discours*, II, pp. 6–8; 'Sur l'état de l'industrie, dans la monarchie française' (1822), in *Discours*, II, pp. 62–3.

[34] See *Bien-être et concorde des classes du peuple français* (Paris, 1848), p. 10: even on the occasion of the abhorred 1848 revolution, 'la patrie ne peut s'empêcher de reconnaître et d'avouer sa race intrépide de Fleurus, de Rivoli, de Zurich et d'Austerlitz; et d'éprouver, en pleurant d'indignation, je ne sais quel espoir et quel orgueil de mère, à travers son affront!'

workers are an essential component of the nation – they have participated in its vicissitudes, share the traits defining Frenchness, and cooperate in the achievement of national goals – and therefore it would be irresponsible to exploit them.

Dupin's recipe for French development as put forward in *Forces productives et commerciales de la France* amounts to the spread of useful knowledge and sound morals, more productive agriculture and a larger industrial sector, and the building of a network of roads, railways, and canals. Since Great Britain provides the best model for all that, emulation of Britain is imperative to 'regain our rank' as honour and *grandeur* dictate. Knowledge of the rival's strength is therefore essential. National power, he explained, is a fact to be assessed in the same way as scientists study a natural phenomenon or a mathematical truth – in both cases, the inner principles should be uncovered and the consequences assessed.[35] As factors in national strength, moral and cultural attitudes proved no exception, and Dupin used statistics and demography to assess not only the state of education in France but also the diffusion of progressive beliefs among present generations.[36] During the Restoration, Dupin was a prestigious figure for precisely the reason that he appraised the place of France in relation to other countries by applying the authoritative tools of science.

Dupin was a genuine Anglophile, especially after the more vivid memories of the war faded away, in the sense that he deeply admired the enemy. His most extensive report on British society is in the third volume (1824) of *Voyages dans la Grande-Bretagne*. Here, as in other minor writings, Dupin argues that 'national character' has been the most important cause of English prosperity. The management of men has been as good as that of things – and man is more effective as a production factor than steampower.[37] The qualities that make up the English character are enterprising industry, forethought, honesty, courage, and firm ambition; and stemming from all of them is 'a cold, steady, and methodical activity' which ends up annihilating the competitors.[38] In a language which occasionally reveals republican residues, Dupin made clear that Britain (or any other country for that matter) would lose its supremacy if 'the useful citizen forfeited his virtues'.[39] The source of English character lies in Britain's stable and liberal institutions, Dupin said almost in a whisper

---

[35] 'Du commerce et de ses travaux publics, en Angleterre et en France' (1823), in *Discours*, I, pp. 281–3, 293, 324–6; 'Introduction d'un nouveau cours', p. 198.

[36] *Forces productives*, I, pp. i–xl.

[37] 'Introduction d'un nouveau cours', p. 196.

[38] *Voyages dans la Grande-Bretagne* (3 vols. in 6 books, Paris, 1820–4). The title of the third volume is *Force commerciale de la Grande-Bretagne* (2 books, Paris, 1824); quotations are from I, pp. xiii–xiv. See also 'Du commerce', pp. 294–6, and 'Introduction d'un nouveau cours', pp. 199–202. Dupin's comparison between the French and the English soldier in vol. I, bk II of *Voyages dans la Grande-Bretagne* (1820), pp. 3–5, is interesting.

[39] 'Du commerce', p. 295.

(there had been efforts to censor the first volume of the *Voyages*). The major faults in French character, on the other hand, were an excess of frivolity and a lack of perseverance, faults which could be amended by science-oriented education. As he also put it, the Frenchman's vivid imagination, which made him clever and brave, brought with it the drawbacks of impulsiveness and a certain lack of businesslike qualities, like firmness and cold blood under difficult circumstances.[40]

Curiously, perhaps, Dupin regarded maintenance (of roads, canals, buildings, machinery, etc.) as a sure sign of the nature of a people's character. A system of constant maintenance had been adopted by enlightened and far-sighted peoples like the English, the Dutch, and the Swiss. The Italians, Portuguese, and Spaniards, on the other hand, intervened only when things were about to collapse. As far as France was concerned, Dupin distinguished between the developed area of the nation – that is the North – where the former system had been adopted, and the underdeveloped South, where the latter had unfortunately prevailed.[41] How to make the South catch up with the North was, in effect, one of his most pressing concerns; in *Forces productives et commerciales de la France* he contended that while climate was not a determinant, the difference was ultimately made by the 'moral energy' of inhabitants.[42]

There was one virtue which epitomized the difference between Britain and France: the ability to associate for useful purposes. Dupin pointed to the enterprising English aristocracy as an example to be followed by its French counterpart. In Britain, the 'spirit of association' has progressed at the same pace as the division of labour, and has become a quintessential part of the 'national character'. In France, extensive state intervention makes a similar development difficult. He chiefly had in mind the construction and maintenance of roads and canals.[43] The social and political byproducts of association were as important as its economic achievements. Following the assumption that it had been association that reunited politically divided England after the Glorious Revolution, Dupin hoped that the same would happen in France. The country was desperately in need of a larger measure of social cohesion to counteract its permanent political turmoil. Association creates those 'ties among all classes on the basis of common interest' which are prerequisite to both political stability and economic performance. The latter is in fact impossible outside the collaboration of all.[44] The ultimate reason for Dupin's regret of the Napoleonic years was

---

[40] *Forces productives*, I, p. 71. See also 'Introduction d'un nouveau cours', pp. 196–7, and *Crise commerciale de 1839* (Paris, 1839), pp. 27, 39–40.
[41] *Force commerciale*, I, pp. 139–40.
[42] *Forces productives*, II, pp. 249–51.
[43] 'Analyse des discours prononcés dans l'Assemblée'; 'Du commerce', pp. 307ff.; *Force commerciale*, I, *passim*.
[44] *Force commerciale*, I, pp. xxiv–v; 'Introduction d'un nouveau cours', p. 198; *Crise commerciale*, pp. 12–16.

that in that period the French had united in the common striving for greatness, however despotic the leadership might have been.[45] A comparison between a well-trained industrial personnel and the army was almost inevitable. Both industrial production and the military were instruments for French supremacy; both were fuelled by patriotism and led by science; furthermore, both provided fair fields for merit, talent, and, ultimately, social advancement.[46] Successive French economists would take up the point.

4   The economic construction of nationhood: Italy

A shift in the focus of 'virtue' towards economic performance was not limited to Gioja and Dupin. In Italy, once the revolutionary momentum had run out of steam, the principles of economic science appeared a useful means of attacking past egalitarian excesses and legitimizing the new, Thermidorian state of affairs. This is illustrated by the trajectories of two authors active at the beginning of the century: Vincenzo Cuoco (1770–1823) and Pietro Custodi (1771–1842).

A mild 'patriot' in the Triennium, the Neapolitan Cuoco diffused the term 'passive revolution' through his celebrated *Saggio storico sulla rivoluzione napoletana del 1799* (1801). A journalist in Milan during the first years of the Napoleonic regime, he later served under Murat in Naples as a top-ranking official (1806–14). In Cuoco's opinion, the immaturity of the *popolo* could be combatted by a programme of 'national education' where the pivotal role was played by 'industry' and 'work'. The foundation of a free society is not the basic consumption habits advocated by Rousseauist revolutionaries but the fulfilment of ever increasing needs. Political oppression stems from insufficient resources to meet aspirations; what should be done is not to set limits to needs but to boost productive forces. Contrary to what many believe, the desire to improve the standard of living has often been the cause, rather than the effect, of liberty. 'Virtue' should not be an abstract concept but one and the same thing as 'interest' and 'conformity to national mores'. In current times virtue cannot but be based on 'the love of work', which in Cuoco's views would lead to self-esteem, patriotism, and manly education.[47] As in the case of Gioja, Cuoco's statistical research on a Lombard district is punctuated by entreaties for state intervention, aimed at implementing productivity in all sectors and absorbing the social consequences of economic growth.[48] The analytical apparatus of the *Wealth of Nations* is used to target both rentiers and the idle poor. A crucial distinction between 'wealth' and 'industry'

---

[45] See, e.g., *Essai historique*, pp. 16–17.
[46] 'Cours de géométrie', pp. 347ff.; *Bien-être et concorde des classes*, pp. 44–5, 60.
[47] 'Frammenti di lettere dirette a Vincenzio Russo' (1799), in V. Cuoco, *Saggio storico sulla rivoluzione napoletana del 1799*, ed. N. Cortese (1801; Florence, 1926), pp. 414–16. See Romani, *L'economia politica*, pp. 32–7.
[48] L. Lizzoli [but V. Cuoco], *Osservazioni sul Dipartimento dell'Agogna* (Milan, 1802).

is introduced. The former is dependent on foreign trade and entails wars, idleness, and a craving for foreign luxury goods, whereas the latter is equated with Smithian productive labour and is the only means of a fair distribution of income.[49]

Cuoco's editorship of the official *Giornale Italiano* (1803–6) represented an opportunity to foster the cause of popular education through agriculture and manufacturing. The journal not only reported economic news from both Italy and Europe (what Cuoco called 'statistica'), but also informed about technological developments, told moral tales, preached obedience to the government, and nourished 'Italian' patriotism and pride.[50] The idea behind this venture was that public morality had its main source in economic qualities, and hence the journal, in stimulating people's industry, would 'create public spirit' – which Italy as a prospective nation was badly in need of. Cuoco regarded it as an essential requirement for modernization. Granted that nations emerged from the trials of production and international economic rivalries, this could not go without loyalty, obedience, enterprise, and a sense of duty on the citizens' part.[51] Cuoco, like Gioja, had a clear understanding of Italian backwardness, and, again like Gioja, he considered the relationship between the economic and the moral as the crux of the Italian matter.

In view of Cuoco's awareness that the Revolution and Napoleon had given Italy an unparalleled opportunity to catch up with modernity after a long period of decline, it may look paradoxical that the world of ancient polities continued to provide him with a language as well as a network of concepts. This is fully evinced by his *Platone in Italia* (1804–6), a series of parables about the state of contemporary Italy masked as a recently discovered manuscript of the time of Greek colonies in Italy. In a letter to Napoleon, Cuoco presented the book as a piece of anti-Jacobin polemics: it is time, he wrote, to depict antiquity as it really was rather than as Rousseau or Mably wanted us to believe it. A eulogy of self-improvement through economic pursuits (that is in agriculture, in view of the setting) is the core message of the *Platone* too.[52]

Pietro Custodi had been a fervent Jacobin during the Triennium. Later on, he was co-opted into the Napoleonic administration, and, over the period 1803 to 1805, edited the monumental collection of *Scrittori classici italiani di economia politica*, whose fifty volumes contain much of what Italians had so far written

---

[49] *Statistica della Repubblica italiana*, ed. V. Gatto (1802–3; Rome, 1991). See also a manuscript fragment transcribed as an appendix to F. Tessitore, *Lo storicismo di Vincenzo Cuoco* (Naples, 1965), pp. 183–4. For Cuoco's criticism of the Poor Laws and his proposal for confinement of the idle, see *Osservazioni*, pp. 74–92.

[50] See 'Programma' [of the *Giornale Italiano*] (1803), in V. Cuoco, *Scritti vari*, ed. N. Cortese and F. Nicolini (2 vols., Bari, 1924), I, pp. 3–12.

[51] *ibid.*; 'Lo spirito pubblico' (1804), in *Scritti vari*, I, pp. 115–24.

[52] *Platone in Italia*, ed. F. Nicolini (1804–6; 2 vols., Bari, 1924), esp. II, pp. 84–91ff. For Cuoco's letter to Napoleon, see *Scritti vari*, II, p. 324.

on economic subjects. The collection aroused much interest and succeeded in bringing political economy back to the order of the day. Custodi intended the collection both as a sort of criticism of the revolutionary past (including his own) and, at the same time, as a means of carrying on the political battle for the national *Risorgimento*. Political economy was attuned to the new historical phase. As he explained in the introduction to the first volume, political economy would be indispensable to the new statesmen who were intending to carry out the urgent tasks of economic, social, and juridical modernization. However, it was needed by society, too, finally relieved as it was from the uncertainties of revolution and war. Once the greatest innovators in the fields of agriculture, manufacturing, and banking, the Italians still had the fibre to become 'rich, powerful, praiseworthy, and praised'; the means of regaining their former status was the application of their economists' teachings as well as the emulation of the leading countries. As he also put it, the Italians, 'despite accidental diplomatic circumstances which create apparent divisions in their country', were the sons of a common motherland, and it was time their country was brought up to the level of prosperity of other nations; this was the core legacy of the eighteenth-century masters of economics. By publishing them, Custodi felt he was acting like 'a gun-dealer who has supplied weapons to an army'. The kind of patriotism he upheld was economic in character, in the belief that behind a renewed economic vigour, the nation's political emancipation could be glimpsed. The Triennium, on the other hand, turned out to have been marked by a disastrous political abstractness: 'We dreamt that political institutions could be created, like fairy castles, with empty phrases and a wave of the hand. And from all this, after six years of civilian unrest, massacres, and looting, we have been left only with the decline of our principles and a cruel, even if useful, disenchantment.'[53]

Custodi's collection succeeded both in making political economy an essential component of national pride, and, together with the writings of authors like Gioja and Cuoco, in establishing a link between political and economic aspirations. A modernizing attitude to economic life took up a manifest political meaning in 1815–48, nourishing the project of federal unification constructed 'from below'. It was thought that social and economic progress in each of the regional states, especially if associated with the liberalization of trade within Italy, would lead ultimately to political emancipation. This was a time when articles about railways, canals, scientific agronomy, machinery, and so

---

[53] 'Proemio dell'editore' (1803), in *Scrittori classici italiani di economia politica* (50 vols., Milan, 1803–16), I, pp. ix–xviii, quotation on p. xiv. See also Custodi's preface to R. E. Haller, *Rapporto al Primo Console della Repubblica francese su le rendite e le spese pubbliche dell'anno IX* (Milan, 1801), p.ii. See D. Donnini Macciò and R. Romani, 'All Equally Rich: Economic Knowledge in Revolutionary Italy, 1796–1799', *Research in the History of Economic Thought and Methodology*, 14 (1996), pp. 23–49.

on, filled the columns of the newly established journals of 'useful knowledge' (*cognizioni utili*), while scientists from the whole peninsula met regularly to discuss applied science issues.[54] In practice, and in sharp contrast with Rousseauist inspiration, patriotism and civic virtue became equated with investment in agriculture, new business ventures, the founding of a savings bank or a Bell–Lancaster school, or writing a pamphlet advocating free trade. In this context, Custodi's message was emblematically taken up by a follower of Gioja exiled in England, Giuseppe Pecchio, who published a summary of Custodi's volumes in 1829. Pecchio emphasized the link between political economy and liberal reforms, defining the former as 'another name for liberty' and maintaining that 'the theorems that lead to wealth lead to liberty as well'. Pecchio coined a definition which gained wide currency: political economy was 'the science of patriotism'.[55] The failure of the 1848 revolutions marked the end of this political phase and paved the way for Piedmontese expansionism.

5 The economic inadequacy of the French: *industrialisme* and after

In France, Napoleonic and post-Napoleonic political economy is a more multifaceted phenomenon than its Italian counterpart. However, the demise of republicanism and the correlated rise of industrialism were widely shared; before it was incorporated into the heart of the Saint-Simonian doctrine, this shift is clearly recognizable in the *idéologues*, as recent scholarship has stressed.[56] The replacement of virtue with *travail* is particularly unambiguous in Rœderer, eager to find a solid basis for liberty and property. Granted that the time-absorbing practice of republican virtues clashes with the pursuit of individual interests, and that love of wealth is a natural passion which engenders activity, industry, and thrift, Rœderer turns to a concept of work as productive of moral, social, and political 'ordre'. His eulogy of the wonderful effects of *travail* is uncompromising: work brings about 'social virtues in their full expression', thus making society possible.[57]

---

[54] See the path-finding contribution by K. R. Greenfield, *Economics and Liberalism in the Risorgimento: a Study of Nationalism in Lombardy 1815–48* (Baltimore, 1965).

[55] G. Pecchio, *Storia dell'economia pubblica in Italia* (Lugano, 1829). See M. Isabella, ' "Una scienza dell'amor patrio": Public Economy, Freedom and Civilization in Giuseppe Pecchio's Works (1827–1830)', *Journal of Modern Italian Studies*, 4 (1999), pp. 157–83.

[56] See M. James, 'Pierre-Louis Rœderer, Jean-Baptiste Say, and the Concept of *industrie*', *History of Political Economy*, 9 (1977), pp. 455–75; T. E. Kaiser, 'Politics and Political Economy in the Thought of the Ideologues', *History of Political Economy*, 12 (1980), pp. 141–60; C. B. Welch, *Liberty and Utility: the French Idéologues and the Transformation of Liberalism* (New York, 1984); B. W. Head, *Ideology and Social Science: Destutt de Tracy and French Liberalism* (Dordrecht, 1985).

[57] 'Cours d'organisation sociale fait au Lycée en 1793', in P. L. Rœderer, *Œuvres* (8 vols., Paris, 1853–9), VIII, pp. 203, 298–9, 264–6.

In the course of his effort to divorce republicanism from the notion of heroic virtue and frugality, Destutt de Tracy turns to a view of society which is economically founded and determined. Exchange is said to be 'the source of all moral sentiments' and therefore traders, 'like all other industrious men', are models of 'all moral habits'. A people moulded on the traders' example 'would be the most virtuous of all'.[58] After stating that 'la liberté, c'est le bonheur', he explains that if the most despotic king administered justly and efficiently, his subjects would enjoy a maximum of happiness and thereby a maximum of liberty. As Destutt de Tracy proceeds to specify, it is the satisfaction of wants and desires that motivates a good organization of society. Even private 'moral pleasures' to a very large extent result from effective economic organization, namely, from 'the good order of things'.[59] As for public virtues, 'I love and admire those who do good [*font du bien*]', he wrote, 'but if everybody just avoided doing evil, all things would go well'.[60]

Relying largely on the analytical basis provided by Say's *Traité d'économie politique*, the *idéologues* disparaged idlers and rentiers in harsh terms. There was the idea that economic efficiency required full social cooperation ('everyone is useful to everyone', in Say's words), and that the social division of labour could supply the glue necessary to restore social harmony.[61] Overall, then, the seeds of later 'industrialist' views were certainly planted by the *idéologues*. Basically, they untied the knot between political participation, on the one hand, and industry leading to a moderate *aisance*, on the other: by unbinding the potentiality of economic enterprise, they dismissed the role of republican virtues in politics. The earlier focus on virtuous consumption changed into a focus on virtuous production.

At the beginning of the Restoration there emerged wide agreement about *industrie* as the organizing principle of society. Its chief proponents were the editors of the *Censeur européen* Charles Dunoyer and Charles Comte, and Saint-Simon with his associates; but Chaptal and the young Adolphe Blanqui could also be mentioned, with Constant as a philosophical founding father.[62] Even if these writers differed in many respects, they agreed on the following set of principles. 'Industry' included all forms of utility-pursuing

---

[58] A.-L.-C. Destutt de Tracy, *Commentaire sur l'Esprit des Lois de Montesquieu* (1806; Paris, 1819), pp. 357–9.

[59] *ibid.*, pp. 148–50, 280 and fn.

[60] *ibid.*, p. 359.

[61] Welch, *Liberty and Utility*, pp. 84–7; Head, *Ideology and Social Science*, pp. 129–48; Kaiser, 'Politics and Political Economy', p. 156. Charles Ganilh held views strikingly similar to those of the *idéologues* in his *Des systèmes d'économie politique* (2 vols., Paris, 1809); see esp. I, pp. 1–62, where he provides a thorough demonstration of 'the morality of wealth'.

[62] As regards Chaptal, see his *Quelques réflexions sur l'industrie en général, à l'occasion de l'exposition des produits de l'industrie française en 1819* (Paris, 1819). Chaptal contributed to *L'industrie*. As regards Blanqui, who contributed to the *Producteur*, his works of the 1820s show unmistakable signs of Saint-Simonism. Later on, Blanqui recanted the doctrine in 'Coup

activity. Both morals and politics were seen to originate from it – it was to the progressive unfolding of industry that Europe owed its *mœurs* as well as the degree of liberty it enjoyed. As it was co-extensive with peace, *industrialisme* suited post-Napoleonic France particularly well: the industrial spirit was seen as in complete contrast to the 'martial' and 'ancient' code it was supposed to supersede. Some *industrialistes* asserted that by indicating the outdated model of the ancient republics, eighteenth-century philosophers had prompted the warlike attitude of the revolutionaries; the ensuing anarchy was fully exploited by the much-detested Napoleon.[63] In the views of the *industrialistes*, productive abilities should be the only criteria of social hierarchies. The distinction between *producteurs* and *oisifs* represented the fundamental social divide. Since a society shaped along 'industrialist' lines was yet to develop in France, this literature is largely exhortative and pedagogical in tone. Overall, the most remarkable feature of *industrialisme* is its comprehensiveness, in not only dictating the rules of politics and the economy, but also serving as a philosophy of history. Say's brand of *industrialisme*, founded on the clear distinction between politics and economics, seems therefore of a different character.[64]

The replacement of republican virtue with economic enterprise is most clearly noticeable in Saint-Simon and his circle, to which so many French economists owed their fundamental inspiration. A representative text is Augustin Thierry's 'Politique des nations et de leur rapports mutuels', published in *L'industrie* in 1817. With Rousseau as his target, Thierry looks for the causes of 'national glory'. Commercial peoples, he argues at length, have always defeated warlike ones because industry is a much more effective source of independence, self-confidence, solidarity, and love of freedom than republican patriotism and martial education (Thierry was referring to Britain, Venice, Holland, Lombardy, and the United States). Modern societies rest on the exchange of goods, Thierry concluded, and the work of each citizen is the fundamental means of solidarity and social cohesion.[65] As Saint-Simon made clear, 'the need and love of liberty originate from industry; they necessarily grow together, and liberty can be strengthened by industry alone'.[66]

The concept of *industrie* was the backbone of a social, moral, and political doctrine which was intended to heal France of the revolutionary wounds. As

d'œil sur l'état actuel de l'économie politique', *Revue mensuelle d'économie politique*, 4 (1835), pp. 529–60. Industrialist themes run through many economic works of those years; see, e.g., Ganilh's rejection of the *esprit de conquête* (alongside the advocacy of protectionist measures) in his *La théorie de l'économie politique* (2 vols., Paris, 1815), II, p. 465.

[63] See esp. *Le censeur européen*.

[64] For the character of that distinction, and for the criticism levelled against Say by Saint-Simon and Dunoyer, see P. Steiner, 'Politique et économie politique chez Jean-Baptiste Say', *Revue française d'histoire des idées politiques*, 5 (1997), pp. 23–58.

[65] 'Politique des nations et de leur rapports mutuels', *SSO*, I, part II, pp. 50, 86.

[66] 'Conclusion' (1817), *SSO*, I, part II, p. 210.

Rousseauesque republican virtue was meant to provide social cohesion, the *industrialistes* believed that the failure of the Revolution in that crucial respect, as mirrored by a succession of ineffectual paper constitutions, imposed a shift towards the economic dimension of society. Successful businessmen being natural leaders, the republican legislator's charisma and eloquence should now be replaced by the impersonal authority of sound social hierarchies, while the economic arena was deemed capable of teaching all the qualities the new type of statesman should have. Basically, citizens' subjection was exchanged for a secure fulfilment of needs.

Although after the 1820s 'virtue' and related issues no longer figured in French economic literature, and understandably so considering the wide consensus about their rejection previously reached, the span of influence of 'virtuous industry' in the Restoration has yet to be noted. Among the causes of a popularity which is impossible to document in full here,[67] there was the role of *industrialisme* as vehicle of a key argument of far-reaching impact, which is to be found at its clearest in the first issues of the *Censeur européen*. In the foreword, the editors stated that the abandonment of the project of the *Censeur* (1814–15), which had concentrated on the criticism of government and had not been inspired by *industrialisme*, was due to the realization that peoples' attitudes played a decisive role in politics. The revolutionary events had spotlighted the ignorance and vices of the French, who, rather than adopting the industrious way, had cherished the obsolete values of ancient republics. Institutional engineering had proved impotent in the face of ideals of economic equality and the belief that wealth could spring from laws. The prominence given to military ideals over 'civil courage' entailed the impossibility of liberty because this consisted of 'an unwavering will to fulfil one's duties in all circumstances'; whenever this will was missing, men were slaves. On a more prosaic plane, the years 1789-1814 had witnessed a fierce race for public appointments and jobs at the expense of productive interests.[68] Comte and Dunoyer adopted the 'industrial virtue' standpoint as a response to this interpretation of theirs of the Revolution. While revolutionaries like Sieyès intended to bring French institutions up to a par with the progress of society and human mind, it may be argued that the *Censeur européen* put forward an almost opposite argument: it had been the French who had lagged behind the level of *industrialisme* reached in 1789. And the prospects for France were particularly gloomy, in view of the strength there of the Europe-wide tendency of *industriels* towards aristocratic habits and the ransacking of public

---

[67] For evidence of the diffusion of a diluted Saint-Simonism in liberal journalism 1815–30, see chapter 4 below.

[68] See in particular 'Avant-propos', *CE*, 1 (1817), pp. i–viii, and C. Comte, 'Considérations sur l'état moral de la nation française, et sur les causes de l'instabilité de ses institutions', *CE*, 1 (1817), pp. 1–92. For a comprehensive account of the journal's experience, see E. Harpaz, '*Le Censeur Européen*: histoire d'un journal industrialiste', *Revue d'histoire économique et sociale*, 37 (1959), pp. 185–218, 328–57.

wealth once professional success had been achieved.[69] Comte and Dunoyer held that they were inaugurating a perspective which radically conflicted with that adopted by eighteenth-century philosophers, who, it was commonly believed, had regarded good *mœurs* as a direct product of a free government. Whether in its *industrialiste* version or not, the idea that citizens' flaws lay somehow at the root of France's constant turmoil grew to be a commonplace in a number of later writers, both minor and major (most notable among the latter being Tocqueville and Taine). What follows is chiefly concerned with the economic aspects of that idea.

The moral and political commitment of French economists, particularly evident in those who after 1841–2 gathered round the *Journal des économistes* and the Société d'Économie Politique, came from an acute contrast between normative precepts and the reality of France. Their ideal world was ruled by three tenets: the principle of population, Say's law, and the productivity of all types of labour; in accordance with these tenets, which presupposed self-reliance and equality when confronted with the hardships of industrial effort, economists advocated free trade and the state's neutrality in the struggle for life. Because they turned self-restraint, thrift, diligence, and energy into optional means of success, protectionism and state intervention were regarded as synonymous with privilege and blatant injustice. As this perspective clashed with the mercantilistic policies carried out under both the Restoration and the July Monarchy, the contrast nourished a pugnacious attitude. The theme of the economic inadequacy of the French and that of French statism mingled into an unrelenting polemic, where the two motifs alternated as cause and effect. In the eyes of the free traders who hegemonized the scene after 1830, the non-accomplishment of the industrialist project was largely due to an insufficient amount of industrial morality, the source of this recurrent theme of French economic discourse being (and this was not by chance) Dunoyer in his *L'industrie et la morale* (1825). As a rule, Dunoyer argued, the only oppression peoples suffer comes from 'their ignorance and their bad habits'. Industrialism can become reality only as long as it takes possession of the people's minds, and the French situation is discouraging in this respect. On the other hand, Dunoyer acknowledged that in the face of French protectionism, centralization, and unenlightened state intervention, 'a people led as if it were a child [*ainsi conduit comme par la main*]' could not but show a weak spirit of enterprise.[70] This is the true cause of socialism in France, many *Journal des économistes*

---

[69] C. Dunoyer, 'Considérations sur l'état présent de l'Europe', *CE*, 2 (1817), pp. 97ff.

[70] *De la liberté du travail* (1845), in C. Dunoyer, *Œuvres* (3 vols., Paris, n.d.), I, p. 273 (this work includes the 1825 book as its first part). Constant criticized Dunoyer's approach by pointing to the responsibility of governments for the 'vices' of 'nations': 'De M. Dunoyer et de quelques-uns de ses ouvrages' (1826), in B. Constant, *Ecrits politiques*, ed. M. Gauchet (Paris, 1997), pp. 654–78. That the economic education of the public was France's most pressing concern had been insisted on by Say: Steiner, 'Politique et économie'.

authors maintained: freedom being the only origin of moral habits, state intervention results in ever increasing demands, demoralization, and ultimately socialism.[71]

It is against such a background that authors like Dunoyer, Blanqui, Faucher, and Chevalier became tireless observers of the economic qualities of peoples in comparison with the French. 'Each people understands better what it lacks by seeing what other peoples enjoy', one observed.[72] This is a political economy focused on policy issues and made up of travel reports. Everything being already fully demonstrated at the analytical level, many French contended, it was time to proceed to the application of economic truths.[73] It should already be clear that Dupin, who did not lack a proper philosophy of the industrialist type, albeit bereft of certain Saint-Simonian corollaries, contributed to the shaping of this mode of economic writing. In focusing on the human element as the crucial factor for development, Dupin's statistical investigations of France and Britain were seminal pieces of fieldwork, which served as a model for the inquiries of the younger economists.

The point about the economic flaws of the French is originally brought home by Blanqui. He believed that the French government of his day was on the whole ahead of the French people, and that 'the errors of the administration reflect those of the public'. He complained that sluggish entrepreneurs and idle capitalists did nothing but demand more state intervention, while peasants were ignorant of new agricultural techniques as well as reluctant to pool their small plots. The bulk of the industrial workers were too poor to be economically far-sighted and politically moderate.[74] This situation was of great concern to him, because there was 'a fact that dominates the whole of modern political economy', that is, the 'moral capital of each people'.[75] The difference between, say, the British and the Spanish economies should in the final analysis be ascribed to differences in moral capital. A concise definition of *capital moral* is given as follows: 'the development of intelligence, the diffusion of useful knowledge, and the suitability of each for his task and his job'.[76] In

---

[71] See the book by the first editor of the *Journal des économistes*, Louis Reybaud: *Etudes sur les réformateurs ou socialistes modernes* (1840; 5th edn, 2 vols., Paris, 1856), I, pp. 32–7, 298.

[72] A. Blanqui, *Voyage d'un jeune français en Angleterre et en Ecosse* (Paris, 1824), p. xvii.

[73] See, e.g., the opening article of the first issue of the *Journal des économistes*: L. Reybaud, 'Introduction', 1 (1841), pp. 1–12.

[74] *Cours d'économie industrielle 1836–1837* (3 vols., Paris and Versailles, 1837–9), *passim*. On the relationship between government and citizens in France, see I, p. 30, and II, pp. 19–20. Blanqui also resorted to the old argument that the French upper classes, contrary to the British ones, held industrial and commercial activities in contempt: *Cours d'économie industrielle 1838–1839* (Paris, 1839), pp. 82–4.

[75] *Cours 1836–1837*, I, p. 13. But see also his admittance that 'l'infériorité industrielle ne dépend pas toujours des fautes des populations, mais souvent de conditions différentes de position, de climat et de direction gouvernementale': I, pp. 22–3.

[76] *ibid.*, I, p. 161.

developing this concept, Blanqui had in mind not only an educational system that met France's needs, but a more comprehensive process that affected the roots of Frenchness itself. The habits of the French, as well as their industrial skills, needed improving, as he tirelessly repeated that it was the practical and enterprising character of the Anglo-Saxons that accounted for the economic performances of Great Britain and the United States.[77] A revolution in habits and ways of thinking was the fundamental pre-requisite of French growth. New roads and canals, for example, could boost the country's performance only on condition that 'l'esprit' of the citizens made them ready to take such a chance.[78]

As Dupin's case suggests, the craving for an economic *revanche* over Britain was a complex feeling, hardly new, and hardly reducible to thunderous appeals to the French producers. Pride about the allegedly specially French road to industrial civilization could easily mingle with signs of an inferiority complex, political arguments were often put forward to either oppose or reinforce economic reasoning and statistical figures, and merciless self-criticism was as widespread as destructive reports on British life. Nevertheless, there was a unifying theme: French economists commonly held that the social cost to Britain of its supremacy had been too great. Léon Faucher's *Etudes sur l'Angleterre* (1845) is a case in point, an example of a widely shared interpretation of Britain as dominated by an 'aristocratic principle'. Faucher argued that its social organization rested on privilege and inequality, whereas France was the land of 'democracy' and equality. Accordingly, the British industrial sector was the preserve of a few families, so that a new type of feudalism had arisen. The prevention of new entries had proved a necessary measure in order to avoid gluts; but this measure did not succeed in relieving massive destitution. The English character, which was energetic but proud and unsociable, matched the socio-econonomic organization. The Englishman needed to be inserted in a hierarchy because he was the least multifaceted type in the world, 'bearing the division of labour in his inner self'. Hence the necessity of large-scale manufactures, which made men focus on minor details. In contrast with Britain, small-scale manufactures located in the countryside were regarded by Faucher as 'natural' to his idea of the French character: egalitarian, sociable, family-oriented, and inventive.[79] There underlay Faucher's comparison the distinction between the economic geniuses of Britain and France, almost a commonplace in both countries from the eighteenth century onwards. The story went that the former nation excelled in producing machine-made staples of general use, and the latter in quality goods – 'fancy articles and

---

[77] See, e.g., *ibid.*, I, pp. 133–7.
[78] *Cours 1838–1839*, p. 429.
[79] *Etudes sur l'Angleterre* (1845; 2 vols., Paris, 1856), esp. I, introduction, and pp. 345–6, 508–11, 536; II, pp. 88–204.

trinkets', in McCulloch's scornful words.[80] This distinction was made in detail by Lauderdale at the beginning of the nineteenth century, and stayed to mark either nation's economic identity throughout the following decades. The reason for this contrast, charged as it was with nationalistic pride and political resonances, was usually thought to lie in the different attitudes and skills of the workforce.[81]

Another travelling economist, former Saint-Simonian Michel Chevalier, held more combative views than Faucher's, and contrasting notions of French dispositions. Chevalier's *Lettres sur l'Amérique du Nord* (1836) documents his discovery, made during a stay of two years in the USA, that Americans were Englishmen 'exaggerated' as regards enterprise. Americans were conquering a continent by means of perseverance, determination and inflexible will, which were the qualities that characterized the Anglo-Saxon race and made it best suited to the task. 'When it is proposed to subdue nature', the Anglo-Saxon is 'our superior', he wrote. Another facet of American man was that he was 'deeply imbued with the sentiment of order'. Religious zeal associated with widespread education and material well-being made American democracy free from the spirit of revolt, while people were fully able to govern themselves. 'How and under what form shall we be able to make the innovations of the English race our own?', Chevalier unremittingly wondered over the whole course of his career. To him, character could be thought of as an effect of circumstances, but each people had certain characteristics which education developed rather than created. In practice he made national character act as a self-determined force which affected the contemporary course of events.[82]

No government, Chevalier argued in 1847, can be blamed for people's ignorance and apathy, for governments commonly reflect citizens' attitudes.[83] He posits the principle that policies must be calculated to fit those attitudes.[84] In general, there exist two main natures in the human race: the active and the passive. The American people show the greatest proportion of the active

---

[80] Crouzet, *De la supériorité de l'Angleterre*, pp. 105–19. That the commodity structure of industrial output in the two countries differed along these lines is confirmed by historians: see pp. 337–41 of Crouzet's book, and P. O'Brien and C. Keyder, *Economic Growth in Britain and France 1780–1914* (London, 1978), pp. 160–8.

[81] Lauderdale, *An Inquiry into the Nature and Origin of Public Wealth* (1804; 2nd edn, Edinburgh, 1819), pp. 269–365.

[82] *Lettres sur l'Amérique du Nord* (3rd edn, 3 vols., Bruxelles, 1838), esp. I, p. 14; II, p. 177; III, pp. 14–15 (*Society, Manners, and Politics in the United States*, ed. J. W. Ward (1839; Gloucester, Mass., 1967), p. 10).

[83] This was particularly true in the case of representative governments: 'Question de la population', *Journal des économistes*, 16 (1847), pp. 221–2.

[84] See, e.g., *Essais de politique industrielle: souvenirs de voyage. France, République d'Andorre, Belgique, Allemagne* (Paris, 1843), pp. 193ff. Here Chevalier argued that the highly advanced reform plan implemented by the Austrian Emperor Joseph II had clashed with his subjects' 'tempérament essentiellement doux et bon, opposé à la précipitation'.

type, and consequently self-government suits them very well; but in France there are many more passive citizens, so that a strong central government and a social order based on the principle of hierarchy have proved necessary. The best thing would be to have the productive sectors organized 'on the model of the army'. 'Someday, with the help of hierarchical association, we shall have an industrial organization even better than that of the English and the Americans', for their individualism brings about excessive competition and lack of social solidarity.[85] France had to maintain the national hallmarks that had made it different in essence from Great Britain, and become the main bulwark against the seemingly irresistible rise of Protestant nations. France's Latin and Catholic character was expressed by an accentuated sociability – 'we do not feel that we live unless we are part of a whole' – and by noble sentiments and enthusiasm.[86]

Chevalier's recipes for France were aimed not only at regaining the edge in international competition, but also at solving the problem of domestic turmoil. French society was in danger – 'it rested on foundations of quicksands' – because of persistent working-class discontent. Thus, for instance, the imperialist policies he suggested obeyed the imperative of domestic 'order', in the unoriginal sense that they were conceived as the means of reaping social cohesion through the expansion of national power.[87] But to leave military exploits aside, in striking similarity with a statement by Rœderer, industrial production appeared to Chevalier as the single moralizing force at hand.[88] The pursuit of material well-being entailed qualities, knowledge, and beliefs which, together with the interests it created, played an important conservative role in society. On a broader plane, the wealth, national power, and scope for measures of social protection that modern industry brought about amounted to the conditions for a peaceful absorption of 'democracy', namely the rise of the masses to a share of political power. But, even in this new age of industry, railways, and democracy, there remained a fundamental need for the subordination of the masses, which only 'religious faith' could ensure.[89]

---

[85] I am quoting from some notes not included in the American edition: *Lettres sur l'Amérique*, I, pp. 322–3; III, 251–6. In his *Cours d'économie politique* (1842–50; 2nd edn, 3 vols., Paris, 1855–66), Chevalier devoted more attention to credit, means of transport, and natural resources than to character in accounting for the American development. For Chevalier's fascination with the military model of organization, a fascination equally felt by Auguste Comte (another former Saint-Simonian), see A. Vinokur, 'Political Economy Between Faith and Works: Saint-Simonism and the Case of Michel Chevalier', *Economies et sociétés*, 20 (1986), pp. 188, 200–1.

[86] *Lettres sur l'Amérique*, II, pp. 244–5; III, pp. 98–100.

[87] The sentence on quicksands is in *De l'industrie manufacturière en France* (Paris, 1841), p. 38. Chevalier dreamed of France dominating all the Latin countries as well as Northern Africa. See, e.g., *Des intérêts matériels en France* (1838; 6th edn, Paris, 1843), p. 150, and *Le Mexique ancien et moderne* (Paris, 1863), pp. 492ff.

[88] Chevalier, *Des intérêts matériels*, p. 3; Rœderer, 'Cours d'organisation sociale', p. 265.

[89] See, e.g., *Lettres sur l'Amérique*, III, pp. 78–9; *Essais de politique*, pp. 92–3, 205, 287.

6   Concluding remarks: Victorian character and the eighteenth-century legacy

In troubled social and political contexts, Gioja and Dupin advocated industrialization on the English model together with the adoption of Franklin's ethics. An economy-oriented model of morality became both an inescapable requisite of growth and a way forward from the ruinous and outdated form of public morality characterizing the revolutionary events. But, granted that the standard against which to assess economic attitudes should be looked for in Britain, what were its features?

It scarcely needs observing that in turn-of-the-century Britain there was no situation of political turmoil and social flux even loosely comparable to the French Revolution and its aftermath. Republicanism as a set of connected views about politics was not unfamiliar to the educated mind, but there was no need for 'virtue' to be turned into an anxious appeal to economic performance. A peculiar state of affairs informed the prevailing attitude towards economic growth, so that it differed sharply from Continental perceptions. First, British economists had no reason to be preoccupied with the energy and skills of the workforce. Confidence in the superior qualities of the available human capital was not shaken until the 1850s (when the achievements of the American and Prussian educational systems became the order of the day). Second, a basic difference, which helps to account for the comprehensiveness of Continental political economy, and in particular for its disproportionate moral and political side, derived from Britain's competitive advantage. Political economy from Smith to McCulloch and Senior was responding to the intellectual as well as practical challenges which stemmed from recent developments in the economy; Gioja and Dupin, on the other hand, were pointing to the road to wealth and national power which their countries would hopefully take. That is to say, much of French and Italian political economy was marked by a prefiguring, pedagogical character.

To come to the British delineation of the 'economic man', it has been noted that in Victorian Britain 'work was the chief sphere in which moral worth was developed and displayed'.[90] The Victorian 'gospel of work' resulted from a harmonious blend of religious, political, and economic values, each element reinforcing the others. This was a conception in which lowbrow and middlebrow culture was in agreement with theology, political economy, and philosophy. The qualities which made up 'character' – self-restraint, self-reliance, independence, industry, thrift – had a common source in the view that

---

[90] S. Collini, 'The Idea of Character: Private Habits and Public Virtues', in his *Public Moralists* (Oxford, 1991), p. 106. For a classic treatment of the Victorian glorification of work, see W. E. Houghton, *The Victorian Frame of Mind 1830–1870* (1957; New Haven, Conn., and London, 1970), pp. 242–62; for the religious background, see B. Hilton, *The Age of Atonement: the Influence of Evangelicalism on Social and Economic Thought* (Oxford, 1988).

industrial exertions were a 'blessing' in themselves, because profoundly moral in nature. Hence the 'means' counted more than the 'end' (that is, wealth), and work and its concomitants (like competition) were man's proper sphere for self-realization. In one of his eulogies of the economic virtues of the British, McCulloch referred to Ferguson's *Principles of Morals and Political Science* (1792) as his inspiration on this point about means and ends;[91] however, another Scotsman, and a more influential one, David Hume, had provided a secularized version of the same view before. But there was a difference: Hume's 'The Stoic' portrayed a philosophical ideal, attainable only by the few, whereas Ferguson was considering the lot of men of all ranks. Significantly, both philosophers maintained that 'vigorous industry', morally precious as it was, could not in any event replace the practice of 'social virtues'.[92] Later, Malthus would place individual morality right at the analytical core of classical political economy. Over the first half of the nineteenth century, in an atmosphere of austere individualism engendered by the evangelical revival, both Malthusian morality and disciplinary concerns did much to obscure the prior emphasis on public virtues and participation. It immediately emerges, even on an examination as superficial as this, that this 'economic man' was a product of peculiarly British circumstances. Hence importing it onto the Continent could not but prove an arduous task, to the point of necessitating the simultaneous evocation of both the riches and the national greatness resulting from the adoption of the new morality.

By pointing to the transformation of virtue along economic lines and by tracing some of its possible legacies, I have not put forward an all-embracing interpretation. There were economists in both Italy and France who do not fit easily into my frame, the most notable among them being Say, Rossi, and Bastiat.[93] Besides, there arises a more general question about the permanence, asserted by some scholars, of a civic humanist inspiration drawn from eighteenth-century (and eventually classical) sources in nineteenth-century European thought. John

---

[91] A. Ferguson, *Principles of Morals and Political Science* (1792; repr. edn, 2 vols., New York and London, 1978), I, pp. 248–55, quoted in J. R. McCulloch, *The Principles of Political Economy* (1825; 5th edn, 1864; repr. edn, New York, 1965), pp. 22–5. For McCulloch on the manufacturing abilities of his countrymen, see esp. 'Rise, Progress, Present State, and Prospect of the British Cotton Manufacture', *ER*, 46 (1827), pp. 1–39. For a sensational eulogy of the 'instinct to accumulation' as an end in itself and 'one of the greatest sources of happiness', see N. W. Senior, *Industrial Efficiency and Social Economy*, ed. S. L. Levy (2 vols., London, 1928), I, pp. 68–9.

[92] 'The Stoic' (1742), in D. Hume, *Essays Moral, Political, and Literary*, ed. E. F. Miller (Indianapolis, 1987), pp. 146–54.

[93] Rossi and Say, however, dealt with many of the themes considered in the chapter. For example, see Rossi's treatment of the spirit of association in his *Cours d'économie politique* (2 vols., Brussels, 1840–2), pp. 60–78. For Rossi's view that 'il faut se résigner à avoir les institutions qu'exige la manière actuelle de voir et de sentir du peuple', see his 'De l'étude du droit dans ses rapports avec la civilisation et l'état actuel de la science', *Annales de législation et de jurisprudence*, 1 (1820), p. 38.

Stuart Mill in particular has recently been seen in a civic humanist light.[94] The question is especially relevant in view of chapter 4, where it is argued that a concern with public spirit was a unifying theme of the liberal thought of the French Restoration.

The economists dealt with in this chapter utterly rejected republicanism under the simultaneous impact of perceived Continental backwardness and the memories of Terror-fuelling Rousseauism. Other turn-of-the-century authors somehow retained elements of the terminology, and some images and concepts, of republicanism: Say, Staël, and Sismondi are three remarkable examples. Forcing all authors into a straitjacket of unreserved opposition to republican motifs seems therefore wrong. More remarkably, once the observer drops the option of a republican form of government as focus, 'civic' arguments are seen to crop up again and again in nineteenth-century Europe, and in particular in France. Clearly enough, it is important to distinguish between the revolutionary legacy, rejected by most, and more general participatory arguments.

The Revolution was a watershed because it attempted to put the traditional republican and civic humanist discourse into practice and failed, in a tragic and shocking way. It ensued that after the Revolution a reference to civic participation did not automatically relate to a ready-made, well-established idiom; on the contrary, it needed inserting within an original framework to be meaningful. To neglect this – that civic humanism as a system of political thought dissolved as a result of 1793–4 – leads to a subtle misrepresentation of the legacy of the eighteenth century. The mentioned nineteenth-century civic arguments may indeed have their sources in eighteenth-century authors (Rousseau usually excepted) or even earlier ones, but the perception of the implications of previous writers' motifs was different. It is important to avoid giving the impression of a certain outdatedness to the 'civic' inspiration, or, at any rate, of viewing that inspiration in isolation from the vital connection between a writer and the questions posed by his or her society.

In liberal London or Paris, civic participation could be either a fact or a hope, but in both cases it was too basic, general, and comprehensive an idea to be made dependent on a single political language, albeit stretching back for centuries, and especially under representative institutions which not only required participation by definition but participation of a new type, congruent with the characteristics of modern societies. There was an acute need for public virtues in the light of phenomena like the extension of the franchise, decentralized administrative institutions, the rise of labour, international competition, or public

---

[94] See, e.g., J. W. Burrow, *Whigs and Liberals: Continuity and Change in English Political Thought* (Oxford, 1988), esp. ch. 4. For Tocqueville as a civic humanist, see B. J. Smith, *Politics and Remembrance: Republican Themes in Machiavelli, Burke, and Tocqueville* (Princeton, 1985), pp. 155–250; A. S. Kahan, *Aristocratic Liberalism: the Social and Political Thought of Jacob Burckhardt, John Stuart Mill, and Alexis de Tocqueville* (Oxford and New York, 1992).

opinion in the age of mass literacy. As a result, the discourse on civic virtues was constantly reinvented according to varying contexts and problems – two elements which, in a sense, are the actual innovations to look for. That no revolution occurred in the tool box does not necessarily entail a persistent vitality of the language of civic humanism, but refers first of all to the very long story of the question it was called to tackle. Yet because it was a question whose attributes changed between, say, the days of Cicero and those of Hume and then Tocqueville, there was much below the surface of nineteenth-century arguments which was 'new': for instance, the shift from virtue to industry documented in this chapter, or the perspectives induced by the 'social sciences' considered later in the book. In short, elements of civic humanism may sometimes have been resorted to (in view of the continuing educational primacy of the classics, the opposite would be surprising), but their content should be redefined each time because both the textual and the historical contexts varied. What is important is the new twist imposed on an old idiom according to the writer's needs.

4 The French Restoration dispute over mores and Tocqueville

A recent book by Larry Siedentop has drawn attention to the sources of the idea of *mœurs* in Tocqueville's *De la démocratie en Amérique*. According to Siedentop, Tocqueville found in the French debate of the 1820s a clear view of the historical and political primacy of society over government, and made this perspective the groundwork of his own reflection. Hence Tocqueville's concern with the 'quality of the citizenry', a theme where he 'reached the highest ground of modern political theory'. By pointing to participation and its moralizing effects he resurrected the ideal of civic spirit, but in a liberal form rather than in classic terms. Siedentop also argues that Tocqueville differentiated himself from Terror-shocked Restoration liberals, who distrusted and feared participation as a means of creating public morality.[1] In endorsing the contextualization of Tocqueville operated by Siedentop, this chapter will investigate the various usages of the notion of *mœurs* in the political thought of Restoration France, the ultimate goal being a better understanding of Tocqueville's stance in *De la démocratie en Amérique* (specifically considered in section 5).

It can safely be argued as an introductory point that *mœurs* were pivotal in French political discourse between 1815 and 1830. Two reasons can be given for this. The first is the centrality of the relationship between mores and institutions to most period accounts of the Revolution. The lower classes in particular, even apart from their appalling ferocity during the Terror, puzzled Restoration writers for their decisive role, which seemed to result from their novel political independence. There was a feeling that a terrible and mysterious force, the French *peuple*, was lying dormant, and nobody could safely interpret their attitudes nor predict their next move.[2] Namely, the Revolution cast fundamental doubt on the identity of the mass of the French, while simultaneously bringing to light their potential as an independent political power.

A second reason for the prominence of *mœurs* came from the peculiarities of the political struggle. The liberals considered the new constitution, the

---

[1] L. Siedentop, *Tocqueville* (Oxford and New York, 1994), esp. pp. 20–41, 66–8, 138–47.
[2] 'Qu'il est affreux de penser que ce peuple qui nous entoure ... peut cacher sous un calme apparent tant de facilité par instants à faire ou à souffrir le mal': C. Rémusat, 'La Révolution française' (1818), in his *Passé et present: mélanges* (2 vols., Paris, 1847), I, p. 100.

Charte, as evidence of the acknowledgement in principle of the 'new social interests' formed by the Revolution, and thereby fought a battle in the name of the *Charte* against conservative governments which denied those interests. During the Restoration *la société* came prominently to the fore as a bone of contention;[3] and it is remarkable that the 'revolutionary interests' were more often than not subsumed by their advocates under abstract notions like 'public opinion', 'public spirit' and 'mores'. It was not just that these notions served to refer to those interests, although they certainly did, but that middle-class interests and opinions tended to become one and the same thing – which is unsurprising – and even that the former were obscured by the latter – which is perhaps unexpected. It is true that under the umbrella of the term 'revolutionary interests' there figured political and cultural 'interests', like freedom of the press, besides those related to tangible issues, like the title to the property previously owned by the Church or the *émigrés*. But it was a general feature of Restoration political literature to leave out a sociological identification of ranks in favour of general statements in terms of mores following the pattern: the French (or the *peuple*) being *a* and *b*, they want *x* and do not want *y*. Relatedly, the political debate was marked by a moral tone, which contributed to the attribution of a largely independent dynamic to constructs like national character, *mœurs*, and public opinion.

1   The *Ultras*

A first set of authors to consider is the *Ultra* group led by Maistre and Bonald. Both first elaborated their views in the 1790s as responses to the revolutionary events. The idea that constitutions were divinely ordained, ancestral handicrafts was the cornerstone of their thinking: if a religion, a set of institutions, and consequently a 'national character' had been associated with a nation since the origin of time, they became permanent features which there was no point tampering with. In the spirit of the ancients, nations were thought to follow an inescapable life cycle, so that, when their constituent elements came to an end, they died. The interest of Bonald and Maistre's views does not lie in their neo-medieval philosophical framework, though, but in how they bent it to encompass the Revolution.

Bonald depicted the Revolution as the final episode in 'the alteration of national character' which had occurred since the Regency. The manly disposition focusing on public interests, as described by Corneille, had been gradually supplanted by the 'voluptuous mores' spread by the epicurean philosophy of Voltaire.[4] Besides this kind of high-sounding polemic intended for the upper

---

[3] L. Siedentop, 'Two Liberal Traditions', in A. Ryan, ed., *The Idea of Freedom* (Oxford, 1979), pp. 153–74; P. Rosanvallon, *Le moment Guizot* (Paris, 1985), pp. 44–5ff.
[4] *Théorie du pouvoir politique et religieux dans la société civile* (1796), *BOC*, I, cols. 439–42; 'Réflexions sur les questions de l'indépendance des gens de lettres' (1805), *BOC*,

ranks, a special concern with the moral condition of the masses was typical of the *Ultras*. Habits, not ideas; memories, not reflections; sentiments, not thoughts: this is the material of which ordinary Frenchmen should be made for Bonald (and Maistre). 'Prejudice' was posited as the foundation of public morality. Accordingly, Bonald's 'national character' was a matter of traditional attachment, of affections and sensitivity, not of reason, and it amounted in practice to immemorial habits of political loyalty and religious devotion. Therefore, a true national character was an impossibility in 'popular states', highly unstable by definition.[5] He judged that in critical times 'national character' was an efficacious last resort for a state precisely because of the moral strength that sentiments and habits could arouse.[6] So keen was Bonald on commending traditional values that he bluntly stated that he preferred drunkenness to atheism.[7]

Oscillation between condemnation and absolution of the French is a leading, albeit subterranean, thread of Maistre's *Considérations sur la France* (1797).[8] The Revolution was seen as the necessary punishment after a century of vice and impiety. Nobody was innocent of the crimes of the Revolution – in particular, France as a whole was guilty of the death of Louis XVI even if the actual perpetrators were few in number. Yet some seventy pages later, he maintained that the French had just been misled by a small number of scoundrels and were now willing to welcome back their king. Even if tactical reasons may have played a part here, there was no real contradiction. It is the French character itself that makes a counter-revolution likely once a spark is set alight. The true 'nature' of the French is in fact to be cowardly in the face of power, passive, and apathetic, although brave in battle. Apart from the moral degeneration of recent occurrence, they really are '*homines ad servitutem natos*', always ready to follow the leader of the day as the Revolution abundantly proved.[9] Switching to the historical mode, Maistre argues that 'the ancient French constitution'

III, cols. 1029–50; and 'De l'éducation publique' (1819), *BOC*, III, cols. 1207–34. On the progressive corruption of *mœurs*, see also Montlosier, *De la monarchie française* (3 vols., Paris, 1814), esp. II, pp. 79–96. Montlosier reconstructed the greatness of French character and mores under aristocratic rule; see A. Omodeo, *Studi sull'età della Restaurazione* (1946; Turin, 1970), pp. 33–7.

5 *Théorie du pouvoir politique*, cols. 437–52; 'Sur les préjugés' (1810), *BOC*, III, cols. 803–10. Maistre held similar views: see in particular *Etude sur la souveraineté* (1794–6), in J. de Maistre, *Essai sur le principe générateur des constitutions politiques* (Lyon, 1924), esp. pp. 155–8 (on prejudice), 245–9 (on republics). Ironically, Bonald's comment on national character in popular states is an adaptation of the view, diffused in the eighteenth century, that a national character could not firmly establish itself in a despotic country because of the lack of regularity in the action of government.

6 *Théorie du pouvoir politique*, cols. 437–8.

7 'Sur les préjugés', col. 810.

8 This is equally true of Bonald: see for instance *Théorie du pouvoir politique*, cols. 440–1, 446–7.

9 J. de Maistre, *Considérations sur la France* (1797; Geneva, 1980), pp. 71–3, 106, 127–8, 147–57. 'Rien n'égale la patience de ce peuple qui se dit *libre*. En cinq ans, on lui a fait accepter trois constitutions et le gouvernement révolutionnaire', p. 148.

rested on those two original features of national character, religious sentiment and the love of monarchy; in contrast, the British and Americans have plenty of 'public spirit', that is love of liberty, because 'they were born to be free'.[10] Each nation had its own mission, in Maistre's views, and France's was the universal dominance of opinion and taste through its language and literary style. But France had fulfilled its destiny only until the age of Louis XIV, when the virtues of national character reached their climax – afterwards, 'the infamous Regency' brought about a moral 'gangrene'.[11]

This sets the background to a standpoint, which, replicated by many, became familiar to Restoration writers irrespective of their political beliefs. Bent on waging war against written constitutions, which in his views opened the door to popular sovereignty, Maistre was led to reverse the direction of the causal relationship between government and 'national character'.

Is it said that government makes mores? I deny it expressly. On the contrary, it is mores that make governments. No doubt, they mutually assist each other, thus creating what I could call a *virtuous circle*; yet the first impulse, the generating principle, always comes from mores and national character. Granted that Lycurgus and his extraordinary government acted on the character of the citizens and transformed them into other men, the Spartans accepted this government with full knowledge of the facts, and in absolute cold blood and freedom: and, certainly, a very large amount of both wisdom and energy was needed to want Lycurgus' laws.[12]

The view that national character shapes political institutions (although both elements are ultimately of divine origin) entails that 'the social contract is a wild dream', for 'despotism is as natural and legitimate for one nation as democracy is for another'.[13]

With sure intuition, Maistre takes issue with a commonplace notion – the demoralizing effects of despotism on citizens – which in effect supported a large part of the French Enlightenment's discourse on *mœurs*. Maistre contends that the example of the Asians, tirelessly made by all 'modern preceptors of revolt' since Montesquieu, would not do because the Asians naturally match that form of government and were great and energetic under it until it degenerated. No nation owes its character to its government; the opposite is true, with political institutions reinforcing the tendencies of national character over the course of time. To accuse a government of debasing its people is therefore absurd. When for some reason the match between government and character

---

[10] *ibid.*, pp. 69, 136; 'Trois fragments sur la France' (1794), in J. de Maistre, *Ecrits sur la Révolution* (Paris, 1989), pp. 81–5, 88–9; *Etude sur la souveraineté*, pp. 152, 280; *Essai sur le principe générateur des constitutions politiques* (1809), in *Essai sur le principe générateur*, pp. 21–2.

[11] See esp. 'Trois fragments', pp. 71–80, and *Etude sur la souveraineté*, pp. 329–31.

[12] 'Trois fragments', p. 81. For Bonald's position, see *Théorie du pouvoir politique*, cols. 420–36ff.

[13] Maistre, *Etude sur la souveraineté*, pp. 109–10.

is broken up, a political crisis occurs and the nation is in danger of dissolving for good.[14] This is clearly what Maistre believed to have happened in 1789–99. The lesson to be drawn was that politics was divinely arranged, and therefore human action could not be effective. It is worth noting that the *peuple* he talked about were still an indistinct mass of subjects; no part was played in his scheme of things by modern ideas of civil society.[15] Yet, *Ultras* and liberals shared in the acknowledgement of the insufficiency of purely political schemes to heal France's wounds and, in particular, in a distaste for constitutional experiments. Where to go from this common starting point led them in different directions.

In view of their religious background and mode of thinking, it came naturally to *Ultras* writers to represent the political struggle of the Restoration as one between clashing principles, with those of the Reformation and eighteenth-century philosophy on the one side, and Catholicism and tradition on the other. This provided a rich soil for a concern with the morality of the 'multitude', albeit of limited originality. Lamennais's polemic against the atheistic 'democracy' ruling France made much of the accusation of spreading materialistic mores. The people were 'degraded' by the irreligious climate in terms of ignorance, vice, and corruption of family life; furthermore, in their blind search for low pleasures the people could easily develop a 'ferocious instinct' and become 'bloodthirsty'. Self-interested individuals were necessarily isolated as an 'anarchy of beliefs' characterized public life. Lamennais's big target was the public provision of education, which in his view represented a deathblow to public and private morality.[16] It is remarkable, in this as in other similar reconstructions, that the citizenry was in practice considered a passive subject, receiving shape and direction from external principles, whether good or bad.

2   Thierry, Michelet, and two ways of discussing French dispositions

To reassess the French identity many Restoration authors turned to history. In this section, Thierry and the early writings of Michelet will be considered. Thierry's explanatory model is well known: the origin of contemporary struggles should be traced back to the conquests of the Middle Ages, when the two

---

[14] *ibid.*, pp. 221–3, 317–27. On Asian character, see also Maistre's *Les soirées de Saint-Pétersbourg* (1821; 2 vols., Geneva, 1993), I, pp. 140–1.

[15] See *Etude sur la souveraineté*, p. 104: 'Il y a eu un *peuple*, une civilisation quelconque et un souverain aussitôt que les hommes se sont touchés. Le mot de *peuple* est un terme relatif qui n'a point de sens séparé de l'idée de la souveraineté: car l'idée de *peuple* réveille celle d'une agrégation autour d'un centre commun, et sans la souveraineté il ne peut y avoir d'ensemble ni d'unité politique.'

[16] *De la religion, considérée dans ses rapports avec l'ordre politique et civil* (1825–6), in F. de Lamennais, *Œuvres* (3 vols., Brussels, 1829–30), II, pp. 7–114, esp. pp. 17–35.

'races' in conflict crystallized two opposite patterns of civilization. The Gauls set up urban communities whose values were equality and labour, while the Franks became feudal barons, warlike and domineering. The Revolution was nothing but the last episode in this war between 'two peoples'. Thierry's writings on French history amount to a eulogy of *la roture*, that is 'the Roman or bourgeois class' or 'the nation' in its entirety. In France as elsewhere in Europe, he maintained on the basis of Staël's *Considérations sur la Révolution française* that liberty was ancient and privilege new.[17] Interestingly, he remarks that the original distinction of 'races' faded away after some generations but was replaced by one of *mœurs*. The middle class of the *communes* was industrious (Thierry was Saint-Simon's secretary in 1814–17), talented, energetic, and with 'a confused sense of social equality'. Their history was one of self-government, popular assemblies, elected magistratures, and local pride.[18] Hence the French people had not, as the establishment historians claimed, been submissive right up to the Revolution; on the contrary, the true ancestors of the modern French were the *roturiers*, characterized by qualities of defiance and bravery that made them figures to take pride in rather than in the outlandish heroes of antiquity.[19] It would be difficult to imagine a more complete overturn of Maistre's stance.

Although Michelet was much less focused on 'races' than Thierry, he too made much of France's Celtic origin. There developed a Celtic internationalism mainly expressed by a strong condemnation of British rule in Ireland. Both historians believed – and it was a crucial denunciation given their frameworks – that 'races' did not mix in Britain because of inflexible English pride: in Michelet's words, 'the Saxon's son' can now be found 'engaged in machine-breaking or killed in Manchester by the sword of the Yeomanry'.[20] Michelet struck a bombastic note in his writings of the early 1830s, a note emphasized by his Carlylean style. He had written *Introduction à l'histoire universelle*, he explained, to show why France was the leading nation of humanity. France's supremacy resulted from a survey of European national characters, evaluated on the grounds of racialist and historical considerations. Biased perceptions and old stereotypes play the lion's share. In agreement with Maistre, Michelet sees the typical feature of the French as their proselytizing attitude, nourished by

---

[17] 'Sur l'antipathie de race qui divise la nation française' (1820), and 'Coup d'œil sur l'histoire d'Espagne' (1820), both collected in A. Thierry, *Dix ans d'études historiques* (Paris, 1835), pp. 291–300, 355.

[18] *Lettres sur l'histoire de France* (Paris, 1827), p. 233; 'Sur les libertés locales et municipales' (1820), in *Dix ans d'études*, pp. 268–70.

[19] *Lettres sur l'histoire*, pp. 2–9, 253, 404; 'Sur les libertés locales', p. 270: 'hommes de la liberté, nous aussi nous avons des aïeux'.

[20] *Introduction à l'histoire universelle* (1831), *MOC*, II, p. 252. The reference is to the 'Peterloo' riot in Manchester in 1819. For Michelet's early views on 'races', see the first two volumes of *Histoire de France* (1833), *MOC*, IV, esp. bk I. In Thierry, Celtism also entailed a fascination with Walter Scott's Highlanders. Both Thierry and Michelet believed in the physiological basis of races.

their naive enthusiasm for what is good and beautiful. But the image of modern Frenchmen that emerges from Michelet's pages is not as straightforward as that of Thierry, as Michelet attempted to save not only the people but the whole past of France. The nation's original 'democratic genius' is curiously said to have eventually taken the form of absolute monarchy, while no criticism of the Old Regime (nor, for that matter, of other periods of French history) is put forward.[21]

The bedrock of Michelet's historical argument is the depiction of the French as men destined for collective action. To apprehend their character graphically, he wrote, 'do not consider the isolated individual but the masses', during, for instance, a battle or a ball. On these occasions 'this living dust' takes up its ultimate import and reveals itself as 'wonderfully beautiful'. The July Revolution, when 'society did everything' in the absence of recognizable leaders, was the most recent proof of this attitude. But it would be inconceivable if separated from the ideas of 'order' and 'unity' which also informed the French people.[22] France's 'general spirit' was the abstract idea of the *patrie* as an entity which encompassed and ennobled individual lives.[23] This propensity for 'communion' mirrored Michelet's view of France as 'a person', a highly centralized spiritual unity created by 'social and political action' through the progressive overcoming of its different races, climates, and soils. Along the trajectory which begun with Montesquieu, Michelet stands out for the war he waged in the names of liberty and spirit against 'the fatalism of race and climate'.[24] He viewed civilization as stemming from the struggle between natural determinism and human 'liberty'. The final outcome would be the unity of man with man, with nature, and with God. The history, the people, and the soil of France would reach a condition of perfect integration. As one interpreter has written, 'Michelet strove for a *symbolic fusion* of the different entities occupying the historical field.'[25] A proper relationship between government and citizens vanishes into a progressing spiritual unity, matching political and geographical unity.

Thierry and Michelet are taken to represent one of the options of progressive culture, that is, the reconstruction of national character with the bricks of history, more or less supported by factual evidence. Obviously enough, this is not closet history; it is expressed in a tendentious, metaphorical and impressionistic style, whose material is the pedigree of the 'true' France, the France of the people. The

---

[21] *Introduction à l'histoire*, esp. pp. 250–1. See also the harmonious portrait of French history in the first four books of *Histoire de France*, which strikingly contrasts with English racial conflicts fuelled by oppression and injustice.

[22] *Introduction à l'histoire*, pp. 250–7.

[23] *Histoire de France*, pp. 383–4; *Introduction à l'histoire*, pp. 247–8ff.

[24] The majority of the writers supporting liberal reform paid little if any attention to climate, and some denied its effect altogether. Overall, climate was not an issue in Restoration France.

[25] H. White, *Metahistory: the Historical Imagination in Nineteenth-Century Europe* (Baltimore and London, 1973), p. 150.

distinction that Michelet and Thierry suggest, and which is relevant throughout the chapter (and the book), is that between the supplying of unwarranted and static characterizations of ancestral national attitudes, on the one hand, and the functional notion of mores, potentially applicable to all countries where a representative system exists, on the other. To anticipate, one of the reasons why Tocqueville's approach is of interest today is that it managed without factors like race, climate, or biased historical reconstructions, mastering *mœurs* purely on a 'civic' basis. Tocqueville's type of analysis has obvious advantages to modern eyes, provided that relative criteria are adopted. To begin with, that the method of *De la démocratie en Amérique* was deductive has been noticed by Furet.[26] Second, even Tocqueville's reflections on *mœurs* served a domestic purpose, as the overlapping of a universalistic and systematic mode with his concern about France is a typical feature of *De la démocratie en Amérique*. Another consideration is that Tocqueville himself was elaborating established images of national characters; for instance, the French passion for equality in preference to liberty had been the substance of many tirades before *De la démocratie en Amérique*.[27] In other words, a dynamic functional viewpoint may share something with a static approach based on alleged national characteristics, for, to a certain extent, the matter itself makes similar 'contaminations' likely. Advocating participation in a given country can hardly go without the recognition of certain mental and behavioural constants, which may prove difficult to explain in purely environmental terms, and thereby to view as temporary; add to this Tocqueville's use of historical analysis with its unavoidable medium- or long-term perspective. National stereotypes are pervasive, and it proved impossible even to Tocqueville to avoid their influence.

Chevalier's *Lettres sur l'Amérique du Nord* (see chapter 3), published one year later than the first volume of *De la démocratie en Amérique*,[28] and which put forward a political agenda equally centred on *mœurs*, can be taken as a term of comparison to illustrate the above difference in approach. Although 'Tocquevillian' themes abound in the *Lettres*, Chevalier's views on mores differ remarkably from those held by the Norman aristocrat. Chevalier's national characters are fixed for all practical purposes, that is, they take up a

---

[26] 'Le système conceptuel de *De la démocratie en Amérique*', in F. Furet, *L'atelier de l'histoire* (Paris, 1982), p. 250. See also P.-P. Royer-Collard to Tocqueville, 29 Aug. 1840, *TOPC*, XI, p. 93.

[27] In addition to the writings of the *doctrinaire* group of which this was a paramount tenet, see, e.g., P. L. Rœderer, 'The Spirit of the Revolution of 1789' (written 1815, published 1831), in his *The Spirit of the Revolution of 1789 and Other Writings on the Revolutionary Epoch*, trans. M. Forsyth (Aldershot, 1989), esp. pp. 6–7; B. Constant, review of Staël, *Considérations sur les principaux événements de la Révolution française, MF*, 2 (1818), pp. 316–25; C. Dunoyer, *L'industrie et la morale considérées dans leur rapports avec la liberté* (Paris, 1825); M. Desloges, review of Droz, *Application de la morale à la politique, LG*, 1 (1826), pp. 298–9.

[28] But many letters appeared in the *Journal des débats* from November 1833 onwards.

naturalistic quality which reduces their interaction with institutions to a minimum. His Saint-Simonian background induces a global perspective, a schematic but supposedly operational classification of peoples following the defining criteria of modernity. In comparison, Tocqueville is restrained, namely, more concentrated on a fundamental concern for France's political stability, admittedly shared with Chevalier. As regards Chevalier's conclusions, the extent of their difference from those of Tocqueville can be measured by Chevalier's view of the impossibility of individualism in Catholic countries on national character grounds.[29] This inference was made possible by his taking national characters as immutable facts. From my angle, Chevalier is important for the neatness and straightforwardness of his use of national character in support of a hierarchical society; his bold statements probably accounted for the success of the *Lettres* as well as of his other books. (In addition, he systematized pivotal elements of French nationalist rhetoric into a coherent vision of modernity, authoritarian and aggressive, which became an arsenal for the use of opposition parties, as, unexpectedly, Tocqueville himself demonstrated in many speeches and writings advocating a foreign policy that fulfilled France's 'mission'.)

The approach in terms of national character contrasts, at least in principle, with that in terms of public spirit endorsed not only by Tocqueville but by some distinguished liberal thinkers of the Restoration as well. The features of the public spirit outlook will emerge from an analysis of that most evocative of forerunning texts, Turgot's *Mémoire sur les municipalités* (1775, first published 1787). In this celebrated proposal for the creation of assemblies in villages and towns, cantons, and provinces, as well as of a general assembly, Turgot links representative institutions to a reform in the perception of public life and duties. Widespread tax evasion and the regular demands of municipalities and groups for exclusive privileges, to the detriment of other localities and groups, are the most blatant symptoms of a deficiency in the feeling of belonging to a community. The want of social bonds (*liens sociaux*) entails the isolation and the purely egoistic concerns of each individual, besides the isolation of the *états* between them; as he wrote, 'there is no public spirit because there are no visible and known common interests'.[30] The progress of a 'spirit of union' is expected to derive not simply from the new assemblies but also from the diffusion of *lumières*, which figure as a condition for their success. Accordingly, Turgot devises a plan for the establishment of an educational system intended 'to form citizens'. 'Mores are the first bond of nations; the first foundation of mores is instruction about the duties of man in society imparted from childhood.'[31] The proposed 'Council for national instruction' would spread a more austere and

---

[29] According to Chevalier, Protestantism was an indispensible requisite of individualism: *Lettres sur l'Amérique du Nord* (3rd edn, 3 vols., Brussels, 1838), III, pp. 98–100.

[30] See the *Mémoire* in *TO*, IV, pp. 574–621; the quoted sentence is on p. 577. The text was actually written by Dupont de Nemours, Turgot's life-long friend, following Turgot's directions.

[31] *ibid.*, p. 579.

noble tone throughout society, but above all it would induce honest and zealous conduct in public life.

For Turgot, the tasks of self-government would consist of the apportioning of taxes, the implementation of policies in the areas of public works and poor relief, and the management of inter-institutional relations. A more efficient and more equitable administration would result inasmuch as matters would be in the hands of those who are directly concerned; much-needed social bonds would form in parallel with the discussion of subjects of common interest.[32] In the case of public works, Turgot observes that the present miserable state of country roads is due to both a poor 'public spirit' and the absence of bodies collecting and organizing the will of citizens, rather than to a lack of money.[33]

A more general effect of Turgot's scheme would be the affirmation of new standards of social worth. In his intention, the system of assemblies should induce an appraisal of citizens exclusively on the basis of their utility to the state; by this means French society would become a cohesive entity in the name of a renewed idea of 'public good'.[34] Turgot's target is clear: in the perspective of the *Mémoire* the financial exemptions of the aristocracy and the clergy appear even more 'disgraceful'. These bodies refuse to give help to the common *patrie*, namely, to perform a deed which amounts to the criterion for actual greatness.[35] Turgot concludes by envisaging 'a new people', morally regenerated through public instruction and the example of wise discussions on serious subjects held in the assemblies.[36] The gist of the text is a series of connected statements: first, that decentralization is instrumental in effective administration; second, that participation is the key to decentralization; and, third, that participation requires public spirit, that is, mores informed by a sense of the common interest. As will be shown, Turgot's motifs recur again and again in the nineteenth-century literature on public spirit – in particular, although the *philosophes* were quite rarely cited during the Restoration, so relevant a precedent in France's recent history could hardly fail to influence the authors considered in what follows.

3 The necessity of public spirit, or the liberal stance

This section is devoted to those major writers who more easily fall within a modern definition of 'liberal' thought; the following will address liberal journalism. Here, reference will be made to Chateaubriand, Constant, and Guizot, but Staël's position will also be recalled on occasion. The inclusion of Chateaubriand in the

[32] *ibid.*, pp. 581–3.
[33] *ibid.*, pp. 590–1.
[34] *ibid.*, p. 619.
[35] *ibid.*, pp. 592–4.
[36] *ibid.*, pp. 620–1. It should be specified that only landowners would be admitted to the assemblies; and that these would have no political function.

'liberal' camp can be questioned; but, unlike Bonald for instance, he accepted the new constitution, and opposed the regime as 'an obscure despotism' after his dismissal from the Villèle government in June 1824. A first point to consider is that many liberals ascribed the misdeeds of the Revolution to a wrong match between governments and faulty or immature *mœurs*. The origin of this view lies in the influence of the *idéologues* in the Directory years, as Staël in particular shows with the utmost clarity in *Des circonstances actuelles qui peuvent terminer la Révolution* (1798); Constant had accounted for the Terror along the same lines in *Des réactions politiques* (1797).[37] The list of those who in various ways pointed to the fundamental role of collective mentalities and opinions in the Revolution includes *idéologues* like Rœderer and Destutt de Tracy, young essayists like Rémusat, Charles Comte, and Dunoyer, public moralists like Jouy, and masters of social thought like Saint-Simon.[38]

But it is Chateaubriand who deserves closer examination in this respect, for his early views on mores had a bearing on his proposal for government *selon la Charte* after 1815. In *Essai sur les révolutions* (1796, republished 1826), he criticized eighteenth-century philosophers who aimed to create *mœurs* by law. It was the other way round that made sense. Mores represented the accordance or disaccordance of people's behaviour with 'the inner sense' which recommended the pursuit of what was good and honest. In practice, *mœurs* were seen by Chateaubriand as the positive effects of religion and morality upon citizens' ideas and behaviour, and for this reason the proper basis of laws. When mores were sound, politics should be a reflection of the current ethical codes. What happened in corrupt times was that legislators cultivated the hope of 'remaking men through laws'. The course of civilization testified that as *lumières* progressed, *mœurs* worsened; and he explained the course of the Revolution in this way, with special reference to secularism.[39]

[The Revolution] came above all from the progress of society towards, at the same time, enlightenment and corruption; this is why so many excellent principles and an

---

[37] For Staël, see chapter 2 above; B. Constant, *Des réactions politiques* (Paris, an V [1797]), pp. 1–2; for a later account, see Constant's review of Sauquaire-Souligné's *Trois règnes de l'histoire d'Angleterre, La Minerve*, 6 (1819), pp. 568–76. For a comment, focused on Constant's 'modèle de l'anachronisme', see M. Gauchet, 'Constant, Staël et la Révolution française', in F. Furet and M. Ozouf, eds., *The French Revolution and the Creation of Modern Political Culture* (3 vols., Oxford, 1989), III, pp. 159–72.

[38] As regards Rœderer, a late text is 'The Spirit of the Revolution of 1789', esp. pp. 5–13; A.-L.-C. Destutt de Tracy, *Commentaire sur l'Esprit des Lois de Montesquieu* (Paris, 1819), pp. 146–8; Rémusat, 'La Révolution', pp. 105–8; for Comte and Dunoyer, see the writings considered in chapter 3 above; E. Jouy, *La morale appliquée à la politique pour servir d'introduction aux observations sur les mœurs françaises au XIXe siècle* (2 vols., Paris, 1822), esp. II, pp. 313–20; C. H. de Saint-Simon, 'Lettres à un Américain' (1817), *SSO*, I, pp. 138–202 (for Saint-Simon on public spirit, see 'Comparaison entre l'état politique de l'industrie en France et l'état politique de l'industrie en Angleterre' (1817), *SSO*, II, pp. 55–6).

[39] *Essai historique, politique et moral, sur les révolutions*, *COC*, I, pp. 55–6, 115, 165, 171–4, 202–3.

equal number of fateful consequences are to be found in the Revolution. The former derived from an enlightened theory, and the latter from corrupt mores. This is
the very cause of the apparently incomprehensible spectacle of crimes grafted onto a
philosophical trunk – this is the view that I have sought to demonstrate throughout
this *Essai*.[40]

The lamentable divorce between *lumières* and *mœurs*, a view clearly inspired
by Rousseau, constituted for Chateaubriand the problematic dimension of
public morality in the wake of the collapse of traditional values. Although
Chateaubriand progressively reconciled himself to civilization, his political
writings of the Restoration advocated 'ancient mores', and religion in particular, to counterbalance the spirit of independence and *raison* embodied in
representative institutions. His acceptance of these rested on the acknowledgement of the changed beliefs and attitudes of the French as a result of the spread
of *lumières*.[41]

Outside France, Chateaubriand in *Voyage en Amérique* anticipated
Tocqueville's account of the contrast in 'political education' between the United
States and the American republics of 'Spanish origin. Their different 'national
characters' rested on the divergent elements which had informed their
'national origins'. Unlike the North Americans, the Southern American peoples lacked the 'instinct for liberty' needed for republican government, and this
instinct could only emerge over time through traditions, *lumières*, examples,
social equality, and common interests.[42] Behind these judgements there lay
the abandonment of his previous option for a type of liberty characterized as
'the daughter of mores and virtue' in favour of one that was 'the daughter of
lumières and reason'. Chateaubriand explained that, since it was in the nature of
mœurs to deteriorate in ages of despotism or luxury, the kind of liberty resting
on them would always be precarious, whereas *lumières* progressed indefinitely.
This new stance was related to a preference for the mores of the moderns over
those of the ancients.[43]

Considering the importance of *mœurs* for the interpretation of the recent
past, it is not surprising that a main tenet of Restoration liberals was that representative institutions could not be effectual without an animating spirit in the
citizenry.[44] The political battle of the Restoration reflected this preoccupation,
with crucial issues ultimately revolving around the relationship between the will

[40] *Essai*, p. 165, fn. In an editorial comment on this passage (1826), he wrote: 'Si j'ai écrit quelque
       chose de bon dans ma vie, il faut y comprendre cette note', p. 165.
[41] *Réflexions politiques* (1814), *COC*, V, esp. pp. 44, 57; *De la monarchie selon la Charte* (1816),
       COC, V, pp. 137–9.
[42] *Voyage en Amérique*, ed. R. Switzer (1827; Paris, 1964), pp. 401–37.
[43] *ibid*., pp. 65–6, 412–14.
[44] However, the enhancement of social bonds through administrative decentralization, and re-
       lated appeals to public spirit characterized the conservatives' programme as well. See C.-H.
       Pouthas, 'Les projets de réforme administrative sous la Restauration', *Revue d'histoire
       moderne*, 1 (1926), pp. 327–9.

and opinions of citizens, of which the liberal party in particular claimed to be the genuine interpreter, and the institutions established by the *Charte*. Two distinct phases can be identified in the progressives' strategy. The first was predominantly defensive, and saw the liberals engaged in asserting the suitability of the French for representative government. A chapter in Staël's *Considérations sur la Révolution française* (published 1818) was aptly entitled 'Are the French made to be free?', and her answer could not but be affirmative. In the second phase the liberals were on the offensive, in an attempt to denounce the limited representativeness of existing arrangements in the face of the new 'revolutionary interests', that is the interests prompted by the Revolution and allegedly sanctioned by the constitution. Hence the *Ultras* rather than the liberals would appear as the real subversives. The language of interests often gave way to that of mores, so that it was in the name of an enlightened public opinion that demands were most frequently voiced. This second phase implied the logical and political primacy of society over political arrangements, an idea which soon became a cornerstone of liberal discourse. Here two authors stand out: Guizot and Constant.

In Guizot's view, granted that governments emanate from societies, the 'moral state' of a people has significant sway over its political situation.[45] He takes issue with the one-sidedness of the previous century on this point: 'if it is true to say that governments make peoples, then it is equally true that peoples make governments'. The Revolution itself, which focused on changing the material organization of life, eventually relied on 'ideas, sentiments, and inner individual attitudes' to achieve its goal.

> [The Revolution] set out to reform the social state by means of the moral state. Therefore, the Revolution should have acknowledged the moral state not only as distinct from, but also, to a certain extent, as independent of the social state; it should have recognized that situations and institutions were not all, nor decided all in the lives of peoples; that other causes could modify, oppose, and even overcome situations and institutions; and that, if the outside world influences man, he in turn influences the outside world.[46]

Specifically, Guizot points to the tremendous effectiveness of ideas (*opinions*) in the modern world. Collective entities like peoples follow ideas, whereas interests are relevant to individuals only; not to mention that, as in the case of the

---

[45] See *Des moyens de gouvernement et d'opposition* (Paris, 1821), pp. 5–7, 165–71; *Essais sur l'histoire de France* (Paris, 1823), pp. 81–3ff.; *Histoire de la civilisation en France* (5 vols., Paris, 1829–32), IV, pp. 362–3. For comments which stress Guizot's particular interaction of the social with the political dimension, see Rosanvallon, *Le moment Guizot*, pp. 35–63; in M. Valensise, ed., *François Guizot et la culture politique de son temps* (Paris, 1991), see C. Lefort, 'Guizot théoricien du pouvoir', pp. 95–110, and A. Kahan, 'Guizot et le modèle anglais', pp. 219–31, esp. pp. 220–6. See also Royer-Collard in P. B. de Barante, *La vie politique de M. Royer-Collard* (2 vols., Paris, 1861), II, pp. 130–6.

[46] *Histoire de la civilisation en France*, I, pp. 42–4, 140–2, quotation on pp. 141–2 (*The History of Civilization*, trans. W. Hazlitt (London, 1846), p. 348; trans. modified).

purchasers of *biens nationaux*, interests and opinions usually go together.[47] Another tenet of importance from this angle is the definition of nations predominantly in terms of shared ideas and sentiments rather than 'exterior' organization.[48]

The background of Guizot's two pamphlets of 1821 and 1822 denouncing the looming control of parties over the judicial system was the traumatic revolutionary experience. This had amounted to 'a state of dissolution and war' bringing about a 'terrible suspension of society' and hence the invasion of politics into the domains of all other powers.[49] Conversely, Guizot argues, the Restoration governments pledged to implement 'justice', that is, to protect the 'general needs' of society. When the dividing line of politics appears to crystallize as a contrast between party rule on the one hand and 'justice' on the other, the educational role of a fair judicial system emerges as crucial. In the process of accustoming citizens to respect each other's interests and rights, the management of criminal justice provides an invaluable opportunity:

If men of all ranks and opinion are treated according to equity and law, the public will take up the habit of thinking that all things should be managed according to equity and law. If there is a place where political bias and party spirit count for nothing, political bias and party spirit will become discredited and weakened elsewhere, too. Society asks for a refuge and a hope … Give justice a firm support point [*point d'appui*], and it will march from there to the conquest of all things, of government as well as of public spirit.[50]

'Social bonds other than those of fear, and other fears than those of blood' are required. The most effective force which keeps society together, as well as ordered and developing, is 'public spirit'; to the point where, as in Holland, there exists 'a public sentiment so general and imperious, it is certain that the goal to which it is directed will be achieved'.[51] Today society is such that the government is half-defeated 'when the public judges that it is in the wrong'. The government's grip should therefore slacken, for social order is naturally maintained by refined

---

[47] *Des moyens de gouvernement*, esp. pp. 135–41. The primacy of opinions over interests was explicitly affirmed by other authors, like Rémusat, 'La Révolution', pp. 112ff.; J. Fiévée, *Des opinions et des intérêts pendant la Révolution* (Paris, 1815); C. L. Le Sur, *La France et les français en 1817* (Paris, 1817), pp. 155–6; and F.-R. de Chateaubriand, 'De la morale des intérêts et de celle des devoirs' (1818), in Chateaubriand's *Grands écrits politiques*, ed. J.-P. Clément (2 vols., Paris, 1993), II, esp. pp. 538–43.

[48] 'Moral unity' was deemed more important and effective than political unity, which would remain weak until there was a common morality to support it: *Histoire de la civilisation en France*, IV, pp. 3–5; see also *Histoire de la civilisation en Europe* (1828–30; 6th edn, Paris, 1856), p. 210.

[49] *Des conspirations et de la justice politique* (1821), in F. Guizot, *Des conspirations et de la justice politique. De la peine de mort en matière politique* (Paris, 1984), p. 23. Guizot's father, too, had been a victim of the Terror.

[50] *ibid.*, p. 81.

[51] *ibid.*, pp. 17, 19 and fn.

mores, work habits, and the widespread understanding of general interests; as 'social constitution' has changed, so should modes of governance.[52] Guizot's tragedy, similar in many ways to that of other Restoration liberals, was his awareness of the weakness of the communal fabric in the name of which he was opposing the conservative governments. That weakness, whose origins Guizot finds in the peculiarities of French feudalism, means that neither 'moral beliefs' nor 'habits' are likely to come to the aid of liberty. Not all popular convictions and attitudes are commendable. Many Frenchmen are suspicious of all 'superiorities', even of the 'natural' ones, and incline to 'permanent revolt'. There is a mixture in the national disposition of 'pride and *mollesse*', shown by unbounded ambition and infinite desires divorced from the strong will and energy required to fulfil them.[53] Guizot speaks of an awkward association between civic inertia and the habit of being 'spectators' of glorious deeds as a legacy of the Napoleonic years. The demoralizing impact of 1799–1814 was a commonplace of liberal literature.

The blend of ardour and softness [*mollesse*], of taste for action and idleness in execution, of search for emotions and aversion to effort, which is the moral state of France in the political realm nowadays, comes from there. This is a condition of impatience and weakness at the same time, which makes us hardly bear rest but dislike work, which makes us despise a monotonous life and therefore diverts us from the active duties of citizenship. Bonaparte committed the crime of exalting and depressing us at the same time.[54]

A characteristic feature of the post-1814 society is that 'everything is obscure and confused although nothing is disordered or violent'. Guizot means that the revolutionary turmoil that had blurred the distinction between legitimate and illegitimate interests, as well as between good and evil morals, still casts its shadow over the nation; yet now, in spite of the fact that the French are inexperienced at the exercise of liberty and thereby make mistakes, society is calm. The restored monarchy found an ordered polity, not a lawless chaos.[55] Nevertheless, the order established by Napoleon was fragile because unsupported by 'guarantees', both in the institutional and in the moral fields. In the latter, 'a real and profound evil' resulted from a twofold want: of 'a resolute sentiment of law [*droit*]', and of deep-seated religious beliefs. What Napoleon looked for, and succeeded in establishing, was 'discipline bereft of moral rule, and obedience in the context of indifference'. Despotism invariably brings about corruption of law, yet Napoleon managed to strike a serious blow not only at the power

---

[52] *De la peine de mort en matière politique* (1822), in Guizot, *Des conspirations*, pp. 87, 166.
[53] *Du gouvernement représentatif* (Paris, 1816), p. 62; *Des moyens de gouvernement*, pp. 161, 208–10, 349, 355–6ff.
[54] *Des moyens de gouvernement*, pp. 236–7. On the dark side of the national character, see also *Histoire de la civilisation en Europe*, pp. 30–1.
[55] *De la peine de mort*, pp. 129, 133.

to resist but also at the thought of resistance, which is the root of a 'moral life'.[56] By revitalizing the two 'guarantees', the Bourbon governments should be recreating 'the moral order' which alone can support 'the external order'; but, fearful of liberty and toleration, they are failing to do so.[57]

Guizot argues in *Des moyens de gouvernement et d'opposition* that the 'passions' of the people should be cautiously managed to make them functional to the liberal cause. The French certainly need rest after years of political strife, but they should also be offered opportunities to practice civic virtues at the local level. Once in charge of the concrete, circumscribed businesses of their region or town, the citizens would emerge from their isolation and learn the arts of association and discussion with specific tangible aims in view. In the process, the social qualities of a superior kind (*des supériorités*) characterizing 'a natural aristocracy', required by liberal France, would appear.[58] As he noted elsewhere, 'liberty is participation': both rights and liberties would wane 'where liberties are not rights, and rights are not ways of exerting power'.[59]

As far as the theory of the sovereignity of society is concerned, Constant's work is obviously fundamental, first of all for the celebrated contrast he drew in 1814 between the military and commercial spirits. In his view, the unfettered growth of modern societies followed a reassuring pattern leading to the independence and welfare of citizens. Arguably, Constant's notion of the ultimate convergence of social tendencies to the liberal programme relieved him of a large part of the concern with French attitudes which other liberals exhibited.[60] His literary works as well as his private papers disclose an unflattering view of the French.[61] Yet the model of commercial society enabled Constant to ignore the national defects, and place *mœurs* within a comprehensive framework, a politico-philosophical system which took full shape in the *Commentaire sur l'ouvrage de Filangieri* of 1822–4.

In both *De l'esprit de conquête* and *Principes de politique*, Constant endorses the form of 'patriotism' which originates from local circumstances and traditions. With the aims of opposing both Napoleonic centralization and philosophers' abstract conceptions, he places a high value on 'habits', 'memories',

---

[56] *ibid.*, pp. 134–5.
[57] *ibid.*, pp. 135–40.
[58] *Des moyens de gouvernement*, pp. 264–9; *Essais*, pp. 42–5. The writing and reading of history could also spread civic awareness: *Histoire de la civilisation en France*, IV, pp. 27–8. For themes similar to Guizot's, see P. B. de Barante, *Des communes et de l'aristocratie* (Paris, 1821), where it was argued that the political system served to protect and regularize the 'empire des mœurs', p. 92.
[59] *Essais*, pp. 50–1.
[60] See, e.g., *De la doctrine politique qui peut réunir les partis en France* (1816), in B. Constant, *Cours de politique constitutionnelle* (2 vols., Paris, 1872), II, pp. 300–2.
[61] See F. Tilkin, 'L'image des nations européennes dans les écrits personnels de Benjamin Constant', in S. Balayé and K. Kloocke, eds., *Le groupe de Coppet et l'Europe 1789–1830* (Lausanne and Paris, 1994), pp. 67–81.

'local pride', and 'specific social bonds' (*liens particuliers*) as vehicles of civic education and active love of the polity. Laws can be good or bad, but this is much less relevant than the 'spirit' in which they are obeyed: if laws manage to touch an inner chord in the citizens by their connection with cherished traditions, any law can hardly fail to produce some good. But, Constant continued, the mania for uniformity has led governments to waste the moral 'treasure' of local patriotism, with the result that congested capital cities preside over provinces bereft of autonomous life.[62] To him as to Guizot, 'public spirit' rather than interests is the independent social variable. When the former is annihilated by despotism, the latter suffer from the paralysis of eagerness and forethought.[63]

Constant wishes to make reform policies dependent on public opinion, that is to point to the necessary harmony between ideas and institutions. Any acceleration in the pace of reform has in fact proved disastrous, he held with special reference to the Revolution.[64] What a legislator should really care about is not rapidity but graduality of change; since the march of men is progressive, the legislator's task amounts to following 'the minute alterations which take place in the moral nature'.[65] This way of addressing the problem of *mœurs* was Constant's hallmark, and was fully developed in the *Commentaire*.[66] In *De l'esprit de conquête*, he applied this approach to the necessity of respecting local laws, institutions, and *souvenirs*: since the past had deep roots in all 'moral beings', these roots could not be severed 'without pain'. But in the operational *Principes de politique* he argued, in agreement with Staël but perhaps in contradiction with himself, that the French would become wise and calm, and 'a spirited feeling for political life' would develop, as long as free institutions were set up.[67] Religion was deemed necessary to create a 'common morality'.[68]

The *Commentaire sur l'ouvrage de Filangieri* shows a refinement and a radicalization of Constant's previous views. Having dismissed the idea of locality-inspired patriotism and laws, Constant insists on the universal suitability of the same minimal set of basic laws to match purely negative government functions. Public opinion figures as a direct expression of the 'masses of the people', where legitimate power ultimately lies, and opinion faces government as a totally independent force. Legislators should restrain themselves, for they have

---

[62] *De l'esprit de conquête et de l'usurpation* (1814), in B. Constant, *Ecrits politiques*, ed. M. Gauchet (Paris, 1997), pp. 164–71, 287–90; *Principes de politique* (1815), in *Ecrits politiques*, pp. 428–9.

[63] *De l'esprit de conquête*, pp. 236ff.; *Commentaire sur l'ouvrage de Filangieri* (2 parts, 1822–4; published as vol. VI of G. Filangieri, *Œuvres*, 6 vols., Paris, 1822–4), I, pp. 76–8, 290, 296ff.

[64] *De l'esprit de conquête*, pp. 279–84; see also *Des réactions politiques*.

[65] *De l'esprit de conquête*, pp. 289–90.

[66] See M. Gauchet, 'Benjamin Constant: l'illusion lucide du libéralisme', in Constant, *Ecrits politiques*, pp. 12–110, esp. pp. 64–74.

[67] *Principes de politique*, pp. 351–9, 393, 404–7, 419, 440, 494–7.

[68] *ibid.*, pp. 474ff.

no special knowledge superior to that of the citizens. Being mere expressions of social relations, laws cannot induce virtuous mores, although, if oppressive, they can destroy the public spirit which is the nation's animating principle. Its function is to protect society from the encroachments of government. Public spirit basically consists of a free press, a feeling of belonging and participation (however imaginary), and religious morality. Britain testifies to the efficacy of public spirit in preserving liberty, in spite of mercantilistic policies and the persecution of Catholics:

> The citizens' energetic character has been preserved, for they have not been disinherited from participation in the administration of public affairs; this participation, although almost imaginary, gives the citizens a sense of their importance which keeps their activities going [*entretien leur activité*]; so that England, even if ruled by Machiavellian cabinets and quite corrupt Parliaments from Sir Robert Walpole to the present day (with a few exceptions), has nevertheless upheld the language, habits, and many of the advantages of liberty.[69]

Spain, in contrast, has experienced the most destructive of despotisms, that which suffocates the press as well as political rights; as a result, 'the nation is dead'. To curb opinion entails the slackening of all human faculties, as the *lumières* are their common foundation and the polity is the 'proper sphere' of *lumières*. 'It follows that governments that kill opinion and seek to encourage interests . . . discover that they have annihilated both.'[70]

In concluding the *Commentaire*, Constant explains that a night-watchman government is the only possible solution to the long-standing problem of the relationship between political power and public opinion. If a government took positive action, in fact, one of two possible cases would ensue. The first was that, if 'absurd laws' had been enacted in earlier times, their repeal would be indefinitely postponed on the pretext of the insufficient maturity of citizens. The example Constant made was that of pre-revolutionary France. The second case occurred when a government launched a reform programme for which the people were unprepared. Pombal's reforms in Portugal and those of the Constituent Assembly were representative of this mistake.[71] Consequently, Constant advocated 'the government of opinion', that is one where opinion posited goals which were later to be guaranteed by institutional developments. For Constant was convinced that public opinion was always progressive, whereas governments had a vested interest and a greater propensity to make mistaken evaluations than the citizens.

> The opinion of a people results from the individual opinion of each, separated from the private interests which falsify it to each citizen; interests which, by meeting in this

---

[69] *Commentaire*, I, p. 73.
[70] *ibid.*, I, pp. 73–7.
[71] *ibid.*, II, pp. 278–82.

common centre, fight and destroy one another. On the other hand, the government or legislator experiences private interests in their full intensity.[72]

Furthermore, laissez-faire policies had significant potential for self-education and therefore self-help. Constant specified that the government should refrain from influencing the opinion of the 'ignorant class'.[73]

French political thought up to the July Revolution went no further than this. French *mœurs* and public opinion came eventually to be equated with those of a 'commercial society', whose dynamic was viewed, at least in principle, as totally independent of that of governments dominated by an anachronistic spirit of conquest. This model lost much of its significance after 1830, when middle-class values got the upper hand. Reflecting this, Tocqueville's analysis shifted the focus once again towards the hard facts of French bourgeois mentality, which Constant had certainly not exalted but had somewhat veiled. As regards the mode of approach, though, it has emerged that Tocqueville could find in his immediate predecessors well-polished examples of the 'civic' way.

4   Liberal journalism and the implementation of the *Charte*

A survey of the liberal camp would not be complete if consideration was not given to a set of writers (some better known than others) active mainly in journalism, a profession which has come to be seen as the vehicle of a 'younger' generation whose attitude and beliefs differed from those characterizing the generation of Staël and Constant.[74] Yet any precise assessment of the generation gap is difficult to make. Constant himself was a star of Restoration journalism. In August 1814, in the *Journal des débats*, he first made a point which was to characterize much of the liberals' journalistic polemic. His argument was constructed thus: we are now enjoying some liberal measures, such as a free press; their educational effects are already perceptible, as the French appear calmer, more loyal and animated, and more reflective than they have been for twenty years; hence, far from being repealed, those liberties must be extended and entrenched.[75] The rationale of Constant's position was, to quote the title of another article of his, that 'political liberty is essential to civil liberty', so that attempting to put public *mœurs* on the right track other than through a consummation of the constitution would be in vain.[76] Constant's key move lay in assuming what could be either an

[72] *ibid.*, II, pp. 288–301, quotation on p. 290.
[73] *ibid.*, pp. 299–301.
[74] See A. B. Spitzer, *The French Generation of 1820* (Princeton, 1987), and F. Diaz, 'Successo e crisi del liberalismo nella Francia del primo Ottocento', *Rivista storica italiana*, 106 (1994), pp. 262–304.
[75] *Journal des débats*, 4 Aug. 1814, in B. Constant, *Recueil d'articles 1795–1817*, ed. E. Harpaz (Geneva, 1978), pp. 144–5.
[76] 'La liberté politique, essentielle à la liberté civile', *Mercure de France*, Oct. 1815, in Constant, *Recueil d'articles 1795–1817*, pp. 254–9.

opinion or a hope – that the French were rapidly improving in accordance with the progress made by liberal institutions – as a fact. The following analysis of some representative reviews will exemplify the wide diffusion of this argument.

Preliminarily, however, it should be noted that a movement among liberals away from despondency was under way in the 1820s, as illustrated by the revision of the interpretation of the Revolution put forward in Staël's *Considérations*. J. C. Bailleul's detailed critique of the book (1818) was followed by the histories of Thiers and Mignet (in 1823 and 1824 respectively). According to these authors, a constitution on the English model (the solution advocated by Staël) had not been a possibility given the circumstances of 1789–99, and, more importantly, the Terror was not an explosion of criminal folly but a tragic concomitant of the titanic struggle waged by the Convention to rescue the Revolution from dangerous internal and external threats.[77] It ensued that the Revolution, cleared of the disturbing mixture of characteristics depicted by Staël, could appropriately become the foundation stone of a new French identity, the date of birth of a new nation founded on liberty. Given this perspective, many reservations were dropped and the perception of the French changed as a result.

Liberal journalists and reviewers diffused a rosy image of their countrymen because this served egregiously the needs of the political platform. Constant set the tone by reiterating on many occasions that he saw the nation 'full of an enlightened patriotism' and 'directed by an admirable reason', but that the French would revert to the bad attitudes of the past if the government embraced a reactionary course.[78] The conservatives proved to be the actual revolutionary party not only by regularly attacking the rights established by the *Charte* but also by refusing to recognize the conversion of the people to moderate and gradual politics, on the one hand, and to economic enterprise, on the other. Liberal and mild institutions, Constant continued, have changed our 'character': the gay, outrageous country of the past has turned into a serious and practical one, which cares about its interests and expresses its will in an ordered and effective way.[79]

---

[77] J. C. Bailleul, *Examen critique de l'ouvrage posthume de Mme la B^{nne} de Staël ayant pour titre: Considérations sur les principaux événements de la Révolution française* (2 vols., Paris, 1818); A. Thiers, *Histoire de la Révolution française* (1823–7; 10 vols., Paris, 1828); F. A. M. Mignet, *Histoire de la Révolution française depuis 1789 jusqu'en 1814* (2 vols., Paris, 1824). See Omodeo, *Studi*, pp. 253–77.

[78] See, e.g., 'Des élections, du ministère, de l'esprit public et du parti libéral en France', *MF*, 4 (1818), p. 15. Constant's parliamentary speeches are also relevant; see, e.g., 'Sur la loi d'exception contre la liberté individuelle' (1820), in B. Constant, *Œuvres*, ed. A. Roulin (Paris, 1964), pp. 1278–9, 1284–6. On Constant as a journalist and the reviews he inspired, see E. Harpaz, *L'école libérale sous la Restauration: le 'Mercure' et la 'Minerve' 1817–1820* (Geneva, 1968).

[79] 'Des accusateurs de la France', *MF*, 7 (1819), pp. 154–60; 'De l'état constitutionnel de la France', *La Renommée*, 1 (1819), in B. Constant, *Recueil d'articles: Le Mercure, La Minerve et La Renommée*, ed. E. Harpaz (Geneva, 1972), pp. 1236–7. For the virtues of the 'classe intermédiaire', see the speech 'Sur le projet de loi relatif à la police de la presse' (1827), in *Œuvres*, pp. 1351–2, where Constant summarized his argument thus: 'La tyrannie peut s'accomoder de prolétaires et de grands seigneurs; la classe intermédiaire lui est fatale.'

By striking this chord, Constant aimed to deny the conservatives' recurrent denunciations of looming revolutions and the ensuing proposals for restriction of rights. Related to this, the new portrait of the French permitted the triggering of an important rhetorical device, namely the appropriation of 'the nation' to the liberal cause. It rapidly became stereotypical to invoke the will of the citizenry to support a point, with the journalist or politician evidently claiming to be its reliable interpreter. Within a paradoxical political context where the opposition strove to defend the constitution and the party in office strove to subvert it, a free press was defended by liberals not only as a fundamental right but also as the single channel through which 'the nation' could be heard and political mistakes thereby avoided.[80] Although, of course, this is an essential mechanism of the representative mode of governance, its application in Restoration France was never devoid of controversy. While some regularly praised 'the nation', others regularly blamed and feared it.

Constant's approach was echoed in the journals he inspired. In the case of *La Minerve française*, the rehabilitation of the French was made easier by a longing for national greatness fuelled by memories of the heroism of Napoleonic armies. Besides a recurrent image of the people as thoughtful, anti-revolutionary, and, in particular, committed to the defence of the existing liberties, there lurked a eulogy of the French based on superior military and civil prowess. The commonplaces of French character were turned upside down as selected episodes of the recent wars were invoked to demonstrate that the 'new' Frenchmen could indeed be resilient, patient, and consistent. The people that had gone through the Revolution were 'destined for glory' because 'all the momentous events and alternations of success and misery have toughened their souls and given national character a fresh strength'.[81]

A major writer of both the *Mercure de France* and the *Minerve* was Etienne Jouy, a novelist and playwright of republican leaning who described the national mores in dozens of articles built around the (imaginary) peregrinations of an 'Ermite de la Guyane' through all of France.[82] Reflecting a renewed interest in the provinces on the part of the Parisian press, Jouy's *historiettes* focused on the

[80] See, e.g., 'Sur la loi d'exception contre la liberté de la presse' (1820), in Constant, *Œuvres*, p. 1338. On the *Charte* as the palladium of French liberty, and the crucial role of freedom of the press and trial by jury within it, see the detailed analysis by J. D. Lanjuinais, *Constitutions de la nation française* (2 vols., Paris, 1819). See also J. D. Lanjuinais, 'De quelques écrits pour et contre la Charte, la loi des élections et le droit de pétition', *RE*, 5 (1820), pp. 122–8, 309–14.

[81] P.-F. Tissot, 'Sur la constance du peuple français dans les revers', *MF*, 6 (1819), pp. 560–8, quotation on p. 563. See also J.-M. de Norvins, 'De la Révolution française', *MF*, 4 and 5 (1819), pp. 549–58, 111–19; P.-F. Tissot, 'Sur l'exposition des produits de l'industrie française', *MF*, 7 (1819), pp. 229–37, 401–16.

[82] See Harpaz, *L'école libérale*, pp. 11, 163–9. Jouy, who was admitted to the Académie Française in 1815, became mayor of Paris for a few days after the July Revolution, and was later appointed curator of the Louvre.

growing industry and strengthening liberal principles of the middle ranks, while paying special attention to the contrasting memories of the Napoleonic wars and the White Terror. Contemporary *mœurs* were also the subject matter of his two-volume *La morale appliquée à la politique* of 1822. This work, although heavily indebted to Helvétius and Condorcet, is interesting for the primacy ascribed to 'public spirit' in the making and unmaking of nations (Jouy's source was the traditionally republican link between public virtues and liberty), and, particularly, for a full account of the change of mores occurring after the moral corruption induced by the institutions of the old order was brought to an end by the Revolution. French *mœurs* have been totally regenerated, Jouy contended, by a fairer distribution of wealth and education as well as by milder laws; the character of the lower classes and that of women have especially improved.[83] The progress of liberty cannot fail to create good attitudes because liberty is intimately bound up with morality and *lumières*, and for this reason it brings about a comprehensive emancipation of civil society.[84]

Jouy's book was favourably reviewed, with special praise given to the chapters on French *mœurs*, in the *Revue encyclopédique* of Marc-Antoine Jullien.[85] This was an outstanding intellectual venture consisting of book reviews both on the natural sciences and on economic and political subjects; it pledged itself to a civilizing mission very much in a Saint-Simonian spirit. The stance that Jullien advocated – that science and industry should be the fields of peaceful and cosmopolitan activity after two decades of European upheaval – was closely associated with the new image of Frenchmen. A diluted Saint-Simonism provided theoretical backing to that image, in fact, as Saint-Simonian motifs flourished in the *Minerve*, the *Globe*, and other reviews. While, in Jullien's words, the social relevance of science and industry in all countries was 'the remarkable phenomenon of the age' and its effects amounted to 'a torrential river', the French were credited with behaving in accordance with it.[86] Reference was made to a new concern with economic enterprise, taken to represent a more general attitude of practicality and sobriety; an attitude which Saint-Simonism helped to set in the dynamic context of civilization.

Saint-Simonian principles and catchwords appear tailored to serve the needs of liberal agitation. The Saint-Simonian argument that work was 'a fertile principle of social life and morality' became the rationale behind the new mores of the French. It followed, for instance, that the social standing of the aristocracy

---

[83] *La morale appliquée à la politique*, II, pp. 320–80.
[84] *ibid.*, e.g. I, p. xxiv; II, pp. 311–12ff., 326, 337, 384.
[85] The anonymous review was published in vol. 16 (1822), pp. 54–62.
[86] See esp. M. A. Jullien, 'Coup d'œil général sur la Revue Encyclopédique', *RE*, 9 (1821), pp. 5–25. Jullien (1775–1848) was *commissaire des guerres* under Robespierre and later worked in the military administration under Napoleon. Jullien's career was punctuated by arrests and periods of exile; before founding the *Revue encyclopédique*, which he directed until 1830, he had created *L'indépendant*, later to become *Le constitutionnel*.

could not but be drastically undermined by a denunciation of its parasitism carried out with all the arguments and authority of 'social science'. Although 'paradoxical' and 'extreme' in his conclusions, many journalists held, Saint-Simon had grasped the motive force driving modern society – 'work considered as both the yardstick of the value of men and the source of human dignity' – and there was nothing visionary in it.[87] The *Charte*, then, came to be interpreted by many liberals as a sanctioning of the advent of a social regime founded on industry and civil equality, with the conservatives attempting to block the matching between social and political change. The political and social scientific viewpoints cooperated to foster an appreciative depiction of the French, although *industrialisme* also served the divergent purpose of spotlighting the flaws of Frenchmen (see the previous chapter on the economists).

A Saint-Simonian inspiration lay at the roots of the *Globe*, the leading and most sophisticated *revue* of the period, where it was repeatedly spelled out how the fundamental function of work was the creation of the 'independent individual who wills, acts, and suffers'.[88] Yet, unlike the *Minerve* and the *Revue encyclopédique*, the *Globe* was Anglophile and influenced by the *doctrinaires*, and for these reasons it appears more restrained in the praise of national virtues. For instance, the *Globe* paid much attention to Dunoyer's polemic against the French 'passion des places', as there was a general agreement with Dunoyer's idea that the ruled as well as the rulers should improve; and it was in the *Globe* that Rémusat first published his attack on the moral degeneration of the upper classes.[89] However, in these same texts it was also maintained that the moral condition of the middle and lower classes was rapidly progressing through the discipline of industrial exertion and the stimulus of better and more varied consumption. Judgements became increasingly approving regardless of the economic sphere as the *Globe* begun turning from its original cultural interests towards politics.

The position of the *Globe* remained more nuanced than that of other journals partly because of a concern with the education of the lower class. Charles Dupin's freelance contributions focused on the need for instruction and education not in the abstract but on the basis of statistical evidence. The moral potential of work was not sufficient to bring about both a peaceful polity and economic growth, as figures established a clear connection between the degree of achievement of these goals in various areas of France and the state of primary

---

[87] J. B. Huet, review of Saint-Simon, *Du système industriel*, *RE*, 10 (1821), pp. 326–30; C. Rémusat, 'De l'industrie et de la liberté', *Tablettes universelles* (1823), in *Passé et present*, I, pp. 190–203; 'Nécrologie: M. Henri de Saint-Simon', *LG*, 2 (1825), pp. 595–6.

[88] T. Duchâtel, 'De l'économie politique en France', *LG*, 1 (1824), p. 141. See also T. Duchâtel, review of Bonald, *De la famille agricole*, *LG*, 3 (1826), pp. 250–2.

[89] See the following articles expounding and commenting on Dunoyer's ideas: 1 (1824), pp. 203–4; 2 (1825), pp. 878–80, 974–6; 3 (1825), pp. 10–11; see also 3 (1826), pp. 298–9. C. Rémusat, 'Des mœurs du temps', *LG*, 2 (1825), pp. 1014–15, in *Passé et present*, I, pp. 349–55.

education.[90] Religion, too, was expected by the *Globe* to play a major role, in line with the teaching of the economists Malthus and Chalmers.[91] Yet Dupin went further, first by using crime statistics to argue, against Catholic harangues, for the superiority of current mores over those of the past and then by attempting a statistical demonstration of the imminent rise to dominance of a 'new' generation over the 'old' one.[92] Dupin characterized the younger citizens as full of respect for public rights and economic forces, having been brought up to practice 'social virtues' and 'civic courage' – in sharp contrast with the attitude of the previous generation. It followed that a silent but irresistible revolution was taking place, led by 'the ideas of the age'. This kind of 'revolution' alone could appeal to moderates like Dupin and the *Globe* authors. Two points are worth stressing: first, the mix of statistics and Saint-Simonism *en sauce Dupin* to which this review resorted in order to posit the suitability of the French to liberal institutions; second, that even the sober *Globe* in the end went too far, crediting the nation with an unlimited amount of 'liberal' qualities. This can be taken as a sign that the rehabilitation of the French was in the air.

The general election of November 1827 that defeated Villèle's government seems to have been a watershed for the *Globe*. It asserted in a celebratory mood that the election campaign testified to the emergence of a class of men who were 'able and committed, energetic and wise', and who associated in order to monitor local governments and the administration. These courageous Frenchmen were said to come from the ranks 'between the aristocracy and the people [*peuple*]'. The citizens have finally 'taken the initiative', in contrast with the 'vain words' and complaints without action of the past; the government does not look like an 'abstract being' any longer as the electoral frauds organized by the prefects have been targeted. Even Staël's question was taken up: yes, the *Globe* answered, the France of 1827 has shown by its innumerable individual sacrifices that it is capable of putting the public before the personal interest. What everybody should specially understand is that representative institutions are not automata but need 'a force to push them'. Now, resting on our laurels would be dangerous, the review warned; the notorious national defect of lack of perseverance has to be overcome, and, to accomplish this, the British provide a tremendous model of tenacity and civil courage.[93] Alongside this enthusiastic acknowledgement of the rise and aptitude of a vanguard, the *Globe* held an

---

[90] C. Dupin, 'Sur les rapports de l'instruction et de la moralité en France', *LG*, 4 (1827), pp. 397–9.

[91] T. Duchâtel, 'De la condition des classes inférieures de la société' (review of Chalmers, *The Christian and Civic Economy of Large Towns*), *LG*, 4 (1826), pp. 183–4, 219–21.

[92] C. Dupin, 'Des crimes et des délits avant et depuis la Révolution', *LG*, 3 (1826), pp. 527–8; C. Dupin, 'La génération ancienne et la France nouvelle', *LG*, 5 (1827), pp. 65–68 (this is a commented extract from the introduction to Dupin's *Forces productives et commerciales de la France*).

[93] 'France', *LG*, 6 (1828), pp. 169–70. See also 'Des conseils généraux de départements', *LG*, 6 (1828), p. 725.

image of the *pays*, that is of the mass of the French, as calmly and moderately advocating liberty and order under the Bourbons.[94]

Before passing on to Tocqueville, it is germane to mention three examples of treatments of traditionally 'Tocquevillian' themes drawn from the *revues*. First, Alexandre de la Borde's two articles of 1819 on municipal organization will be briefly considered. As well-informed pieces presenting a polished, unblemished picture of English decentralization and indicating it as a model for France, these articles laid out a fundamental element of the liberal platform in an archetypal way. Participation at the local level is seen by la Borde as the ultimate cause of the wealth, power, and liberty of England. From my angle, the essential point is the link established between 'public spirit' – consisting of civic solidarity, association, understanding of public interests, and a passion for justice – and participatory institutions. The class embodying English public spirit is the middle class, whose dignity and self-awareness result from service as constables or jurors. An important consequence of the local, part-time, and non-stipendiary character of administrative positions, as well as of their rotation, is the absence of post-hunting in England. The general lesson England teaches is that the qualities of the citizens make the constitution work efficiently, smoothly and cheaply, or, in other words, that a widespread concern for public affairs provides an inestimable 'moral and political' guarantee.[95]

That equality rather than liberty was cherished by their countrymen was common knowledge for the *doctrinaires* and those within their sphere of influence. However, views differed as to the interpretation of this alleged datum. Less pessimistic than his friends Royer-Collard and Barante, who ascribed the weakness of the social fabric to the isolation of equal individuals, and thereby advocated a prominent role for the 'social superiorities' in local politics and associative ventures, the journalist Rémusat looked on the bright side of equality.[96] Writing in 1826, he defined the 'social state' of France as a 'democracy' whose spirit rested on a distinction between *mœurs* and opinions: while the former were more uniform than those of all other countries, the latter diverged. Rémusat's intention was to argue that even the aristocracy had democratic *mœurs* (in their private transactions, or for sharing the national *sociabilité*, or for the value given to work) in spite of their political views – 'even the friends of the past belong

[94] 'Du pays et du ministère', *LG*, 7 (1829), pp. 545–6. In *LG*, see also, e.g., 'France', 6 (1828), pp. 361–2; 'France', 6 (1828), pp. 819–20; 'France', 7 (1829), pp. 195–6; 'France', 7 (1829), pp. 241–2; 'France. Le nouveau ministère', 7 (1829), pp. 503–4.

[95] See the two untitled survey articles in *RE*, 1 (1819), pp. 59–83, 264–81. See also A. de la Borde, *De l'esprit d'association dans tous les intérêts de la communauté* (2nd edn, Paris, 1821). La Borde (1773–1842) was a soldier in the Austrian army from 1789 to the mid-1790s, and a diplomat under Napoleon; during the Restoration he had two spells as a deputy.

[96] See Royer-Collard in Barante, *La vie politique de M. Royer-Collard*, II, pp. 130–7ff., 224ff.; Barante, *Des communes et de l'aristocratie*, esp. pp. 3–23; see also C. Rémusat, review of Barante, *Des communes et de l'aristocratie*, *LG*, 7 (1829), pp. 131–2.

to this century'. This situation testified to the happy state of the nation, dominated by a 'sentiment' of justice rejecting class prejudices and aiming at social cohesion and political tranquillity.[97]

The third instance of a 'Tocquevillian' subject is the political relevance of religion according to Constant. In that remarkable piece, the preface to *De la religion* (1824), Constant criticizes utilitarianism and asserts that liberty requires exaltation, virtue, and sacrifice, which he relates to a 'religious sentiment' consisting in essence of the feelings of infinity, piety, nature and beauty. This sentiment alone can lead men to do great and noble deeds and thus fulfil their nature.[98] In this context, which may or may not contradict other tenets of his, there figures an implicit but transparent indictment of the behaviour of the French between 1789 and 1814. Even if this censure does not come as a surprise to the readers of other writings by him, here Constant gave the full picture; this is the comprehensive critique which, although possibly implied, did not occur in the political texts.

Constant's interpretation was that the French had followed the precepts of a 'rightly understood self-interest' (*intérêt bien entendu*, an expression which Tocqueville would also use) and for this reason had been unable to found a free polity. 'This indifference, this servility, this persistence of a calculating attitude, this versatility in finding pretexts – is this another thing than a rightly understood self-interest?' A dominant concern with order and property prevented the Revolution from becoming the scene of generalized plundering but, at the same time, made legal assassinations easier. Hence there occurred a moral degradation which was expressed by servility in the face of a violent power and a *frondeur* behaviour when the government was moderate. The marriage of a daughter or the career of a son were put before patriotism and moral principles in the name of prudence. A natural effect of a rightly understood self-interest is the isolation of each individual, Constant continued, but human dust turns into mud when the storm comes. 'Institutions are mere forms when nobody wants to sacrifice himself for them. When tyranny is overthrown by selfishness, this does nothing but divide the spoils of tyrants.'[99] Tocqueville would argue that the 'rightly understood self-interest' of the Americans succeeded in making public-spiritedness the interest of each. Tocqueville's Americans can be seen as a solution to Constant's anxiety about the strict moral requirements of liberty.

Scratch the surface, then, and one discovers that Constant, the most brilliant of journalists, came to contradict the rosy image of Frenchmen which he himself had helped to construct. It is true that the Frenchmen he was talking

[97] C. Rémusat, 'De l'égalité', *LG* (1826), in *Passé et present*, I, pp. 355–64.
[98] *De la religion considérée dans sa source, ses formes et ses développements* (1824–7; bk 1, Lausanne, 1971), pp. 9–26. The ideas in the preface had appeared in at least one article: 'De la religion et de la morale religieuse', *MF*, 5 (1819), pp. 583–90.
[99] *De la religion*, pp. 15–26, quotations on pp. 20, 24.

about were those of 1789–1814, but one is at a loss as to how their successors could be blessed with 'religious sentiment'. In the end, the question about the civic attitude of the French received no positive answer from liberals in 1815–30 and stayed to bewilder and anger political thinkers. If the press presented an appreciative front, the search for a deeper layer of opinion cannot induce equally unanimous conclusions. What really counts is the way in which national identity themes are put to use, so that it is the complimentary reinvention of the French which is distinctive of the Restoration; but the suspicion that in some cases the logic of liberal argument pushed reservations aside finds textual support not only in Constant but also in the very book that ideally inaugurated the post-revolutionary phase, Staël's *Considérations*, which presented a favourable view of the French which was likely to differ from Staël's real opinion (see chapter 2).[100] Not to mention those who were cautious or openly critical, like the economists dealt with in chapter 3, or Guizot and other *doctrinaires* with their analyses of the equality of isolated and self-interested citizens. If a degree of propaganda in the handling of *mœurs* confirms previous findings about the inherent pliancy of this and similar notions, it is the total relevance of the subject within the Restoration debate that has ultimately emerged from my account.

5   Tocqueville

It is now generally admitted that many cornerstones of *De la démocratie en Amérique* were first lain by *doctrinaires* like Royer-Collard or Guizot.[101] Tocqueville's consideration of the 'social state' as an explanation for political institutions was no novelty. From my angle too, the originality of *De la démocratie en Amérique* stems more from the quality of the assemblage than from its single building blocks. In agreement with other authors considered here, Tocqueville's concept of the social state eventually amounted to the prevailing set of attitudes and ideas. What was the defining trait of democratic societies? A 'passion for equality', was his famous answer.[102] This passion

---

[100] In replying to Chateaubriand's *De la monarchie selon la Charte*, Constant wrote in 1816: 'Il ne faut pas déshonorer vingt-sept années de notre histoire, vingt-sept années durant lesquelles . . . ont a vu des hommes de tous les partis donner de sublimes exemples de courage, de désintéressement, de fidélité à leurs opinions, de dévouement à leurs amis, et de sacrifice à leur patrie. Il ne faut pas présenter la nation . . . comme une race servile et parjure, coupable d'avoir joué tous les rôles, prêté tous les serments' (*De la doctrine politique*, p. 288).

[101] In addition to Siedentop's works, see C. Rémusat, 'De l'esprit de réaction: Royer-Collard and Tocqueville', *Revue des deux mondes*, 35 (1861), pp. 777–813; L. Diez del Corral, 'Tocqueville et la pensée politique des Doctrinaires', in L. Diez del Corral et al., *Alexis de Tocqueville: livre du centenaire 1859–1959* (Paris, 1960), pp. 57–70; and Rosanvallon, *Le moment Guizot*.

[102] For a comment, see Furet, 'Le système conceptuel', esp. pp. 241–9, and P. Manent, *Tocqueville et la nature de la démocratie* (Paris, 1982), pp. 20–3. Furet speaks of Tocqueville's 'égalité

was part of a network of collective beliefs, which Tocqueville usually called *mœurs*. By that term he meant 'the whole moral and intellectual condition of a people'.[103] As Drescher has pointed out, aristocratic society was equally defined in terms of 'habits of mind'.[104] After Siedentop and other commentators, textual evidence is hardly needed to support the point about the pivotal role of *mœurs* in *De la démocratie en Amérique*.[105] The recurrence of Tocqueville's appeals to the explanatory power of widespread beliefs and ideas, as well as of people's 'instincts', 'habits', and 'perceptions', is equally striking in 'Etat social et politique de la France' and *L'Ancien Régime et la Révolution*.[106] Even his explorations in political economy pointed to the centrality of the interaction between public morality and economic forces.[107]

It is not just that *mœurs* are fundamental in *De la démocratie en Amérique*, but that there is little else there, the book's purpose being the attempt at a total moralization of social dynamics achieved through a radicalization of the perspective of previous writers. There is no lack of declarations of intent in Tocqueville's corpus: for example 'the more I study ... the cause of the changes in this world, the more I remain convinced that everything in politics is nothing but consequence and symptom, except for the ideas and sentiments reigning among a people, which are the true causes of everything else'.[108] In striking similarity with another extreme moralizer of political discourse, Chevalier, there lay behind Tocqueville's approach the idea that society could not escape destruction 'if the moral tie is not strengthened in proportion as the political tie is relaxed'.[109] In consonance with this goal of his, all the basic elements of his view of democracy fall within moral or intellectual categories. I am referring to both his agenda – how to associate the passion for equality with a 'passion for liberty' – and his recommendations – enhanced religious feeling and civic education through participation. That is not to say that laws and political institutions play no part in Tocqueville's system, nor that they have no influence on mores. But laws and institutions are considered only for their effects

des conditions' as a normative rather than a descriptive concept, as a 'passion sociale' and an ideology rather than a statistical fact.

103 *DA*, I, part IV, ch. 2, p. 300.
104 S. Drescher, *Dilemmas of Democracy: Tocqueville and Modernization* (Pittsburgh, 1968), pp. 27–8.
105 See B. J. Smith, *Politics and Remembrance: Republican Themes in Machiavelli, Burke, and Tocqueville* (Princeton, 1985), pp. 155–250; J.-C. Lamberti, *Tocqueville and the Two Democracies* (Cambridge, Mass., 1989), pp. 55, 187ff., 237–8; A. S. Kahan, *Aristocratic Liberalism: the Social and Political Thought of Jacob Burckhardt, John Stuart Mill, and Alexis de Tocqueville* (Oxford and New York, 1992), ch. 4.
106 See F. Furet, *Penser la Révolution française* (Paris, 1978), ch. 2.
107 Tocqueville's writings on pauperism are in *TOPC*, XVI, pp. 117–61.
108 Tocqueville to Bouchitté, 23 Sept. 1853, in A. de Tocqueville, *Œuvres complètes*, ed. G. de Beaumont (9 vols., Paris, 1861–6), VII, pp. 299–300.
109 *DA*, I, part II, ch. 9, p. 308 (*Democracy in America*, trans. F. Bowen and P. Bradley (1 vol., 2 parts, London, 1994), I, ch. 17, p. 307).

on people's mental habits, which are the determinants of a nation's political fortunes.

Interpreters of Tocqueville have not fully apprehended the radicality of his project. Tocqueville was a political moralist rather than a political scientist relying on induction or a forerunner of sociology. He built a system of political thought on the basis of moral judgement. The degree of confusion that exists about this possibly derives from passages like that at the opening of chapter 3 of volume I:

> Social condition [*état social*] is commonly the result of an event, sometimes of laws, oftener still of these two causes united; but when once established, it may justly be considered as itself the source of almost all the laws, the usages, and the ideas which regulate the conduct of nations: whatever it does not produce, it modifies. To become acquainted with the legislation and the mores of a nation, therefore, we must begin by the study of its social condition.[110]

But the straightforward dependence of mores upon social arrangements is called into question by the very picture of the democratic social condition as a state of mind which contributes with the utmost efficacy to the maintenance of society's democratic character. The citation conveys a wrong impression then. Hundreds of pages of *De la démocratie en Amérique* support the view that the democratic social condition in itself does not form mores, or at least not the good ones. Whereas 'individualism' appears to be a direct consequence of the democratic condition, patriotism and public spirit are brought about by 'external' factors like religion and municipal freedom.

As far as the French debate on mores is concerned, Tocqueville efficaciously assembled previously disjointed elements under the aegis of the dichotomy between aristocratic and democratic societies. Exemplary evidence is offered by his treatment of the type of 'public spirit' appropriate to each of the two societies. Granted that 'instinctive patriotism', that is attachment to birthplace and ancient customs, is a thing of the aristocratic past, he depicts a peculiarly democratic 'patriotism of reflection'. This is of a less generous and ardent, but eventually more fruitful and lasting, form, which blurs into the personal interests of the citizen. Concern for the polity reflects each citizen's awareness of the inextricable link between his own welfare and that of the community at large. 'Rational' patriotism springs from knowledge and good laws, and tends to be identified with the exercise of civil rights.[111]

Against this background, Tocqueville provided a graphic portrait of 'public spirit' in France in the long aftermath of the Revolution.

---

[110] *DA*, I, part I, ch. 3, p. 45 (*Democracy in America*, I, ch. 3, p. 46; trans. modified).

[111] *DA*, I, part II, ch. 6, pp. 245–8. See D. S. Goldstein, 'Alexis de Tocqueville's Concept of Citizenship', *Proceedings of the American Philosophical Society*, 108 (1964), pp. 39–53.

Epochs sometimes occur in the life of a nation when the old customs of a people are changed, public morality is destroyed, religious belief shaken, and the spell of tradition broken, while the diffusion of knowledge is yet imperfect and the civil rights of the community are ill-secured or confined within narrow limits. The country [*patrie*] then assumes a dim and dubious shape in the eyes of the citizens; they no longer behold it in the soil which they inhabit, for that soil is to them an inanimate clod; nor in the usages of their forefathers, which they have learned to regard as a debasing yoke; nor in religion, for of that they doubt; nor in the laws, which do not originate in their own authority; nor in the legislator, whom they fear and despise. The country is lost to their senses . . . and they retire into a narrow and unenlightened selfishness. They are emancipated from prejudice without having acknowledged the empire of reason; they have neither the instinctive patriotism of a monarchy nor the reflecting patriotism of a republic; but they have stopped between the two in the midst of confusion and distress.[112]

In this situation of transition from one type of patriotism to the other, the citizen is indifferent to such things as 'the condition of his village, the police of his street, the repairs of the church or the parsonage', which he views as unconnected with himself; pride for communal ownership and a spirit of improvement are unknown; everything is expected to come to him from the government; and, servile in front of the 'pettiest officer', he is only waiting for an opportunity to break the law.[113] Tocqueville held that the tendency towards democracy had progressed in the worst possible way in France. The most powerful, clever, and moral classes of the nation had made no preparation for democracy, which was abandoned to its 'wild instincts' like a child without 'parental guidance'. Its existence 'was seemingly unknown when suddenly it acquired supreme power'. Its excesses during the Revolution weakened it; afterwards an institutional framework still aristocratic in character was set up. The 'democratic revolution' which had occurred in society was not carried to completion through the implementation of the laws, mores, and ideas required to bring out the advantages of democracy.[114]

As regards America, its structure of government could be operated only by educated and experienced citizens, as its failed adoption in Mexico demonstrated.[115] The lesson America taught amounted to the absolute relevance of *mœurs* as the real foundation and moving force of governments.[116] In comparing Tocqueville to, say, Staël, one measures the change that had occurred in the French scene in two decades: while Staël expected a representative government to create good mores, Tocqueville, building on the basis

---

[112] *DA*, I, part II, ch. 6, p. 246 (*Democracy in America*, I, ch. 14, pp. 242–3).

[113] *DA*, I, part I, ch. 5, pp. 93–4. On 'individualism' in democracies, see *DA*, II, part II, chs. 2–7, pp. 105–26ff. Post-revolutionary aristocracy, however, is deemed not just blameless but altogether virtuous: *DA*, II, part III, ch. 11, pp. 217–18.

[114] *DA*, I, introduction, pp. 5–6.

[115] *DA*, I, part I, ch. 8, pp. 169; part II, ch. 5, pp. 235–6; part II, ch. 9, pp. 319–23.

[116] *DA*, I, esp. part II, ch. 9, pp. 299–323.

of Restoration thought, entertained no such hope, and few did after him. The eighteenth-century tradition came to an end, and, in parallel, the necessity to couple free institutions with appropriate, responsible conduct became an established truth. *De la démocratie en Amérique* is entirely devoted to illustrating this twofold argument, and, for this reason, is a milestone in my story. Tocqueville sanctions the transition from a perspective focused on the moralizing potential of liberty to one focused on public spirit as a condition for effective liberty. The following passage is memorable:

> Local institutions are to liberty what primary schools are to science; they bring it within the people's reach, they teach men how to use it peacefully and enjoyably, and how to embrace it as a habit. A nation may establish a free government, but without municipal institutions it cannot have the spirit of liberty. Transient passions, the interests of an hour, or the chance of circumstances may create the external forms of independence, but the despotic tendency which has been driven into the interior of the social system will sooner or later reappear on the surface.[117]

To characterize Tocqueville's brand of 'civic' thinking, an important element is the anxious emphasis he placed, first, on the epoch-making change represented by the collapse of the old society, and, second, on the risks that liberty was running as a consequence. These risks originated from a moral vacuum: now, 'everything seems doubtful and indeterminate in the moral world'. Not only has religion lost its previous influence, but also the kind of 'parental affection' linking rulers to their subjects has vanished as a consequence of 'the tumult of revolution' – the throne is no longer surrounded by the people's 'respect'. As nothing seems capable of mitigating the extremities of power, in the near future Europe might experience forms of despotism so oppressive as to be without parallels in history. In such a situation, granted that the single alternative is between tyranny and an ordered democracy, 'my aim has been to show, by the example of America, that laws, and especially mores, may allow a democratic people to remain free'.[118] The consideration of social circumstances, however, complicates matters. In a country (like France, arguably) where the traditional aristocratic society has collapsed, the lack of emancipating mores and beliefs goes with the lack of the material conditions necessary to sustain them:

> What strength can even public opinion have retained when no twenty persons are connected by a common tie, when not a man, nor a family, nor chartered corporation, nor class, nor free institution, has the power of representing or exerting that opinion, and when every citizen, being equally weak, equally poor, and equally isolated, has only his personal impotence to oppose to the organized force of the government?[119]

---

[117] *DA*, I, part I, ch. 5, p. 59 (*Democracy in America*, I, ch. 5, p. 61; trans. modified).

[118] *DA*, I, part II, ch. 9, pp. 326–30 (*Democracy in America*, I, ch. 17, p. 329; trans. modified).

[119] *DA*, I, part II, ch. 9, p. 328 (*Democracy in America*, I, ch. 17, p. 328).

Characteristically, the means by which Tocqueville envisages overcoming these concrete obstacles is a spiritual one. The people's awareness of the danger is expected to lead to 'great sacrifices' for the cause of the gradual growth of appropriate mores and institutions.[120]

Citizens' participation is essential, but it requires supplying them 'with experience', and inspiring them 'with the feelings which they lack in order to govern well'. France faces two necessary tasks: introducing democratic institutions, and 'imparting to all the citizens those ideas and sentiments which first prepare them for freedom and afterwards allow them to enjoy it'.[121] A public spirit suited to the democratic state ideally consists of love and respect for the laws, mutual confidence between all classes, recognition of public duties, and a propensity to voluntary association.[122] But it is inherent in the democratic mind to set some obstacles to the achievement of these qualities, like the 'envy' which makes the people reject the ablest and most distinguished citizens as rulers.[123] As Tocqueville's overall message is that democracy needs checks and direction to combine liberty with equality, so his notion of public spirit, unlike Constant's conception of the interaction between public opinion and institutions, is pedagogically oriented in his desperate search for moralizing factors. He was led by the principles that, first, 'there is no true power among men except in the free union of their will', and, second, that 'without ideas held in common there is no common action' to point to 'patriotism and religion' as the only two possible motivations behind a stable democracy.[124] The efficacy of religion is the prime object of eulogy throughout *De la démocratie en Amérique*.[125]

Tocqueville attempted to put his theories to work in the political arena. As a deputy (1839–50), he eventually became a respected figure in French politics, as his ministerial appointment of 1849 demonstrates. But, although his parliamentary speeches and political journalism abounded with public morality themes (some being specially designed to deal with them), he failed to get his message across, a fact which he was painfully aware of.[126] His recommendations focused on fostering 'the highest ideas and passions' to heal the nation of its indifference, materialism, individualism, and unbelief. As regards the means, there was a policy of *grandeur* which went so far as to

---

[120] *DA*, I, part II, ch. 9, p. 329.
[121] *DA*, I, part II, ch. 9, pp. 329–30 (*Democracy in America*, I, ch. 17, p. 330; trans. modified).
[122] *DA*, I, introduction, p. 7.
[123] *DA*, I, part II, ch. 5, pp. 203–5.
[124] *DA*, I, part I, ch. 5, p. 94; II, part I, ch. 2, p. 16 (*Democracy in America*, I, ch. 5, p. 93; II, bk I, ch. 2, p. 8). Incidentally, Tocqueville was at pains to distinguish modern democracies from those of antiquity.
[125] See, e.g., *DA*, I, part II, ch. 9, pp. 301–15; II, part I, ch. 2, pp. 16–19; part I, ch. 5, pp. 27–34; part II, chs. 15–17, pp. 149–57.
[126] See, e.g., Tocqueville to Beaumont, 22 Nov. 1842, *TOPC*, VIII, bk I, p. 487; to L. de Kergorlay, 19 Oct. 1843, *TOPC*, XIII, bk II, pp. 128–9; to Beaumont, 9 Sept. 1850, *TOPC*, VIII, bk II, p. 296.

contemplate a war against Britain, as well as decentralizing measures.[127] He also upheld 'educational freedom', namely the establishment of Catholic schools and universities.[128]

These efforts were not only ineffective, but also conservative in character. During the Restoration, the primacy of society had served to oppose privilege. But when Tocqueville, in accordance with his intellectual stance, ascribed the cause of political corruption to the nation's bad mores, one does wonder what sort of political programme he had in mind. He was confronted with the new regime's narrow and unsteady political basis, with the government swaying as it liked the votes in the provinces, and with the breaking up of parties in the Chamber enabling the government to secure a majority through the granting of personal favours. To account for all this, he wrote:

> Only those who neglect the history of free countries do not know that political virtue is not to be found in their rulers, whose ambition, egoism, and lack of principles are only limited by public opinion. Rulers usually have the amount of honesty which is forced upon them by mores [*mœurs publiques*]. Rulers cannot but be what the nation compels them to be, and therefore their vices and weaknesses are to be especially imputed to the nation.[129]

Tocqueville's denunciation of the passivity of the French was usually associated with a condemnation of illiberal institutions and practices; but in the end his arguments absolved politicians and laid the blame for France's instability and corruption on the citizens.[130] Although this may have been a fully respectable interpretation, it could hardly avoid implying an elitist standpoint, if not a sus-picion of indirectly favouring legislative inertia. There were also difficulties inherent in the stance itself: post-hunting for instance, a traditional polemical theme since the Revolution, was on one occasion made to bear disproportion-ate responsibilities.[131] Furthermore, it can be argued that what Tocqueville was really fighting over was the kind of passions actually held by Frenchmen, not their lack of passions as he claimed. On a broader plane, his prescriptions, like those of many others who have attempted to translate a judgement about

---

[127] On Tocqueville's colonialism and belligerence, besides the texts collected in *TOPC*, III, there is a famous exchange with Mill (1840–2) in *TOPC*, VI, pp. 330–8; see also *DA*, II, part III, ch. 22, p. 274. See T. Todorov, *Nous et les autres: la réflexion française sur la diversité humaine* (Paris, 1989), pp. 219–34.

[128] See esp. the 1844 articles collected in *TOPC*, III, bk II, pp. 560–88, with the title 'Polémiques à propos de la liberté d'enseignement'.

[129] 'Lettres sur la situation intérieure de la France' (1843), *TOPC*, III, bk II, p. 96.

[130] Apart from the important 'Lettres sur la situation intérieure', other examples are: 'Quelques idées sur les raisons qui s'opposent à ce que les français aient de bonnes colonies' (1833), *TOPC*, III, bk I, pp. 35–40; 'Notes, 1847?', *TOPC*, III, bk II, pp. 719–28; 'Note pour le Comte de Chambord' (1852), *TOPC*, III, bk III, pp. 465–7.

[131] 'Discussion de l'adresse. Séance du 18 janvier 1842', *TOPC*, II, pp. 197–207; see also 'Notes pour un discours', *TOPC*, III, bk II, pp. 208–12; and *DA*, II, part III, ch. 19, pp. 256–7.

civic attitudes into policies, suffer from the disproportion between the abstract generality of the problem and the necessarily limited range of actual measures, which despite being restricted in efficacy to the long term were invoked in the face of topical events and specific problems.[132]

Although the focus of this chapter is the link between the Restoration thinkers and *De la démocratie en Amérique*, it can be briefly suggested that Tocqueville's other major work deepened the perspective being outlined. In depicting the interaction between institutional reform and collective mentalities before 1789, *L'Ancien Régime et la Révolution* took the history of the latter as its main thread. This emerges not only from certain clear statements about French passions and character as determinants of the nation's political vicissitudes, statements which, extreme as they are, may have been motivated by Tocqueville's bitterness and disillusion after the coup.[133] In fact collective mentalities are the main actors on the stage, for events were said to depend on appraisal by particular classes and groups. More precisely, the Revolution's build-up was marked by mistaken perceptions and judgements, especially on the part of the aristocracy and the middle ranks. There was an exceptional hatred for the feudal system, when in reality the yoke was harsher in other countries where no revolution took place. But the visibility of the social divide was too evident for an equality-loving people. Vanity, individualism, and pride characterized the middle class and kept it apart from the people, with the result that neither solidarity nor public spirit could develop. Post-hunting gained the upper hand over productive investments, and 'this miserable ambition' was more detrimental to agriculture than taxation. The aristocracy, which still considered itself as the leading class, was in reality powerless and isolated; as Tocqueville put it, the aristocracy lived in an 'imaginary society' after allowing the king to take its political rights away and contenting itself with tax exemption and privileges in exchange. But the road the nobles had taken was suicidal, and they were completely unaware of what was looming ahead. As regards the lower ranks, they showed the incapacity of 'slaves' for self-restraint, and related ideas and habits, even when they got rid of their masters.[134] One may form the impression that Tocqueville was projecting his long-standing views of his fellow citizens back into the pre-revolutionary age; not unexpectedly, perhaps, given the thesis of *L'Ancien Régime* about the timing of centralization policies. *L'Ancien Régime* shows Tocqueville's balance between a 'civic' and a 'national character' approach leaning over to the latter side, as an unavoidable consequence of both the lengthened span and the absence of scope for participatory motifs in that period of history.

---

[132] In 'Notes pour un discours' Tocqueville wrote: 'Il est facile d'indiquer des sources de mal plus profondes que celles dont il est question dans la Chambre. Cela est facile, mais faire aboutir cela à de la politique pratique est très difficile', p. 208.

[133] *L'Ancien Régime et la Révolution* (1856), *TOPC*, II, pp. 217, 247–50.

[134] *ibid.*, pp. 99–106, 190, 152–8, 189–90, 245.

De la démocratie en Amérique can be seen as the culmination of the liberal thought of 1815–30, but with a caveat. Tocqueville's concern with *mœurs* had a progressive facet – political participation at the local level, in fact a common demand since Thermidor – but also a more ambiguous, if not altogether conservative, one. In France after 1830, insistence on mores may have served to enhance the intellectuals' self-image but also distanced the possible solutions of problems by moving the focus away from the overdue reform of political abuses and blatant social injustices, for which circumscribed socio-economic analysis and legislative engineering were needed. Tocqueville's spiritualization of politics marked French political conscience for decades to come, paving the way for a French tradition of masters of political passions which includes, for instance, Renan, Taine, and Durkheim, alongside other less worthy writers like Le Bon.

Great Britain

5   Between Whiggism and the science of manners: Britain, 1750–1800

People's characteristics in relation to institutional settings was a subject as important to eighteenth-century Englishmen and Scotsmen as it was to contemporary Frenchmen; yet the assessments offered in the two nations differed remarkably. A factor to consider is the variety of modes for the expression of political opinion in Britain. In France, writing *en philosophe* was a necessity for those who aimed at intervening in the political debate, since more topical and popular modes were not tolerated. Hence philosophy was, among other things, a prime language of politics. In Britain, the philosophical register coexisted side by side with a fairly free expression of political views in the press as well as in books which, albeit foreign to philosophic complications, struck a middle chord between a popular and a conceptualized treatment. Leaving aside the press, obvious differences separated the philosophical approach from that of those who wrote about politics in the light of the issues of the day. Adam Smith's *The Theory of Moral Sentiments* cannot be placed in the same category as Burke's *Reflections on the Revolution in France*. Smith's philosophical detachment in addressing manners and customs shared little with Burke's partisan denunciation of French mentality in the immediate wake of the Revolution. Burke's book is a long pamphlet, Smith's a comprehensive reformulation of the moral problem. There was a frequent contrast in contents, however, which was more important than any dissimilarity in genre, tone, or arrangement. Philosophers showed a complex attitude towards the set of arguments labelled as 'Whiggism'. As the ideological legitimation of the status quo, Whiggism encapsulated the political tradition of the nation, and thereby was the staple of the great majority of political writers.

This distinction between the philosophers and the others, which admittedly is a rough one, is put forward in order to mark out the attempt of some philosophers, most notably Hume, Smith, and Millar, to formulate the relationship between the quality of citizens and institutions within new and comprehensive frameworks. These were the ethics of sympathy and the stadial conception of history. Granted that the most evident thread running through the British eighteenth century is the link between British liberty and British virtue, the philosophers set out to criticize, complicate, and enrich this cornerstone of Whiggism by applying innovative perspectives. The philosophical enterprise brought with it a critique of current ideology. By contrast, the political writers to whom substantial space is devoted in the chapter, Burke and Hazlitt, elaborated Whiggish motifs, each in his own way.[1] High culture was characterized by this dualism, well exemplified by the cross-national agenda and fairly cosmopolitan approach of the Scottish literati, on the one hand, and the fits of anti-French hysteria recurring in less abstract styles of political communication, on the other. This chapter will swing between consideration of philosophic and 'Whiggish' literature. It would be simplistic, however, to suppose that the two were regularly in opposition, as the following sections will show.

1   Whiggism

Among the many different themes and perspectives encompassed by 'Whiggism', the most relevant one for this study is belief in the superiority of the English (or the British) over the French (the other peoples posing no conceivable challenge).[2] This belief was based on a contrast between a people living under a free constitution and one grovelling under a tyrannical government: the former was virtuous, the latter corrupt, with Locke himself providing authority for the depiction of the French as 'slaves'.[3] The connection between French absolutism and French vices was so customarily made as to suggest a relationship of cause and effect; yet an adverse moral judgement was also implicit, as the French appear to have been despised, rather that pitied as victims of unfortunate circumstances. On the one hand, the view that men make governments was certainly not alien to the British mind. On the other hand, a disparaging opinion of the French helped to define the English (British) national identity. This section exemplifies Whiggism through, first, the reconstruction of a more popular debate, and, second, an analysis of a 'philosophic' specimen.

The eleven editions through which John Brown's *Estimate of the Manners and Principles of the Times* (1757) went in two years, as well as the number of reviews and pamphlets it generated, demonstrate the profound, albeit fleeting, impression that the book made on the public.[4] The *Estimate* is a

---

[1] Yet, to indicate that the sketched contrast should be taken with a grain of salt, it is worth recalling that both writers began their careers with philosophic treatises: Burke published *On the Sublime and the Beautiful* in 1756, and Hazlitt his *Essay on the Principles of Human Action* in 1805.

[2] See esp. J. G. A. Pocock, 'The Varieties of Whiggism from Exclusion to Reform', in his *Virtue, Commerce, and History* (Cambridge, 1985), pp. 215–310.

[3] For a survey, see D. Forbes, *Hume's Philosophical Politics* (Cambridge, 1975), pp. 139–53.

[4] 'Nothing could be more popular than that work', Burke later wrote in *First Letter on a Regicide Peace* (1796), *BWS*, IX, p. 192. Brown later added a second volume and an *Explanatory Defence* (1758). The *Estimate* was translated into French with the title *Les mœurs anglaises* (The Hague, 1758), and went through two editions. The second volume was also translated. See D. D. Eddy, *A Bibliography of John Brown* (New York, 1971).

condemnation of the corrupt habits that, in Brown's view, prevailed in England. Leslie Stephen judged it, quite correctly, to be 'a well-written version of the ordinary complaints of luxury and effeminacy which gained popularity from the contemporary fit of national depression'.[5] In effect, Brown, a clergyman of sound Whig principles and a *protégé* of Warburton, was responding to a series of defeats at the hands of the French, at a time when recovery was not yet on the horizon. 'Our publick Miscarriages', Brown stated, are due to the 'Manners or Principles' of the 'leading People'. His premise was that the strength or weakness of a state, its security or the degree of danger it faced, depended on moral attitudes. These had the power to counteract bad laws, while even the best laws could never secure the state when virtue was lacking. Although Brown lamented the rise of 'effeminacy' in the higher ranks, he admitted that the common people were 'much more irreproachable than their Superiors in Station'; the problem was that the 'multitude' was incapable of independent action, being like 'a *lifeless Ball* sleeping in the *Cannon*', waiting to be fired by the aristocracy.[6] The causes of the corruption of the ruling class were misguided education ('the Pupil is not carried on from *Words* to *Things*'), the power of 'factions', and luxury. Granted that the French were equally corrupt, they nevertheless fought bravely, led by a strong feeling of military honour and unimpeded by factions. Contemporary moral crisis aside, however, Brown readily admitted that Britain was still the best country in the world; he could not help affirming that the spirit of liberty, humanity, and justice was alive and well, practised even by the higher ranks.[7]

Brown's blend of Bolingbroke and Montesquieu was given a hostile reception in most quarters. Among the angry pamphleteers there was also one 'Hangman' of 'Rope Alley, Newgate Street'. The debate exposed the rock-solid confidence of the English in themselves, and in the moral and political disposition of the middle and lower orders in particular. Most critics did not deny the corruption of a proportion of the upper ranks, but at the same time forcefully expressed their trust in the 'sour, severe, laborious, spirited, and masculine Briton'. Lavish praise bestowed on the British constitution went hand in hand with unwavering confidence in the bulk of the nation, where the 'spirit of the age' was most in evidence.[8] To explain that the 'middling and common people' were immune to

[5] *DNB*.

[6] *An Estimate of the Manners and Principles of the Times* (2 vols., Dublin, 1758), I, pp. 11, 18, 47–57; II, pp. 12–14.

[7] *ibid.*, I, pp. 13–17, 22ff., 67–75ff., 84–8, 92–128ff.; II, 15–20, 24–6.

[8] All articles and pamphlets were intended to be anonymous; see *The Real Character of the Age* (London, 1757); *The Prosperity of Britain Proved from the Degeneracy of Its People* (London, 1757); review, *Critical Review*, 3 (1757), pp. 338–47; 'Swithin Swing', *Letters to the Estimator of the Manners and Principles of the Times* (London, 1758); O. Ruffhead, review of the second volume, *MR*, 18 (1758), pp. 354–74; review of the *Defence*, *MR*, 18 (1758), pp. 608–15; *Some Doubts Occasioned by the Second Volume of an Estimate . . .* (London, 1758); review of the

depravity and corruption, it was argued that, if under a tyrant subjects were mere 'Hands', a free government appealed to citizens' 'Hearts'. Granted that France was a despotism and hence the French were brutish 'slaves', the conscience of every Briton testified to the covenant creating the nation.[9]

Pride in the middling orders was celebrated by Robert Wallace in a book which is by far the most comprehensive reply to the *Estimate*. Although there are good reasons for complaining of the men of fashion and politeness, Wallace argued, the middle ranks remain the seat of genius and honesty. If liberties were threatened, their cry of alarm would unfailingly be heard throughout the country. It is these ranks that underpin a free constitution, and this is why any comparison with France is out of place. Since a free constitution brings about bold and firm habits of mind in the citizens, 'security and liberty' are the best remedy for corruption. The factor which ultimately generates public virtue in Britain is the greater interest citizens have in the preservation of the constitution.[10] As an anonymous pamphleteer put it: 'it is an error to suppose Religion or Honour necessary to national Union: Interest will serve the Purpose. The more Men have to lose, the more strictly they will join to preserve it.'[11]

The motifs raised in the reception of the *Estimate* were well established. They occurred within a political context which clearly differed from that of France, first, in the greater degree of 'democratization' of the political struggle, and, second, in the moral bedrock represented by a positive national self-image, stemming from the 'Glorious Revolution' and Protestantism. In mid-eighteenth-century Britain, politics had gradually become capable of mobilizing wide sectors of the population through the press, associations, appeals to the people, and extra-parliamentary agitation.[12] Britain was a post-revolutionary society in which, although an oligarchic Parliament controlled politics (more or less effectively), homage was invariably paid to the principles of liberty and

second volume and the *Defence, Gentleman's Magazine*, 28 (1758), pp. 174–7, 211–13, 249–51, 305–7. See also John Gordon, *A New Estimate of Manners and Principles* (Cambridge, 1760–1), esp. pp. iii–xiv. Yet, there were also those who agreed with Brown, either in total or in part: see W. Rose, review of the first volume, *MR*, 16 (1757), pp. 430–43; 'Some Account of an Estimate...', *Gentleman's Magazine*, 27 (1757), pp. 166–71; *A Letter to the Author of the Estimate, on That Part of His Explanatory Defence which Relates to the Universities* (London, 1758); 'Britannicus', *Friendly Admonitions to the Inhabitants of Great Britain...* (London, 1758). See also *Another Estimate of the Manners and Principles of the Present Times* (London, 1769). Commentaries seem to reflect the turn of events in the war, with the bleak prospect of 1757 improving in 1758.

[9] *The Real Character*, p. 33.
[10] R. Wallace, *Characteristics of the Present Political State of Great Britain* (London, 1758). Wallace (1697–1771) was the clergyman, member of the Philosophical Society of Edinburgh, who debated with Hume the populousness of the ancient world.
[11] *The Real Character*, p. 34.
[12] See, e.g., J. Brewer, *Party Ideology and Popular Politics at the Accession of George III* (Cambridge, 1976), and H. T. Dickinson, *Liberty and Property: Political Ideology in Eighteenth-Century Britain* (London, 1977).

independence. There was an entrenched rhetoric concerning the vital political role within the mixed constitution played by 'free-born Britons' or Saxon liberty, with the whole nation being represented, 'virtually' at least, in the law-making process. Thus, the notion of an English (or British) national character conveyed messages and resonances impossible to find in contemporary France, where many still identified *le peuple* with the rabble.

Whiggism is a statement about the English in comparison with the French, but the criteria for judgement were universal in nature. There ensued an ambivalence between the parochialism of conclusions and the generality of standards. It is a main tenet of Adam Ferguson's *Institutes of Moral Philosophy* that any government should suit the character of the people it is made to rule. This character refers to the people's 'degree of virtue, or of other principle, on which the state may rely for the discharge of social and political duties'.[13] Here one has a straightforward affirmation of national character as defined by the amount of civic qualities it exhibits. This perspective represents a marked departure from that which was common in France, in spite of Ferguson's adherence to Montesquieu in other respects. The influence of Montesquieu was in fact decisive for the diffusion there of an idea of national character as an enduring disposition, objectively given through the effects of climate and government, and affecting all spheres of life – for instance, the French were *léger*, the English melancholic, etc. Although this outlook was not absent in Britain, the distinguishing feature was a tendency to appraise national character in the light of its capacity to achieve and defend liberty, and thereby to work free institutions. Not only the French, but also the Italians and the Spanish, were regularly censured for their inability to do so. Actually, public virtues featured in the French debate as well, but only as an ideal to pursue, whereas in Britain they were intended as a fact shaping the British polity.

Ferguson's standard is that of a self-governing democracy, made possible by a 'perfectly virtuous' people, bereft of 'adventitious' social distinctions, and inhabiting a state of limited extent. But he admits that 'no entire nation was ever known to be perfectly virtuous'. Britain is (implicitly) classed as a country of great extent, with a variety of distinctions of ranks – some arising from fortune and birth, some from talent – and where the people include 'the virtuous and the vicious'. The thing to note is that Britain was ruled by public virtue, although not in a pure form. As the *Essay on the History of Civil Society* shows at length, Ferguson envisaged a declining degree of public virtue in Britain, and the *Institutes*, albeit a quite schematic textbook, is equally no panegyric of his compatriots.[14] The French, however, are said (again, implicitly) to be ruled by

---

[13] *Institutes of Moral Philosophy* (1769; repr. edn, London, 1994), pp. 283, 292; quotation on p. 292.
[14] *ibid.*, pp. 293–7.

'vanity'. Ferguson speaks of a people

on whose vanity, and sense of personal importance, rather than virtue, the state must rely for the discharge of the social and political duties. A people amongst whom a continual adventitious subordination takes place, without any example, or any desire, of equality.
Such a people are not fit to govern themselves.
Their subordination must terminate in a prince or monarch.
They require monarchy as a bond of union, and as a source of honour.
While every one attends to what concerns himself, the monarch, for the preservation of his own person and dignities, must attend to the public safety, and public order.
The subordinate ranks will court his favour, and consult their own dignity, by actions, either splendid in themselves, or useful to the state, whilst they are serviceable to the king.
The members of the state are drawn together, and moved in a body, not by their love to the community, or to mankind, but by their veneration for their common superior, and by their expectations from their common source of preferment and honour.
The maxims of honour are not susceptible of sudden changes; and the dignities of family, tho' for the most part conferred by the prince, are hereditary; and therefore independent.
Both these circumstances oblige the prince to govern according to fixed and determinate laws.[15]

The difference between the British and the French is one of nature, not of degree, even if it is true neither that France was a despotism nor that the French were slaves as the Whiggish stereotype would prescribe.

As a pervasive disposition, Whiggism in my sense – free Britons versus servile French – was variously articulated throughout the decades of concern here. The parochialism of Whiggism, however, came under attack from the philosophical quarter. The view was expressed that the difference between the political arrangements of France and Britain was one of degree and not of kind. The mechanism of sympathy provided a foundation to the shaping of characteristics through the social medium. A sophisticated and comprehensive historical method, the approach to 'manners' in terms of economic stages, challenged any simplistic relationship between government and national dispositions, thereby favouring a cosmopolitan outlook. From radicals and conservatives alike, there also emerged positions which, in maintaining that English virtues were being corrupted by an alleged degeneracy of government and a new fondness for luxury, might at first seem to be an alternative to Whiggism. However, before the American Revolution nobody went as far as to believe that, although possibly faulty, the British constitution was anything other than the best on earth. By claiming to have created more democratical and rational constitutions, the American Revolution and, more especially, the French Revolution altered the terms on which the discussion was conducted. At these junctures other peoples were claiming to have created free institutions. The nineteenth-century 'French disease' would not be slavery but political rationalism.

[15] *ibid.*, pp. 297–9.

2   Hume

From 'vulgar Whiggism', to use Duncan Forbes's term, we move on to the champion of its 'sceptical' version, David Hume.[16] Hume's essay 'Of National Characters' (1748) would alone suffice to make him the most suitable candidate to represent the Scottish Enlightenment in my story, but his contribution to the theme of the relationship between government and the quality of the citizenry went far beyond that single essay. The roots of Hume's essay on national characters lie in *A Treatise of Human Nature*. Here he defines 'sympathy' as 'that propensity we have to sympathize with others, and to receive by communication their inclinations and sentiments', however different from our own. It follows that it is to sympathy that we ought to ascribe 'the great uniformity we may observe in the humours and turn of thinking of those of the same nation', rather than to climate, which cannot account for the observed changes in national characters. The force of sympathy is greatly increased by 'resemblance and contiguity' of country, manners, and language.[17] The central place assigned to sympathy confers a fundamental role on 'customs and habits' in Hume's philosophical universe, with education being a facet of these. The 'opinions and notions of things' we learn in our childhood usually prove impossible to eradicate, he asserted, adding: 'I am persuaded, that upon examination we shall find more than one half of those opinions, that prevail among mankind, to be owing to education, and that the principles, which are thus implicitly embrac'd, overballance those, which are owing either to abstract reasoning or experience.'[18]

The core of 'Of National Characters' is a devastating critique of the climatological theory, possibly a rapid response to the *Esprit des lois*.[19] Nine arguments are given to oppose 'the influence of air or climate' over human physiology and hence 'temper'. Basically, the boundaries of national characters coincide with state borders, and not with rivers, seas, or mountains. In addition, a people may change dramatically over time, as the ancient and modern Romans prove.[20]

[16] Forbes, *Hume's Philosophical Politics*. I have faithfully followed Hume in the use of 'English' or 'British' (as I have in all sections of the chapter, with all the authors concerned).

[17] *A Treatise of Human Nature*, ed. L. A. Selby-Bigge and P. H. Nidditch (1739–40; Oxford, 1978), pp. 316–20; see also pp. 427–38, 581–2. See also 'Of the Rise and Progress of the Arts and Sciences', in D. Hume, *Essays Moral, Political, and Literary*, ed. E. F. Miller (1741–77; Indianapolis, 1987), pp. 112, 114; *An Enquiry Concerning the Principles of Morals* (1751), in D. Hume, *Enquiries*, ed. L. A. Selby-Bigge and P. H. Nidditch (Oxford, 1975), p. 229.

[18] *Treatise*, pp. 116–17. See also 'The Sceptic', in *Essays*, pp. 170–1. The crucial theme of the uniformity of human nature in relation to different manners is dealt with in *A Dialogue* (1751), in *Enquiries*, pp. 324–43; see also *An Enquiry Concerning Human Understanding* (1748), in *Enquiries*, pp. 80–96. For a comment on the existence of both a common humanity and a difference among nations, see J. G. Hayman, 'Notions on National Characters in the Eighteenth Century', *The Huntington Library Quarterly*, 35 (1971), pp. 1–17.

[19] This is the view of P. E. Chamley, 'The Conflict between Montesquieu and Hume', in A. S. Skinner and T. Wilson, eds., *Essays on Adam Smith* (Oxford, 1975), pp. 274–305.

[20] 'Of National Characters', in *Essays*, pp. 197–207.

Hume also rejects the North–South cleavage within Europe: a glance at the map reveals that a warm sun could make men either lively or grave, candid or treacherous, refined or savage, as well as their languages either melodious or harsh; and, while the conquests of Northern barbarians should be ascribed to poverty rather than to native courage, the inclinations of Northerners to spirits and Southerners to love may be accounted for on 'moral' grounds.[21] The example of the Jews demonstrates that 'where any set of men, scattered over distant nations, maintain a close society or communication together, they acquire a similitude of manners, and have but little in common with the nations amongst whom they live'. If neighbouring nations have constant intercourse 'they acquire a similitude of manners, proportioned to the communication'.[22] That is to say that 'a sympathy or contagion of manners' makes national characters, Hume's starting point being the imitative nature of the human mind, which 'causes like passions and inclinations to run, as it were, by contagion'. The 'nature' of governments is the most important cause in determining the modes of communication and influence among men. Hume suggests that the 'persons in credit and authority' who first established a government have shaped, by their dispositions and example, the manners of succeeding generations – subsequently, people imbibe 'a deeper tincture of the same dye' through education.[23]

Sympathy applies to any form of social communication, so that, for instance, economic conditions shape manners, as do different professions; the nation is not the only possible setting for uniform manners. On the basis of this framework, so inherently flexible and multisided, Hume makes a 'sceptical' statement that flies in the face of 'vulgar' Whiggism: an English national character does not exist. Since the government is a mixture of monarchy, aristocracy, and democracy, it does not exert any definite influence; all religions are tolerated; the ruling class consists of both landowners and traders; and no coercion is used to make the citizens feel and act in the same way. This is why 'the English, of any people in the universe, have the least of a national character; unless this very singularity may pass for such'.[24] For Hume, national characters are not relevant to political or philosophical thinking. They figure as a fact of life which is worth considering because of its operational value: 'the common people in Switzerland have probably more honesty than those of the same rank in Ireland; and every prudent man will, from that circumstance alone, make a difference in the trust which he reposes in each'.[25]

This is as far as 'Of National Characters' goes. In other writings there are substantial insights into the English national character, which often emerge

---

[21] *ibid.*, pp. 207–15.
[22] *ibid.*, pp. 205–6.
[23] *ibid.*, pp. 202–3.
[24] *ibid.*, p. 207.
[25] *ibid.*, p. 197.

through comparison of the English and the French. The Englishman is said to be conspicuous for modesty, pugnacity, sensibility to 'the blessings of [his] government', straightforwardness, and good sense, though inclined to excess and bereft of delicacy of taste and artistic sensibility. Although the French had *'companionable* qualities' like politeness and wit, and were masters in *'l'Art de Vivre'*, Hume was altogether glad that 'more solid qualities' were honoured in Great Britain.[26] The causes of the two peoples' different attitudes were to be looked for in their political and economic circumstances, which amounted to a contrast between a 'civilized monarchy' like France and a 'republic', a form of government which England resembled in many decisive respects.[27] By setting moral and social standards, forms of government shape the ideal type of the citizen. In a republic 'it is necessary for a man to make himself *useful*, by his industry, capacity, or knowledge', while in a monarchy he is required 'to render himself *agreeable*, by his wit, complaisance, or civility'.

> In a civilized monarchy, there is a long train of dependence from the prince to the peasant, which is not great enough to render property precarious, or depress the minds of the people; but is sufficient to beget in every one an inclination to please his superiors, and to form himself upon those models, which are most acceptable to people of condition and education. Politeness of manners, therefore, arises most naturally in monarchies and courts; and where that flourishes, none of the liberal arts will be altogether neglected or despised.[28]

In France, where 'hereditary riches' make all the difference, honour, favour, and military virtue are sought. Conversely, in England 'present opulence and plenty' are the chief source of social distinction, and the qualities involved in successful commerce and manufacturing flourish, accompanied by corruption and venality. Different 'prejudices' match different types of rule, and each government 'by varying the *utility* of those customs, has commonly a proportionable effect on the sentiments of mankind'.[29]

As already mentioned, Hume made no secret of where his preference lay. He is famous for undermining many pillars of civic republican discourse, but his criticisms harmonized rather than clashed with his option for a 'republican'

---

26 'Of Civil Liberty', p. 91; 'Of the Balance of Power', pp. 338–9; 'Of Eloquence' (variant reading, 1742 to 1768), p. 622, all contained in *Essays*; *Enquiry on Morals*, p. 262. For the English predisposition to 'passionate ardour' and 'furious enthusiasm', see 'Of the Balance of Power', pp. 339–40.

27 'The republican part of the government prevails in England, though with a great mixture of monarchy': 'Of the Liberty of the Press', in *Essays*, p. 12; 'Whether the British Government Inclines More to Absolute Monarchy, or to a Republic', in *Essays*, pp. 47–53, esp. p. 51.

28 'Of the Rise and Progress of the Arts', pp. 126–7 (see on p. 127 the inclusion of England amongst the republics). See also 'Of Eloquence' (variant reading), pp. 621–2. In *A Dialogue* Hume gives a much bleaker image of the French (characterized by adultery, stubborn loyalty to oppressive kings, 'the superiority of the females', duelling, etc.), but the dialogic character of the text may raise doubts about whether this image was actually Hume's.

29 'Of Civil Liberty', pp. 92–3; *Enquiry on Morals*, pp. 248–9.

set of manners in the sense just explained. When arguing for the legitimacy of manufacturing and trade, and hence of 'luxury', he made a case for the moralizing effects of work, especially in manufactures. His reading of the economic sphere entailed nothing less than a new viewpoint on civilization in which *industry, knowledge,* and *humanity,* are linked together by an indissoluble chain'.[30] Yet for Hume there is little room for mechanical inferences, such as an unqualified dichotomy between liberty, work, and wealth on the one hand, and absolute monarchy, idleness, and poverty on the other.[31] He refused to view the contrast between England and France as one between liberty and 'slavery'. But the fact remains that different governments bring about different opinions: 'notwithstanding the efforts of the French, there is something hurtful to commerce inherent in the very nature of absolute government, and inseparable from it'; this is not the commonly alleged insecurity of property, but the lack of honour attributed to commerce.[32]

As regards the role of religion in determining the characters of the English and the French, the essay 'Of Superstition and Enthusiasm' provides a clue. Both attitudes were wrong. The English were typically guilty of the latter, the French were guilty of the former, since they followed 'the Romish church'. The difference was that, while enthusiasm could be reconciled with political liberty, superstition could not. Superstition prompted 'priestly power', enthusiasm opposed it. Much of the latter's fury vanished 'in a little time', unlike the power of the priests, which became ever more effective and dangerous. Another point of contrast was that 'superstition is an enemy to civil liberty, and enthusiasm a friend to it', with the consequence that the former rendered men 'tame and abject' and fitted to slavery, while the latter nurtured 'a spirit of liberty'.[33] It followed that the task of preserving 'the small sparks of the love of liberty, which are to be found in the French nation' fell on the shoulders of a group of enthusiasts, the Jansenists.[34]

---

[30] 'Of Refinement in the Arts', in *Essays,* pp. 268–80, esp. pp. 270–1. See Hume's ideal of 'the man of action and virtue', who acquires things 'by fatigue and industry', and for whom work itself is the chief ingredient of happiness: 'The Stoic', in *Essays,* pp. 146–54; 'Of the Middle Station of Life', in *Essays,* pp. 545–51, esp. pp. 545–8; and *Enquiry on Understanding,* pp. 8–9.

[31] See, e.g., with relation to France, 'Of Civil Liberty'; and, with relation to the welfare of common people in free governments, 'Of Commerce', pp. 265–6.

[32] 'Of Civil Liberty', pp. 92–3.

[33] 'Of Superstition and Enthusiasm', in *Essays,* pp. 73–9. For a definition of 'superstition' which recalls the common Protestant view of Catholicism, see p. 74; for an explicit indication, p. 78. See also *The History of England* (1754–62; 6 vols., Indianapolis, 1983), I, ch. 1, pp. 51–4, and, for a succinct account of Catholicism as the biggest stumbling block to a Stuart succession, see 'Of the Protestant Succession', in *Essays,* p. 510.

[34] 'Of Superstition', p. 79. Note the clear difference between Staël and Hume in their respective views of 'enthusiasm'. The latter writer was reacting against enthusiasm as the defining characteristic of seventeenth-century Puritans, whose interregnum had so severely shocked the governing-class mind that the polemic against enthusiasm continued throughout the eighteenth

The 'national spirit' of the English is a consequence of one the freest governments ever to appear on the face of the earth, and Britain is the 'guardian of the general liberties of Europe, and patron of mankind'.[35] As for the economy, English workers enjoy a measure of happiness that has no equal, thanks to a fair distribution of wealth: 'in this circumstance consists the great advantage of England above any nation at present in the world, or that appears in the records of any history'.[36] In short, if on the one hand Hume criticized the English character – though only on a single issue, that of its inclination to excess through 'passionate ardour' – on the other hand this criticism should be viewed against a quite traditional background, which does not so much qualify his 'sceptical Whiggism' as complements it with standard patterns of political thinking.[37]

This conclusion does not exhaust the implications of Hume's position. He believed in specific cause–effect relationships, not in national characters fixed once and for all. The interaction of historical and political circumstances, as well as of education, customs, and habits, did not lead to the construction of static, or teleological, national portraits but to the understanding of particular manners. For instance, Greek homosexuality came from 'a very innocent cause, the frequency of the gymnastic exercises among that people'.[38] This empirical approach connected with his view that 'the humour or education either of subject or sovereign' took second place to forms of government, laws, and institutions (a stance calculated to dilute the emphasis on civic virtue and 'zeal'). 'Good laws may beget order and moderation in the government, where the manners and customs have instilled little humanity or justice into the tempers of men.'[39]

century. It referred to a quasi-pathological belief in personal inspiration from God as well as to the religious and political consequences of that belief. On the relationship between the English Enlightenment and the themes revolving around enthusiasm in this sense, see J. G. A. Pocock, *Barbarism and Religion* (2 vols., Cambridge, 1999), I, *The Enlightenments of Edward Gibbon*.

[35] 'Whether the British Government Inclines More to Absolute Monarchy, or to a Republic', pp. 49–50 (yet in this passage Hume associated 'a magnificent idea of the British spirit and love of liberty' with a warning about the risks it was threatened by at the moment); 'Of the Coalition of Parties', in *Essays*, p. 495; 'Of the Protestant Succession', p. 508; 'Of the Balance of Power', p. 635 (variant reading, 1752 to 1768). See also *The History of England*, IV, appendix III, p. 370. See Forbes, *Hume's Philosophical Politics*, pp. 150–3.

[36] 'Of Commerce', p. 265.

[37] On the English tendency to extremes, see Forbes, *Hume's Philosophical Politics*, p. 223 and fn. But, granted that this trait was inextricably linked to religious 'enthusiasm', Hume stated that it had been 'under the shelter of puritanical absurdities' that liberty established itself in Britain: *The History of England*, IV, appendix III, p. 368. In his days, the spirit of civil liberty managed 'to purge itself from that pollution': 'Of the Coalition', p. 501.

[38] *A Dialogue*, p. 334.

[39] 'That Politics May Be Reduced to a Science', in *Essays*, pp. 14–31, esp. pp. 18, 25; see Forbes, *Hume's Philosophical Politics*, ch. 7 (entitled 'The primacy of political institutions'), and, for a treatment in the light of the eighteenth-century concept of the legislator, see the important article by D. Winch, 'The Science of the Legislator: the Enlightenment Heritage', in M. J. Lacey and M. O. Furner, eds., *The State and Social Investigation in Britain and the United States* (Cambridge, 1993), pp. 63–91, esp. pp. 73–7. The idea of a 'frail' human nature, especially when applied to public matters, was of great background importance here.

In the end, the relevance of manners to politics was derivative at best. Like 'all moral determinations', they depended on 'fashion, vogue, custom, and law', not to mention 'chance'. Once considered in this perspective, the contrast between the manners of France and England amounted (in *A Dialogue*) to a mere matter of balance: 'we must sacrifice somewhat of the *useful*, if we be very anxious to obtain all the *agreeable* qualities'.[40]

The concept of 'opinion' in Hume, however, undermines any straightforward interpretation of his position. In parallel with the idea that 'a tyrannical government enervates the courage of men, and renders them indifferent towards the fortunes of their sovereign', he maintained that force was always on the side of the governed, so that opinion was the ultimate source of power even under the most despotic and military rule. 'The soldan of Egypt, or the emperor of Rome, might drive his harmless subjects, like brute beasts, against their sentiments and inclination: But he must, at least, have led his *mamalukes*, or *pretorian bands*, like men, by their opinion.'[41] Interest itself, as in 'all human affairs', was subject to the rule of opinion, the antithesis between the two being solved for good, to Hume's mind, by the religious and political struggles of the previous century which had testified to the storming force of 'passion', 'enthusiasm', and 'principle'. A politician who failed to take account of the power of a sense of public justice or other similar 'points of right', would 'prove himself but of a very limited understanding'. Hume distinguished between an 'opinion of interest', concerning the feeling of the advantages or disadvantages brought about by the government, and one 'of right', which judged the legitimacy of existing power and property allocations.[42]

Thus it seems that in spite of all Hume's talk about the primacy of institutions, a door was left open for a contrary position: only suitable views in the citizenry could guarantee liberty. As a statement on the ultimate power of opinion Hume's stance enjoyed immense influence throughout Europe in the eighteenth and in the following centuries. As Hume knew well, opinions are different from manners and national character, with opinions being not so universally endorsed, yet more specific and subject to more rapid change. At the same time, the three notions are contiguous, and later authors would not always distinguish between them. Hume's discussion on public opinion was in all probability informed by

---

See, e.g., Hume's 'Of the Origin of Government' and 'Of the Independency of Parliament', in *Essays*, pp. 37–41 and pp. 42–6.

[40] *A Dialogue*, pp. 333, 339–40 (this is a part of the text which is most likely to represent Hume's own views).

[41] 'Of the First Principles of Government', in *Essays*, pp. 32–3; the quotation on the effects of tyranny is taken from 'That Politics May Be Reduced to a Science', p. 23.

[42] 'Of the First Principles', pp. 33–4, 606 (variant reading, 1741 to 1768); 'Whether the British Government Inclines More to Absolute Monarchy, or to a Republic', p. 51; 'Of the Original Contract', p. 486. On deference to established authority and utility as the two psychological foundations of political obligation, see D. Winch, *Riches and Poverty: an Intellectual History of Political Economy in Britain, 1750–1834* (Cambridge, 1996), pp. 146–7, 194–5.

two background motifs: the spectre of 'enthusiasm' and the question of whether the French people should be viewed as victims or willing slaves.[43] Regardless of this context, the view that consensus always plays a role introduced a degree of ambiguity into Hume's legacy, lending itself to divergent readings. In view of the pivotal importance ascribed to governments in the shaping of the mental universe of citizens, it may be argued that Hume was asserting the irreducible interaction of the two elements, institutional and human. At any rate, the principle was indirectly stated that peoples were always consonant with established governments. Put more strongly, this amounts to a view that it is the people's attitudes that ultimately shape institutions. Admittedly, it could also be argued that Hume's point was devoid of precise conceptual import, simply a memorandum to rulers not to disregard the subjects' will, or an invitation to see representative arrangements as the most solid in the long run, or a hint at the potential dangers to the state deriving from the difficulty in ascertaining the will of the unrepresented sector of the population. The section on Millar will show how the combination of a stadial approach to manners with civic humanist tenets resulted in a comparable tension in the attribution of cause and effect to men or institutions.

3   Smith

Adam Smith's analysis of individual and collective character is a development of Hume's. The two philosophers shared a concern with character formation, with Smith even more disinclined than Hume to apportion praise and blame to the English, the French, or any other modern people. Both authors used the concept of sympathy as a base for the social construction of character, and both pointed to the fundamental role of education in this respect. Additionally, the core of Hume's 'Of National Characters' – the devastating critique of climate and the importance of government – was taken for granted by Smith.

The *Theory of Moral Sentiments* focuses on the idea that it is only in the community and through the community that the general rules of morality can be formed: we are led to them by 'our continual observations upon the conduct of others'.[44] In searching for the judgement of an impartial spectator, men express their willingness to found their seeking of social approval on a standpoint which is common to agent and spectator. 'Virtue' entails an inherent relation to the judgements made by other men. The complement of virtue as a relational concept is Smith's view of society as a closely knit fabric of family, neighbourhood,

---

[43] In France, 'law, custom, and religion concur, all of them, to make the people fully satisfied with their condition': 'Of the Liberty of the Press', p. 10.
[44] *TMS*, III.4.7; more generally, see III.i.1–7. See K. Haakonssen, *The Science of a Legislator* (Cambridge, 1981), pp. 52–61.

and national affections. Only within definite social settings does man fulfil his nature and the moral life take on meaning.[45] An example of the moralizing nature of social contexts is supplied by 'the middling and inferior stations of life', which usually associate professional abilities with moral conduct under the pressure of peer judgement. The success of these 'private men' depends to a great extent upon 'the favour and good opinion of their neighbours and equals; and without a tolerably regular conduct these can very seldom be obtained'. In Smith's society, where everybody is bound to everybody else through sympathy and the 'external' viewpoint of the impartial spectator, the reassuring proverb that 'honesty is the best policy' is guaranteed.[46]

Mutual sympathy works as a 'selection procedure' for the adjustment of character and behaviour to the circumstances of society.[47] In each community, fitting propensities are encouraged and inappropriate ones are deterred through social sympathy and antipathy, respectively. Smith cites as an example the socialization process at school, through which a child learns to moderate his passions in order to gain the favour of his equals.[48] Collective attitudes are of various kinds. There are, first, those that 'we expect' from different professions and different ages.[49] Then there is national character, defined as a people's sentiments concerning the appropriate degree of each quality, and determined by 'that degree which is usual' in a given country at a given time.

That degree of politeness, which would be highly esteemed, perhaps would be thought effeminate adulation, in Russia, would be regarded as rudeness and barbarism at the court of France. That degree of order and frugality, which, in a Polish nobleman, would be considered as excessive parsimony, would be regarded as extravagance in a citizen of Amsterdam. Every age and country look upon that degree of each quality, which is commonly to be met with in those who are esteemed among themselves, as the golden mean of that particular talent or virtue. And as this varies, according as their different circumstances render different qualities more or less habitual to them, their sentiments concerning the exact propriety of character and behaviour vary accordingly.[50]

Since it is certain that all men sooner or later accommodate themselves 'to whatever becomes their permanent situation', national manners rest on national

---

[45] See, e.g., *TMS*, VI.concl.1–7.

[46] *TMS*, I.iii.3.5. On the Smithian 'prudent man', see VI.i.1–16. On religious sects forming circles where conduct can be observed and judged, especially in big cities, see *WN*, V.i.g.12. For comments, see D. Winch, *Adam Smith's Politics* (Cambridge, 1978), ch. 5. On honesty as the best policy, see Hume, *An Enquiry Concerning the Principles of Morals*, pp. 282–3. Among the Scottish philosophers, the centrality of social sentiments and trust in particular was asserted, in terms which might recall Smith, by Kames.

[47] Haakonssen, *The Science of a Legislator*, pp. 58–9.

[48] *TMS*, III.3.22.

[49] *TMS*, V.2.4–6.

[50] *TMS*, V.2.7. See also *Lectures on Rhetoric and Belles Lettres*, ed. J. C. Bryce and A. S. Skinner (1762–3; Oxford, 1983), pp. 198–9.

circumstances.[51] A general distinction is that between civilized nations, where the virtues of humanity are more cultivated than those of self-command, and barbarous nations, where the harsh conditions generate strenuous self-denial and self-command together with a contempt of the humane passions.[52]

'What forms the character of every nation', Smith wrote in the *Wealth of Nations*, is 'the nature of their government.'[53] In the *Lectures on Rhetoric and Belles Lettres* it is said that in describing the character of a nation 'The Government may be considered in the same view as the air of a single person; The Situation, Climate, Customs as those peculiarities which give a distinguishing tincture to the character, and form the same generall out lines into very different appearances.'[54] The effects of democratic and aristocratic government are called to account for 'the temper of the people' influencing the styles of Demosthenes and Cicero, respectively; Smith was referring, in accordance with character formation through sympathy, more to two systems of social relationships and patterns of advancement than to government strictly intended.[55] Education is another factor of character, both individual and collective. Its importance is conveyed by the famous example of a philosopher and a 'common street porter': the two 'characters' do not differ by natural endowment but by 'habit, custom, and education'.[56] In Smithian terms, education amounts to an institutionalized form of the impartial spectator's commands. 'The influence of commerce on the manners of the people' is dealt with in the *Lectures on Jurisprudence*. Granted that commerce brings about 'probity and punctuality', the Dutch are more endowed with these qualites than the English; but this is not due to an original 'national character' as some pretend.[57] Smith was possibly referring to the argument, widespread in mercantilistic literature, which ascribed Dutch prosperity to national dispositions, in the absence of a natural base. He held that 'there is no natural reason why an Englishman or a Scotchman should not be as punctual in performing agreements as a Dutchman'. The true cause lay in 'self interest': when business dealings are frequent, probity proves more advantageous than cheating. Holland being more commerce-oriented than England, Dutch merchants effectively set the tone of morals.[58]

---

[51] *TMS*, III.3.30, V.2.13.
[52] *TMS*, V.2.8–10. For an application of this view, see William Robertson's 'stadial' portrait of the native Americans. Their most telling feature was said to be their extreme independence and lack of sympathy. Savagery ends up as a reversed image of the community based on sympathy, which, one is entitled to conclude on the basis of Robertson's pages, represents the other extremity of the chain of progress. See W. Robertson, *The History of America* (1777), in *Works* (10 vols., London, 1826), where it makes up vols.VIII–X: IX, pp. 84–92.
[53] *WN*, IV.vii.b.52.
[54] *Lectures on Rhetoric*, p. 82.
[55] *ibid.*, pp. 154–62.
[56] *WN*, I.ii.4.
[57] *Lectures on Jurisprudence*, ed. R. L. Meek, D. D. Raphael, and P. G. Stein (1762–6; Oxford, 1978), p. 538.
[58] *ibid.*, pp. 538–9.

The variations introduced by national characters and manners in moral sentiments are limited in scope, however, and hence they are not very important. 'The worst that can be said to happen' is that 'the duties of one virtue are sometimes extended so as to encroach a little upon the precincts of some other.'[59] A well-known feature of the Scottish reading of manners is that it rested on a strong belief that the universal traits of human nature would ultimately prevail over 'custom' and fashion. 'Conjectural' history could not be attempted apart from this belief, which alone made 'conjectures' possible. Sentiments of approbation and dislike, it was remarked, are too regular in their operation to be attributable to the 'capricious' influence of custom, whose force is at best to modify rather than alter human nature. The connection between motives and actions 'is as regular and uniform as that between the cause and effect in any part of nature', according to Hume, whose philosophy did much to establish this view.[60] Confronted with the striking varieties of law, opinion, and habit which their historical analyses revealed, Scottish authors traced them back to the effects of uniform moral principles under the most varied circumstances.[61] For Smith, 'the characters and conduct of a Nero, or a Claudius, are what no custom will ever reconcile us to, what no fashion will ever render agreeable'.[62] It is the 'natural' character, so to speak – the appropriateness of the principles leading the impartial spectator's judgement – that is of paramount importance to the polity, not national character.

The characters of men, as well as the contrivances of art, or the institutions of civil government, may be fitted either to promote or to disturb the happiness both of the individual and of the society . . . What institution of government could tend so much to promote the happiness of mankind as the general prevalence of wisdom and virtue? All government is but an imperfect remedy for the deficiency of these . . . On the contrary, what civil policy can be so ruinous and destructive as the vices of men? The fatal effects of bad government arise from nothing, but that it does not sufficiently guard against the mischiefs which human wickedness gives occasion to.[63]

---

[59] *TMS*, V.2.13.

[60] *An Enquiry Concerning Human Understanding*, p. 88. See fn.18 above.

[61] See, e.g., Kames, *Essays on the Principles of Morality and Natural Religion* (1751; 3rd edn, 1779; repr. edn, London, 1993), pp. 26–46, 92–9; Kames, *Elements of Criticism* (1762; 6th edn, 1785; repr. edn, 2 vols., London, 1993), I, pp. 421–5; Kames, *Sketches of the History of Man* (1774; 2nd edn, 4 vols., 1778; repr. edn, London, 1993), IV, pp. 18–19ff.; Kames, *Loose Hints upon Education* (1781; 2nd edn, 1782; repr. edn, London, 1993), pp. 309, 322–7; A. Ferguson, *An Essay on the History of Civil Society*, ed. D. Forbes (1767; Edinburgh, 1966), part I, sec. 2, pp. 10–15ff.; A. Ferguson, *Principles of Moral and Political Science* (1792; repr. edn, 2 vols., New York and London, 1978), II, pp. 145–54. For Millar, see J. Craig, 'Account of the Life and Writings of John Millar, Esq.', in J. Millar, *The Origin of the Distinction of Ranks* (1771; 4th edn, 1806; repr. edn, London, 1990), pp. xxix–xxx, xxxiv–xli. For Smith, see *TMS*, V.2.14–16.

[62] *TMS*, V.2.1.

[63] *TMS*, IV.2.1.

Given this framework, the mental torpor caused by the division of labour in a commercial society is intolerable because, first, 'the security of every society must always depend, more or less, upon the martial spirit of the great body of the people'; second, 'ignorant and stupid' people are easy prey to 'enthusiasm and superstition'; and, third, they are more prone to rash and uninformed judgements of the government.[64]

A side of Smith's position should be mentioned although it was obliquely posited, namely, that sympathy and the impartial spectator referred to a social divide. On the one hand, Smith cherishes the image of a community of equal neighbours who know one another, who are ready to give help, and who naturally socialize because this is one of the true forms of happiness man can experience. It has been suggested that Smith's ethical theory is 'a defense of ordinary life', with 'sympathetic care' being 'the core of a reasonable and moral community'.[65] On the other hand, there is the corrupt world of the 'man of rank and distinction', who is depicted as scornful of virtues, vain, hankering after power and wealth, and deeming himself above the law.[66] There emerges from Smith's pages a censure of the great, who, in leading their lives apart from the social settings where alone moral sentiments come into existence, wasted the potential for good they held. This contrast amounts to a vantage point from which to assess Smith's criticism of the 'man of system'. His ideal statesman, the 'legislator', embodies a 'public spirit' with humanist undertones and 'feelings of humanity'. These consist of a concern with the happiness of 'our fellow-creatures', or, in more telling words, of an 'immediate sense or feeling of what they either suffer or enjoy'.[67] Even leaders, like great soldiers and sovereigns, should have the sympathy and compassion which arise from social intercourse, and which make public spirit 'more gentle'. Any form of public virtue which is merely abstract, that is which does not spring from a direct apprehension of the needs of the citizens, is dangerous because it is liable to take the forms of factionalism and fanaticism. 'The man whose public spirit is prompted altogether by humanity and benevolence' will adopt a moderate course, will respect the existing arrangements, and, following the example of Solon, will not antagonize 'the confirmed habits and prejudices of the people'.[68] But a serious obstacle to the humanity of rulers is that they are customarily in contact exclusively with 'that impertinent and foolish thing called a man of fashion', the vain men of appearances who set the moral tone in courts and drawing-rooms.[69]

---

[64] *WN*, V.i.f.59–61.
[65] C. L. Griswold, Jr, *Adam Smith and the Virtues of Enlightenment* (Cambridge, 1999), pp. 127, 144.
[66] *TMS*, I.iii.2.4–5, I.iii.3.1–8.
[67] *TMS*, IV.1.11. On the criticism of the man of system, see Haakonssen, *The Science of a Legislator*, pp. 90–2, 97.
[68] *TMS*, VI.ii.2.13–18.
[69] *TMS*, I.iii.3.5–8. See also *WN*, V.i.g.10.

4   The progress of manners: Millar and other Scots

As in the case of French contemporary thought, mid and late eighteenth-century British treatments of national character show traits of a genuine 'discourse', in the sense that authors assembled in various ways viewpoints, ideas and examples of Greek, Roman, and humanist origin. Throughout the eighteenth century assessing the relationship between citizenry and government meant picking and mixing arguments from ancient traditions of thought, which served to articulate the authors' situated goals. The quality of the assemblage could be poor, as not infrequently writers moved indiscriminately across the territories of climate, government, civic humanism, and so on, inevitably ending up with incoherent, self-contradictory statements. Kames's four-volume *Sketches of the History of Man* is a British case in point. As causes of national character and 'manners', race, soil, climate, a free or despotic government, the different stages of social progress, and the alternation of patriotism and luxury all figure there, but relative degrees of efficacy, or modes of interaction are never treated.[70]

Yet the stadial account of 'manners' which accompanied the Scottish theory of stadial progress represented a fresh development of wide influence.[71] Within this framework manners were related to the corresponding stage of economic, social, and political development on which they were thought to depend. Millar adopted this line of inquiry in its most systematic form. Smith made use of the stadial framework in the lectures on natural jurisprudence, but the degree of his adherence to economic causation – his 'materialism' – is disputed.[72] Other authors adopted the stadial approach piecemeal, with some occasionally

---

[70] It should be added that in Britain political and social factors were favoured over physical causes. Apart from Kames's oscillations between race and climate, Ferguson was alone among the major writers in endorsing climate. See Kames, *Sketches*, I, pp. 50–75, 99ff.; II, pp. 51–70; and Ferguson, *Essay*, part III, sec.1, pp. 108–21. For a criticism of Ferguson on climate, see the review of the *Essay*, probably by Gibbon, in *Mémoires littéraires de la Grande Bretagne*, 1 (1768), pp. 54–5. Falconer, Monboddo, Gregory, and Dunbar in particular dealt with race, climate, soil, and human evolution: J. Gregory, *A Comparative View of the State and Faculties of Man with Those of the Animal World* (1765; 6th edn, London, 1774; repr. edn, London, 1994); J. B. Monboddo, *Of the Origin and Progress of Language* (6 vols., Edinburgh, 1773–92); J. Dunbar, *Essays on the History of Mankind in Rude and Cultivated Ages* (1780; 2nd edn, 1781; repr. edn, Bristol, 1995); W. Falconer, *Remarks on the Influence of Climate, Situation, . . . on the Disposition and Temper, . . . of Mankind* (London, 1781).

[71] For a definition of manners, see, e.g., Kames, *Sketches*, I, p. 315: they are 'a mode of behaviour peculiar to a certain person, or to a certain nation'. According to J. G. A. Pocock, 'Edmund Burke and the Redefinition of Enthusiasm: the Context as Counter-Revolution', in F. Furet and M. Ozouf, eds., *The French Revolution and the Creation of Modern Political Culture* (3 vols., Oxford, 1989), III, p. 31, manners are 'the codes and rituals which were ethically necessary when humans were to live socially, in one another's presence'. Then, manners seem to refer to practices more than to mental dispositions – but, in view of the obvious links between the two spheres, a sharp dividing line is difficult to draw.

[72] See A. S. Skinner, *A System of Social Science* (Oxford, 1979), ch. 4; Haakonssen, *The Science of a Legislator*, pp. 181–9; A. Fitzgibbons, *Adam Smith's System of Liberty, Wealth, and Virtue* (Oxford, 1995), pp. 123–6.

speaking of a savage or an agricultural stage, or of the civilizing side-effects of commerce.[73] It is arguable that the stadial constructions of Smith and Millar were refined conceptualizations of a general idea on which many agreed, namely the social origin of manners. Yet, if it would be wrong to confuse stadialism with economic determinism, it would be equally wrong to regard stadialism as a view of historical complexity immune to moral judgement. Its dismissal would be extraordinary, in fact, and Millar's *The Origin of the Distinction of Ranks* is no exception.

Millar outlines his stance in a dense introduction. Different systems of law and government have their causes in

the differences of situation, which have suggested different views and motives of action to the inhabitants of particular countries. Of this kind, are the fertility or barrenness of the soil, the nature of its productions, the species of labour requisite for procuring subsistence, the number of individuals collected together in one community, their proficiency in arts, the advantages which they enjoy for entering into mutual transactions, and for maintaining an intimate correspondence. The variety that frequently occurs in these, and such other particulars, must have a prodigious influence upon the great body of a people; as, by giving a peculiar direction to their inclinations and pursuits, it must be productive of correspondent habits, dispositions, and ways of thinking.[74]

Here Millar posits 'situation' in geographic, economic, and social terms as the determinant of a people's mind, and hence of their political and legislative systems. Clearly then, there exists a 'national character', that is, a set of mental dispositions peculiar to each country. His next step is to argue that, since man has a natural disposition and capacity for improvement, and a similarity of needs and faculties, progress has everywhere followed a uniform stadial pattern. Successive modes of acquiring at first subsistence, and then ease, determine the establishment of property, the cultivation of 'feelings of humanity', and the recognition of rights; together with a gradual liberation from need, complex forms of government arise. These 'effects of improvement' in turn induce suitable alterations in taste, sentiments, and 'system of behaviour'. Millar's conclusion is that 'the character and genius of a nation' should be the same as that of any other nation placed in similar circumstances. For 'accidental causes', however, the manners of a nation may lag behind its material civilization, as happens when a society has remained for a long time at a certain stage, and consequently has become 'habituated to the peculiar manners of that age'.[75]

[73] Generally speaking, the contrast between barbarous and polite societies underlay much of the 'philosophical' thinking in eighteenth-century Britain. For samples of the versatility of the stadial standpoint, besides the cases of Ferguson and Robertson considered below, see Gregory, *A Comparative View*, pp. v–viiff.; Dunbar, *Essays*, essay 1; Falconer, *Remarks on the Influence of Climate*, bk VI; and J. Adams, *Curious Thoughts on the History of Man* (Dublin, 1790).
[74] *The Origin of the Distinction of Ranks*, p. 2.
[75] *ibid.*, pp. 2–5.

The strength and novelty of Millar's approach results from the dialectic between the uniformity of patterns of improvement, on the one hand, and the infinite variety of a country's 'situation', on the other. In this way the simultaneous presence of traits in common with other peoples and national peculiarities can be explained. When contrasted with the static conceptualizations widespread at the time, especially in France, Millar's dialectic has unusual explanatory power.

The above arguments are complemented in Millar by a criticism of the myth of the legislator, allegedly capable of creating collective characters by virtue of singular abilities. It is more likely that all those 'patriotic statesmen' were not 'actuated by a projecting spirit', but by a spirit of moderation; they could not do more than accommodate their measures to the situation and prevailing opinions of their countrymen. The regulations enacted by the celebrated Lycurgus, for instance, matched the primitive manners and barbarity of the Spartans.[76] Millar identifies legislators with 'men of system', and advocates the opposite practice of 'moderate improvements' deviating little 'from the former usage'. His position can be seen as a reflection of the gradualness of human progress, and of the close correspondence between its differing components. In presenting his book as a 'natural history of mankind' (although limited to some subjects: the condition of women, paternal authority, modes of government, and master–servant relationships), Millar meant to stress the subordinate role of the political element when compared with the momentousness of social and economic factors. Montesquieu's theory of the effects of climate through human physiology is also criticized in this introduction; like many other Scots, Millar did not go beyond a belief in the indirect effects of climate, as instanced in the customary story of idleness springing from a mild climate and a fertile soil, with the opposite deriving from a harsh natural environment.[77]

The device Millar employs to trace bygone manners is conjecture: having outlined the characteristics of, say, savage life with respect to economic activity and social organization, he infers the manners of savages from these characteristics. Since a savage is constantly exposed to many dangers and hardships, any refinement of sentiments and pleasures is unlikely to occur, 'the passions of sex' have no scope, and as a result the condition of women is miserable.[78] These inferences may not be novel, but the reader perceives throughout the book that Millar is applying a precise pattern of reasoning. The same causal chains are regularly employed, but no *a priori* scheme limits the appraisal of social and cultural complexity. To continue the example, he shows how the advent of

---

[76] *ibid.*, pp. 5–8. Here Millar agrees with Ferguson, *Essay*, part III, sec. 2, p. 124.
[77] *The Origin of the Distinction of Ranks*, pp. 8–11.
[78] *ibid.*, pp. 15–46. When the progress of manufactures and commerce takes place, with all its social and moral concomitants, women obtain 'that rank and station which appears most agreeable to reason', and this condition shapes women's manners and sentiments accordingly, pp. 88–98.

the practice of taming and pasturing cattle (with related changes in the social structure) led to new views on the intercourse of the sexes; later, the introduction of agriculture altered those views again; and so on.[79] At the same time the stadial scheme is flexibly applied, since it is evident that all 'polished' nations must not have passed through all stages.[80] Millar considered the attachment of men to established habits as a natural characteristic, and thereby stressed how difficult it was to change them under any circumstances.

For Millar, manners are always social manners, in the non-banal sense that the economy, social organization, social ranks, and manners tend to evolve as a whole. The following passage exemplifies well this core stance, and also hints at the two-way causal relationships binding the material with the cultural facets of social life:

When men begin to disuse their ancient barbarous practices, when their attention is not wholly engrossed by the pursuit of military reputation, when they have made some progress in arts, and have attained to a proportional degree of refinement, they are necessarily led to set a value upon those female accomplishments and virtues which have so much influence upon every species of improvement, and which contribute in so many different ways to multiply the comforts of life. In this situation, the women become, neither the slaves, nor the idols of the other sex, but the friends and companions.[81]

A point to be stressed is the 'concrete' nature, so to speak, of what Millar calls 'the character and manners of the people'. He put forward a genealogy of certain mental attitudes (towards women, paternal authority, etc.) by investigating their social foundations, and in so doing distanced himself from the practice of making abstract statements about national characters as all-encompassing portraits of peoples. He focused on specific manners originating from specific aspects of life (but nothing forbade their union *a posteriori* under the umbrella of 'national character'). This analytical approach went with a choice of topics representing the social at its most profound.[82] Underlying all this, there was Millar's choice of an ideal-typical history, independent of particular national histories and utilizing a theoretical model valid for all such histories. It was quite logical for him to write *An Historical View of the English Government* after *The Origin of the Distinction of Ranks*.

Once Millar has been congratulated on his method, which some have regarded as an anticipation of modern 'social scientific' procedures, it remains

---

[79] *ibid.*, pp. 57–66ff.
[80] As Craig paraphrases Millar's lectures on jurisprudence: 'All [nations] have not passed through exactly the same stages of improvement; all have not advanced with equal rapidity; some have remained long stationary at an early period of their course; while others, hurrying on with rapid strides at first, have appeared to repose for a while at a more advanced station, from which they have again proceeded with increased celerity and vigour.' Craig, 'Account', p. xxxvii.
[81] *The Origin of the Distinction of Ranks*, p. 89.
[82] Compare Smith, *Lectures on Jurisprudence*, pp. 141–99, 438–58.

to address his civic humanism. There was a point in the parallel progress of wealth and manners beyond which the two separated and opulence entailed moral corruption through luxury. In his own words, 'there are certain limits beyond which it is impossible to push the real improvements arising from wealth and opulence'. The 'debauchery' of Rome 'at the end of the Commonwealth' was cited as evidence, while France figured as the clearest contemporary illustration – but England was at risk too.[83] A tendency towards voluptuous pleasures characterized all contemporary Europe, the general effect of which was 'to turn the attention, from the pursuits of business or ambition, to the amusements of gallantry; or rather to convert these last into a serious occupation'.[84] The fall into disuse of militias was a more specific consequence, cooperating with 'effeminacy' in the strengthening of monarchical power[85] – a trend which Millar acutely feared, in spite of the antidotes which his own stance had led him to identify. *The Origin of the Distinction of Ranks* features a sketch of the emancipation of labour through the liberating forces of improved agriculture, manufactures, trades, and professions. Whereas the exclusively agricultural economy of 'rude ages' placed most peoples in a state of dependence, inducing submission, veneration for the master, and even pride in their servile obedience, the advent of the 'arts' entailed middle-rank independence and the growth of a free spirit. The insatiable addiction to luxury and idleness of the great would sooner or later reduce them to poverty, in parallel with the rise of 'the frugal and industrious merchant'.[86] But, in spite of the economic foundations of his view of progress, Millar did not trust economic forces to deliver liberty. He kept faith with patriotism.[87] When 'a strong disposition to pleasure' intervened, the positive moral consequences of refinement came to an end, corruption spread, and people were obliged to have recourse to public virtues to put progress back on track. Liberty was not a mechanical product of refinement – liberty did exist in states, like those of antiquity, which had made inconsiderable progress in the arts – although the habits of independence it required were prepared by commerce and manufactures.

In *An Historical View of the English Government* Millar applied his historical and economic approach to the understanding of the 'national characters' of the Scots, the English, and the Irish. He intended to defend both his countrymen and the Irish from English accusations, and to warn the English against the

---

[83] *The Origin of the Distinction of Ranks*, pp. 99–108, 138–9; quotation on p. 101.
[84] *ibid.*, p. 108.
[85] For militias and standing armies, see *ibid.*, pp. 220–5; for Millar's pessimism, see pp. 236–42 (however, in Britain the Revolution 'at last produced a popular government, after the best model, perhaps, which is practicable in an extensive country', p. 240).
[86] *ibid.*, pp. 230–5, 261–81; but see the whole ch. 6, addressing the master–servant relationship.
[87] Patriotism, at any rate, could really flourish only in small states; the liberty enjoyed by the ancient republics testified to this: *ibid.*, pp. 236–40. In *An Historical View of the English Government* (1787; 4th edn, 4 vols., London 1812), Millar dealt with the historical conditions which had made a free government in the extensive British Isles possible.

allure of monarchical patronage. He was at pains to explain that the Scottish traits stigmatized by the English were the unfavourable side of an intelligent and sagacious disposition, induced by 'a state of rudeness and simplicity' which contrasted with the manufactures and commerce of England and the ensuing narrow-mindedness of the people.[88] Apart from any specific conclusion, these pages point to the political importance he ascribed to the mental traits of the three populations of Britain. Their different original 'situations' as well as their different histories had determined their peculiar attitudes. These attitudes could not be subsumed under the English character, and should be given full consideration when devising policies. He endorsed Hume's dictum that every government was founded on opinion, 'the general voice of the community'.[89] The danger of an Anglo-centred perspective was especially relevant in the case of Ireland, as a brief further discussion of Millar in the next chapter will illustrate. While 'manners' figure prominently as effects in his ideal-typical reconstructions, public morality as a political factor fully emerges when he tackles questions of topical relevance.

When wealth turns into 'opulence' the moral register of patriotism comes forcefully into play. There is a fuzzy area in Millar's texts where historical narrative ends and a political argument for modern Britain begins. The substance of that argument appears to be a reflection on the existing set of habits and opinions. The ultimate determinants of political life are in fact patriotism, martial spirit, 'the spirit of liberty', 'courage', 'fortitude', avarice, 'the mercantile spirit', and so on. In France, absolute rule had managed to corrupt the people to the point that they were happy with their condition; this effect was not an exception, but a requisite of despotic government.

The people, in short, must be made to exult in that power by which they are kept in subjection, to regard their own glory as involved in that of their *grand monarque*, and their own debasement and servitude, as compensated by the splendour of his prerogative, and the extent of his dominion. Experience has shewn that by long custom, and by the influence of example, such a national spirit is not unattainable; nay, that sentiments of loyalty and affection to a despot, have, in the history of the world, and even of civilized nations, been more prevalent than a sense of liberty and independence.[90]

Conversely, liberty elevated and dignified a people, and the British government was the best in the world. However, Millar denounced royal patronage as likely

---

[88] *An Historical View*, III, pp. 87–96ff., and IV, pp. 152–3 (on Scottish character); IV, pp. 1–68 (on Irish history; on Irish character, see esp. pp. 8–17, 50–1); IV, pp. 94, 194–200, 212–14, 230ff., 246–53, 371, 375 (on English character). On the dangerous consequences of the division of labour on mental development, see III, pp. 90–1; IV, pp. 145–61. Compare Smith, *Lectures on Jurisprudence*, pp. 539–40.

[89] *An Historical View*, III, p. 329.

[90] *ibid.*, III, p. 350. Compare *Letters of Crito, on the Causes, Objects, and Consequences, of the Present War* (1796), in J. Millar, *Letters of Crito e Letters of Sidney*, ed. V. Merolle (Milan, 1984), pp. 46–50.

to create 'habits of dependence' in 'a mercantile people' like the English – 'by a people of this description, no opportunity of earning a penny is to be lost'. In a commercial country the attitudes of tradesmen – avarice, a 'coarse' honesty, self-interest, lack of solidarity and generosity – were communicated to every member of the community.[91] Patronage must be opposed because it amounted to a serious attack on what appears to be the ultimate variable of politics, 'national character', where this is assessed against the yardstick of civic virtues. Millar extended his analysis to the private sphere, where family life and friendship risked being debased by an all-pervasive utilitarian viewpoint which, in spite of all its adherence to the rules of justice, could not lead to happiness.[92]

Ferguson's *Essay on the History of Civil Society* distinguishes between 'savage' and 'barbarous' nations. The former

have little attention to property, and scarcely any beginnings of subordination or government. [The latter] having possessed themselves of herds, and depending for their provision on pasture, know what it is to be poor and rich. They know the relations of patron and client, of servant and master, and suffer themselves to be classed according to their measures of wealth. This distinction must create a material difference of character, and may furnish two separate heads, under which to consider the history of mankind in their rudest state . . .[93]

The manners, mental attitudes, and habits belonging to these states are reconstructed in historical and anthropological detail, mainly through the reports of Charlevoix and Lafitau on the North American tribes and through Tacitus and other Latin authors. Ferguson deals with the sexual roles, the sense of equality and honour, warlike values, independence, the culture of giving and receiving gifts, phlegm and composure, candour, altruism, and so on, of the 'savage' peoples; and much attention is also paid to the peculiar dispositions of 'barbarians'.[94] But when polished societies come under discussion, this complex and multisided mode of analysis is abandoned, and national characters appear to consist only of the transcendent values of civic humanism which Ferguson cherished in a Christian-Stoic, vitalist version.[95] These values are ahistorical because all societies could not but rest on them, from Greece and Rome to the nations of modern Europe. Even early tribes could not entirely dispense with them after the introduction of private property.[96] The thread running

[91] 'Political Consequences of the Revolution', in *An Historical View*, IV, pp. 69–101, esp. pp. 78–9ff., 94–5; 'The Effects of Commerce and Manufactures, and of Opulence and Civilization, upon the Morals of a People', in *An Historical View*, IV, pp. 174–265, esp. pp. 188–200, 246–8.
[92] 'The Effects of Commerce', pp. 248–53ff.
[93] *Essay*, part II, sec. 2, pp. 81–2.
[94] *ibid.*, part II, sec. 2, 'Of rude nations prior to the establishment of property', pp. 81–96; and part II, sec. 3, 'Of rude nations, under the impressions of property and interest', pp. 96–107.
[95] See D. Forbes, 'Introduction', in Ferguson, *Essay*, pp. xxviii–xxx. For Ferguson's disparagement of 'politeness', see *Essay*, part VI, sec. 4, p. 256.
[96] *Essay*, part II, sec. 3, pp. 102–4; part VI, sec. 1, pp. 241–2.

through the history of civil society is a moral and 'republican' one, regardless, in practice, of stadial differences. What characterizes developed commercial societies in the course of history is a special need for civic values in the face of an increasing 'desire of profit', 'the separation of professions', individualism, hedonism, and 'effeminacy'.

Clearly enough, in addressing polished societies Ferguson had a point to press, while primitive manners allowed for a more scholarly treatment. It is not difficult to identify this point with 'corruption', to which the last two parts of the *Essay* are devoted. The dialectic of patriotism and degeneration is unsuitable for assessing 'savage' communities where 'decay' can have little meaning. There is more than a lack of corruption in early societies, however, since Ferguson places an appreciative emphasis on the 'vigour of spirit' of the primitive man. His energy represents the original foundation of an attitude invariably necessary for maintaining national independence and freedom. A detailed survey of the forms in which savage and barbaric vigour came about is therefore appropriate. But in any state of arts and commerce, the preference for private advantage and pleasure over public concerns looms large; hence the eternal struggle between public virtue and decay becomes an all-encompassing perspective.[97] The introduction of property is the real divide – 'the individual having now found a separate interest, the bands of society must become less firm'.[98] This criterion being inadequate to organize the study of history proper, Ferguson's account of the progress of civilization looks like a philosophy of history, and, at times, it takes up the character of a jeremiad calling for moral regeneration.[99]

A celebrated application of stadial tenets is the fourth book of William Robertson's *History of America* on the native Americans. The same work, however, begins with a history of the European 'spirit of discovery' since the Egyptians, in which a materialist approach was clearly not Robertson's goal. Linking developments in the spirit of discovery to economic and social arrangements proved problematic when refined ages were addressed. He progressively abandoned that perspective and made the vicissitudes of that spirit relatively independent of social circumstances.[100] Robertson was a consummate historian in the classic mould rather than one of the 'sociological' branch of the Scottish Enlightenment; however, a dividing line between conjectural and narrative history may be difficult to draw, not least in view of the versatility of stadial–materialist theory, which was variously diluted. There is a basic Scottish position on the relationship between 'manners' and society, with

---

[97] See also Ferguson's application of these views to Roman history: *The History of the Progress and Termination of the Roman Republic* (1783; 5 vols., Edinburgh, 1813).
[98] *Essay*, part II, sec. 3, p. 98.
[99] For an example of Ferguson's jeremiads, see *ibid.*, part VI, sec. 3, pp. 252–3ff. For comments, see R. B. Sher, *Church and University in the Scottish Enlightenment* (Edinburgh, 1985), pp. 43, 206–12; Pocock, *Barbarism*, II, *Narratives of Civil Government*, pp. 330–1, 346–8.
[100] *The History of America*, VIII, pp. 1–60.

'national character' being apparently the compound result of the set of manners embraced by a people. Robertson's *View of the Progress of Society in Europe* neatly expresses the tenets of this position. The pivotal idea is this: 'the characters of nations depend on the state of society in which they live, and on the political institutions established among them'. An important corollary of this is that 'the human mind, whenever it is placed in the same situation, will, in ages the most distant, and in countries the most remote, assume the same form, and be distinguished by the same manners'.[101] As products of social structures, all established customs, even the most absurd, are firmly rooted in minds, and thereby 'the bare promulgation of laws and statutes' cannot change them.[102] Rather, manners change by virtue of the same interrelated forces pushing European refinement forward: commerce, security of property, a taste for liberty, science, literature, etc. Typically, manners are effects, but also secondary causes, of the progress of civilization.[103] From this set of views – underpinned by the Scots' dilution of the power of climate (Ferguson is an exception) – a cosmopolitan outlook took shape quite naturally.[104]

5   Burke and his enemies: prejudice and reason in a revolutionary age

The target Burke had in mind in writing the *Reflections on the Revolution in France* might have been either radicals like Price or Whigs like Fox, or both, but in any case it is certain that the American and French revolutions precipitated a way of thinking on political affairs which, although held by a minority, and stemming from well-entrenched sources, Burke deeply disliked. With authors like Price, Paine, Priestley, and Godwin, there occurred a radicalization of

---

[101] *The Progress of Society in Europe* (1769; Chicago and London, 1972), p. 154. For an English reference, see Gibbon on the Germans in *The History of the Decline and Fall of the Roman Empire* (1776–88; 12 vols., London, 1820), I, ch. 9, pp. 344–83; for a general statement, see IV, ch. 26, pp. 333–5.

[102] Robertson, *The Progress of Society*, p. 47.

[103] *ibid.*, esp. p. 22. Compare K. O'Brien, *Narratives of Enlightenment: Cosmopolitan History from Voltaire to Gibbon* (Cambridge, 1997), pp. 135, 137–41.

[104] Hume was in the company of Robertson, Kames, and Smith in revising the definition of France as under despotism, and of the French as slaves. For these three authors, France was an absolute monarchy where some liberties were at worst tolerated, politeness was upheld, and industry was not unknown. See, e.g., Kames, *Essays upon Several Subjects Concerning British Antiquities* (1745; 2nd edn, 1749; repr. edn, London, 1993), pp. 200–1; Kames, *Loose Hints*, pp. 302–3; Robertson, *The Progress of Society*, pp. 131–3; Smith, *WN*, IV.iii.c.12–3, IV.vii.b.52, V.i.g.19, V.ii.k.78. The cosmopolitanism of Dunbar's *Essays* also deserves mention. That is not to say that national bias (especially in the form of common knowledge) was consistently avoided; even Smith, admittedly in the most unprovincial of contexts, characterized the French 'genius' through 'perspicuous description and just arrangement' but spoke of 'the original and inventive genius of the English'. 'Letter to the *Edinburgh Review*' (1755), in A. Smith, *Essays on Philosophical Subjects*, ed. W. P. D. Wightman (Oxford, 1980), pp. 248–9.

Lockean and Humean premises combined with a deep suspicion of state action. These writers not only argued that government was a trust, but also that rulers were nothing but the servants of the people. As for the influence of Hume, the idea of the primacy of public opinion was given a combative turn, deriving logically from radical premises on the nature of government. The radicals' stance on the qualities and role of the citizenry can be outlined with reference to the group as a whole.[105]

The old idea that 'the dispositions and manners of men depend more than we can well conceive on the nature of the government to which they are subject' was originally emphasized by the radicals through the rationalistic theory of morals and knowledge to which they subscribed.[106] Granted that despotism debased and liberty exalted human character, this was because personality was shaped by circumstances (an idea substantiated by the psychological associationism of Hartley), among which government was particularly powerful. In political as well as all other fields, if confronted with the right sort of experience, man would develop the right habits and attitudes. Everybody would naturally follow virtue and rectitude if free from restraint; the wicked were such because, far from being self-directed, they were under a base external control. As Price put it: 'no one who acts wickedly acts as he likes, but is conscious of a tyranny within him overpowering his judgement and carrying him into a conduct for which he condemns and hates himself'.[107] Hartley's associationism provided a theoretical foundation for the radicals' faith both in progress and in education. As Godwin in particular insisted, intellectual enlightenment entailed sure effects: 'show me in the clearest and most unambiguous manner that a certain mode of proceeding is most reasonable in itself or most conducive to my interest, and I shall infallibly pursue that mode'.[108] By hindering the practice of 'righteousness', despotism made the pursuit of a religious life more difficult, a fact of special relevance for a group which had constitutional links with Dissent. Religious implications apart, it was agreed that without a feeling of liberty, security, and independence, improvements in science, the economy, or any other section of activity were impossible. 'Political liberty' came to be understood

[105] But on radicalism as a 'blanket label' see J. C. D. Clark, *Revolution and Rebellion* (Cambridge, 1986), pp. 97–103.

[106] The quotation is taken from R. Price, *The Evidence for a Future Period of Improvement in the State of Mankind* (1787), in R. Price, *Political Writings*, ed. D. O. Thomas (Cambridge, 1991), p. 164.

[107] *Additional Observations on the Nature and Value of Civil Liberty* (1777), in Price, *Political Writings*, p. 81. In parallel, the essence of liberty is the autonomy and independence of the individual: 'to be free is to be guided by one's own will; and to be guided by the will of another is the characteristic of servitude' (R. Price, *Observations on the Nature of Civil Liberty* (1776), in *Political Writings*, p. 26).

[108] W. Godwin, *Enquiry Concerning Political Justice and Its Influence on Morals and Happiness*, ed. F. E. L. Priestley (1793; 3rd edn, 1797; repr. edn, 3 vols., Toronto, 1946), I, p. 445. See also, e.g., R. Price, *A Discourse on the Love of Our Country* (1789), in *Political Writings*, pp. 181–2.

as the guarantee of 'civil liberty', the set of natural rights through which man experienced self-fulfilment.[109]

In a free polity, where every person practised 'self-direction' and 'self-government' and tried to improve himself intellectually and morally, vigilance over possible encroachments of liberty was an everyday duty for all. Although government was a determinant of character, public virtue was necessary to establish and maintain a free government. It was a consequence drawn from Locke that 'if a people would obtain security against oppression, they must seek it in themselves and never part with the powers of government out of their own hands. It is there only they can be safe.'[110] Being a member of a community entailed 'participation':

if we see our country threatened with calamity, let us warn it. If we see our countrymen proud and insensible to the rights of mankind, let us admonish them. If the demon of corruption is poisoning the springs of legislation and converting the securities of public liberty into instruments of slavery, let us point out to them the shocking mischief, and endeavour to recover them to a sense of their danger. It is true we may be able to do but little in this way. But in this case every little is of unspeakable consequence, and if no one would neglect the little in his power much might be done.[111]

This statement suggests that if the 'sense of the people' was the bulwark of liberty, there were sinister interests at work in the state. To counter them, only the traditional free spirit of the English would do. The dangers came from the Test and Corporation Acts, public debt, patronage, septennial parliaments, standing armies, colonial repression, and offensive wars. In the very critical situation the people were called on to face, Price judged that 'indifference' and 'irreligiosity' had already seriously impaired determination to resist abuses.[112] On the other hand Priestley, who rejoiced in the spirit of the revolutionary events of the seventeenth century, held that if the English were confronted with a government turned tyrannical they would do 'what Englishmen are renowned for having formerly done in the same circumstances'.[113] Although views differed as to the state of public virtues, there was no doubt as to where the secret of a free community lay.

It is worth pausing at this point to comment on the wide diffusion, demonstrated by many of the authors considered so far in this chapter, of the idea of a moral 'corruption' threatening British liberty. This perspective seems to have complemented, rather than replaced, Whiggish pride (with which even Price, for one, was tainted), in the obvious sense that a fall from grace requires a previous

---

[109] See esp. J. Priestley, *An Essay on the First Principles of Government* (1768; 2nd edn, London, 1771), pp. 1–72.
[110] Price, *Additional Observations*, p. 83.
[111] R. Price, *A Fast Sermon* (1781), in *Political Writings*, pp. 112–13.
[112] See, e.g., Price, *Observations*, p. 30.
[113] Priestley, *An Essay*, p. 67.

state of grace.[114] The current, Whiggish notion of English character focused on an ethic of civil vigilance and resolution which almost by definition exposed itself to corruption. It is arguable that the number of those who *warned* against a possible degeneration was higher than the number of those who lamented the actual occurrence of it; but of course this is a grey area where dividing lines are difficult to draw. The influence of particular events on perceptions of moral decay also deserves mention, with the effect of the American war or the Middlesex election operating in the opposite direction to that of Louisbourg or Waterloo. In this respect, the achievement of Burke's *Reflections* was to supply a reading of the French Revolution – an event potentially leading, and with unprecedented force, to an indictment of the British constitution – which neutralized that critical potential and confirmed the English in their traditional sense of superiority over the French.

The characteristics of British 'corruption' differ from the feeling of decay experienced in France at the time. After Bolingbroke and Swift's denunciations of the 'monied interest', the language of virtue and corruption in Britain had to a remarkable extent an economic or 'material' ring. The *philosophes*, in contrast, did not abandon an essentially moral territory. In Britain, the growth of a commercial society induced fears which came to be articulated through the idiom of civic humanism, which served to voice demands for specific measures (like education or a militia), rather than to reject commercial society altogether. In France, civic humanism was a form of moral protest, the reservoir of moral examples against which contemporary misery could be assessed. At bottom the British were warning of a possible future degeneration ('effeminacy') in a context of national elevation and prosperity, while the French were lamenting both a current degradation of moral standards and the loss of the power and prestige the nation had suffered since the golden age of Louis XIV.

The radical posture, largely stemming from the dissenting experience of marginalization, served to support, alternatively, self-defence and extra-parliamentary agitation for reform. The contrast with the world of Burke – private secretary to political patrons, party man and parliamentary politician – could hardly be sharper. There is a revealing passage in *Thoughts on the Present Discontents* listing the social groups that could legitimately have a say in politics. In appealing to 'the opinion of the people', namely 'the natural strength of the kingdom', against the king and his 'junto', he mentioned 'the great peers, the leading landed gentlemen, the opulent merchants and manufacturers, the substantial yeomanry'.[115] Party was for him a matter of personal connections,

---

[114] See Price's early text *Britain's Happiness, and the Proper Improvement of It* (1759), in *Political Writings*, pp. 1–13; on the French being 'proud of their monarchs, even when they are oppressed by them', see J. Priestley, *Lectures on History and General Policy* (1788; London, 1826), pp. 337–48, quotation on p. 342; and see the section on Hazlitt below.

[115] *Thoughts on the Present Discontents* (1770), *BWS*, II, p. 282.

cemented by gentlemanly honour, fidelity, and friendship; and 'patriotism' amounted to a combination of 'public and private virtues', in the sense that the social intercourse of gentlemen was requisite for the creation of political links.[116] By contrast, in radical politics 'people' referred not only to the middle ranks but also to the upper strata of the 'inferior class'. This was in accordance with the humble origins of radical authors, whose fathers were staymakers (Paine), cloth-dressers (Priestley), or Dissenting ministers (Price, Godwin, Burgh, and Hazlitt).[117] It is a remarkable occurrence in British politics that until 1789 Burke could occasionally be found fighting side by side with Price's artisans.[118]

Burke's approach to the relationship between men and government was not uniform. The *Reflections* inaugurated a second phase. In his writings on America, the character of the colonists figures as one of the circumstances which made their revolt difficult to subdue. It was in view of their 'fierce spirit of liberty' that Burke recommended a reconsideration of British policies in America, in obeisance to the general rule that the 'character and situation of a people must determine what sort of government is fitted for them'.[119] The task of representative institutions was not 'to force the public inclination', but only to give 'the general sense of the community' a sanction and 'a technical dress'. Far from being the matter of abstract speculation, free government was in essence 'moral prudence and natural feeling', namely, respect for the ideas about liberty a people held regardless of their truth.[120] As he put it, the American question was not whether the Americans' disposition deserved praise or blame, but 'what, in the name of God, shall we do with it?'[121] This doctrine of the primacy of a people's beliefs over politics from above was associated with the idea of the impotence of laws to establish liberty where people were corrupt: since politicians could only be 'true samples of the mass', they mirrored the mass's virtues and vices.[122] Finally, in his pieces on America as well as in other perorations of his, Burke admonished his audiences for the risk of losing the traditionally English spirit of liberty if the measures he advocated were not

[116] *ibid.*, pp. 314–20.
[117] Incidentally, Richard Burke was a Dublin attorney.
[118] For Pocock, 'Varieties of Whiggism', p. 276, it is a plausible historical interpretation that 'the Whig regime, even at its most oligarchic, possessed a liberal flexibility that the ancien régime lacked'.
[119] 'Speech on Conciliation with America' (1775), *BWS*, III, pp. 119, 136; *Letter to the Sheriffs of Bristol* (1777), *BWS*, III, p. 316. The causes of the 'disobedient spirit in the colonies' were: English descent, Dissenting religion (in the North), education, local legislative assemblies, a will to emphasize the contrast with the slave condition (in the South), and the distance from the motherland. 'Speech on Conciliation', pp. 119–25. See C. P. Courtney, *Montesquieu and Burke* (Westport, Conn., 1975), pp. 91–106.
[120] *Letter to the Sheriffs*, pp. 315, 317–19. For similar views, see 'Speech on Opening of Impeachment' [of Hastings] (1788), *BWS*, VI, pp. 301–3, 345–6.
[121] 'Speech on Conciliation', p. 125.
[122] *Letter to the Sheriffs*, p. 327; 'Speech on Conciliation', pp. 130–1.

taken – 'a great alteration in the national character', he typically warned, would ensue.[123]

These views of Burke on the role of collective dispositions can be interpreted as a variation, albeit momentous, on the Humean theme of public opinion.[124] But in the *Reflections on the Revolution in France* there figures a eulogy of British institutions which, in projecting their antiquity back into an atemporal dimension of 'old establishments', 'antient usage', 'settled law', 'experience', and 'a slow but well-sustained progress', introduces a new motif into the eighteenth-century discourse on national character. Supported by a mode of writing which makes much of suggestion and image, he speaks of a venerable, organically grown English political experience, upon which layers of national character have matured as both effects and causes. Projecting national characteristics back in time was not new, of course, but the peculiarity of Burke's operation lies in the *ad hoc* reinvention of a past, as vague and even mythical as the Saxon mixed government evoked by some, but tailored to counter the political rationalism of the French (and British) revolutionaries with their faith in paper constitutions. Unlike those who in the previous decades had found a free and democratical 'ancient constitution' in the English past, and had portrayed the English accordingly, Burke's myth was unconditionally conservative, and his English were men of stubborn traditionalism.

With the aim of opposing the metaphysical criteria adopted by the French to rebuild the state, Burke's first step is to argue that the English constitution

has emanated from the simplicity of our national character, and from a sort of native plainness and directness of understanding, which for a long time characterized those men who have successively obtained authority amongst us. This disposition still remains, at least in the great body of the people.[125]

What is peculiarly Burkean is the consideration of English straightforwardness not as a virtue in itself, but as a virtue to the extent that it has been embedded in the nation's historical achievements. National characteristics cannot but be ancestral because they draw their sanction from the past, when their effects on events unfolded, and, simultaneously, they took shape in relation to events;

---

[123] *Letter to the Sheriffs*, pp. 328–9; 'Speech on Conciliation', p. 127; 'Speech on Opening of Impeachment', pp. 271–2; and the speech of 7 May 1789 on the impeachment of Hastings, in E. Burke, *Works* (8 vols., 1854–69), VII, pp. 448–9.

[124] In the early historical writings there are sparse hints at a roughly 'conjectural' determination of manners. See *An Abridgment of English History* (1757), *BWS*, I, pp. 348–9, 357–8, 391–3, 429–31 (on the attitudes common to 'all barbarians'), 456–7 (on the similarity of manners in Europe brought about by the diffusion of feudal rule). For Burke's endorsement of the Scottish conceptualization of manners, see J. G. A. Pocock, 'The Political Economy of Burke's Analysis of the French Revolution', in his *Virtue, Commerce, and History*, pp. 193–212.

[125] *Reflections on the Revolution in France* (1790), *BWS*, VIII, p. 141. There may be a Humean influence in Burke's reference to the role played by the character of leaders; however, as argued below, this motif matched Burke's picture of the mass of the people as an amorphous body.

it is through a gradual historical process, that is, that national characteristics have revealed themselves. 'Time is required to produce that union of minds which alone can produce all the good we aim at.'[126] If collective virtues need the sanction of time, continuity is the attribute marking English history and, with it, the English character. Because our disposition is sluggish and resists innovation, 'we still bear the stamp of our forefathers' of the fourteenth century for 'generosity and dignity of thinking'. Unlike the French, 'we preserve the whole of our feelings still native and entire, unsophisticated by pedantry and infidelity'.[127]

In dealing with the English past Burke hardly distinguishes between a spiritual sphere of attitudes and beliefs on the one hand, and concrete national institutions, on the other: the history of England is a whole where partitions are neither possible nor appropriate. Hence he carelessly shifts references from a disposition (the Englishman's respect for hierarchy, for instance) to the underlying thing (England's established social structure), and vice versa. Since the constitution has developed slowly and by gradual accretions, beliefs and institutions have been inextricably and constantly combined, and for this reason neither can properly be indicated as cause or as effect. This is a harmonious universe where the monarchical sentiment of the people matches the existing monarchical establishment, the Anglican Church corresponds to a widespread religious faith, and so on. Additionally, apart from Burke's organicism, applying definite chains of causes and effects falls outside the symbolic and evocative mood of the *Reflections*:

We fear God; we look up with awe to kings; with affections to parliaments; with duty to magistrates; with reverence to priests; and with respect to nobility. Why? Because when such ideas are brought before our minds, it is *natural* to be so affected; because all other feelings are false and spurious, and tend to corrupt our minds, to vitiate our primary morals, to render us unfit for rational liberty; and by teaching us a servile, licentious, and abandoned insolence, to be our low sport for a few holidays, to make us perfectly fit for, and justly deserving of slavery, through the whole course of our lives.[128]

A series of paragraphs in the first-person plural illustrates the beliefs underlying the political state of England. Actually, they are 'prejudices', Burke proudly contends, and cherished as such. The English are in favour of 'an established church, an established monarchy, an established aristocracy, and an established democracy, each in the degree it exists, and in no greater'.[129] By diffusing sublime and lofty principles, the Church of England moralizes political life and restrains popular demands. As for the elements of which the political balance

---

[126] *ibid.*, p. 217.
[127] *ibid.*, p. 137. See Pocock, 'Edmund Burke', p. 23.
[128] *Reflections*, pp. 137–8.
[129] *ibid.*, pp. 138, 142.

consists, all of them share in the feelings of service and responsibility which religion consecrates; all of them 'continue to act on the early received, and uniformly continued sense of mankind'.[130] Given this highly moralized picture of public life, the English are said to view the state as what links generations together, 'keeps the action of men in a certain course', and sets 'the test of honour' so that moral principles can be 'early worked into the habits'. All these functions would be impaired if the state was not an object of reverence but could be modified without due caution, according to 'the fancy of the parties'. By adhering to these principles both the educated and the uneducated 'move with the order of the universe', namely they follow 'the common nature and common relation of men'.[131] Through their membership of an ancestral community the English achieve a truth which is given in nature as the fulfilment of man's assignment on earth: 'they conceive that He who gave our nature to be perfected by our virtue, willed also the necessary means of its perfection – He willed therefore the state – He willed its connexion with the source and original archetype of all perfection.' Burke insists that these views are not merely his own, but the general and uninterrupted opinion of the English 'from very early times to this moment'.[132]

Burke's critics made much of his eulogies of prejudice as the best mover of men, a view flying in the face of radicals with their belief in human perfectibility through reason. Paine, for one, denied that men 'must be governed by fraud, effigy and show' and asserted 'the irresistible nature of truth'. Prejudices about government coming from education and habit 'are nothing': people are attached to prejudices in the belief that they are true, so that, as soon as they realize their mistake and apply reason and reflection, prejudice is gone. Therefore, all men are fit for freedom, and human nature is vicious only to the extent that tyranny has corrupted it. Paine contended that to be free was a matter of will, a lesson any individual could learn through the honest pursuit of his interest, which induced 'a knowledge of his rights' and the recognition that fear alone supported despotism.[133]

In *A Letter to a Member of the National Assembly*, Burke reasserted the decisive importance of the human material for the shaping of policies – 'I must know the power and disposition to accept, to execute, to persevere', that is, 'I must see the men.'

Without a concurrence and adaptation of these to the design, the very best speculative projects might become not only useless, but mischievous. Plans must be made for men. We cannot think of making men, and binding nature to our designs. People at a distance must judge ill of men. They do not always answer to their reputation when you approach

[130] *ibid.*, pp. 142–5, quotation on pp. 142–3.
[131] *ibid.*, pp. 145–9.
[132] *ibid.*, p. 149.
[133] T. Paine, *Rights of Man*, ed. H. Collins (1791; Harmondsworth, 1985), pp. 157–8, 174, 208, 210.

them. Nay, the perspective varies, and shews them quite otherwise than you thought them.[134]

In the case of France, Burke related the people's unreadiness for liberty to their unwillingness to restrain their appetites and passions through the 'controlling power' of 'moral instruction'.[135] This check could not come from the masses, but only from an aristocracy, because no multitude left to itself can tolerate any control, regulation, and 'steady direction whatsoever' in their inordinate desire for power.[136] Properly speaking, 'the people' as distinct from a number of loose individuals exist only by virtue of the discipline imposed by an aristocracy.[137] The gulf between Burke's oligarchic and Paine's democratical perspectives could hardly be wider, while the hopes raised by the French Revolution lent this contrast dramatic practical relevance.

The French Revolution created an urgent need among the English for a more closely defined self-image. If, to paraphrase a commentator, it was impossible after 1789 to remain sceptical, this was particularly so with respect to the special qualities required to operate free institutions.[138] With Burke, the focus shifted from an active public spirit based on ardour, independence, and devotion to the polity to a different set of qualities. The French could not be depicted as willing slaves any longer, since they had rebelled; but they could plausibly be shown to be a people dominated by a spirit of system, bereft of the attitudes which should go with representative institutions. These qualities were attachment to the national tradition, religious faith, deference, moderation, prudence, sobriety, plainness, and a practical attitude best exercised and illustrated in economic enterprise. Burke put the task assigned to this set of characteristics very clearly: 'our people will find employment enough for a truly patriotic, free, and independent spirit, in guarding what they possess, from violation. I would not exclude alteration neither; but even when I changed, it should be to preserve.'[139] The risk of decay did not result from lack of renovation, but from rashly conceived innovation.

Actually, by positing Britain as a standard of political continuity and religious and social deference, Burke was working a sort of miracle – for few of his contemporaries held such a rosy image, although nearly every writer agreed that the British constitution was the best in the world. It is arguable that the central features of eighteenth-century British thought were ultimately motivated by a concern with the sources of political instability present in Britain – Hume is

---

[134] *A Letter to a Member of the National Assembly* (1791), *BWS*, VIII, p. 326. See also *First Letter on a Regicide Peace*, pp. 193–4.
[135] *A Letter to a Member of the National Assembly*, p. 332.
[136] *An Appeal from the New to the Old Whigs* (1791), in *Works*, III, p. 362.
[137] *ibid.*, pp. 364–70; see also *First Letter on a Regicide Peace*, p. 199.
[138] D. Miller, *Philosophy and Ideology in Hume's Political Thought* (Oxford, 1981), p. 194.
[139] *Reflections*, p. 292.

only the most transparent case in point.[140] The century had been marked by the questions related to the Hanoverian succession, the Jacobite uprising, persistent ministerial instability, the increasing power of the Crown, the Middlesex election, and dissension about the American colonies. Although of varying and perhaps decreasing constitutional relevance, all these issues had a strong impact on the British mind. The notion, traceable to classical sources, that a free government entails a degree of agitation and discontent due to the clash of opinions was common knowledge, but it did not suffice to allay widespread anxiety.

This chapter began with a distinction between the philosophic approach and the 'vulgar' Whiggism of political literature at large. There was in particular an unbridgeable gap between the philosopher, sceptical and cosmopolitan, and the journalist, passionate and xenophobic.[141] The succeeding century would witness a reduction in that gap, in a context of shifting sociological conditions for intellectual work. If journalism became 'philosophical', some philosophers were not in favour of cosmopolitanism. It is emblematic that Mill's broad-minded perspective found its most inveterate enemies among literati like Carlyle. One of the new material circumstances was the rise of the great reviews, the *Edinburgh* and the *Quarterly* in particular. These catered for a wide public and were instrumental in blurring the boundaries between 'philosophical' and 'vulgar' opinion. If I had to cite a single intellectual development underlying the new 'middle' mode, I would point, unoriginally, to the remarkable persistence of Burkean tenets.[142] The subject of the next section, William Hazlitt, was a high-quality journalist and, overall, a transitional figure, an admirer of Napoleon wavering between an awareness of the 'vulgarity' of a nationalistic outlook and the plain fact that he really did not like the French.

6   Hazlitt

One of Staël's closest English friends was Henry Crabb Robinson, an intimate of Lamb, Coleridge, Wordsworth, and Southey.[143] Hazlitt was also numbered among his friends, but the two parted company as a consequence of Hazlitt's attacks on Wordsworth. However, Robinson had no difficulty in conceding that Hazlitt 'was an extraordinary man'.[144] A philosopher, painter, art critic, journalist, historian, and a Dissenter and political radical all his life, Hazlitt became from circa 1813 onwards the 'leading critic on the liberal side', a

---

[140] See esp. G. Giarrizzo, *David Hume politico e storico* (Turin, 1962), and Sher, *Church and University*.
[141] See J. Black, *The English Press in the Eighteenth Century* (London, 1987).
[142] On Burke's nineteenth-century reputation, see S. Collini, D. Winch, and J. Burrow, *That Noble Science of Politics* (Cambridge, 1983).
[143] 'As the valued friend of great men his name will survive': *DNB*.
[144] H. Crabb Robinson, *Diary, Reminiscences, and Correspondence* (3 vols., London, 1869), I, p. 63.

fact which was 'of incalculable importance in determining the tone of English cultural life in the second quarter of the century'.[145]

Of Hazlitt's two reviews of *De l'Allemagne*, the first supports both Staël's opinion of the Germans and her grouping of national literatures, while the second serves mainly as a vehicle for Hazlitt's own criticism of Lockean philosophy. As part of 'the best analysis that has been given of the literary and philosophical productions of the modern Germans', their contemplative disposition is justly singled out, and traced back to the political and social situation of the German states. Staël's felicitous style combines classic and romantic elements – the two classes of literature which she has 'so well distinguished as characteristic of different nations' – in a way that shows her not only as a Frenchwoman but also as 'the daughter of Susan Kürchod [Suzanne Curchod, a devout Calvinist]'.[146] There were meaningful similarities between Hazlitt and Staël: both took Rousseau as their starting point, and both rejected utilitarianism and materialism in the name of higher principles. Hazlitt's 'romantic' credentials were impeccable. It is curious that the two authors I take as introducing the nineteenth century are a French hater of Napoleon and one of his very few English supporters – one who was so shocked at the news of Waterloo that he got dead drunk and disappeared from circulation for many days.[147]

While Staël was perhaps the last eighteenth-century cosmopolitan, Hazlitt saw a 'natural antipathy' between the English and the French which made mutual understanding 'hopeless'.[148] This aversion was a case of a general rule: 'there are certain moulds of national character in which all our opinions and feelings must be cast, or they are spurious and vitiated'. Each nationality reasoned its own way because of 'something in the juices and the blood'; a Frenchman could not admire Shakespeare or an Englishman understand Kant.[149] Hazlitt's own travels taught the same lesson in a different guise – the *Journey through*

[145] M. Butler, *Romantics, Rebels and Reactionaries: English Literature and Its Background 1760–1830* (Oxford, 1981), p. 169. It has been argued that by 1807 Hazlitt became a 'constitutional Whig' in his 'practical politics': J. Kinnaird, *William Hazlitt Critic of Power* (New York, 1978), pp. 107–9ff. There is a very perceptive account of his reactions to Burke in D. Bromwich, *Hazlitt: the Mind of a Critic* (New York and London, 1983), ch. 8.

[146] Originally published in the *Morning Chronicle*, 13 Nov. 1813, the review I have been drawing from has been collected in *HCW*, XIX, pp. 5–9. The second review of *De l'Allemagne*, equally from the *Morning Chronicle* but of February and March 1814, is in *HCW*, XX, pp. 12–36. On Mme Necker, 'who spread a little Protestant seriousness among the *monde*', see S. Schama, *Citizens: a Chronicle of the French Revolution* (Harmondsworth, 1989), pp. 88–9.

[147] R. Blythe, 'Introduction', in W. Hazlitt, *Selected Writings*, ed. R. Blythe (Harmondsworth, 1982), p. 22.

[148] *The Plain Speaker* (1826), *HCW*, XII, pp. 327–8.

[149] *Characteristics: in the Manner of Rochefoucault's Maxims* (1823), *HCW*, IX, pp. 216–17; *Plain Speaker*, p. 324, fn. One of Hazlitt's favourite areas for comparison between the French and the English was painting technique, which for him pointed straight to the respective national characters; see, e.g., an article which contains autobiographical elements: 'On Means and Ends' (1827), *HCW*, XVII, pp. 212–26.

France and Italy (1826) concludes with the view that 'however delightful or striking the objects may be abroad, they do not take the same hold of you, nor can you identify yourself with them as at home'. It was not simply because a foreign language was, in his view, an insuperable barrier that a full sentimental life was impossible abroad, where one ran the risk of becoming 'a mongrel'.[150]

Hazlitt's first work of notice, the *Essay on the Principles of Human Action* of 1805, sketches the contrast between the French and the English in terms that would provide a 'philosophical' basis for a number of later comparisons. In short, the French do not let specific objects impress their minds: 'from whatever cause it proceeds, the sensitive principle in them does not seem to be susceptible of the same modification and variety of action as it does in others'. Their limited spectrum of feelings cannot match 'the different degrees and kinds of power in the external objects', a characteristic which cooperates with their 'quickness of perception' to induce a sort of impatience in their reactions to things. Insufficient time was devoted to each impression: the French 'do not grapple with the object'. This peculiarity of the senses causes 'levity', inconsistency, and a predilection for abstract thinking. French character originates from attributing an equal importance to words and things – 'all their feelings are general'.[151] The final step was to make French levity synonymous with moral indifference, but this he postponed to later writings.

In the *Essay*, Hazlitt went on to say that the English were a mirror image of the French. The English are a 'heavy people', that is, slow to be moved by an object (and hardly at all by words), but, when this does happen, the impression has a deep and lasting effect and evokes 'a number of other impressions in it'. Indifferent to general conceptions, an Englishman retains only individual images, about which he broods.[152] As Hazlitt wrote in the *Journey*, the English rejoice in 'the conflict with external matter' as the moment when they really feel alive; they appreciate only the material qualities of 'solidity, inertness, and impenetrability' in things. Hazlitt went to some lengths to explain that 'they require the heavy, hard, and tangible only, something for them to grapple with and resist, to try their strength and their unimpressibility upon'.[153] Hence there emerged an English national character that Hazlitt liked, a set of qualities originally stemming from the Reformation and then passed on to inform the struggle against the Stuarts: 'manly independence of spirit', sturdiness, plainness, straightforwardness, and discipline. To him, this character was

---

[150] *Notes of a Journey through France and Italy*, HCW, X, pp. 302–3. For information about this and other travels of his, see S. Jones, *Hazlitt: a Life* (Oxford, 1989), esp. ch. 16.

[151] I am drawing from a long footnote on the French in *Essay on the Principles of Human Action*, HCW, I, pp. 24–6.

[152] *ibid.*, p. 26, fn.

[153] *Notes of a Journey*, p. 242.

naturally republican.[154] Hazlitt took an obvious pride in the fact that 'we are of a stiff clay, not moulded into every fashion, with stubborn joints not easily bent', in spite of the Englishman's almost grotesque want of refinement and artistic drawbacks in music and painting.[155] The religious origin of as sound a national character, and in particular the role of the vernacular Bible (the 'one great lever' of English liberty), were missed by French revolutionaries: 'perhaps a reformation in religion ought always to precede a revolution in the government'.[156]

Thus in Hazlitt there figures a historical, albeit schematic, explanation of national character associated with the one given in terms of 'moral sentiments' in the *Essay*. In addition, at times he seems to endorse a climatological and physiological set of causes; and there are also clear traces of a civic humanist perspective, with its stress on virtue and independence.[157] In the end, neither definite nor general theories of the causes of national character are advanced. A thing to note, bearing in mind the *Essay*, is the breakdown of Hume's solution of the possible contrast between a human nature deemed universal and the evident variety of manners and values. Hume judged all men to be driven by the same motive forces of interest and sympathy, forces which took different forms according to circumstances which prompted this or that view of utility and pleasure. With his depictions of the French and English ways of thinking, Hazlitt abandoned Hume's position of a uniform human nature, though he did so only implicitly, by assertions rather than connected arguments, and contradicted by the *Essay* itself, imbued as it is with Scottish philosophy. He ended up writing (in *The Plain Speaker*) that the French 'are affected by things in a different manner from us, not in a different degree'.[158] He did not provide any substantial reason for such a view, in spite of the display of philosophical apparatus. He adopted the distinction first drafted in the *Essay* as a background fact, to add a philosophical resonance to his criticism of French art, manners, and history.

---

[154] *The Life of Napoleon Bonaparte* (1828–30), *HCW*, XIII, pp. 46–8, 56. The *Life* makes up vols. XIII–XV.

[155] *Lectures Chiefly on the Dramatic Literature of the Age of Elizabeth* (1820), *HCW*, VI, pp. 191–2.

[156] *Life of Napoleon*, XIII, p. 56. For a comment, see T. Paulin, *The Day-Star of Liberty: William Hazlitt's Radical Style* (London, 1998), pp. 17–23.

[157] For his evaluation of the effects of climate and innate dispositions, see *The Round Table* (1817), *HCW*, IV, pp. 43, 45–6; *Plain Speaker*, pp. 144, 169–78 (where the traditional North–South distinction is carried to remarkable extremes of vulgarity and impudence), 230–41; 'Farington's Life of Sir Joshua Reynolds' (1820), *HCW*, XVI, pp. 193–6. Hazlitt preferred physiognomy to phrenology, which he criticized at length in *Plain Speaker*, pp. 137–56, and in 'Phrenological Fallacies' (1829), *HCW*, XX, pp. 248–55. Classic republicanism, which contributes significantly to his image of English character, surfaces for instance in Hazlitt's impatience with 'mechanical refinement', 'softness', 'effeminacy', and 'licentiousness'.

[158] *Plain Speaker*, p. 328.

There are passages in Hazlitt's works where the French are abused for not having 'fixed principles or real character'.

The French mind never identifies itself with any thing, but always has its own consciousness, its own affectation, its own gratification, its own slippery inconstancy or impertinent prolixity interposed between the object and the impression. It is this theatrical or artificial nature with which we cannot and will not sympathise, because it circumscribes the truth of things and the capacities of the human mind within the petty round of vanity, indifference, and physical sensations, stunts the growth of imagination, effaces the broad light of nature, and requires us to look at all things through the prism of their petulance and self-conceit. The French in a word leave *sincerity* out of their nature (not moral but imaginative sincerity), cut down the varieties of feeling to their own narrow and superficial standard, and having clipped and adulterated the current coin of expression, would pass it off as sterling gold.[159]

Hazlitt showed no doubt that a right cast of mind was necessary to the successful establishment of free institutions. He conceded that the Revolution had given the French the spirit of liberty and Napoleon military ambition, but neither had lasted long. 'Both of these gave an energy and consistency to their character, by concentrating their natural volatility on one great object. But when both of these causes failed, the Allies found that France consisted of nothing but ladies' toilettes.'[160] Hazlitt's verdict that the French would never be free until they understood English poetry is indicative of an approach which did not refrain from open scorn and derision.[161]

Yet this vulgar Whiggism coexisted side by side with another line of argument, more original and interesting. Hazlitt's portrait of the English was in fact two-edged, with the negative aspects occasionally outweighing the positive ones. His *Examiner* piece 'Character of John Bull' affirmed the Englishman's stupidity, credulity, irritability, and delight in a 'bugbear', that is an object of hate and confrontation. 'In short, John is a great blockhead and a great bully', who

boasts of the excellence of the laws, and the goodness of his own disposition; and yet there are more people hanged in England than in all Europe besides: he boasts of the modesty of his countrywomen, and yet there are more prostitutes in the streets of London than in all the capitals of Europe put together. He piques himself on his comforts, because he is the most uncomfortable of mortals; and because he has no enjoyment in society, seeks it, as he says, at his fireside, where he may be stupid as a matter of course, sullen as a matter of right, and as ridiculous as he chuses [*sic*] without being laughed at. His liberty is the effect of his self-will; his religion owing to the spleen; his temper to

---

159 *ibid.* For another specimen of Hazlitt's attacks, see 'Schlegel on the Drama' (1816), *HCW*, XVI, pp. 88–9.
160 *Political Essays* (1819), *HCW*, VII, p. 86. See also *Life of Napoleon*, XV, pp. 205, 258; 'On Means and Ends', pp. 217–18. Hazlitt ascribed even the Terror to national character: *Life of Napoleon*, XIII, pp. 55–6, 120.
161 *Notes of a Journey*, p. 162.

the climate. He is an industrious animal, because he has no taste for amusement, and had rather work six days in the week than be idle one.[162]

In part at least this bleak portrait was motivated by political considerations, filtered through the journalistic quarrels in which Hazlitt was frequently involved. It was a recurrent accusation of his that the English lent themselves to becoming 'the dupes of quacks and impostors', namely the editors and authors in the *Quarterly*, *Blackwood*, and *John Bull*. Public opinion was now under the control of 'half a dozen miscreants', who, building on the anti-revolutionary policies of successive governments, had nearly succeeded in extinguishing the traditional English virtues.[163] English simplicity and plainness could be easily manipulated: as 'dry and plodding' people used to deal with 'matter', they could hardly conceive of anybody telling lies and thought that 'all they hear or read must be true'.[164]

Hazlitt also discussed the idea of national character in terms which are bound to perplex the reader of much of the above. As his disparaging remarks on the French went hand in hand (sometimes in the same piece) with a critique of English insularity, so his statements about the inevitability of a national mental framework were accompanied by a consideration of the problematic place of national character in the contemporary mind. Both the French and the English characters, Hazlitt wrote, are more complex than either side think, and 'nothing can be more ridiculous indeed than the way in which we exaggerate each other's vices and extenuate our own'. He went even further: 'our contempt for others proves nothing but the illiberality and narrowness of our own views'.[165] With paradoxical nonchalance, he explained French parochialism by alleging that they were too conceited and self-centred to do justice to other peoples, while maintaining that the English laughed at foreigners because, 'from their insular situation, they are unacquainted with the manners and customs of the rest of the world'. This was regrettable, because much could be learnt by 'contact and collision' with other nations in order to test opinions that were often endorsed only by 'instinct'. 'By visiting different countries and conversing with their inhabitants, we strike a balance between opposite prejudices, and have an average of truth and nature left.' That a variety of national tastes and dispositions is a source of good is denied only by those who attempt to impose an allegedly

---

162 *The Round Table*, pp. 99–100. See also, at least, 'Queries and Answers; or the Rule of Contrary' (1827), *HCW*, XX, pp. 149–50; 'Manners Make the Man' (1829), *HCW*, XX, pp. 220–3; and 'English Characteristics' (1829), *HCW*, XX, pp. 247–8.
163 *Notes of a Journey*, pp. 244–7; *Plain Speaker*, p. 322; *Life of Napoleon*, XIII, pp. 48–9; 'On Public Opinion' (1828), *HCW*, XVII, pp. 306–8; etc. On the attacks Hazlitt encountered, see J. O. Hayden, *The Romantic Reviewers 1802–1824* (London, 1969), pp. 204–15.
164 'Queries and Answers', p. 150. See also 'Character of the Country People' (1819), *HCW*, XVII, pp. 66–71.
165 *Table-Talk* (1821–2), *HCW*, VIII, p. 307; *Characteristics*, p. 215.

universal standard on the world at large – a reference to the French that was transparent.[166]

The diary of Hazlitt's journey in France and Italy and a later article, 'Travelling Abroad', mark a further step in his self-interrogation of the legitimacy and inherent ambivalence of national manners and taste. In these works, the origin of national prejudice is traced to the impossibility of admitting 'two standards of moral value according to circumstances', and to a related reluctance to acknowledge the worth of others. 'Our self-love is annoyed by whatever creates a suspicion of our being in the wrong; and only recovers its level by setting down all those who differ from us as thoroughly odious and contemptible.'[167] The French are dirty, we often complain; 'but when we find that they are lively, agreeable, and good-humoured in spite of their dirt, we then know not what to make of it'. Talking about national characters implies a flawed process of abstraction: anything odd or absurd met with in France is taken to represent the country, whereas similar connections are not established in England. We seize upon our carefully selected examples of Frenchness – one of those chosen by Hazlitt is a bag lady met by the roadside in Paris, another is a beggar boy hitting his monkey – 'with avidity and delight'. But we do not notice a well-fed, strongly built, huge man because he does not match our idea of France as the land of *soup-maigre*, *sabots*, and 'scare-crow figures'. Hazlitt comments: 'it is strange we cannot let other people alone who concern themselves so little about us'. But it is difficult, 'I confess', to avoid prejudices, despite their easily noticeable negative effect on our 'happiness' and understanding.[168] With all this self-awareness and self-criticism, the fact remained that Hazlitt in France could hardly come to terms with the French, and in particular with things like the Parisian way of coach driving, or road maintenance, or the chaotic walking along the *boulevards* – trifles, perhaps, but clearly considered by Hazlitt indications of more serious flaws.[169]

The beauties of Italy broke the deadlock in Hazlitt's mind. Italy was perceived as an unreal land, a land of imagination where national rivalries lost their *raison d'être* in the face of nature and the artistic legacies of the past.[170] What, in the part of the *Journey* dealing with France, almost amounts to an obsession with

---

[166] *Characteristics*, pp. 215–17.
[167] *Notes of a Journey*, p. 138; 'Travelling Abroad' (1828), *HCW*, XVII, pp. 335–6. This article originally appeared in the *New Monthly Magazine*; here it figures on pp. 332–44.
[168] *Notes of a Journey*, pp. 138–45.
[169] *ibid.*, pp. 143–4, 155–6. Similar examples are the Frenchman taking his dog into the coach with him, or his total occupation of window space when he wishes to see something, unmindful of the other travellers' need for air: 'Travelling Abroad', p. 337.
[170] On Italy, besides the Italian part of the *Journey*, see 'Travelling Abroad', pp. 343–4. Hazlitt's reaction to Italy falls within a fairly standard pattern for foreign travellers and observers, to whom Italy looked like *la terra dei morti*, the land of the dead – Hazlitt wrote: 'their cities are the cities of the dead'. On the image of Italy in the eighteenth and nineteenth centuries, see F. Venturi, 'L'Italia fuori d'Italia', in *Storia d'Italia* (6 vols., Turin, 1972–6), III, pp. 987–1481.

conflicting national attitudes, turns into a more relaxed and descriptive mood as Hazlitt traverses the dizzying slopes from Mont Cenis to Susa. As he wrote, 'in other places I forget myself, but in France I am always an Englishman'.[171] His remarks on the Italian character, even when critical, are dispassionate in tone ('musical people', 'sons of nature', 'childish', 'insolent waiters', etc.); a republican recipe for national recovery is also devised for the natives' use.[172]

Hazlitt, in conclusion, saw an antithesis between the French and the English, but almost against his will. He was both vulgar in his contempt for the French, and sceptical in his search for a deeper truth behind the national diversities of manners and taste. Hazlitt, as a radical of Dissenting stock, could not advocate the matchless merits of the British constitution. But he could hardly do without some idea of an English spirit of liberty, albeit corrupted as a consequence of the wars waged against revolutionary France and Napoleon. Hazlitt's quest was a particularly frank and honest swan song for eighteenth-century cosmopolitanism, however qualified one may think it was. More generally, he poses a question about the potentially thin boundary between the identification of a national frame of thought and xenophobia.

With Hazlitt we enter the nineteenth century, the age of cultural nationalism. National characters are not assessed by such universal criteria as civic virtue, martial spirit or corruption; they are depicted afresh, so to speak, in the awareness that the character of each nation is rooted in a specific cultural reality, impossible to reproduce elsewhere. National stereotypes may remain the same, but a portion of the universalism involved in the philosophical premises which were typical of the eighteenth century is lost. Hazlitt's portraits of the French and the English were not new in essence – that the former were gay and the latter sturdy was commonplace – but they were infused with a spirit of indelible contrast, a spirit made possible by the identification of 'Frenchness' and 'Englishness' as entrenched cultural entities. Sadly, at the time of the Napoleonic wars, few would regard Europe as Gibbon had done, as 'a great republic, whose various inhabitants have attained almost the same level of politeness and cultivation'.[173] As the previous chapter indicates, however, and as will be shown in those that follow, the approach in terms of cultural nationalism did not go unchallenged throughout the century.

[171] 'Travelling Abroad', p. 344.
[172] *Notes of a Journey*, pp. 256–7.
[173] Gibbon, *Decline and Fall*, VI, ch. 38, p. 407.

6 British views on Irish national character, 1800–1846

1 Introduction

Despite the long-standing reputation of the Victorians for showing contempt towards the Irish, recent scholarship has drawn a more complex and nuanced picture which acts as a liberating insight for my research.[1] I aim to extend this reassessment back to the hitherto under-documented period between the Act of Union and the Famine, and in the process to argue that, in discussing Irish character, early and mid-nineteenth-century British authors made use of a theme that was central to their political universe, the relationship between a free constitution and the moral adequacy of its citizens. The Irish case provides a vantage point from which to survey the varying ways in which this relationship was upheld.

In accordance with nineteenth-century usage, what is meant by the term 'Irish character' is the traits and attitudes exclusively of the Irish peasantry. The psychological traits and the detectable behaviour that made up the 'Irish character' were not in question at the time. All agreed on its warm-heartedness, inquisitiveness, and social disposition; whereas, on the dark side, its indolence, proneness to fight and riot, inclination to lawlessness, and lack of forward thinking were commonly mentioned. Even the Irish writers, Protestant and Catholic, added little substantial to the stereotype,[2] which, however, marked a significant step beyond the 'wild Irishman' whose echoes still resound through Hume's

---

[1] Those who, following in the footsteps of L. P. Curtis, Jr, *Anglo-Saxon and Celts: a Study of Anti-Irish Prejudice in Victorian England* (Bridgeport, Conn., 1968), have asserted the continuity of anti-Irish feeling have been opposed, in various ways, by S. Gilley, 'English Attitudes to the Irish in England, 1780–1900', in C. Holmes, ed., *Immigrants and Minorities in British Society* (London, 1978), pp. 81–110; D. G. Paz, 'Anti-Catholicism, Anti-Irish Stereotyping, and Anti-Celtic Racism in Mid-Victorian Working-Class Periodicals', *Albion*, 18 (1986), pp. 601–16; and R. F. Foster, *Paddy and Mr Punch: Connections in Irish and English History* (London, 1993), pp. 171–94.

[2] For a sample, see R. Bell, *A Description of the Condition and Manners as Well as of the Moral and Political Character, Education, & c. of the Peasantry of Ireland . . .* (London, 1804), esp. pp. 13–25, 34–5 (this is a collection of articles of unusually high literary quality, detail, and penetration); J. W. Croker, *A Sketch of the State of Ireland, Past and Present* (London, 1808), pp. 27–37 (this work went through some twenty editions, and was republished in 1884); S. Barlow, *The History of Ireland, from the Earliest Period to the Present Time* (2 vols., London,

History of England. The perceived image of the Irish had in fact undergone a slight but decisive shift over the course of the eighteenth century.[3] In the decades of concern here, some long-noticed qualities succeeded in making an impact on the stereotype. Even the most thunderous Tory reviewer had to acknowledge that the Irish had certain virtues, like hospitality, courage, or fondness for family affections. Despite this, political discourse overwhelmingly dealt with Irish faults, constant reference being made to their notoriety. The new stereotype credited the Irish with virtues of a chiefly 'private' nature, which to political or economic observers were likely to appear less relevant than their very 'public' vices. It is generally true that national images are part of textual traditions, where continuity is predominant, and that therefore the establishment of new shades of meaning always proves difficult.

Commentators differed, not only as to the emphasis laid on one or other of the above features, but, more crucially, as to the causes of them. A fundamental divide was at play: was Irish character due to history – was it the result of centuries of oppression and demoralization – or to primordial, quasi-natural causes – to Celtic descent and immemorial habits? This dilemma, which the Irish debate exemplarily encapsulates, lies at the heart of the notion of national character itself. It is true that some authors thrived on the tacit blurring of history into nature and vice-versa. A case in point was that, according to many, the civilizing influence of the Reformation had failed to extend to Ireland because of the savage state of the natives: by arguing so, an historical event became inextricably linked to the image of Irish ancestral barbarism. Nevertheless, the dilemma between historical and original characteristics was to a certain extent inescapable.

The features of Irish character were focused through comparison not only with the English character but also with the Scottish, there definitely being three actors on the stage rather than simply two. Yet it is difficult to notice any uniform view that accords with the provenance of the commentators; political standpoints largely predominated over any other consideration. On the

---

1814), II, pp. 419–30; G. L. Smyth, *Ireland: Historical and Statistical* (3 vols., London, 1844–9), III, pp. 14–33. For a general comment, see the perceptive essay by D. Kiberd, 'Irish Literature and Irish History', in R. F. Foster, ed., *The Oxford History of Ireland* (Oxford, 1992), pp. 230–81.

[3] See D. Berman, 'David Hume on the 1641 Rebellion in Ireland', *Studies: an Irish Quarterly Review*, 65 (1976), pp. 101–12; Voltaire's attitude is also revealing of eighteenth-century hostility to the 'religious fanaticism' of Irish rebels: G. Gargett, 'Voltaire and Irish History', *Eighteenth-Century Ireland*, 5 (1990), pp. 117–41. The 'transformation of the stereotypical Irishman in the period following the Restoration from a half-human savage into a ridiculous and contemptible gimcrack Englishman' has been documented by D. Hayton, 'From Barbarian to Burlesque: English Images of the Irish c.1660–1750', *Irish Economic and Social History*, 15 (1988), pp. 5–31. Some Irish qualities already figure in Tudor literature: D. B. Quinn, *The Elizabethan and the Irish* (Ithaca, NY, 1966), pp. 89–90, 150–1. For a comprehensive account, see J. T. Leerssen, *Mere Irish & Fíor-Ghael: Studies in the Idea of Irish Nationality, Its Development and Literary Expression Prior to the Nineteenth Century* (Amsterdam and Philadelphia, 1986), esp. ch. 2.

other hand, there is no evidence whatsoever that Irishness, however defined, had a bearing on the characterization of British identity. Even those who praised Irish warmth and spontaneity, in favourable contrast with English or Scottish attitudes, could hardly avoid viewing the Irish as 'others'. The Union notwithstanding, Ireland continued to be perceived as an obstinately rebellious province which had to be healed of its many wounds before any true contribution to the national polity could be contemplated. The contrast with Scotland could not be more striking, as many contemporaries observed.

2   Scottish philosophy and Whig politics: the *Edinburgh Review*

An account in social and historical terms of the Irish peasant's lack of industrious habits was given by Arthur Young in 1780, and his views remained influential well into the succeeding century.[4] Above all, elements of a social and historical environmentalism occurred in the *Edinburgh Review*. In the face of the reassertion of accusations of Catholic criminal cunning by exponents of the Ascendancy in the wake of the 1798 rebellion, the publication took a radically divergent stand.[5] Burke's *Letter to Sir Hercules Langrishe* provided the conceptual frame of reference that the Edinburgh reviewers needed for a campaign against the remaining Catholic disabilities; the campaign mingled with a defence of Irish character, which, in Burke's view, had been intentionally impaired by the penal laws. What Burke had in mind, however, was the moral attitude of the Catholic gentry, the lower classes being largely outside his concerns.[6] But the 1798 revolt, and, on a larger scale, the French Revolution, shifted the focus of interest towards the peasantry, whose state of mind now became the subject of intense interest. After the Act of Union, and during the Napoleonic wars, the loyalty of Ireland came prominently to the fore – and the complaint about insufficient knowledge of Irish affairs became a regular feature of British commentaries.

A glance at the leading document of Ascendancy opinion immediately after 1798 is useful in assessing the relevance of the *Edinburgh Review* approach. In writing his *Memoirs of the Different Rebellions in Ireland* (1801), Richard Musgrave's hidden task was to play down the disturbing fact that the United Irishmen who sparked off the revolt of 1798 arose from an alliance between Catholics and Protestants. In accordance with a long-established pattern, the recent upsurge is depicted as a religious war, prompted by the Catholic priests.

---

[4] A. Young, *A Tour in Ireland 1776–1779*, ed. A. W. Hutton (1780; 2 vols., Dublin, 1970).
[5] I use the expression 'Protestant Ascendancy' to describe Irish Protestants, more especially Anglicans and landlords. However convenient the term is, it nonetheless conceals significant differences in Ireland's ruling class: see J. Spence, 'The Philosophy of Irish Toryism, 1833–52', PhD thesis, University of London (1991).
[6] *Letter to Sir Hercules Langrishe* (1792), *BWS*, IX, pp. 594–639.

Granted that peace and security 'depend on the morals of the lower class of the people', no autonomous will is ascribed by Musgrave to the Irish peasants, who are represented as mere puppets whose strings are in the hands of priests. 1798 is seen merely as the latest, inevitable outcome of the political disloyalty and moral wickedness inherent in Catholic tenets. Ireland's perpetual state of rebellion could only be soothed by new English settlements.[7]

In Britain, those who opposed Musgrave's line of argument could not help supplying a different explanation of the Irishman's faults. While Burke offered ready-made arguments for Catholic emancipation, it was the Scottish philosophers' stadial conception of history that became the theoretical background to progressive accounts of Irish character. Millar, in particular, had treated Irish mores along 'materialist' lines in a previously unpublished paper on 'The Government of Ireland' contained in the posthumous edition of *An Historical View of the English Government* (1803). In this paper – overall, a carefully argued denunciation of English policy towards Ireland – Millar opposes the view held by many English writers that the native Irish were 'disgraced by a greater portion of barbarity and ferocity, than the rude inhabitants of other countries'. Irish customs 'exhibit that striking resemblance of lines and features, which may be remarked in the inhabitants of every country before the advancement of arts and civilization'. The only peculiarity of Irishmen is that the continual 'acts of injustice and oppression' perpetrated by English governments have made the Irish character focus on 'political and religious disputes' in preference to more pragmatic concerns. The Irishman mocked on English stages for his 'bulls' and blunders is an unfair caricature, Millar continued, of an 'ardent and vehement' temper, of 'a disposition open, forward, undesigning, and sincere, little corrected by culture'.[8] Most importantly, Millar's treatment made the religious factor less consequential. This now appeared as a secondary and late element.

Millar's approach to national character, which in *An Historical View* was applied to English and Scottish attitudes as well, was expounded by Jeffrey in his account of the book, and was adopted by many contributors to the *Edinburgh Review*.[9] As regards Ireland, there ensued the position that 'a state of barbarity as to manners, sentiments, and habits of life' had necessarily resulted from the general and extreme poverty of the Irish.[10] The notion that mores follow from

[7] *Memoirs of the Different Rebellions in Ireland* (3rd edn, 2 vols., Dublin, 1802), quotation from I, p. xiv.
[8] 'Review of the Government of Ireland', in J. Millar, *An Historical View of the English Government* (4th edn, 4 vols., London, 1812), IV, pp. 7–9, 49–52. The stadial view of Irish manners is traceable to Hume's *History of England* as well, but buried under gloomy depictions of Irish atrocities.
[9] Jeffrey's review is in *ER*, 3 (1803), pp. 154–81; see esp. pp. 165–8.
[10] J. Mill, 'State of Ireland', *ER*, 21 (1813), pp. 342–3. Mill had already dealt with Irish affairs: see the 'Preface by the translator' and the 'copious notes' in C. Villers, *An Essay on the Spirit*

the level of civilization naturally merged with that other Scottish tenet, that government is a most effective factor in the shaping of habits and dispositions. Leading Edinburgh reviewers like Jeffrey, Smith, Napier, Mackintosh, Hallam, and Mill agreed in ascribing the dark side of the Irish character to 'the infamous policy of the English'. In particular, although most of the penal laws had been repealed between 1772 and 1793, the persistence of both their social effects and the mores they had brought about was often pointed to. As Mackintosh wrote in 1812, circumstances are such as to take away from the Catholics 'skill and industry, hope and pride'.

The helotism of the Catholic, which either breaks his spirit or excites his rage, in either case equally unnerves his arm, and devotes his fields to barrenness. Men are only just, when they are justly dealt with; and those who are looked down upon as slaves, must look up to their masters as tyrants. The sense of degradation, as well as that of insecurity, extinguishes industry, either by subduing the activity of the human mind, or by converting it into destructive fury.[11]

Equally unanimous among the reviewers was the claim that hostility to Popery had turned into a convenient screen behind which the Ascendancy had cloaked its policy of social exclusion and economic exploitation. 'As soon as you make the Irish happy, you will break the charm of the priest', for superstition is invariably found associated with wretchedness and poverty.[12] With increasing awareness over these decades, the Irish question came to be seen by the Edinburgh reviewers as essentially a social and economic one; the repeal of the remaining Catholic disabilities in 1829, which brought to an end a phase of intense interest in Irish affairs, certainly reinforced the trend.

Malthus's article of 1808 marked a breakthrough in this direction. He famously demonstrated that 'indolent and turbulent habits' resulted from the effects of the 'potato system' on fertility rates via the labour market. Malthus's next step is very significant, for he identified English rule as the main factor in the Irish reliance on the cheapest and humblest sort of food. Despotism, he argued in typical eighteenth-century jargon, invariably annihilates to a great extent individual importance and dignity. It follows that full emancipation of Catholics is necessary to induce 'an elevation in the character and condition

and *Influence of the Reformation of Luther . . . Translated, and Illustrated with Copious Notes,* by *James Mill* (London, 1805).

[11] J. Mackintosh, 'Wakefield's *Ireland*', ER, 20 (1812), p. 352; and see 2 (1803), pp. 398–402 (Smith); 8 (1806), pp. 116–24 (Napier); 8 (1806), pp. 311–36 (Hallam); 11 (1807), pp. 116–44 (Jeffrey); 34 (1820), pp. 320–38 (Smith); 46 (1827), pp. 433–70 (Jeffrey). Sydney Smith in particular wrote regularly on Irish affairs. Bentham, too, subscribed to the *Edinburgh Review* interpretation: *Principles of the Civil Code* (1802), in J. Bentham, *Works*, ed. J. Bowring (11 vols., Edinburgh, 1843), I, p. 317.

[12] Mill, 'State of Ireland', p. 363. Irish character shows a basic similarity to Hindu character as depicted by Mill in *The History of British India* (3 vols., London, 1817), I, pp. 312–15. Mill's Hindus are passionate, imaginative, 'sharp and quick of intellect', but also indolent and passive.

of the lower classes of society', and, with it, a taste for the comforts of life. While Catholic disabilities remain, no system of education can possibly work in Ireland, argued Malthus against the Irishman J. W. Croker.[13]

Theoretically, Malthus provided the most articulate explanation for the Irish moral situation. The point was later brought home by fellow economists McCulloch and Senior, who both elaborated on the necessity of inspiring the Irishman with a more refined taste which led him to aspire to a less coarse diet. The desired change in the indolent habits of the people was in their opinion to result from interventions designed both to render labour more productive and to reduce the prices of many conveniences through lighter taxation.[14] The political economists, in subsuming the Irish question under 'scientific' categories, never failed to oppose fatalistic as well as religious-minded views. In Senior's article of 1844 an explicit hint of the way in which 'material' and 'moral' evils interact is given, with the 'moral evils' being insecurity, ignorance, and indolence, which have been brought about by the 'material evils', namely want of capital and absence of small proprietorship. The moral evils have in turn made the material evils more severe. In particular, the Irish tendency to violence and resistance to law – their 'most prominent' and 'more mischievous' trait – has deterred British capital from being employed in Ireland. Although such a trait is seen as ensuing from the misuse of law perpetrated by the English, and ignorance and indolence too are accounted for on the same lines, Senior makes clear that it is now imperative for the Irish to practise the virtues of self-help in order to break their 'circle of calamities'.[15]

It was generally understood by the Edinburgh reviewers that certain Irish traits did hinder social and economic development, but education was viewed as an effective remedy. However, some inconsistencies surface. Sydney Smith, for instance, inserted a sharply worded criticism of Irish character into one of his pleas against English policy in Ireland.

The Irishman has many good qualities: He is brave, witty, generous, eloquent, hospitable, and open-hearted; but he is vain, ostentatious, extravagant, and fond of display – light in counsel – deficient in perseverance – without skill in private or public economy – an enjoyer, not an acquirer – one who despises the slow and patient virtues – who wants the superstructure without the foundation – the result without the previous operation – the

---

[13] 'On the State of Ireland', in *The Works of Thomas Robert Malthus*, ed. E. A. Wrigley and D. Souden (8 vols., London, 1986), IV, pp. 23–43, esp. pp. 40–2 (originally in *ER*, 12 (1808), pp. 336–55). Malthus wrote a second article on Ireland, here on pp. 47–67.

[14] See, e.g., J. R. McCulloch, 'Ireland', *ER*, 37 (1822), pp. 60–109, esp. pp. 95–6; N. W. Senior, 'Ireland', *ER*, 79 (1844), pp. 189–266, esp. pp. 205–9. On the genesis of Senior's article, endorsed by all Whig leaders, see P. H. Gray, 'British Politics and the Irish Land Question, 1843–1850', PhD thesis, University of Cambridge (1992), pp. 61–5.

[15] Senior, 'Ireland', pp. 196–209. For an assessment of the economists' approach to Ireland, see the classic study by R. D. Collison Black, *Economic Thought and the Irish Question* (Cambridge, 1960).

oak without the acorn and the three hundred years of expectation. The Irish are irascible, prone to debt, and to fight, and very impatient of the restraints of law. Such a people are not likely to keep their eyes steadily upon the main chance, like the Scotch or the Dutch.

Textual evidence supports the view that Smith believed this character to be 'original', predating the 'system of atrocious cruelty and contemptible meanness' established by the English and to which Irish backwardness is 'directly chargeable' even if the national character 'contributes something'.[16] Generally speaking, it can hardly be maintained that the Edinburgh reviewers were unreservedly sympathetic to the Irish peasantry; they were attempting to achieve objectivity on a political question by bringing it under the cold eye of the social analyst. The problem is that a solid layer of moral principles constituted the foundation of social knowledge in those decades; which seems to explain why scathing remarks on Irish character sometimes spring up like weeds alongside sociological arguments. A particularly puzzling example is McCulloch's *A Dictionary, Geographical, Statistical, and Historical* (1841–2), with its neat contrast between a socio-economic analysis of Ireland's evils and the unexpected vehemence of the ensuing portrait of Irish habits.[17] Senior is another case in point: both his Irish journals and his post-Famine articles abound with deprecatory remarks on 'that most un-English society' and its people. Large cracks in the veneer of social analysis become visible. In the long and intricate history of Irish distress nothing is more striking, Senior wrote in 1849, 'than the intimate connection of much of that distress with the carelessness, the inactivity, and the improvidence of the sufferers'.[18]

In the wake of the Act of Union, the Edinburgh reviewers were not alone in playing down national character as a major cause of Irish backwardness. Most travellers associated stern condemnation of British policy with a socio-economic explanation of the defects of the Irish character. The London barrister, George Cooper, who toured Ireland in 1799, made use of both the Scottish theory of history and the concept of despotism and its effects associated with Montesquieu. It is maintained that the Irish peasantry's dispositions – its 'extraordinary indolence' for instance – are similar to those of 'all nations who have been seen in a state of ignorance and barbarity'. 'Gothic' Catholic tenets and oppressive colonial governments have combined to demoralize the Irish, who, largely incapable of restraining their intense passions, have become easy prey to mean and ferocious vices. By introducing good government and justice

---

[16] Smith, 'Ireland', pp. 334–5.
[17] J. R. McCulloch, *A Dictionary, Geographical, Statistical, and Historical* (2 vols., London, 1841–2), II, pp. 35–52, esp. pp. 48–50.
[18] 'Relief of Irish Distress in 1847 and 1848' (*ER*, 1849), in N. W. Senior, *Journals, Conversations and Essays Relating to Ireland* (2 vols., London, 1868), I, p. 230; see also pp. 212–16, 236. Senior's familiarity with national character issues is evidenced by 'France, America, and Britain' (*ER*, 1842), in his *Historical and Philosophical Essays* (2 vols., London, 1865), I, pp. 1–139.

into Ireland, not only would most faults of the national character be eliminated, but the Irish would show their suitability 'for the highest attainments in moral or intellectual excellence'. The energy and intensity of the Irish character stands no comparison anywhere: 'strong passions awaken the faculties, and suffer not a particle of the man to be lost'.[19]

A similar point of view is adopted by Joshua Kirby Trimmer in his writings of 1809, 1812, and 1822. Trimmer was an Englishman who went to Ireland to set up a brickworks on behalf of the Board of Ordnance. The following statement by him is not uncommon in the travel literature of the period.

I went there with my mind prejudiced with the prevalent idea that the manners of the lower order of people were radically and incorrigibly depraved, and that it did not arise from any exterior causes, by the gradual removal of which their condition might be ameliorated, and their manners improved. Whether, in changing my opinion, in consequence of a short residence amongst them, I have formed a truer estimate of their character, it will be for the public to determine.[20]

To many writers, the Irish appeared polite, cheerful, and clever. In spite of their tragic situation, they enjoyed family affections with a warmth unknown to the English. The purity of their sexual life was another common matter for congratulation.[21] Late in the period of concern here, the moralizing and disciplining effects of both the Repeal and the Temperance Movements were largely acknowledged (even if the political message of the former was opposed by most British onlookers).[22]

The work that probably did most to replace the stereotype of the 'wild Irishman' with a more sympathetic and, at the same time, more detailed picture was Edward Wakefield's *An Account of Ireland, Statistical and Political* (1812).[23] His two bulky volumes depicted all facets of Irish life, seasoning

[19]   G. Cooper, *Letters on the Irish Nation* (London, 1800), pp. 34–51, 53–75, 125–48. See also J. C. Curwen, *Observations on the State of Ireland* (2 vols., London, 1818), where Ireland was viewed as a 'pastoral nation' whose development via 'the introduction of refinements' had been blocked by political and economic factors. Curwen was a Cumbrian businessman and MP.

[20]   J. K. Trimmer, *A Brief Inquiry into the Present State of Agriculture in the Southern Part of Ireland* (London, 1809), p. 1. Trimmer wrote also *Further Observations on the Present State of Agriculture, and Condition of the Lower Classes of the People, in the Southern Parts of Ireland* (London, 1812), and *Observations on the Present State of Agriculture . . . to which Are Added Further Observations Relating to the Same Subjects* (London, 1822).

[21]   See, e.g., Curwen, *Observations, passim* (and I, pp. 171–2, on Irish women); Mr and Mrs S. C. Hall, *Ireland: Its Scenery, Character, & c.* (3 vols., London, 1841–3), esp. II, pp. 314–15, on Irish women (but, while Mr Hall was English, Mrs Hall was Irish); J. Grant, *Impressions of Ireland and the Irish* (2 vols., London, 1844), esp. II, pp. 183–5.

[22]   See, e.g., Hall, *Ireland*, I, pp. 33–47; An English Traveller, *A Visit to the Wild West, or, a Sketch of the Emerald Isle* (London, 1843); Grant, *Impressions of Ireland*.

[23]   The work rapidly gained a reputation for objectivity and knowledgeability. Edward Wakefield (1774–1854) was a farmer at Romford and later a land agent in London. His mother was the Quaker philanthropist, traveller, and writer Priscilla Wakefield; and one of Edward's sons was the Edward Gibbon Wakefield mentioned below. Edward was a long-standing friend of Mill and Place and was employed by Ricardo as his land agent.

arguments and figures with travel notes, reminders of the principles of political economy, and geographical descriptions. Many core points in Malthus's analysis recur in his pages. Wakefield considered his work to be a continuation of Young's: he fully endorsed Young's concern with the educative, disciplining, and improving role of landlords, whose deficiencies in Ireland occasioned both writers' bitter laments. The Irish peasant is portrayed as a victim of the harsh treatment he receives and especially of the system of tenancy. 'The progress of national misfortune' is summarized thus: 'oppression deadens every generous feeling in the mind, and begets apathy and idleness; idleness is the parent of want; want gives birth to discontent, and discontent produces anarchy, resistance to the laws, and rebellion.'[24]

A notable characteristic of Wakefield's narrative is the effort to shift attention away from the religious divide. There are three elements in his strategy. First, he does not identify Catholics exclusively with peasants, as most authors implicitly or explicitly do. He stresses the existence, social relevance, and loyalty of other groups: the 'gentlemen of landed property' and the middle-class graziers. Second, Wakefield reverses the direction of influence between Catholic priests and their flocks: in contrast to Musgrave, the latter control the former. Third, Wakefield tends to speak of a comprehensive and truly 'national' Irish character, that is inclusive of all classes and faiths. Although he mentions the 'character of industry and enterprise' which marks the people of Ulster in sharp contrast with the rest of the country, he extends the range of the usual stereotype. Typical negative characteristics like garrulousness, prodigality, 'thoughtless habits', violence, impetuosity, vanity, and a propensity to extremes – in short, a 'want of restraint upon their passions' – are seen to be shared by Protestants and Catholics alike.[25]

3   The Tory press

Some support for a less biased image of the Irish came from an unexpected quarter, the Tory press. Neither *Blackwood's Edinburgh Magazine* nor the *Quarterly Review* devoted themselves unreservedly to a defence of the Ascendancy. The extreme views expressed in *Quarterly Review* by mavericks such as Robert Southey and William Sewell were successfully counteracted by more pragmatic articles. Excess of population, non-resident landowners, and cottage farming figured among the causes of Irish dispositions; Catholicism was by no means their single source.[26] Poulett Scrope mounted a passionate campaign for an Irish poor law and a plan of public works which relied heavily on the social account of Irish idleness. 'The curse of Ireland is the general want of employment

---

[24] *An Account of Ireland, Statistical and Political* (2 vols., London, 1812), I, pp. 262–3.
[25] *ibid.*, II, pp. 542–66, 571, 794–7, 805–6.
[26] See, e.g., G. Taylor, 'Population of Great Britain and Ireland', *QR*, 53 (1835), pp. 56–78; J. Miller, 'State of Ireland', *QR*, 56 (1836), pp. 219–77.

for its inhabitants, and their consequent idle and unproductive vagrancy, habits of plunder, occasional starvation, disease, despair, and turbulence.'[27] The proposition that 'a finer race of men than the Irish peasantry, more nobly gifted and more generously disposed, is not to be found upon the habitable globe', was reannounced in the pages of the *Quarterly*.[28] Ireland was not a regular topic for *Quarterly* reviewers, who nevertheless attempted to set up a bulwark against the Edinburgh offensive on Catholic emancipation. A circumstance of note is the division of opinion on this key issue within the Tory camp, with Castlereagh and Canning supporting emancipation and Wellington and Liverpool opposing it.

Blackwood's seems to be another matter. It prided itself on being 'the only Irish magazine' and published dozens of pieces on Irish affairs, mostly by representatives of the Ascendancy. A peak of interest occurred in the 1820s, when Catholic emancipation was at issue. A notable contributor was Horatio Townsend of Cork, who most assiduously voiced the usual grievances of the Anglo-Irish on the depraved mentality of the peasants. The whole of Townsend's assessment of Irish evils rested on the necessity of a 'moral reformation' – that is, the emulation of English prudence, industry, honesty, and decorum – viewed as a prerequisite to material improvement. Irishmen, he argued, should give up blaming English oppression for 'their own defects, imperfections, and vices'. The 'ancient superstition' of Catholicism was seen to lurk behind the mischievous side of Irish character.[29] A more 'British' editorial line was also upheld, blending the denunciation of an all-powerful Popish plot with condemnation of landowners' rapacity and negligence. In the words of leading journalist David Robinson, the Irish peasants are 'religious fanatics, and political revolutionists, as well as savages', but this is the fault neither of England, as Whig propagandists claimed, nor of the landlords. Intellectually, the lower classes are the 'slaves' of Catholic priests regularly connected to 'profligate demagogues'; the peasantry is in fact not 'a people acting from settled principle' but an indistinct populace whose mind is shaped by the educated.[30] Although Robinson's analysis focused on how to replace the influence of the priests with that of a proto-English class of landowners, his more immediate and realistic task was to reaffirm the validity of the religious divide in the face of conciliatory Whig policy. Thus those facets of Irish character not directly related to the alleged Popish agitation, such as laziness, were unclamorously accounted for on the

---

[27] G. Poulett Scrope, 'Senior's *Letter on the Irish Poor'*, *QR*, 46 (1832), p. 400. See also G. Poulett Scrope, 'Irish Poverty', *QR*, 55 (1835), pp. 35–73. Tories with humanitarian sympathies, like M. T. Sadler, often shared the environmentalist perspective: see Sadler's *Ireland; Its Evils, and Their Remedies* (London, 1828), pp. 17–18.

[28] G. A. A. Dealtry and J. T. Coleridge, 'The Church in Ireland', *QR*, 31 (1825), p. 523.

[29] H. Townsend, 'The Irishman, I', *BM*, 14 (1823), pp. 544, 549.

[30] Quotations from D. Robinson, 'Ireland', *BM*, 15 (1824), p. 280; and from D. Robinson, 'On What General Principles Ought Ireland to Be Governed?', *BM*, 25 (1829), p. 63.

basis of the dispiriting circumstances.[31] Later on, Catholic conspiracy and Whig complacency continued to recur in *Blackwood's*, but the review's gradual shift of focus towards parliamentary politics resulted in the eventual disappearance of the earlier national character themes.[32]

Religion-induced standpoints play the main role in Southey's *Quarterly Review* article (1828) as well. Catholicism, it is contended, takes full advantage of both peasant distress and a primeval attitude to vice and murder. '*Occisio, combustio, devastatio*': the whole history of Ireland is comprised in these three words.[33] In a similarly mystic vein, Oxford clergyman William Sewell turned Irish character into apt material for the restoration of a 'pure and holy form of Christianity', or, more mundanely, for an anti-modern society founded on deference. Sewell elaborated at length on a set of characteristics whose potential usefulness had already been noticed by other contemporaries: the Irishman's childlike docility and gratitude, his fatalism, gregariousness, and impetuosity. He is a warm-hearted creature who is made 'for loyalty and religion', whereas the English are a 'pudding and ale' people leaning dangerously towards 'a spirit of independence' nourished by political economy. It follows that, while the mode of influencing Englishmen is through their head, 'the way to govern an Irish peasant is through his heart'. Paternal rule of the feudal type, associated with occasional doses of military discipline and fortified by the sober religious tenets of Protestantism, would succeed in keeping the Irish 'under rule'.[34]

Having surveyed both Whigs and Tories, an overall evaluation can be offered.[35] A first point to consider is the prevalence of a historical perspective. Variously detailed reconstructions of Anglo-Irish relations over the centuries constituted the main vehicle for assessments of Irish character.[36] Although

---

[31] Robinson, 'Ireland', pp. 272, 274, 276, 291. On the one hand, Robinson's criticism of the absentees went as far as advocating the confiscation of their land; on the other, his antipathy towards the Irish populace surfaces in various contexts: see, e.g., his 'Notes on the United States of America', *BM*, 24 (1828), pp. 626–7.

[32] *Blackwood's* turned from politics to literature as its prevailing interest. After 1829, there appeared a notable article by the historian Archibald Alison: 'Ireland', 33 (1833), pp. 66–87, 223–42, 338–57, 561–82, and 36 (1834), pp. 747–67.

[33] 'The Roman Catholic Question in Ireland', *QR*, 38 (1828), pp. 535–98, quotation from p. 543. Perhaps also 'Ireland: Its Evils and Their Remedies', *QR*, 38 (1828), pp. 53–84, is by Southey. More moderate views on the Irish are expressed in R. Southey, *The Life of Wesley* (2nd edn, 2 vols., London, 1820), II, pp. 256–63.

[34] W. Sewell, 'Romanism in Ireland', *QR*, 67 (1840), pp. 120–1; W. Sewell, 'Sketches of the Irish Peasantry', *QR*, 68 (1841), pp. 340, 350, 369–70.

[35] As regards another important review, the radical *Westminster*, there is very little to report. The Irish question seems to have held no special interest. The review opposed the introduction of a poor law in Ireland in the late 1820s and early 1830s.

[36] In a late specimen of historical environmentalism, Charles Greville wrote: it is impossible 'to form a fair and impartial judgement upon Irish affairs ... without knowing, and keeping studiously in view, the whole course of Irish history'; earlier events are in fact 'linked with succeeding transactions in an unbroken chain of connection'. C. C. F. Greville, *Past and Present Policy of England Towards Ireland* (London, 1845), p. 14.

historical writing strictly intended will be (cursorily) dealt with in section 6 below, it can already be pointed out that, as far as the historical treatment was concerned, the Whig, *Edinburgh Review* stance had the advantage over Tory interpretations. Centuries of English wrongdoings, tirelessly re-examined under the aegis of a prestigious historical method, guaranteed the plausibility of an environmentalist account of Irish character, and, with it, the legitimacy of a reformist agenda. The Whig 'Justice to Ireland' campaign of 1835–41, which Lord John Russell saw as focused on 'a disposition of mind favourable to the Irish people', is a case in point.[37] More regular and fair information also contributed to a more favourable climate of opinion, in parallel with the progressive growth of a tolerant attitude towards Catholicism. Yet, all these influences were to a certain extent counterbalanced by others, as the next section will show.

4   A grey area: political economy, race, and religion

The causal relationship between Catholicism and poverty was firmly established long before the decades of concern here. But this theme progressively gained strength throughout the first half of the nineteenth century. A general reason for this was the link established in mainstream political economy between 'scientific' principles and the agents' moral habits – the point was that in the absence of the latter the economy would not work properly. The role of the principle of population was paramount in this respect, as the admittedly extreme case of Thomas Chalmers, a leading figure of a group of 'evangelical' political economists, shows at length. In the evidence he gave to a committee on the state of Ireland (1830), Chalmers reaffirmed his fundamental belief that 'character is the cause, and . . . comfort is the effect'. What the Irish economy needed was moral improvement, aimed at bringing about a change in marriage habits along Malthusian lines. Purely economic measures would prove ineffective after a short lapse of time, while a poor law would have an irretrievably demoralizing effect. The Scottish case served to show that moral improvement could be obtained through education, and, in particular, through religious education centred on non-compulsory 'Scriptural classes'.[38]

Whatever the influence of evangelical economics, a retributive element of Malthusian origin, recent scholarship has convincingly argued, was part and

---

[37] See Lord J. Russell, *The Government of Ireland. The Substance of a Speech Delivered in the House of Commons on Monday, April 15th, 1839* (London, 1839), esp. p. 16, where the theme of Irish character is tackled.

[38] 'Evidence Before the Committee of the House of Commons on the Subject of a Poor Law for Ireland' (1832), in T. Chalmers, *Dr Chalmers and the Poor Laws*, ed. G. Kerr and G. Chalmers Wood (Edinburgh, 1911), pp. 63–235. For Chalmers's view of the Irish, see his *The Doctrine of Christian Charity Applied to the Case of Religious Differences* (Glasgow, 1818), pp. 40–2.

parcel of social and economic thought.[39] This holds true even if many dismissed the religious side of the matter, and most introduced a time lag between an increase in well-being and population. Senior, for one, made the most of self-helpism in his *Letter* against an Irish poor law. Here, welfare is depicted as being entirely dependent on 'industry' and 'forethought'. He gave abundant excerpts from Chalmers's evidence, 'the most instructive, perhaps, that ever was given before a Committee of the House of Commons'.[40] However, the main point made by such writers as Chalmers, Senior, and Whately – the negative moral effects of a legal provision for the poor – was universally valid. Therefore, although retributive economics called for a definite view of Irish character, the discussion revolved around a mechanism of human nature and not specific national characteristics. Ireland was only the worst possible guinea pig.

The Irish were held in low esteem from another economic perspective: the alleged pivotal role of the human factor in the ongoing civilization of new countries. That certain 'races' seemed fit for the task – that is, that they showed unremitting vitality and energy in the face of titanic challenges, being capable of moulding nature to their will – was, for many, indisputable evidence of their superiority. The celebration of Anglo-Saxonism through an economic-minded pattern of thought where 'race' referred to ancestral identity rather than biological traits was boosted by a Frenchman, Chevalier, who published his famous *Lettres sur l'Amérique du Nord* in 1836, while in Britain, the first to upgrade the traditional theme of the supremacy of Britons in all things economic in accordance with the new international scenario was Oxford economist Herman Merivale.[41] As far as Ireland is concerned, the scathing remarks of economist and colonizer Edward Gibbon Wakefield are representative of widely held opinion: 'the hordes' of Irish emigrants to North America were 'virtually slaves' because of 'their servile, lazy, reckless habit of mind' in the midst of 'the energetic, accumulating, prideful, domineering

---

[39] See B. Hilton, *The Age of Atonement: the Influence of Evangelicalism on Social and Economic Thought* (Oxford, 1988); P. Mandler, 'Tories and Paupers: Christian Political Economy and the Making of the New Poor Law', *Historical Journal*, 33 (1990), pp. 81–103; A. M. C. Waterman, *Revolution, Economics and Religion: Christian Political Economy, 1798–1833* (Cambridge, 1991).

[40] N. W. Senior, *A Letter to Lord Howick, on a Legal Provision for the Irish Poor* (London, 1831). The 1833 commission, presided over by Richard Whately, opposed a poor law on the usual moral grounds but viewed the flaws in the Irish character as due to the lasting effects of the penal laws: 'Third Report from His Majesty's Commissioners for Inquiring into the Condition of the Poorer Classes in Ireland', *Parliamentary Papers*, 30 (1836), pp. 7–8.

[41] See the series of articles on colonization issues which Merivale published in the *Edinburgh Review* since 1839. However, in assessing Irish habits Merivale adopted a firm environmentalist stance: laziness and recklessness were the eventual product of landowners' greed, that is of their advantage on the labour market, and could be overcome by productive investments in agriculture. H. Merivale, *Five Lectures on the Principles of a Legislative Provision for the Poor in Ireland* (London, 1838).

Anglo-Saxon race'.[42] Feelings like these probably owed something to Irish immigration to Britain, universally regarded by economists as a potential cause of lower wages.[43]

Both the meaning and the use of the term 'race' were so loose that not only physical characteristics, but also climate, language, and perhaps also religion and primitive mode of government, seem to have contributed to its definition. 'Race' was a catchword which resists any attempt at deconstruction; its range of application was mobile and indistinct.[44] It can hardly be ascertained whether 'race' was used in the sense of type, that is to designate one of a limited number of permanent forms, or in the sense of lineage and common descent.[45] The two meanings appear closely interrelated as long as 'race' turns into an operational notion in the hands of historians, economists, travellers, etc. Then, the regular suggestion 'race' transmitted was an allusion to unchangeable ancestral characteristics.

The period of interest here witnessed the progressive rise of 'race' to the status of paradoxically self-evident folk term after the heated debates about Celts and Goths of the last third of the previous century. The ever more definite characterization of the Anglo-Saxons did not imply that the cause of the Celts was deserted. The historian of the Anglo-Saxons, Sharon Turner, one of the first 'Germanists' of notice, appreciated the genius and sensibility of 'the great Celtic race', ancient Irish barbarity being equated to that of the Anglo-Saxons.[46] Pinkerton's anti-Celtic racialism being kept alive by books like John MacCulloch's, some antiquaries and ethnologists committed themselves to its refutation, even when, as in the case of George Chalmers's *Caledonia*, nothing like a eulogy of the Celts was put in its place.[47] James

[42] E. G. Wakefield, *A View of the Art of Colonization* (London, 1849), pp. 84, 175. Travellers in the United States often sketched an unflattering image of Irish immigrants; see, e.g., F. Marryat, *A Diary in America with Remarks on Its Institutions* (1839; New York, 1962), pp. 395–6.

[43] G. Cornewall Lewis's official *Report on the State of the Irish Poor in Great Britain* (London, 1836) depicted the immigrants as 'the most efficient workmen', p. 79.

[44] This imprecision was fully recognized by the middle of the century: C. Bolt, *Victorian Attitudes to Race* (London and Toronto, 1971), pp. ix–x.

[45] The distinction is put forward by M. Banton, *Racial Theories* (Cambridge, 1987), pp. 1–64.

[46] S. Turner, *The History of England from the Norman Conquest, to the Accession of Edward the First* (London, 1814), pp. 240, 242.

[47] J. MacCulloch, *The Highlands and Western Isles of Scotland* (4 vols., London, 1824), IV, pp. 250–98. Among his critics, see J. Browne, *A Critical Examination of Dr MacCulloch's Work on the Highlands and Western Isles of Scotland* (Edinburgh, 1825), and T. Price, *An Essay on the Physiognomy and Physiology of the Present Inhabitants of Britain* (London, 1829). G. Chalmers, *Caledonia: or, a Historical and Topographical Account of North Britain* (1807–26; 8 vols., Paisley, 1887–1902), I–II. C. O' Halloran, 'Golden Ages and Barbarous Nations: Antiquarian Debate on the Celtic Past in Ireland and Scotland in the Eighteenth Century', PhD thesis, University of Cambridge (1991), is a good introduction to the debate. Robert Knox's *The Races of Men* (1850) marked the end of a widely observed truce between Saxons and Celts. See R. Horsman, 'Origins of Racial Anglo-Saxonism in Great Britain Before 1850', *Journal of the History of Ideas*, 37 (1976), pp. 387–410.

Cowley Prichard, the father of British ethnology, explained the degradation of the Irish along environmentalist lines, as they had been exposed for centuries to hunger and ignorance, the 'two great brutalizers of the human race'.[48] The Welshman Thomas Price (himself a believer in races, but environmentally determined) wrote that, whatever their racial stock, the Irish should be more appropriately classified as *'the well-fed*, and *the ill-fed'*.[49]

The above is merely a tentative exploration of unbounded territory. But, in order to assess the place of 'race' in the discourse on Irish society, its careless, everyday use in various contexts is more relevant than the treatments offered by self-appointed specialists. There was a grey area in the British attitudes to the Irish, where the ambiguities of both race and religion served, either together or in turn, to express feelings and attitudes which were very much part of the context I wish to reconstruct. In this section, Celtic race and Catholic religion are chiefly dealt with in relation to their alleged influence on economic life.

Brazen conclusions are drawn on the basis of 'race' – religion is entirely neglected – by the 'commissioner' of *The Times*, Thomas Foster, who collected his articles written on the eve of the Famine in *Letters on the Condition of the People of Ireland*. Here is a blatant case of a preconceived view masquerading as the outcome of a five-month tour of Ireland. The evidence supplied by several official reports being hard to ignore, Foster endorses in its entirety the *Edinburgh Review* economists' analysis of the effects of existing forms of tenancy on the habits of the population. In particular, Foster notes that the lack of improvements by the tenants is due to the landlords' eventual appropriation of benefits. At this point, a treatment of Irish destitution in terms of the inferiority of the Celts in comparison to the Ulster Saxons is brought into play and given pre-eminence.[50] Although Foster's collection of newspaper articles may be dissimilar to the more refined literature which it is the purpose of this chapter to examine, in acting as a reminder of the notorious approach to Irish affairs of the most influential of British papers, it may serve to place the more up-market texts in the proper perspective.

The relative wealth of Ulster was traditionally connected to the Protestant faith of its inhabitants. Henry Inglis was the only one who argued against that connection explicitly and at length. He efficaciously reminds the reader of the areas where sustained growth is associated with Catholicism but on the whole his arguments seem unconvincing. The Scottish origin of the Ulstermen gave rise to a character fit to business, wrote Inglis, which has made all the difference between the North and the rest of Ireland; in those wealthier areas, Catholics too enjoy well-being thanks to higher wages and continuous employment.[51]

---

[48] Quoted in G. W. Stocking, Jr, *Victorian Anthropology* (New York, 1987), p. 63.
[49] Price, *An Essay*, p. 103.
[50] T. C. Foster, *Letters on the Condition of the People of Ireland* (London, 1846).
[51] H. D. Inglis, *Ireland in 1834* (2 vols., London, 1834), II, pp. 212–18, 251, 267, 324. See Black, *Economic Thought*, p. 157.

Ascribing poverty to laziness and, in turn, laziness to Catholicism evoked a sort of primordial note which few Protestants refrained from striking. But some were more cautious and self-restrained than others, English and Scottish authors as a rule being among the former. In the 1820s, most of them simply alluded to the link between Catholicism and idleness as a matter of course, and did not credit it with decisive effects. In view of later outspokenness, it is arguable that the struggle for Catholic emancipation played a part in inducing a low-profile approach. The Anglo-Irish, in contrast, were always heavy-handed.[52]

In 1835, Cobden tackled the religious divide thoroughly: Catholicism had made the Irish genius unsuited to 'the eager and persevering pursuit of business'. If it can be proved that 'the Protestant is, more than the Catholic faith, conducive to the growth of national riches and intelligence, then there must be acknowledged to exist a cause, independent of misgovernment, for the present state of Ireland, as compared with that of Great Britain, for which England cannot be held altogether responsible'. Irishmen have clung tenaciously to their savage characteristics of ancient days because everywhere in Europe Catholics abhor change, Cobden concluded on the basis of a short survey.[53] It is in the unrestrained manifestation of the passions – 'in the vehement display of natural feeling' – that the Irishmen's main fault seems to lie. This results in a 'ferocious and lawless community' where 'filth, depravity, and barbarism' are exhibited on a large scale.[54] This evident fragility of Cobden's celebrated cosmopolitanism is confirmed by his American diaries, where he remarks that the Irish are everywhere the same: 'the same passions – the same cunning – the same love of fun and drink – the same proneness to riot and fight'.[55]

As for Cobden's practical proposals, they are more or less in line with those put forward by progressive writers. He does not call for the conversion of Catholics, possibly because he says that only their persecution has kept their faith alive (but he argues that the true aim of the reform of tithes would be to induce more enlightened views on religious matters).[56] Cobden's case seems to a certain extent to conform with the pattern noticed in section 2: perhaps the

---

[52] See, e.g., R. M. Martin, *Ireland Before and After the Union with Great Britain* (London, 1843), pp. 189–94, where the self-help precepts of the Bible were contrasted with the various 'excuses for idleness' offered by Catholicism. Martin wrote also *Ireland, as It Was, – Is, – and Ought to Be* (London, 1833).

[53] *England, Ireland, and America* (1835), in R. Cobden, *The Political Writings* (London, 1878), pp. 25–7. Cobden's point on the economic superiority of Protestant countries was accepted by G. Cornewall Lewis, 'The Irish Church Question', *London Review*, 2 (1835), pp. 252–4, but much softened in a later reprint: G. Cornewall Lewis, *On Local Disturbances in Ireland* (London, 1836), pp. 387–91. The first essay in this book ('Irish Disturbances', pp. 1–340) is a detailed account of Irish agricultural violence along social and political lines.

[54] Cobden, *England*, p. 31.

[55] E. Hoon Cawley, ed., *The American Diaries of Richard Cobden* (New York, 1969), p. 125. Cobden's *European Diaries 1846–1849*, ed. M. Taylor (Aldershot, 1994), show the same anti-Catholic bias.

[56] Cobden, *England*, pp. 28–30.

Irish are despised but this feeling does not enter into policy prescriptions. The fact is that the full emancipation of Catholics took away from the progressive writers not only a powerful argument in defence of the Irish, but also, and perhaps more importantly, the association of their cause with a battle for civil rights. Since little if any improvement in their habits seemed to come to light in successive years, political environmentalism lost momentum to a significant extent.

It is not by accident that Cobden was an enthusiast of phrenology to the point of finding Combe's *Constitution of Man* 'like a transcript of my own familiar thoughts'.[57] Combe denied the influence of circumstances and in particular of government on both individual and national character, preferring to ascribe them to observed regularities in 'size, form, and constitution of the brain'. A chapter of Combe's *A System of Phrenology* is probably the most telling polemic in this respect.[58] Although the phrenological movement appears to us as a distinct forerunner of the scientification of social thought which took place after the mid century, its appeal to contemporaries lay primarily in its being the most radical of the available languages of morals. Phrenology made possible the expression of certain moral perspectives. There was an urge in Britain, which went beyond phrenological circles, to belittle environmental causation in favour of the full independence and responsibility of individuals. One wonders whether young Cobden's animal spirits were stirred by phrenologists' pan-moral utopia: the whole of society to be reconstructed along retributive lines. The scientification of morality advocated by Combe meant that the sphere of ethical judgement became all-pervading. On the one hand, politics is reduced to the choice of rulers with the right skulls; on the other, the degree of liberty a people can enjoy is determined by the relative development of 'the faculties of Benevolence, Veneration, and Conscientiousness'.[59] Behind the smokescreen of anatomical innatism the actual contents of this utopia are unbounded John Bullism, stretched to cover the whole social compact.

Once removed from the sphere of politics to be placed under the umbrella of 'science', nothing can protect the Irish from the violence of a gloomy stereotype. Not surprisingly, the analysis of their skulls reveals the usual personality traits,[60] while an explanation of Ireland's political misfortunes is promptly supplied.

Hierarchies and constitutions do not spring from the ground, but from the minds of men: If we suppose one nation to be gifted with much Wonder and Veneration, and little Conscientiousness, Reflection and Self-Esteem; and another [i.e. Scotland] to possess

---

[57] Quoted in J. Morley, *The Life of Richard Cobden* (London, 1920), p. 93.

[58] G. Combe, *The Constitution of Man Considered in Relation to External Objects* (1828; 8th edn, Edinburgh, 1847), pp. 193–6, 256; G. Combe, *A System of Phrenology* (1825; 4th edn, 2 vols., Edinburgh, 1836), II, pp. 726–67.

[59] G. Lyon, 'Essay on the Phrenological Causes of the Different Degrees of Liberty Enjoyed by Different Nations', *Phrenological Journal*, 2 (1824–5), p. 607.

[60] Anon., 'Cursory Remarks on Ireland', *Phrenological Journal*, 2 (1824–5), pp. 161–77.

an endowment exactly the reverse; it is obvious that the first would be naturally prone to superstition in religion, and servility in the state; while the second would, by native instinct, resist all attempts to make them reverence things unholy, and tend constantly towards political institutions, fitted to afford to each individual the gratification of his Self-Esteem in independence, and his Conscientiousness in equality before the law.[61]

Ulster prosperity, an anonymous contributor to the *Phrenological Journal* contended, must be ascribed to a different shape of the population's brains – hence the linen manufacture.[62] The huge success of *Constitution of Man* notwithstanding, phrenology as a system of thought did not gain access to the higher circles of British culture. Yet phrenology unrefinedly and shamelessly expressed certain postures that were in the air at the time.

5   Dewar and nineteenth-century national character

Daniel Dewar's *Observations on the Character, Customs, and Superstitions of the Irish* (1812) is dedicated to Thomas Brown, who succeeded Stewart in the Edinburgh chair of Moral Philosophy. Like Brown, Dewar, who at the time he wrote was yet to be admitted to the Church of Scotland, held a professorship in Moral Philosophy.[63] His book is an extensive and quite brilliant application of the ideas of Hume, Smith, Stewart, and Malthus to the Irish case – with a crucial twist though, as will be shown in due course. Dewar too praises the Irish for their inquisitiveness, shrewdness, and 'ardent love of kindred and of country', and blames political and economic circumstances for their defects.[64] Dewar's point about the education of the Irish forms the theoretical and political core of the book, which carries further the alliance between social environmentalism and education noticed earlier.[65] Once the government has done its part – once the disabilities are taken away and the fruits of industry secured – Irishmen are expected to go through a process of education aimed to make them suitable for representative institutions.

By comparing the Irish to their sister people, the Scottish Highlanders, whom he regards as a model, Dewar comes to the conclusion that the difference is ultimately accounted for by the lack in the former of both 'enlightened education'

---

[61] Combe, *A System of Phrenology*, II, p. 731. Yet Irish indolence is due to long periods of unemployment, Combe argues on p. 767, fn.

[62] 'Cursory Remarks', pp. 176–7.

[63] Dewar taught at the University and King's College, Aberdeen. In 1819 he was translated to Tron Church, Glasgow. He wrote *Elements of Moral Philosophy, and of Christian Ethics* (2 vols., London, 1826), and co-authored *A Dictionary of Gaelic Language* (Glasgow, 1831).

[64] The one-volume work is divided into two parts, each with separate pagination; for what is referred to in the text, see *Observations on the Character, Customs, and Superstitions of the Irish* (London, 1812), I, pp. 21–85.

[65] Another Scot, Christopher Anderson, discussed at length the Irish need for education: see his *Memorial on Behalf of the Native Irish* (London, 1815), and *Historical Sketches of the Native Irish and Their Descendants* (1828; 2nd edn, Edinburgh, 1830).

and 'moral and religious instruction'. Taken together, these are 'omnipotent' principles of improvement, as Adam Smith and Malthus have demonstrated.[66] To expedite the propagation of enlightened education, Gaelic-speaking teachers could be introduced from Scotland, as well as Bell-Lancaster schools, and, as far as religious teaching is concerned, the 'pure morality of Christianity' would be diffused through the Bible; the 'prejudices of the natives', however, must not be offended.[67] Dewar's agenda stems from his awareness of the power of habits on behaviour as well as from his view that 'national prejudices' can continue in all their force long after the institutions from which they had arisen are forgotten. The Irish question amounts to establishing popular habits and beliefs which, as in Scotland, 'come in aid of the sober dictates of reason and philosophy, and give energy and effect to the enlightened deductions of the sage, and the generous efforts of the legislator'.[68] Dewar ends up putting forward the rule that any successful plan of reform is the effect, rather than the cause, of 'national intelligence and improvement', and reference to the ignorant French people unprepared to change in 1789 is made to prove the point.[69] Thus Dewar is maintaining that historically determined national characters are to be considered an independent force for all practical purposes.

At this point it is appropriate to take a step backward. In eighteenth-century Britain, as the previous chapter has shown, there were some perspectives capable of inducing assessments of the relationship between people and government that were strikingly different from the assessment provided by Millar. Together with the Whiggish pride in the English genius imbuing political culture at large and the ambiguities of Hume, both the civic humanist tradition (as heralded by Adam Ferguson for instance) and Burke's writings on the American question pointed, or might have been interpreted as pointing, to a proper national character as a prerequisite rather than a consequence of a free government. The fear of moral corruption with political decline as its consequence was pervasive; it was felt even by some of those who made a stadial study of manners, Millar included. As for Burke's *Reflections*, they spread a vision of the British constitution in which the moral qualities of the people appeared inextricably embedded in the institutional and legislative framework. This chapter illustrates how a tension between a social and political account of collective character, on the one hand, and a perspective affirming the moral determination of society and politics, on the other, continued to mark the British mind in the nineteenth century. The problem was that, as a logical consequence of the 'moral' approach, the government held to suit Ireland was a junta rather than the British constitution.

---

[66] *Observations*, I, pp. 30, 138, 156–7; II, pp. 67ff.
[67] *ibid.*, II, pp. 66–145.
[68] *ibid.*, II, pp. 8, 13, 15.
[69] *ibid.*, II, p. 128.

In the light of British evidence, one wonders if the thesis holds – and it is a thesis that is regularly put forward, albeit usually in an almost incidental way – that the eighteenth century witnessed a socio-political causation while the nineteenth century reversed the direction of influence between government and national character. Perhaps it does, but it is a matter of degree, rather than of a neat sequence of the two approaches. The eighteenth-century French scene looks more straightforward in that it featured a more marked predominance of the political factor; although this was not infrequently combined with climate, a factor pulling in the opposite direction. Before 1789, the political argument was a powerful weapon in the anti-absolutist polemic waged by the *philosophes*, who could use it to censure at the same time the regime and the moral atmosphere of French society. The contrast between Britain and France becomes striking once the 1790s are considered, with the former country being characterized by Burke's message and the latter by the political rationalism of the revolutionaries. In both nations, the cosmopolitanism of the Enlightenment vanished with the end of the Napoleonic wars, to be replaced by different forms of cultural nationalism. This transformation was more marked in France, defeated and anxious to catch up, than in Britain. Chevalier, among the economists, and Michelet, among the historians, well illustrate the relationship which existed between cultural nationalism and the approach affirming the primacy of a people's attitudes over institutions. It is worth stressing, however, that neither were civic values of a universal nature unknown to the nineteenth century, nor cultural nationalism to the eighteenth.

As far as Britain is concerned, the topicality of Irish affairs, together with a long-standing enmity for a people geographically so close but resembling the self-image of the English turned upside down, make Irish character an ideal test for the detection of the steps through which environmentalism came gradually to be abandoned. The period 1800–50 witnessed both the ambiguities of the advocates of environmentalism and the constant attacks it underwent. It is doubtful whether Richard Chenevix's two-volume *Essay upon National Character* (1832) exerted any influence: although pointing to the 'moral' direction, the work is messy and clumsy.[70] Rather, it is plausible to indicate Carlyle and Macaulay as links between successive generations, albeit in the awareness that they elaborated traditional Whiggish motifs. The approach in terms of the ascendancy of national character would only gain the upper hand in the second half of the century, with the tentative breakthrough represented by Spencer's *Social Statics* (1850) and Bagehot's *Letters on the French Coup d'Etat of 1851* (1852).

---

[70] For this interesting figure of chemist, phrenologist, and journalist, see R. Cooter, *The Cultural Meaning of Popular Science: Phrenology and the Organization of Consent in Nineteenth-Century Britain* (Cambridge, 1984), pp. 57–9.

If I had to fall back on a general hypothesis to account for the progressive independence of national character from governing institutions, I would ascribe it to a series of factors relating to the processes of enlargement of 'society', with the emergence of the modern concept of nation as one of these factors, and the French Revolution as another. Intended purely as a theoretical frame of wide generality, one can say that over the period 1750–1850 authors progressively expanded the boundaries of 'society', and, with it, those of the political community. The sway of an ever more dominant 'society' over politics was in consequence emphasized; the concept itself of a representative government encapsulates this development. Add to this that the British, French, and Italian 'societies' on occasions became charged with a potential for orderly liberty and economic growth, in stark contrast to these countries' suffocating governments. Hence the growing independence of national character from institutions after 1815 would be a reflection of the advent not exactly of mass politics, but of a standpoint which could not ignore the new, post-1789 political role not only of the middle class but also, in some cases at least, of the lower ranks. Yet, the timing of French and British politics is very different, so that John Bull would predate Marianne by fifty years or thereabouts. It is indicative of this lag that while for many French *philosophes* of the mid eighteenth century national aristocracies were the natural bearers of national traits, contemporary English texts have revealed a widespread awareness that they should be drawn from 'the middling and common people'. Within this framework, the point concerning Ireland is that, whereas peasants' mores figure in all British accounts of Ireland since Giraldus Cambrensis, their relevance to political discourse should be seen as a relatively recent occurrence. In the literature being surveyed, the Irish peasantry is said to have a distinctive character which marks it out from the peasantries of other nations and, related to it, a political behaviour independent of the will of those who ought to be its natural leaders. The peasantry is definitely one of the conscious forces in Irish politics even though its records are kept by others.

The role of 'public spirit' in the political cultures of Britain and France qualifies the progress of the character-makes-government approach. As indicated in the previous chapter, the participatory qualities subsumed under the label public spirit came to be incorporated into the established definition of English (or British) character. Whiggism entailed a view of the role of citizens in the making and workings of institutions, a view lasting over the whole period 1750–1850 and beyond, of potentially universal application. In France, many liberals held a functional reading of the notion that dispositions determine institutions, in the sense that they placed much emphasis on the universal need for public spirit as a concomitant of representative government rather than on a specifically French version of it. Hence it is pertinent to make a distinction within the camp of the nineteenth-century upholders of the ascendancy of men over institutional engineering: to urge a modelling of the constitution on a certain idea of, say, Frenchness is not the same thing as to question the practice of devising constitutions regardless of the qualities required to operate them.

6   Carlyle and Macaulay

The British writer who did most to prepare the ground for the change in perception was probably Carlyle. 'Signs of the Times' amounted to a manifesto for a spiritualist vision of society and history phrased as a denunciation of the 'Mechanical Age'. In the political domain, the mechanical age was said to consist of a blind faith in the efficacy of institutions, namely, of a belief that if you 'contrive the fabric of law aright' the spirit of freedom 'will of herself come to inhabit it' without any further effort. To counter this belief, Carlyle argued against Smith and Bentham that, first, 'our happiness depends on the mind which is within us, and not on the circumstances which are without us', and, second, that mind and history with it were ultimately determined by something he called 'faith', 'Moral Force', or 'Idea'. It followed that 'it is the noble People that makes the noble Government; rather than conversely'.[71] Since style counted for much of the fascination that his ideas held for contemporaries, this quite long passage is worth quoting:

The deep, strong cry of all civilised nations, – a cry which, every one now sees, must and will be answered, is: Give us a reform of Government! A good structure of legislation, a proper check upon the executive, a wise arrangement of the judiciary, is *all* that is wanting for human happiness. The Philosopher of this age is not a Socrates, a Plato, a Hooker, or Taylor, who inculcates on men the necessity and infinite worth of moral goodness, the great truth that our happiness depends on the mind which is within us, and not on the circumstances which are without us; but a Smith, a De Lolme, a Bentham, who chiefly inculcates the reverse of this, – that our happiness depends entirely on external circumstances; nay, that the strength and dignity of the mind within us is itself the creature and consequence of these. Were the laws, the government, in good order, all were well with us; the rest would care for itself![72]

A detailed treatment of Carlyle's contribution cannot be given here, but an overview of his remarks on Irish character may suffice to make my general point. *Chartism* is the relevant text – the same where free rein was given to the mystique of Anglo-Saxonism.

The use of the term 'Sanspotatoes' to designate the Irish peasantry is actually not proof of a derisive attitude on Carlyle's part. Such a typical efflorescence of

[71] 'Signs of the Times' (1829), in T. Carlyle, *Critical and Miscellaneous Essays* (7 vols., London, 1888), II, pp. 239–40, 242–4.
[72] *ibid.*, p. 239.

language points to English wrongdoings in Ireland. In his perspective, however, it is not material needs alone that mark the fate of men on Earth, while the most disruptive effects of injustice concern the moral sphere.

For the oppression has gone far farther than into the economics of Ireland; inwards to her very heart and soul. The Irish National character is degraded, disordered; till this recover itself, nothing is yet recovered. Immethodic, headlong, violent, mendacious: what can you make of the wretched Irishman? . . . A people that knows not to speak the truth, and to act the truth, such people has departed from even the possibility of well-being. Such people works no longer on Nature and Reality; works now on Phantasm, Simulation, Nonentity; the result it arrives at is naturally not a thing but no-thing, – defect even of potatoes. Scarcity, futility, confusion, distraction must be perennial there. Such a people circulates not order but disorder, through every vein of it; – and the cure, if it is to be a cure, must begin at the heart: not in his condition only but in himself must the Patient be all changed. Poor Ireland! And yet let no true Irishman, who believes and sees all this, despair by reason of it.[73]

But the cause of Irish degradation seems to be forgotten in the abusively worded portrait of Irish immigration to Britain which follows. Further on, the identity of 'Might and Right' is argued against Thierry. It comes to mind, then, that for Carlyle English rule of Ireland is a historical necessity its operational brutality notwithstanding, the ultimate curse of the 'noisy vehement Irish' being their geographical nearness to the 'strong silent' Anglo-Saxons. Yet Carlyle's pity for the Irish as well as his attack on English policies seem heartfelt, however unstereotyped their phrasing. Later, Ireland would take up even a symbolic meaning in his eyes: 'Ireland really *is* my problem; the breaking point of the huge suppuration which all British and all European society now is', he wrote in the diary of his 1849 journey.[74]

The depiction of the Irish as a people which 'knows not to speak the truth' expresses a deeply ingrained belief of his, as *Cromwell* makes clear. The same theme returns: the Irish are 'unveracious', that is, false in thought because they have 'parted company with Fact'. They have refused to listen to the 'harsh story' which 'Fact' tells; a story which concerns not only the necessity to bend to the yoke but also the Irish's perpetual inability to become strong by imposing discipline on themselves. Cromwell has therefore come to Ireland 'like the hammer of Thor' to re-establish the difference between 'Good' and 'Evil'.[75] In Carlyle's conceptual network, 'Facts' are also the unerring laws of

---

[73] *Chartism* (1839), in *Critical and Miscellaneous Essays*, VI, p. 126.
[74] *Reminiscences of My Irish Journey in 1849*, ed. J. A. Froude (London, 1882), p.v. For his visits to Ireland, see F. Kaplan, *Thomas Carlyle: a Biography* (Cambridge, 1983), pp. 334–47. A merciful reference to the Irish peasants is in *The French Revolution*, ed. K. J. Fielding and D. Sorensen (1837; Oxford, 1989), p. 442.
[75] T. Carlyle, *The Letters and Speeches of Oliver Cromwell*, ed. S. C. Lomas (1845; 3 vols., London, 1904), I, pp. 459–60, 462. Kaplan has written that for Carlyle 'history is an avenging arrow from God': *Thomas Carlyle*, p. 225.

Nature against which man has to prove himself, his virtue and strength lying in the work he does and not in the words he utters. Work always agrees with fact. The 'talent of silence' that peoples like the English and the Romans have shown is sure proof of their consonance with both Nature and History.[76]

That environmentalist accounts of Irish character by and large failed to have a lasting influence on British opinion became progressively manifest after the promising campaign which led to Catholic emancipation in 1829. The fragility of that stance came tragically to full light during the Famine, when providentialist and retributive explanations of the potato failure – seen as 'the judgement of God on an indolent and unself-reliant people' – held sway over attitudes towards relief policy.[77] As Mill argued when criticizing the proclamation of a day of General Fast for Ireland (24 March 1847), it proved disastrously true that there were few things more practically mischievous 'than giving the countenance of authority to the religious notions characteristic of a rude age'.[78]

The field of historical writing provides exemplary evidence of the shift from environmentalist to 'spiritualist' views, and in particular to an aggressive ideology of Anglo-Saxonism. It is not an overstatement to say that Macaulay's *History of England* marks the end of a phase in which some of the traditional Irish grievances were finally acknowledged. Millar's interpretation of Irish character had been adhered to by Hallam, who argued that Ireland would have developed as Scotland did but for the English conquest. The other noteworthy history of England of the first half of the century was written by the Catholic Lingard in a conciliatory spirit, evidenced by the mild tone and the almost equal amount of blame apportioned to the two sides. Earlier in the century, another English Catholic historian, Francis Plowden, had gone as far as postulating that the Irish character was suited to the Union.[79] William Godwin certainly did his

---

[76] *Past and Present* (1842; London, 1888), pp. 134–43. On Carlyle's 'facts', see Kaplan, *Thomas Carlyle*, p. 343. In a *Spectator* article, Carlyle proposed to organize Irish peasantry into military corps: S. Heffer, *Moral Desperado: a Life of Thomas Carlyle* (London, 1995), pp. 265–6.

[77] See the following contributions by P. H. Gray: 'British Politics'; ' "Potatoes and Providence": British Government Responses to the Great Famine', *Bullán*, 1 (1994), pp. 75–90; 'Ideology and the Famine', in C. Póirtéir, ed., *The Great Irish Famine* (Dublin, 1995), pp. 86–103. See also Hilton, *The Age of Atonement*, pp. 108–14. The quotation is by Charles Trevelyan, permanent under-secretary at the Treasury, cited in Hilton, *The Age of Atonement*, p. 113.

[78] 'The General Fast' (1847), *MCW*, XXIV, p. 1075. On J. S. Mill's forty-three *Morning Chronicle* articles on Ireland (1846–7), where he contended that peasant proprietorship was the solution because it could heal the two main vices of Irish character, idleness and reproductive improvidence, see in particular L. Zastoupil, 'Moral Government: J. S. Mill on Ireland', *Historical Journal*, 26 (1983), pp. 707–17. Mill's first clash with Carlyle occurred over Ireland in May 1848. Faced with Carlyle's claim that England had a civilizing mission, Mill strongly denied it in the light of centuries of English misrule: 'England and Ireland' (1848), *MCW*, XXV, pp. 1095–100. Mill was replying to T. Carlyle, 'Repeal of the Union', *The Examiner*, 29 April 1848, pp. 275–6.

[79] See respectively H. Hallam, *The Constitutional History of England from the Accession of Henry VII to the Death of George II* (2 vols., London, 1827), II, pp. 699–770; J. Lingard, *A History of*

best to defend Cromwell's *res gestae* in Ireland, though not to the extent of either approving of English rule overall or ignoring the Irishman's many virtues. In *History of Ireland and the Irish People*, Samuel Smiles denounces English oppression with the utmost force, and, correspondingly, Irish character appears to him to have been debased by past anarchy and a perpetual state of war. Yet contemporary Irishmen offer 'a sublime moral spectacle' of devotion and self-sacrifice through the Temperance and Repeal movements, thus indicating that 'regeneration is at hand'.[80] There were some stains in the picture as well. The most serious one was probably Carlyle's *Oliver Cromwell*; another was the highly successful *History of Europe from the Commencement of the French Revolution* (1833–42) by Archibald Alison, where Irish character was deemed to be irreconcilable with representative government.[81] It should be recalled that the Celtic descent that Alison complained about was in the same years eulogized by Thierry and Michelet in parallel with an indictment of British policies towards Ireland. The rise of Celticism in French historiography has to be taken into account, whatever the influence that the French climate of opinion might have exerted in Britain.

The religious divide, effectively played down by most of the aforementioned historians,[82] was revived by Macaulay in the context of extensive recourse to national characters (and other more or less metaphysical historical subjects) as explanatory devices.[83] But, he observes, religion was not the only difference between the natives and the settlers of English and Scottish origin: they were 'two populations, locally intermixed, morally and politically sundered'. Different races, languages, and 'stages of civilisation', in addition to 'strongly opposed' national characters, had determined a 'strong antipathy'[84] – so strong

---

England from the First Invasion by the Romans to the Accession of Henry VIII (8 vols., London, 1819–30); and F. Plowden, *An Historical Review of the State of Ireland* (2 vols., London, 1803), esp. I, pp. 1–7.

[80] W. Godwin, *History of the Commonwealth of England* (4 vols., London, 1824–8); S. Smiles, *History of Ireland and the Irish People, Under the Government of England* (London, 1844), esp. pp. iii–iv, 20. William Cobbett's denunciation of the Reformation (on both sides of the water) was isolated: *A History of the Protestant Reformation in England and Ireland* (2 vols., London, 1829).

[81] A. Alison, *History of Europe from the Commencement of the French Revolution . . . to the Restoration of the Bourbons* (vols. 1–2, 1833; 6th edn, 10 vols., Edinburgh, 1844), esp. III, pp. 692–706. On Alison, see M. Bentley, 'Victorian Historians and the Larger Hope', in M. Bentley, ed., *Public and Private Doctrine* (Cambridge, 1993), pp. 134–40.

[82] George Brodie too deserves mention in this respect: see his *History of the British Empire, from the Accession of Charles I to the Restoration* (4 vols., Edinburgh, 1822), I, pp. 441–9; III, pp. 157–9. See also Greville, *Past and Present Policy*. On the other hand, S. Turner's *The Modern History of England* (4 vols., London, 1827–9), written in opposition to Leland, stresses the role of the Catholic Church in the Irish rebellions.

[83] J. Clive, *Thomas Babington Macaulay* (London, 1973), pp. 105–24.

[84] T. B. Macaulay, *The History of England from the Accession of James II* (5 vols., London, 1849–1855), II, pp. 128–31.

as to lead Macaulay to endorse Cromwell's policy of 'extirpation'. A parallel
between the Irish and the American Indians figures both in the *Essays* and in
the *History*.[85]

The character of the Irish is depicted by Macaulay according to two logically
different but continuously overlapping perspectives. On the one hand there is
the quasi-natural Celtic descent, ancestrally showing 'the susceptibility, the vivacity, the natural turn for acting and rhetoric, which are indigenous on the
shores of the Mediterranean Sea'. On the other, historical factors like underde-
velopment and the resilience of Catholicism are called to account for the lack
of mental cultivation, diligence, and forethought, as well as for the 'Helot feeling', of the Irishman; English rule was 'the dominion of wealth over poverty,
of knowledge over ignorance, of civilised over uncivilised man'. The blurring
of the two perspectives – entailing a 'natural' sanction of a historical course –
turns Irish history into a self-fulfilling prediction, as demonstrated by the failed
acceptance of the Reformation. As the Irish 'were some centuries behind their
neighbours in knowledge', they did not embrace the new faith; additionally, as
the Reformation was in fact an insurrection of the 'great German race', of the
peoples speaking a 'Teutonic' language, the Irish were naturally excluded.[86]

The Irish character is evaluated against the yardstick of the Scottish. In the
Essays, the comparison serves to exemplify that the human stuff may, as in
Scotland, 'supply in a great measure the defects of the worst representative
systems', constitutions being means and not ends. A similar capacity is out
of the question in Ireland. In the *History*, the Scots are said to possess 'all
the qualities which conduce to success in life' whereas the Irish have those
which make a people 'interesting'.[87] Perhaps more remarkably, the portrait of
the ancient Highlanders follows more strictly stadial lines and is much more
sympathetic than that of their fellow Celts the Irish.[88] Although the following
comment is arrogant almost to the extent of caricature, no such ray of hope is
ever shone onto the Irish.

There was therefore even then evidence sufficient to justify the belief that no natural
inferiority had kept the Celt far behind the Saxon. It might safely have been predicted
that, if ever an efficient police should make it impossible for the Highlander to avenge
his wrongs by violence and to supply his wants by rapine, if ever his faculties should

---

[85] 'Sir William Temple' (1838), in T. B. Macaulay, *Critical and Historical Essays*, ed. F. C.
Montague (3 vols., London, 1903), II, p. 262; *The History of England*, IV, p. 115. See also
'Social and Industrial Capacities of Negroes', *ER*, 45 (1826), p. 405. Macaulay wrote in 'Sir
William Temple', p. 262, that 'it is in truth more merciful to extirpate a hundred thousand human
beings at once and to fill the void with a well-governed population, than to misgovern millions
through a long succession of generations'.

[86] *The History of England*, I, p. 66; II, pp. 127–31, 134.

[87] 'Burleigh and His Times' (1832), in *Critical and Historical Essays*, I, pp. 468–70; *The History
of England*, I, pp. 65–6.

[88] *The History of England*, III, pp. 304–9.

be developed by the civilising influence of the Protestant religion and of the English language, if ever he should transfer to his country and to her lawful magistrates the affection and respect with which he had been taught to regard his own petty community and his own petty prince, the kingdom would obtain an immense accession of strength for all the purposes both of peace and of war.

The difference between the two Celtic peoples is accounted for by 'the better qualities of an aristocracy' which the Highlanders showed.[89]

[89] *ibid.*, III, pp. 308–9. For a comment on Macaulay's attitude, see N. Lebow, 'British Historians and Irish History', *Eire-Ireland*, 8 (1973), pp. 32–5 (although the paper suffers from an oversimplistic interpretative line). A few years later, R. H. Inglis Palgrave took a radically divergent stand on English dealings with Irish and Scots: *The History of Normandy and of England* (4 vols., 1851–64; Cambridge, 1921), IV, pp. 208–11, 492–4.

Part II

1850–1914

7 The demise of John Bull: Social sciences in Britain, 1850–1914

1 Introduction: the social scientific perspective

This chapter and the following one investigate the role of national character within the framework of the 'social sciences'. Granted that it would be unrealistic to assume that those who with growing assurance styled themselves social scientists completely broke with previous approaches and ideas, it is equally undeniable that a new intellectual framework gradually took centre stage, and that, together with the fragmentation and professionalization of social knowledge, it had momentous consequences. An evolutionist perspective, which informed most of the 'social sciences' at this early juncture, was instrumental in bringing about new viewpoints. Fundamental among these was a fresh relevance of the collective dimension of life: after Darwin, individual self-interest pure and simple could hardly be considered rational behaviour in view of the needs of the social organism as a whole. Largely as a result of this viewpoint, which accorded with the coming into being of more intricate and sophisticated patterns of social interdependence, the grounds on which both national character and public spirit were assessed shifted.

A distinction between old and new perspectives is thus crucial to my argument in this second part of the book. A clear-cut differentiation between the 'scientists' and the 'humanists' proves out of place in view of figures like Bagehot or Taine, who seemingly belonged to both groups. There has been considerable confusion and disagreement in the historians' attempts to achieve a non-teleological definition of social science that could comprehend the breakthrough of 1870–1900 or thereabouts.[1] The traditional textbook distinction

---

[1] Tocqueville and Marx, and sometimes Montesquieu, are customarily considered active in the tradition of sociological thought by historians of the discipline: see, e.g., the classic treatment, admittedly aware of the risks of anachronism and de-contextualization, by R. A. Nisbet, *The Sociological Tradition* (New York, 1966), where Montesquieu is not taken into account; and that, less astute methodologically, by R. Aron, *Les étapes de la pensée sociologique* (Paris, 1967), where Montesquieu receives lengthy attention. At the time when sociology was establishing itself, however, views about its task and boundaries differed remarkably; in the three volumes of the London *Sociological Papers* (1905–7) there are sixty-one definitions of sociology: P. Abrams, *The Origins of British Sociology: 1834–1914* (Chicago and London, 1968), p. 3.

serves to identify the 'social scientists' only by rule of thumb. Spencer and Durkheim would be numbered among the scientists, but not Bryce and Renan – in practice, this may just mean that the authors' self-definitions are upheld. But a research programme inspired by and modelled on the natural sciences is probably an appropriate dividing line, even if such a feature was hardly a novelty *per se*. In any case, what is relevant here is the emergence of new foci on national character, rather than the labelling of authors or the testing of their claims to scientificity. Accordingly, social scientific approaches are defined as those which marked a difference in the treatment of the relationship between institutions and the quality of the citizenry in the years 1850–1914; a difference found to derive from, first, the view of society as a functional whole, and, second, the adoption of more refined tools for social investigation. The textbook classification of social scientists largely overlaps with that entailed by this definition, thus indicating that my use of the category 'social science' rests on traditional ground.

The importance of collective attitudes to the first wave of social scientists is attested to by *prima facie* evidence. From approximately mid century, it became a widespread assumption that the age was witnessing a consolidation of the economic achievements of the previous decades; that the combined forces of applied science, industrial organization, and modern means of transport had overcome long-established constraints in production and consumption; and, accordingly, that a scenario of eventual well-being for all was not chimerical. But, in parallel, one notices a recurrent complaint about the inadequacy of men to the new environment. A number of viewpoints, often dependent on the evolutionary perspective, were devised to analyse this problem. To mention just a few, Durkheim's *De la division du travail social* and *Le suicide* addressed the insufficient development of moral and social bonds in the face of the ever-progressing division of labour; Spencer's sociology made much of the slow process of adaptation of human attitudes and desires to new spheres of action; and many political scientists focused on the lower classes' lack of the civic virtues required by the enlargement of the franchise. Further examples are the anthropologists who dealt with the theory of 'survivals', that is the continuation of past states of mind long after the disappearance of the conditions which gave rise to them, and the economists throughout Europe who expressed concern at the disparity in pace between technical advance and moral and cultural progress. Most blatantly, eugenics presented itself as a straightforward solution to the problem of under-achievers and of human performance in general.

The perception of a gulf between dispositions and material forces was fuelled by 'democracy'. Although there were differences of timing and in other respects, in both Britain and France liberal principles and the corresponding institutional machinery came to be seen as settled questions in the face of the phenomena which 'democracy' designated: not only the sharing of power with the lower classes but also the advent of a mass society and its concomitants, like a new wave of urbanization, new public utilities and facilities, organized parties and trade unions, factory reform, working-class leisure, and a popular press. Society had fully emerged, to use the terminology of part I; this emergence multiplied the spheres of application of public spirit, and thereby made the inspiration of civic awareness in citizens' hearts both more urgent and more problematic. In France, public morality remained an object of keen interest through the turmoil of the mid century into the Third Republic, which in the views of many authors failed to induce a change in political habits and social behaviour. In Britain, a similar preoccupation gathered momentum from a tangle of causes: prominent among these were a concern with the workings of political democracy, the new responsibilities of citizenship in urban settings, and the growing social conscience of the intelligentsia. As will be shown in chapter 9 with reference to both British and Italian writers, 'democracy' provided the context for a conception of public spirit which could not be reduced to that of Tocqueville and Mill.

In this chapter, the question of the novelties brought about by the 'social sciences' in Britain is specifically addressed. The chapter concentrates on the emergence of a model of social environmentalism along 'social scientific' lines against rival claims. A preliminary consideration is that it is difficult to over-estimate the importance of ideas of national character in British culture in the second half of the century.[2] What was previously largely implicit – that nations are in the final analysis founded on the attitudes of citizens – was made explicit, and not infrequently turned into the fulcrum of those over-comprehensive theories of civilization which characterized the period. Some writers continued the eulogy of the Anglo-Saxon 'race', but now in the context of imperialistic rivalries; Dilke and Kidd are cases in point. As will be argued in full with reference to Froude, many authors made great play of an idea, race, which they were neither able nor willing to define even in the broadest terms.[3] One of these authors, James Bryce, even acknowledged its inherent emptiness.[4] A second

---

[2] See S. Collini, *Liberalism and Sociology: L. T. Hobhouse and Political Argument in England 1880–1914* (Cambridge, 1979), pp. 28–30; and, by the same author, 'The Idea of Character: Private Habits and Public Virtues', in *Public Moralists* (Oxford, 1991), pp. 91–118. More generally, see many scattered remarks in S. Collini, D. Winch, and J. Burrow, *That Noble Science of Politics* (Cambridge, 1983).

[3] See, e.g., E. A. Freeman, 'Race and Language', *Contemporary Review*, 29 (1877), pp. 711–41, esp. 724–32, 739–40; J. Bryce, *The Relations of the Advanced and the Backward Races of Mankind* (Oxford and London, 1902); J. Bryce, *Race Sentiment as a Factor in History* (London, 1915). G. W. Stocking, Jr, *Victorian Anthropology* (New York, 1987), pp. 63–4, comments on the wide acceptance of Lamarckism: 'Given the belief that the habitual behavior of human groups in different environments might become part of their hereditary physical makeup, cultural phenomena were readily translatable into "racial" tendencies.' In what follows, the term 'racialism' will connote a non-biological notion of race.

[4] Bryce, *The Relations*, p. 9; Bryce, *Race Sentiment*, pp. 3–4, 18.

group of writers, of which Spencer will be taken as a first example, dealt with national character issues within the environmentalist framework provided by an evolutionary perspective that went a long way towards shaping the 'social sciences'. These two groupings do not exhaust the complexity of the British panorama, however, while certain issues (like certain writers) cut across their boundaries. If a single general view, endorsed by authors from all quarters, marked the years 1850–1900, it would be the view of liberty as a state of mind, the role of institutions being accordingly played down. This pervasive conception, which reversed the teaching of Hume's 'Of National Characters', took various guises but eventually the 'social sciences' put forward new viewpoints which altered the scenario for good: this is the interpretative line argued here. The beginning of the twentieth century seems to have been a watershed with respect to the establishment of a 'scientific' social environmentalism. Earlier on, what will be referred to as the 'inner liberty doctrine' held the field, as the next section will illustrate.

2   Liberty is in the minds of the free

The rationale of H. T. Buckle's history of civilization (1858–61) can be summed up in the three 'selfs' which, in his view, alone make liberty possible: 'self-discipline, self-reliance, and self-government'.[5] With Buckle, a radical, 'the people' figure as the exclusive holders of these allegedly typically English virtues. Following in the footsteps of a radical tradition which comprised Hazlitt, E. Bulwer Lytton, Cobden, J. S. Mill, Samuel Laing, Samuel Smiles, and George Combe, Buckle laid emphasis on two tenets in particular.[6] The first was that countries that had 'the form of liberty without its spirit' were doomed to failure. The second was that governments could not civilize nations, and legislators were not the cause of social progress.[7] The essence of the doctrine of inner liberty is condensed in these two assumptions, which would be endorsed by a number of writers from different standpoints. In the hands of Buckle, the doctrine is used to account for English civilization, as the independence and 'lofty bearing' of the people were instrumental in the avoidance of that French trap, the 'spirit of protection'.

[5] H. T. Buckle, *History of Civilization in England* (2 vols., London, 1858–61), I, p. 575. Buckle's declared dismissal of morality as a factor in favour of intellectual proficiency proves specious in the course of the book. Buckle's targets were the 'theological spirit', the excessive claims of politics, and state intervention.

[6] All of the cited have been considered but Bulwer Lytton and Laing – for Smiles see below in this chapter. For the novelist and MP Edward Bulwer Lytton, see his *England and the English*, ed. S. Meacham (1833; Chicago and London, 1970). For Samuel Laing the elder (1780–1868), the radical Scot, and not the namesake who was a railway director and a scientific popularizer (1812–1897), see esp. his *Notes of a Traveller, on the Social and Political State of France, Prussia, Switzerland, Italy, and Other Parts of Europe* (London, 1842).

[7] Buckle, *History of Civilization*, esp. I, pp. 453–8, 567–70, 605–17; II, pp. 130–5.

Walter Bagehot, with Carlyle, was perhaps the most influential proponent of the doctrine in its conservative version. As the two previous chapters have documented, the pride in Britain's liberty could serve either progressive or conservative purposes with equal efficacy. To take a step backwards, Brougham's famous speech of 1832 is emblematic of the use of Whiggish motifs within a progressive agenda. To the supporters of the Reform Bill it was germane to give an account of the middle class as moral and responsible. Brougham spoke of 'the people', that is the middle classes, as 'the genuine depositaries of sober, rational, intelligent, and honest English feeling'. And continued: 'Unable though they be to round a period, or point an epigram, they are solid, right-judging men, and, above all, not given to change . . . Grave, intelligent, rational, fond of thinking for themselves, they consider a subject long before they make up their mind on it; and the opinions they are thus slow to form they are not swift to abandon.' In other words, the middle classes showed 'a dogged love of existing institutions': this very Burkean trait made them fit for representation.[8] Under different circumstances, this same image of genuine, plain right-mindedness became the raw material for both Carlyle's Anglo-Saxon myth and Bagehot's eulogy of deference; Buckle's emphasis on the independence of Englishmen was a matter of degree and not of a different idiom. The view that English liberty rested on the moral grounds represented by a traditional set of virtues was common to all. Of course, varying choices from that set made the difference. If radicals like Buckle stressed self-reliance and public spirit, Brougham adopted Burke's anti-revolutionary reformulation of English character, and Bagehot went as far as making submissiveness the defining trait of the nation.

Bagehot was a staunch proponent of the idea of national character, to the point of founding on it the political destinies of both England and France.[9] 'With a well-balanced national character', he wrote in 1852, 'liberty is a stable thing'; conversely, 'paper is but paper', and 'the best institutions will not keep right a nation that *will* go wrong'. Liberty requires certain qualities which the English have and the French do not; and, for all practical purposes, national characters are unchangeable.[10] This simple message was put forward in two basic variants. In *The English Constitution*, the elitist model of government of Britain was said to hang on the deferential character of the masses (and favourably contrasted to the democratic model of the United States). By addressing the irrational deference of the English (elsewhere called their 'real sound stupidity') at the time of the second enlargement of the franchise, Bagehot was unmasking the radicals' sturdy Englishman to put in his place a vision of the lower and middle

[8] H. Brougham, *Speeches* (4 vols., Edinburgh, 1838), II, pp. 599–601.
[9] See J. Burrow, 'Sense and Circumstances: Bagehot and the Nature of Political Understanding', in Collini, Winch, and Burrow, *That Noble Science*, pp. 161–81.
[10] *Letters on the French Coup d'Etat of 1851, BCW*, IV, pp. 49–50. But see *Physics and Politics* (1872), *BCW*, VII, pp. 34, 134.

orders as 'narrow-minded, unintelligent, incurious'. They revelled in the 'theatrical' elements of the constitution. It was because 'great communities are like great mountains – they have in them the primary, secondary, and tertiary strata of human progress' that the British constitution included 'mystic', 'occult', and 'brilliant' components, intended to make an impression 'by appealing to some vague dream of glory, or empire, or nationality'. The gist of *The English Constitution* is that the English are not able to elect a parliament; if you doubt, he suggests, 'go out into their kitchens'.[11]

The second variant of Bagehot's view on national character is put forward in the ambitious *Physics and Politics*. This is an attempt to explain the origin and workings of national characters on the basis of history and biological evolutionism, with Lamarckian heredity and unconscious imitation serving to account for both national and class differences.[12] The adoption of the evolutionist apparatus provided Bagehot with a framework within which the notion of national character, of long-standing concern to him, could receive a comprehensive and authoritative treatment. Since Buckle had claimed to dismiss moral causes as factors of progress, he is at pains to specify that the consideration given to hereditary transmission does not exclude the action of moral forces: 'it is the action of the will that causes the unconscious habit; it is the continual effort of the beginning that creates the hoarded energy of the end; it is the silent toil of the first generation that becomes the transmitted aptitude of the next'.[13] The horrors of the French Revolution are said to be a case of 'atavism', namely, of a relaxation of social customs inducing a return to primitive passions; the French and the Irish are specially prone to this instability.[14] As regards the English, his conclusion is that the 'practical Englishman' may be 'stupid' to talk to, but excels in 'this great union of spur and bridle, of energy and moderation'. Idiosyncratic and extreme minds are biologically primitive, while the 'animated moderation' which characterizes the English is the quality most suited to modern society. They know 'when to pull up' – to this 'rough instinct' the success of England in the world is to be ascribed.[15]

At the time of Britain's unchallenged greatness, when many pressing political and social problems appeared to have been surmounted, the chord more generally struck could hardly fail to be a self-congratulatory one. Heavily influenced by German scholarship, the 'Oxford School' of historians celebrated the

---

[11] *The English Constitution* (1865–7), *BCW*, V, pp. 208–9. The sentence on stupidity is in *Letters*, p. 51.

[12] For Bagehot's theory of national character in *Physics and Politics*, see esp. pp. 34–40, 64–80, 100. Perhaps mindful of Hume, in this work Bagehot made unconscious imitation a crucial mechanism in the shaping of national character; the point would later be taken up by French and Italian crowd theorists and sociologists. For his Lamarckian account of classes, see pp. 21, 84 and *passim*.

[13] *ibid.*, p. 22.

[14] *ibid.*, pp. 104–5.

[15] *ibid.*, pp. 122–33.

uninterrupted progress of England as guaranteed from the very beginning by the qualities of the Teuton 'race'. (Admittedly, Stubbs's argument was much more elaborate than Green's and Freeman's.)[16] A distinct Francophobia correlated with this 'liberal racialist' version of Whiggish history, which, in embracing the theory of primitive Germanic freedom, rested on an ancestral notion of national character. 'New and foreign elements have from time to time thrust themselves into our law', Freeman wrote, 'but the same spirit which could develope [*sic*] and improve whatever was old and native has commonly found means sooner or later to cast forth again whatever was new and foreign'.[17] The English had the characteristics of 'the German race to which they belonged': love of freedom and equality, a sense of justice, and independence – in short, the virtues of self-government.[18]

J. S. Mill's qualified contribution to the doctrine of inner liberty took two forms.[19] First, in *Logic*, he declared his intention to give scientific status to the idea of national character as the pivot of scientific politics, although his 'ethology' failed to materialize. His discovery that 'there exist universal laws of the formation of character' entailed that a separate science of government was an impossibility, because government was 'most mixed up, both as cause and effect, with the qualities of the particular people or of the particular age'.[20]

[16] J. W. Burrow, *A Liberal Descent: Victorian Historians and the English Past* (Cambridge, 1981), pp. 97–151. But even for Stubbs 'the nation did not derive its independent character and its freedom from the constitution; the constitution was the expression of the national capacity for freedom': C. Parker, *The English Historical Tradition Since 1850* (Edinburgh, 1990), p. 43.

[17] E. A. Freeman, *The Growth of the English Constitution* (London, 1872), p. 19.

[18] J. R. Green, *A Short History of the English People* (1874; London and Toronto, 1915), pp. 2–4. That 'the character of a nation determines in great measure the form and vitality of the state' was an axiom to another historian, Lord Acton: 'Nationality' (1862), in his *The History of Freedom and Other Essays*, ed. J. N. Figgis and R. V. Laurence (London, 1907), p. 297.

[19] For recent comments on Mill's ethology and views on character, see L. S. Feuer, 'John Stuart Mill as a Sociologist: the Unwritten Ethology', and J. M. Robson, 'Rational Animals and Others', both collected in J. M. Robson and M. Laine, eds., *James and John Stuart Mill Papers of the Centenary Conference* (Toronto, 1976), pp. 86–110, 143–60; G. Becattini, 'Pensiero economico e pensiero politico nell'Inghilterra vittoriana: il ruolo cruciale di J. S. Mill', *Il pensiero politico*, 15 (1982), pp. 28–47; G. Becattini, 'J. S. Mill fra economia politica e scienza generale della società', in G. Basevi et al., *Scritti in onore di Innocenzo Gasparini* (2 vols., Milan, 1982), I, pp. 83–94; S. Collini, 'John Stuart Mill and the Philosophic Method', in Collini, Winch, and Burrow, *That Noble Science*, pp. 127–59; H. M. Clor, 'Mill and Millians on Liberty and Moral Character', *Review of Politics*, 47 (1985), pp. 3–26; J. Carlisle, *John Stuart Mill and the Writing of Character* (Athens, Ga., and London, 1991); and P. Smart, 'Mill and Nationalism: National Character, Social Progress and the Spirit of Achievement', *History of European Ideas*, 15 (1992), pp. 527–34. On Mill on citizenship, see below chapter 9.

[20] *A System of Logic Ratiocinative and Inductive* (1843), *MCW*, VIII, pp. 846–7, 859, 863–74, 904–7; quotations on pp. 864, 906. 'The character, that is, the opinions, feelings, and habits, of the people, though greatly the results of the state of society which precedes them, are also greatly the causes of the state of society which follows them; and are the power by which all those of the circumstances of society which are artificial, laws and customs for instance, are altogether moulded', p. 905.

Second, he affirmed the doctrine in famous writings, among which *Considerations on Representative Government* stands out. Here there is the memorable
statement that 'if we ask ourselves on what causes and conditions good government in all its senses, from the humblest to the most exalted, depends,
we find that the principal of them, the one which transcends all others, is the
qualities of the human beings composing the society over which the government
is exercised'.[21]

At the root of the relevance Mill ascribed to public spirit there was seemingly
his rejection of Owen's 'fatalist' view of character;[22] for participation is to Mill
very much a matter of self-improvement and self-education as well as of political
or administrative agency. As early as 1831, in 'The Spirit of the Age', he congratulated the English people on their training themselves in the qualities of self-
government, and in particular in the spirit of association.[23] His polemic against
the misery of the acquisitive English disposition softened in later years, when it
became increasingly clear to him that 'the active, self-helping character is not
only intrinsically the best, but is the likeliest to acquire all that is really excellent
or desirable in the opposite type'.[24] It is probable that Louis Napoleon's seizure
of power influenced his views about the French character, which may have represented an alternative to English greed. Increasingly, French character appeared
to him not only subject to 'the double education of despotism and Catholicism'
but also seriously degraded by centralization.[25] Arguably, Mill's own brand of
public spirit embraces the man-made, history-made three requisites of a free and
stable society as put forward in 'Coleridge': 'restraining discipline', a feeling of
loyalty, and an active principle of social cohesion. The first requisite accustoms
the citizenry to subordinate private impulses to general ends; the second consists
of attachment to something permanent in the constitution (such as a common
God, the laws, or some political principle); and the third aims at the creation of
a feeling of common interest.[26] *Considerations on Representative Government*
was written in support of an approach to politics mediating between pure constitutional engineering and government as an organic product of the *Volksgeist*.
In this text Mill deals with the interaction between human types and institutions
while carefully avoiding sweeping rules and unwarranted generalizations – his
line being, basically, that if public virtues are needed to establish representative
institutions, these have the power to educate the people.[27] He stresses the value

---

21 *Considerations on Representative Government* (1861), *MCW*, XIX, p. 389.
22 The character of man 'is formed by his circumstances . . . but his own desire to mould it in a
    particular way, is one of those circumstances, and by no means one of the least influential':
    Logic, p. 840.
23 'The Spirit of the Age' (1831), *MCW*, XXII, pp. 314–15.
24 *Considerations*, p. 409.
25 *ibid.*, pp. 408–9; 'Centralisation' (1862), *MCW*, XIX, pp. 583, 594, 605, 608–9.
26 'Coleridge' (1840), *MCW*, X, pp. 133–6 (also quoted in full in *Logic*, pp. 921–4).
27 *Considerations*, esp. pp. 374–82. See Collini, 'John Stuart Mill', esp. pp. 148–56.

of participation in general and the civic virtues of the English in particular; these virtues make them fit for representative government.[28]

The present survey concerns the prevalence of a broad outlook, irrespective of details and, in particular, of causes – which justifies the inclusion of the environmentalist Mill as well as racialists and other mystics. The wide acceptance of the unifying 'doctrine' (albeit impossible to document to its full extent here) seems more telling about the British mind than a precise categorizing of authors according to the nature of their approach. However, one cannot disregard the fact that Mill was at pains to distinguish himself from Carlyle-like spiritualism, in which he never indulged. The advocacy of the dependence of national character on circumstances, Mill asserted, placed him in the tradition of thought inaugurated by Helvétius.[29] This claim is substantiated in the parts of the *Logic* devoted to ethology. Race was not exactly his stock-in-trade either, although he sporadically resorted to the notion, on one occasion with ample reference to the Irish.[30] Mill apart, a handling of the idea of inner liberty that was both cautious and consistent was quite rare, especially in the more down-market literature where that idea was regularly embraced. For instance, distinctively Carlylean overtones, although diluted and popularized, were coupled with a Teutonist rhetoric in the version by Samuel Smiles, the radical journalist turned apostle of self-help. Smiles found difficulty neither in extending the precepts of individual self-help to make up the character of the nation as a whole, nor in presenting character as the true origin of Britain's liberty and wealth.[31]

In a Millian vein, James Bryce's *American Commonwealth* portrayed the Americans as a people of 'unconscious philosophers', whose good sense and patriotism remedied the faults of the political machinery.[32] 'Public opinion', namely the leading political ideas and habits, is the key to the whole American polity. Public opinion is the 'reflection and expression' of a national character said to be generous, hopeful, independent, self-reliant, practical, and moral, qualities owed to a large extent to political discussion.[33] A habit of judging the conduct of affairs has induced a strong sense of personal responsibility and independence associated with moderation. The sway of democracy as a form of government over the American genius has been overrated, Bryce writes against Tocqueville, since in the United States 'it is not simply the habit of voting but the briskness and breeziness of the whole atmosphere of public life, and the

---

[28] *Considerations*, pp. 412, 421.
[29] 'Bentham' (1838), *MCW*, X, p. 110.
[30] The Irish are dealt with in racial terms in 'Michelet's *History of France*' (1844), *MCW*, XX, pp. 235–7.
[31] See S. Smiles, *Self-Help* (1859; London, 1997), where there are 'Carlylean' sentences like this: 'the noble people will be nobly ruled, and the ignorant and corrupt ignobly', p. 3. See also *Character* (1871; London, 1997).
[32] *The American Commonwealth* (1888; 2 vols., London, 1889), e.g. I, p. 301; II, p. 412.
[33] *ibid.*, II, pp. 243–54.

process of obtaining information and discussing it, of hearing and judging each side, that form the citizen's intelligence'.[34]

The outstanding economist of the post-Millian age, Alfred Marshall, held a vision of civilization as the outcome of national and racial 'spirits'. To him, English freedom sprang from the same ancestral qualities that secured free enterprise for the nation.[35] With regard to the role of human types in economic civilization, there are three strands in Marshall's 1890 *Principles*. First, one finds an economic history whose protagonists are races and national characters – a history, as Parsons noted, of amazing narrowmindedness and superficiality in which Carlyle, Spencer, and Hegel are made easy.[36] Second, there is an unequivocal endorsement of national characters as ultimate determinants of economic growth. They were deemed to depend on race and climate, but also on the prevalent forms of economic life. Third, a concern with the elevation of the moral and intellectual standards of the workers is posited as what gives economic studies 'their chief and their highest interest'. Other economists' contentions were less sweeping than Marshall's. According to Oxford professor and colonial expert Herman Merivale, the question about how far character is the product of institutions 'is scarcely a practical one'. The effect of institutions is at best 'gradual and slow, to a degree which little suits the impatience of political theorists'. Granted that liberty is the most powerful factor of growth in new communities (much land is available in Southern Russia, for example, but Germans prefer to migrate to America), not all dispositions are suited to it. Anglo-Saxons are the best colonists because active qualities are balanced by moderation and sound religious and moral feelings.[37]

Among the 'social scientists', the social psychologist William McDougall stated as a scientific law that institutions (for example, a parliament) could not be successfully imitated by other nations (for example, Russia or the South American states) until the underlying ideas and sentiments became widespread.[38] The sociologist Benjamin Kidd found the French and in general the Latin races lacking those 'altruistic feelings' which had made democracy work in England.[39] The anthropologist James Hunt took up the legacy of the phrenologists and Robert Knox and reiterated their views about Celtic political inferiority and

[34] *ibid.*, I, pp. 4, 11; II, pp. 327, 612–16.

[35] A. Marshall, *Principles of Economics* (London, 1890), p. 37.

[36] T. Parsons, 'Economics and Sociology: Marshall in Relation to the Thought of his Time', *Quarterly Journal of Economics*, 46 (1932), p. 335. For a more nuanced judgement, see D. Winch and S. Collini, 'A Separate Science: Polity and Society in Marshall's Economics', in *That Noble Science*, pp. 328–9. A detailed treatment can be found in R. C. O. Matthews and B. Supple, 'The Ordeal of Economic Freedom: Marshall on Economic History', *Quaderni di storia dell'economia politica*, 9 (1991), pp. 189–213.

[37] H. Merivale, *Lectures on Colonization and Colonies* (1841; 2nd edn, rev. and enl., London, 1861), pp. 657–8.

[38] W. McDougall, *An Introduction to Social Psychology* (London, 1908), pp. 341–2.

[39] B. Kidd, *Social Evolution* (London, 1894), esp. pp. 297–301.

Saxon liberty.[40] In McDougall and Kidd, as in other social scientists, a fresh preoccupation with the inner roots of national power and efficiency tended to replace, or combine with, the preoccupation with the mental sources of liberty; this adjustment in argument matched a parallel adjustment in the climate of opinion and in the political agenda, with the Boer war acting as a catalyst to set off widespread fears of decline.

In spite of the citations one can pile up, the inner liberty doctrine was to be stated in a more indirect way, if any, as a result of the endorsement of the evolutionary theory. This in fact entailed, in Wallas's graphic words, the transfer of the cause of development 'from within to without'.[41] Although Spencer, for one, voiced the dependence of liberty on national character in *Social Statics*, overall the doctrine was subordinated (by Spencer himself, too) to the broader question of the evolution of morals in connection with social growth. There emerged a quite common way of inserting collective morality within the evolutionary framework, focused on the interaction between social forms and innate instincts. Utilitarian psychology was rejected in the face of a new conceptualization of man and society as inextricably related organisms, calling, on the one hand, for recognition of the original, pre-rational motives at the basis of conduct, and, on the other, for an understanding of changes in attitudes induced by the social environment.

Darwinism induced a shift in the foundations of moral discourse. To authors like Ritchie and Leslie Stephen, the problem was how to account for higher moral conceptions in the context of the survival of the fittest, a quest which led to the reconstruction of ethics as interwoven with evolution in an open-ended process based on biological and social inheritance. Character, they argued, was moulded by this process and thereby by what was, in broad terms, environment. As the century wore on, the Whiggish complacency of a Bagehot was replaced by the search for a rationale for moral agency and conscious progress. Ritchie's issue was not to discriminate among nations according to their spiritual capacity for representative government but to to make room for reform by positing men's conscious effort as one of the factors of evolution.[42] The stance Stephen articulated amounted to an intrinsic connection between moral law and society, in the sense that morality was not deemed right or wrong in the abstract but expressed 'the most effective qualities of character which can be developed in a given agent to make him an efficient member of society'. It was a universal principle

[40] In *Anthropological Review*, 6 (1868), see Hunt's 'Knox on the Celtic Race', pp. 175–91, and 'Knox on the Saxon Race', pp. 257–79. R. Knox, *The Races of Men* (1850; London, 1862).

[41] G. Wallas, 'A Criticism of Froebelian Pedagogy' (1901), in his *Men and Ideas* (London, 1940), p. 137.

[42] D. G. Ritchie, *Darwinism and Politics* (1889; London, 1895). As for the protagonists of 'sociocultural evolutionism', Tylor, Lubbock, and McLennan, who felt a need for 'reassurance that processes whose origin was purely natural would somehow lead to a moral outcome', see Stocking, *Victorian Anthropology*, pp. 222–4.

that 'a man is virtuous or the reverse so far as he does or does not conform to the type defined by the healthy condition of the social organism'. As Stephen also put it, morality was the sum of the preservative 'instincts' of a society.[43] As a result of these major changes in perspective, the inner liberty doctrine lost its centrality.

3   Froude's *The English in Ireland*

The high fortunes of some crucial Carlylean tenets in the second half of the century make J. A. Froude a suitable yardstick against which to measure the impact of the 'social sciences'. Tacitly put to work by Macaulay, Carlyle's frame of reference was endorsed unconditionally by Froude, a historian, journalist, novelist, and in general a public figure of outstanding renown and influence. To continue the line of inquiry of chapter 6, the focus of attention will be his *The English in Ireland in the Eighteenth Century* (1872–4), a book which, in conjunction with Froude's American lectures on the same subject, created a stir in two continents.[44] Collective mentalities figure prominently in his writings from the very beginning of his career, even in unexpected contexts. What Newman and the other Tractarians were trying to do, Froude argued in his sensational *The Nemesis of Faith* (1849), was to 'unprotestantize' the country and thereby to produce a wholly different kind of national character from that which had led England to greatness. That is not to say that he viewed religion as the determinant of collective dispositions, although it certainly played a part. Long before the Reformation the English had shown their superior qualities resulting from ancestral Anglo-Saxon stock.[45] Froude's version of the doctrine that the attitudes of peoples make all the difference is to be evaluated in the context of the absence of any attempt on his part to explain these attitudes rationally, that is, to search for the causes of the racialist predispositions he alleged. This absence is the more remarkable in view of Froude's declared cult of facts and noteworthy archival work.[46]

With typically Carlylean proclivity, Froude made indiscriminate use of 'the passion and resolution of brave and noble men' as a criterion for truth. By an odd twist of logic, the sides in a dispute were deemed good or bad not by their own worth but according to the (alleged) moral fibre of those who endorsed them – he went as far as to remark that 'where the wise and

---

[43] L. Stephen, *The Science of Ethics* (London, 1882), pp. 168, 217, 396–7. See also F. Pollock, 'Evolution and Ethics', *Mind*, 1 (1876), pp. 334–45.

[44] See D. MacCartney, 'James Anthony Froude and Ireland: a Historiographical Controversy of the Nineteenth Century', *Historical Studies*, 8 (1971), pp. 171–90.

[45] *The Nemesis of Faith* (1849; London, 1988), pp. 150–1.

[46] For Froude as 'an avowed disciple of Ranke, determined to extend the scope of his sources as far as he could', see J. Kenyon, *The History Men: the Historical Profession in England since the Renaissance* (Pittsburgh, 1983), pp. 115–25.

good are divided, the truth is generally found to be divided also'.[47] Here we have much more than an evocative personalization of historical narrative, more, that is, than a rhetorical device. The metamorphosis of innate virtues into historical criteria points to the essence of Carlylism as the doctrine of a free hand in politics and morals. Froude's detection of moral worth is, apparently, all that is needed to explain past, present, and future events – outside formal requirements, no genuine evidence is given in support of the historian's quasi-religious authority.

As a not unexpected inference, Froude held that if a people were divided, reckless, and ignorant they could not be trusted with representative institutions. In a country, say Ireland,

there are brave men, and there are cowards, and the wise man is generally braver than the fool. Suppose in any community, two-thirds who are cowards vote one way, and the remaining third will not only vote, but fight the other way. What becomes of the voting theory? The brave and the determined minority will rule the timid and the undetermined.[48]

A consequent assumption might have been that powerful individuals and peoples were always right; this assumption would have set an evaluating criterion of a verifiable type, though a questionable one. But Froude reversed the equation: 'nature . . . has allotted superiority of strength to superiority of intellect and character'. This is why innumerable Irish defeats over the centuries testified to an ineradicable 'racial' weakness.[49] History merely confirmed the dictates of a providential nature.

Froude's three-volume *The English in Ireland* amounts to a provocative and abusively worded account of Anglo-Irish relations from the conquest to the Union, albeit associated with a denunciation of English policies (alternately judged either too harsh or too soft). The thread of the narrative is the view of the Irish as bereft of 'the habits of self-command' required by liberty; it follows that they must be treated firmly for their own good. The Irish permanently agitate and regularly revolt, but, lacking the qualities which alone can secure victory, their patriotism is mere 'words' and their insurrections occasions for pillage, personal revenge, and treachery. It was therefore in accordance with a law of historical necessity that the Normans, who were 'born rulers of men',

---

[47] 'The Influence of the Reformation on the Scottish Character' (1865), in J. A. Froude, *Short Studies on Great Subjects* (4 vols., London, 1877–83), I, pp. 155–6, 180; see also p. 187. For Froude's philosophy in a nutshell, see 'Calvinism' (1871), in *Short Studies*, II, pp. 1–59.
[48] 'Ireland Since the Union' (1872), in *Short Studies*, II, pp. 516–17.
[49] *The English in Ireland in the Eighteenth Century* (3 vols., London, 1872–4), I, pp. 2, 4–5, 11, quotation on p. 5; see also pp. 22–3. On 'outcomes as vindications' in Froude, see Burrow, *A Liberal Descent*, p. 273. There are also environmentalist views here and there; see, e.g., 'Ireland Since the Union'. On Froude's paradoxical fascination with Ireland and the Irish, see S. Gilley, 'English Attitudes to the Irish in England, 1780–1900', in C. Holmes, ed., *Immigrants and Minorities in British Society* (London, 1978), p. 90, and Burrow, *A Liberal Descent*, p. 262.

came 'to take direction of them'.[50] But this 'incurable' Irish race 'would neither resist courageously, nor . . . honourably submit'.[51] To Froude, the single effective campaign was that of Cromwell, for he provided real leadership and pursued stern policies. The many weak, conciliatory, and vacillating governments, on the other hand, had cherished Irish self-government, with mischievous consequences. Mingled with a severe condemnation of Irish landlords and English protectionists, one finds a characteristic chapter ironically entitled 'Irish Ideas' supplying abundant evidence of homicide, theft, massacres of Protestants, and various other forms of ferocious and barbarous behaviour.[52]

Like Carlyle, Froude saw silence as an external sign of achieved self-control or, to borrow his term, 'manliness'; related to this, he contended that 'the better kind of men' meddled in politics only in critical times, when, Cincinnatus-like, they leave the works assigned to them by nature. Professional politics was only for the vain and restless.[53] Froude's nostalgia for organic communities was an important element of his Carlylean portrait of the English as a chosen people who shifted effortlessly from private to public virtues – a people as proficient at work as implacable at war, and the more truly so because reluctant to deploy all their terrible strength. Class differences were watered down by an author who looked back with envy at the 'moral beauty' of medieval peasants' lives;[54] all ranks of the English people partook of a quasi-mythical status sanctioned by history. Reformation-inspired Elizabethan seamen, 'self-taught and self-directed' because 'the free native growth of a noble virgin soil', were Froude's favourite instances of plebeians with the right stuff.[55] In spite of his complaints about contemporary decay, his Victorian audiences could not but revel in the continuity in moral inspiration which, Froude showed, underpinned national history. In the age of oncoming democracy, the heroism of plain men was probably a more effective piece of myth-making than the eulogy of heroes as leaders, a type of literature which, at any rate, Froude's history could certainly complement.

Froude's volumes on Ireland met with sharply divided reactions in England. The supporters' camp included *The Times, Pall Mall Gazette, Edinburgh Review*, and the *Quarterly Review*, whereas the *Saturday Review, Spectator, Athenaeum, MacMillan's Magazine, British Quarterly Review, Fortnightly Review*, and the *Contemporary Review* were among the opponents. When one

---

[50] *The English in Ireland*, I, pp. 15–17.
[51] *ibid.*, I, p. 12.
[52] *ibid.*, I, pp. 408–45.
[53] *ibid.*, III, pp. 2–3. In the important article 'England's Forgotten Worthies' (1852), Froude wrote that, to the Elizabethan sailors, 'their profession was the school of their nature, a high moral education which most brought out what was most nobly human in them': *Short Studies*, I, p. 448. For Lecky's remark about the term 'orator' in Froude's vocabulary as synonymous with 'complete political fatuity', see 'Mr Froude's English in Ireland', *MacMillan's Magazine*, 30 (1874), pp. 170–1.
[54] 'The Influence of the Reformation', pp. 157–60.
[55] 'England's Forgotten Worthies'; see Burrow, *A Liberal Descent*, p. 272.

comes to the issue of race and character, however, the two sides appear more balanced than a mere count of the periodicals would suggest. The supporters' front was united in pointing the finger at the Irish character as the root of all evils. In his 'impartial' and 'moderate' account, Froude had demonstrated beyond doubt the incapacity of the Irish for self-government (and thereby for Home Rule); in view of their inherent helplessness, *The Times* wrote, 'things would scarcely have been better' even if our ancestors had acted differently.[56] That old Whig tenet just rediscovered by Bagehot – that 'a representative system can only be managed by mutual forbearance, moderation, and respect' – was endorsed with unwavering assurance by these reviewers as the last word of political science.[57] That unfitness for self-government was a strong argument is proved by its acceptance by some of those who on the whole rejected Froude's reconstruction, like the reviewers of the *Saturday Review* and the *Athenaeum*.[58] A serious defence of Irish character was mounted only in the *British Quarterly Review*.[59] The accounts by the Irishmen John Elliot Cairnes and William Lecky largely eschewed the issue, only to show some embarassment when compelled to tackle it.[60] An article by Goldwin Smith intended as a reply to both Froude and Father Burke, his most vociferous Irish critic, asserted the unsuitability of the Irish for self-government on the grounds of racialist dispositions and lack of practice.[61] Although references to Celtism and Anglo-Saxonism were occasionally made, the reception of Froude's volumes was marked by most reviewers' idea of liberty as a plant which slowly grows in 'bosoms' and 'hearts' – a Burkean motif, not necessarily related to racialist preconceptions.

4   Spencer on social environmentalism

Spencer's sociology was doubtless as prejudiced as Froude's history (and he held little sympathy for the Irish either).[62] The evolutionary process depicted by this founding father of the social sciences is a teleology through and through, to the effect that in this respect no dividing line can be drawn between the

---

[56] *The Times*, 4 April 1874, p. 10; see also 8 Nov. 1872, p. 7.

[57] See *Pall Mall Gazette*, 27 April 1874, pp. 11–12, and 8 May 1874, pp. 11–12; T. Croskery in *ER*, 137 (1873), pp. 122–53, and 139 (1874), pp. 468–506 (quotation on p. 476); W. R. Greg in *QR*, 134 (1873), pp. 169–85, and J. L. Whittle in *QR*, 136 (1874), pp. 498–526.

[58] *Saturday Review*, 34 (1872), pp. 553–4, 698–700, 735–7; *Athenaeum*, no. 2351, 16 Nov. 1872, pp. 629–30; no. 2425, 18 April 1874, pp. 517–18; no. 2426, 25 April 1874, pp. 557–9.

[59] See 57 (1873), pp. 484–511 (but I suspect that its author was Irish).

[60] Cairnes's review is in *Fortnightly Review*, 16 (1874), pp. 171–91; Lecky replied to Froude in *MacMillan's Magazine*, 27 (1872–3), pp. 246–64, and 30 (1874), pp. 166–84 (see p. 169 for Lecky's views on Irish character; but see also p. 261 in the first of his reviews).

[61] G. Smith, 'The Irish Question', *Contemporary Review*, 21 (1872–3), pp. 503–28. Smith also wrote *Irish History and Irish Character* (Oxford, 1861).

[62] For Spencer's view of the Irish, see *Social Statics* (1850; London, 1868), p. 255; 'A Theory of Population', *Westminster Review*, 57 (1852), p. 500; and *The Principles of Sociology* (1876–97; 2nd edn, 3 vols., London, 1877), I, p. 67.

historian and the sociologist. Furthermore, especially in the light of *Social Statics*, it might be argued that Spencer endorsed an evolutionary variant of the inner liberty doctrine. Yet a closer look at his writings reveals momentous differences in approach. Initially, *Political Institutions* (1882), which is the fifth part of the *Principles of Sociology*, will be considered.

Although the right racial characteristics were deemed prerequisite for the emergence of an 'industrial society', race as a growth determinant was either played down or ignored altogether in favour of social environmentalism whenever Spencer analysed the later stages of development. He held as a fundamental tenet that 'a necessary relation exists between the structure of a society and the natures of its citizens'. In *Political Institutions*, Spencer devised the ideal types of the two basic social forms, the 'militant' and the 'industrial', and inferred from these types the corresponding character traits. The war-oriented militant society produces a temperament which is patriotic, loyal, brave, and honourable, but vengeful and with little consideration for the life and property of others. Work is despised and considered the business of women and slaves. Spencer was at pains to point out that a militant society brought about a mental state of 'passive acceptance and expectancy', and thereby a lack of individual initiative. With the soldier's obedience to commanders posited as a model pattern of social behaviour, there is generated a belief that the power of government is boundless. Where everything is done by public agencies, businesses cannot but be routinely managed, and industry and enterprise obliterated.[63]

In contrast, industrialism in Spencer's meaning entails 'a strong sense of individual freedom, and a determination to maintain it'; respect for the claims of others; and 'humane sentiments'. The defining characteristic of an industrial community is not the prevalence of economic concerns *per se*, but the form of social co-operation, which is voluntary and structured through contract relations. In the absence of a centralized, suffocating regulation from above, people have the chance to cultivate both the qualities of self-help and those of justice and altruism. The free pursuit of peaceful activities stimulates the self-consciousness and independence which make man capable of holding his ground and, at the same time, of relating to other people in a co-operative and sympathetic way. Illegal power is resisted, and state intervention is restricted to a minimum, by citizens whose values are freedom of thought, individual initiative, and benevolence. While aggressiveness decreases, philanthropy grows, and feelings of respect and love pervade domestic relations.[64]

Since Spencer thought that the Western societies of his time were a blend of the two ideal types, the two sets of characteristics were said to be mingled there. A severe critic of English mores, at this point of his account Spencer did not

[63] *Political Institutions* (1882; repr. edn, London, 1996), pp. 682–90, quotations on pp. 682, 689.
[64] *ibid.*, pp. 718–27.

miss the opportunity to observe that his fellow citizens were much inferior to some uncivilized tribes as far as the 'industrial' virtues were concerned.[65] At the same time, he did believe England better placed in the evolutionary scale between pure militancy and pure industrialism than any other Western country, America included.[66] Since the determination to be free was a major evaluative criterion of his, some traditional anti-French motifs figure in his writings; and he did not like Germany either, of course. But it is indicative of his broader, ultimately non-Whiggish framework of thought that in *Political Institutions* what he praised the English for was a higher than average decrease in loyalty, credulousness, patriotism, and aggressiveness as well as a superior enterprising spirit.[67] Granted that the sources of Spencer's conception of a worthy character should be looked for not in the Whig mainstream, but in its radical branch from Price to Buckle,[68] that conception amounts to a quite peculiar mix of traits.

Spencer's analysis, albeit schematic, represents a way forward from national character as a static, original, and vaguely accounted-for notion. In narratives like Froude's, national character figures as an inexplicable and barely defined *deus ex machina* acting behind the scenes, whose mystery just adds to its power. That collective mentalities are subject to change seems to fall beyond the range of possibilities; arcane entities do not change. By means of a comprehensive model of social causation, Spencer put forward an alternative approach. On the one hand, the evolutionist perspective combined with the dichotomy between militancy and industrialism provided him with a flexible and powerful pattern of explanation of collective attitudes, a pattern in principle inductively testable by fellow researchers. On the other hand, the focus shifted from national histories to an abstract model of development applicable to all communities. There was nothing peculiarly French in the French character, then: its flaws just resulted from a more backward stage in 'industrial' terms.

That Spencer's ideal types are biased in accordance with his advocacy of laissez-faire is obvious, but this is not the point. To repeat, radical innovations do not occur in the history of national character; as regards the social determination of collective dispositions, there has been no lack of instances in the previous chapters. But the new intellectual climate induced by Darwinism did have an impact, as society came to be apprehended as an autonomous whole, with its own natural laws gaining primacy over politics. The role played by social factors in the shaping of mentalities was redefined and systematized. The idea was that, as collective dispositions were a constituent part of the social organism, or

---

[65] *ibid.*, p. 722.
[66] See, e.g., *Social Statics*, pp. 117–18, 428–9; *Political Institutions*, pp. 723, 726; 'The Americans' (1883), in *Essays: Scientific, Political, & Speculative* (1891; repr. edn, 3 vols., London, 1996), pp. 471–92, esp. pp. 476–7.
[67] *Political Institutions*, pp. 722–7.
[68] See J. D. Y. Peel, *Herbert Spencer: the Evolution of a Sociologist* (London, 1971).

even, in Spencer's case, the essential expression of evolution, they too followed definite laws and could therefore be systematically and comprehensively accounted for. True, Spencer himself muddled the sociological coherence of the outlined model, as will be argued immediately below. Nevertheless, a perspective like Spencer's invites contrast not so much with Hume's classic stance as with Tocqueville's much later dichotomy between aristocracy and democracy, which remained quintessentially political in spite of his efforts not to neglect social dynamics.

Spencer's two ideal types of society are crystallizations of the process of human evolution. He was a Lamarckian, that is, he believed that acquired characteristics were transmitted to successive generations by biological inheritance. His faith in progress ultimately rested on this conception; conversely, he accounted for hindrances and delays with the insufficient adaptation of men to evolving social conditions. He spoke of the ongoing 'moulding and re-moulding of man and society into mutual fitness', for life was 'the continual adjustment of internal relations to external relations'.[69] Specifically, the mechanism of adaptation works thus:

if an individual is placed permanently in conditions which demand more action of a special kind than has before been requisite, or than is natural to him – if the pressure of the painful feelings which these conditions entail when disregarded, impels him to perform this action to a greater extent – if by every more frequent or more lengthened performance of it under such pressure, the resistance is somewhat diminished; then, clearly, there is an advance towards a balance between the demand for this kind of action and the supply of it.[70]

The habits thus formed are passed on to the successive generation, in accordance with the law, valid for both individual and social organisms, that 'functional equilibrations generate structural equilibrations'.[71] The motor of progress is, in the social domain as anywhere else, an ever-increasing 'differentiation' of functions, division of labour being a prominent example.[72]

Since advances in intelligence and morals consist of more varied and complete adjustments to circumstances, both knowledge and moral feelings are of necessity relative to the current stage of evolution. This explains why a primitive people may show attachment to a despot: in connection with the exigencies of militancy, the people's mental state requires a harsh rule. As for religion, the same people not only needs, but also cherishes 'a celestial rule that is similarly harsh', full of dreadful ideal penalties. An effective adaptation exists between

---

[69] Quotations from *The Data of Ethics* (1879; repr. edn, London, 1996), p. 246.
[70] *First Principles* (1862; 3rd edn, 1870), pp. 505–6.
[71] *ibid.*, p. 508.
[72] See 'Progress: Its Law and Cause' (1857), in *Essays*, I, pp. 8–62. But see also the article where Spencer argued that the pressure of population was the stimulus to progress: 'A Theory of Population'.

established institutions and beliefs, on the one hand, and the dispositions of citizens, on the other; in theory even the most oppressive of governments, or the most absurd of religions, can be necessary to the social equilibrium. Hence Spencer's point is that sudden change causes mischief; in each community a balance between progressive and conservative tendencies should always be preserved, because both are necessary.[73]

Spencer envisages a mutual shaping of men and institutions (both social and political) rather than a social determination of personality pure and simple. As stated in a research programme of 1876, there exists a reciprocal influence between 'the characters of men and the characters of the societies they form'.[74] In dealing with the industrial society, he writes that if its relations mould the thoughts and sentiments of men, these, in turn, determine 'social arrangements into corresponding forms'.[75] To qualify this interaction, which in itself merely asserts that social development is a result of men's actions, an important difference is introduced. In militant societies, the adaptation of men to a constant state of war is pursued by the community through education, custom, and opinion; this is an indispensable process aimed at preserving the life of individuals. But in industrial societies, where the individual 'owns himself', a contrary mechanism is in place as 'society has now to be moulded by the individual to suit his purposes'. Having lost its nature of coercive organization, society is now a medium for the peaceful activities of each citizen: 'there remains no power which may properly prescribe the form which individual life shall assume', and hence men, unconstrained, naturally adjust to the higher requirements of the social state.[76] That is, men carry out processes of further differentiation which at the same time stimulate the heightening of social attitudes. An industrial society is the ideal place where men construct their social environment, and, in doing so, perfect themselves as social beings. Yet there is the fundamental proviso that the 'discipline' of evolution presides over the course of society and the moral development of individuals; Spencer's argument cannot make room for an independent and creative role for men, but only for a predetermined course of action.

The key idea of human adaptation to social circumstances is double-edged: since men do adjust over the long term, Spencer's model is based on social causation, but the absence of coercion in modern societies renders adaptation a possibility, rather than a certainty, once a closer focus is brought in. If adjustment does not occur, environmentalism is unavoidably contradicted, although only to the extent that men stick to former ways of living rather than reacting positively

---

[73] *First Principles*, pp. 116–23.
[74] 'The Comparative Psychology of Man' (1876), in *Essays*, I, pp. 353, 369.
[75] *The Principles of Sociology*, I, p. 589.
[76] *The Principles of Ethics* (1879–93; 2 vols., Indianapolis, 1978), II, pp. 272–5, quotation on p. 274.

to the current stimuli. That failed adaptation is not a rare eventuality is accounted for on the basis that the nature that men inherit from 'an uncivilized past' is 'still very imperfectly fitted to the partially civilized present'.[77] It emerges that character is Spencer's most substantive concern, on the grounds that the possibility of defective adjustment turns collective dispositions into the crucial factor of progress for all practical purposes.

As Spencer abandons abstract theorizing for topical issues, his argument splits in two. The first motif is that his recurring complaints about insufficient adaptation – which means inadequate sense of responsibility, energy, independence, benevolence, co-operative attitude, etc. – at times point to this insufficiency as the cause of social arrangements (especially in his early works). Dishonesty in trade was one of his favourite examples. In *Social Statics*, the monetary arrangements of communities were determined by the morality of their members, to the effect that metallic currencies were appropriate for dishonest, and banknotes for honest, communities. 'The ratio of paper to coin', Spencer wrote, 'will vary with the degree of trust individuals can place in one another', irrespective of state interventions.[78] In his 1859 essay 'Morals of Trade', he ascribed the 'system of commercial cannibalism' of contemporary England to the average English character 'placed under special conditions', a situation for which he blamed the imperative of material development which blinded the age.[79] In all his writings he brought forward evidence showing 'how far the mass of men are from fitness for free institutions': for example, the trade unions' practice of boycotting non-unionist workers denied personal independence.[80] A frequent theme is that institutions are unable to bring about social improvement: 'the defective natures of citizens will show themselves in the bad acting of whatever social structure they are arranged into'.[81] Men, Spencer typically affirmed, are not pliable at will; reforms do not work if imposed without due preparation on people 'undisciplined in freedom'. Institutions and laws just mirror national habits and opinions and governments should not try to accelerate the pace of growth.[82]

The second motif is Spencer's polemic against the debasing effects of state intervention on character. There is no 'strongest' reason for restricting the range of government actions.[83] In view of the fervour of his laissez-faire convictions, this polemic encapsulates at best his combination of evolutionary ethic with political stand; to his eyes it probably constituted the most important inference to be drawn from his evolutionary construction. The essential consideration is that

[77] *ibid.*, II, pp. 277, 315.
[78] *Social Statics*, pp. 433–40, quotation on p. 433.
[79] *Essays*, III, pp. 113–51.
[80] *The Principles of Ethics*, II, p. 315.
[81] *The Man versus the State* (London, 1884), p. 43.
[82] See, e.g., *Social Statics*, pp. 270–4, 505–16; 'The Social Organism' (1860), in *Essays*, I, pp. 265–307; *Political Institutions*, pp. 749–50.
[83] *The Principles of Ethics*, II, p. 271.

for Spencer political institutions tend to lose their functions to the extent that minds evolve towards an ever fuller endorsement of 'industrial' virtues. Man is thought to develop towards an ideal state in which he would spontaneously refrain from infringing other people's rights, that is, without the need for institutional coercion. Until this stage is reached, laws (like manners and religions) amount to 'controlling agencies'.[84] In fully grown industrial societies, the only institutions Spencer assigned positive tasks to were the 'natural' ones, namely those which spontaneously grew out of the social fabric.[85] The mechanism through which the government's influence works is as follows. The principle of survival of the fittest requires that the moulding of attitudes occurs (or fails to occur) through the unimpeded exercise of faculties, but 'over-legislation' as a response to social change induces disuse of faculties and hence 'a re-moulding of the average character' for the worse. Character becomes 'deformed' as a consequence of its adjustment to 'artificial arrangements'.[86] What 'hotheaded philanthropy' is leading to is a disavowal of the connection between conduct and its consequences, 'a redistribution of benefits irrespective of desert' whose effects are discouragement of industry, bodily and mental degeneracy, and eventually 'communism and anarchism'.[87]

This tangle of assumptions gives Spencer's environmentalism a peculiar turn, and waters down to some extent the neatness of the departure which his sociology marked. It will be argued in a later chapter that even Spencer's utopian side has an important part to play in my story. In the next sections, other specimens of the social scientific perspective will be offered, though no pretence at completeness is made.

5   A new framework: McDougall, Wallas, and others

In 1914, Alexander Shand published *The Foundations of Character* as a stepping stone to the establishment of a systematic and cumulative science of character, both individual and collective. Shand, who rejected associationism, intended nevertheless to fulfil Mill's promise of a fully fledged ethology.[88] In this 'study of method', Shand defined character as the organization of emotions

---

[84] *The Data of Ethics* is the relevant text here. But see also 'Manners and Fashion' (1854), in *Essays*, III, pp. 1–51, and 'Absolute Political Ethics' (1890), in *Essays*, III, pp. 217–28.
[85] In *Essays*, III, see 'Over-legislation' (1853), pp. 236–7, and 'Specialized Administration' (1871), pp. 401–44.
[86] *The Man versus the State*, p. 62; *The Principles of Ethics*, II, p. 278.
[87] *The Principles of Ethics*, II, pp. 289–92.
[88] For the differences between Mill and Shand, who moved away from Mill's 'intellectualistic' model of character, see D. E. Leary, 'The Fate and Influence of John Stuart Mill's Proposed Science of Ethology', *Journal of the History of Ideas*, 43 (1982), pp. 153–62. Shand (1858–1936) was admitted to the Bar in 1887; he held no academic appointments. He was one of the founders of the British Psychological Society in 1901. The distinction between sentiment and emotion informing *The Foundations of Character* was first made in an article of 1896. The book went through several editions.

and sentiments according to 'organic' psychological laws. Viewing emotions as dynamic forces pursuing ends, he set out to analyse each of them (like anger, disgust, joy, etc.) in isolation from the others. Sentiments were attitudinal systems organizing emotions in comprehensive and permanent mental structures. The material of the new science – to be found in literature, proverbs, and maxims – should be processed and made available to future researchers.[89] In fact, to a modern reader the book looks like a lengthy, indigestible discussion of preliminary issues on the basis of evidence that is always questionable.

In spite of its shortcomings, Shand's book was intended to apply to character a 'scientific' approach modelled on the natural sciences. At the juncture of 1914, drawing inspiration from them was scarcely a novel perspective. Identifying an object called 'culture or civilization', and studying its evolution dispassionately and by means of a 'scientific method, with its stringency of argument and constant check of fact' had been practised by British ethnologists since the 1860s at least.[90] A naturalistic–evolutionary viewpoint of society was in the air well before the *Origin of Species*, although Darwinism was instrumental in its almost universal acceptance and diffusion.[91] As far as national character and public spirit are concerned, the social scientific approach manifested itself in various forms, the most blatant of which was the eugenic movement of Francis Galton and Karl Pearson. Rather than following the bio-medical thread, some developments in other, more 'social' areas of influence of the evolutionary message will be considered.

Besides Shand, a thorough analysis of personality came from the social psychologists William McDougall and Wilfred Trotter. Inspired by Darwinism, both claimed to be reacting against the 'intellectualist fallacy' and hence based their theories on instincts and emotions. In his *Introduction to Social Psychology* (1908), McDougall distinguished between instinctual 'dispositions', physical 'temperament', and 'character' as the hierarchical system of socially acquired sentiments and habits. Character rested on the native basis of dispositions and temperament, in the sense that the acquired tendencies interacted with that basis. Temperament, in particular, played a significant part insofar as both certain organs and the nervous tissues determined a number of 'constitutional conditions' of mental life.[92] Within these limitations, McDougall regarded the psychological identity of individuals as a social construction. He distinguished four stages in the 'social genesis of the idea of self': there

---

[89] *The Foundations of Character: Being a Study of the Tendencies of the Emotions and Sentiments* (London, 1914).

[90] Quotation from E. B. Tylor, *Primitive Culture* (2 vols., London, 1871), II, p. 409. On the method of anthropology, see Stocking, *Victorian Anthropology*, esp. pp. 76–7.

[91] See J. W. Burrow, *Evolution and Society* (Cambridge, 1966), pp. 19–21; G. Jones, *Social Darwinism and English Thought* (Sussex, 1980), ch. 1.

[92] *An Introduction to Social Psychology*, pp. 116–20. McDougall borrowed Shand's theory of sentiments as 'an organised system of emotional tendencies', p. 122.

were, first, instinctual activities modified by pleasure and pain; second, further modifications were induced by the existing system of punishments and rewards; third, conduct was determined by anticipation of social praise and blame; and, fourth, there were elite-conceived moral ideals, which, irrespective of the social environment, could succeed in setting original standards of behaviour.[93] He juxtaposed the gregarious masses to the morally innovative elites who made all the difference in social evolution.[94] National characteristics were in the main expressions of cultural, political, and social traditions which each generation acquired via 'imitation', as Gabriel Tarde had shown.[95]

If the reader is inclined to doubt the truth of these statements, let him make an effort of imagination and suppose that throughout a period of half a century every child born to English parents was at once exchanged (by the power of a magician's wand) for an infant of the French, or other European, nation. Soon after the close of this period the English nation would be composed of individuals of French extraction, and the French nation of individuals of English extraction. It is, I think, clear that, in spite of this complete exchange of innate characters between the two nations, there would be but little immediate change of national characteristics. The French people would still speak French, and the English would speak English . . . The religion of the French would still be predominantly Roman Catholic, and the English people would still present the same diversity of Protestant creeds. The course of political institutions would have suffered no profound change, the customs and habits of the two peoples would exhibit only such changes as might be attributed to the lapse of time . . . And we may go even further and assert that the same would hold good if a similar exchange of infants were affected between the English and any other less closely allied nation, say the Turks or the Japanese.[96]

The stance on character put forward in the *Introduction* was later filtered through what may be defined as an idealistic premise. McDougall sketched the agenda of social psychology in the relevant chapter of *Psychology: the Study of Behaviour* (1912), a Home University Library textbook where the main lines of his reflection are neatly posited. In view of the wariness of the *Introduction*, these pages assume special importance.[97] His starting assumption is the existence of 'over-individual or collective minds' which condition all collective actions in highly organized societies; the rationale behind such a

---

[93] *ibid.*, p. 181.

[94] *ibid.*, pp. 85–7, 217–20, 296–301, 326–8, 341–5.

[95] *ibid.*, pp. 329–31. McDougall affirmed that the illustration of 'the nature of collective mental processes' fell outside 'the plan of this volume' (pp. 320–1), but he contradicted himself in practice. As he made explicit in a later writing, his treatment of individual volition accounted for collective attitudes as well: 'The Will of the People', *Sociological Review*, 5 (1912), pp. 89–104, esp. pp. 90–3.

[96] *An Introduction to Social Psychology*, pp. 330–1.

[97] He later admitted that, as some critics had remarked, there was little *social* psychology in the *Introduction*: W. McDougall, *The Group Mind: a Sketch of the Principles of Collective Psychology with Some Attempt to Apply Them to the Interpretation of National Life and Character* (Cambridge, 1920), preface.

view was pretty uncommon in Britain: 'the actions of the society are, or may be, very different from the mere sum of the actions with which its several members would react to the situation in the absence of the system of relations which renders them a society'.[98] Each individual mind is moulded 'at every point' by the intellectual and moral tradition which informs society. This process takes place through 'suggestion', 'sympathy', and 'imitation', three mechanisms by which innate impulses are directed towards appropriate objects – ranging from language to 'a system of moral sentiments'. The effectiveness of these mechanisms is advocated in parallel with a criticism of both intellectualist and utilitarian explanations of the development of the mind.[99]

McDougall goes on to show how the study of unorganized crowds casts light on the mental workings of organized groups and, by implication, society. Basically, the higher moral and intellectual level of the latter is due to the prominent role in them of natural leaders, as the case of the army typifies; but what he calls 'group-spirit', and again deals with by taking the army as example, is also important.[100] The analysis of organized groups like the tribe, the political party, the trade union, etc., where suggestion, sympathy, and imitation are equally at work albeit on a smaller scale, introduces the consideration of 'the most complex, interesting, and important form of collective mind', namely 'national character'. In the single page that he nevertheless devotes to it, McDougall rejects the view of an average national type and favours an idea of national character as a kind of superindividual soul of the country, the product of history and 'the system of living traditions and institutions'. Given its link with the past, the character of a nation is said to include much more than the sum of each individual's character.[101]

McDougall's notion of a collective spiritual entity served to uphold social environmentalism rather than challenging it; and accounting for a national character in his sense amounted to investigating the influence on attitudes of a

---

[98] And, conversely, 'the thinking and acting of each man, in so far as he thinks and acts as a member of a society, is very different from his thinking and acting as an isolated individual': *Psychology: the Study of Behaviour* (New York and London, 1912), pp. 228–9. In *The Group Mind*, he distanced himself from German idealism, which after 1914 many had linked to German militarism. McDougall cited Maitland and Barker as proponents of a type of idealism which, like his, did not uphold the idea of 'a super-individual consciousness, somehow comprising the consciousness of the individuals composing the group': *The Group Mind*, p. 19. But McDougall's rejection of that idea rested only on its present unverifiability. For a discussion of Oxford idealism (McDougall lectured in that university from 1904) in relation to its concern with national mind and character, see J. Stapleton, *Englishness and the Study of Politics: the Social and Political Thought of Ernest Barker* (Cambridge, 1994), pp. 35–68ff.

[99] *Psychology*, pp. 230–5.

[100] *ibid.*, pp. 235–46. An army's 'group-spirit' amounts to a sentiment of devotion to the army and its representatives in the soldiers, a sentiment reinforced by traditions, symbols, etc. (pp. 244–6).

[101] *ibid.*, p. 247.

country's 'long past' in its concrete expressions. So far so good, but his next step seems in disagreement with much of the above, for he asserts that 'however great the influence of traditions, of institutions, and of economic conditions, in determining the course of life and the success or failure of a nation, the innate qualities of the population will make themselves felt and, in the long run, will exert a preponderant influence over all other factors'.[102] It confusedly emerges that a people's inborn traits constantly exert 'a shaping and selective influence' upon the growth of its culture and institutions; these traits account for a decisive part of a nation's collective mind. Granted this, 'we have an immense field awaiting exploration' since very little truly scientific study of innate dispositions, namely investigation conducted through 'exact observation', has been hitherto carried out. In concluding the chapter, McDougall indicates the most pressing questions requiring answers from future research. Distinguishing in principle between inbred and acquired characteristics is one of these questions; then the mental endowment of each race and people (including the 'Celts' and 'Teutons') should be detailed and explained; and the study of the psychological effects of present living conditions should be carried out. He hinted that the widening gulf in talent and morality between the masses and the elites could be due to innate dispositions.[103]

McDougall's interest in collective characters culminated in his book of 1920, *The Group Mind*, a most comprehensive treatment which, in ideal fulfilment of the line of argument just summarized, is cast along predominantly racial lines. His thesis is that race 'gives a constant bias to the evolution of the social environment, and, through it, moulds the individuals of each generation'.[104] After claiming objectivity and sporting 'scientific' restraint, he draws conclusions sanctioning the crassest of commonplaces about the Irish, the French, about Catholicism and Protestantism, etc. The example of English infants exchanged at birth for French ones is now made to uphold the primacy of original dispositions.[105] Yet in a sense he clung to social psychology. He did not dismiss the viewpoint that individual psychology was intelligible only in relation to the life of societies, which, as 'organic' wholes with their own 'individuality', in large measure shaped the units composing them.[106] Innate racial attitudes were considered in close association with the social environment and in particular with its intellectual and moral traditions, of whose development the progress of peoples wholly consisted.[107]

---

[102] *ibid.*, pp. 248–9.
[103] *ibid.*, pp. 249–51.
[104] *The Group Mind*, p. 118.
[105] 'In the course of perhaps a century there would be an appreciable assimilation of English institutions to those of France at the present day, for example, the Roman Catholic religion would gain in strength at the cost of the Protestant': *ibid.*
[106] *ibid.*, pp. 1–10, 213.
[107] *ibid.*, p. 269.

McDougall's dissection of character has political overtones – even apart from the elitist beliefs expressed in all his writings, his 'scientific' view of the English as the most culturally homogeneous people appears related to his advocacy of a strong sentiment of nationality in the face of sectional bodies like the trade unions.[108] Yet his 1908 treatise does not carry an overt political message; McDougall's remarks are scattered and obliquely posited to the effect of seeming incidental. As an intended piece of natural science, the book considered all men irrespective of nationality. To pass judgement on specific sections of humanity thereby required a switch to the particularist mode, but in terms which did not contravene the rules of scientificity. Eugenics seems to have met this exigency.[109] In a context where even animism had to be demonstrated through 'empirical science',[110] scientific reserve is more telling than occasional political outspokenness; one perceives that McDougall viewed a contrast of sorts between his scientific role and the freewheeling expression of social and political preferences.[111]

Although much less influential than McDougall's 1908 volume, Trotter's articles look more modern by virtue of a quasi-Freudian thesis.[112] Ignoring national fences, Trotter posited two mental types, the stable and the unstable, as produced by the 'herd instinct' in modern communities. This amounted to a biological instinct of 'gregariousness', which he deemed necessary for the effective functioning of the human mind.[113] Although 'suggestibility' was man's feature underlying both mental propensities, the stable individual rationalized the conflict between the herd's lofty moral teaching and reality, whereas the unstable one failed to do so. A nation where the stable personality prevailed was energetic but narrow-minded and reluctant to change; and where the other type dominated it was sceptical, apathetic, and unsteady although adaptable and 'sensitive'. A quick reference was made to the ancient Romans and Jews, as well as to the contemporary Japanese, as examples of peoples of the former kind. Their great willpower as well as their hardness contrasted with the traits of the unstable, resulting from 'the thwarting of the primary impulses to action

---

[108] *An Introduction to Social Psychology*, pp. 344–5; 'The Will of the People', esp. p. 103.
[109] See W. McDougall, 'A Practicable Eugenic Suggestion', *Sociological Papers*, 3 (1907), pp. 55–80.
[110] W. McDougall, *Body and Mind: a History and Defense of Animism* (London, 1911).
[111] On McDougall's flawed commitment to objective psychology, see M. Steininger, 'Objectivity and Value Judgements in the Psychologies of E. L. Thorndike and W. McDougall', *Journal of the History of the Behavioral Sciences*, 15 (1979), pp. 263–81.
[112] In fact, Trotter was acquainted with Freudian psychology (he was a close friend of Ernest Jones, Freud's biographer). Trotter and McDougall are equated with conservative thinkers by R. N. Soffer in 'New Elitism: Social Psychology in Prewar England', *Journal of British Studies*, 7 (1969), pp. 111–40, and in *Ethics and Society in England* (Berkeley, 1978), pp. 217–51. Yet, D. P. Crook, *Darwinism, War and History* (Cambridge, 1994), p. 148, holds that 'unusually for a crowd theorist, Trotter's politics were left of centre'.
[113] 'Herd Instinct and Its Bearing on the Psychology of Civilised Man', *Sociological Review*, 1 (1908), pp. 227–48.

resident in herd suggestion by the influence of an experience which cannot be disregarded'.[114]

Trotter regrets the blame which eugenicists and more generally 'the mentally resistant class' put on the unstable, presented as eccentrics or deficient in temper. He is inclined to see both mental illnesses and alcoholism as reactions to instability. In modern times the unstable are on the increase, Trotter maintained, but this would not necessarily be a problem if men managed to readjust the interplay between environment and mind (he speaks of the 'mental environment') with the aim of reaping the best from either type. The sensitivity to feeling and experience of the unstable can be valuable to society; they have a potential for 'intercommunication', a necessary requisite of human development, which a 'disorderly environment' is unable to liberate without transforming it into a quasi-pathological symptom. Since suggestibility entails an equal acceptance of both unreasonable precepts and 'rational verifiable knowledge', lasting progress can only be achieved through 'the extension of the rational method to the whole field of experience', so that irrational beliefs would not be assumed.[115] In Trotter's dichotomy there might be implied a criticism of the one-sidedness of English character, of which determination, enterprise and manliness were traditional staples.

By identifying 'the two great mental types found in society' and not using them to typify nations, Trotter's analysis implicitly questioned the legitimacy of national character as a unit of group psychology and, by extension, of social thought. His approach is akin to McDougall's in assuming a close interaction between environment and instinctual dispositions. With a difference, though, for Trotter emancipated himself from the racial encumbrance; he derided 'the facile doctrines of degeneracy, the pragmatic lecturing on national characteristics, on Teutons and Celts, on Latins and Slavs, on pure races and mixed races, and all the other ethnological conceits with which the ignorant have gulled the innocent so long'.[116] But when in 1916 he enlarged upon his position in a book and applied it to the war situation, German character was deemed to centre around 'a primitive type of the gregarious instincts – the aggressive', while German society was equated to a 'wolf pack'.[117]

A point to note in the approach brought about by the social sciences is a tendential change of subject. The 'people' whose dispositions social scientists most often talked about were neither 'the English' in general nor the abstractly conceived middle classes but the urban skilled and unskilled workers

---

[114] 'Sociological Application of the Psychology of Herd Instinct', *Sociological Review*, 2 (1909), pp. 36–54, quotation on p. 49.
[115] *ibid.*, pp. 46–54.
[116] Quoted in H. C. Greisman, 'Herd Instinct and the Foundations of Biosociology', *Journal of the History of the Behavioral Sciences*, 15 (1979), p. 366.
[117] *Instincts of the Herd in Peace and War* (London, 1916), p. 191. The book was republished many times, most recently in 1953.

empirically apprehended. A representative document is the volume edited by Charles Masterman, *The Heart of the Empire* (1901). A core group of contributors with direct experience of social work addressed the 'new city race' which inhabited crowded and unhealthy districts and which, these authors maintained, lamentably contrasted with the previous working-class type (said to be physically healthy, religious, energetic, and steady). The new men were physically weak and mentally excitable and voluble, and were leading a dull and monotonous life with purely materialistic goals. The English, regretted Masterman, cannot be apprehended any longer within 'some large framework of meaning' since this ever-growing part of the population is neither eager to get on nor reactive and responsible, neither devoted to intellectual pursuits nor nurturing the spark of religious sentiment. The urban worker is just 'acquiescent' with a mood of 'a certain fatuous cheerfulness'. It was a sign of the changing times that Masterman, in order to mark out the spiritual void of English labour, went as far as congratulating the French working classes on their 'devotion to abstract ideas'.[118]

A similar sense of astonishment pervades Hobson's *Psychology of Jingoism*, where the running thread is a bitter comparison between old 'John Bull' and the national dispositions as revealed by the Anglo-Boer war.[119] Urban life had induced 'a surface smartness, an alertness of manipulation of ideas within a narrow area of interest and experience', and eventually 'a neurotic temperament' which fed on the waves of excitement generated by the press. 'Jingoism is the passion of the spectator, the inciter, the backer, not of the fighter.'[120] The new characteristics Hobson pointed out, and which applied to both the educated and the uneducated, were credulity, brutality, vainglory, and lack of sense of humour.[121] To support his polemic, Hobson made use of crowd psychology and in particular of Le Bon's idea of 'regression': 'the British nation became a great crowd, and exposed its crowd-mind to the suggestions of the press'.[122] It may have been a legitimate inference, then, that crowds behaved in the same way everywhere in the industrial world, because life in large cities had determined mental patterns which were stronger than national habits and traditions. From a different angle, *Jingoism* exemplifies the growing realization

---

[118] C. Masterman, 'Realities at Home', in C. Masterman, ed., *The Heart of the Empire* (London, 1901), pp. 1–52. See also in the book the essays by R. A. Bray, 'The Children of the Town', pp. 111–64, and G. M. Trevelyan, 'The Past and Future', pp. 398–415. During the First World War, Masterman was the head of the government propaganda office which waged 'the war of the professors'.

[119] *The Psychology of Jingoism* (London, 1901), esp. pp. 32, 34. For background, see G. R. Searle, *The Quest for National Efficiency* (Berkeley, 1971), and P. Clarke, *Liberals and Social Democrats* (Cambridge, 1978), esp. pp. 90–4.

[120] *The Psychology of Jingoism*, pp. 6–9.

[121] *ibid.*, pp. 21–66. For a reminder of traditional English attitudes, see pp. 44–5.

[122] *ibid.*, p. 19. See M. Freeden, 'Hobson's Evolving Conceptions of Human Nature', in M. Freeden, ed., *Reappraising J. A. Hobson* (London, 1990), pp. 54–73.

that states of minds, now analysed in the light of instinctual propensities and crowd sentiments, were highly sensitive to manipulation.

There was a widespread feeling among those who embraced the social sciences that civilization was entering a novel phase. Wallas's *Human Nature in Politics* reflects the consciousness that a new set of political conditions had arisen as a response to the enlargement of the franchise and the phenomena of mass society. Relatedly, the new psychology of impulses and instincts invited a reformulation of man's motives. The book is devoted, under the aegis of William James, to the systematic reconstruction of politics upon a theory of human nature eschewing the 'intellectualist fallacy'. In order to avoid abstract thinking and correspondingly to make accurate predictions, this is a necessary task, Wallas commented. As he also put it, political institutions should be made to adapt to 'the actual facts of human nature'.[123]

In the book, an analysis of the instincts relevant to politics (affection for the powerful, fear, longing for property, etc.) is conducted in association with the consideration of 'man's political environment'. Wallas approves of parties because these are 'something which can be loved and trusted', and for this reason they fulfil a function required by human nature.[124] In fact, on the basis of evidence supplied by laboratory tests, he unveils mass political opinion as the product of 'non-rational inference' insofar as political symbols and ideals are cherished for their emotional contents. For example, a nation is an image consciously built by statesmen on symbols and 'a common inheritance of passionate feeling' with the aim of creating a sufficient basis of patriotism.[125] The goal of politics is 'to create as much meaning as possible' because 'human emotions must have something to attach themselves to'.[126]

Granted that it is possible to construct an average human type by the empirical detection of persistent traits, there occur differences in the practical outcomes of innate inclinations due to the influence of environment. To assess these variations – which can be mathematically calculated – is the special problem of politics. Since many variables are simultaneously at play, each case is complex and different from all others. The study of history should complement knowledge of 'the facts of the human type'.[127] A political thinker, Wallas warned, 'should be constantly on his guard against generalisations about national or racial "character" ', since this may alter very rapidly in the modern world.

National habits used to change slowly in the past, because new methods of life were seldom invented and only gradually introduced, and because the means of communicating

[123] *Human Nature in Politics* (London, 1908), pp. v, 12–29, 83, 167.
[124] *ibid.*, pp. 82–4ff.
[125] *ibid.*, pp. 59–81.
[126] *ibid.*, pp. 79, 82.
[127] *ibid.*, pp. 121–36, 149.

ideas between man and man or nation and nation were extremely imperfect; so that a true statement about a national habit might, and probably would, remain true for centuries. But now an invention which may produce profound changes in social or industrial life is as likely to be taken up with enthusiasm in some country on the other side of the globe as in the place of its origin . . . Under these new conditions . . . English indifference to ideas or French military ambition are habits which, under a sufficiently extended stimulus, nations can shake off as completely as can individual men.[128]

To make the use of national character even more problematic, Wallas noticed the increasing ethnic heterogeneity of states and empires.[129] To him, generalizations about collective dispositions were examples of the abstract reasoning which he wanted to ban from politics to be replaced by 'quantitative' arguments. For instance, in discussing the methods to be used by Poor Law commissioners, Wallas denied the validity of considering the average characteristics of the population; rather, individuals should be arranged 'in "polygons of variation"' according to their nervous and physical strength, their ' "character" ', and the degree to which ideas of the future were likely to affect their present conduct.[130]

In *Human Nature in Politics* Wallas embraced a view of politics as a technique, both psychological and statistical, although he explicitly rejected the exploitation of irrationality in advocating a scientific education intended to make people conscious of their own mental processes. His recommendation of eugenics had a similar 'technical' connotation.[131] (Wallas's successive work, *The Great Society*, would strike different chords.) The deepened, 'scientific' knowledge of character he endorsed was not made to impinge on the aims of parties or the policies of government, but on a more effective implementation of whatever platforms they chose. This book exemplarily points to a relationship between the advent of political 'science' and politics as shaped by mass behaviour and opinion. The ensuing approach entails the rejection of a notion as vague as national character, replaced by a psychology capable of accounting for the traits of the man in the street. The abstract question whether attitudes or institutions get the upper hand loses relevance to Wallas's politician, bent on calculating the effects of specific circumstances on character with the aim of concerting a measure or of winning an election.[132]

[128] *ibid.*, p. 137.
[129] *ibid.*, pp. 277–84ff.
[130] *ibid.*, pp. 159–60.
[131] *ibid.*, pp. 180–98ff., 292–4.
[132] The publication of an *Ethological Journal* from 1905 to 1929 (but with a gap 1914–22) should also be mentioned. Edited by Bernard Hollander, MD, and associated with a London-based Ethological Society, the journal lacked academic support and led a lacklustre life under the aegis of the odd mix of phrenology, heredity, and eugenics of its editor. There appeared articles on the national characters of the Japanese, Irish, Hungarians, Americans, Jews, etc. A. R. Wallace was a member of the Society, with C. Lombroso and M. Nordau as corresponding members.

6   The demise of economic man: Marshall and Hobson

As mentioned in chapter 3, British classical political economy had endorsed a certain idea of collective attitudes, centred around the so-called 'gospel of work'. As regards national character proper, the universal validity of both the framework and the tools of analysis of political economy in principle enabled economists to do without notions like national character. J. S. Mill's insertion of it within the body of economic theory cannot be said to be representative,[133] whereas it is true that numerous writings on policy issues do consider national characters. Ricardo's model testifies to the abstract nature of the analytical core of economic knowledge (although few texts were as dry as his *Principles*); and this trend continued, and deepened, with the advent of marginalism. As anticipated, there is a momentous stumbling block in Marshall. Yet neither he nor his fellow economists developed the racialist line of inquiry expressed in the chapters on economic history which open the *Principles*, as both preferred to pursue another aspect of Marshall's concern with human types, the elevation of the workers' mental life.[134] After mid century the gospel of work appeared untenable, in fact, inasmuch as growing affluence made leisure an option for the middle classes and trade unions mobilized support for shorter hours. Displacing the gloomy philosophy of work and thrift and asserting more varied lifestyles of higher intellectual quality involved a momentous application of social science to collective mentalities; in the following pages consideration will be given to Marshall and Hobson.

With Marshall, it was the favourable economic situation that prompted the change in emphasis. He viewed his age as a period of unprecedented wealth and prosperity which offered precious margins for an acceleration of reform. Once the basic needs were more or less being met, it became possible to foster the development of the 'higher mental faculties' which would bring about a 'noble and refined life'. The qualities Marshall specially targeted were a higher sense of duty, altruism, and a taste for beauty in nature and the arts; more generally, he aimed at 'a fullness of life' made possible by workers' 'mental growth'.[135]

It was a fundamental tenet of Marshall's thought that 'some strenuous exertion' or at least 'some hard work' was necessary to the moulding of a sound character. Yet the balance between the qualities induced by work and those made

---

[133] Reflections on national mentalities are scattered through the *Principles of Political Economy*, and in particular the chapter entitled 'On What Depends the Degree of Productiveness of Productive Agents' (bk I, ch.7), is largely concerned with them.

[134] Yet it was not until the fifth edition (1907) of the *Principles* that the historical section was moved from the text of bk I to appendix A. See also Marshall's late *Industry and Trade* (1919; London, 1923).

[135] 'The Future of the Working Classes' (1873), in A. Marshall, *Memorials*, ed. A. C. Pigou (London, 1925), pp. 101–18; *Principles*, pp. 2–4. See also 'Co-operation' (1889), in *Memorials*, pp. 238–9.

possible by leisure needed redressing.[136] He took on 'the sacrifice of the individual to the exigencies of . . . production', arguing that the pursuit of wealth was a 'noble aim' only as long as it supplied the necessaries 'for life and culture'.[137] However, the two sets of faculties, the industrial and the non-industrial, could be distinguished only for the sake of argument, to the effect that the enrichment of personality ultimately strengthened industrial growth. Marshall typically maintained that what modern business needed most was moral and physical 'vigour', that is 'general abilities' like 'sagacity', 'energy', 'self-mastery', 'mental activity', 'judgement', etc.[138] These qualities could hardly be divorced from the mental refinements which reform targeted, as the following passage indicates.

The physical superiority of the English race over all others that have lived as largely as we are doing a town life, is due to a great extent to the games in which our youth exercises its physical faculties for the sake of exercising them: the religious, the moral, the intellectual and the artistic faculties on which the progress of industry depends, are not acquired solely for the sake of the things that may be got by them; but are developed by exercise for the sake of the pleasure and the happiness which they themselves bring . . . We ought then to inquire whether the present industrial organization might not with advantage be so modified as to increase the opportunities which the lower grades of industry have for using their mental faculties, for deriving pleasure from their use, and for strengthening them by use.[139]

Ideally, work should become a source of 'happiness' through 'healthful exercise and development of faculties', and enterprise should be presided over by the forces of association and social sympathy.[140] More practically, Marshall pointed out that a chain of favourable effects was likely to be triggered by higher wages: these brought about more labour efficiency together with habits of self-respect, and hence significant economic advantages in the medium term. And all should work less – a temporarily diminished production would be of little import, he contended.[141] The 'energizing influence' of hope and self-respect which was the backbone of Marshall's economics of reform proves indistinguishable from his vision of growth.[142]

[136] Compare H. Sidgwick, *The Principles of Political Economy* (1883; 3rd edn, 1901; repr. edn, London, 1996), p. 520, where he stuck to the view that 'human beings generally have a tendency to overvalue leisure as a source of happiness'. See also L. Stephen, 'The Morality of Competition', in his *Social Rights and Duties* (2 vols., London, 1896), I, pp. 133–73.

[137] Marshall, *Principles*, pp. 182, 305.

[138] *ibid.*, pp. 260–79.

[139] *ibid.*, p. 308. See also 'The Future of the Working Classes', p. 118. The quoted passage is intended by Marshall as an application of Spencer's views on the development of faculties by use.

[140] 'The Old Generation of Economists and the New' (1897), in *Memorials*, p. 310.

[141] *Principles*, pp. 295, 731.

[142] 'The Old Generation', pp. 310–11.

The issue of the length of the working day was specially linked to Marshall's concern with leisure and consumption. Constantly, he lamented the ostentatious patterns of consumption of the rich, but 'even the working classes buy many things that do them little good and some things that do them harm'.[143] This wasteful expenditure should be redirected towards, first, standard goods of a better and more artistic quality, and, second, goods intended to provide the public with 'higher forms of enjoyment'. Museums, parks, playgrounds, a healthy environment in towns, and the preservation of nature in the immediate outskirts of towns are Marshall's recurring examples of this second class of goods and thereby of the conditions under which 'the people generally would be so well nurtured and so truly educated that the land would be pleasant to live in'.[144] Marshall is inclined to lend an active role to communities with respect to patterns of consumption: 'it would be a gain if the moral sentiment of the community could induce people to avoid all sorts of display of individual wealth'.[145] Marshall expected not only the workshop but society at large to mould characters, so that previously irrelevant aspects of communal life were charged with positive potentialities. His depiction of the workers in the context of society – as plain a conception as it may seem today – helped to relegate economic man to economic modelling at its most abstract.[146]

Nobody voiced the demand for a new type of man more radically than Hobson in his essay 'Character and Society' (1912) and in *Work and Wealth* (1914). The indictment of the 'Victorian personality' they contain – an indictment

[143] Quotation from 'Social Possibilities of Economic Chivalry' (1907), in *Memorials*, p. 324.
[144] *Principles*, pp. 181–3; 'Social Possibilities', p. 345. See also 'Where to House the London Poor' (1884), in *Memorials*, pp. 142–51.
[145] *Principles*, pp. 181–2. On the importance of public opinion as an economic force, see J. K. Whitaker, 'Some Neglected Aspects of Alfred Marshall's Economic and Social Thought', *History of Political Economy*, 7 (1975), pp. 171–5.
[146] Marshall's frame of reference was endorsed by many contributors to the *Economic Journal*, which he did not edit but to some extent controlled. On its pages, that men should turn from means to ends figures as a recurring formula to express the ultimate goal of reform. See esp. J. Bonar, 'Old Lights and New in Economic Study', 8 (1898), pp. 431–53, and H. Llewellyn Smith, 'Economic Security and Unemployment Insurance', 20 (1910), pp. 513–29. As part of the journal's support of economic reform, it was important to demonstrate that shorter hours did not result in more drinking or other disgraceful activities but in a more varied, intellectually gratifying, and thereby nobler life. Marshall's pupil and colleague S. J. Chapman associated a shorter working day with a 'full living' for all; a life where 'social intercourse', 'variety of experience', 'contact with nature', and 'intimacy with life as a whole' became possible. See also J. Rae, 'The Eight Hours Day in Victoria', 1 (1891), esp. pp. 36–42; F. S. Nitti, 'The Food and Labour-Power of Nations', 6 (1896), pp. 30–63; S. J. Chapman, 'Hours of Labour', 19 (1909), p. 372. See N. Jha, *The Age of Marshall* (London, 1973), pp. 107–8. J. S. Nicholson's nervous defence of 'labour as an element of duty and spiritual well-being' testifies to a common knowledge which, at least in principle, rejected the 'economic man' in favour of the 'all-around man': J. S. Nicholson, 'Inaugural Address to the Scottish Society of Economists', 7 (1897), p. 543; see C. Gide, 'Has Cooperation Introduced a New Principle into Economics?', 8 (1898), p. 504. C. Devas, 'Lessons from Ruskin', 8 (1898), p. 35, defined Ruskin as 'the hammer of the economic man'.

carried out through principles of universal application – comprises a fully fledged prefiguration of its alternative. That environment moulds character, Hobson contended, is a dangerous half-truth; 'true sociology' teaches that a constant interaction between the two actually takes place. It is therefore a proper task to draw a picture of the personality best fitted 'not merely to fall in with the new arrangement of life foisted upon them by modern external forces, but to give out intelligent energy in making these arrangements and in putting reasonable order into what otherwise would seem a "blind" unfolding of some secret "cosmic" function' which is as likely to enslave man as to liberate him.[147]

A brief review of Hobson's steps prior to the works referred to should start with his defiant statement of 1889 that, under-consumption being the cause of the social question, the ultimate responsibility rested with 'the most respectable and highly extolled virtue of thrift'.[148] His comments on the East London Jews are another example of Hobson's scant respect for traditional economic virtues. Having come to believe that the way forward from under-consumption lay in the workers' contractual capacity to hang on to a higher standard of living, the Jews' acceptance of a lower than customary wage was a slap in the face. They embody, he wrote, the economists' 'economic man'. Being 'steady, industrious, quiet, sober, thrifty', the London Jews are the very people to be encouraged 'from the point of view of the old Political Economy'. But they are 'void of social morality', as shown by their proneness to undersell their fellow workers as well as by their using their 'superior calculating intellect' to take advantage 'of every weakness, folly, and vice' of the society in which they live.[149] Alongside these critical motifs, Hobson elaborated the issue of quality in economic life – quality of consumption and work, but also quality of personal and communal life through leisure, education, co-operation, and 'comradeship' – which became progressively prominent from *The Evolution of Modern Capitalism* (1894) on.[150]

Hobson, who not unexpectedly saw an inextricable link between an individualist philosophy and the blind advocacy of self-helpist precepts, rejected the former on the basis of a radically organicist view of society and the latter by sound environmentalism coupled with principles of social

---

[147] 'Character and Society', in P. L. Parker, ed., *Character and Life* (London, 1912), p. 56. For a survey of the debate on character and reform at the turn of the century, see M. Freeden, *The New Liberalism: an Ideology of Social Reform* (Oxford, 1978), pp. 170–94.

[148] J. A. Hobson and A. F. Mummery, *The Physiology of Industry* (1889; repr. edn, London, 1992), pp. 99, 182. This posture seems to soften in J. A. Hobson, *The Problem of the Unemployed* (1896; repr. edn, London, 1992), pp. 92–3.

[149] *Problems of Poverty* (London, 1891), pp. 59–60. Hobson was probably drawing from Beatrice Webb's account of the London Jews originally contributed to C. Booth's *The Life and Labour of the People of London* (1889), and republished in S. Webb and B. Webb, *Problems of Modern Industry* (London, 1898), pp. 20–45; see esp. pp. 42–5.

[150] *The Evolution of Modern Capitalism* (London, 1894), esp. pp. 368–83.

justice.[151] In this last respect, almost as a preliminary to the writings on character, he successfully challenged that pillar of Victorian mentality, the view that assistance saps responsibility and independence.[152] As far as organicism is concerned, he directed attention to the interaction of minds which created a common will, thought, and consciousness in each society.[153] In operating through a refinement of rooted instincts, man's reason brings about an increasing integration of each individual into the 'wider organism'.[154] Social organicism provides the ultimate reasons for reform – in their present state, the economy, the government, and people's dispositions clash with the preservation and well-being of the social aggregate – as well as indicating the direction of change – minimization of the 'vital costs' of production, socialization of industry, a democracy with a 'head' of skilled officials, and a more other-oriented personality. The crux of the matter is that for Hobson only the 'organic standpoint' makes sympathy possible.

In man regarded as individual it is very difficult to recognise any possibility of a disinterested motive, because all such motives are ruled out *ex hypothesi*. But regard the individual man as subject to the dominant control of some wider life than his, that of race, society, humanity or kosmos, and the difficulty disappears. He becomes capable of 'disinterested' curiosity, 'disinterested' love, 'self-sacrifices' of various kinds, because he is a centre of wider interests than those of his own particular self.[155]

Given the 'organic' imperative of forwarding the survival and advance of the community 'regarded as a conscious whole', Hobson stressed the individual's duties to the polity (rather than his or her rights) in both the political and economic spheres.[156]

To come to Hobson's views on model personality, the customary image of an average 'John Smith' needed revising because the old type of character had

---

[151] See esp. *Physiology of Industry*, pp. 103–16; *Problem of the Unemployed*, pp. 74–88; *Work and Wealth: a Human Valuation* (1914; repr. edn, London, 1992), pp. 12–17, 307–8, 349–60.

[152] 'The Social Philosophy of Charity Organisation', *Contemporary Review*, 70 (1896), pp. 710–27.

[153] On the one hand, 'there is not a school, a church, a club, even for the lightest and most recreative object, embodying some purpose or idea and the common pursuit of it, which does not impress a common character upon its members': 'The Re-Statement of Democracy', *Contemporary Review*, 81 (1902), p. 265. On the other, 'the individual feeling, his will, his ends and interests, are not entirely merged in or sacrificed to the public feeling, will and ends, but over a certain area they are fused and identified, and the common social life thus formed has conscious interests and ends of its own which are not merely instruments in forwarding the progress of the separate individual lives, but are directed primarily to secure the survival and psychical progress of the community regarded as a conscious whole': 'The Re-Statement of Democracy', pp. 265–6.

[154] *Work and Wealth*, pp. 355–7.

[155] *ibid.*, p. 356.

[156] On organicism and political participation, see esp. 'The Re-Statement of Democracy'; on work as a duty for all, see *The Evolution of Modern Capitalism*, pp. 379–80, and later writings as well.

degenerated into a 'neurotic' state due to 'an excessive premium on adaptiveness'. A coarse, hard, grasping attitude had resulted from decades of unconstrained economic transformation. Laissez-faire individualism was based on the notion that

a sound society required nothing more than a set of these hard-headed, intelligent, self-centred monads, each vigorously asserting his rights, pursuing his separate material interests, and caring nothing for the rights and interests of his neighbours. Under the providential order of the universe, from this constant clash of competing self-interests there was to emerge a social harmony. There is now no need to expose the theoretical and practical falsehood of this conception of society.[157]

Modern sciences show that a healthy self separated from 'that living and growing thing we call society' cannot exist. Sociability and solidarity are natural attributes of man, forms of self-expression which make a community really strong and wealthy. Far from being efficient, in fact, a society of self-contained individuals is in danger of dissolution for lack of balance and generosity – especially in critical times, when a dose of self-sacrifice is required.[158] In contrast to the selfish type, a 'true' individuality based on psychological stability and social dispositions would resist 'collective suggestion' and the propensity 'to think and feel in swarms'; a lack of both solidity and 'wider sympathy' lies at the basis of 'collective obsessions of the mob-mind' like jingoism.[159]

A balanced personality, Hobson continued in his sketch of 'our ideal man of progress', will thrive on a shorter and more creative working day and on the effects of the emancipation of women on family life. Leisure is for the exercise of 'capricious and unordered impulses', for, in a Millian spirit, 'eccentricities and extravagancies'; it is for 'play', and not just for rest. 'Friendship, play, and nature' are fundamental, for a society where everything is carefully regulated cannot be an ideal. The rationale of this stance is that proper leisure raises 'the banner of revolt against the tyranny of industry over human life'.[160] In this 'strenuous age', Hobson wondered, how can citizens make the most of home life, social activities, political participation, and the opportunities of education and friendship? 'Most of the growing public expenditure which the modern State or City lays out upon the amenities of social life, the apparatus of libraries, museums, parks, music and recreation, is half wasted because industry has trenched too much upon humanity.'[161] To counterbalance the specialization in the workplace, more and qualitatively better leisure is needed to keep the worker 'human'. A net economic benefit would eventually ensue from education and, paradoxically perhaps, from 'idleness' itself. Quoting Wordsworth and

---

[157] 'Character and Society', pp. 71–2.
[158] ibid., p. 72–5.
[159] ibid., pp. 57, 77–82.
[160] ibid., pp. 85–104; Work and Wealth, pp. 228–49, quotation on p. 241.
[161] Work and Wealth, p. 236; see also pp. 248–9.

Thoreau, but in contrast with a century of mainstream moral thought, Hobson praises the virtues of idleness: excessive 'calculation into life' has caused it to be forgotten that novel thoughts often originate from 'seasons of vacancy and reverie'. Talent is more common than is usually believed, and forms of play are momentous ways to nurture it. His general idea is that machine production and democracy give the chance of overthrowing 'the domination of Industry over the lives, the thoughts, and the hearts of men'. The issue is posited in the terms of the inversion of means and ends between the pursuit of wealth and men's lives, an inversion which in Hobson takes up a decidedly humanist, Ruskinian flavour.[162] Besides society, nature too gives meaning to human life. In 'Character and Society', Hobson's final point is about man being part of nature rather than its master: as the most sophisticated of animals, he owes his finest faculties to continuity with 'the general creative energy that pulses through nature'.[163]

In rejecting the economic man, Marshall and Hobson could rely on insights by Mill, Ruskin, Spencer, Arnold, Hobhouse, and all the others who from mid century had variously objected to the current model personality. It is no accident that themes and claims similar to Marshall and Hobson's figure in the writings of other major social scientists: for instance, McDougall analysed the tendency to play, while Spencer and Wallas advocated leisure.[164] The time was definitely ripe for a relaxation of the gospel of work. For the comprehensiveness of its treatment and the liberating force of its new model of man, Hobson's stance in particular assumes an emblematic value. In the years preceding 1914 the set of qualities which had made up the English character in the past – self-restraint, energy, independence, enterprise, and thrift – was no longer deemed sufficient and, if not associated with social propensities, was thought to have disruptive effects. At the root of this recognition there was above all the social evolutionary perspective. (T. H. Green's philosophy was probably another major influence.) Evolutionism entailed a new conception of human nature – much more instinctual and composite than that of the utilitarians – to be grasped within society as the norm-giving environment proper to men.[165] In McDougall's emphatic words, there emerged a vision that made men and institutions 'nodes or meeting points of all the forces of the world acting and reacting in unlimited time and space'.[166] As Sidney Webb put it, 'it was

---

[162] 'Character and Society', pp. 96–100; *Work and Wealth*, pp. 237–44, 289–90ff.

[163] 'Character and Society', pp. 102–3.

[164] The advocacy of leisure is in Spencer, 'The Americans'; and in G. Wallas, *The Great Society* (London, 1914), pp. 380–9 (Wallas came to share Hobson's fundamental inspiration, in addition to a number of other specific points; see, e.g., his review of *Work and Wealth* in *The Nation*, 15, 27 June 1914, pp. 495–6); a discussion of 'the tendency to play' is in McDougall, *An Introduction to Social Psychology*, pp. 107ff.

[165] See L. Stephen, *The English Utilitarians* (1900; repr. edn, 3 vols., Bristol, 1991), esp. I, pp. 297–307.

[166] McDougall, *The Group Mind*, p. 2.

discovered (or rediscovered) that a society is something more than an aggregate of so many individual units – that it possesses existence distinguishable from those of any of its components'.[167]

The advent of the social sciences coincided with a perception of men and women as ends in themselves rather than, as before, means to allegedly higher ends such as liberty, political stability, national power, Christian salvation, or economic growth. Hobson and Marshall did not sacrifice people's well-being to, respectively, the ideal of socialism and the exigencies of British industry, insofar as a better quality of life comprehensively intended was to them a goal *per se*. To speak up against the onesidedness of the workers' experience, what Marshall and Hobson did was to put themselves in their shoes, for the spiritual needs of the educated were thought not to differ from those of the mass. Hobson's ideal personality would suit not only John Smith but everybody. A focus on organic impulses gave life a broader scope than utilitarianism did; the consideration of leisure and rest, in particular, undermined the abstractness of Victorian values by adding a dimension which really turned 'hands' into men. All these circumstances engender a feeling in the modern reader that, at this juncture, some questions which are still with us began to be approached in a spirit not dissimilar from our own. Signally, disentangling personality from an exclusive concern with work is a legacy of social Darwinism which, once its bearing is transposed from blue to white collars, remains of importance today.

The 'Victorian personality' proved remarkably resilient in the face of changing social environments and the gradual weakening of religious sentiments. For a significant instance, traditional attributes like a practical bent, self-reliance, and law-abidingness coexist with the advocacy of a 'full man' in the portrait of the English offered by Ernest Barker's *National Character* (1927).[168] Yet, what the social scientific critics of Victorian virtues were attempting at the turn of the century was not a redefinition of English identity *per se* but an apprehension of the personality capable, everywhere, of coping with the pressures of mass production and civilization, and, additionally, of directing society on the right track. There was an intrinsic universalist bias in social Darwinism which marked the origins of the social sciences, even if some betrayed this inspiration. John Bull was not entirely dismissed by social scientists: Kidd, for one, strove to update and reinforce the stereotype by injecting racialism and democratic instincts into the old form of Protestant-sourced morality.

The social sciences were devising *models* of social behaviour which effectively cut across national boundaries – a development made possible by a

---

[167] S. Webb, 'The Historic Basis of Socialism', in G. B. Shaw, ed., *Fabian Essays* (1889; 1948; repr. edn, London, 1996), p. 53.

[168] E. Barker, *National Character and the Factors in Its Formation* (1927; London, 1939). See Stapleton, *Englishness and the Study of Politics*, esp. pp. 118–21.

set of intertwined causes which it is now appropriate to restate. Perhaps the most important of these causes is the adoption of a naturalistic viewpoint: societies were no longer the battlegrounds of political values and philosophies, but the objects of fact-based study. Since they were organisms, societies could be systematically studied within a broad evolutionary frame which qualified their uniqueness. The inductive characterization of this viewpoint went with a cumulative, professionalized idea of knowledge. Another major cause was the operational recognition of the fragmentation of society into groups and classes, a recognition clashing with the inclusiveness of the idea of nation. Since Montesquieu, authors had only occasionally bothered to specify the social classes that they had in mind when talking about the temperament of the nation. As argued earlier in the book, in both Britain and France after 1789 the idea of a national character customarily implied reference to all ranks, primarily in the sense of asserting the extension of political relevance to the middle and lower classes. A certain ambiguity was inherent to the message and constituted much of its efficacy. The social sciences made this ambiguity impossible, at least potentially, by analysing clearly defined classes and groups, which as a rule had their counterparts in other countries. Add to this that in Britain large sectors of the intelligentsia were fully aware of social cleavages and in favour of reform, an attitude which could not but induce suspicion towards aggregative notions like national character.

This is why national character is intrinsically a conservative concept: it groups together winners and losers in an indiscriminate manner. Its rejection, however, may appear perplexing to some even today. In principle, the standpoint of the social sciences (as traced in this chapter) ultimately entails that we are all everywhere the same, because equally moulded by irresistible social circumstances which are more or less alike in all industrialized countries and rapidly conforming to the Western model elsewhere. Contrastively, an appeal to national (or regional, municipal, etc.) character would be an attempt to re-establish a dimension where men and women are in control of their social environment by virtue of their cultural traditions, that is, of what is more specifically human, personal, and indispensable to the apprehension of the world outside the self.[169] Although the sharpness of the contrast is only due to the sake of clarity, the point is that there may still be a need for the rash conclusions and reassuring

---

[169] See, e.g., J. Michelet, *Le peuple* (1846; Paris, 1946), pp. 232–3: 'une âme de peuple doit se faire un point central d'organisme; il faut qu'elle s'asseoie en un lieu, s'y ramasse et s'y recueille, qu'elle s'harmonise à une telle nature ... C'est une force, pour toute vie, de se circonscrire, de couper quelque chose à soi dans l'espace et dans le temps, de mordre une pièce qui soit sienne, au sein de l'indifférente et dissolvante nature qui voudrait toujours confondre. Cela, c'est exister, c'est vivre. Un esprit fixé sur un point ira s'approfondissant. Un esprit flottant dans l'espace, se disperse et s'évanouit ... Le plus puissant moyen de Dieu pour créer et augmenter l'originalité distinctive, c'est de maintenir le monde harmoniquement divisé en ces grands et beaux systèmes qu'on appelle des nations.'

stereotypes supplied by national characters. They seem to have the potential to meet the demand for communal identity which social science finds difficult to handle. The dubious status of national character is reflected by its being, on the one hand, a regular presence in journalism and popular culture, and on the other an academic oddity, kept at arm's length by most but not infrequently called into play under many disguises.

8   Durkheim's collective representations and their background

The previous chapter dealt with a change in the study of national character in Britain, a change brought about by the reorganization of social thought which took place in the period 1870–1900 or thereabouts. This was not a revolution, but an acceleration towards a 'scientific' – that is, a more systematic, rigorous, comprehensive, and cautious – approach. Among the phenomena accompanying this acceleration were the universal adoption of inductive methods and techniques, at least in principle; the division of labour between social disciplines as well as the separate constitution of each of them, in both scientific and institutional terms; and a systematic and cumulative practice. To list in summary the principal results of social scientific research concerning collective character, one can point to the rise of more cogent and definite forms of environmentalism based on the evolutionary theory; to the establishment of a broader psychological framework, featuring more refined concepts; to the acknowledgement of the changing nature of collective characteristics; to the attention paid to classes and groups irrespective of national boundaries; and to the revision of the stereotype of the Englishman. Behind all this, there lay an awareness of the new mass dimension of social life; a purely individualistic framework began to be deemed insufficient to account for certain peculiarly modern phenomena. In short, as the psychological characteristics of the men in the street assumed ever more importance in all respects, the study of collective attitudes became raised, in the eyes of its protagonists at least, to the level of a true science.

In France, this line of development was endorsed by Durkheim and his school to the point of making the Spencers or McDougalls look like popularizers. The issue which the new science of sociology was called to address, however, remained that which had occupied the French mind in the previous decades: how to generate social cohesion, and thereby political stability.[1] Since the 1790s, institutional engineering had proved an ineffective way to deliver the regular workings of representative institutions; hence the stress on the human factor so

[1]   See G. Hawthorn, *Enlightenment and Despair: a History of Social Theory* (1976; Cambridge, 1987), p. 114, and S. Lukes, *Emile Durkheim: His Life and Work* (Harmondsworth, 1973), pp. 195–9.

common among French authors. The novelty of Durkheim's sociology is to be measured by the yardstick of the French tradition of thought about *mœurs* and public spirit. Accordingly, before addressing Durkheim, it is appropriate to briefly sketch what happened after Tocqueville.

1   The civic tradition and Taine

The growth of habits of civic participation, free discussion and personal responsibility through local self-government, associationism, and trial by jury stayed at the core of liberal thinking after 1848. Universal suffrage and Louis Napoleon's regime merely made matters more momentous and urgent. Late in the 1860s, Prévost-Paradol spoke of the 'deadly discouragement and deep weariness' which had taken possession of the French. Indifferent and apathetic, they had forgotten that moral causes determined the fate of nations, for a healthy society rested on the constant and voluntary sacrifice of personal interests to collective ones.[2] As Prévost-Paradol put it, the question was to identify the factors that induced men to refrain from selfish acts which they knew would go unpunished but would eventually result in the disintegration of the polity. These factors were religion, duty, Tocqueville's interest rightly understood, and honour. But only the first and the last could be grasped by ordinary Frenchmen, and, given the progressive weakening of religion, it was often simple fear of public dishonour that halted the hand of the bank clerk or made soldiers loyal and brave.[3] Even the 'point of honour' was in danger in contemporary France, however, owing to the corrupting spectacle of a 'triumphing iniquity'. Assuming that honour amounted to the idea that ends do not justify means as well as a full acceptance of the rules of the games, a series of revolutionary, that is illegal, governments had taught an opposite lesson. The bad example set in the political world had infected private morality, so that wealth was applauded, whatever the means by which it had been achieved. Prévost-Paradol was outraged by the political attitude of the better off: in France, wealth did not entail independence as in Britain, but its holders invariably complied with the government's will both in Parliament and at the local level. As regards the working classes, he commented disparagingly on their favourite doctrine of unlimited state action.[4]

To foster self-government, associationism, and individual responsibility, the influential Edouard Laboulaye updated the American myth.[5] He kept in good

[2] L. A. Prévost-Paradol, *La France nouvelle* (1868; 2nd edn, Paris, 1868), pp. 336, 349.
[3] *ibid.*, pp. 350–9.
[4] *ibid.*, pp. 360–71.
[5] See his *Histoire politique des Etats-Unis d'Amérique* (3 vols., Paris, 1855–66), and the best-selling *Paris en Amerique* (Paris, 1863), a fictional portrayal of the political, religious, and educational freedom of the United States. When Tocqueville died in 1859, 'the torch of the American School' passed to him: O. Rudelle, 'France and the American Experience, 1789–1875', in R. C. Simmons, ed., *The United States Constitution: the First 200 Years* (Manchester, 1989), p. 106. Laboulaye was a politician and a professor at the Collège de France.

repair the idea that liberty is valueless if unrelated to a 'moral rule' entrenched in man's heart and soul; for in the political vicissitudes of a nation as well as in the moral life of an individual, an 'inner guide' is required. Political forms are relatively unimportant. His analysis pointed to two morality-creating factors suggested by the American example: religion and education.[6] Laboulaye declared the French fit for representative institutions, against those who deemed them devoid of the spirit as well as the *mœurs* of liberty (though at times he shared Tocqueville's opinion: 'there is no country where equality is so willingly taken for liberty'). Laboulaye's confidence rested, first, on the tendencies towards freedom and association inherent in economic enterprise, and, second, on the consideration that the civic qualities of the French were still untried, buried as they had been under the discouraging weight of extensive state control.[7]

The flaws of the French were the subject of persistent complaints by contemporary economists, with the demoralizing effects of state intervention remaining an associated motif. Late in the century, the polemic gained fresh momentum from low fertility rates, which most imputed to a selfish and conservative mentality. Emile Levasseur, the doyen of economic historians, blamed customs like late marriages and dowries, and attitudes like post-hunting and a penchant for luxuries. It turns out that these *mœurs* mirrored the growth of 'democracy', which, Levasseur argued, in France was dangerously mingled with a 'revolutionary spirit' undermining social solidarity.[8] In the economic sphere, he went on, the moral crisis France was experiencing was revealed by an eagerness to consume and a reluctance to perform hard work.[9] The most authoritative economist of the age, Paul Leroy-Beaulieu, put forward as 'the most important' consequence of a stationary population that children reared in small families became self-indulgent and timid, reluctant to embark on risky ventures like innovative businesses or colonization.[10] In contrast, the Anglo-Saxons continued to be depicted by many economic writers as paragons of energy, dedication, and indomitable spirit. In the 1870s, there was also a resurgence of the motif

---

[6] See 'L'éducation en Amérique' (1853), esp. pp. 171–3, and 'L'Amérique et la Révolution française' (1850), pp. 304–5, both collected in E. Laboulaye, *Etudes morales et politiques* (Paris, 1862).

[7] 'L'Etat et ses limites' (1860), pp. 85, 99; and 'La liberté antique et la liberté moderne' (1863), pp. 133–6, both collected in E. Laboulaye, *L'Etat et ses limites* (1863; 4th edn, Paris, 1868). For Laboulaye's apprehensions, see 'Alexis de Tocqueville' (1859), in *L'Etat et ses limites*, p. 154, and also pp. 157, 161, 178, 180.

[8] E. Levasseur, *La population française* (3 vols., Paris, 1889–92), esp. III, pp. 222, 297–303, 492. That 'democracy' acted as a factor of reproductive restraint was widely acknowledged. Far from being a blind critic of democracy, Levasseur welcomed social and political reform, but kept faith with free contract as the primary form of social bond.

[9] *ibid.*, II, pp. 516–17.

[10] P. Leroy-Beaulieu, *Traité théorique et pratique d'économie politique* (4 vols., Paris, 1896), IV, p. 628; see also his 'La question de la population et la civilisation démocratique', *Revue des deux mondes*, 143 (1897), pp. 883–4.

of Protestant economic superiority in the writings of the Belgian Emile de Laveleye.[11]

However, it was rare that national self-criticism and even Anglophilia did not coexist with feelings of patriotism and pride for the achievements of French civilization. There were also some who stuck to the idea of French primacy. Auguste Comte's *Système de politique positive* confirmed his previous criticism of Britain and the British, and reiterated that the French were destined to act as the *avant-garde* of the reorganization of Western societies along 'positive' lines.[12] Comte's political objective consisted of a reform of *mœurs*. It was not just that institutions were founded on opinions and customs, but that a new morality alone was capable of determining radical change; politics became secondary in the face of the 'spiritual reorganization' led by philosophers. Comte spoke of the 'organization of public spirit' and public opinion, and of a regeneration of mentalities through the development of *sociabilité*. It was because of its superior sociability that the proletariat was indicated as the agent of 'positive' reform. Comte's hostility to an acquisitive and performance-oriented personality led him to associate material success with 'intellectual mediocrity and moral imperfection', since energy, prudence, and perseverance sufficed to achieve it – that is, success was a matter of simple 'character' – while the superior qualities springing from the 'heart', like sympathy, generosity, solidarity, abnegation, etc., played no part.[13] In making mores central to social and political life within the framework of an emphatically 'scientific' project, Comte appears to be a forerunner of Durkheim in a crucial sense; on the other hand, the extremely limited sway of Comte's politico-moral conception proper over French thought hardly needs recalling.

The way in which Hippolyte Taine falls within the Tocquevillian tradition of civic responsibility (a tradition which could also be labelled Guizotian, or Constantian for that matter) is peculiar. Taine coupled a concern with public spirit, especially manifest in *Les origines de la France contemporaine*, with an attempt at a grand theory of national character full of Montesquieuvian and Hegelian resonances. That is not to say that Prévost-Paradol or Laboulaye did not have opinions on the French national character – even in these 'civic' writers there was no lack of bitter references to lasting French characteristics like vanity, frivolity, or servility. But these defects were regarded as a political (or economic) datum, an unfortunate occurrence whose remedy was looked for in religion, legislative reform, and education; they were not the findings of

---

[11] E. de Laveleye, *Le Protestantisme et le Catholicisme dans leur rapports avec la liberté et la prosperité des peuples: étude d'économie sociale* (Brussels, 1875).

[12] For Comte on Britain, see *Cours de philosophie positive*, ed. M. Serres, F. Dagognet, A. Sinaceur, and J.-P. Enthoven (1830–42; 2 vols., Paris, 1975), II, pp. 406–33, 511–24ff., 694–5; *Système de politique positive* (1851–4; 4 vols., Paris, 1912), IV, pp. 490–4.

[13] *Système de politique*, I, pp. 131–2.

a comprehensive science of collective character. The focus was on how well suited certain French inclinations were to representative institutions, rather than on the forces, whether historical or natural, shaping attitudes in a general, broad scenario. In brief, the civic approach was characterized by two features contrasting with other viewpoints circulating in France. First, there was a plea for virtues of universal nature and applicability, irrespective of any alleged Frenchness. Second, effects rather than causes were in the foreground, and, more specifically, no reference was made to either natural–physical factors (like climate, or human physiology) or ethnic determinants (that is, non-biological notions of race). However, as Taine shows, the civic approach was not always to be found in its 'pure', ideal-typical form.

Taine's travel report on England accounts for superior English industry, energy, and even morality with a climate which excludes in principle a pleasurable life. Although lacking physiological intricacies, Taine's frame of reference differs little here from Montesquieu's contrast between North and South.[14] Yet Taine, who claimed to be above all a psychologist, soon elaborated on such a basis.[15] The text for which he was first hailed as an authority on collective attitudes by the French public was the introduction to his *Histoire de la littérature anglaise* (1864). Here, he postulated a historiographical revolution aimed at bringing to light collective psychologies, which he saw as the explanatory principles of civilizations. Each of these was moulded by the pervasiveness of a specific 'productive element' of a psychological nature. Taking on eighteenth-century philosophy, Taine wrote: today we know that 'the moral structure of a people and an age is as particular and distinct as the physical structure of a family of plants or an order of animals'.[16] A 'system' presides over the organization of sensations and ideas in the mind of each people, assembling into a definite pattern the various ways in which men recall their 'representations', or 'images', of things. Representations may be sharp or blurred, violent or calm, comprehensive or focused, and so on. How a people connects a specific representation to universal conceptions is decisive for the shaping of its civilization, as the characteristics of representations eventually determine those of language, religion, art, etc.[17]

Taine identified three causes determining these 'primordial differences' in mental organization: 'race', 'milieu', and 'moment'. Although Darwin is cited (and Lamarck hinted at), Taine's 'race' refers to the innate propensities of arcane human aggregates like the 'Arians', the 'Germans', the 'classic races',

---

[14] *Notes sur l'Angleterre* (written 1861–2; Paris, 1872).
[15] For Taine's claim, see E. Boutmy, *Taine, Scherer, Laboulaye* (Paris, 1901), p. 8, and S. Barrows, *Distorting Mirrors: Visions of the Crowd in Late Nineteenth-Century France* (New Haven, Conn., and London, 1981), p. 87.
[16] *Histoire de la littérature anglaise* (1864; 5 vols., Paris, 1892), I, p. xii.
[17] *ibid.*, I, pp. xix–xxii, xxxix–xlv.

etc. 'Milieu' means the natural and social circumstances which either alter or reinforce the racial basis; again with Montesquieuvian resonances, climate is said to have been fundamental in bringing about differences within the Arian peoples. Since the effects of milieu and race are cumulative and progressive, 'moment' is the situation determined by them at a given time, when new events may intervene to reshape the existing 'spirit'.[18] Clearly, the introduction to the *Histoire de la littérature anglaise* is an odd text.[19] Of a purely methodological character, it puts forward the criteria to appraise just about every event in history, and in less than fifty pages. Furthermore, Taine's manifesto makes the totally unwarranted claim to be devising a set of natural laws, which are certain and capable of predictions. Sainte-Beuve and Stendhal figure as the best examples of authors who have treated sentiments 'as naturalists and physicists'; that is to imply that the psychological laws of civilizations are to be looked for in literature above all.[20]

Whatever its intrinsic improbability, the fact that the introduction was widely quoted, and the three factors of collective attitudes considered as a useful approximation, suggests a more cautious evaluation.[21] In fact the five volumes of the *Histoire* are intended as an application of the tenets stated in the introduction, while the psychological and physiological mechanisms of 'images' account for much of Taine's two-volume *De l'intelligence* (1870). It is true, as Taine's disciple Emile Boutmy wrote, that the *Histoire* 'is less what its title indicates than an analysis of the English soul and spirit throughout the centuries'.[22] Race, milieu, and moment are called into play to account for English civilization: the 'national traits' are seriousness, melancholy, energy, passion, realism, and 'the feeling of inner things'. Taine's masterful chapter on Carlyle contains a revealing tribute to German culture, where Taine seemingly found the idea of civilizations as wholes presided over by a single 'inner quality'.[23] In *De l'intelligence*, psychology is studied with a view to the broad framework: 'an historian deals with applied psychology, a psychologist with general history'.[24] Here Taine, who

---

[18] *ibid.*, I, pp. xxiii–xxxv.
[19] 'Un tel chaos conceptuel et terminologique est rare': C. Evans, *Taine: essai de biographie intérieure* (Paris, 1975), p. 401.
[20] Taine, *Histoire*, I, pp. xliii, xlv–viii.
[21] Taine's disciple, Boutmy, wrote in *Taine*, p. 9: 'Les jeunes gens de ce temps-là, aujourd'hui des vieillards, se rappellent la profonde émotion causée par ces pages mémorables. Il sembla que la critique littéraire, jusque-là livrée à la fantaisie, s'appropriait les procédés, s'élevait à la dignité d'une science exacte. L'avènement de la nouvelle méthode fut salué avec transport.' See J. van Ginneken, *Crowds, Psychology, and Politics 1871–1899* (Cambridge, 1992), ch. 1 (Taine's 'influence in France and abroad was overwhelming', p. 47). But in 1906 there appeared a book by Paul Lacombe entitled *La psychologie des individus et des sociétés chez Taine, historien des littératures* (Paris), which mercilessly criticized the whole construction from the viewpoint of Tarde's psychology.
[22] Boutmy, *Taine*, pp. 8–9.
[23] Taine, *Histoire*, V, pp. 268–81.
[24] *De l'intelligence* (2 vols., 1870), I, p. 8.

always adopted the mantle of science, emphasizes the physiological basis of sensations and 'images' on the basis of laboratory evidence.

With the shock of 1870–1 fixed in his mind, Taine devoted the core chapters of the first volume of *Les origines de la France contemporaine* to the principle which, in his view, had shaped French culture and thereby determined the course of French history since the eighteenth century. The 'classic spirit' was an abstract and universalistic mode of reasoning which had originated from the conversations at court and in the *salons* in the seventeenth and eighteenth centuries. Its component elements, intended to please the courtier's taste, were a literary and oratorical tone; the avoidance not only of technical but also of specific terms; an exclusive concern with the abstract, the simple, and the general; a disregard for the complexity of reality; and a deductive habit modelled on mathematics. The ensuing criticism of eighteenth-century philosophy shaped Taine's judgement of the Revolution, which was basically Burkean. In their endorsement of abstract ideals, the revolutionaries had been unable to apprehend both the living roots of the old institutions and the psychological traits of real men. A *raison raisonnante* had obscured the fact that in 1789 'twenty million people and more had hardly passed the mental state of the Middle Ages'. The import of Taine's argument was clear: a constitution which would last had to be devised on the basis of the people's character as well as on their collective past. 'It is therefore necessary', he wrote, 'to reverse the usual method and understand [*se figurer*] the nation before writing the constitution.'[25]

The anthropological pessimism so evident not only in the crowd theorists, whom Taine inspired, but also in Durkheim, informs the narration of revolutionary violence which makes up *La Révolution*. The natural man, as Taine defined him, was an irrational savage, and the social man may well be hardly better – the constraints of civilization may fail to curb instincts. Furthermore, manual workers are inherently incapable of apprehending general ideas, which they always combine with passions, instincts, and prejudices; the resulting mixture may be explosive. For example, the idea of popular sovereignty ignited the eternal reservoir of lower-class ferocity and rapacity during the revolutionary turmoil. All this was made worse by French excitability and sociability, or, as Taine put it, by the lack of that 'natural ballast' which more phlegmatic peoples have.[26]

The civic side of Taine emerges from a successive volume of *Les origines*, where both the revolutionary and the Napoleonic regimes were apprehended as expressions of the classic spirit. This went with the view that the revolution had failed for lack of public spirit, especially at the local level. Whereas

[25] *Les origines de la France contemporaine*, I, *L'ancien régime* (Paris, 1876), pp. ii–iii, 278; and more generally pp. 240–328.
[26] *ibid.*, pp. 312–16, and *Les origines de la France contemporaine*, II, *La Révolution* (3 vols., Paris, 1878–85).

revolutionary legislators took the high quality of the citizenry for granted, the French were actually 'exceedingly sensitive', inexperienced, impatient, intractable, and excitable. Additionally, under the revolutionary governments the passions of the people had become embittered:

[at the juncture of 1799] each brought personal bias and resentment into the performance of his duties; to prevent him from being unjust and mischievous demanded a tightened curb. All sense of conviction, under this regime, had died out; nobody would serve gratis as in 1789; nobody would work without pay; disinterestedness had lost all charm; ostentatious zeal seemed hypocrisy; genuine zeal seemed self-dupery; each looked out for himself and not for the community; public spirit had yielded to indifference, to egotism, and to the need of security, of enjoyment, and of self-advancement. Human materials, deteriorated by the Revolution, were less than ever suited to providing citizens – they simply afforded functionaries.[27]

One of the worst outrages perpetrated by the Revolution was the obliteration of the ancient provinces – 'the accumulated work of ten centuries' – replaced by 'factitious agglomerations of juxtaposed inhabitants'. Before they were cut apart by the scissors of the *géomètre* and prefects took control, local societies were veritable reservoirs of spontaneous co-operation and political education; each *petite patrie* aroused zeal and devotion to the public interest, besides opening up opportunities for talent and ambition. Now all this has been lost, in obeisance to the principle of universal symmetry.[28] The model of dependent functionaries, not of enterprising and participating citizens, has been presented to the people by successive regimes, and the French have effortlessly endorsed it. Napoleonic France was the 'masterpiece' of classic spirit. Since co-operative activities became unfeasible, especially on a local basis, public life in a society of equals turned into a competition for places and honours, with the state as umpire.[29] Taine stressed how the doctrine of popular sovereignty denied the differences (geographical, economic, social, educational, etc.) which alone made local co-operation significant. The problem was that equality suited the French character perfectly.[30]

Taine deployed a vibrant attack on the post-Napoleonic state for continuing the policy of supplanting 'the special and spontaneous bodies'. Many precious 'organs' of society had either atrophied, been absorbed or turned out to be abortive. By paralysing individual effort, the stranglehold of associations entailed both the fading of social virtues and political passivity and subservience. Taine set out to extol co-operation, independence, enterprise, local affections,

---

[27] *Les origines de la France contemporaine*, III, *Le régime moderne* (2 vols., Paris, 1891–4), I, p. 123 (*The Modern Regime*, trans. J. Durand (2 vols., London, 1891), I, p. 96).
[28] *ibid.*, I, pp. 395–6.
[29] *ibid.*, I, pp. 155–89, 298–352.
[30] *ibid.*, I, pp. 300–2, 358–97.

patriotism, and, more generally, 'diversity and change'.[31] It is unfortunate but true, he said, that in the mass of men individual interests get the upper hand over social ones; this is why the role of the state is crucial. By being just or unjust, liberal or oppressive, the legislator is in fact responsible for the weakening or the strengthening of the social instinct, which to Taine appeared as the only realistic political device.[32] But Napoleonic centralization was upheld by all successive regimes, only to be made worse by universal suffrage and local taxation.[33]

Aside from Taine's peculiar construction, the civic approach should be viewed alongside 'nationalistic' and 'scientific' perspectives. The nationalistic perspective, which may be traced back to Michelet's *Le peuple*, amounted to a reflection on Frenchness on the basis of *Blut und Boden* elements. The Renan of *La réforme intellectuelle et morale* may be viewed as a mild representative of this current, in which Brunetière may also be numbered. The scientific perspective was fuelled by a flourishing school of social psychology, which included Boutmy, Le Bon, Fouillée, Ribot, Marie, Paulhan, and others. The claimed scientific nature and method of their analyses was the unifying trait of this group, whose members differed widely in other respects. But a figure like the geographer Vidal de la Blache, for example, was influenced by both Michelet and the social scientists; the above bipartition far from exhausts possible analysis of the situation, whose special feature was the psychological turn which characterized this early stage of social sciences in France. The influence of Taine – by 1899 the six volumes of the *Origines* had gone through eighty-nine printings in all – largely accounts for this feature.[34] In combining a 'scientific' frame of reference with a focus on France's political instability, as the Commune renewed the fears of 1793 and 1848, Taine set the tone of the younger generation's work. Once his *œuvre* is considered as a whole, the 'social scientific' tradition of Montesquieu and Comte appears to have met the civic tradition of Constant and Tocqueville through the marriage of history and psychology. Taine's scientific credentials were repeatedly questioned (most famously by the historian Alphonse Aulard), but his sway ultimately rested on the updating of an existing trend in French culture towards a focus on mental dispositions.

---

[31] *ibid.*, I, pp. 141–54.

[32] *ibid.*, I, pp. 354–8.

[33] Taine expressed the spirit which ought to have informed local life thus: 'Nous sommes ensemble, dans le même bateau; le bateau est à nous, et nous en sommes l'équipage. Nous voici tous pour le manœuvrer nous-mêmes, de nos mains, chacun à son rang, dans son poste, avec sa part, petite ou grande, dans la manœuvre': *ibid.*, I, p. 397.

[34] Barrows, *Distorting Mirrors*, p. 91, fn. The lasting legacy of Victor Cousin, who made psychology central to academic philosophy, should also be considered. For Durkheim's appreciation of Taine's rationalist empiricism, see C. Tarot, *De Durkheim à Mauss, l'invention du symbolique* (Paris, 1999), pp. 107–9.

2   Durkheim: *mœurs* the object of a positive science

For Durkheim, too, what and how people thought was more important than any material arrangement. The view of society as a proper 'being', irreducible to a sum of individuals, was his starting point.[35] As he wrote as early as 1885, society has 'its life, *conscience*, interests, and destiny'. Individuals were linked by 'ideal bonds' supplied by society, like language and the rules of reasoning, and even the substance of our evaluations depended on the prevailing *mœurs* and tastes. As a result, each people had its own 'character'.[36] In another early review, Durkheim argued that law depended on *mœurs*; that these determined the 'organic structure' of society as well; and that the study of psychic phenomena should therefore be at the heart of sociology.[37] He defined *mœurs* as 'a crystallization of human conduct' on the grounds of public utility. Not only were law and morality created unintentionally by these 'collective habits', these 'subconscious sentiments', but also institutions, with Durkheim explicitly taking sides with the critics of *raison raisonnante*.[38] His advocacy of a science of *mœurs* entailed viewing morality as an indispensable social function, whose task was to make man understand that he was not 'a whole, but a part of a whole'. In each society, current morality was the result of a long evolution; we had to abide by it because men had found nothing better in centuries 'of pain and toil'. It would be puerile to claim to know better than human experience itself.[39]

Durkheim's programme of 1888 began with a critique of what it is tempting to view as the foundation of the classic spirit, namely the idea of a man-made society, the product of 'art and reflection'; a critique, incidentally, which recalls the eighteenth-century attacks on the 'man of system'. To Durkheim, once it was accepted that society was a human artefact, a belief in the possibility of altering it at will would follow. The extreme complexity of real societies, the difficulty of devising their laws, and the limitations of what we would call methodological individualism suggested an opposite approach. He made a plea

---

[35] Durkheim's intellectual trajectory was not rectilinear, and this is why the exposition will follow a rough chronological order. On the changes in some fundamental tenets which occurred after *De la division du travail*, see B. Lacroix, *Durkheim et le politique* (Montreal, 1981), ch. 2. But, although the concept of collective representation was not employed before the turn of the century, an analysis from the viewpoint of *mœurs* reveals significant continuities in Durkheim's quest.

[36] Review of Schäffle, *Bau und Leben des sozialen Körpers*, *Revue philosophique*, 19 (1885), pp. 84–5, 91.

[37] Review of Gumplowicz, *Grundrisse der Soziologie*, *Revue philosophique*, 20 (1885), pp. 627–34.

[38] 'La science positive de la morale en Allemagne' (1887), in E. Durkheim, *Textes*, ed. V. Karady (3 vols., Paris, 1975), I, pp. 275–6, 281ff., 342–3.

[39] *ibid.*, pp. 278, 326, 336, 342–3. For Durkheim, Wundt and Leslie Stephen in particular had attempted a science of *mœurs*. See also 'La philosophie dans les universités allemandes' (1887), in *Textes*, III, pp. 460–6.

for an inductive, localized, and cautious study of 'social facts', in contrast with Spencer's construction of a grand philosophical system.[40] When listing more specifically the tasks of sociology, he mentioned first the investigation of 'social psychology' as expressed by 'shared ideas and sentiments'. Moral maxims and beliefs, languages, religions, political doctrines, legends, etc., which guaranteed 'the unity and continuity of collective life', were of a psychological but not individual nature. They should be studied as natural phenomena ruled by laws and cause–effect relations.[41]

Keeping in mind the distinction between the viewpoint of mores and that of national character, the latter appears secondary in these early writings. The notion of *mœurs* is more appropriate to the narratives of a theoretical and methodological nature Durkheim engaged in. It is the binding function of mores which is stressed, not their being hallmarks of specific societies.[42] The difference between his perspective in these writings and that of many previous exponents of the public spirit tradition lies in Durkheim's focus, which encompasses more ground than the workings of political institutions insofar as it regards the degree of cohesion of a society. This function of *mœurs* is one of the shifts in outlook defining scientific sociology.

A non-evaluative standpoint appears implicit in Durkheim's position, as, in contrast to Comte, he acknowledged the plurality of social types. That is not to say that Durkheim's sociology was purely descriptive, but only that the logic of the science of *mœurs* as functional elements entailed a check on the expression of judgements concerning both other nations and domestic political issues. Unlike most French writers since Montesquieu and Voltaire, Durkheim did not comment significantly on Britain and the British; nor on the traits of other peoples, except in his wartime pamphlets.[43] In spite of his involvement in the campaign in favour of Dreyfus, he always spoke of French politics indirectly, namely as a sociologist. His concern in his celebrated intervention against Brunetière was the same as in the scientific writings: 'all that societies require in order to hold together is that their members fix their eyes on the same end and come together in a single faith'.[44] Durkheim's ambition to turn

---

[40] 'Cours de science sociale: leçon d'ouverture', *Revue internationale de l'enseignement*, 15 (1888), pp. 24–5, 28–9, 36ff.

[41] *ibid.*, pp. 42, 45–6. For his opinion of Lazarus and Steinthal's *Völkerpsychologie*, see p. 42; on institutions as functions of social life, see p. 45. On the same page he wrote: 'la morale est même de toutes les parties de la sociologie celle qui nous attire de préférence et nous retiendra tout d'abord'.

[42] On Durkheim's functionalist perspective, see *ibid.*, pp. 43–5.

[43] There is a footnote on the peculiarities of English social structure in *De la division du travail social* (Paris, 1893), bk II, ch. 3, pp. 312–13.

[44] 'L'individualisme et les intellectuels' (1898), in E. Durkheim, *La science sociale et l'action*, ed. J. C. Filloux (Paris, 1970), p. 268 ('Individualism and the Intellectuals', trans. S. and J. Lukes, in *Durkheim on Religion*, ed. W. S. F. Pickering (London and Boston, 1975), p. 64). See also *Les règles de la méthode sociologique* (Paris, 1895), pp. 174–5, 178–9.

morality into a science by considering it a social fact is a key move, whose effects would become progressively more marked as time went by. He would set up the *Année sociologique* as a workshop where systematic, cumulative, and unbiased research on collective attitudes was supposed to take the place of general and tendentious statements; henceforth, a scientific viewpoint would form and downgrade all others as non-scientific, the sphere of novelists and journalists. Granted that this was not the end of national character talk even for Durkheim himself, his project inaugurated a new phase in comparison with Taine's impressionistic and literary–philosophical standpoint.

Having said that Durkheim was an innovator, it must be conceded that he kept faith with the traditional denunciations of French character and mental habits. The 1888 inaugural lecture ends on a familiar note, although his criticism draws a particular form and cogency from the sociological apparatus. In France, he wrote, collective spirit has become weak in parallel with the triumph of the *moi*. Each Frenchman imagines himself as self-sufficient, and, unrestrained, aims to succeed in life by following only his own desires and beliefs. This attitude is exactly what sociology is designed to oppose in teaching the 'organic' interdependence of all; a 'social mass' in fact surrounds and 'permeates [*pénètre*]' each individual.[45] In another text, and in a Tainesque spirit, he called his compatriots 'unconscious Cartesians' for their abhorrence of complexity. This cast of mind induced neglect of the 'nature of things' and hence a belief in revolutionary methods.[46]

So far, writings prior to Durkheim's first book, *De la division du travail social*, have been examined; in that work, the social dimension of morality was given full scope. Morality, now unreservedly equated with *mœurs*, was defined as 'a network of bonds [*réseau de liens*]', as well as all that was a 'source of solidarity'.[47] With the focus on the conditions of social cohesion, these conditions, of a morphological origin, were immediately translated into mental attitudes. Durkheim's idiom is that of 'sentiments', 'psychic types', 'states of conscience', and so on. The point he wished to make against Spencer and utilitarianism regarded the nature of modern society, which, although presided over by division of labour, remained nevertheless essentially moral in character: 'nous sommes liés', he urged, we are connected.[48]

The introduction of *conscience collective* in *De la division du travail* served to elucidate the rationale of social solidarity by referring to the set of sentiments whose infringement defined a crime in the context of the type of social state which, in Durkheim's terminology, was characterized by 'mechanical

---

[45] 'Cours de science sociale', p. 48.
[46] 'La philosophie dans les universités', pp. 454, 461, 482–3, 485–6.
[47] *De la division du travail*, conclusion, pp. 448–9.
[48] See esp. *ibid.*, bk I, ch. 7, pp. 249–51 (the quotation is on p. 251); conclusion, pp. 448–60.

solidarity'.[49] However, there figures a definition of *conscience collective* as an independent reality, which not only contains no reference to social solidarity, but neatly posits *conscience collective* as a scientific concept, and seemingly a very important one, without mentioning any restriction on its use.

The totality of beliefs and sentiments common to average citizens of the same society forms a determinate system which has its own life; one may call it the *collective* or *common conscience*. No doubt, it has not a specific organ as a substratum; it is, by definition, diffuse in every reach of society. Nevertheless, it has specific characteristics which make it a distinct reality. It is, in effect, independent of the particular conditions in which individuals are placed; they pass on and it remains. It is the same in the North and in the South, in great cities and in small, in different professions. Moreover, it does not change with each generation, but, on the contrary, it connects successive generations with one another. It is, thus, an entirely different thing from particular *consciences*, although it can be realized only through them. It is the psychical type of society, a type which has its properties, its conditions of existence, its mode of development, just as individual types, although in a different way. Thus understood, it has the right to be denoted by a special word. The one which we have just employed is not, it is true, without ambiguity. As the terms, collective and social, are often considered synonymous, one is inclined to believe that the collective *conscience* is the total social *conscience*, that is, extend it to include the whole psychic life of society, although, particularly in advanced societies, it is only a very restricted part. Judicial, governmental, scientific, industrial, in short, all special functions are of a psychic nature, since they consist in systems of representations and actions. They, however, are surely outside the common *conscience*.[50]

The gist of the definition is the reference to an average set of sentiments; correspondingly, it was the similarities in psychic life that characterized the 'mechanical' form of solidarity, much in the same way as the 'organic' form rested on differences.[51] *Conscience collective* was designed to match one of the two types of social cohesion Durkheim identified, contrastively, as the past and the present. But the dichotomy was subsequently tacitly dropped.[52]

In tune with the distinction made in the above citation between collective and social *conscience*, Durkheim spoke elsewhere of the relative indefiniteness and obscurity of *conscience collective*, whereas 'the representations that derive from the state' were clear and self-conscious. As an aggregate of specialized and technical bodies, the state provides knowledge which clearly exemplifies the contents of 'social *conscience*'. The principal function of the organs of the

---

[49] *ibid.*, bk I, chs. 1–3, pp. 71–136ff.

[50] *ibid.*, bk I, ch. 2, pp. 84–5 (*The Division of Labor in Society*, trans. G. Simpson (New York and London, 1965), pp. 79–80; trans. modified). As many commentators have observed, the fact that *conscience collective* may be translated either as collective 'conscience' or 'consciousness' reflected the interplay that Durkheim saw between these two elements. To preserve this feature, I have left *conscience collective* untranslated.

[51] *ibid.*, bk I, ch. 3, pp. 139–40.

[52] See G. Gurvitch, 'Le problème de la conscience collective dans la sociologie de Durkheim', in his *La vocation actuelle de la sociologie* (2 vols., Paris, 1969), II, pp. 13–20.

state is not to act but to 'co-ordinate ideas and sentiments', that is 'to think', for, 'strictly speaking, the state is the very organ of social thought'.[53] Sociology was intended to play an enlightening role in this context.[54]

Unoriginally, Durkheim viewed French political instability (as well as the 'social question') as a moral problem. He proposed as a solution, at least in the medium term, the creation of new institutions, the *corporations*, together with other pieces of legislation similarly expected to lay the foundation for a superior morality. One might detect an ambivalence in his view of the role of institutions: although thinking in terms of collective *conscience* and sentiments, Durkheim would resort to the legislator to influence minds, and, by doing so, deny the primacy of the mental dimension. But, although he chose for himself the point of view of collective morality, he took for granted the mutual influence of the material and the ideal (of which *De la division du travail* is a case in point). Not only did education make up the other half of his recommendations; but the new legislation he demanded seems to have been dependent on the spread of new ways of thinking among the population, and in particular of conscious deliberation and a critical spirit as embodied by democratic governments. The defining trait of democracy was the fully cognizant form of allegiance it made possible, thanks to a constant flow of communication between the citizens and the state; in this sense, the state did not exert an influence on people as an exterior force as the two became interlinked in some way.[55]

3   Durkheim: from *mœurs* to representations

Basically, a representation is something external perceived or impressed upon the individual. In *Le suicide*, individual psychology is seen as dominated by collective beliefs, concepts, and sentiments, originating from the very fact of human aggregation. Durkheim's insistence on the *sui generis* reality of 'collective representations', that is, their being external to individuals, began here.[56] Collective representations were 'things', and should be studied as such. Famously, he contended that social life was 'made up of representations', and, accordingly, that sociology amounted to collective psychology. For instance, religion was a system of representations of a collective type, because religion

---

[53] See the 1890–1900 lectures published as *Leçons de sociologie: physique des mœurs et du droit*, ed. H. N. Kubali (Paris, 1969), pp. 79–90, esp. pp. 86–7.

[54] On the potentiality of sociology, see 'Cours de science sociale', p. 48; *Les règles*, pp. 174–5; *Le suicide: étude de sociologie* (1897; Paris, 1930), bk II, ch. 2, pp. 170–2; 'Détermination du fait moral' (1906), in E. Durkheim, *Sociologie et philosophie*, ed. C. Bouglé (1924; Paris, 1963), pp. 85–90.

[55] On democracy, see *Leçons de sociologie*, pp. 110–41.

[56] *Le suicide*, bk III, ch. 1, pp. 350–63.

was of necessity a social phenomenon; more evocatively, Durkheim added in one of his unfortunate lapses into mysticism, it was a 'way of thinking of the collective being'.[57]

The adoption of collective representations did not entail a rejection of *conscience collective*, which, as a term to express the average sentiments of a society, was not peculiarly Durkheimian (in spite of the claim quoted above) but very much the stock in trade of French social scientists. Unlike collective representation, *conscience collective* was not elaborated on by Durkheim, and was often used carelessly. Representation was far from being Durkheim's original coinage, either. In addition to its adoption by Taine, Renouvier, and other French philosophers, the term was in current use among German intellectuals, like Wundt and Simmel, some of whom were likely to have influenced Durkheim.[58] One of the reasons why Durkheim introduced collective representation was probably its superior analytical manageability, for while *conscience collective* expressed a given mental condition of society, it did not help the sociologist to concentrate on specific ideas.[59] Collective representation did not suffer from the vagueness inherent in mean notions. Another characteristic of collective representation has already been hinted at: unlike an average *conscience collective*, it pointed directly to the superindividual nature of society and social productions, the fulcrum of Durkheim's science. Since representations like religion, language, or logical categories were intrinsically shared with others, they were social regardless of the individuals who held them. Therefore collective representations could be aptly treated as things.

There was also a difference in meaning between the two concepts, which seems to allude to the imminent thematic change in Durkheim's research. In *Le suicide*, he made a distinction between two types of social viewpoint, the 'average' and the 'collective', with, I would argue, the former being captured by *conscience collective* and the latter by collective representation. The difference lay in the mediocrity of 'average' in comparison with 'collective' morality, which alone was responsible for the achievements of civilizations. The *sui generis* reality of social life referred to the gap between the 'vulgar' morality of an average individual and the morality of the whole, sanctioned by laws

---

[57] *ibid.*, bk III, ch. 1, p. 352.

[58] 'Representation' had largely replaced 'idea' in most French philosophical writings by the 1890s: J. I. Brooks III, 'Analogy and Argumentation in an Interdisciplinary Context: Durkheim's "Individual and Collective Representations"', *History of the Human Sciences*, 4 (1991), p. 228. 'Collective representation' seems to have have been introduced by Espinas.

[59] Compare Lukes's point that *conscience collective* 'was insufficiently analytical for his purposes subsequent to *The Division of Labour*': *Durkheim*, p. 6. By contrast, Nisbet thinks that both collective and individual representations 'are descriptive, rather than analytical, concepts and serve to emphasize the role of society and its codes rather than to clarify interactive processes': R. A. Nisbet, *Emile Durkheim* (Englewood Cliffs, NJ, 1965), p. 59. Gurvitch, 'Le problème de la conscience collective', simply omits any mention of collective representations in favour of *conscience collective*.

and public opinion, and activated in full during historical phases of creative exaltation.[60] Granted that society was an entity independent of individuals, it had a morality of its own which was irrespective of, and superior to, the mean of individual moralities. In the light of this distinction, the study of religious representations, of which most of Durkheim's successive work consisted, falls within the 'collective' viewpoint but it does not square with *conscience collective*.

However, to place much emphasis on the shift from one concept to the other may be specious. In contrast with the reading just put forward, it is defensible that the *conscience collective* could be constructed by assembling the collective representations of all social facts of relevance.[61] Collective representations of ordinary things are fully admissible. Since the category 'collective representation' remains *per se* general and over-comprehensive, and an account of its relationship with *conscience collective* was never offered, nothing guarantees that the contrast between average and collective just sketched was always present in Durkheim's mind when he used these terms, which easily lend themselves to loose application. In spite of this, since this contrast matches the evolution of his research, it provides a valuable clue as to how this most puzzling facet of his sociology must be interpreted.

The differences between the science of *mœurs* (of which *De la division du travail* is a specimen, with *Le suicide* as a transitional work) and the research on religion carried out by using collective representation are not obvious. 'Religion' came for Durkheim to hold a wider meaning than usual, being defined as 'a system of collective beliefs and practices that have a special authority'. With or without temples and priests, 'religion' was the social glue, and no community could do without a form of it.[62] The sacred was defined in 1899 as the

---

[60] *Le suicide*, bk III, ch. 1, pp. 356–60. See also 'Jugements de valeur et jugements de réalité' (1911), in *Sociologie et philosophie*, pp. 121, 123, 132–8; review of Jérusalem, *Soziologie des Erkennens*, *AS*, 11 (1906–9), p. 45: 'Nous touchons ici à une erreur qui est encore trop répandue et que nous considérons comme la pierre d'achoppement de la sociologie. On croit trop souvent que ce qui est général est social et, inversement, que le type collectif n'est autre chose que le type moyen. Tout au contraire, il y a entre ces deux types une distance immense. La conscience moyenne est médiocre, tant au point de vue intellectuel que moral; la conscience collective, au contraire, est infiniment riche puisqu'elle est riche de toute la civilisation.' See also *Le socialisme*, ed. M. Mauss (1895–6; 2nd edn, Paris, 1971), pp. 41–2, 49–50.

[61] For an interpretation along these lines, see P. Bohannan, '*Conscience collective* and Culture', in E. Durkheim et al., *Essays on Sociology and Philosophy*, ed. K. H. Wolff (New York, 1964), p. 82. On the other hand, Parsons has made a sharp distinction between *conscience collective* and collective representations: while the former was a set of common beliefs and sentiments, the latter emanated from a common reality, and hence it was this substratum that was shared. T. Parsons, *The Structure of Social Action* (1937; Glencoe, Ill., 1949), ch. 9. See also the differences indicated by Lukes, *Durkheim*, pp. 4–8.

[62] 'L'individualisme', pp. 270–1. See also 'De la définition des phénomènes religieux' (1899), in E. Durkheim, *Journal sociologique*, ed. J. Duvignaud (Paris, 1969), esp. pp. 160–3, for an indirect demonstration.

set of representations produced by that particular being, society: 'it includes all sorts of collective states, common traditions and emotions, feelings which have a relationship to objects of general interest, etc.; and all those elements are combined according to the appropriate laws of social mentality'. Conversely, profane things are 'those which each of us constructs from our own sense data and experience'.[63] Individualism (in Durkheim's sense) was the only possible modern version of 'religion'. Studying 'religions', therefore, appears in principle like another wording for the science of *mœurs*, rather than a change of direction. Given the cohesive function of both mores and 'religion', the two seem to be almost synonymous.

From the turn of the century onward, however, Durkheim concentrated on primitive religions, and the shift towards anthropological literature created a hiatus between his practice of social science and the science of *mœurs*. This was due to his fascination with a subject more esoteric than, say, the division of labour, and very distant in time from contemporary France; but there was also a shift in Durkheim's concerns. By pointing to the religious origins of modes of classification among primitive peoples, what Durkheim (and Mauss) were setting out to achieve was a different conceptualization of modern science, whose social nature and relation to religion and morality were to be fully acknowledged. It would follow that social life had suffered no traumatic gaps over the centuries, for science, morality, and religion not only shared concepts and procedures, albeit at different degrees of refinement, but originated from the same source, namely the human capacity for 'collective thought' beyond the individual's standpoint. At the same time, these three most important forms of 'impersonal' thinking would all be encompassed and made to testify to Durkheim's sociology; all this within the relatively limited scope of this research.[64] In other words, the study of religion in its primitive forms seemed to him, first, to suggest a truce between science and religion of particular relevance to modern France, and, second, to be the best support for that crucial claim of his, the *sui generis* reality of collective productions, irreducible and superior to individual volition. Through these works it became even more manifest that,

---

[63] 'De la définition des phénomènes religieux', pp. 162–3 ('Concerning the Definition of Religious Phenomena', trans. J. Redding and W. S. F. Pickering, in *Durkheim on Religion*, p. 95). For a detailed comparison between the sacred and the moral, see 'Détermination du fait moral'. See also H. Hubert and M. Mauss, *Mélanges d'histoire des religions* (Paris, 1909), p. xvi. The elaboration of the 'morale laïque' is of relevance here; see esp. Durkheim's lectures of 1902–7 collected as *L'éducation morale*, ed. P. Fauconnet (Paris, 1925).

[64] See esp. E. Durkheim and M. Mauss, 'De quelques formes primitives de classification: contribution à l'étude des représentations collectives', *AS*, 6 (1901–2), pp. 66–72, and E. Durkheim, *Les formes élémentaires de la vie religieuse* (1912; Paris, 1960), conclusion, pp. 593–638, esp. pp. 613–38. See also Hubert and Mauss, *Mélanges*, preface. For Durkheim's view that religion contained, from the beginning, though in a diffused state, all the elements of collective life, see the prefatory note in *AS*, 2 (1898), pp. iv–v; and also *Leçons de sociologie*, pp. 174–97.

while psychology dealt with the individual, the realm of sociology was the set of 'moral milieux' which made up collective mentality as a social artifact.[65]

To return to representations, the 1898 article devoted to them largely consists, rather disappointingly, of preliminary work, with Durkheim bent on clearing the ground of antithetical theories. One finds a critique of the 'psycho-physiological school', which denied the existence of states of mind independent of the neural substratum, and a defence of the thesis that representations can be unconscious.[66] The article confirms the independent reality of representations, said to react directly upon each other and combine according to their own laws. Although in origin strictly related to the features of the social substratum from which they derive, collective representations, once created, have the power to induce new ones autonomously.[67] Durkheim wrote one year later: 'it is quite natural for this collective mind to see reality in a different way from us, because its nature is of a different order. Society has its own mode of existence which is peculiar to it; correspondingly, its own mode of thought.'[68]

In the late *Les formes élémentaires de la vie religieuse*, Durkheim's customary reticence about the concept of collective representation did not prevent him from enlarging on it a little. Here, not only does he cite religion, language, the categories of understanding, or other elaborate systems as examples of collective representations, but also the national flag and a priceless postage stamp. The rationale is that man 'adds to the immediately given data of senses, and projects his sentiments and impressions upon things'. Ideas do constitute reality in society, where 'idealism applies almost literally'; objects 'disappear' into an 'ideal superstructure', a 'comprehensive symbolism'.[69] Elsewhere, he maintained that things, both economic and moral–religious, 'have no value in

---

[65] See, e.g., 'La sociologie et son domaine scientifique' (1900), in *Textes*, I, pp. 28–30. In 1905, Durkheim wrote that the science of morality was the science he had devoted himself to for twenty years or so; see the translation of this short piece, first published in *La revue*, in *Durkheim: Essays on Morals and Education*, ed. W. S. F. Pickering (London, 1979), p. 35. For a suggestion of continuity in Durkheim's subject, see 'Détermination du fait moral', pp. 54–5, where he called his Sorbonne course later published as *Leçons de sociologie* a course 'sur la science des mœurs, théorique et appliquée'.

[66] 'Représentations individuelles et représentations collectives' (1898), in *Sociologie et philoso-phie*, pp. 2–25 (on the psycho-physiological school), 25–32 (on unconscious representations).

[67] 'Représentations individuelles', pp. 42–3. Created by society, collective representations also shape it; for an example of interaction, see Durkheim and Mauss, 'De quelques formes primi-tives', pp. 25–8, about the effects of categories over the organization of clans. See also Hubert and Mauss, *Mélanges*, p. xxxviii.

[68] 'De la définition des phénomènes religieux', p. 162 ('Concerning the Definition of Religious Phenomena', p. 95). See *L'éducation morale*, p. 98: 'la société . . . se pense'.

[69] *Les formes élémentaires*, bk II, ch. 7, pp. 325–7; see also conclusion, pp. 603–4; and 'Jugements de valeur', esp. pp. 137–8. On the relationship between collective representations and symbols in Durkheim, see Tarot, *De Durkheim à Mauss*, pp. 212–25, 236–44, although Pickering's analysis, which is more faithful to Durkheim's texts, seems preferable: *Durkheim's Sociology of Religion* (London, 1984), p. 281. Unlike Tarot, Pickering is inclined to equate symbols with collective representations.

themselves' but only 'in relation to states of mind', for 'values are the product of opinion'.[70] The radical nature of Durkheim's 'idealism' – to use his own term – becomes apparent, and the continuity view which characterized his analysis of categories – unchanged in essence in passing from the religious to the scientific domain – becomes clearer. If facts are not 'hard' but partake of the nature of the mind, and the thread that connects and gives meaning to them is purely mental, the great service of religions lay in their production of the first representations of the relationship between things, an achievement from which modern science started.

Durkheim's course of lectures on moral education casts light on discipline as the essential social attribute. As Aron in particular has stressed, Durkheim viewed isolated human nature as dominated by egoistic passions; hence the fundamental role of social aggregations in morality.[71] Discipline could be instilled in the minds of men – in the form of 'public opinion' for example – only on condition that they were members of a group. At the same time, 'a spirit of discipline', albeit 'founded on reason and truth', was put forward as the essential condition for any form of communal life.[72] Appropriately, the definition of 'social fact' in *Les règles de la méthode sociologique* was what coerces the individual.[73] Discipline was a 'system of representations', whose dictates individuals obeyed because of the 'sacred' nature of the entity from which those dictates emanated, that is, society. In this perspective, 'character' amounted to self-control (individuals interiorized social rules). There are hints that the personality-shaping power of discipline applied to peoples as well.[74] Although Durkheim's conceptualization of collective mentalities did change over the decades, social cohesion remained the goal they were made to deliver.

Discipline does not exhaust social morality. Having reiterated that each moral system is a function of the underlying social organization, Durkheim points to the ideal of perfect morality which each society conceives, and comments: this ideal type 'is the keystone of the whole social system and gives it its unity'.[75] He sketches the profiles of two opposite 'moral temperaments', applicable to both individuals and peoples as extreme types. There is, first, the personality ruled by duty, rational and strong-willed although cold and stiff. Second, there is the

---

[70] 'Détermination du fait moral', pp. 82–3.
[71] R. Aron, *Les étapes de la pensée sociologique* (Paris, 1967), pp. 317–405. For a specimen of Durkheim's position, see 'L'éducation: sa nature et son rôle' (1911), in E. Durkheim, *Education et sociologie*, ed. P. Fauconnet (Paris, 1922), pp. 50–9.
[72] *L'éducation morale*, p. 103; *Les règles*, p. 152.
[73] *Les règles*, p. 19.
[74] 'L'éducation', pp. 55–6; *Les formes élémentaires*, bk II, ch. 7, pp. 296–8; *L'éducation morale*, pp. 50–3 (an example previously given concerned a people).
[75] 'Détermination du fait moral', pp. 81–2. This point is often made, for instance in *L'éducation morale*, p. 99, and in 'L'évolution et le rôle de l'enseignement secondaire en France' (1906), in *Education et sociologie*, p. 143.

passionate character, reluctant to comply with rules but capable of great deeds, albeit occasionally. Durkheim holds that in a given society either temperament can predominate.

When a people has achieved a stage of equilibrium and maturity, when the various social functions, at least temporarily, are articulated in an ordered fashion, when the collective sentiments in their essentials are incontestable for the great majority of people, then the preference for rule and order is naturally preponderant ... On the other hand, in times of flux and change, the spirit of discipline cannot preserve its moral vigour since the prevailing system of rules is shaken, at least in some of its parts. At such times, it is the other element of morality, the need for some objective to which one can commit oneself – in a word, the spirit of sacrifice and devotion – that becomes the spring [*ressort*], par excellence, of morality.[76]

It is possible that Durkheim was contrasting the English to the French, in addition to pointing out the correlation between a situation of *anomie* (or its opposite) and the corresponding mental attitude. But, even if one conceded that the temperamental dichotomy was about the two peoples, his idea of a national character would amount here to a reversible assemblage of moral propensities subject to the current social arrangements.

The 'European societies' were passing through a phase where discipline counted less than the attachment to suitable collective ideals. To make people pursue these ideals (Durkheim considered not just patriotism but also the cosmopolitan values of humanity), it was appropriate that men always created inner representations of things, because representations implied a personal, 'egoistic' element which somehow altered the nature of what would otherwise seem purely 'altruistic'. The point was that, given a type of man as socialized as that he depicted, there was no sharp separation between self-oriented and other-oriented sentiments.[77] As regards Durkheim's analysis of the French contemporary mind, overall the theme of social discipline was not really differentiated from that of collective ideals, as the country evidently needed both.

Durkheim's subtle contempt for his compatriots surfaces through an implicit but transparent parallel between the psychology of children and that of the French. Both managed to be fond of novelties and stay essentially unchanged – paradoxically, the most revolutionary of peoples was routine-loving. With the French, habits were always stronger than impressions, which were invariably ephemeral.[78] At the origin of French character there was the 'Cartesian' spirit, which had spread among all ranks, and generated a simplistic viewpoint on social reality – references to Taine's 'classic' spirit are absent, but the epithet 'Cartesian' implied more or less the same. This attitude was expressed above

---

[76] *L'éducation morale*, pp. 115–16 (*Moral Education*, trans. E. K. Wilson and H. Schnurer (New York and London, 1973), pp. 100–1; trans. modified).
[77] ibid., pp. 116–18, 237–50ff., esp. pp. 246–7, 261–2.
[78] ibid., pp. 155–7.

all by a predominant individualism, of necessity amoral; among its more momentous consequences, there were a lack of associative spirit and the crisis
of collective ideals.[79] As regards the means for reforming the French 'mental
constitution', the difficulty Durkheim met, and frankly recognized, is typical of
all mentality-oriented thought. Having set the problem as how to give citizens
'the taste for collective life', he admitted that only the regular practice of associationism could achieve this; but this practice needed a corresponding opinion
as its prerequisite. Education was the only way to break the circle.[80]

Critical remarks like these, however, coexisted with national pride. France
was seen as a 'being' whose history had developed without breaks along progressive lines, and according to an impersonal 'force of things'. All societies
were first and foremost a set of ideas and sentiments – a *conscience* – so that
it was the 'national character' of France, as evidenced through history, that the
morality educator should teach in the end.[81] 'Now, what is the history of a
people if not the genius [*génie*] of that people developing through time?' The
feature of the French 'spirit' that Durkheim especially wanted to be taught in
schools was its universality: 'we think for humanity'. This was why in France
patriotism and cosmopolitanism sometimes seemed to combine. But, although
the universalist attitude should be preserved, it was urgent to rid it of its cocoon
of Cartesian rationalism, which entailed a 'simplistic geometrical' standpoint.[82]

Durkheim did give a course on the making of French character, albeit in the
form of a history of pedagogy, later published as *L'évolution pédagogique en
France*.[83] He was well aware of the broad scope of the subject – 'almost a
history of French spirit' – and of its main connection – 'the history of pedagogy
and collective ethology are, in effect, closely linked'.[84] The national passions
for order and uniformity are explained as effects of precocious and radical
centralization, while the Cartesian attitude proper is said to derive from the
education imparted in Jesuit schools. The French have no taste for a free and
varied way of life, and tend to class people and things in preconceived patterns,
because all moral and institutional diversities were rashly obliterated during the
process of state making. The Jesuits held, and taught, a general and abstract view
of man, narrowed into a series of types inherited from antiquity which were
bereft of historical, social, or geographical traits. There ensued an inability
to apprehend what is complex and changeable, and a focus on 'the abstract,
the general, and the simple'. This disposition marked the French mind from

---

[79] *ibid.*, pp. 286–300.
[80] *ibid.*, pp. 266–70. See also 'L'éducation'.
[81] *L'éducation morale*, pp. 315–19.
[82] *ibid.*, pp. 319–23, quotation from p. 319 (*Moral Education*, p. 278).
[83] *L'évolution pédagogique en France*, ed. M. Halbwachs (1938; 2nd edn, Paris, 1969). The course
on 'L'histoire de l'enseignement en France' started in 1904–5 and continued to be taught by
Durkheim until the war.
[84] *ibid.*, p. 5.

the seventeenth century to the Napoleonic age – passing through Corneille's heroes, the atomistic individualism of the Enlightenment, and the revolutionary Declaration of Rights.[85]

Acknowledging the faults of the national disposition, Durkheim argued, is a necessary condition for real change, which cannot but be based on educational reform, for 'spirit takes the form of the things it thinks of'. The French are used to representations of 'elementary, simple, and cramped [*exiguës*] things' only, and to a bias for abstractions regardless of the fact that the objects of representations ought to be 'realities objectively given outside the spirit'.[86] The study of history, science, and classical languages has the potential to bring French rationalism down to earth, by shaping a mental attitude which accepts the 'irreducible complexity' and 'infinite richness' of reality.[87] From this survey of the pedagogical thought of the nation it comes out that French character consists of a set of collective representations – it could hardly be otherwise, since men cannot but represent their social reality to themselves. A further inference can be drawn. In France, the ways of thinking of the elites came in the course of time to inform the mentality of the whole country. To adopt the dichotomy outlined above, the representations of the few, which constituted a 'collective' viewpoint, were eventually shared by all, a fact which may call for an 'average' viewpoint (and hence for *conscience collective*). As Durkheim explained in *Le suicide*, each 'average man' has a perception of the moral forces presiding over society, but only a very dim one.[88] But some men are not as *moyen* as the others, in the sense that the representations of the leading classes figure as the cause which first sets those forces in motion. In the final analysis, Durkheim's (and Taine's) 'national character' is a product of the intellectuals, of their grasping, or failure to grasp, the progressive tendencies moulding the mind at a given moment.[89]

Education reflects the advance made in this direction. In each society, a 'system of education' imposes itself on individuals with irresistible strength. This system consists of customs and ideas which are for the most part the product of previous generations; hence schools are an expression of the *esprit national*.[90] In France, a new educational ideal should be posited; a new 'pedagogical faith' framed in the light of the 'exigencies of the present' should guide

---

[85] *ibid.*, pp. 142–5, 311–17. On abstract characters in French literature, compare Taine, *L'ancien régime*, pp. 254–62.

[86] *L'évolution pédagogique*, pp. 145, 315, 365.

[87] *ibid.*, pp. 366–98.

[88] *Le suicide*, bk III, ch. 1, pp. 356–60.

[89] 'Ce qui lie les hommes en société, c'est une commune manière de penser, c'est-à-dire de se représenter les choses. Or, à chaque moment de l'histoire, la manière de se représenter le monde varie suivant l'état où sont parvenues les connaissances scientifiques ou qui passent pour telles ...': *Le socialisme*, p. 120.

[90] 'L'éducation', pp. 41–3; 'Nature et méthode de la pédagogie' (1911), in *Education et sociologie*, pp. 78–80.

teachers.[91] Historical precedents are fundamental in this respect, because the actual existence in the past of a pedagogical alternative to the humanist ideal would testify to a need of the social organism. The study of nature, embodying a reaction against the Jesuits' practice, was sanctioned by the educational reforms of the Revolution (which was not totally dominated by a Cartesian spirit, *pace* Taine), and it was later upheld by Saint-Simon and Comte. Hence a current of 'realistic pedagogy' is not alien to France, and in its full development and application lies the way out of the national impasse.[92]

Although Durkheim put forward not only a science of *mœurs* but also an idea of French character, the two viewpoints were kept separate, as the latter figures only in the courses. Yet a common inspiration underlies all his texts: the criticism of the classic spirit, a line of argument which did not go without the endorsement of some Burkean motifs. Durkheim, like many other French authors of the age, appears to have negotiated as well as he could a path between an urgently necessary criticism of his own country and a strong love for its tradition and culture. Even the Revolution had not been a real break in the course of a national history which was in the end a reason for pride, in view of France's unique contribution to civilization.[93]

The concept of collective representation at root denied a rigid and all-embracing national character. Possibly, the two approaches related to different modes of discourse. On the one hand, the theme of Frenchness pertained essentially to the sphere of practice, educational and thereby political; on the other hand, the study of particular collective representations was the task of pure science (so to speak). There is a difference between, say, Durkheim's moral education courses and the writings on primitive religion, in spite of his confidence that the former were as scientifically founded as the latter. But the two domains – that of French character and that of specific representations – overlapped, most remarkably because the concept of collective representation was applied in both. The inevitability of this application ensues not only from the fact that French traits derived from the representations of intellectuals, but also from the twofold dimension of collective representation. As both a necessary, ordinary mechanism of the human mind and the vehicle of civilization, collective representation was a very broad form of thinking.

In Durkheim there is the attempt to develop sociology apart from non-scientific considerations, with the discourse on French mentality ambiguously borrowing from the scientist's apparatus – ambiguously because the ways in

---

[91] 'L'évolution et le rôle de l'enseignement', pp. 143–58.
[92] *L'évolution pédagogique*, pp. 318–64. On Taine's view of the Revolution, see *ibid.*, pp. 335ff.
[93] *L'éducation morale*, pp. 317–18. For continuity in French history, see *L'évolution pédagogique*, esp. pp. 18–24. For Durkheim's pride in France's achievements and national greatness, see, to the exclusion of wartime writings where this feeling is paramount, 'L'individualisme', pp. 273–5.

which certain representations came to be shared by most, and in general the laws governing collective representations, were never spelled out. The confinement of national character themes to the lecture-room shows that they were not essential to his sociological project. The principles of sociology were universal in scope, as the situation of *anomie* that Durkheim viewed as the core of the French question went much beyond the boundaries of France, which just happened to be hit harder than other countries. While he analysed the origins of collective productions like religion and the logical categories, he did not deal either with less structured but politically more topical representations, or with the modern transformations of the representations he studied. To this choice of subject matter, which mirrors his concern with the 'infinitely rich' ground covered by the 'collective' (rather than average) viewpoint, should be added Durkheim's interest in the idea of 'civilization' as a supra-national moral environment. What results is a research programme about the conceptual aspects of civilizations – that is, considered in their 'higher' representational features – where national characters play no part.[94] In this perspective, the peculiarity of Durkheim's contribution would lie in the effort to show how a *specific* feature of a given social milieu articulates with a *specific* collective representation.[95]

Although deeply influenced by the French tradition of civic virtue in his dealing with *mœurs*, Durkheim's organicism, perhaps together with his gloomy view of human nature, induced a break with the Tocquevilles or Constants. To Durkheim, society was a matter of 'obscure forces' and vital functions, where good *mœurs* counted first and foremost for their cohesive potential; what he stressed was discipline, not participation. *Qua* sociologist, he identified social phenomena of which citizens were not in control, and which they had no power, unaided by a sociology-conscious state, to modify. That is not to say that the quality of the citizenry was immaterial, but that the theoretical framework of sociology did not leave room for the unconstrained shaping of society from below. The truly social mind, the mind of the whole that is, lay in state agencies rather than in any association of a private nature. To account for Durkheim's imperviousness, one should consider that he was a self-conscious

---

[94] On the study of civilizations, see Durkheim's introduction to the review section on civilizations in *AS*, 5 (1900–1), p. 168: 'il y a dans chaque civilisation une sorte de tonalité *sui generis* qui se retrouve dans tous les détails de la vie collective'. See also E. Durkheim and P. Fauconnet, 'Sociologie et sciences sociales' (1903), in *Textes*, I, pp. 150–3. For a later reappraisal, see Durkheim and Mauss's 'Note sur la notion de civilisation', *AS*, 12 (1909–12), pp. 46–50, where a civilization was defined as 'une sorte de milieu moral dans lequel sont plongées un certain nombre de nations et dont chaque culture nationale n'est qu'une forme particulière', p. 48.

[95] For a brilliant example of Durkheim's method, apart from his own contributions, see H. Hubert, 'Etude sommaire de la représentation du temps dans la religion et dans la magie' (1905), in Hubert and Mauss, *Mélanges*, pp. 189–229. On this work by Hubert, see F.-A. Isambert, 'Henri Hubert et la sociologie du temps', *Revue française de sociologie*, 20 (1979), pp. 183–204.

scientist in the line of Montesquieu and Comte, rather than a liberal political thinker. Durkheim's approach entailed that collective representations were true because they reflected 'the nature of things'.[96]

Durkheim marked a real methodological difference in comparison with the standards of the age, especially in his works on religion where the socio-political problems of France were not directly at issue. Rigorous and imaginative at the same time, he did not content himself with generalities; his research was constantly in progress, cumulative, and based on a scrupulous verification of facts. Again, this is no small achievement when measured by the yardstick of his contemporaries' practice, as the next section will show, and it is in this context that Durkheim's approach deserves to be called scientific.

4   Durkheimians and others: the debate on sociology and psychology

The characterization of society through habits, ideas, and sentiments was widespread among French social scientists.[97] The shocks of the defeat and the Commune reinforced an existing trend towards an apprehension of society in non-material terms, with social science as the new vehicle of this persistent outlook: material conditions having changed so radically between 1793 and 1871, what else but the shape of minds could account for the perpetual turmoil? The alleged coming-of-age of the scientific study of collective characters often resulted in the advocacy of a 'psychological approach'. Taine was a fundamental inspiration, first, in pointing to the spiritual–psychological nature of civilizations, second, in claiming scientific status, and, third, in delineating the 'classic spirit'. It was commonly maintained that this spirit had pervaded all ranks, so that a continuity between the Jacobins and the socialists in the light of a common 'character' looked like the veritable thread connecting the recent history of France.

Taine's example may also have given rise to the lack of rigorousness of many social scientists, whose methodological coherence, caution in drawing conclusions, and attention to fact leave much to be desired. Their definition as 'metaphysical and spiritualist positivists' seems quite appropriate.[98] The most

[96] See, e.g., *Les formes élémentaires*, conclusion, pp. 623–6.
[97] In addition to Le Bon, Boutmy, Fouillée, and Ribot mentioned in the next paragraph, the number of social scientists who viewed society as an essentially mental phenomenon, or at any rate emphasized its spiritual dimension, includes Vidal de la Blache and the school of human geography, Vacher de Lapouge and the 'anthroposociologists', the historian Henri Berr and his school, the sociologists René Worms, Paul Lacombe, Jacques Novicow, Alfred Espinas, Edmond Demolins and many other Le Playists, the social psychologists Frédéric Paulhan, Charles Letourneau, Auguste-Armand Marie, and others.
[98] J. Benrubi, *Les sources et les courants de la philosophie contemporaine en France* (2 vols., Paris, 1933), II, p. 610 (but Benrubi was referring to the French philosophers of the interwar period).

blatant instance is probably Le Bon. His mix of racialism, millenarianism, and Burkeanism (via Taine) had as its cornerstone the view that the course of history was determined by beliefs and faiths crystallized into racial characteristics. In practice, history came to be shaped by the contrast between Latins and Anglo-Saxons, in their customary typologies.[99] Le Bon's fully fledged, intemperate use of racial and national characters shows many affinities with the school of 'anthroposociology' led by Vacher de Lapouge. To Boutmy, climate was the main factor of civilizations and national characters, a thesis especially manifest in his report on England, where Taine's Montesquieu revived through comparisons between Northerners and Southerners and remarks on physiology.[100] A self-styled expert on national characters, Alfred Fouillée, who wrote *Psychologie du peuple français* (1898) and *Esquisse psychologique des peuples européens* (1903), confusingly combined Taine's race and milieu not only with Tarde's mechanisms of influence and suggestion but also with Durkheim's idea of social morphology. Théodule Ribot, professor of experimental psychology at the Sorbonne and the Collège de France, appears unable in his *L'hérédité psychologique* to negotiate the path of a definite and cogent argument between the conflicting claims of environmentalism and heredity.[101] It would not be difficult to lengthen this survey.

At the turn of the century, the Durkheimian school emphasized the scientific nature of social thinking. Scientific standards were set and taken seriously, thus helping to determine both the kind of projects to be carried out and everyday research practices. These standards served to distinguish between true scientists and dilettanti. There was a substantial difference between the perspective of the group of the *Année sociologique* and that of most of the others, a difference which had two sides. First, the Durkheimians had an approach which was comprehensive, capable of adaptations, and respectful of facts. Second, their enterprise was genuinely collective and hence cumulative, so that they could afford to pause for thought rather than always jumping to conclusions. Yet, to make up the whole difference, there is another element to consider, although its bearing is difficult to assess. Boutmy and Fouillée, to put forward two critical examples, were infinitely less powerful thinkers than Durkheim. While even a master like Taine looks at times like a charlatan, the theoretical originality of these two authors is just about zero, and their treatments often poor. Although the crowd theorists were more innovative, they did not in general offer comprehensive theories, and when they did, these turned out to be of very limited

---

[99] Le Bon's relevant works are *Les lois psychologiques de l'évolution des peuples* (Paris, 1894), and *La psychologie des foules* (Paris, 1895).

[100] E. Boutmy, *Essai d'une psychologie politique du peuple anglais au XIXᵉ siècle* (Paris, 1901). Boutmy's account of the Americans is more balanced, with room made for the influences of economic life and Anglo-Saxon public spirit besides climate: *Elements d'une psychologie politique du peuple américain* (Paris, 1902).

[101] T. Ribot, *L'hérédité psychologique* (1871; 2nd edn, Paris, 1882), esp. pp. 119–37.

novelty.[102] Superior talent may or may not bring with it fitting methodological choices, but in the case at hand it helps to explain the formation of a veritable Durkheimian school and the practices that teamwork made possible.

In the *Année sociologique*, the review section, compiled with an ambition to completeness, was often of as much moment as the articles. Sub-sections followed the boundaries of the various research fields and comprised both short notices and longer pieces.[103] The reviews of the literature on collective psychology and related topics were dominated by a cautious note.[104] In confirming that 'sociology is collective psychology', Paul Fauconnet, a close collaborator of Durkheim, stated nonetheless that many questions collective psychologists were dealing with were too complex to be successfully considered at the time. Because sociology was a progressing science, it could afford to ignore for the time being the problems it could not address; this attitude was by far preferable to 'a restless and vagrant [*vagabonde*] curiosity'. Fauconnet's position was typical. Granted that the study of collective psychology should consist of the analysis of collective representations, the group of the *Année sociologique* agreed that a science of collective representations – of the ways in which they came into existence, developed, and disappeared – was still to be initiated. For the moment then, the proper task was to prepare material by research on specific collective representations like myths, legends, religions, languages, and sciences.[105]

This was the official position of the Durkheimian group, and as such was repeated many times in the journal apropos of ambitious works expounding crowd, 'ethnic', and other types of group psychology, as well as depicting specific national characters, episodes of *Kulturgeschichte*, race traits, and so on. As Celestin Bouglé put it in reviewing a book stating the dependence of the mind on society: 'to show, through the comparative analysis of facts, how a certain intellectual habit was born out of a certain social situation would be more useful than affirming once again that reason is a product of the polity'.[106] The avowal of the pillars of Durkheimism alternated with a circumspect posture. Dominique Parodi warned against taking analogies between individual and

---

[102] It is often argued that Tarde's sociology, whose basic unit was the individual, was the only possible French alternative to Durkheim and his school.

[103] For an insider's view, see Mauss's manuscript 'An Intellectual Self-Portrait' (1930), in P. Besnard, ed., *The Sociological Domain: the Durkheimians and the Founding of French Sociology* (Cambridge and Paris, 1983), esp. pp. 142–4.

[104] The relevant labels changed many times, ranging from 'Sociologie psychologique et spécifique', 'Ethologie collective', and 'Personnalité individuelle et personnalité collective' to 'La mentalité des groupes' and 'Psychologie sociale'. Reviews of interest can also be found under other, non-specific, headings.

[105] P. Fauconnet, reviews of Rossi, Sighele, and Tarde, *AS*, 5 (1900–1), esp. pp. 162–6. See also by Fauconnet the review of Brinton, *The Basis of Social Relations*, *AS*, 7 (1902–3), pp. 186–90.

[106] C. Bouglé, review of De Roberty, *Sociologie de l'action*, *AS*, 11 (1906–9), p. 47.

collective 'souls' as scientific demonstrations.[107] In Mauss's opinion, Wundt's collective psychology was not social enough, that is, it treated social organizations as 'derived' (rather than primary) and took the 'unorganized mass of individuals' as its starting point; hence Wundt's preference for the notion of 'soul' over collective representations.[108] Paul Lapie criticized Fouillée for being content with generalities in his *Psychologie du peuple français*.[109] Bouglé's review of Boutmy on England proposed to replace the 'natural milieu' with a changing 'human milieu' as the main factor of mentality.[110] A similar substitution, but with instincts as the overburdened factor, was suggested by Bouglé in reviewing McDougall.[111] Hubert stated it bluntly: race 'is not a scientific problem'.[112] In commenting on Burckhardt's *Griechische Kulturgeschichte*, the same Hubert wondered about the fuzzy boundaries of ethology and history, and defined the former as a 'quintessence' of the latter, but very difficult to capture.[113]

However, Durkheim himself recognized the future need to grasp those unifying elements of great comprehensiveness of which national character was one (and civilization was another). Either individual or collective, character 'is the central and permanent nucleus which links together the various moments of life and makes the flow [*suite*] and continuity of it'.[114] An article by Lapie, 'Ethologie politique', discussed two ways of dealing with national character, the individualist–psychological and the sociological. Only the latter was the method of science, which neither Taine, Boutmy, nor Fouillée managed to attain, because, instead of systematically looking for manifestations of national character in social institutions (like religion for example), they focused on a non-existent average individual. The article is a thorough denunciation of the three authors' confused, self-contradictory, and vague thinking; clearly, Lapie's goal was to mark a difference as well as a point of no return. Far from being a 'literary genre', political ethology was a 'science' aiming at laws of coexistence and succession, and was part of a 'concrete sociology'. Although knowable only through the study of institutions, national character could help to understand them better, as well as to evaluate practical questions in education

---

[107] D. Parodi, review of Rossi, *Psicologia collettiva*, *AS*, 4 (1900), pp. 131–4.

[108] M. Mauss, review of Wundt, *Völkerpsychologie*, *AS*, 10 (1905–6), pp. 210–16, esp. p. 216, and 11 (1906–9), pp. 53–68, esp. p. 58.

[109] P. Lapie, review of Fouillée, *Psychologie du peuple français*, *AS*, 2 (1898), p. 555.

[110] C. Bouglé, review of Boutmy, *Essai d'une psychologie politique du peuple anglais*, *AS*, 5 (1900–1), pp. 177–83.

[111] C. Bouglé, review of McDougall, *An Introduction to Social Psychology*, *AS*, 11 (1906–9), pp. 38–40.

[112] H. Hubert, review of Colajanni and Finot, *AS*, 9 (1904–5), p. 167.

[113] H. Hubert, review of Burckhardt, *Griechische Kulturgeschichte*, *AS*, 7 (1902–3), pp. 191–3.

[114] E. Durkheim, introduction to section: 'Civilisation en général et types de civilisation', *AS*, 5 (1900–1), p. 168. See also Fauconnet, review of Brinton, p. 190.

and politics. On these premises, Lapie judged Taine's concept of representation as misleading, because *a priori* and purely formal, that is neglectful of the nature of the objects perceived; moreover, all three writers had failed to study the laws of the combination of representations and characteristics into a whole.[115]

An author greatly influenced by Durkheim, Lucien Lévy-Bruhl, tried to improve on collective representations. Beside representations and 'beliefs [*croyances*]', taken together as 'images and ideas linked in a certain way', he posited 'sentiments' as vehicles of the varying imperative character of representations and beliefs. That is, in each individual *conscience* the strength of representations was not determined by their clarity but by their 'imperativity', expressed by sentiments of different intensity. In spite of their fleeting nature, sentiments should be analysed in parallel with representations and beliefs.[116] To show that the evolution of collective sentiments was slower than that of collective representations and beliefs, Lévy-Bruhl gave the example of property, still perceived in a traditional way in spite of widespread criticism; only when this criticism managed to establish a connection with collective sentiments would it become effective. These proved difficult to change because they could be 'represented' only through other sentiments. The objective knowledge provided by sociology was the only antidote to a blind submission to sentiments.[117] Lévy-Bruhl's introduction of sentiments earned him a rebuke from Fauconnet in the *Revue philosophique*: the notion is 'obscure', and, at all events, sentiments are bereft of autonomous evolution.[118]

At the time of the launch of the *Année sociologique* the relationship of sociology to psychology had been a matter of controversy between Durkheim, on the one hand, and Bouglé and Lapie, on the other.[119] Apart from a spirited correspondence, the terms of the discussion can be grasped from some published pieces.[120] Being one of the core Durkheimians, Bouglé's case is of particular importance. His *Les sciences sociales en Allemagne* (1896) documented the psychological approach which, in his view, pervaded social thinking in both Germany and France, with only one notable exception: Durkheim. Taking issue with *De la division du travail* and *Les règles de la méthode sociologique*,

---

[115] P. Lapie, 'Ethologie politique', *Revue de métaphysique et de morale*, 10 (1902), pp. 490–515.
[116] L. Lévy-Bruhl, *La morale et la science des mœurs* (Paris, 1903), pp. 227–35ff.
[117] *ibid.*, pp. 249–85.
[118] P. Fauconnet, 'La morale et la science des mœurs', *Revue philosophique*, 57 (1904), pp. 72–87, esp. pp. 84–7. See also the self-referential review by Durkheim in *AS*, 7 (1902–3), pp. 380–4. See L. Lévy-Bruhl, 'La morale et la science des mœurs. Réponse à quelques critiques', *Revue philosophique*, 62 (1906), pp. 1–31 (but he did not reply to Fauconnet).
[119] See the important article by P. Besnard, 'La formation de l'équipe de l'*Année sociologique*', *Revue française de sociologie*, 20 (1979), pp. 7–48.
[120] The relevant letters are in Besnard, 'La formation de l'équipe', pp. 32–44, and in Durkheim, *Textes*, II, pp. 393–402.

Bouglé contested the idea that social phenomena were always reflected in 'exterior things' like laws or rules. Rather, the essence of social facts was their psychological dimension, and thereby introspection was needed for their understanding.[121] A few months later, convinced by Durkheim that his reading had been partial at least, Bouglé set out to defend him precisely from Charles Andler's accusation of dismissal of psychology. Here Bouglé confirmed that social reality consisted of 'states of *conscience*'; it was because 'social forms' were 'known, loved, interpreted' by minds that they really became social.[122]

Bouglé's friend Lapie shared the same perspective: 'societies are systems of ideas', and 'the causes of social facts are reasoned arguments [*des raisonnements*]'.[123] Lapie, too, was wary of some of Durkheim's methodological statements. The analytical axis of Lapie's book *Les civilisations tunisiennes*, subtitled *Etude de psychologie sociale*, was a comparison between the character of the Muslims and that of the Jews. In reviewing the book, Durkheim pointed to Lapie's simplistic definitions of the two temperaments and the disproportion between these and the wide range of effects they were supposed to determine.[124] (As shown, Lapie later became a critic of not dissimilar specimens of methodological naivety.) The impasse was broken when Lapie came to acknowledge that in *Le suicide* and elsewhere Durkheim was making 'concessions' – he was in fact stressing the distinction between individual and collective psychology. Bouglé took Durkheim's article on representations in this sense. The piece 'will undoubtedly serve to clear up some misunderstandings arising from Durkheim's previous methodological publications'. It is now apparent, Bouglé continued, that the exteriority and independence of social facts do not entail that they are material, and that 'a special psychology', that is 'collective in the proper sense', should be the backbone of sociology.[125] Nevertheless, anyone expecting to find an application of collective representations to modern societies in Bouglé's *Les*

---

[121] *Les sciences sociales en Allemagne: les méthodes actuelles* (Paris, 1896), pp. 142–72. Bouglé put forward a comprehensive methodological critique of Durkheim but his alleged rejection of psychology was the core of it. This critique rested on some of Durkheim's statements in *Les règles de la méthode sociologique*, like the definition of social fact (*Les règles*, p. 19) and that of causality (p. 135). However, Bouglé observed that Durkheim was writing as a psychologist when dealing with *conscience collective*: *Les sciences sociales*, p. 151.

[122] C. Bouglé, 'Sociologie, psychologie et histoire', *Revue de métaphysique et de morale*, 4 (1896), p. 366. See also Bouglé's review of Patten, *The Relation of Sociology to Psychology*, *AS*, 1 (1897), pp. 156–9. Besnard holds that Bouglé's *Les sciences sociales*, although dated 1896, appeared in reality in October or November 1895 ('La formation de l'équipe', p. 12, fn.). For the limitations of Bouglé's position, see W. P. Vogt, 'Un Durkheimian ambivalent: Célestin Bouglé, 1870–1940', *Revue française de sociologie*, 20 (1979), p. 127: 'Bouglé n'explicite pas la nature du lien entre une introspection *individuelle* du sociologue et une psychologie *sociale*.'

[123] P. Lapie, 'L'année sociologique 1895: la morale sociale', *Revue de métaphysique et de morale*, 4 (1896), p. 361.

[124] E. Durkheim, review of Lapie, *Les civilisations tunisiennes*, *AS*, 2 (1898), pp. 557–9.

[125] C. Bouglé, review of Durkheim, 'Représentations individuelles et représentations collectives', *AS*, 2 (1898), pp. 152–5.

idées égalitaires: étude sociologique (1899) will probably be disappointed. Collective representations do not play a part in the book, as Bouglé's starting point is much more commonsensical than Durkheim's: a 'social idea' (like equality) is one that is commonly accepted by the individuals who make up a society. The main thesis, too, is simple, although indisputably Durkheimian. The egalitarian idea would spread as an effect of an extension of the morphological boundaries (the social 'quantity') and the progress of communications ('density').[126]

5   Afterword

The *Année sociologique* group dissolved after the deaths of Hertz in 1915, of Durkheim in 1917, and of Hubert in 1927. A team working together was a necessary condition for the development of the Durkheimians' research programme, for only the amassing and cataloguing of facts legitimated their striving after a grand theory of collective representations. The want of this requisite might account for the chequered fortunes of collective representations after the war. But it is arguable that collective representations had been insufficiently conceptualized to be widely adopted as a research tool. It was the genius of Durkheim, the fresh framework of sociology, and the practice of methodological rigour that imparted intellectual tension to a notion which, in itself, was no novelty and could not be, given its generality. For instance, the idea of a psychology 'sans moi' could be, and was, traced back to Herbart.[127]

Durkheim's legacy was variously interpreted by his fellow workers after the war, if not denied altogether.[128] The war acted as a watershed after which, in Mauss's words, 'everything had collapsed'.[129] For example, Hubert and Mauss, who before 1918 had been 'jumeaux de travail', dealt very differently with nationality. Hubert wrote and lectured about the Celts and the Germans. Although his works rest on a very solid linguistic and archaeological basis, there are assertions that recall Michelet or Renan: the Celtic peoples shared 'a soul' of sensitivity, individualism, and passion for general ideas, but lacked

---

[126] C. Bouglé, *Les idées égalitaires: étude sociologique* (Paris, 1899), p. 30 and *passim*.

[127] Bouglé, *Les sciences sociales*, pp. 39–40. Herbart's fundamental work on the theoretical concept of the self is *Psychologie als Wissenschaft neu gegründet auf Erfahrung, Metaphysik und Mathematik* (1824–5).

[128] Having said that an extensive inquiry about the post-1918 scene has not been made, it is true that collective representations were not absent from the writings of Durkheimians in the interwar period: see, e.g., M. Halbwachs, *Evolution des besoins dans les classes ouvrières* (Paris, 1933); M. Halbwachs, *Les causes du suicide* (Paris, 1930); and F. Simiand, *Le salaire, l'évolution sociale, et la monnaie* (3 vols., Paris, 1932).

[129] Mauss, 'An Intellectual Self-Portrait', p. 141. On the Durkheimian legacy between the world wars, and the schism which occurred between a philosophical (Lapie, Bouglé, Davy, Parodi) and a sociological (Mauss, Simiand, Granet, Halbwachs) reading of the master, see J. Heilbron, 'Les métamorphoses du durkheimisme, 1920–1940', *Revue française de sociologie*, 26 (1985), pp. 203–37.

political sense. These features still inform modern France, Hubert commented admiringly; a nation is in essence a common way of thinking and feeling.[130] For Mauss, nations were peculiarly modern phenomena defined above all by the political participation of citizens. His manuscript 'La nation' (1919–20) focused on the 'superstitious attraction' to a strongly marked 'national character' which modern peoples showed. Each people was eager to differentiate itself through elements like race, language, or civilization. Mauss pointed out how this 'conscious formation of national characters' clashed with the fast developing uniformity of societies and cultures, a process which he warmly endorsed. National mentalities were becoming alike in the direction of the 'unity of the human spirit'.[131] In short, his very un-Durkheimian point was that the prevailing collective representations about nationality – to use a term, collective representation, that Mauss did not employ here – were wrong.

In taking up the *Année sociologique* in the 1920s, Mauss detailed a programme which, far from clarifying the analytical potential of collective representations, further obscured it. His concern was how to grasp society as a whole, and the 'total man' with it, after years, he commented, spent in studying isolated sections of this whole by means of narrow-ranging disciplines. This concern takes three directions, whose relationships are confused. First, *conscience collective* is defined as the whole of which collective representations are parts. But, second, any distinct idea of collective representation vacillates when Mauss lumps them and social practices together into 'social physiology', and asserts that a connection with an act (*acte*) is inherent to a true collective representation; 'act' appears to range from communication to behaviour. Third, room is made for a study of peoples which addressed the 'essence', 'individuality', or even the 'quiddité' of societies: the task of 'collective ethology' is to consider the relationships between all social phenomena.[132]

As Durkheim left it, the concept of collective representations may have looked rather like a tortuous route to the study of primitive religions and, more generally, to the origins of modern thought. 'Mentalité' was a term Durkheim did use but caution in the handling of broad generalizations was paramount. It is commonly accepted that Lévy-Bruhl broke with this prudent approach in a series of books on the 'mentality' of uncivilized peoples which began as early as 1910 and

---

[130] H. Hubert, *Les celtes* (2 vols., Paris, 1932), I, pp. 1–24; II, p. 336.

[131] The text is in M. Mauss, *Œuvres* (3 vols., Paris, 1969), III, pp. 571–625. See also the speech on nationality Mauss gave in 1920, and then published: *Œuvres*, III, pp. 626–34. For a comment on Mauss on the idea of nation, see Tarot, *De Durkheim à Mauss*, pp. 177–83.

[132] M. Mauss, 'Rapports réels et pratiques de la psychologie et de la sociologie' (1924), in his *Sociologie et anthropologie* (Paris, 1973), pp. 283–310. The 'total man' is an 'average man', pp. 305–6. M. Mauss, 'Divisions et proportions des divisions de la sociologie' (originally published in *AS*, n.s., 2, 1927), in *Œuvres*, III, esp. pp. 183–4, 186–8, 201–18, 225, 228–32.

continued in the interwar decades.[133] To highlight very briefly some features of Lévy-Bruhl's work may help to understand what Durkheim did *not* do. First, by referring to an all-embracing 'primitive mentality' (made up of collective representations) to be found anywhere, Lévy-Bruhl substantially loosened the link between a specific representation and a specific social organization.[134] In fact he put forward statements so general that they could hardly prove testable. Second, to take up the distinction previously made, he dealt with what amounted to an average type (Durkheim's *conscience collective*), whereas after *De la division du travail* Durkheim had steered himself towards the 'collective' type (the 'higher' representations which expressed the progress of man). Third, having ossified collective representations into a mentality, he viewed this as the fundamental determinant of social life: explicitly or implicitly, the interaction of the material and the ideal was lost in favour of a one-way direction of influence.[135] Fourth, Lévy-Bruhl's notion of 'sentiments' resurfaced in many forms to express the strong emotional and instinctual side of the pre-logic mentality. 'Sentiments' were finally transformed into the 'category' presiding over the perception of the supernatural.[136]

Pace Durkheim, from the point of view of a social scientist of today the most 'scientific' piece of work of the years 1870–1914 was probably André Siegfried's *Tableau politique de la France de l'Ouest* (1913). On the basis of electoral behaviour, analysed via statistics, diagrams, and maps, Siegfried aimed to assess the 'political temperament' of the French West. The book is astonishingly modern in its conception: given a precise task, a circumscribed research field, and thorough processing of data, Siegfried was able to draw conclusions which necessitated a minimum number of hypotheses. These related to the connections to be made between social, economic, demographic, and religious variables, on the one hand, and electoral behaviour, on the other. His analysis revealed that the determinants of political choices did not lie in political ideas proper but in something more comprehensive which he called 'temperaments', which synthesized such factors as viewpoints on society, ways

---

[133] For a balanced assessment of Lévy-Bruhl's writings on primitive thought, see E. E. Evans-Pritchard, *Theories of Primitive Religion* (Oxford, 1965), pp. 78–99. Commentators agree in viewing Lévy-Bruhl rather than Durkheim as the moving force behind the elaboration and diffusion of the idea of *mentalité* which has informed twentieth-century French historical writing. See P. Burke, 'Strengths and Weaknesses of the History of Mentalities', *History of European Ideas*, 7 (1986), pp. 439–51; and G. E. R. Lloyd, *Demystifying Mentalities* (Cambridge, 1990). The enduring influences of Michelet, Berr, and Vidal de la Blache should also be carefully evaluated.

[134] On the relationship between mentality and collective representations, see esp. *Les fonctions mentales dans les sociétés inférieures* (Paris, 1910), pp. 1–24. See also *La mentalité primitive* (1922; 4th edn, Paris, 1925).

[135] The meaning of 'institution' became so broad that it included hunting, fishing, religious ceremonies, illnesses, births, etc. See *Les fonctions mentales*, part III.

[136] See *Le surnaturel et la nature dans la mentalité primitive* (1931; Paris, 1963).

of reacting to events, attitudes to life, sentiments, and so on. Nevertheless Siegfried admitted that there were limits to a causal analysis of temperaments, and he pointed to 'the mystery of ethnic personalities' as an 'admission of defeat'.[137] Siegfried, too, who in 1950 wrote the stereotype-laden *L'âme des peuples*, did not completely escape the French way of approaching social science.[138]

[137] A. Siegfried, *Tableau politique de la France de l'Ouest* (Paris, 1913), esp. pp. 364–5, 496–8.
[138] (Paris, 1950).

9 Socializing public spirit, 1870–1914

1 Tales of everyday life

To be real, civic qualities must inform common behaviour; this is why small things have the potential to reveal basic attitudes. Not infrequently, certain minor mores seem to set the tone of communal life. Observers perceive that, say, the apparent unwillingness of some peoples to queue is deep-rooted – with some reason, one might trace it back to habits of distrust of authority and amoral self-advancement formed through centuries – and that it tells a truth about those peoples. Mores of this kind may be directly observed or experienced by writers, a circumstance which alone accounts for much of their impact. This chapter begins with a sample of (allegedly) meaningful occurrences, brief stories whose common rationale will be made clear later on.

There was a certain hospital in which the custodians used to take home with them the food of the patients and even the sheets of the dying, recounted the Italian historian Pasquale Villari. The 'secret poison' of Italian society, he explained, is the conviction that even under a free government doing one's own duty is not the principal means to get ahead.[1] The aftermath of the *Risorgimento* has witnessed 'the triumph of the incompetent' and the corruption of politics under the aegis, customary in Italy, of a 'double norm' for public and private life.[2] Italians consider politics to be not only different from, but also contrary to morals, although science and history have demonstrated that public virtues are the only safe basis for nations and governments. How is it possible to create a modern polity, Villari wondered, when society 'does not suggest anything' and expects everything to be done by the government?[3]

Another Italian, the pedagogue, philosopher, and political thinker Aristide Gabelli, imputed the low 'civil education' of his fellow citizens to Catholicism. In contrast to Protestantism, Catholicism induced individual irresponsibility and

---

[1] P. Villari, *La guerra presente e l'Italia* (Florence, 1870), pp. 27, 31. Villari corresponded with Mill for eighteen years.

[2] 'Di chi è la colpa? o sia la pace e la guerra' (1866), in P. Villari, *Le lettere meridionali ed altri scritti sulla questione sociale in Italia* (Florence, 1878), pp. 229–52. For Villari on the historical causes of Italy's moral state, see esp. *Niccolò Machiavelli e i suoi tempi* (1877–82; 2nd edn, 3 vols., Milan, 1895–97), esp. III, pp. 375–87.

[3] *La guerra presente*, p.34; 'Di chi è la colpa?', p. 234.

moral apathy through an education instilling the primacy of abstract thought over observation, and of exterior behaviour over the shaping of character; Italians took their undisciplined selves rather than the external world as the gauge of behaviour.[4] This attitude was exemplarily reflected by their deficient work ethic. Italians seem condemned to take up their jobs by a hostile destiny, as if their true occupations should be totally different. When you ask for a stamp at the post office, 'you have to wait for the employee to finish an animated conversation about hunting with his three or four colleagues, a conversation which of course makes it impossible to assist you'. The waiter at the *caffè* seems absorbed in business other than that which you, 'relying on appearances', think proper to him. Office clerks, railway staff, shop assistants, cabmen, etc. seem 'in contemplation of a less unjust fortune' which ought to have made them bankers or professionals. Hence a buoyant carelessness and thoughtlessness: when a Roman says 'I am coming', you have to wait for half an hour. People are everywhere beautiful, good, and nice, but they seem to repeat 'do not bother me'. The problem is, Gabelli commented, that a modern society is a complex arrangement where everybody is linked to everybody else in a number of ways, and therefore it cannot do without the predictable and ordered cooperation of its citizens. Everywhere in the civilized world, 'living by unconscious feelings and fugitive impressions with the soul in the eyes and without any forethought' has disappeared, thanks to stricter laws, a hard life of work and order, and a greater need for steadiness and thrift – but the Italians have remained 'the good-time guys [*buontemponi*] of Europe'.[5]

In *The Data of Ethics*, Spencer sets out to demonstrate that altruism is a law of evolution. Individual welfare is dependent on due regard for the welfare of others, and the more so the more a community advances. A modern society is characterized by a network of mutual obligations and services. For instance, we rely on efficient producers for the low price of the goods we buy; on responsible patients for not spreading their diseases; and on reliable employees for the punctual delivery of messages. 'Yesterday the illness of [a] child due to foul gases, led to the discovery of a drain that had become choked because it was ill-made by a dishonest builder under supervision of a careless or bribed surveyor.' A less serious case is that of 'railway passengers who, by dispersed

---

4   See esp. by Gabelli: *La questione religiosa in Italia* (Milan, 1864); 'L'educazione vecchia e la nuova principalmente nei collegi' (1868), in A. Gabelli, *L'istruzione in Italia*, ed. P. Villari (2 vols., Bologna, 1891), I, pp. 3–48; 'Metodo di insegnare in relazione colla vita' (1873), in *L'istruzione in Italia*, I, pp. 85–117. On Villari and Gabelli as exponents of the early phase of Italian positivism, see the classic study by E. Garin, 'Metodo e concezione del mondo nel positivismo', in E. Garin et al., *Cultura e società in Italia nell'età umbertina* (Milan, 1981), pp. 163–88.

5   'Metodo di insegnare in relazione colla vita', pp. 88–95; 'Prefazione', in Ministry of Agriculture, *Monografia della città di Roma e della campagna romana* (2 vols., Rome, 1881), I, p. xviii. For a comment on Villari and Gabelli as public moralists, see R. Romani, *L'economia politica del Risorgimento italiano* (Turin, 1994), pp. 228–41.

coats', make people believe that 'all the seats in a compartment are taken when they are not'.[6] As a specimen of behaviour which sparks long chains of unintended consequences, the tipping of railway porters particularly raises Spencer's indignation.

While the porter, expecting sixpence from some wealthy-looking man entering a first class, is fussing about in the compartment arranging his bundle of rugs, and parcels, and umbrella, in the rack, or is coming back from the van to tell him his portmanteau and gun case have been duly placed in it, two or three others are kept waiting – a shabby-looking person with bag in hand, from whom probably not a penny will come, or a widow with a cluster of children and miscellaneous belongings, who is agitated lest the train should start without her. So that the richer passenger's seeming generosity to the porter, involves ungenerosity to other passengers.[7]

Worst is to come, because the postponed accommodation of the non-tipping passengers has kept the train waiting; since this happens at every large station, delay steadily increases; the eventual result is the 'chronic unpunctuality' of the service and the ensuing possibility of collisions.[8]

Children's vaccination and the maintenance of drains figure as examples of the interrelatedness of modern life in Huxley's critique of Spencer's laissez-faire. Considering that it was impossible for anyone to do something wrong without damaging all his fellow citizens, the extension of state duties was necessary. Social organization is comparable to 'the synthesis of the chemist' by which 'independent elements are gradually built up into complex aggregations'. Not only laws, but also manners, are in the final analysis contracts aimed at self-restraint.[9] (Spencer, too, spoke of religion, laws, and manners as 'controlling agencies'.)[10] The natural laws presiding over society and the cosmos amounted to the rules of a 'mighty' game, a game 'infinitely more difficult and complicated than chess'; yet everybody should grasp them, and above all a knowledge of 'sociology' was required, because 'the machinery of society' was very delicate.[11]

To the historian E. A. Freeman, the law represented a commonwealth which was the object of 'patriotism' and thereby the source of public morals. This was why citizens had to abide by the law even in minor matters. Take the case of

---

[6] *The Data of Ethics* (1879; London, 1996), pp. 210–11.
[7] *The Principles of Ethics* (1879–93; 2 vols., Indianapolis, 1978), II, pp. 321–3, quotation on p. 322.
[8] *ibid.*, pp. 322–3.
[9] 'Administrative Nihilism', in T. H. Huxley, *Critiques and Addresses* (London, 1873), pp. 3–32, quotation on pp. 20–1.
[10] H. Spencer, 'Manners and Fashion' (1854), in his *Essays: Scientific, Political, & Speculative* (1891; 3 vols., London, 1996), III, pp. 1–51.
[11] In *The Major Prose of Thomas Henry Huxley*, ed. A. P. Barr (Athens, Ga., and London, 1997), see 'A Liberal Education; and Where to Find It' (1868), p. 209, and 'Science and Culture' (1880), pp. 237–8.

smoking in railway carriages where this is forbidden. 'Sometimes a man will ask if his fellow-passengers have any objection to his smoking, just as he might ask for any trifling favour; he does not see that he might as reasonably ask whether his fellow-passengers have any objection to have [*sic*] their pockets picked.' Instead of handing him over to the guard, the other passengers often show an understanding attitude. The conception of the public viewpoint which people hold is lamentably poor, Freeman commented.[12]

Both Tarde and Wallas noticed the silence prevailing in crowded omnibuses in Paris and London respectively. 'To a *provincial* disembarked in Paris, nothing looks more odd, more against nature than the view of omnibuses full of people who carefully refrain from talking to each other', for in the countryside everybody chats with everybody else. Tarde, who was bent on establishing conversation as a principal medium of public opinion, explained the urbanites' behaviour in terms of the increased 'intensity' of 'the need for conversation' in many situations, a fact which made people seek protection when possible from the flow of words.[13] Wallas drew a similar conclusion, although in the light of the perception of human nature brought about by Darwinism: Londoners did not talk to casual neighbours because 'certain facts in our inherited nature make us shrink from the effort involved in acquiring every few minutes a new acquaintance'. In cities 'as crowded as beehives' we feel the need to 'fence ourselves' in obedience to an instinct which harks back to our ape-like ancestors.[14]

All the above specimens have something in common: at a micro-level, and in an urban setting, reference is made to a set of characteristics – honesty, competence, reliability, efficiency, vigilance, participation, and privacy – deemed necessary to social life in view of the increased physical contiguity and functional interrelatedness of men. The focus is on how well suited the citizens are to the operation of social mechanisms, rather than, as it was with public spirit advocates, on how suited they are to the functioning of representative institutions. To differentiate this 'social' approach from that of public spirit, the qualities thus contextualized are labelled 'civism'. This chapter is devoted to a delineation of its meaning and fortunes in Britain. Two Italian examples will also be provided to illustrate the role of 'civism' in a country differently circumstanced. First, it is appropriate to enlarge on the new setting for the practice of public virtues which civism refers to.

2   Civism

'Civism' evolved out of the public spirit viewpoint which ran through the nineteenth century. As Mill's formulation exemplarily shows, public spirit entailed

---

[12] E. A. Freeman, 'Public and Private Morality', *Fortnightly Review*, 13 (1873), pp. 405–28.
[13] G. Tarde, *L'opinion et la foule* (Paris, 1901), pp. 141–2.
[14] 'Darwinism and Social Motive' (1906), in G. Wallas, *Men and Ideas* (London, 1940), pp. 92–3.

that the basis of good government had to be looked for in the 'virtue and intelligence of the human beings composing the community'. This held true with respect to the administration of justice – witnesses should not lie, and judges should not take bribes; to municipal administration – the disinterested participation of citizens was required; to a representative system – electors should vote responsibly; to a representative assembly – where the self-control of its members proves necessary; and to government – whose action could be disrupted by personal rivalries. Generally speaking, 'whenever the general disposition of the people is such, that each individual regards only those of his interests which are selfish, and does not dwell on, or concern himself for, his share of the general interest, in such a state of things good government is impossible'.[15] Mill pointed to the obstacles represented by a lack of obedience, the contrary fault of 'extreme passiveness', a 'spirit of locality', and the French vices of post-hunting and care for equality but not liberty.[16] By concentrating on the effective workings of representative institutions, Mill's concern was evidently one of a political nature.

Civism differs from Mill's public spirit on three grounds. First, the novelty of turn-of-the-century civism is its social characterization. This type of public spirit is not just about Mill's political duties but about the arrangements required to make a mass society work. In a transforming urban environment, the combination of larger-scale economic activities with new spheres of activity and behaviour – brought about by leisure, more varied patterns of consumption, mass provision of services, new forms of associative life, improved education, newspapers, and so on – entailed a degree of interrelatedness previously unknown. Hence there was a novel emphasis on the quality of citizenship as an indispensable means for the smooth workings of large, complicated societies. How 'the others' were perceived and acted upon became fundamental in crowded and sensitive settings. Admittedly, any sharp distinction between the social and political elements would be out of place; even independently of the myriad of points where social behaviour touches on the political, the psychology of city dwellers appeared to many contemporaries to be related to the advent of democratic politics.[17]

---

[15] *Considerations on Representative Government* (1861), *MCW*, XIX, pp. 389–90.

[16] *ibid.*, pp. 415–21. For this side of Mill's thought, see B. Semmel, *John Stuart Mill and the Pursuit of Virtue* (New Haven, Conn., and London, 1984); J. W. Burrow, *Whigs and Liberals: Continuity and Change in English Political Thought* (Oxford, 1988); G. W. Smith, 'Freedom and Virtue in Politics: Some Aspects of Character, Circumstances and Utility from Helvétius to J. S. Mill', *Utilitas*, 1 (1989), pp. 112–34; H. S. Jones, 'John Stuart Mill as Moralist', *Journal of the History of Ideas*, 53 (1992), pp. 287–308; E. F. Biagini, 'Liberalism and Direct Democracy: John Stuart Mill and the Model of Ancient Athens', in E. F. Biagini, ed., *Citizenship and Community: Liberals, Radicals and Collective Identities in the British Isles, 1865–1931* (Cambridge, 1996), pp. 21–44.

[17] For example, Mill's concerns had social repercussions. See, e.g., the comparison between the tradesman whose morality can be effectively checked by public opinion in a small society, and

The second element characterizing civism is the circumstance just referred to, democratic politics. As a consequence of its development, there opened up new perspectives for responsible citizenship and social co-operation. Yet many viewed the rise of organized parties as a threat to independent thought and thereby the fulfilment of civic duty. This view, considered along with the higher standard of living enjoyed by the upper strata of the working class, made some writers regard how to overcome manipulation and lack of interest as the central question, whereas to Mill's generation the problem had been the want of knowledge and leisure deriving from deprivation and overwork. However, the relaxation of previous constraints made the criticism of the gospel of self-help (considered in chapter 7) possible, and British civism represents a development of that criticism.

The third element of differentiation from previous ideas of public spirit is the relevance of the micro-dimension. The tales told in the first section were not mere illustrations of a theory but an essential part of the theory itself. The phenomena which made up civic life became too various and disparate to be subsumed under a few principles without loss. Some of these phenomena were entirely new experiences (like vaccination, a holiday, or a tram trip) which did leave a mark on the social imagination. In other words, micro-histories were neither anecdotes nor examples – neither bonuses which added a vivid or personal touch, nor explanatory tools – since the micro-physics of everyday life often managed to capture more about the dynamic of interrelatedness than any abstract concept could.[18] Micro-histories appealed to the personal experience of the reader, and for this reason were likely to be particularly effective. As British civism emerged from the union between a moral concern of religious origin and the social scientific perspective, so a grand theoretical framework was not lacking, either. However, all things considered, what is public spirit socially intended as but a micro-physics of justice? The Italians in particular endorsed this programme, judging by their attempts to spread (what they regarded as) the Anglo-Saxon credo condensed into the slogan 'honesty is the best policy'. Admittedly, none of the authors considered assessed civism as a development in the public spirit tradition. But the exigency that civism expressed was elaborated on in a variety of ways, even within frameworks as conflicting as Spencer's individualism and Fabian socialism.

3   Socializing public spirit: from Spencer to the Fabians

In accordance with his early Quaker background as well as his radical, middle-class views, Spencer viewed retribution as the only possible teaching agency:

his counterpart 'in the crowded streets of a great city' where 'marketable qualities' become the key to success: 'Civilization' (1836), *MCW*, XIX, pp. 132–3.

[18] Mixing the general and the particular is now customary in political philosophy. See, e.g., Michael Walzer's theory of 'social goods' in *Spheres of Justice* (Oxford, 1983).

'the only cure for imprudence is the suffering which imprudence entails'.[19] The importance of a strong moral fibre is paramount in *Social Statics*: 'Where the character is defective, intellect, no matter how high, fails to regulate rightly, because predominant desires falsify its estimates.'[20] Yet Spencer carried the radical tradition of Cobden or Buckle to a utopian extreme which, paradoxically, implied a denial of the stern traits of the 'Victorian personality'. There is a 'civic' side in Spencer's sociology, expressed not chiefly by appeals to political participation and vigilance, but by the drawing up of a philosophical warrant for a society of responsible and enterprising citizens, increasingly capable of giving others their due. As indicated in chapter 7, to Spencer social progress amounted to the gradual adaptation of men's minds to circumstances and to the corresponding relaxation of coercive measures. His adherence to Lamarckianism gave substance to the view that 'the perfect man alone can realize the perfect state'.[21] If penalties on improvidence were not mitigated by the government, the development of attitudes was guaranteed by the course of evolution. Remarkably, the traditional bedrock of hard work, duty, and thrift was not viewed as the final stage of moral evolution. His theorizing is of a positively prefiguring nature, centring around the 'law of equal freedom', which stated that the only possible limit to the upholding of personal rights was their infringement upon the like claims of others; the law was only imperfectly carried into effect in his time. The law was first formulated in *Social Statics*, but received its full communal import only in later writings.

Spencer does not depict individuals as atoms but as united by a 'pro-ethical sentiment' nurtured by the pressures of public opinion in the context of a growing 'social self-consciousness', that is the consciousness of the social aggregate that each individual holds.[22] This disposition reflects the fact that, in contrast with 'those rude groups in which men lead lives so independent that they severally take the entire results of their own conduct', in developed societies 'fellow men become more and more implicated in our actions'.[23] The 'private combinations' that for Spencer characterize and constitute industrial societies have the potential to meet all social needs and functions by appealing not only to self-interest but to sympathy as well. Sympathy presides over churches, hospitals, 'charitable agencies', schools, scientific societies, etc. The range of sympathy is finite, in the sense that it applies to the social relations surrounding each citizen – hence the decentralized character of the private associations informed by it. As with all 'natural' organizations, they develop gradually if there is a

---

[19] *Social Statics* (1850; London, 1868), p. 386.
[20] *ibid.*, p. 383.
[21] *ibid.*, pp. 263–4.
[22] *Principles of Ethics*, I, pp. 367–9; 'The Morals of Trade' (1859), in *Essays*, III, pp. 113–51.
[23] *Principles of Ethics*, I, p. 515.

function for them.[24] Spencer's 'industry', in being inherently opposed not only to aggressiveness and war but also to dishonesty, 'revengefulness', and 'untruthfulness', was not only an economic and sociological category but also a blueprint for a better communal life.[25]

Education and the diffusion of knowledge do not fit men for industrial society for 'it is essentially a question of character'. The suitable character is expected to observe the law of equal freedom, which prescribes, first, opposition to 'every illegitimate act, every assumption of supremacy, every official excess of power, however trivial it may seem'. A second prescription is respect for the claims of others – a principle denied, for instance, by the railway tycoons who in America elevated the urban railways without compensating the owners of nearby properties.[26] Whereas the survival of the fittest required that one being achieved its end at the expense of other beings, a crucial part of Spencer's ethics dealt with the highest forms of conduct, characterized by the satisfaction of all parties involved through co-operation for social ends, and hence by a complete and harmonious fulfilment of the law of equal freedom in a thoroughly developed industrial society.[27] Although this conduct was an ideal which would take much time to realize, the 'absolute ethics' of altruism suited to the final stage of the adaptive process was the yardstick for evaluating the 'relatively right' during the transitional phases.[28]

To be adopted as a standard, altruistic conduct 'must be conceived not in a vague and shifting way, but definitely and consistently'[29] – a task which Spencer undertook in *The Data of Ethics*. Theoretically, an industrial society might rest on the bare fulfilment of contracts, but it would fall short of 'that highest degree of life which the gratuitous rendering of services makes possible'. Since altruism is as natural and necessary as egoism, a concern for the improvement and welfare of others amounts to a good utilitarian policy (as the examples given in the first section of the chapter served to demonstrate). The quality of life of each individual would suffer if altruism and public spiritedness were missing, and this is why evolution prescribes them as the ultimate form of adaptation. Justice is not enough – societies also need the 'beneficience' by which men

[24] 'Over-legislation' (1853), in *Essays*, III, pp. 254–6; 'Specialized Administration' (1871), in *Essays*, III, pp. 432–7; *Principles of Ethics*, II, pp. 405–9; *Political Institutions* (1882; London, 1996), p. 703. See M. W. Taylor, *Man versus the State: Herbert Spencer and Late Victorian Individualism* (Oxford, 1992), pp. 179–80. For a contrasting view, see M. Richter, *The Politics of Conscience: T. H. Green and His Age* (1964; Lanham, Md, 1983), p. 23: 'Spencer's elaborate system marks the extreme limit of concern for gain and the denial of obligation between man and man.'

[25] See, e.g., *Political Institutions*, pp. 726–7.

[26] 'The Americans' (1883), in *Essays*, III, pp. 475–9.

[27] *The Data of Ethics*, pp. 17–18; *Political Institutions*, pp. 244–7.

[28] *The Data of Ethics*, pp. 271–5; 'Absolute Political Ethics' (1890), in *Essays*, III, pp. 217–28.

[29] *Principles of Ethics*, II, p. 490.

'complete one another's lives'.[30] Altruism was envisaged to permeate all social relations. Altruism

> may be expected to attain a level at which it will be like parental altruism in spontaneity – a level such that ministration to others' happiness will become a daily need – a level such that the lower egoistic satisfactions will be continually subordinated to this higher egoistic satisfaction, not by any effort to subordinate them, but by the preference for this higher egoistic satisfaction whenever it can be obtained.[31]

As for the mores that were thought to substantiate the law of equal freedom, Spencer devised a programme aimed at 'rationalizing social usages' whose pillar was a denunciation of overwork. In an early article, he held that the pressure of population, which lay at the root of human improvement, tended progressively to fade, to the effect that eventually men would perform no more than 'a normal and pleasurable activity'.[32] Thirty years after writing these words, he denounced the American habit of overworking by pointing, on the one hand, to the physical injury caused by a high-pressure life, and, on the other, to the loss of the capacity for relaxation and pleasure. Overwork was socially inefficient and eventually disruptive. Spencer called for 'a revised ideal of life' which responded to the end of the race for the conquest of nature.[33] He had little sympathy for the moral tone of the times, which, much in Mill's spirit, he judged to be characterized by an indiscriminate admiration for wealth and success. Yet Spencer aimed to differentiate himself from previous critics of Victorian character like Mill, who, in his inaugural address at St Andrews, had argued that life was for learning and working. The reverse was actually true, with learning and working serving to make life complete.[34] A broader difference is also discernible: Spencer's plea for relaxation directed attention to a social necessity whose neglect risked jeopardizing civilization, while Mill was speaking to the elites, whom he invited to cultivate 'a sense of perfection' to become 'the future intellectual benefactors of humanity'.[35] Spencer the organicist sociologist could not agree with Mill that 'individuality is the same thing with development'.[36]

---

[30] *The Data of Ethics*, pp. 146–9, 187–218.
[31] *ibid.*, p. 243; see also the whole of ch. 14, and *Political Institutions*, ch. 19. Spencer's view of the future of the human race was shared by A. R. Wallace: 'The Origin of Human Races and the Antiquity of Man Deduced from the Theory of "Natural Selection"', *Anthropological Review*, 2 (1864), pp. 158–70, esp. pp. 169–70 (but he would later amend the utopianism of this vision). On Victorian altruism, see S. Collini, 'The Culture of Altruism: Selfishness and the Decay of Motive', in his *Public Moralists* (Oxford, 1991), pp. 60–90.
[32] 'A Theory of Population', *Westminster Review*, 57 (1852), p. 500.
[33] 'The Americans'.
[34] *ibid.*, pp. 484–7. On overwork, see also *Principles of Ethics*, I, pp. 525–30, 561–2.
[35] J. S. Mill, 'Inaugural Address Delivered at the University of St Andrews' (1867), *MCW*, XXI, esp. pp. 255–7.
[36] *On Liberty* (1859), *MCW*, XIX, p. 267.

Granted that 'an unwritten law enforced by opinion is more peremptory than a written law not so enforced', Spencer sketched the forms of social intercourse to match the future 'growth of human nature into harmony with the social law'.[37] He wages a comprehensive polemic against the 'ascetic bias' spread by both religion and education, but appropriate only to times of militancy. He defends rest, the pleasures of the table, moderate drinking (useful 'in the abnormal states established in many by overwork'), a variety of amusements, and in general he approves of 'the pursuit of pleasure for pleasure's sake'.[38] 'Such satisfactions serve to raise the tide of life, and taken in due proportion conduce to every kind of efficiency.'[39] Yet sanguinary spectacles like boxing (but also 'the brutalities of football matches') keep alive the barbarous instincts, and hence they 'profoundly vitiate social life'.[40] Spencer advocates 'a protestantism in social usages' against the tyranny of existing conventions – 'I am sick of this standing about in drawing-rooms, talking nonsense, and trying to look happy.' He is in favour of informal and spontaneous gatherings of friends and views the rules presiding over a 'ten o'clock "at home"' as a specimen of unnecessary authority.

You see young gentlemen feeling whether their ties are properly adjusted, looking vacantly around, and considering what they shall do next. You see ladies sitting disconsolately, waiting for some one to speak to them, and wishing they had the wherewith to occupy their fingers. You see the hostess standing about the doorway, keeping a factitious smile on her face, and racking her brain to find the requisite nothings with which to greet her guests as they enter . . . Intellect and feeling are alike asphyxiated. And when, at length, yielding to your disgust, you rush away, how great is the relief when you get into the fresh air, and see the stars! How you 'Thank God, that's over!' and half resolve to avoid all such boredom for the future![41]

Spencer's proposals for a reform of mores are detailed, ranging from choice in marriage to the discharge of the responsibilities of parenthood, from the 'follies of fashion' to the 'extravagant outlays for funerals'. In many circumstances, he judged, happiness and health are decreased by a concern with extrinsicalities and appearances.[42] His analysis was guided by the view that the interconnection of men made a complete separation between the individual and social ethics impossible: 'conduct of which the primary results are purely personal, has often secondary results which are social'.[43]

Viewed from this citizenship angle, Spencer, the staunchest of the advocates of laissez-faire, appears to have shared in a crucial motif of his rivals.

[37] *Political Institutions*, p. 329.
[38] *Principles of Ethics*, I, pp. 525–30, 533–7, 539–44, 555–62.
[39] *ibid.*, I, p. 556.
[40] *ibid.*, I, pp. 559–60.
[41] 'Manners and Fashion', esp. pp. 30–51, quotation on p. 41.
[42] *Principles of Ethics*, esp. I, pp. 570–2, 575–84; II, pp. 416–17, 420–3.
[43] *ibid.*, I, pp. 522–3.

'Community' and 'citizenship' were the hallmarks of a variety of social reform theorists like the Fabians, the New Liberals, the Marshallians, etc. It is
peculiar of the British scene that civism was predominantly seen through the
lenses of social reform, and that the assertion of the social dimension of life took
up a comprehensive and politically charged form. As individualism, not seldom
expressed in crude variants, had been an ideological pillar in the Victorian age,
so the reaction against individualism was radical. The dynamic of functional
interrelatedness was interpreted by means of the idea of community, which was
on the one hand a theoretical construction, a vision to pursue, and on the other a
pivot of progressive platforms. Community rested on the view that solidarity and
co-operation, rather than self-interest and competition, should inspire all social
relationships; any different arrangement would sanction injustice and eventually destroy society. Three major influences lay at the root of this development:
the idealist teaching of T. H. Green, the British tradition of trade unionism and
socialism, and the evolutionary perspective as encapsulated in social science;
at the core of all of which there was the welfare of society as the new ethical
horizon.[44] The relaxation of the imperative of self-reliance which had marked
earlier British thinking – a core condition for any development in the communal direction – took place within a momentously transformed framework of
thought.

In a transitional figure like Sidgwick one finds a stepping stone to citizenship
in the social sense, but in conjunction with a sharp limitation of its scope.
Sidgwick recognized that the citizens of a state should have 'a consciousness
of belonging to one another, of being members of one body, over and above
what they derive from the mere fact of being under one government'; yet the
purpose served by the 'cohesive force' he was appealing for was 'to resist the
disorganising shocks and jars which foreign wars and domestic discontents
are likely to cause from time to time'. However essential was their function,
Sidgwick's understanding of these bonds ('vaguely implied in the term Nation')
did not extend to the social sphere proper.[45] The social reformers' 'community',
in contrast, was the setting of mutual recognition, where responsible citizens
pursued co-operative tasks in the light of the 'common good'. That is, collective
goals did occur, and were to be achieved by conscious thought and action, not
by the invisible hand, while community life was informed by an altruistic spirit
of service stemming from 'sympathy'.

---

[44] On Green and his sway, see D. Nicholls, 'Positive Liberty, 1880–1914', *American Political
Science Review*, 56 (1962), pp. 114–28; Richter, *The Politics*; S. Collini, 'Sociology and Idealism in Britain 1880–1920', *Archives européennes de sociologie*, 19 (1978), pp. 3–50. For an
introductory assessment on socialism and community, see E. Yeo and S. Yeo, 'On the Uses
of "Community": from Owenism to the Present', in S. Yeo, ed., *New Views of Co-operation*
(London and New York, 1988), pp. 229–58.
[45] H. Sidgwick, *The Elements of Politics* (1891; 3rd edn., 1908; Bristol, 1996), pp. 222–5.

Since some features of the Fabians' programme – like the prominent roles of the state and professional expertise, and the opposition to plans for workers' control – went in a contrary direction, the fact that they shared the idea of community testifies to its relevance within the social reformist discourse. In the Fabians' more theoretical writings 'community' figures as the subject of reform: first of all, as an increasingly self-conscious organism, and then as the manager of both national and municipal services, the administrator of surpluses, and the organizer of production; on more pragmatic occasions, community amounts to the seat of local government. Certain assumptions underpinned the centrality of this notion. As men's rights are social rather than natural, so full self-realization can be obtained only through the social medium. As Ritchie maintained, each citizen of this ideal community is willing to recognize the claims of others upon himself or herself.[46] Beatrice Webb pointed in particular to 'a new spirit of fellowship' expressed through a variety of democratic associations.[47] The community is characterized, in Sydney Olivier's words, by 'an intricate tissue of social consciousness extremely sensitive to all kinds of anti-social, or immoral, action'.[48] Sidney Ball spoke of the common good 'which gives to our particular work its meaning, its quality, and its value'. Ball referred to the connection between art and economics established by Ruskin, Morris, and others, who had set 'quality' as an economic question; in this light, the scope of reform should be much wider than the betterment of a purely material standard of living.[49] The environmentalist view of character formation held by Robert Owen was opportunely rediscovered. According to Beatrice Webb, Owen had set the goal of economic life – 'a noble character in the citizen' – and pointed to a reformed society as the means of achieving it – 'democracy as a form of association'.[50]

The rationale behind Fabian community was twofold. There was, first, the exigency of an efficient and fair functioning of society. This was a 'social organism', in which each citizen was not an independent unit but a unit cooperating in the workings of the whole.[51] The twist the Fabians (and other social reformers) imparted to this familiar notion was that the current organization of society not only made a conscious and effective fulfilment of functions impossible for the greatest number, but also threatened the foundations of associative life.

[46] 'The Ultimate Value of Social Effort' (1889), in D. G. Ritchie, *Studies in Political and Social Ethics* (London, 1902), p. 181.

[47] B. Potter, *The Co-operative Movement in Great Britain* (London, 1891).

[48] S. Olivier, 'The Moral Basis of Socialism', in G. B. Shaw, ed., *Fabian Essays* (1889; 1948; repr. edn, London, 1996), p. 105.

[49] S. Ball, 'The Moral Aspects of Socialism', *International Journal of Ethics*, 6 (1895–6), pp. 294, 299–303.

[50] Potter, *The Co-operative Movement*, esp. pp. 18–31, 35–9, 219–40.

[51] See, e.g., S. Webb, 'The Historic Basis of Socialism', in Shaw, *Fabian Essays*, p. 54; S. Webb, 'The Difficulties of Individualism' (1891), in S. Webb and B. Webb, *Problems of Modern Industry* (London, 1898), pp. 229–33. See A. M. McBriar, *Fabian Socialism and English Politics 1884–1918* (Cambridge, 1962), pp. 157–9.

'A community in which some members are overworked while others can get no work at all is *ipso facto* unhealthy.'[52] The excessive length of the working day has a disruptive effect on parenthood, as well as on the relationship between husband and wife. 'It is not in this way', Sidney Webb averred, 'that a nation obtains capable men and women, self-reliant citizens, able to take their places in the world as the self-governing members of a mighty empire.'[53] As regards the wealthy, parasitic minority which does not contribute anything to the community, the equal obligation of all the able-bodied to serve it was a driving force of Fabianism. From this angle socialism was intended as 'a method of social selection according to social worth' in the widest sense.[54] A reformed social environment would provide opportunities for 'progress in the sense of public duty', which is 'our hope and our real aim'.[55] Ideally, there would arise a mutual obligation between the individual and the community, with the latter accepting certain protective responsibilities and the former practising the virtues of citizenship. This position was nicely exemplified by the Webbs' summary of the Minority Report of the Poor Law Commission: granted a 'corporate responsibility', the citizens faced 'new and enlarged obligations' with regard to education, conduct, and health.

> It is ... an inevitable complement of this corporate responsibility, and of the recognition of the indissoluble partnership, that new and enlarged obligations, unknown in a state of *laisser faire*, are placed upon the individual – such as the obligation of the parent to keep his children in health, and to send them to school at the time and in the condition insisted upon; the obligation of the young person to be well conducted and to learn; the obligation of the adult not to infect his environment, and to submit when required to hospital treatment.[56]

The second viewpoint on community, distinguishable from the first only for explanatory purposes, stemmed from socialism as a moral ideal. As Sidney Webb put it, on the ethical side socialism 'expresses the real recognition of fraternity, the universal obligation of personal service, and the subordination of individual ends to the common good'.[57] In nurturing an 'inferior' and 'narrow' type of character, private property and competition were destructive of the

[52] S. Webb and H. Cox, *The Eight Hours Day* (London, 1891), p. 6.
[53] *ibid.*, p. 146. 'An Eight Hours Day will for the first time put into the hands of thousands of working men an opportunity of becoming competent for the duties of citizenship', p. 151.
[54] Ball, 'The Moral Aspects', p. 320. For a criticism of the view that the Fabians were in favour of eugenics, see G. R. Searle, 'Eugenics and Class', in C. Webster, ed., *Biology, Medicine and Society 1840–1940* (Cambridge, 1981), pp. 217–42.
[55] Webb, 'The Difficulties of Individualism', p. 253; see also S. Webb, 'The Reform of the Poor Law' (1890), in *Problems of Modern Industry*, pp. 156–91, where he wrote: 'In that creation of individual character, which is the real goal of all collective effort, the time has come for a new departure', p. 158.
[56] S. Webb and B. Webb, *English Poor Law Policy* (1910; London, 1963), pp. 318–19.
[57] S. Webb, *Socialism in England* (London, 1890), p. 10.

'social ethics' indispensable to a 'happy social life'.[58] Granted that this goal was not just around the corner, neither was it an unwarranted aspiration. A fuller life required a basis in 'the concrete relations of life'; the people were learning how to use their electoral weight to effect the regulation of economic activities; and the process liberated new interests, curiosities, and propensities in men and women.[59] The demand for a reduction in working hours – a paramount battle for the Fabians – springs from 'the strongly-felt desire for additional opportunities for recreation and the enjoyment of life'. Moulded by 'wider education' and 'increased prosperity', the working classes of the Fabians' day are said to differ from the previous generation content to work, eat, and sleep: they realize that life is many-sided, and long for amusement and education.[60] Leisure lays the basis for an 'expansion of life' which encompasses citizenship, and which constitutes the ultimate end of socialism.

In late Victorian and Edwardian Britain, community and citizenship were variously apprehended by social reformers according to background and purposes. But 'community' remained as a repository of the claims of humanity against deprivation and misery. 'Community', regularly charged with positive overtones, in the final analysis meant 'we, the people' – although in view of their origins many of its spokespersons were decent enough to refer to 'them'. In spite of their idealistic features, community and citizenship owed much to the example set by the everyday virtues of plain men associated in trade unions, temperance societies, or local councils. This is why at times the British version of civism seems to have more to do with good neighbourly relations than with the management of the country, and the former was actually a condition for the latter. However cosy it looked, though, British citizenship rested on significant historical changes: the reform policies implemented by governments since Gladstone's first ministry, a new wave of associationism, and the spirit of service which took possession of a sizeable proportion of the educated classes. The utopia was a concrete one, in being a projection of allegedly existing tendencies onto a not too distant future whose mobilizing potential should not be underestimated. According to Hobhouse, 'an ideal is as necessary to the reformer as the established fact is to the conservative'.[61] However, due to its insertion within a framework as abstract and comprehensive as community, which rested in essence on prefiguration, the socio-civic transformation of collective character could hardly fail to suffer from excessive generalization and loose boundaries.

[58] Olivier, 'The Moral Basis', pp. 107–20; Webb, 'The Difficulties of Individualism', pp. 242, 248–9.

[59] Ball, 'The Moral Aspects', esp. pp. 306–7; Webb, 'The Difficulties of Individualism', pp. 246–7.

[60] Webb and Cox, *The Eight Hours Day*, pp. 1–3, 147–8. On the peculiarities of G. B. Shaw's position among the Fabians, see McBriar, *Fabian Socialism*, pp. 82–92.

[61] L. T. Hobhouse, 'The Ethical Basis of Collectivism', *International Journal of Ethics*, 8 (1898), p. 139.

4   Socializing public spirit: Hobhouse, Hobson, and Wallas

To Hobhouse, the 'common good' at which the community aimed was the growth of men and women 'as thinking, feeling, active beings'.[62] As the highest form of social bond, 'citizenship' figured as a concise term to express the conditions in which the self-realization of one did not cramp that of another. Hobhouse criticized Mill for his distinction between self-regarding and other-regarding actions: 'there is no side of a man's life which is unimportant to society, for whatever he is, does, or thinks may affect his own well-being, which is and ought to be matter of common concern, and may also directly or indirectly affect the thought, action, and character of those with whom he comes in contact'.[63] A harmonic development of society was Hobhouse's lodestar, as guaranteed, first, by the existence of an inner 'harmonizing power' leading to the self-discipline and growth of individual personality, and, second, by the postulated possibility of a non-conflictual line of social development. His view of harmony, unlike that of the 'older economists', entailed 'actual support' in order to determine conditions such as 'not merely to permit but actively to further the development of others'.[64]

As the higher life is 'inclusive of others', a principle of mutual recognition shapes the sphere of rights. The possibility of social harmony rests on a shared understanding of social interdependence, as in the case of car driving: 'the liberty of the motor-car to use the roads may, and often does, go so far as to impair the liberty of any other class of vehicle or the liberty of pedestrians to use the same road for their purposes'. An excess of liberty on the part of some contradicts the rights of all others. Any motorist wants to reach his destination quickly, but this may endanger pedestrians, including motorists themselves as pedestrians. To cite another example, Hobhouse upholds the right to walk along the street without 'being pushed off the pavement into the mud' by a hurrying passer-by. Rights are justified expectations, not solely founded on law, since some rights are unrecognized by law, but on the 'common good' as dictated by the moral consciousness. But the duties called for by situations where free-riding is possible (he mentions the closing times of shops, too) have to be compulsorily enforced.[65]

Hobhouse dismisses as proper standards of morals what he calls 'external' agencies like self-interest: external, that is, to 'character' as determined by

---

[62] *Morals in Evolution* (2 vols., London, 1906), I, pp. 70–1. See also *Liberalism* (1911), in L. T. Hobhouse, *Liberalism and Other Writings*, ed. J. Meadowcroft (Cambridge, 1994), pp. 61–4.

[63] *Liberalism*, p. 58.

[64] *ibid.*, pp. 59, 62. On the non-conflictual character of community relations in Hobhouse, see S. Collini, *Liberalism and Sociology: L. T. Hobhouse and Political Argument in England 1880–1914* (Cambridge, 1979), pp. 126–7, 146, and *passim*.

[65] *Social Evolution and Political Theory* (New York, 1911), pp. 190, 194–8. The passage about the expectations of an 'impartial person' as a criterion for defining rights has a Smithian flavour, p. 197.

the interaction of an instinctual basis with a definite 'social tradition'.[66] The solidarity, self-sacrifice, care for the weak, and in general the other-regarding feelings which characterize the family provide Hobhouse's template (although self-reliance is also deemed important). In a word, he upholds 'the natural movements of kindness'.[67] A man who is a nuisance to his neighbours should be taught to discipline himself rather than be punished.[68] State intervention does not sap character because in a democratic regime laws (which sanction intervention) result from the combined efforts of the citizens themselves – the state is no different from a friendly society or a trade union, and state action amounts to an effect of a 'heightened sense of collective responsibility'.[69] In contrast with the morally blind course of natural selection, the citizens' evolving consciousness of purpose constituted Hobhouse's principle of social progress. The increasingly rational control of the environment testified to a growing 'dominance of mind' in social affairs.[70] The 'social mind' is defined as the ideas operative in a community, serving to direct the life, both mental and practical, of individuals. It is a tissue of psychological forces 'that arises from the operations of masses of men, and moulds and is in turn remoulded by the operation of masses of men'. The more developed the social mind, the more conscious it is of society as a whole.[71]

Hobhouse's brand of civism makes much of the sharing of moral feelings. When an issue stirs some impulse within us, we are able to dissipate 'the patter of the street' and make an independent moral judgement, which immediately becomes an element of a wider opinion.

For no sooner has the judgement escaped us – a winged word from our own lips – than it impinges on the judgement similarly flying forth to do its work from our next-door neighbour, and if the subject is an exciting one the air is soon full of the winged words clashing, deflecting or reinforcing one another as the case may be, and generally settling down towards some preponderating opinion which is society's judgement on the case.[72]

Individual views are modified as a result of this socialization of personal opinion, for discussion has some sort of effect on each participant. In a nutshell, this is the way in which society prepares itself for 'some new departure'. Hobhouse wrote: 'we have here in miniature at work every day before our eyes the essential

[66] *Morals in Evolution*, I, pp. 12–17.
[67] 'The Ethical Basis', pp. 153, 155–6; *Social Evolution*, pp. 47–8. See Nicholls, 'Positive Liberty', pp. 125–7. A link between Spencer's treatment of altruism and Hobhouse's failure to provide a plausible 'natural' explanation for the progress of altruism is established by G. Hawthorn, *Enlightenment and Despair: a History of Social Theory* (1976; Cambridge, 1987), pp. 108–11.
[68] *Liberalism*, p. 59.
[69] *Social Evolution*, pp. 191–2; *Liberalism*, p. 64.
[70] *Morals in Evolution*, II, p. 284.
[71] *Social Evolution*, pp. 94–101, quotation on p. 98.
[72] *Morals in Evolution*, I, p. 15.

process by which moral judgements arise and grow'.[73] Yet the prefiguration of a communal future did not go without an awareness that the growth of society had altered the conditions of public morality.

As society becomes larger and more complex many of its obligations become more remote and impersonal. Losing their direct application to our neighbour whom we see, our charity and our sense of justice are diluted and lose their strength. Our sympathies cease where our imagination fails to reach, and the great fabric of government is apt to become an inhuman machine advancing blindly over the living flesh and blood that happens to come in its way.[74]

The whole of Hobson's work was aimed at demonstrating that an economic system based on selfishness was not only unjust but also inefficient in a broad sense, on the grounds that it did not stimulate social qualities, wasted workers' abilities and talents, and led to periodic crises. A prime condition of a healthy community was an 'organic' connection between work and enjoyment in the life of every individual. To Hobson as to the Fabians, the attempt, whether of an individual or a class, 'to escape the physical and moral law which requires the output of personal exertion as the condition of wholesome consumption' should never be successful.[75] This condition being met, the productive system comes to be envisaged as 'a great cooperative process for the mutual aid of members of society'.[76] Better and securer conditions of employment 'would sow the seeds of civic feeling and social solidarity'; in particular, more leisure is a prerequisite of popular self-government, whose foundation is the spare time and energy which people need to equip themselves for it. Among the enriching opportunities opened up by leisure there also figured the activities which came with membership of churches, trade unions, clubs, recreational societies, and so on. By taking part in associations like these, the citizen would contribute to the community as surely as he did in his economic capacity.[77]

Radical economic reform would bring about a co-operative 'social soul', which would compensate for the relative lack of individual incentives resulting from large-scale public intervention and for the unavoidable dullness of many jobs – this is the outcome of Hobson's discussion on whether human nature is sympathetic enough to respond satisfactorily to a 'sound and equitable' environment.[78] Whereas the competitive system demoralized, public control of the production of standardized goods would reveal 'the social meaning of industry' to its operators, that is, they would accept the social ends as their own.[79] The

[73] *ibid.*
[74] *ibid.*, II, p. 283.
[75] *The Evolution of Modern Capitalism* (London, 1894), p. 379.
[76] *Work and Wealth: a Human Valuation* (1914; London, 1992), p. 250.
[77] *ibid.*, pp. 248–9.
[78] *ibid.*, pp. 283–8.
[79] *ibid.*, pp. 293–4, 301–6.

progress of civilization, as Hobson saw it, amounted to a growing awareness of interrelatedness, with the 'secret threads of social feeling' to be used for 'the weaving of the fabric of social institutions'.[80] He believed in the 'instinctive wisdom of the people'; this wisdom – wide, deep, and obscure – exhibited 'the urge of an inner flow of psycho-physical energy'.

We may go further and suggest that advancing reason in the individual animal may consist in a growing sympathy and syn-noesis with the operations of the wider organism. Must not this be what happens when what we term reason endorses and reinforces the instinctive actions of specific preservation and well-being, substituting reflection for impulse, plans for customs, orderly and changing institutions for blind ordinances whose authority is gregarious imitation or superstitious prestige? ...May not then the whole process of the rationalisation of man be regarded as a bringing of the individual man into vital communion of thought and feeling with the thoughts and feelings of the race, of humanity, perhaps of the larger organic being of the kosmos?[81]

Disinterested feelings become possible once individuals are inserted within a wider universe of meaning than their own selves.[82] But a serious problem is posed by the likely attitude of the officials to be placed at the top of the socialist bureaucracy. It is a characteristic of higher bureaucrats, in fact, to think and behave as masters in their own businesses rather than public servants, and to treat both lower-grade functionaries and the public accordingly. It follows that unless their 'pride of caste' is dispelled and a contact with the people's claims is established, the necessary social spirit in the masses would not arise.[83]

So far, civism has been intended as, on the one hand, the outcome of reforms whose implementation would meet the demands of interrelatedness, and, on the other, as an already existing attitude, pointing to the direction of social evolution. A millenarian trait was clearly at play, in spite of the universal criticism of Marx's prophetical determinism. But there were reformers for whom the spread of civism in Britain could not be taken for granted, and who in fact deemed the citizenry so anxiously unhappy as to suggest an ongoing 'disintegration' of the human material of society. This was the starting point of Wallas's *Great Society*. Its conclusion was a plea for 'social inventions' which enabled working-class people to regain control of their lives. Wallas listed, for instance, country walks, the Boy Scouts, improved 'sitting and cooking' habits, and rational forms of socialization for 'youths and maidens' in the urban environment. 'How, in the typical tenement, is a certain measure of privacy to be secured for

---

[80] *ibid.*, p. 307.
[81] *ibid.*, pp. 351–6, quotation on pp. 355–6.
[82] *ibid.*, e.g. p. 356.
[83] *ibid.*, pp. 286–8. The solution lies, first, in a reduction of the salary gap between top and lower officials; second, in the chance for the children of the poorer classes to enter all grades of public service; and, third, in effective publicity and criticism, pp. 287–8.

an unmarried daughter, either spending the day at home or coming home after her work?'[84] This and similar questions were prompted by the destruction of traditional village customs, and made urgent by the degrading setting in which the lower classes spent their lives (gambling, drink, 'music-halls', 'halfpenny romances', 'suggestive films', street gangs, the nervous strain of those eager to be 'respectable', and other factors were cited).[85] The advent of the Great Society, a 'general change of social scale', accounted for the deterioration of life Wallas described. Now, the social environment had an 'intimate connection with all sides of human existence'; but this had negative psychological consequences.[86] At its most profound, the increased complexity and pervasiveness of society generated a 'feeling that we have lost grip over the course of events'.[87] The emotional separation of people from their communal roots caused widespread and deep 'unhappiness' by seemingly entailing a surrender to 'blind forces'.

Rather than seeing contemporary social transformation as an opportunity for a 'total' form of citizenship, Wallas saw it as the denial of the possibility of community. Accordingly, unlike Spencer, Hobhouse, and Hobson, he had no fully fledged theory to superimpose on actual communal life. He traces 'public spirit' back to the natural dispositions of 'Love and Pity' for fellow human beings, and, asserting that society is held together by these dispositions, points to more complete information, better education, and the study of psychology as factors in their growth and diffusion.[88] Psychology helps people to understand others by rendering intelligible signs like 'the tired mother snapping at her tired child, the weak smile of the dreamy youth, the intense self-consciousness of the two talkers who are "showing off" to the other inmates of the omnibus'.[89] Civism remained problematic, though. The demoralization and isolation of most people was exemplified by the passive reading of newspapers, which had largely taken the place of the formative practice of conversation.[90] In spite of all his suggested remedies (including the creation of discussion groups), the gap between the 'Cornish fishermen' who worked unhurriedly in an environment they themselves had created and the 'unknown crowd which makes the solitude of London' was hard to bridge.[91] Perhaps not many Londoners were consciously unhappy, but the 'harmony of the whole being' which constituted happiness was clearly wanting there, in spite of the parks, libraries, and galleries which Wallas had campaigned for.[92]

---

[84] *The Great Society: a Psychological Analysis* (London, 1914), pp. 376–80, quotation on p. 377.
[85] *ibid.*, pp. 65–70.
[86] *ibid.*, p. 3.
[87] *ibid.*, p. 344.
[88] *ibid.*, pp. 145–65.
[89] *ibid.*, p. 161.
[90] *ibid.*, pp. 298–303.
[91] *ibid.*, pp. 7, 161.
[92] *ibid.*, pp. 7–8.

5   A step backward: Bryce and political duties

To reformers like Hobson or Hobhouse, democracy appeared to be a requisite of 'community'; the democratic nature of the political framework was taken for granted and the focus was on social justice. However, democracy was still the prime issue for a wider circle, worried at the prospect of the uneducated replacing the 'governing class' at the helm of the state. A body of literature which addressed the conditions for the workings of democracy ensued, and it is striking how often these conditions amounted to 'civic' recommendations. This literature, of a prevalently political character, was related in a variety of ways to the social conception of civic duties documented in what precedes.

Those who opposed democracy altogether could not do so without questioning the public spirit of the lower classes. Maine went so far as to shake that pillar of English civic identity, the ability of plain men to serve as jurors. His case against democracy rested on the view that the masses were too ignorant to understand their true interests, and were incapable of exercising volition, prone to 'levity of assent' and party manipulation, and, finally, stubbornly conservative.[93] Rousseau in particular was deemed responsible for the principle of abstract equality of men, but Bentham, too, had misunderstood human nature:

He overestimated its intelligence. He wrongly supposed that the truths which he saw, clearly cut and distinct, in the dry light of his intellect, could be seen by all other men or by many of them. He did not understand that they were visible only to the Few – to the intellectual aristocracy. His delusion was the greater from his inattention to facts which lay little beyond the sphere of his vision. Knowing little of history, and caring little for it, he neglected one easy method of assuring himself of the extreme falseness of the conceptions of their interests, which a multitude of men may entertain.[94]

Maine's anti-democratic stance was of universal validity rather than depending on British circumstances. Because of their 'popular' implications, he rejected nationality and race as principles of political legitimacy as well as of historical explanation, while arguing that political cohesion was guaranteed only by past or present common subjection to royal power.[95]

The main British representative of the literature on the conditions of democracy, James Bryce, partly attributed the civic qualities of the Anglo-Saxons to the Teutonic legacy.[96] Whatever the origin of the citizens' capacity for independent thought, responsible voting, and participation, however, he regarded these

---

[93] H. S. Maine, *Popular Government* (London, 1885), esp. pp. 89–91.

[94] *ibid.*, p. 86. On Rousseau and Bentham, see *ibid.*, pp. 127–95, and H. S. Maine, *Ancient Law* (1861; 3rd edn., London, 1866), pp. 87–92ff. On the division of opinion among the Benthamites as to the capacity of the people to recognize their own interest, and the peculiar conservatism of figures like Austin, Greg, or Lowe in the second half of the century, see A. V. Dicey, *Lectures on the Relation Between Law and Public Opinion in England During the Nineteenth-Century* (London, 1905), pp. 160–4.

[95] *Popular Government*, pp. 27–8.

[96] *The American Commonwealth* (1888; 2 vols., London, 1889), I, pp. 25, 563; II, pp. 328.

characteristics as required by the very idea of a democratic polity. Bryce argued all the way from his 1867 essay on democracy to *The Hindrances to Good Citizenship* of 1909 that a democratic government presupposes certain qualities in the mass of the citizens in order to 'recoil from the mere demagogue'.[97] This was Bryce's core argument, whose clear Tocquevillian origin is further emphasized by Bryce's subject matter of 1888, *The American Commonwealth*.[98] The continuity with Mill's position is also evident, in spite of several differences in treatment and in particular of a change in tone: Mill was hopeful, while Bryce either was not, or thought it more responsible to give the impression that he was not. In 1867, though, the extension of the franchise was recommended on the grounds that 'the many' now possessed 'those things which are the bases of political power', namely 'knowledge, self-respect, and the capacity for combined action'. The Bill had to pass because 'the social progress of democracy has outrun its political progress'.[99]

Bryce's outlook became more uneasy as time went by. In modern societies, he argued Bagehot-like, obedience does not rest on reason but on indolence, deference, and sympathy – in one word, on imitation. The average man has a disposition to follow rather than to be independent, especially in large democracies, where to differ from the mass requires special nerve; even in England, love of liberty has always been a comparatively 'feeble passion'. The problem is that democracy requires, ideally, a habit of rational compliance founded on 'an independent reason, conscience, and will'. What a 'reasonable optimist' may hope for in practice is not that ordinary men would ever manage to master details, but that they attain a capacity for the judgement of general issues.[100]

In the tidy *Hindrances to Good Citizenship*, Bryce made a case for 'intelligence, self-control, conscience', with the last term meant to indicate a sense of civic duty.

> The citizen must be able to understand the interests of the community, must be able to subordinate his own will to the general will, must feel his responsibility to the community and be prepared to serve it by voting, working, or (if need be) fighting. Upon the extent to which these civic capacities are present in the community, the excellence of its government will generally depend.[101]

But 'the citizens have failed', and the causes are 'indolence, personal self-interest, party spirit'. As regards the first, Bryce considers the growth of an

---

[97] 'Flexible and Rigid Constitutions' (1884), in J. Bryce, *Studies in History and Jurisprudence* (2 vols., Oxford, 1901), I, p. 189.

[98] See J. Bryce, 'The Historical Aspect of Democracy', in G. Brodrick et al., *Essays on Reform* (London, 1867), pp. 239–78, for references to Tocqueville.

[99] *ibid.*, p. 272.

[100] 'Obedience', in *Studies*, II, pp. 1–48, esp. pp. 24, 31. On the democratic ideal of the 'intelligent independence of the individual voter', see Bryce's preface to M. Ostrogorski, *Democracy and the Organization of Political Parties* (London, 1902), pp. xliv–xlv.

[101] *The Hindrances to Good Citizenship* (1909; New Haven, Conn., 1919), p. 7.

'indulgent spirit' which rules out 'indignation', the fact that each individual has a very small share in government in large states, the increased pressure to conform, the distraction of new leisure activities, and various forms of neglect (to vote, to serve in office, to reflect upon public affairs, and to help the less competent). By way of contrast, he cites Sidgwick's return trip to Cambridge from Davos to vote, although he knew that his side had an ample majority.[102] Self-interest sways democratic politics above all by the effects of the 'power of money' over 'the leading class', which is also the 'tone-setting class'. The fading of the moral standard is a most serious problem, for, 'eating into the national character', it destroys 'the very sentiments to which the reformer has to appeal'.[103] Party politics becomes a hindrance to civic duty if and when it replaces passion or habit for independent thought – far from turning into ends, parties should remain means to 'truth'.[104] As for Bryce's proposed remedies, these focus on education (and moral education in particular), the moral leadership of superior men through an enlightened public opinion, and a sense of pride in the national tradition.[105]

Reading Bryce after Hobhouse or Hobson, one has the impression that the gospel of citizenship Bryce preaches addresses unrelated individuals. In Bryce's pages there is no sense of real social bonds at work, nor of possible positive influences of imitation (which seems to be of slackness only).[106] Apparently, democracy has no goals of itself (say, equality, co-operation, or welfare) capable of arousing citizenship, and it is only a matter of increased numbers. The British constitution was made possible by the right mix of qualities ('legal-mindedness', 'conservative temper', and 'intellectual freshness and activity') which was present in the elites, while the educational effects of the constitution could not but shape the upper classes' dispositions only – then democracy arrived with its unreasonable demands.[107] If some form of mass involvement is an inescapable necessity considering the extension of the franchise, in view of the moral situation of the people this involvement brings fearsome problems; to Bryce citizenship is in the end a question of how to cope with an emergency, namely a question of order and power, not of some 'good life'. Democracy entails a danger to liberal values, and citizenship is intended as a way out, albeit of uncertain efficacy. Although ultimately endowed with appropriate qualities, Bryce's Americans suffer from 'the fatalism of the multitude': each individual feels impotent in the face of the majority and acquiesces in its decisions not because of its Tocquevillian 'tyranny' but out of a sense of 'the insignificance of

[102] ibid., pp. 20–42.
[103] ibid., pp. 43–74, quotation on p. 68.
[104] ibid., pp. 75–104.
[105] ibid., pp. 105–34.
[106] He just mentions 'the diffusion among the educated and richer classes of a warmer feeling of sympathy' towards 'the less fortunate': ibid., p. 132.
[107] 'Flexible and Rigid Constitutions', pp. 185–93.

individual effort'.[108] An existential condition like this, which Bryce did not confine to the Americans, was hardly a promising basis for any government which attempted to do without men with exceptionally high levels of independence, competence and knowledge.

At various levels of abstraction, 'citizenship' was talked about by many in Britain at the turn of the century. Lectures were held and textbooks were written about its principles. A citizen being one who 'has a voice in the government',[109] the idealist philosopher John MacCunn observed that 'democracy adds a new ethical, as well as political, significance to the home, the school, the industrial organization, the religious society'.[110] In this didactic literature, 'democracy' came to refer not only to the direct political relevance of the lower strata's beliefs and its attached duties, but also to a mass society whose workings prescribed certain views and actions in a variety of domains. Granted that a proper exercise of citizenship was deemed a *conditio sine qua non* for the success of democratic government, self-appointed teachers of civics placed emphasis on the responsibilities associated with mass interrelatedness in both private and public life.[111] Constant changes in economic and social conditions call for a high degree of adaptability together with a spirit of service to the community, one educator wrote.[112] To both pragmatic teachers and social scientists, citizenship was equally essential, as an idea suspended somehow between description, injunction, and prefiguration.

6   Turiello and Ferrero

As the enthusiasms of 1859–61 waned in the face of momentous problems, the Italian ruling class anxiously wondered about the place of Italy in a transforming world. The leading lights of the *Risorgimento*, liberty and nationality, had to be quickly adapted to an age of democracy, social reform, increasing military budgets, industrial mass production, and aggressive colonialism. Suddenly confronted with social discontent as well as the race for power among countries, Italians felt that they had no choice but to model their nation on Germany and Britain – the fate of Spain and Greece, on the one hand, and of France,

---

[108] *The American Commonwealth*, II, p. 302. See also 'Obedience', pp. 40–1; *Hindrances*, pp. 23–5.

[109] H. O. Newland, *A Short History of Citizenship and Introduction to Sociology* (London, 1904), p. 11.

[110] J. MacCunn, *The Making of Character: Some Educational Aspects of Ethics* (Cambridge, 1900), p. 103.

[111] See, besides the texts already cited: J. E. Thorold Rogers, *The British Citizen* (London, 1885); O. Browning, *The Citizen: His Rights and Responsibilities* (London, 1893); J. MacCunn, *Ethics of Citizenship* (Glasgow, 1894); and, more generally, M. E. Sadler, ed., *Moral Instruction and Training in Schools* (2 vols., London, 1908), with a short contribution by Wallas (I, pp. 308–11).

[112] M. E. Sadler, 'Introduction', in Sadler, *Moral Instruction*, I, pp. xv, xxiv.

on the other, warned against the feasibility of other options.[113] With Northern Europe as a yardstick, the list of what Italy lacked became necessarily long, but one motif seems to have predominated: the lamentable state of the civic conscience.

Analysis of the Italian case will be limited to the consideration of two books, one by the Neapolitan Pasquale Turiello (1836–1902), and the other by the Turin-based Guglielmo Ferrero (1871–1942). Turiello's two-volume *Governo e governati in Italia* (1882) is now regarded as a classic of the literature devoted to the 'Southern question' and, more generally, of Italian nationalism; Ferrero's *L'Europa giovane: studi e viaggi nei paesi del nord* (1897) was a reportage about Northern Europe which caused some stir. Both authors held definite ideas of the Italian character – a product of climate and history for Turiello, and a specimen of the Latin race for Ferrero – but national character *per se* was not the focus of their attention. Rather, emphasis was placed on the wide range of social consequences which the Italian character had, in terms recalling the present-day 'communitarian' analysis of the Italian *malaise*.[114] Whereas in Britain the political bearing of civism was somewhat indirect, connected as it was to ideal views of community, in Italy social morality issues were more 'concrete' and topical. As for the two authors' quite static views of Italian mentality, it may be suggested that in a new and fragile country images of collective identity, albeit critical, were to some extent requested by the circumstances: there was a pressing need to define the antecedents, the present state, and the foreseeable future of a diverse body of citizens whose unification under a single government was to continue to be perceived as a challenge for a long time. The *Risorgimento* had been marked by an exaltation of Italian achievements aimed at rebuking the disparaging views of the Italian stock regularly put forward by foreigners since the *Esprit des lois*. After 1861, the very name *italiani* took up moving resonances, evoking memories which spanned from ancient Rome to the genius of Cavour but, at the same time, were rarely bereft of sectional interests and thereby controversy. As the backward state of some areas of the peninsula at the time of unification was a shocking surprise to many patriots, so the resilience of corrupt habits and attitudes under a representative government appeared puzzling.

The starting point of Turiello's reflection was that the Italians, and Southerners in particular, had an individualistic nature, which made it difficult for

---

[113] For a comprehensive account, see F. Chabod, *Italian Foreign Policy: the Statecraft of the Founders*, trans. W. McCuaig (Princeton, 1996).

[114] See R. D. Putnam, *Making Democracy Work: Civic Traditions in Modern Italy* (Princeton, 1993). See also how Leopoldo Franchetti, a student of the Italian South contemporaneous to Turiello, is put to use by Diego Gambetta in 'Mafia: the Price of Distrust', in D. Gambetta, ed., *Trust: Making and Breaking Cooperative Relations* (London, 1988), pp. 158–75.

them to 'proceed alongside the others'.[115] 'Loose' (*disciolti*) Italians seldom
endured moral bonds beyond those of the family. They associated by necessity
rather than through mutual confidence, and within any organization always distinguished between 'protectors' and 'protected'. 'In a civil environment which
has been in a state of disintegration for centuries', the institutions of the new
state were not openly and straightforwardly operated, for people preferred resorting to cliques (*clientele*) of a personal character based on the exchange of
favours.[116] In the Southern regions, people are not used to a state 'not created to
the advantage of one or a group' and show 'a barbaric intolerance' towards the
impersonal rule of law. With each individual regarding the others as devoid of
'the sense of limit and communal co-operation, and inclined to take advantage',
administrative and political institutions can hardly be perceived as benevolent
agencies of the common good.[117] Crime arose naturally from the lack of an
effective institutional network reacting with the peasants' hunger for land; the
Neapolitan mafia, the *camorra*, was often linked to political cliques and enjoyed
strong support among the population.[118]

The moral situation had severe consequences on economic life to the point of
blocking both reform and growth in the South. In the countryside, ancient ha-
treds between peasants and landowners, together with the 'ethnological' lack of
self-control of both, made impossible any reformist project that envisaged their
co-operation – 'they cannot face each other with any degree of confidence'.[119]
However, the same peasant who regularly cheats on his landowner is perfectly
honest in his dealings with unknown persons. In towns, the lower classes are
not at all lazy nor dishonest – in Naples, unlike in Turin, nobody jumps off the
tram to avoid paying the fare, and the populace has no 'natural' disposition to
theft. But each party to an exchange is always afraid of being swindled, with
predictable effects on efficiency. The habit of lying is 'like a feint in fencing':
a form of self-defence.[120] Turiello's criticism of the middle classes is stern.
Exploitation and artifice were their favourite means of getting on, whereas 'effort and a frank co-operation with others' did not look like an option. Granted
that a habit of distrust and cunning was a 'capital defect of the Italian temperament', the lack of manufacturing ventures was imputed to the 'poor mutual confidence of the well-to-do'. Turiello commented: 'It is a historical and
well-deserved destiny that a people of cunning individuals can record many

---

[115] *Governo e governati in Italia* (2 vols., Bologna, 1882), I, p. 123, and *passim*. Turiello, a
journalist and teacher, fought under Garibaldi in 1860–1 and 1866–7. Villari criticized Turiello
for imputing too much to national character: 'L'Italia giudicata da un meridionale' (1883), in
P. Villari, *Le lettere meridionali*, ed. F. Barbagallo (Naples, 1979), pp. 193–220.

[116] See, e.g., *Governo e governati*, I, pp. 147–8.

[117] *ibid.*, I, pp. 328–9, 378–410, quotation on p. 394.

[118] *ibid.*, I, p. 71–86.

[119] *ibid.*, I, pp. 201–2.

[120] *ibid.*, I, pp. 205–15.

individual achievements, but meet with regular collective defeats when confronted with those who are stronger because more disciplined.' Whereas manufacture and commerce languished, usury thrived: a sure indication of a propensity to distrust, and dominate, the others.[121]

There is much else in Turiello's book, namely a detailed study of local politics
and a conservative programme of administrative reform to match military education and expansion abroad. Many of his recommendations appear motivated
by the necessity to restrain the native disposition. But however conservative his
proposals and however excessive his faith in the explicative power of national
character, there is an earnest demand for justice at all levels in Turiello. The
newspapers of the Neapolitan provinces were a main source of information for
him, to the effect that his book abounds with micro-stories of passivity, neglect,
corruption, illegality, and intimidation. Roads, he reports, had become tracks
through lack of maintenance. In Basilicata, there was one local council that did
not meet for three years. It was not rare that unfranchised citizens were fined two
or even three times as much as the legal amount. The owner of the single grind-
ing mill in an area was also in charge of collecting the tax on flour, and thereby
could easily cheat customers out of the tax; having bribed the local government,
he had succeeded in stamping out the competition of a rival mill. Common lands
were regularly appropriated by those few individuals who controlled the municipality. In one village, the teacher was illiterate. In another, the mayor was
the brother of the local MP, the mayor's uncle was the teacher, and his cousin
tax-collector and secretary of the municipality – and so on, for Turiello's record
of grievances is extremely long.[122] In a situation like this, a plea for civism is
a plea for a micro-physics of justice. Rights and duties are interpreted in their
everyday contexts, and even minor acts of favouritism or unfairness, if repeated,
if perceived as part of a system, disrupt the roots of society. These roots are
thought to be moral in nature, and amount to hope, trust, and motivation. This
'moral' viewpoint was widely diffused in post-1861 literature, as shown both
by the works on the Italian South by Villari, Franchetti, Sonnino, or Fortunato
(informed by a 'civic' perspective similar to Turiello's), and by the writings of
social scientists. Ranging from the group of economists led by Luzzatti to the
social psychiatrists of the school of Lombroso, social scientists analysed the
defects of national dispositions in the light of their respective specialisms.[123]

---

[121] *ibid.*, I, pp. 215–28, quotation on p. 217. For a suggestive comparison, see A. Pagden, 'The
Destruction of Trust and Its Economic Consequences in the Case of Eighteenth-Century
Naples', in Gambetta, *Trust*, pp. 127–41.

[122] See, e.g., *Governo e governati*, I, pp. 267–9.

[123] On Turiello and the other *meridionalisti* of his time, see M. L. Salvadori, *Il mito del buon-
governo: la questione meridionale da Cavour a Gramsci* (Turin, 1960), and A. Asor Rosa,
'La cultura', in *Storia d'Italia Einaudi* (6 vols., Turin, 1972–6), IV, *Dall'unità ad oggi*, part 2,
pp. 909–25. On the economists, see Romani, *L'economia politica*, pp. 201–41. On Lombroso
and his school, see R. Villa, 'Scienza medica e criminalità nell'Italia unita', in *Storia d'Italia*

Turiello was a relatively secluded character; Ferrero was much more on the public stage. As a young man, he was a close disciple of Lombroso, and co-authored with him *La donna delinquente* (1893) (translated as *The Female Offender* in 1895). A journalist of socialist leaning, he became a world-famous popularizer of Roman history with *Grandezza e decadenza di Roma* (1902–7), to the point of being invited to the White House by Theodore Roosevelt. Following his opposition to fascism, he was nominated for a Nobel prize in 1923–6 and held a chair in contemporary history in Geneva from 1930. His bibliography is fifty pages long, and many of his books (chiefly on politics and history, with forays into political sociology and the philosophy of history) have been translated into several languages.[124] In *L'Europa giovane*, the work which according to Gaetano Mosca revealed Ferrero as a 'phenomenon', he recounted his travels in Britain, Germany, Scandinavia, and Russia through the lenses of his Lombrosian background.[125] Half travel diary and half sociology, the book was intended for a wide public.

Ferrero ascribed to Taine the old distinction between 'Latin' and 'German' races around which *L'Europa giovane* revolves. But, thanks to his Lombrosian background, Ferrero did innovate by making sexual morality central to that distinction, thus reviving a standpoint largely suppressed in the nineteenth century but important to Montesquieu and other *philosophes*. According to Ferrero, the root of all the other psychical differences between the two races lay in the colder and less precocious sexual drive of the 'Germans'. Sporting his medical expertise, Ferrero guided the reader through a series of details about the orgiastic South and the sublimated North which were arousing enough to have been a likely cause of the book's success. Unlike those seats of pubescent innocence, Oxford and Cambridge, university towns in the South of Europe are crowded with 'armies of prostitutes'; in the South, there exists a kind of smile unknown in the North, 'the smile of lust', widely practised even in educated circles; the 'extraordinary custom' of the Finnish sauna would be unthinkable in Italy or Spain; in these countries, crimes originating from passions go unpunished, amidst the approval of the population; and so on.[126] As far as public virtues are

Einaudi: Annali, VII, *Malattia e medicina* (Turin, 1984), pp. 1143–78, and D. Pick, *Faces of Degeneration: a European Disorder, c.1848–c.1918* (Cambridge, 1989), pp. 111–50. On sociology, see F. Barbano and G. Sola, *Sociologia e scienze sociali in Italia 1861–1890* (Milan, 1985).

[124] For a concise biography, see the entry by P. Treves in *Dizionario biografico degli italiani* (50 vols., Rome, 1960–), XLVII, pp. 16-27. For an account of his collaboration with Lombroso, see L. Bulferetti, *Cesare Lombroso* (Turin, 1975), esp. pp. 340–51. L. Salvatorelli et al., *Guglielmo Ferrero: histoire et politique au XXe siècle* (Geneva, 1966), has a bibliography on pp. 139–89.

[125] G. Mosca, 'Il fenomeno Ferrero', *La riforma sociale*, 7 (1897), pp. 1017–31, 1135–64. Mosca is a stern critic of Ferrero's simplistic and over-comprehensive explanations of social attitudes, but appreciates the acumen of single observations and the cohesiveness of the whole work. *L'Europa giovane* was republished in 1904 and 1946, and translated into Croatian in 1918.

[126] *L'Europa giovane: studi e viaggi nei paesi del Nord* (1897; Milan, 1904), pp. 123–76.

concerned, he argues that the physiological and nervous exhaustion induced by a busy sexual life makes a strong commitment to work and communality impossible. In contrast, the British and the Germans have healthy and ordered family lives, and thereby efficient economies and strong social bonds.[127]

Never afraid of a bold conjecture, Ferrero drew a number of consequences from his main thesis, skilfully mixing micro- and macro-considerations. The social superiority of the German race rested on 'duty' and 'conscience'. These things are 'both little and big'; ultimately, they are the material that makes up a satisfactory social order. None of the organizations which provide the strength of modern society – government, industries, railway networks, banks, parties, scientific institutions, etc. – can do without the conscientious effort of each one of their component members. Take a clerk in a German post-office, obstinately trying for a week to identify the addressee of a letter; he senses his job as a duty and a responsibility, connected to the welfare of all others.[128] Unfortunately, duty is for pleasure-driven Italians something extraordinary and theatrical, whereas for the Northern peoples it is just humble, methodical, everyday practice – and the latter type of performance is exactly what modern society requires from the average citizen.[129] The heroes of the age are the punctual employee, the concierge who will not forget a delivery even if untipped, the scrupulous teacher, the worker who does not slacken when the overseer turns his back, the army officer who complies with the rules, the inspector who does not postpone his visits, and so on.[130] Italians also lack 'collective spirit' – the 'power to extend ourselves for each other' in joint ventures, but also 'co-ordination' and 'subordination' – and this is another serious setback in view of the needs of civilization.[131] At bottom, what the 'German' societies have to teach is that intellectual brilliance is less important than 'moral sense', and that the amount of it in the masses is the ultimate factor; 'German' greatness lies in 'a huge number of humble virtues put together'.[132] It is indicative of the explanatory relevance Ferrero gave the micro-dimension that, in order to epitomize the contrast between the artistic Latins and the methodical 'Germans', he resorted to biscuits and pastries: in London, the biscuits are very good because machine-made, whereas the pastries are hardly edible because produced in small workrooms.[133]

In the political realm, the contrast is between Latin caesarism and 'German' social democracies. Caesarism is a system of spoliation through taxation, where the productive classes have no real representation and state revenue serves to

---

[127] ibid., pp. 177–216.
[128] ibid., pp. 184–6.
[129] ibid., pp. 186–203.
[130] ibid., pp. 186–7.
[131] ibid., pp. 377–8.
[132] ibid., pp. 422–3.
[133] ibid., pp. 192–4.

maintain useless colonies, an army of do-nothing bureaucrats, rapacious businessmen, and corruption on a mass scale. Ancient Rome was the 'colossal masterpiece of this genre'.[134] In comparison, industrial capitalism seems to Ferrero
to generate solidarity and justice through association and meritocracy.[135] But
he was well aware that economic competition was a 'battlefield' leaving many
wounded on the ground. He pointed to a development which is a good instance
of his physiologically minded form of civism. Britain showed that unmarried
women – whom he called, in English, 'spinsters' – became the grass roots of all
charity movements by reason of insuppressible maternal impulses. In a treatment oscillating between mockery and admiration, Ferrero speaks of a 'third
sex' of women who, unmarried and childless by choice or necessity, develop
strong passions for social causes and the protection of the weak. The spinsters
are a 'pathological phenomenon', though put to good use as 'a numerous body
of nurses' bent on healing social scars. Suppression of motherhood was the
prime condition for the occurrence of this 'lay and free' type of nuns.[136]

It is appropriate that this history of national character should conclude with a
work like Ferrero's whose format, assertive style, and rough-and-ready conclusions seem to allude to the retrogression which national character progressively
underwent through the twentieth century – reflecting how from being the secret of civilizations and the medium of a scientific study of societies, national
character changed into a matter for popularizers and journalists.[137] However,

---

[134] *ibid.*, pp. 203–11.
[135] *ibid.*, pp. 417–23.
[136] *ibid.*, pp. 315–47.
[137] Actually, there has been no lack of attempts at 'scientific' notions of national character after
1914; and it may be a worrying consideration that national character regularly re-emerged in
times of war. In the first instance, the main lines of a history of national character since 1914 can
be reconstructed through a series of entries in social science dictionaries and encyclopedias.
See, e.g., A. A. Roback, 'Character', in *Encyclopaedia of the Social Sciences* (15 vols., London,
1930–5), III, pp. 335–7; G. A. De Vos, 'National Character', in *International Encyclopedia
of the Social Sciences* (17 vols., London and New York, 1968), XI, pp. 14–19; 'Carattere
nazionale', in L. Gallino, *Dizionario di sociologia* (Turin, 1978), pp. 94–8. For a comprehensive bibliography, see P. Boerner, ed., *Concepts of National Identity: an Interdisciplinary
Dialogue* (Baden-Baden, 1986), pp. 193–225. On the use of national character themes in
wartime in the twentieth century, as both propaganda and 'science', I refer the reader to the
literature on the 'professors' wars' in particular countries. In addition, see M. Mead, 'The Study
of National Character', in D. Lerner and H. D. Lasswell, eds., *The Policy Sciences* (Stanford,
1951), pp. 70–85; M. Mead, 'National Character', in A. L. Kroeber, ed., *Anthropology Today*
(Chicago, 1953), pp. 642–67. As regards Britain, on Barker and other British writers on national
character in the interwar period and beyond, see J. Stapleton, *Englishness and the Study of
Politics: the Social and Political Thought of Ernest Barker* (Cambridge, 1994). As regards
France, a particular venture should be mentioned. In ideal continuation of the intense work in
the 1920s and 1930s by A. Siegfried, P. Gaultier, A. Joussain, F. Roz, and others, a *Revue de la
psychologie des peuples* began publishing in 1946. Although a provincial venture – the journal
emanated from an institute based in Le Havre – it enjoyed prestigious academic support. A
book by its founder, Abel Miroglio, had gone through three editions by 1965: *La psychologie
des peuples* (1951; Paris, 1965).

this Lombrosian let loose North of the Alps substantiated his own 'scientific' conception of Italian attitudes through vivid comparisons with the state of the civic feeling in other countries; in so doing, Ferrero helped to keep alive the myth of the North, a model against which the progress of Italy has constantly been assessed.

Conclusion

1   From *esprit général* to civism

Throughout the period 1750 to 1914, national self-criticism prevailed in France, often associated with the advocacy of an English model of political and economic behaviour; on the other side of the Channel, in contrast, the national attitudes were commonly eulogized and the French character disliked. The book has revolved around this axis, in itself a reflection of the two nations' different histories. However, French sensitivity to suggestions from abroad did not avert a large dose of nationalism, in which the French were akin to the British.

The eighteenth century witnessed a different reception in the two countries of the motifs inherited by antiquity and the Renaissance, with the diffusion of climatology in Britain effectively blocked by Hume's strictures. Civic humanist themes, on the other hand, achieved wide currency in both nations, while social environmentalism was enhanced in Britain by stadial history and the concept of sympathy. The delineation in early and mid-nineteenth-century France of a model of civic participation as most necessary in the post-revolutionary situation found no counterpart in Britain in the same period – arguably because the virtues of civic participation were taken for granted, lying as they did deep at the core of Whiggish identity, as seen not only through radical eyes like Hazlitt's but also through those of a Froude or a Freeman. With regard to public spirit, it is tempting to summarize the contrast between the two countries as one between aspiration and description. In the final decades of the period examined, the criticism of the moral basis of Victorian society induced British pleas for a 'fuller life'. A widespread advocacy of more balanced personalities – the acknowledged insufficiency of 'hard-headed, pushing, self-centred monads', in Hobson's words – came as an answer to both the new opportunities and the new pressures brought about by democracy and mass production. After one hundred and fifty years when the human element had been viewed as a means for higher ends (liberty and wealth, basically), there eventually developed a concern with the alienation of individuals in the wake of the achievement of those ends. Again, the two nations differed. If Britain took the path of 'civism', that is, of the social dimension of citizenship, France with Durkheim took that of social science, that is in his case, of a careful reconstruction of the representations of which collective mentalities consist. In the halcyon days of social scientific thought, Durkheim and his school tried harder than anyone to go beyond the political instrumentality of collective characters.

The inherent complexity of the idea of national identity has emerged. The implications of eighteenth-century *esprit général* differ from those of nineteenth-century 'national character', a concept which eventually evolved into a manifold idea of civism. Yet only a lifeless and exterior history of the images of peoples suggests itself as an alternative to a treatment that makes the contextualized instrumentality of collective mentalities the focus of analysis. At the same time, the discussion of collective attitudes in historical settings has appeared to relate to a general and constant preoccupation of social thinking. As has been asserted, 'all theorizing in the social sciences builds, implicitly or explicitly, upon conceptions of human behaviour'.[1] That political and economic institutions could not be viewed in isolation from the people operating them, and hence that conceptual categories were needed to assess collective attitudes, constituted a common starting point for the authors considered.

National character, on the one hand, and public spirit and civism, on the other, have been concentrated on as two modes, historically interrelated, of talking about public dispositions. The former mode defines the traits of a people on a (usually) long chronological horizon; this definition supplies ready-made answers to specific issues. Here the national divides are quintessential, in the sense that one people is said to accomplish things which other peoples cannot. The latter mode posits a set of behavioural and mental standards as requisite for the achievement of certain goals, regardless of all-encompassing national identities. Accordingly, the qualities concerned have no predetermined geographical boundaries. In so sharp an arrangement as this, the distinction is of course idealtypical: it has been shown how in practice the two modes could go together in the same writer. The diversity of motifs involved in the two modes explains why a story that began with the effects of climate has ended with civism – and why the bricks used to build current depictions of national mentalities are often of heterogeneous provenance.

2   The political culture approach

The careless usage of terms like 'national identity' in many textual contexts has always puzzled me: how can educated people refer to such an inherently vague conundrum, a generalization which irresponsibly overlooks class and group

---

[1] D. C. North, *Institutions, Institutional Change and Economic Performance* (Cambridge, 1990), p. 17.

distinctions? How is it possible to remain unaware that these alleged national identities are by their own composite natures subject to rapid change? In the late 1980s and early 1990s, I was struck by the magnitude and apparent relevance of the 'national identity' issue within the American debate over the loss of the national competitive advantage, with special regard to the corresponding increase in Japanese imports. The 'cultural' side of that debate, which figured journalists and academics alike, swung between sheer xenophobia, recognitions of national peculiarities, and appeals to people to work their fingers to the bone.[2]

Americans could have been inoculated against the national identity line of argument, though, for since the 1950s the concept of national character has repeatedly been the object of destructive criticism on the part of American social scientists. Conversely, this very criticism testifies to the regular resurgence of a concept whose roots lie deep in American culture. One particular episode of this story is worth mentioning, not only because it is relevant in itself but also because it consists in a shift from national character to 'political culture' which has familiar traits. What many social scientists reacted to after 1945 was the work carried out on modern peoples by anthropologists like Ruth Benedict and Margaret Mead, work which began as part of the social science war effort. Mead's *And Keep Your Powder Dry* (1942) and Benedict's *Chrysanthemum and the Sword* (1946), on American and Japanese character respectively, are the most famous examples of a literature which flourished in the 1940s and 1950s under the aegis of the 'culture and personality' approach.[3] The interrelatedness of all elements, both cultural and behavioural, within each social system was a main tenet of this approach; as Mead put it: 'attitudes toward the hearth, the soil, and the country, toward rulers and enemies, are very highly

---

[2] It is representative of the climate of opinion that the bestselling novelist Michael Crichton attached a bibliography on the Japanese challenge to the thriller *Rising Sun* (London, 1992), which deals with a murder case in the context of growing Japanese control of key American industries; in this bibliography (pp. 353–5), one finds titles like C. V. Prestowitz, Jr, *Trading Places: How We Are Giving Our Future to Japan and How to Reclaim It* (New York, 1989), and J. Fallows, *More Like Us: Putting America's Native Strengths and Traditional Values to Work to Overcome the Asian Challenge* (Boston, 1989). For an example of misguided patriotism from a distinguished academic, see L. Thurow, *Head to Head: the Coming Economic Battle Among Japan, Europe, and America* (London, 1993). Of course, the debate was not limited to interventions of this kind.

[3] For reconstructions and bibliographies, see M. Mead, 'The Study of National Character', in D. Lerner and H. D. Lasswell, eds., *The Policy Sciences* (Stanford, 1951), pp. 70–85; M. Mead, 'National Character', in A. L. Kroeber, ed., *Anthropology Today* (Chicago, 1953), pp. 642–67; G. Gorer, 'National Character: Theory and Practice', in M. Mead and R. Métraux, eds., *The Study of Culture at a Distance* (Chicago, 1953), pp. 57–82; G. A. DeVos, 'National Character', in *International Encyclopedia of the Social Sciences* (17 vols., London and New York, 1968), XI, pp. 14–19; R. Wilkinson, *American Social Character: Modern Interpretations from the '40s to the Present* (New York, 1992). Mead's protégé, the British anthropologist Geoffrey Gorer, wrote on the American, Russian, and English national characters; see, e.g., *Exploring English Character* (London, 1955).

patterned and can be shown to fit into the coherent character structure of the people'.[4] In parallel, emphasis was placed upon the peculiarities of each cultural tradition.

The basic criticism levelled at this approach was over-generalization. It was pointed out, for instance, that the existence of a 'basic personality' in a given society is questionable; that class differences cut across cultural and national boundaries; and that changes in behaviour related to social change may occur without necessarily invoking changes in personality traits.[5] Members of the separate disciplines, including many anthropologists, found the 'culture and personality' approach, and national character with it, too vague and impressionistic. The *International Encyclopedia of the Social Sciences* defined descriptions in terms of national character as 'grotesque' and sneered at 'the use of anthropomorphic categories of analysis'.[6] In a balanced article, David Riesman pointed out the different features of his *The Lonely Crowd*, which equally attempted to make the linkage between a psychoanalitic approach and certain historical questions. *The Lonely Crowd* focused on specific social strata in a specific historical setting, he remarked, and analysis 'did not move outward from individuals toward society, but rather the other way round'. Generally speaking, 'the differences among men that will increasingly matter will not arise from geographical location'.[7]

At this point, there emerged an alternative concept in political science which resembles in inspiration the public spirit perspective dealt with in the chapters above: 'political culture'. Almond and Verba's *The Civic Culture* (1963), a questionnaire-based study of political attitudes in five nations, was a seminal point of reference. 'We are concerned in this book', the authors wrote, 'with a number of classic themes of political science: with what the Greeks called "civic virtue" and its consequences for the effectiveness and stability of the democratic polity; and with the kind of community life, social organization, and upbringing of children that fosters civic virtue.'[8] Faced with the post-war establishment of a host of new nations, on the one hand, and the communist challenge, on the other, Almond and Verba pointed to an appropriate 'political

---

[4] Mead, 'The Study of National Character', p. 85.
[5] See, e.g., D. Riesman, 'Psychological Types and National Character: an Informal Commentary', *American Quarterly*, 5 (1953), pp. 325–43; A. Inkeles and D. J. Levinson, 'National Character: the Study of Modal Personality and Sociocultural Systems', in G. Lindzey, ed., *Handbook of Social Psychology* (2 vols., Reading, Mass., 1954), II, pp. 977–1020; DeVos, 'National Character'.
[6] H. Eulau, 'Political Behavior', in *International Encyclopedia of the Social Sciences*, XII, p. 209.
[7] 'The Study of National Character: Some Observations on the American Case' (1958), in D. Riesman, *Abundance for What? and Other Essays* (New York, 1965), pp. 555–73, quotations on pp. 565 and 573.
[8] G. A. Almond and S. Verba, *The Civic Culture: Political Attitudes and Democracy in Five Nations* (Princeton, 1963); I am quoting from the abridged edition (Boston, 1965), p. IX.

culture' as a necessary requisite of a democratic regime; at the same time, they stressed the difficulty of transferring what was a matter of 'attitude and feeling', of subtle cultural components that is, to countries where these were not indigenous. In the authors' reconstruction, Britain and the United States provide the yardstick against which the progress of Italy, Mexico, and Germany on the road towards a genuine 'civic culture' is measured. This is defined as a culture of pluralism and moderation, consensus and diversity, participation and trust.

Almond and Verba acknowledge an influence of the culture and personality approach on their work, and recognize the interdependence of political qualities and general cultural characteristics. Essentially the political culture approach is said to differ on the grounds of manageability and focus, and in the consequent possibility of empirical testing.[9] In practice, however, the book saps the very foundations of the culture and personality viewpoint. The data collected through five thousand interviews enable the authors to investigate the crucial question of whether the differences in political culture observed in the five countries vary according to national or status patterns, whatever the country. Education, for instance, appears to have a marked cross-national impact, although variously distributed over the different aspects of civic culture; Almond and Verba can put forward as an empirically tested rule that 'the higher the educational level, the less difference there is among nations'.[10]

The Civic Culture is a wide-ranging attempt to analyse the abstract, composite, and slippery beliefs making up national 'political styles' – things like interpersonal trust, the 'affective commitment to the political system', or value orientations – through extensive empirical evidence. This methodological option guaranteed the establishment of the political culture approach as a tool of political science. Contrastively, the concept of national character emerged from the project as a casualty, at least as regards the study of politics. On the one hand, sample surveying techniques can hardly be employed to apprehend a notion as general as national character; on the other, national character is not in fact at issue, for what counts in any country is the same set of civic qualities. In the opinion of its advocates, political culture as a more 'restrictive' concept occupied part of the ground previously allocated to national character – a view that, in principle, might reduce the contrast between the two approaches to one of scope rather than genre.[11] But a major problem with national character, Lucian Pye argued, was the tendency 'to treat all behavior as essentially interrelated so that analysis might leap from toilet training to high level policy making and

---

[9] *ibid.*, pp. 9–13.
[10] *ibid.*, pp. 161–7, 319ff.
[11] L. W. Pye, 'Introduction: Political Culture and Political Development', in L. W. Pye and S. Verba, eds., *Political Culture and Political Development* (Princeton, 1965), p. 8.

back again with little sense that the political life of a society might have its own rules and the capacity to filter out some attitudes while accentuating others'.[12]

The contrast between national character and political culture appears related to the progressive specialization and professionalization of social thought, and to the accompanying modifications in intellectual outlook and working framework. Be that as it may, the ground lost on this occasion by the national character perspective was substantial. The concerns behind the idea of political culture, diffused from eminent quarters, contributed significantly to the present-day marginalization (or occultation or disguise) of national character in history and the social sciences. The parallel influence of the emphasis placed on civic attitudes by students of political culture hardly needs mentioning. Yet, the story is far from being over; even a critic like Riesman believed that 'there will remain for a long time differences in national character just as great as differences in character arising from occupation and class'.[13] From my angle, this American episode is significant in confirming a finding of this book, namely the recurrence of what are basically two ways of dealing with citizens' attitudes.

3   The scientific and the moral

Disentangling the subjective and the biased from the socially objective is the promise made by the social sciences, at least as Durkheim, Weber, and many others have intended them. Yet to attempt this goal with respect to collective, and especially national, identities must be regarded as an extremely challenging task, despite the progress unquestionably made by Durkheim himself and later by many other social scientists.[14] Collective identities have turned out to be closely tied to political, economic, or intellectual causes. For instance, if one stands for the communitarian ideal, the citizens of a 'community' quite unavoidably become charged with positive overtones which all readers perceive; the same holds for other ideals in relation to other entities like the French or the English, the working or the middle classes. Another hindrance to scientific detachment is that resorting to national identities typically peaks in critical times, when outside enemies or rivals seem to gain the upper hand, and consequently a redefinition of national values appears urgent. The mentioned American reactions to Japanese manufacturing performance and the debate on Englishness during the Thatcher years in Britain, whose 'identity' was allegedly threatened by the European Union, are recent cases in point.

---

[12] L. W. Pye, 'Culture and Political Science: Problems in the Evaluation of the Concept of Political Culture', in L. Schneider and C. M. Bonjean, eds., *The Idea of Culture in the Social Sciences* (Cambridge, 1973), p. 68.

[13] Riesman, 'The Study of National Character', p. 572.

[14] It is significant that the cautious approaches put forward by social scientists in both Britain and France were swept aside in 1914–18 under the pressure of propaganda, often by the social scientists themselves. Durkheim is the most notable example.

There are of course milder standpoints, less ideologically determined, like that expressed almost incidentally by Michael Walzer in this passage about political community as the place where

Language, history, and culture come together (come more closely together here than anywhere else) to produce a collective consciousness. National character, conceived as a fixed and permanent mental set, is obviously a myth; but the sharing of sensibilities and intuitions among the members of a historical community is a fact of life.[15]

How can one deny the truth of this minimal, 'thin' argument? In the introduction to this book, it was hinted at the Janus-like nature of the idea of collective identities: it is, at the same time, right and wrong. It is right because, yes, it is 'a fact of life' that the members of a community share opinions and sentiments; but it is wrong since, on closer scrutiny, not all groups within the community are likely to hold the same 'sensibilities and intuitions', nor with the same degree of energy, nor for the same span. In actual fact, disagreements about fundamentals are far from rare in spite of common social membership. Hence the fact of life referred to by Walzer, to be taken as a fact, requires qualification; yet qualifying it can hardly avoid introducing political judgements and thereby jeopardizing its status of fact.

I am not hypothesizing an ideal form of social knowledge from which political motivations and values are excluded. As stimuli to research, these have proved to be a necessary part of the social scientific enterprise. But even the type of scientific objectivity attainable in the social field is particularly difficult to achieve when one is confronted with the inescapable tension between a necessarily limited basis of empirical evidence and the magnitude of the generalizations involved. Here a distinction emerges, for the willingness or lack of willingness to put subjective beliefs in the place of evidence provides a demarcation line in our culture. Whereas bold generalizations about national characters seem to be required by the public and are in fact supplied by the media, the academic community as a rule refrains from them; national identity talk can also be found in the area between the two discourses, an area where demonstration standards are relaxed and a subjective bias is not unwelcome. It is likely that popularizers appreciate that 'virtually every popular generalization about nations is at best only a half truth', but that they nevertheless feel content about it.[16] As regards social scientific investigations like that by Almond and Verba, the use of sample surveying techniques should not obscure, first, the problems inherent in sampling, second, their indispensable supplementing with history,

---

[15] M. Walzer, *Spheres of Justice: a Defense of Pluralism and Equality* (Oxford, 1983), p. 28.

[16] The quotation is drawn from a review article by T. Zeldin, who expresses a kind of common position among professional historians, suspicious of generalizations which conceal variations: 'Ourselves, as We See Us', *The Times Literary Supplement*, 31 Dec. 1982, pp. 1435–6. See also Peter Burke's review of Schama's *The Embarrassment of Riches* in *London Review of Books*, 12 Nov. 1987, pp. 13–14.

psychology, and sociology, and, third, the consequences of political bias. In the case of *The Civic Culture*, where an ideological stand is openly taken, the first and, possibly, third points led to the obscuring of the American racial question: failure to deal with the political attitudes of minorities entailed disregard for the fact that for some Americans the civic culture had not yet arrived.[17]

The methodological pitfalls of treatments of collective mentalities depend, in the final analysis, on the very reason why those treatments are carried out. It is arguable that the link between morality and society constitutes the core of the notion of national or civic character; and morality is a subject of momentous consequence but which scarcely lends itself to 'scientific' approaches. Nobody would deny that there is an ineffable moral tension pervading (to a greater or lesser extent) society; an amalgam of histories, cultures, and practices as well as an awareness of communal bonds which ultimately rest on moral grounds. The problem is that the moral bedrock of society is not a fact, but a perception. To both a greedy Anglo-Irish landowner and a righteous Fabian, for example, notions of collective identity served to come to terms with this elusive reality. Under changing historical circumstances, national and civic character themes have provided a point of reference designed to expand the boundaries of the political (or the economic) towards the moral. If this is the intellectual need that national character has fulfilled, its contents fall of necessity outside the domain of precision, while its study cannot eschew a degree of subjectivity.

The stance of those who are critical of their fellow citizens has usually proved to be more consciously moral in tone than that of those who sing their compatriots' own praises. Critics have often applied the public spirit mode, and given vent to personal perception and experience, whereas national eulogists typically resort to traditional material laden with stereotypes and always questionable historical assumptions. The act of criticizing the mores of one's nation is brimming with moral significance, underpinned by reference to a superior standard of behaviour. Yet there is the risk of forgetting the incessant interaction of the social–institutional with the moral–cultural element, and, relatedly, of taking excessive pleasure in playing the earnest judge of less earnest or less aware fellow citizens. Tocqueville is a case in point with reference to both risks. At any rate, the setting of higher civic standards, often through an appeal to foreign models, is a very important stimulus to the everyday task of constructing the polity from below, on the basis of the responsible behaviour of each citizen.

As a possible contribution to the evolving self-awareness of contemporary social thought, this book indicates the remarkable extent to which, between Montesquieu and Hobson, the view was held that society consisted of a network of ideas, sentiments, and beliefs interacting with institutions. The history of what

---

[17] A. I. Abramowitz, 'The United States: Political Culture under Stress', in G. A. Almond and S. Verba, eds., *The Civic Culture Revisited* (Newbury Park, Calif., 1989), pp. 180–4.

national character encompassed has pointed to public sentiments as a constant concern of the Anglo-French mind. Hence what intellectual history can provide is, on the one hand, a series of specimens of the interplay between the sphere of 'the given' and that of ideas, together with a claim about the legitimacy of this interplay, in spite of its problematic nature; on the other hand, it can offer a cautionary tale about the traps lain along the way.

Index

Alison, Archibald, 225
Almond, Gabriel A., 338–9, 341
Andler, Charles, 300
Arbuthnot, John, 9
Aristotle, 8, 25, 30, 84, 94
Arnold, Matthew, 267
Aron, Raymond, 289
Augustine, Saint, 9
Aulard, Alphonse, 279

Bagehot, Walter, 220, 231, 235–6, 241, 245
Bailleul, Jacques-Charles, 141
Ball, Sidney, 316
Barante, Prosper Brugière de, 146
Barker, Ernest, 1, 268
Bastiat, Frédéric, 119
Benedict, Ruth, 337
Bentham, Jeremy, 97, 222, 324
Blanqui, Adolphe, 110, 114–15
Bodin, Jean, 9
Bodmer, Johann Jakob, 13
Bolingbroke, Henry St John, Viscount, 161, 187
Bonald, Louis de, 123–4, 132
Bonstetten, Charles-Victor de, 79
Bouglé, Célestin, 297, 298, 299–301
Boutmy, Emile, 276, 279, 296, 298
Brougham, Henry, 235
Brown, John, 160–1
Brown, Thomas, 218
Brunetière, Ferdinand, 279, 281
Bryce, James, 232, 233
  on America, 239–40
  on democracy, 324–7
Buckle, Henry Thomas, 234, 235, 236, 247, 311
Burckhardt, Jacob, 298
Burgh, James, 188
Burke, Edmund, 10, 63, 82, 90, 159, 160, 184, 187, 191–3, 203, 204, 219, 220, 235
  on American character, 188–9

Reflections on the Revolution in France, 189–91
Burke, Thomas N. (Father Burke), 245

Caesar, 76
Cairnes, John Elliot, 245
Callot, Emile, 30
Cambrensis, Giraldus, 221
Canning, George, 210
Carlyle, Thomas, 1, 7, 193, 220, 225, 235, 240, 242, 244, 276
  on Irish character, 222–4
Carnot, Lazare-Nicolas-Marguerite, 99
Castlereagh, Robert Stewart, Viscount, 210
Cato, Marcus Portius (of Utica), 76
Cavour, Camillo di, 328
Chalmers, George, 214
Chalmers, Thomas, 145, 212, 213
Chaptal, Jean-Antoine-Claude, 110
Chardin, Jean-Baptiste-Siméon, 28
Charlevoix, Pierre-François-Xavier de, 182
Chastellux, François-Jean de, 36, 60–1
Chateaubriand, François-Auguste-René de, 131–3
Chenevix, Richard, 220
Chevalier, Michel, 93, 114, 149, 213, 220
  and Tocqueville, 129–30
  on national character, 116–17
Cicero, Marcus Tullius, 95, 121, 173
Cobden, Richard, 234, 311
  on Irish character, 216–17
Coleridge, Samuel Taylor, 193
Combe, George, 217, 234
Comte, Auguste, 274, 279, 281, 293, 295
Comte, Charles, 80, 110, 112–13, 132
Condillac, Etienne Bonnot de, 36, 67
Condorcet, Marie-Jean-Antoine-Nicolas Caritat de, 61–2, 66, 67, 143
Constant, Benjamin, 63, 84, 85, 86, 102, 110, 131, 134, 153, 279
  as journalist, 140–2

on French character, 147–8
on public spirit, 137–40
Cooper, George, 207–8
Corneille, Pierre, 123, 292
Coyer, Gabriel-François, abbé, 36
Croker, John Wilson, 206
Cromwell, Oliver, 223, 225, 226, 244
Cuoco, Vincenzo, 106–7, 108
Curchod, Suzanne, 194
Custodi, Pietro, 106, 107–8, 109

D'Alembert, Jean-Baptiste Le Rond, 23, 36
Darwin, Charles, 231, 275
Daunou, Pierre-Claude-François, 66–7
Demosthenes, 100, 173
Descartes, René, 30
Destutt de Tracy, Antoine-Louis-Claude, 110, 132
Dewar, Daniel, 218–19
Diderot, Denis, 21, 27, 36, 49–51
Dilke, Charles Wentworth, 233
Drescher, Seymour, 149
Dreyfus, Alfred, 281
Du Bos, Jean-Baptiste, 9, 28
Dunoyer, Charles, 110, 112–13, 132, 144
Dupin, Charles, 93, 114, 115, 118, 144–5
as civic humanist, 99–101
on England and the English, 104–6
on manufacturing, 101–4
Durkheim, Emile, 1, 5, 6, 156, 232, 271, 272, 274, 277, 296, 297, 298, 299, 300, 301, 302, 303, 336, 340
on collective representations, 284–9
on *conscience collective*, 282–4
on French character, 289–95
on mores, 280–2

Faucher, Léon, 93, 114, 115–16
Fauconnet, Paul, 297, 299
Fénelon, François de Salignac de la Mothe, 9
Ferguson, Adam, 119, 219
on national character, 163–4
on manners, 182–3
Ferrero, Guglielmo, 328, 331–4
Fontenelle, Bernard Le Bovier de, 9
Forbes, Duncan, 165
Fortunato, Giustino, 330
Foster, Thomas Campbell, 215
Foucault, Michel, 7, 97
Fouillée, Alfred, 279, 296, 298
Fox, Charles James, 184
Franchetti, Leopoldo, 330
Franklin, Benjamin, 98, 118
Freeman, Edward Augustus, 237, 307–8, 335

Froude, James Anthony, 233, 245, 247, 335
on English character, 244
on Irish character, 242–4
Furet, François, 129

Gabelli, Aristide, 305–6
Galen, 30
Galton, Francis, 252
Garat, Joseph Dominique, 67
Gibbon, Edward, 200
Gioja, Melchiorre, 93, 106, 107, 108, 109, 118
as economist and statistician, 96–9
on mores, 95–6
Gladstone, William Ewart, 318
Godwin, William, 184, 185, 188, 224
Goguet, Antoine-Yves, 36
Green, John Richard, 237
Green, Thomas Hill, 267, 315
Guizot, François-Pierre-Guillaume, 131, 134–7, 138, 148

Hallam, Henry, 205, 224
Haller, Berthold, 13
Hartley, David, 185
Hazlitt, William, 160, 188, 193, 234, 335
and Staël, 193–4
on English character, 195–8
on French character, 194–7
on national character, 198–200
Hegel, Georg Wilhelm Friedrich, 240
Helvétius, Claude-Adrien, 49, 51–3, 62, 64, 67, 84, 143, 239
Herbart, Johann Friedrich, 301
Hertz, Robert, 301
Hippocrates, 30
Hobhouse, Leonard Trelawney, 267, 319–21, 323, 324, 326
Hobson, John Atkinson, 6, 261, 268, 323, 324, 326, 335, 342
on civism, 321–2
on jingoism, 258–9
on model personality, 263–7
Holbach, Paul Heinrich Dietrich d', 36, 51, 53, 57–9, 64
Hubert, Henri, 298, 301–2
Hume, David, 1, 4, 64, 119, 121, 159, 181, 185, 192, 196, 201, 218, 219, 234, 248, 335
'Of National Characters', 165–6
on English and French characters, 166–70
on public opinion, 170–1

Hunt, James, 240
Huxley, Thomas Henry, 307

Inglis, Henry D., 215

James, William, 259
Jeffrey, Francis, 63, 87–8, 89, 91, 92, 205
Jouy, Victor-Joseph-Etienne de, 132, 142–3
Jullien, Marc-Antoine, 143

Kames, Lord (Henry Home), 176
Kant, Immanuel, 194
Kidd, Benjamin, 233, 240–1, 268
Knox, Robert, 240

La Borde, Alexandre de, 146
Laboulaye, Edouard, 272–3, 274
La Bruyère, Jean de, 12
Lafitau, Joseph-François, 182
Laing, Samuel, 234
Lamarck, Jean-Baptiste de, 275
Lamb, Charles, 193
Lamennais, Hugues-Félicité-Robert de, 126
Lapie, Paul, 298–9, 300
La Porte, Joseph de, 31
Lauderdale, Earl of (James Maitland), 116
Laveleye, Emile de, 274
Law, John, 23
Le Bon, Gustave, 156, 258, 279, 296
Lecky, William Edward Hartpole, 245
Leroy-Beaulieu, Paul, 273
Levasseur, Emile, 273
Lévy-Bruhl, Lucien, 299, 302–3
Lingard, John, 224
Liverpool, Earl of (Robert Banks Jenkinson),
    210
Locke, John, 12, 160, 186
Lombroso, Cesare, 330, 331
Louis XIV, 23, 35, 47, 125, 187
Louis XVI, 124
Louis Napoleon, see Napoleon III
Luzzatti, Luigi, 330
Lycurgus, 178
Lytton, Edward Bulwer, 234

Mably, Gabriel Bonnot de, 36, 46, 47, 48,
    51, 58, 94, 97, 107
  on French history and character, 37–9
  on peuple, 53–7
Macaulay, Thomas Babington, 7, 220, 224,
    242
  on Irish character, 225–7
MacCulloch, John, 214
McCulloch, John Ramsay, 116, 118, 119,
    206, 207

MacCunn, John, 327
McDougall, William, 240, 257, 267, 298
  Introduction to Social Psychology,
    252–3, 256
  Psychology, 253–5
Machiavelli, Niccolò, 8, 9, 61, 99
Mackintosh, James, 63–4, 86, 88–9, 205
Maine, Henry Sumner, 324
Maistre, Joseph de, 123, 124–6, 127
Malthus, Thomas Robert, 119, 145, 209,
    218, 219
  on Ireland, 205–6
Marie, Auguste-Armand, 279
Marshall, Alfred, 1, 240, 267, 268
  on character reform, 261–3
Marx, Karl, 322
Masterman, Charles, 258
Mauss, Marcel, 287, 298, 301, 302
Mead, Margaret, 337
Merivale, Herman, 213, 240
Michelet, Jules, 126, 127–9, 220, 225,
    279, 301
Mignet, François-Auguste-Alexis, 141
Mill, James, 205
Mill, John Stuart, 1, 6, 120, 193, 224, 233,
    234, 251, 261, 267, 313, 319, 325
  on inner liberty, 237–9
  on public spirit, 308–9, 310
Millar, John, 159, 171, 219, 224
  as civic humanist, 179–82
  on Irish character, 204
  on manners, 176–9
Monge, Gaspard, 99, 101
Montesquieu, Charles-Louis de Secondat de,
    1, 4, 6, 7, 12, 19–21, 38, 41, 42, 47, 48,
    49, 53, 61, 62, 67, 76, 79, 84, 94, 125,
    128, 161, 163, 178, 207, 269, 275, 279,
    281, 295, 296, 331, 342
  on esprit général, 24–31
  on French mores, 22–4
  reviewed, 31–7
Morelly, 36
Morris, William, 316
Mosca, Gaetano, 331
Muralt, Béat-Louis de, 13–14, 43
Musgrave, Richard, 203–4, 209

Napier, Macvey, 205
Napoleon I, 72, 79, 80, 82, 99, 103, 107,
    111, 136, 194, 197, 200
Napoleon III, 238, 272
Narbonne, Louis de, 85
Necker, Jacques, 82, 92
Necker de Saussure, Adrienne-Albertine, 92
Newman, John Henry, 242

Olivier, Sydney, 316
Owen, Robert, 238, 316

Paine, Thomas, 184, 188, 191, 192
Parodi, Dominique, 297
Parsons, Talcott, 240
Paulhan, Frédéric, 279
Pearson, Karl, 252
Pecchio, Giuseppe, 109
Peter the Great, 39
Pinkerton, John, 214
Plato, 8, 30
Plowden, Francis, 224
Pocock, John, 3
Polybius, 30
Pombal, Sebastiao José de Carvalho y
    Mello, 139
Prévost-Paradol, Lucien-Anatole, 272, 274
Price, Richard, 184, 185, 186, 188, 247
Price, Thomas, 215
Prichard, James Cowley, 215
Priestley, Joseph, 184, 186, 188
Pye, Lucian, 339

Racine, Jean, 87
Raynal, Guillaume-Thomas-François, 36,
    46–8
Rémusat, Charles de, 132, 144, 146–7
Renan, Ernest, 156, 232, 279, 301
Renouvier, Charles, 285
Ribot, Théodule, 279, 296
Ricardo, David, 261
Richelieu, Armand-Jean du Plessis de, 82
Riesman, David, 338, 340
Ritchie, David George, 241, 316
Robertson, William, 183–4
Robespierre, Maximilien-François-Isidore
    de, 64, 67
Robinson, David, 210
Robinson, Henry Crabb, 193
Rœderer, Pierre-Louis, 66, 109, 117, 132
Roosevelt, Theodore, 331
Rossi, Pellegrino, 119
Rousseau, Jean-Jacques, 21, 27, 36, 66, 94,
    97, 99, 107, 120, 133, 194, 324
    and nationalism, 43–6
    on mores and public opinion, 39–41
    on original characters, 41–3
Royer-Collard, Pierre-Paul, 146, 148
Ruskin, John, 267, 316
Russell, Lord John, 212

Sainte-Beuve, Charles de, 276
Saint-Simon, Claude-Henri de Rouvroy de,
    110, 111, 127, 132, 144, 293

Say, Jean-Baptiste, 110, 111, 113, 119, 120
Scrope, George Poulett, 209
Senior, Nassau William, 118, 206, 207, 213
Sewell, William, 209, 211
Shaftesbury, Lord (Anthony Ashley Cooper),
    12–13
Shakespeare, William, 73, 87, 194
Shand, Alexander, 251–2
Sidgwick, Henry, 315, 326
Siedentop, Larry, 122, 149
Siegfried, André, 303–4
Sieyès, Emmanuel-Joseph, 112
Simmel, Georg, 285
Sismondi, Jean-Charles Simonde de,
    79, 120
Skinner, Quentin, 3, 7
Smiles, Samuel, 225, 234, 239
Smith, Adam, 102, 118, 159, 177, 218,
    219, 222
    Theory of Moral Sentiments, 171–3, 175
    on human nature, 174–5
    on national character, 172–3
Smith, Goldwin, 245
Smith, Sydney, 205, 206–7
Solon, 8, 40, 50, 62, 175
Sonnino, Sidney Costantino, 330
Southey, Robert, 193, 209, 211
Spencer, Herbert, 220, 232, 234, 240, 241,
    267, 281, 282, 323
    on civism, 306–7, 310–14
    on evolution, 248–51
    on militant and industrial societies,
    245–8
    on mores, 313–14
    on social environmentalism, 245–51
Staël-Holstein, Anne-Louise-Germaine
    Necker de, 1, 120, 127, 132, 134, 138,
    140, 141, 145, 148, 151, 193, 194
    *Considérations sur la Révolution
    française*, 80–4
    Corinne, 76–9
    writings of the 1790s, 64–70
    on English character, 73
    on French character, 74, 81–3
    on national character, 70–3
    on political morality, 64–6, 69–70, 74–6
    on public spirit, 67–8, 83–4
    on Russian character, 79–80
    reviewed, 85–92
Stendhal (Henry Beyle), 276
Stephen, Leslie, 161, 241–2
Stewart, Dugald, 218
Strabo, 30
Stubbs, William, 237
Swift, Jonathan, 187

Tacitus, 182
Taine, Hippolyte, 1, 113, 156, 231, 282,
    285, 290, 292, 295, 296, 298, 299,
    331
  on national character, 274–7
  on public spirit, 277–9
Tarde, Gabriel, 253, 296, 308
Thatcher, Margaret, 340
Thierry, Augustin, 111, 126–7, 128, 223,
    225
Thiers, Louis-Adolphe, 141
Thoreau, Henry David, 267
Toqueville, Charles-Alexis de, 1, 27, 84, 113,
    121, 122, 129–30, 133, 140, 146, 147,
    233, 239, 248, 272, 273, 279
  as politician, 153–5, 156
  on aristocratic and democratic mores,
    150–3
  on the social state, 148–50, 155
Townsend, Horatio, 210
Trimmer, Joshua Kirby, 208
Trotter, Wilfred Batten Lewis, 252, 256–7
Turgot, Anne-Robert-Jacques de
  on Montesquieu, 32–3
  on public spirit, 130–1
Turiello, Pasquale, 328–30, 331
Turner, Sharon, 214

Vacher de Lapouge, George, 296
Verba, Sidney, 338–9, 341
Vidal de la Blache, Paul, 279
Villari, Pasquale, 305, 330
Villèle, Jean-Baptiste-Séraphin-Joseph de,
    132, 145
Voltaire (François-Marie Arouet), 27, 33–6,
    39, 48, 123, 281

Wakefield, Edward, 208–9
Wakefield, Edward Gibbon, 213
Wallace, Robert, 162
Wallas, Graham, 241, 267, 308
  Great Society, 322–3
  Human Nature in Politics, 259–60
Walzer, Michael, 341
Warburton, William, 161
Watt, James, 101
Webb, Beatrice, 316
Webb, Sidney James, 267, 317
Weber, Max, 2, 340
Wellington, Duke of (Arthur Wellesley), 210
Whately, Richard, 213
Wordsworth, William, 193, 266
Wundt, Wilhelm, 285, 298

Young, Arthur, 203, 209